MATISSE

IN SEARCH OF TRUE PAINTING

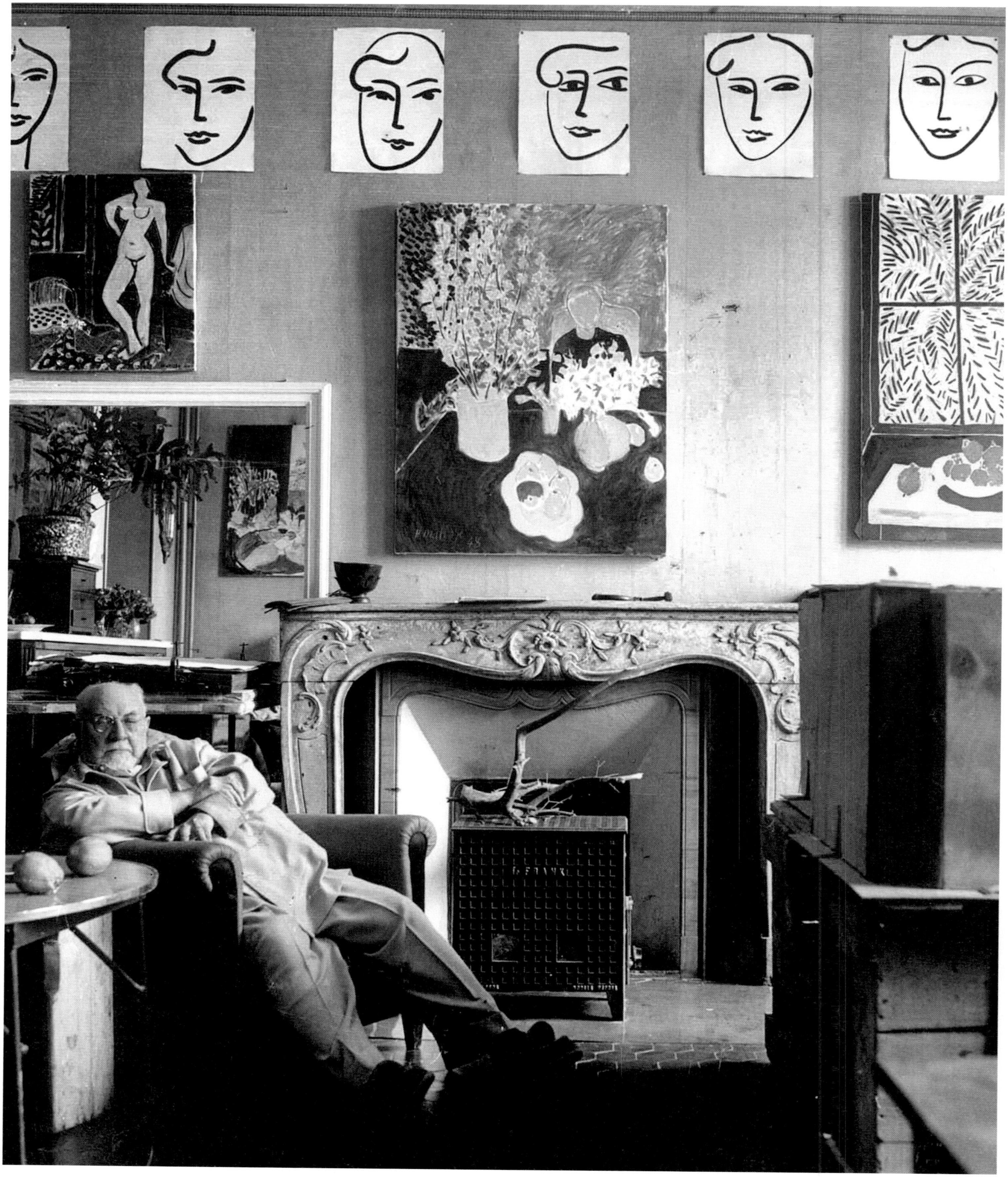

MATISSE

IN SEARCH OF TRUE PAINTING

Edited by Dorthe Aagesen and Rebecca Rabinow

With essays by Dorthe Aagesen, Stephanie D'Alessandro, Cécile Debray, Isabelle Duvernois, Jack Flam, Claudine Grammont, Rémi Labrusse, Doïna Lemny, Isabelle Monod-Fontaine, Kasper Monrad, Rebecca Rabinow, Samantha Rippner, Kathrine Segel, Hilary Spurling, and Alastair Wright

YALE UNIVERSITY PRESS | LONDON

This catalogue is published in conjunction with an exhibition held at the Statens Museum for Kunst, Copenhagen, 14 July–28 October 2012, and at The Metropolitan Museum of Art, New York, 4 December 2012–17 March 2013. An earlier version of the exhibition was presented at the Centre Pompidou, Musée National d'Art Moderne, Paris, 7 March–18 June 2012.

This publication is made possible by The Andrew W. Mellon Foundation.

Published by Yale University Press, London, by arrangement with The Metropolitan Museum of Art, New York.

Edited by Margaret Donovan
Designed by Susan Marsh
Production by Christopher Zichello
Bibliography by Jean Wagner, with the assistance of Judith Calder
Translations from the French by Jane Marie Todd and from the Danish by René Lauritsen

Typeset in Fournier and Gotham
Printed on 135 gsm GardaPat Kiara
Separations by Professional Graphics, Inc., Rockford, Illinois
Printed and bound by Die Keure, Bruges

ISBN 978-0-300-18857-8 (hbk)

A catalogue record for this book is available from the British Library.

JACKET ILLUSTRATIONS: (front) *Young Sailor I*, 1906. Collection of Sheldon H. Solow (cat. 10); (back) *Young Sailor II*, 1906. The Metropolitan Museum of Art, New York, Jacques and Natasha Gelman Collection, 1998 (cat. 11)

FRONTISPIECE: Michel Sima. Matisse in his studio at the Villa Le Rêve, Vence, 1948 (fig. 92, detail)

PAGE VI: Matossian. Photographed stage of *The Dream*, 1940 (fig. 80c)

To the memory of Claude Duthuit (1931–2011),
who loved, respected, and tirelessly
fostered an appreciation for the art of his grandfather Henri Matisse

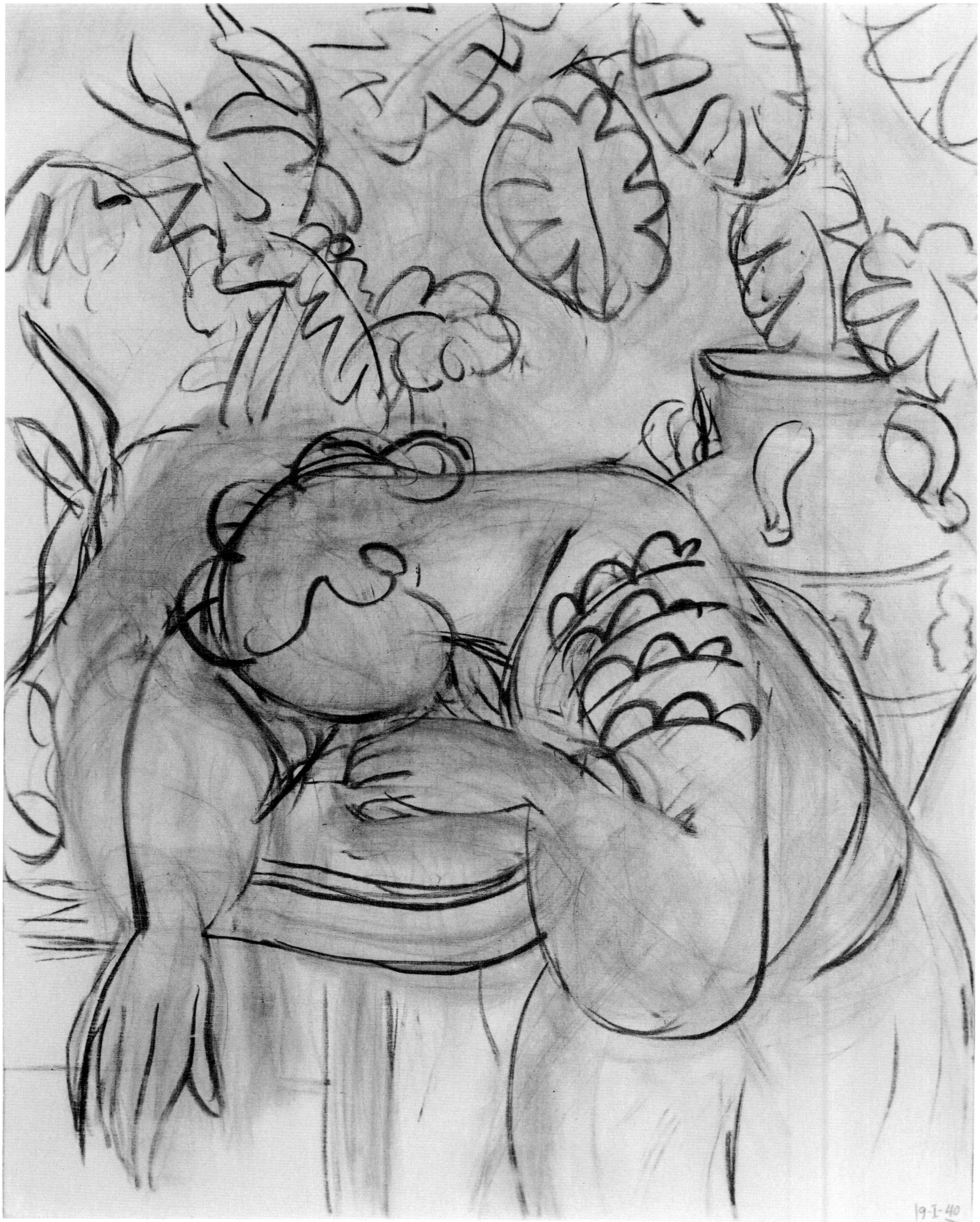
19-I-40

CONTENTS

DIRECTORS' FOREWORD

Young Sailor II, *Le Luxe II*, and *Nasturtiums with the Painting "Dance" I*—three paintings from the collections of the Statens Museum for Kunst and The Metropolitan Museum of Art—raise essential questions that this exhibition and catalogue aim to address. As their titles suggest, each work has a corresponding "double": a nearly identical composition painted on an identically sized canvas. Though it is well known that Henri Matisse frequently painted repetitive images, precisely what drove him to use this method has never before been studied in depth. Reuniting the artist's pairs, trios, and series offered us the opportunity to investigate his motivation as well as the innovative ways in which he continually pushed the boundaries of his painting.

In 1949 the critic Clement Greenberg called Matisse "the brush-wielder and paint-manipulator *par excellence*, the quiet, deliberate, self-assured master who can no more help painting well than breathing." Unbeknownst to Greenberg, painting did not, and never had, come easily to Matisse. Throughout his career, he constantly hesitated, questioned, repainted, and reevaluated his work. He used his completed paintings as tools, repeating compositions in order to compare effects and gauge his progress. Each painting in the present exhibition was reexamined in this new context, and as a result much has been learned about Matisse's process and about the pictures themselves.

We thank the authors of the catalogue for sharing their expertise, and we warmly acknowledge Curators Dorthe Aagesen at the Statens Museum for Kunst and Rebecca Rabinow at The Metropolitan Museum of Art, who organized this exhibition for our institutions.

Our gratitude is extended to the Archives Matisse, which offered us critical guidance and assistance in this endeavor.

We also acknowledge the Centre Pompidou, Musée National d'Art Moderne, Paris, and especially President Alain Seban, Director Alfred Pacquement, Vice-Directors Brigitte Leal and Didier Ottinger, and Curator Cécile Debray for their partnership in connection with this project and for their essential loans.

We are particularly thankful to our lenders, who recognized the significance of their pictures within the context of the exhibition and who agreed to share them with our audience.

At the Statens Museum for Kunst, we are obliged to the Augustinus Foundation, the Knud Højgaard Foundation, the Kandinsky Foundation, and the Beckett Foundation for their generous support of the exhibition. Thanks are also due to the Danish Ministry of Culture for their involvement in the project. At the Metropolitan Museum, we are grateful to Jane Carroll and Diane and James Burke for making the exhibition possible and to The Andrew W. Mellon Foundation for this publication. The Georges Lurcy Charitable and Educational Trust is to be acknowledged for supporting the educational programming associated with the exhibition. We would also like to recognize the Federal Council on the Arts and the Humanities for granting an indemnity for this project.

KARSTEN OHRT
Director, Statens Museum for Kunst

THOMAS P. CAMPBELL
Director, The Metropolitan Museum of Art

ACKNOWLEDGMENTS

The Matisse family and the Archives Matisse have been unstinting in their support of this exhibition. In continuing the work of her late husband, Claude, Barbara Duthuit has been a gracious source of encouragement. Georges Matisse assisted us with image-related requests and went to exceptional lengths to help us achieve accurate color reproductions. We thank him along with his brother, the photographer Michael Matisse. Wanda de Guébriant shared her vast knowledge of Matisse's oeuvre and working methods; all the authors of this volume owe her a debt of gratitude.

Our understanding of Matisse's method of painting in pairs and series has been enriched by the scholars Stephanie D'Alessandro, Yve-Alain Bois, John Elderfield, Jay M. Fisher, Jack Flam, Isabelle Monod-Fontaine, Kasper Monrad, Jeff L. Rosenheim, Gary Tinterow, and Jeffrey Weiss, as well as by the authors represented here.

Furthermore, we would like to acknowledge the following individuals from lending institutions, archives, foundations, and libraries who were particularly helpful as we researched and planned for the exhibition: Laura Albans, Isabelle Alonso, Sylvain Amic, Katarina Andersson, Helga Kessler Aurisch, Martin Beisly, Thomas Bompard, Jean-Philippe Bonilli, Igor Borodin, Emily Braun, Kim Broker, Cheryl Brutvan, Alessandra Carnielli, Olivier Cousinou, Nicholas Cullinan, Delphine Dannaud, François Delcroix, Anne Delebarre, Patrice Deparpe, Virginie Devillez, Daniele Devynck, Jerry Dobrick, Judith Dolkart, Maggie Edwards, Michelle Elligott, Moriah Evans, Hanne Finsen, Gwenaëlle Fossard, Ilda François, Flavia Frigeri, Cathy Gicquel, James T. Glisson, Lukas Gloor, Michelle Harvey, Jodi Hauptman, Margareta Helleberg, Catherine Herbert, Joseph Holbach, Michèle Hornn, Adrienne Jeske, Eik Kahng, Katharina Katz, Simon Kelly, Albert Kostenevich, Anette Kruszynski, Frederik Leen, Jay Lemire, Karen Levitov, Harriet Loffler, Isabelle Maeght, Diane Mallow, Nils Messel, Maria Isabel Molestina, Camille Morando, Iris Müller-Westermann, Tanja Narr, Johanna Holm Norrvik, Nykia Omphroy, Mina Oya, Anniina Pääkkönen, Jennifer Paoletti, Suzanne Penn, Florence Perez, Christine Poullain, Donald Prochera, Anne-Catherine Prud'hom, Chin Yeow Quek, Victoria Reed, Joseph Rishel, Anne Roquebert, Elaine Rosenberg, Katherine Rothkopf, Jennifer Schauer, Iris Schmeisser, Shannon Schuler, Nicole Simões da Silva, Rachel Sloan, Véronique Sorano-Stedman, Per Jonas Storsve, Valérie Sueur-Hermel, Dominique Szymusiak, Vérane Tasseau, Michael Taylor, Ann Temkin, Jennifer Tobias, Lilian Tone, María Molestina Triviño, Dominique Vasseur, Sara Vignale, Trish Waters, John Welter, Oliver Wick, Francesca Wilmott, Maria Zetterberg, and Nina Zimmer.

Ultimately, this exhibition is indebted to the thirty-five public institutions and eight individuals who so generously permitted us to share works from their collections with our visitors. The show debuted at the Centre Pompidou, Musée National d'Art Moderne, Paris, in early March 2012 as "Matisse: paires et séries" under the leadership of Director Alfred Pacquement, Curator Cécile Debray, Assistant

Curator Doïna Lemny, curatorial assistant Elsa Urtizverea, and production manager Cathy Gicquel.

We are most appreciative that our directors—Karsten Ohrt at the Statens Museum for Kunst and Thomas P. Campbell at The Metropolitan Museum of Art—were unwavering in their support for the project.

In New York, David Nash of Mitchell-Innes & Nash kindly shared his expertise by providing third-party values required for the United States Government Indemnity application.

At the Statens Museum for Kunst, the exhibition was planned with the advice of Peter Nørgaard Larsen, Jørgen Wadum, Michael K. Hansen, Kim Gundersen, Berit Anne Larsen, and Lise Korsgaard. Gitte Kikkenberg administered the schedule and budget, while Thor Nørmark Larsen arranged loans and transportation. Conservation and technical examinations were carried out by Kathrine Segel, Troels Filtenborg, and Pauline Lehmann Banke. Annemette Fogh, Annette Bjørg Koeller, and Sille Haahr-Aasmul contributed to the production of the Danish version of the catalogue. Elisabeth Topsøe planned the exhibition design. Mette Houlberg Rung was closely involved in the curatorial process and prepared educational materials with the assistance of Louise Springborg and Pernille Feldt. Jacob Helbo Bøstrup Jensen provided essential curatorial assistance throughout the planning of the show, aiding with both research and practical matters. Thanks also go to colleagues at the Department of Collections and Research for their interest, encouragement, and thought-provoking discussions.

At The Metropolitan Museum of Art, Associate Director for Exhibitions Jennifer Russell provided helpful advice and assistance. The exhibition was planned with the additional guidance of Meryl Cohen, Martha Deese, Kirstie Howard, and Linda Sylling. Mary Clare McKinley, an efficient and valued member of the curatorial team, worked on every aspect of the exhibition and catalogue, both as a researcher and administrator. Conservators Isabelle Duvernois, Shawn Digney-Peer, Michael Gallagher, Rachel Mustalish, and Marjorie Shelley shared insights regarding a variety of conservation issues. We also thank Anthony Askin, Carrie Rebora Barratt, Kay Bearman, Barbara Bridgers, Catherine Brodsky, Jennie Choi, Aileen Chuk, Erin Coburn, Nina McN. Diefenbach, Jeff Elliott, Maria Fillas, Robyn Fleming, Peggy Fogelman, Sarah Higby, Cynthia Iavarone, Marci Kwon, Michael Langley, Paco Link, Ann Matson, Missy McHugh, Mary McNamara, Sandie Peters, Emily Rafferty, Rachel Robinson, Brooks Shaver, Rebecca Tilghman, Elyse Topalian, Yer Vang, and Sheena Wagstaff, who all contributed in important ways.

This catalogue is a testament to the dedication of the Metropolitan Museum's Editorial Department, working in tandem with their counterparts at the Statens Museum for Kunst. Mark Polizzotti was a passionate advocate for the book, as was Sven Bjerkhof. The texts were skillfully shaped and edited by Margaret Donovan, without whose tireless efforts the book would never have been realized. Christel Hollevoet-Force and Mary Chan spent months constructing provenances and exhibition histories, which were adroitly organized and styled by Jean Wagner. Christopher Zichello managed the production and supervised the separation of the images, which were ordered by Jane S. Tai with the help of Crystal Dombrow and Ling Hu. The elegant design was created by Susan Marsh. Our thanks also extend to Gwen Roginsky, Peter Antony, Michael Sittenfeld, Robert Weisberg, and Jennifer Van Dalsen.

DORTHE AAGESEN AND REBECCA RABINOW

LENDERS TO THE EXHIBITION

BELGIUM

Brussels, Royal Museums of Fine Arts of Belgium, 60

DENMARK

Copenhagen, Statens Museum for Kunst, 14, 16, 30, 40

FINLAND

Vaasa, Tikanoja Art Museum, 32

FRANCE

Albi, Musée Toulouse-Lautrec, 58

Le Cateau-Cambrésis, Musée Matisse, 28

Montpellier, Musée Fabre, 57

Nice, Musée Matisse, 51

Paris, Centre Pompidou, Musée National d'Art Moderne, 4, 12, 13, 26, 29, 56, 59, 64

Paris, Centre Pompidou, Musée National d'Art Moderne, on extended loan to the Musée des Beaux-Arts et d'Archéologie, Besançon, 31

Paris, Centre Pompidou, Musée National d'Art Moderne, on extended loan to the Musée d'Orsay, Paris, 7

Paris, Musée de l'Orangerie, 50

GERMANY

Düsseldorf, Kunstsammlung Nordrhein-Westfalen, 6

RUSSIA

Moscow, The State Pushkin Museum of Fine Arts, 20, 55

Saint Petersburg, The State Hermitage Museum, 17, 18

SWEDEN

Stockholm, Moderna Museet, 22

SWITZERLAND

Basel, Fondation Beyeler, 62

Basel, Kunstmuseum Basel, 42

Solothurn, Kunstmuseum Solothurn, 24

Zürich, Fondation E. G. Bührle Collection, 3

UNITED KINGDOM

London, Tate, 23, 52

UNITED STATES

Baltimore, The Baltimore Museum of Art, 2, 45

Chicago, The Art Institute of Chicago, 34

Columbus, Columbus Museum of Art, 44

Houston, The Museum of Fine Arts, 37

New York, The Metropolitan Museum of Art, 11, 19, 35, 49

New York, The Museum of Modern Art, 25, 27

New York, Pierre and Tana Matisse Foundation, 15

Norfolk, Chrysler Museum of Art, 33

Philadelphia, Philadelphia Museum of Art, 39, 47, 48, 53

Saint Louis, Mildred Lane Kemper Art Museum, Washington University in Saint Louis, 1

Saint Louis, Saint Louis Art Museum, 41

Santa Barbara, Santa Barbara Museum of Art, 5

Washington, D.C., National Gallery of Art, 21

Washington, D.C., The Phillips Collection, 61

West Palm Beach, Norton Museum of Art, 43

PRIVATE COLLECTIONS

The Phillips Family Collection, 8

Collection of Sheldon H. Solow, 10

ANONYMOUS LENDERS

9, 36, 38, 46, 54, 63

MATISSE

IN SEARCH OF TRUE PAINTING

INTRODUCTION

Dorthe Aagesen and Rebecca Rabinow

The original purpose of *Matisse: In Search of True Painting* was to conduct a comprehensive study of *Le Luxe I* and *II* (cats. 12, 14). Begun in 1907, these two canvases were created during a ten-year period in which Matisse produced more than a dozen pairs of paintings. Each of these pairs consists of two canvases of the same dimensions that depict the same subjects (albeit with minor alterations), and each work was painted within a few months of the other. It is the formal treatment—the character of the brushwork, surface, colors, and so forth—that most often differentiates the canvases. Seen within the greater context of these pairs, our understanding of *Le Luxe I* and *II* evolved, and the scope of our study was broadened. Ultimately, it became clear that Matisse's pairs are part of a continuum.[1] He repeated images throughout his career, and each repetition (manifested sometimes as a pair and other times as a trio or series) has its own story and circumstances. While this manner of working is certainly not unique to Matisse—repetition and seriality feature in much of Western art—his need to progress methodically from one painting to the next is especially striking. Taken as a whole, it reveals Matisse as an artist who conducted a dialogue with his earlier works, someone who continually questioned himself and his methods in order to, as he put it, "push further and deeper into true painting."[2] Thus, our examination of a single pair of paintings evolved into a fuller presentation dedicated to a particular aspect of Matisse's painting process, one that spans almost five decades.

Early Investigations

Matisse's practice of repeating compositions dates back to the 1890s. As an academically trained student, he was accustomed to copying old master paintings. Copying was regarded not as an empty mechanical procedure but rather as a way of thoroughly analyzing another work of art. The aim was to imitate as painstakingly as possible. The successful copy was considered a significant work of art in itself, potentially as valuable as the model.[3] Matisse and his fellow students certainly painted many copies at the Musée du Louvre, and it was with such a work that Matisse had his first success as an artist. In January 1896 the French State purchased his copy of Annibale Carracci's *Hunt* (1894; Musée de Grenoble) for six hundred francs and sent it to the Grenoble Hôtel de Ville.[4]

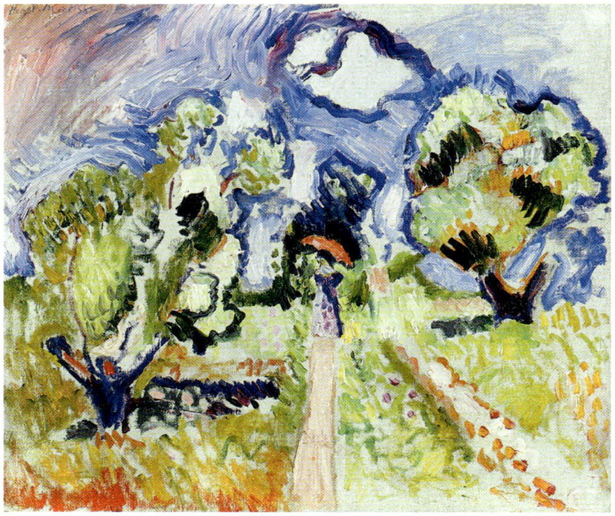

Fig. 1. *Madame Matisse in the Olive Grove*, 1905. Oil on canvas, 18½ x 21⅝ in. (47 x 55 cm). Private collection

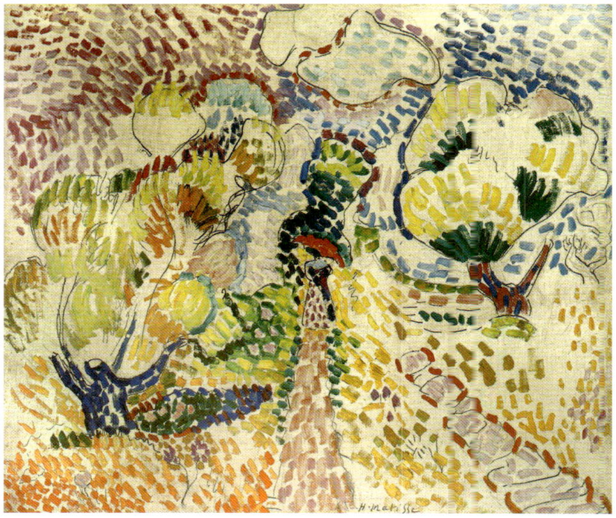

Fig. 2. *Madame Matisse in the Olive Grove*, 1905. Oil on canvas, 18½ x 21⅝ in. (47 x 55 cm). Private collection

The traditional practice of copying supplied Matisse with both a conceptual basis and a methodological background for working with repeated images. While Matisse found much to admire in the Louvre, he was equally receptive to the great variety of artistic styles he encountered in Parisian galleries at the turn of the century.[5] He was particularly intrigued by the work of contemporary artists such as Paul Cézanne (1839–1906), Paul Gauguin (1848–1903), Vincent van Gogh (1853–1890), and Paul Signac (1863–1935). He endeavored to understand their paintings by experimenting with their different styles and methods. How better to become conversant with the strengths and weaknesses of Cézanne and Signac, for example, than to arrange a still-life composition and paint it twice, once in the manner of each artist (cats. 8, 9).[7] These paintings are among Matisse's first deliberately executed pairs: canvases painted about the same time and depicting the same composition in altogether different ways. A similar example can be found in two small landscapes from 1905 that show the artist's wife holding a parasol while strolling through an olive grove in Collioure (figs. 1, 2). The canvases are exactly the same size, but one is painted with broad, Expressionist strokes in the Fauve manner, while the other is rendered in a Divisionist mode.

Of course, an inherent problem in adapting another artist's style, even temporarily, is that it can be interpreted as weakness. Originality has long been considered a necessary attribute of all great European artists. Partly for this reason, French critics during the first years of the 1900s were disheartened by what they perceived as a general lack of inventiveness. They were particularly disturbed to find younger artists copying from the previous generation in superficial and meaningless ways.[6] In June 1904, at the time of Matisse's first solo exhibition, his artistic debts were all too evident. The Danish art historian and critic Carl V. Petersen annotated his copy of the exhibition pamphlet as follows.

> *Still life after Gauguin, landscape after Cézanne, the Seine after Pissarro, interior after Vuillard, a small landscape à la Roussel. Big lunch table à la Cl. Monet's lunch from 68, but with more color, coastal rocks à la Valtat, pointillated* landsc. (*with discretion). Everything heavy, turbid, impure of color, uncertain in its construction, fumbling in intent and yet—talent?*[7]

Did Matisse's paintings contain even a spark of originality? After examining the works on view, the French critic Charles Morice concluded that he could find no "sign of a powerful, creative individuality."[8]

The critical reactions intensified when Matisse presented *Luxe, calme, et volupté* (cat. 7) at the spring 1905 Salon des Indépendants. The painting was criticized for drawing upon too many disparate sources without conveying a clear understanding of any. Matisse's eclecticism, his "chameleon-like versatility," was perceived as undermining the sincerity of his approach.[9] Two years later, in his first published interview, the artist addressed this issue directly: "I have never avoided the influence of others. . . . I believe that the personality of the artist develops and asserts itself through the struggles it has to go through when pitted against other personalities. If the fight is fatal and the personality succumbs, it is a matter of destiny."[10] In response to the critics' accusations, he insisted that an essential trace of his individuality permeated his art: "My personality . . . appeared the same no matter what different states of mind I passed through."[11]

As Matisse pushed himself to find his own means of expression, his efforts began to win him recognition. Once the 1905 Salon d'Automne opened its doors, he was hailed as the leader of the young painters. Although the so-called Fauve style of his art was ridiculed by critics, as well as by the public, his work had caught the attention of a handful of influential collectors and dealers. Afterward, from time to time, Matisse revived the practice of emulating another artist's style. In 1914–15, for example, he painted several portraits of his daughter, Marguerite. One of these, *White and Pink Head* (cat. 29), was created after he had spent time in Collioure with the Spanish Cubist Juan Gris.[12] During this period, Gris was particularly interested in the interplay between positive and negative space as well as in the paring down of forms into geometric shapes. Evidently intrigued by their discussions, Matisse explored these issues in *White and Pink Head* but not in his other representations of Marguerite made at the same time (cat. 28, figs. 48–50).

First Pairs

"Style," or means of expression, would remain one of Matisse's central concerns for years to come. Indeed, it was his exploration of style that sparked the creation of his first true pairs, in which neither painting is entirely indebted to another artist. Upon his return to Collioure in the summer of 1906, he depicted a local teenage fisherman in a work that has all the hallmarks of his own expressive Fauvism (cat. 10). He then executed a second version of the composition on an identically sized canvas, this time employing flat color and deformation to produce a drastically different effect (cat. 11). Unsure of this new direction, Matisse told his friends that *Young Sailor II* had been painted by the local postman.

Over the next ten years, Matisse approached his pairs in a variety of ways. *Young Sailor II* is a free copy, but he used a full-size cartoon (cat. 13) and squaring in the creation of his next major pair, *Le Luxe I* and *II* (cats. 12, 14). Matisse's objective seems to have been to attain a precise relationship between the two versions, yet he intentionally altered elements in the second canvas, changing the contour of one

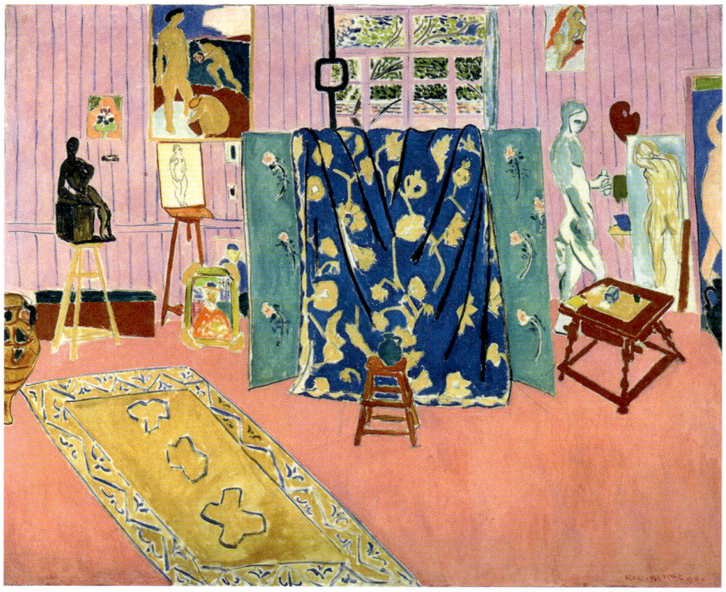

Fig. 3. *The Pink Studio*, 1911. Oil on canvas, 70⅝ x 87 in. (179.5 x 221 cm). The State Pushkin Museum of Fine Arts, Moscow

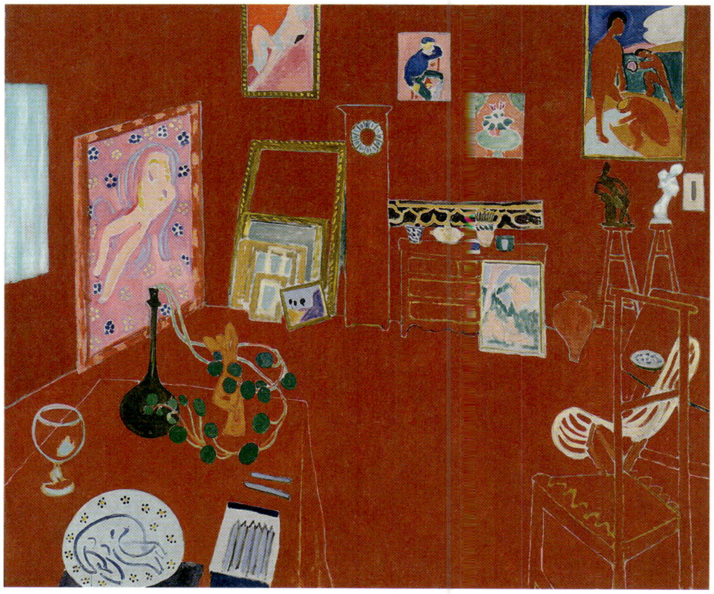

Fig. 4. *The Red Studio*, 1911. Oil on canvas, 71¼ x 86¼ in. (181 x 219.1 cm). The Museum of Modern Art, New York, Mrs. Simon Guggenheim Fund, 1949

figure's back, readjusting another's foot, and so forth. The squaring process did not become part of his typical working method, perhaps because he ultimately found it cumbersome or simply unnecessary.

Painting in pairs offered Matisse alternate solutions to any given pictorial challenge. In most cases he valued both canvases. Some remained unfinished and were kept in his studio, where they served as inspiration. The unfinished version (cat. 15) of *Nude with a White Scarf*, for instance, appears at the upper right of the wall in *The Pink Studio* (fig. 3), while the completed version (cat. 16) is featured in the subsequent *Red Studio* (fig. 4). In essence, Matisse here presents a pair within a pair. Certain pairs made during the early 1910s were the result of Matisse's work on important commissions. On more than one occasion, he showed a large canvas to the Russian businessman Sergei Shchukin only to set it aside and paint a nearly identical but more heavily worked image for Shchukin's Moscow residence. *Dance I* (1909; The Museum of Modern Art, New York) and *Dance II* (1910; The State Hermitage Museum, Saint Petersburg) may be the first instances of this practice, but Matisse is known to have subsequently worked in this manner for other collectors as well.

Back in the fall of 1907, when *Le Luxe I* had first been displayed at the Salon d'Automne, it was presented as a sketch and entitled *Le Luxe (esquisse)*. The creation of an *esquisse* in preparation for a major painting is an exercise steeped in tradition; however, Matisse disregarded the hierarchy that valued the finished picture over the preparatory work. Similarly, in October 1912, when *Nasturtiums with the Painting "Dance" I* and *Goldfish and Sculpture* (cat. 19, fig. 52) were shown at the "Second Post-Impressionist Exhibition" in London—at exactly the same time that the

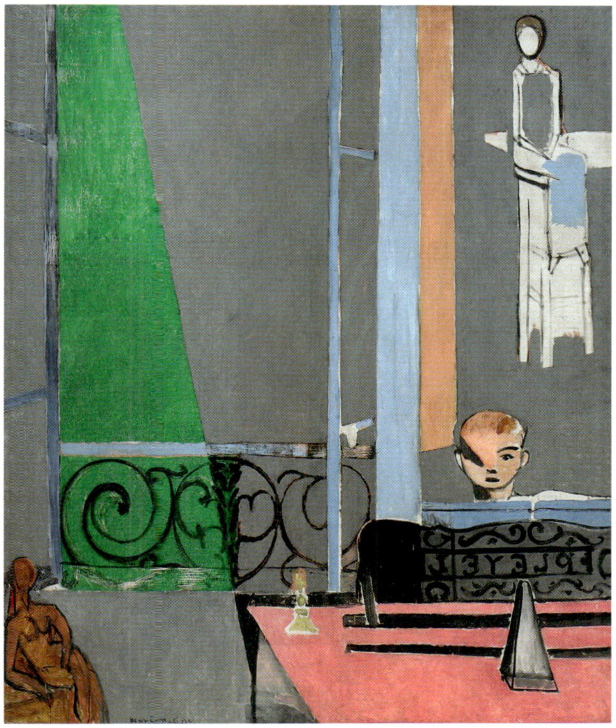

Fig. 5. *The Piano Lesson*, 1916. Oil on canvas, 96½ x 83¾ in. (245.1 x 212.7 cm). The Museum of Modern Art, New York, Mrs. Simon Guggenheim Fund, 1946

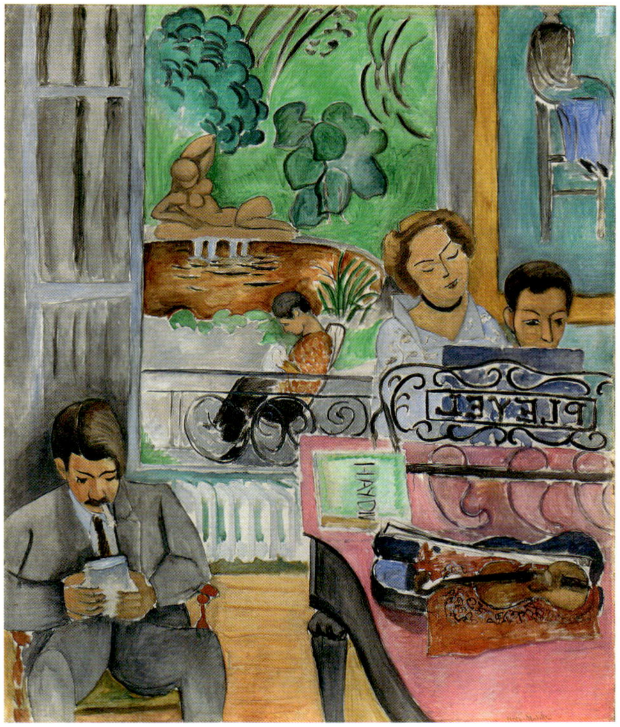

Fig. 6. *The Music Lesson*, 1917. Oil on canvas, 96½ x 83 in. (245.1 x 210.8 cm). The Barnes Foundation, Philadelphia

second versions of both were on view at the Salon d'Automne in Paris (cat. 20 and The Barnes Foundation, Philadelphia)—each of the four paintings was presented as a complete and finished work. Matisse did not draw the public's attention to his pairs and rarely exhibited them together.

Matisse used his pairs of the 1910s to investigate a variety of issues. In paintings such as *Seville Still Life I* and *II* (cats. 17, 18) from 1910–11 and *Interior with Goldfish* and *Goldfish and Palette* (cats. 26, 27) from 1914, he pans out and zooms in on his subject in a cinematic way in order to explore different approaches to a two-dimensional surface and an illusionistic space.

Inevitably, the novelty and usefulness of painting in pairs waned. Canvases such as *The Piano Lesson* and *The Music Lesson* (figs. 5, 6) are among the last instances from the 1910s in which Matisse worked strategically in this manner. John Elderfield has made a compelling case for understanding these canvases within the historical context of World War I,[13] and he and others have written about the striking juxtaposition of geometric abstraction in the earlier canvas with the more immediate naturalism in the second.[14] Matisse later recalled the conflict: "A will to rhythmic abstraction was battling with my natural, innate desire for rich, warm, generous colors and forms."[15]

Painted Repetitions

Painting sessions with the sensual Italian model Laurette over a period of six or seven months in

1916–17 were instrumental in reorienting Matisse as he abandoned the restrictions inherent in painting in pairs and fully embraced larger series. The artist's depictions of Laurette in a green robe on a pink chair with a neutral background (cats. 35, 36) anticipate the "theme-and-variation method" that would characterize much of his subsequent work, in which he repeated a subject while varying the size of the canvas, style, brushwork, and cropping.[16]

One wonders whether it was simply by chance that Matisse's enthusiasm for working in series coincided with his revived interest in Impressionism. In 1917 he traveled to Giverny to meet Claude Monet and, at the end of the year, to Cagnes-sur-Mer to make the acquaintance of Auguste Renoir. Matisse was acutely aware of the popularity of Monet's many series, having witnessed firsthand the crowds headed to see Monet's "Views of the Thames" exhibition at Durand-Ruel in 1904, while his own solo exhibition just down the street at Ambroise Vollard's gallery remained nearly empty. The Impressionist legacy was very much on his mind when he attempted to capture the essence of a light-filled room in a series of paintings executed in Nice in the winter and spring of 1917–18 (cats. 38–40). Similarly, the scores of paintings Matisse made on the Channel Coast during the summer of 1920 resulted from a desire to revisit a motif emblematic of Impressionism. The three largest works in this group feature nearly identical subjects painted on canvases of the same dimensions and are distinguished from one another by slight stylistic modifications (cats. 43–45). Matisse knew that Monet had painted the same chalk cliffs a few decades earlier. Both artists captured subtly different light effects, but while Monet's principal interest lay in the rendering of atmospheric conditions, Matisse's primary concern was presumably the comparison of various pictorial solutions.

The subjects of Matisse's series of the late 1910s and the 1920s are still lifes, odalisques, and hotel interiors. Investigation of stylistic alternatives, no longer the pressing issue, gave way to sequences of related images. Matisse painted and repainted the same rooms, constantly rearranging the furniture and objects, varying colors and patterns, repositioning models, all in order to explore different pictorial effects. Floral arrangements and screens, as well as patterned wallpaper and fabrics, play a major role in these canvases.

Matisse had long repeated his imagery, as can be seen in his views of the Pont Saint-Michel and Notre-Dame Cathedral (cats. 3–5, 23–25, figs. 14, 15, 44), motifs to which he returned for more than a decade. This approach was hardly unique to Matisse; indeed, one is hard pressed to name an artist who has not worked in this manner. In the 1920s and 1930s, the ubiquity of serial creation gained even more attention thanks to advances in art historical scholarship and publishing, including Jacob-Baart de la Faille's four-volume illustrated catalogue raisonné of Van Gogh's oeuvre (1928) and the publication of the first volume of Christian Zervos's Picasso catalogue raisonné (1932).[17]

In 1931 Matisse was honored with an important traveling retrospective at the Galerie Georges Petit, Paris; the Kunsthalle Basel; and the Museum of Modern Art, New York. No early pairs were included, but critics did comment on the serial nature of his more recent work: "In spite of the repetition of subject-matter . . . there is no effect of monotony, every work by Matisse being the solution of a fresh artistic problem. This frequent return to similar themes in different conditions is evidence for, rather than against, his purely artistic originality and fertility."[18]

Not everyone was as complimentary. Admirers of Matisse's more austere, avant-garde paintings felt he

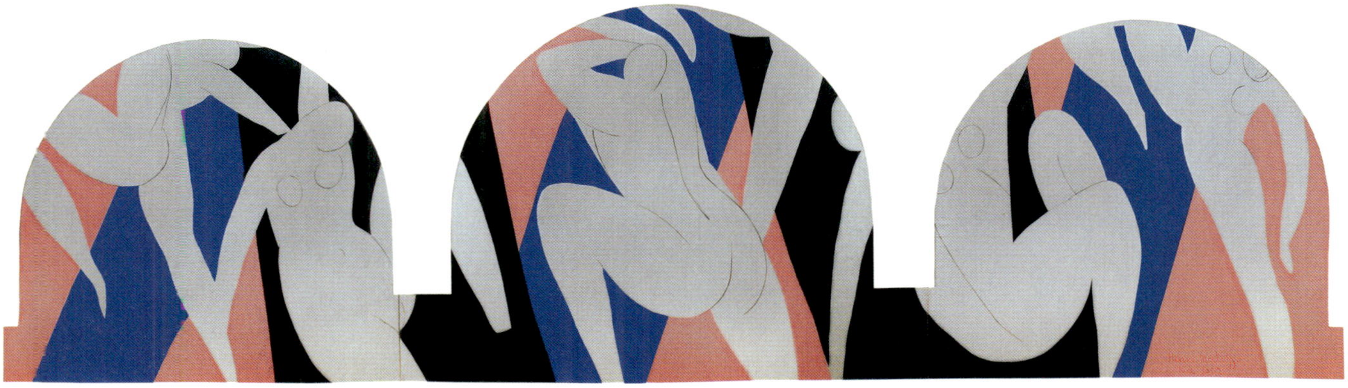

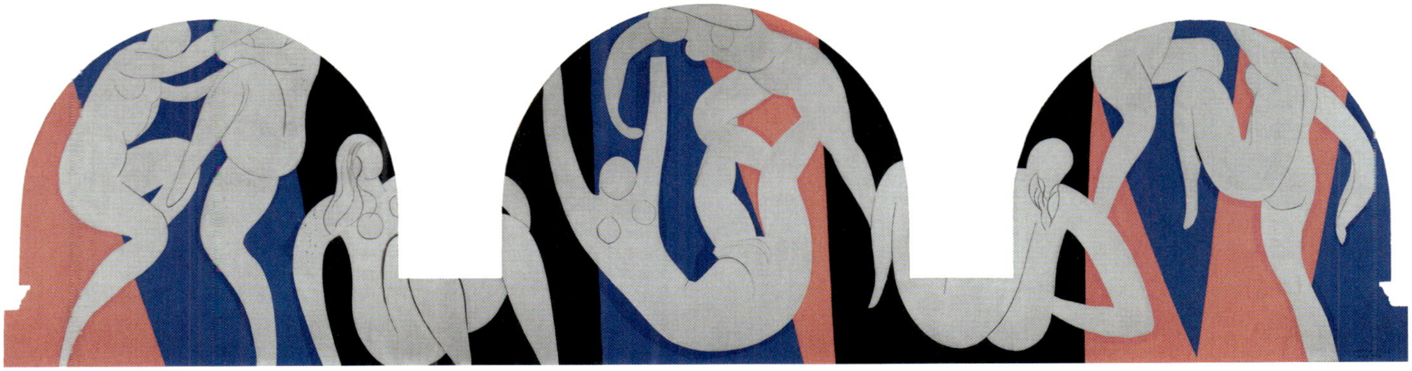

Fig. 7. *Dance*, 1931–33. Oil on canvas (from left to right), 11 ft. 2 in. x 12 ft. 8⅜ in. (340 x 387 cm); 11 ft. 7¾ in. x 16 ft. 4 in. (355 x 498 cm); 10 ft. 11⅞ in. x 12 ft. 10 in. (335 x 391 cm). Musée d'Art Moderne de la Ville de Paris

Fig. 8. *Dance*, 1932–33. Oil on canvas (from left to right), 11 ft. 1¾ in. x 14 ft. 5¾ in. (339.7 x 441.3 cm); 11 ft. 8 in. x 16 ft. 6⅛ in. (355.9 x 503.2 cm); 11 ft. 1⅜ in. x 14 ft. 5 in. (338.8 x 439.4 cm). The Barnes Foundation, Philadelphia

had lost his edge: "That same bourgeois tastelessness which marks so much of Renoir beats out a monotonous fugue in the repetitious arrangements of [his] odalisques against arabesques and in the fortuitous and arbitrary use of ready-made *decors*."[19] Matisse had already begun defending himself from this type of criticism in a 1925 interview in which he provided a broader context for his series, remarking that the old masters "went on re-doing the same painting and always differently. After a certain time, Cézanne always painted the same canvas of the *Bathers*."[20]

Matisse's interest in repeated imagery was not limited to a single medium. It is an essential aspect of his oeuvre, from his sketchbooks to his completed drawings, prints, sculptures, and even his later paper cutouts. In the early 1940s, he developed a drawings project, part of which was published under the title *Dessins: Themes and Variations*, in which the process of creation specifically relied on the principle of seriality (cats. 57, 58).

Photography and Painting

A notable change occurred in Matisse's practice in the 1930s. During the first half of the decade, his attention was focused on the monumental mural, *Dance*, which had been commissioned by Albert Barnes for his residence in the Philadelphia suburbs. (In one sense, the Barnes mural can be viewed as part of an inadvertent "pair"—Matisse had the wrong dimensions for the bays and had to begin again; figs. 7, 8).[21] Shortly before this time, and specifically while he was working on the mural, Matisse hired a photographer to document his work in progress. According to his model and studio assistant Lydia Delectorskaya, the photographer was called in "when, at the end of a session, it seemed to Matisse he had come to the end of his work or he decided he had arrived at a significant stage. . . . Subsequently, he adopted this method for a good many of his pictures and even for some of his charcoal studies which had required a lot of work."[22]

The earliest examples of Matisse's use of photography to capture and preserve his progress date back to the first decade of the twentieth century, when the photographer and art dealer Eugène Druet occasionally photographed Matisse's unfinished works. In 1908, for example, Druet had the opportunity to see Matisse's *Harmony in Red (The Red Room)* (1908; The State Hermitage Museum, Saint Petersburg) at an early stage of development and eagerly offered to photograph it in color at his own expense. Other times, Matisse took the initiative, commissioning photographs when certain paintings had reached a stage he wished to preserve.[23] Photographs were taken of *Dance II* and *Music* (1910; The State Hermitage Museum, Saint Petersburg) while these two decorative panels were being created for Shchukin, and several photographers are known to have captured the development of Matisse's work on *Bathers by a River* (fig. 56).[24]

If the states of any given painting are thought of as a sequence of pictures—all different yet nevertheless related solutions to the same problem—then the photographs of the painting in progress may be considered as yet another example of seriality in Matisse's art. Photography, with its ability to "register and give us documents," as Matisse pointed out in 1908, was the ideal medium to preserve "versions" of an image that would otherwise be lost.[25] For the artist and anyone else fortunate enough to see them, these photographs have the capacity to multiply one canvas into a series, thereby adding a dimension of time and process to the final painting.

Of course, photography had its limitations. All the known photographs of the various states of Matisse's paintings taken in the 1930s and 1940s are small and in black and white. They served less as complete documentation of a given moment in the creation of a work and more as an aide-mémoire for the artist. Matisse addressed their role in a 1945 interview with Léon Degand: "I work from feeling. I have my conception in my head, and I want to realize it. I can, very often, reconceive it. But I know where I want it to end up. The photos taken in the course of the execution of the work permit me to know if the last conception conforms more to what I am after than the preceding ones, whether I have advanced or regressed."[26]

For Matisse, these photographed states also served as visual documentation that could be used to explain his objectives. Around 1910, during the course of a conversation with the Catalan writer J. Sacs (the alias of Felius Elies), Matisse produced a large portfolio full of photographs by Druet to demonstrate "the process of several of his works, begun with utter obedience to the artistic canons of scholastic classicism and transformed progressively by means of successive omissions and deformations

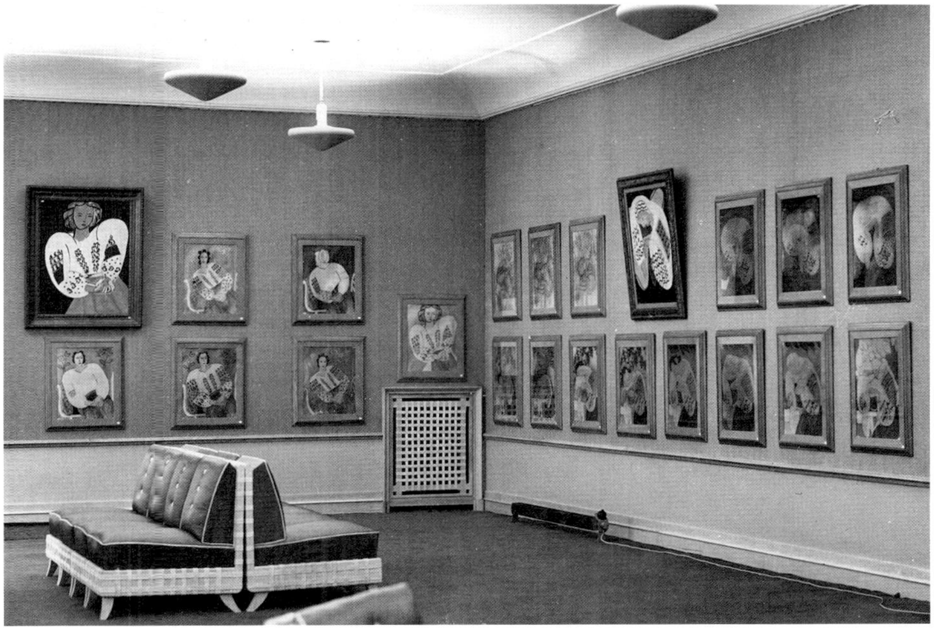

Fig. 9. Marc Vaux. Installation view of *The Romanian Blouse* (fig. 81) and *The Dream* (cat. 54) accompanied by photographed states, Galerie Maeght, Paris, December 1945. Archives Matisse, Paris

until he had obtained a point more or less proximate to his instinctive view of the object or animated being that he wanted to paint."[27]

During the mid-1930s, Matisse shared photographs of the stages of his paintings with collectors, critics, and friends.[28] Documented instances of this effective marketing strategy include the twenty-two photographs of the successive stages of *Large Reclining Nude* (1935; The Baltimore Museum of Art) sent by the artist to Etta Cone in Baltimore and the ten photographs of the stages of *The Large Blue Dress* forwarded to John McIlhenny in Philadelphia (fig. 79a–j).

The inaugural exhibition of the Galerie Maeght in Paris, in December 1945, brought greater public awareness to the photographs documenting the creation of Matisse's paintings. In the aftermath of World War II and the German occupation of France, there was a widespread desire to reassert the cultural hegemony of France. Partly in response, the 1945 Salon d'Automne, which ran from September 28 through October 29, showcased thirty-seven canvases by Matisse, more than half of which had been painted during the war. Five and a half weeks later, six of these paintings reappeared at the Galerie Maeght exhibition, each accompanied by large framed photographs of its earlier states (fig. 9).[29]

Matisse, who was living in Vence at the time, corresponded with Maeght about various aspects of the project, referring to it as "the didactic exhibition."[30] He seems to have either proposed or agreed to the novel concept specifically because it would emphasize the effort that went into each of his paintings. After reading the preface by the young poet Jacques Kober, which had been commissioned for the exhibition brochure, Matisse sent Maeght a telegram expressing his concerns:

> *Haven't I passed the age where I need to be introduced as a painter, which is the point of prefaces? If there is something to write, it should be*

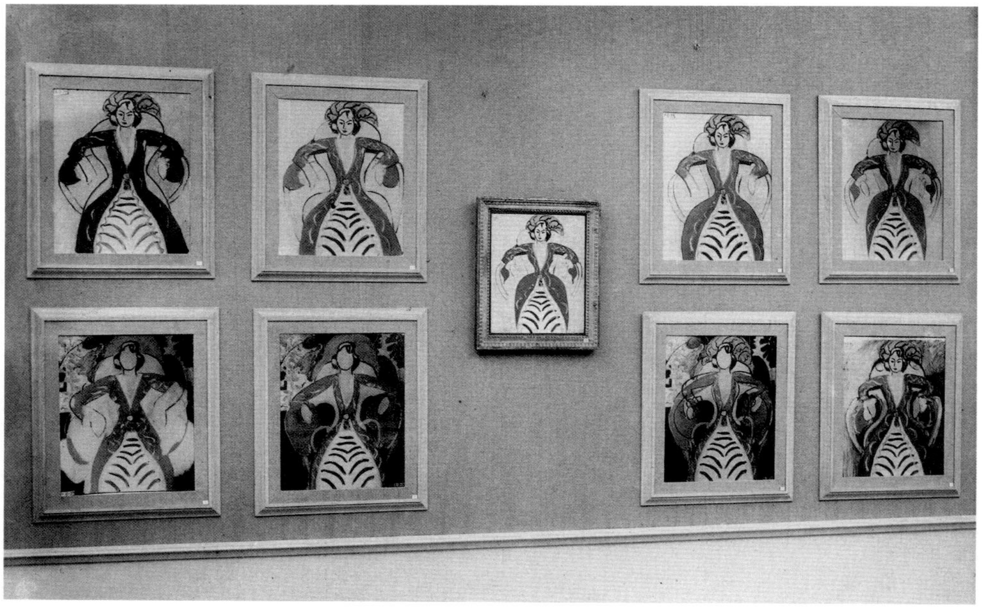

Fig. 10. Marc Vaux. Installation view of *La France* accompanied by photographed states, Galerie Maeght, Paris, December 1945. Archives Matisse, Paris

> *to specifically indicate the unique character of this exhibition. The paintings were just on extended view. The only interest of this exhibition is its didactic character. . . . The only [point] that should be mentioned is the progressive development of the works through their various respective states toward definitive conclusions and precise signs.*[31]

Maeght's response is not preserved, but Matisse followed with another telegram: "It is indispensable to add an *extra notice* to the catalogue clearly indicating the didactic character of this exhibition. Even use my own words about this. Following my personal logic, I continue from one state to another toward conclusive and definitive results."[32]

Matisse was aware that it had been a bold decision to display the photographs, although some of them had already been reproduced. Many artists hid their use of photography as a tool in the painting process out of concern that they would be criticized.[33] Matisse, however, embraced the opportunity to put his process on display and dispel the notion that he was a facile painter who worked spontaneously. Since he was unable to travel to Paris, Delectorskaya arranged to have the photographs reprinted on large sheets of Kodak-Pathé paper.[34] In the case of *La France* (1939; Hiroshima Museum of Art), the painting was actually smaller than the accompanying photographs (fig. 10).

Despite the particularly cold weather and postwar dearth of electricity, the opening was a success and, to Maeght's delight, attracted the poet Louis Aragon, the author François Mauriac, and the artists Albert Marquet and Pablo Picasso, among others.[35] Visitors were fascinated by the display, which elicited comparisons to time-lapse photography and film. Only the most careful observers would have noticed that Matisse's development of a painting from original idea to final canvas was not a smooth progression from naturalism to simplification. In actuality, the photographic prints demonstrated that the paintings were the result of a long, complex process.

By agreeing to present them, the artist tacitly acknowledged that their presence added to the viewer's understanding and appreciation of his work. During the years that followed, Matisse would continue to include a selection of the photographs alongside the final paintings in his exhibitions.[36]

The Vence Studio

The theme of his studio interior, which had played such a key role in Matisse's pictures throughout his career, was addressed again in a series of late paintings, created during the mid-1940s. The nearly eighty-year-old artist painted numerous views from within his studio at the Villa Le Rêve in Vence (fig. 11). These are easily identified by a palm tree outside the window and by glimpses of his own works on the walls. This group of paintings has been interpreted as an experiment with color, in which Matisse "'dilute[d]' the language into a serial effect, testing various color relations on a single motif."[37] Alfred Barr was dazzled by this "great series of large interiors" and identified *Large Red Interior* from 1948 (cat. 64) as the climax and epitome of Matisse's painting from these years.[38] As Isabelle Monod-Fontaine has noted, the painting depicts doubles: two tables, two animal-skin rugs, and two additional rectangular pictures hanging on the walls.[39]

For more than forty years, Matisse used pairs, trios, and series to focus and further his craft and also to continue a dialogue with his earlier paintings. The ultimate goal of the present volume is to encourage thinking about that method. While the duplication of images in the early part of Matisse's career is not a new observation, scholars have never fully agreed upon the purpose of this practice. In the following pages, a diverse group of art historians share their thoughts concerning a variety of individual pairs, trios, and series. There is still much to learn, but it is clear that for Matisse the process of creation was not simply a means to an end but a dimension of his art as important as the finished canvas.

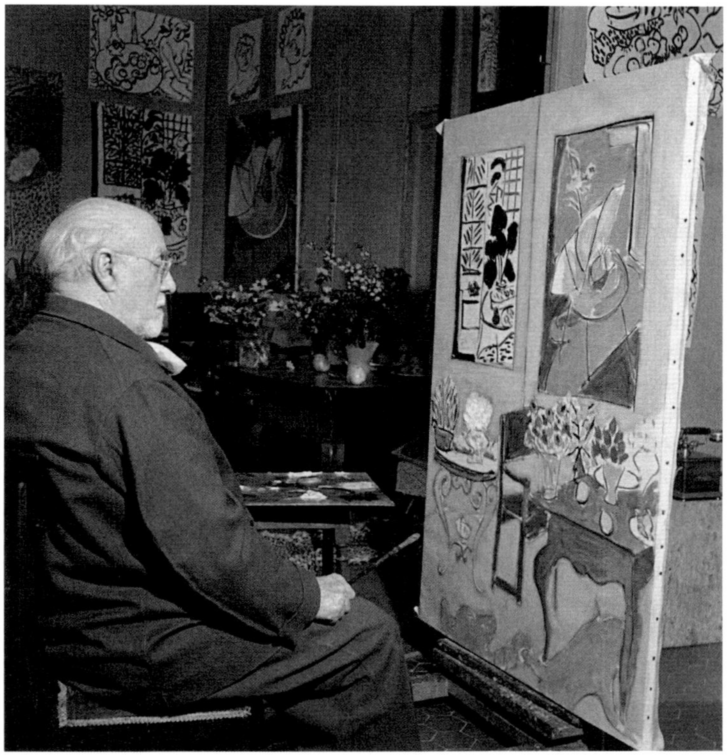

Fig 11. Matisse with *Large Red Interior* (cat. 64), Villa Le Rêve, Vence, 1948

"A PICTURE IS LIKE A GAME OF CARDS"

Claudine Grammont

During his initial attempts at Impressionist painting in the late 1890s, Matisse sometimes created pairs or two versions of a single motif, although the precise method and meaning of such works have yet to be discovered.[1] These two still lifes (cats. 1, 2) painted in Toulouse in the winter of 1898–99 are identical in format and very close in subject matter, but one is more highly worked. It is difficult to say whether they were done concurrently or one after the other, and the situation is further complicated by a similar picture, *Sideboard and Table* (fig. 12), painted at the same time and place but from a different angle and with additional objects.

Jack Flam, the first to make the connection between the two still lifes, has suggested that the work in Baltimore, *Still Life with Compote, Apples, and Oranges* (cat. 2), preceded that in Saint Louis, *Still Life with Compote and Fruit* (cat. 1).[2] Flam considered the main difference between the paintings to be that, in the Saint Louis version, Matisse sought to imitate the effect of light not by Impressionist means but rather through a harmony of pure colors, thus anticipating the advent of Fauvism.[3] To Flam, the sequence of the paintings basically marked a shift from a descriptive, pictorial mode to an abstract, decorative one. He argued that Matisse did not finish the Saint Louis version because such a use of color was beyond him at the time.[4]

The opposite sequence might just as easily be proposed. In that case, Matisse would have organized his composition in the first (Saint Louis) version in terms of simple shapes, corresponding to well-defined zones of color; then, in the second (Baltimore) version, he would have adopted a composition similar in line and color, with local, flat tones, which he gradually covered over.[5] This manner of proceeding, which is not unusual, attests to Matisse's early Neo-Impressionist experiments, undertaken after he had read Paul Signac's "D'Eugène Delacroix au néo-impressionnisme" ("From Eugène Delacroix to Neo-Impressionism," 1898), which had recently appeared in *La Revue blanche*.[6] In this treatise, Signac stressed "the principle of the separation of elements." "Light and color," he wrote, "will be clearly separated, and the painter will give dominance sometimes to the one, sometimes to the other, as he pleases."[7] This pair of Matisses follows that rule, color dominating in the Saint Louis version, light in the Baltimore version.

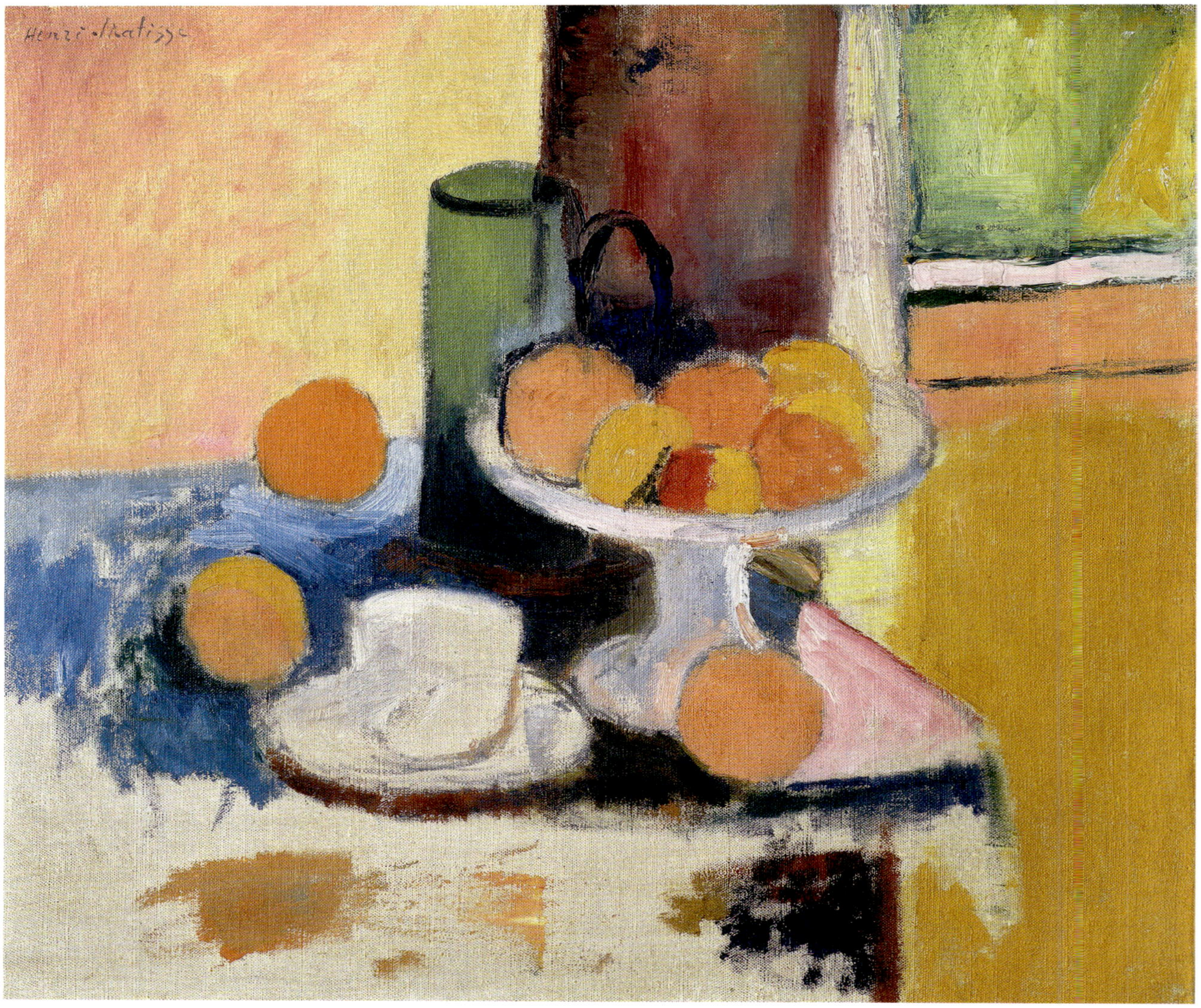

1 | *Still Life with Compote and Fruit*, 1899

Oil on canvas, 18⅛ x 21⅞ in. (46 x 55.6 cm). Mildred Lane Kemper Art Museum, Washington University in Saint Louis, Gift of Mr. and Mrs. Sydney M. Shoenberg, Jr., 1962

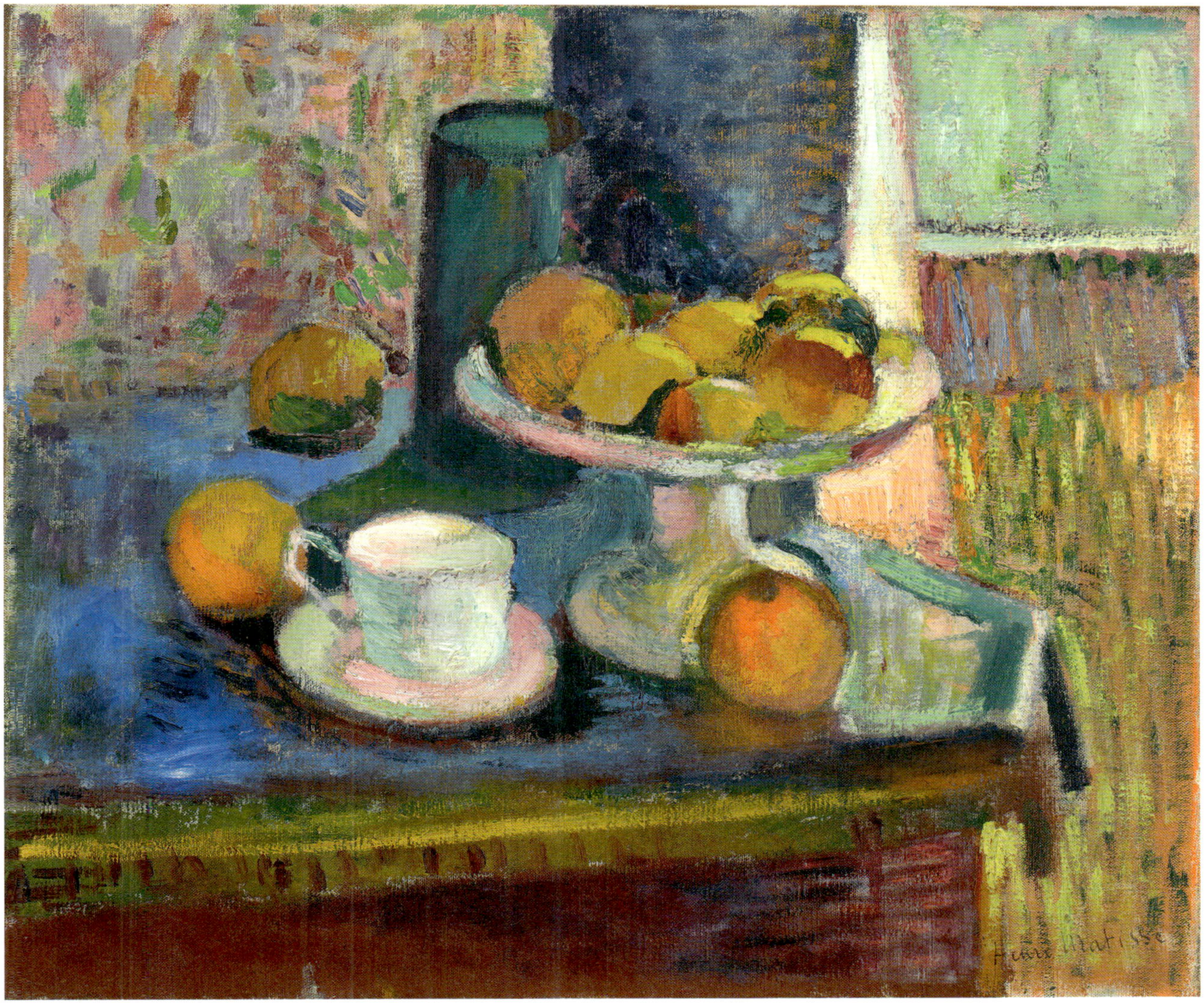

2 | *Still Life with Compote, Apples, and Oranges*, 1899

Oil on canvas, 18¼ x 21⅞ in. (46.4 x 55.6 cm). The Baltimore Museum of Art,
The Cone Collection, formed by Dr. Claribel Cone and Miss Etta Cone of Baltimore, Maryland

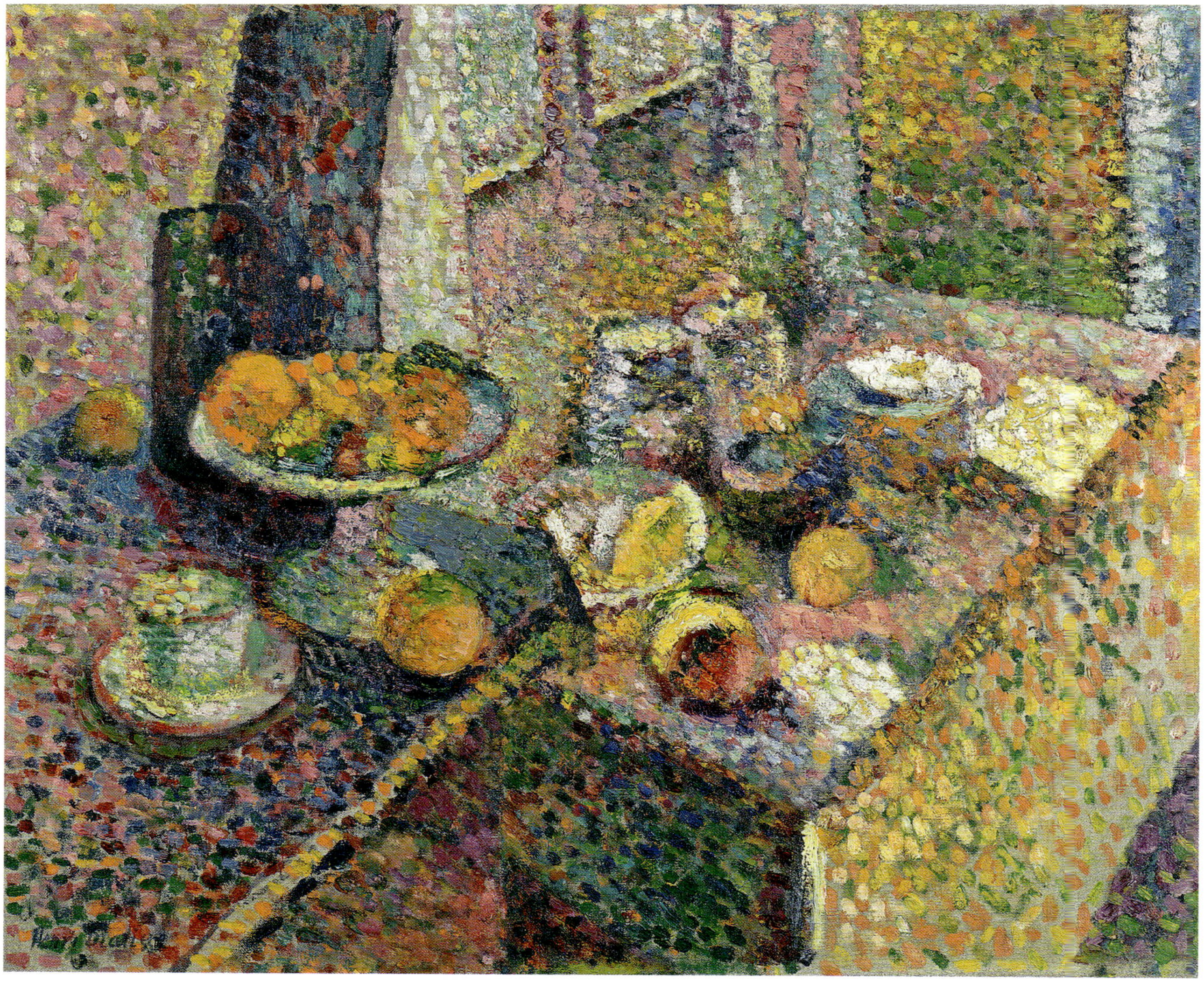

Fig. 12. *Sideboard and Table*, 1899. Oil on canvas, 26⅝ x 32½ in. (67.5 x 82.5 cm). Kunsthaus Zürich, Gift of the Holenia Trust in memory of Joseph H. Hirshhorn, with support from Rolf and Margit Weinberg

Signac also emphasized that the Neo-Impressionist painter must organize the picture plane by planning a linear scheme in correlation with the color scheme.[8] Thus, Matisse would have accomplished that originally in the Saint Louis painting and then retained the organization, albeit latently, in the Baltimore version.

Consequently, the work in Saint Louis would be a sketch for the one in Baltimore. Not only does it have the incomplete appearance characteristic of a sketch, but it also, most significantly, points to the initial idea behind the painting. Traditionally, the term "sketch," unlike "draft," does not connote an "unfinished" work. It merely refers to the first idea—the one most

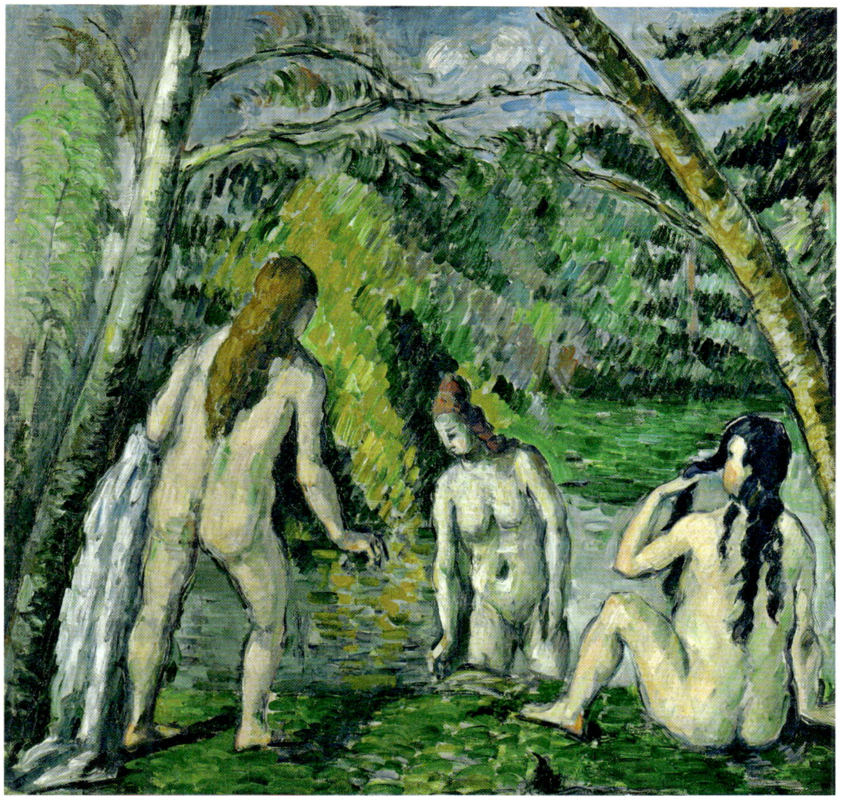

Fig. 13. Paul Cézanne. *Three Bathers*, 1879–82. Oil on canvas, 20½ x 21⅝ in. (52 x 55 cm). Petit Palais, Musée des Beaux-Arts de la Ville de Paris, Gift of Henri Matisse and his wife, 1936

spontaneous and closest to the artist's soul—that must be recaptured in the final picture.[9] In addition, at the same time as he encountered Neo-Impressionist doctrine, Matisse also discovered Cézanne (fig. 13),[10] which led him to reflect on the paradox that a picture might have an "unfinished" quality but not necessarily be incomplete. From that moment on, he granted great importance to the idea of the "sketch."

Of course, Matisse could have quite simply painted over *Still Life with Compote and Fruit*, that first stage, but, as he later explained to the American artist Clara T. MacChesney, it was imperative that the "sketch" be retained to guide him in realizing his final picture.[11] Similarly, his student Hans Purrmann quoted Matisse as once remarking, "A picture is like a game of cards: you must figure from the very beginning on what you will have at the end; everything must be worked out backwards and always be finished before it is begun."[12] Finally, in his own "Notes d'un peintre" ("Notes of a Painter," 1908), the artist stated quite clearly, "For me, all is in the conception. It is thus necessary to have a clear vision of the whole right from the beginning."[13]

Matisse seems to have regarded the duality between the sketch and the final picture as an effective way to analyze the notion of "pairs." In any event, in these two still lifes, this duality also served as a means of putting Neo-Impressionist theory into practice. But even as he did that, Matisse also put the theory to the test, since two systems—Signac's and Cézanne's—were already competing with each other, and he did not yet know whether the two were compatible.

IMPRESSIONISM IN QUESTION

Claudine Grammont

Between 1894 and 1905, Matisse often painted views from his windows at 19, quai Saint-Michel, which overlooked the Pont Saint-Michel to the west and Notre-Dame to the east. It is difficult to establish an exact order for the eight views of the bridge known from this period, especially for those done around 1900.[1] The first, a small work in gray tones from 1895, is a view from the quays.[2] *Pont Saint-Michel, Snow Effect* (cat. 3), painted from the studio, offers a broader, clearly more Impressionistic view. It is rather close to *The Sideboard* (1897; private collection), a large interior scene that the artist exhibited in early 1897, and may be contemporary with that painting.

The year 1897 is considered significant in Matisse's career, marking both his discovery of Impressionism and his initial attempts at painting in that style. The artist's first contacts with Impressionism most likely occurred during his second visit to Brittany, in the summer of 1896, when he met the English painter John Peter Russell, a close friend of Monet.[3] During the following winter, his friend Henri Evenepoel wrote that Matisse "is doing Impressionism at the moment and now swears only by Claude Monet";[4] in the spring of 1897, Matisse and Pissarro met for the first time. But it was really only in the summer of 1897 at Belle-Île-en-Mer that Matisse began to attempt Impressionist landscapes. Modifying his palette, technique, and method of work, he also began to paint in pairs.

The title of *Pont Saint-Michel, Snow Effect*, with its reference to the aesthetics of effect, reinforces the work's close connection to Impressionism.[5] Pursuing the effect of light in all its atmospheric subtleties and variations momentarily encouraged Matisse to be "only an eye," as in Cézanne's well-known characterization of Monet. While snow is undoubtedly extremely difficult to paint,[6] Matisse had already had experience in depicting whiteness in the bouquet of guelder roses at the center of *The Sideboard*. In the Pont Saint-Michel painting, however, the static quality of that interior gives way to a more active effect, captured in the movement of the barges and their plumes of smoke, in the distant factories and the silhouettes of passersby.

That quality of motion is what differentiates *Pont Saint-Michel, Snow Effect* from later paintings of the same subject. In one of these (fig. 14), the handling of the medium and surface dominates, and the colors are

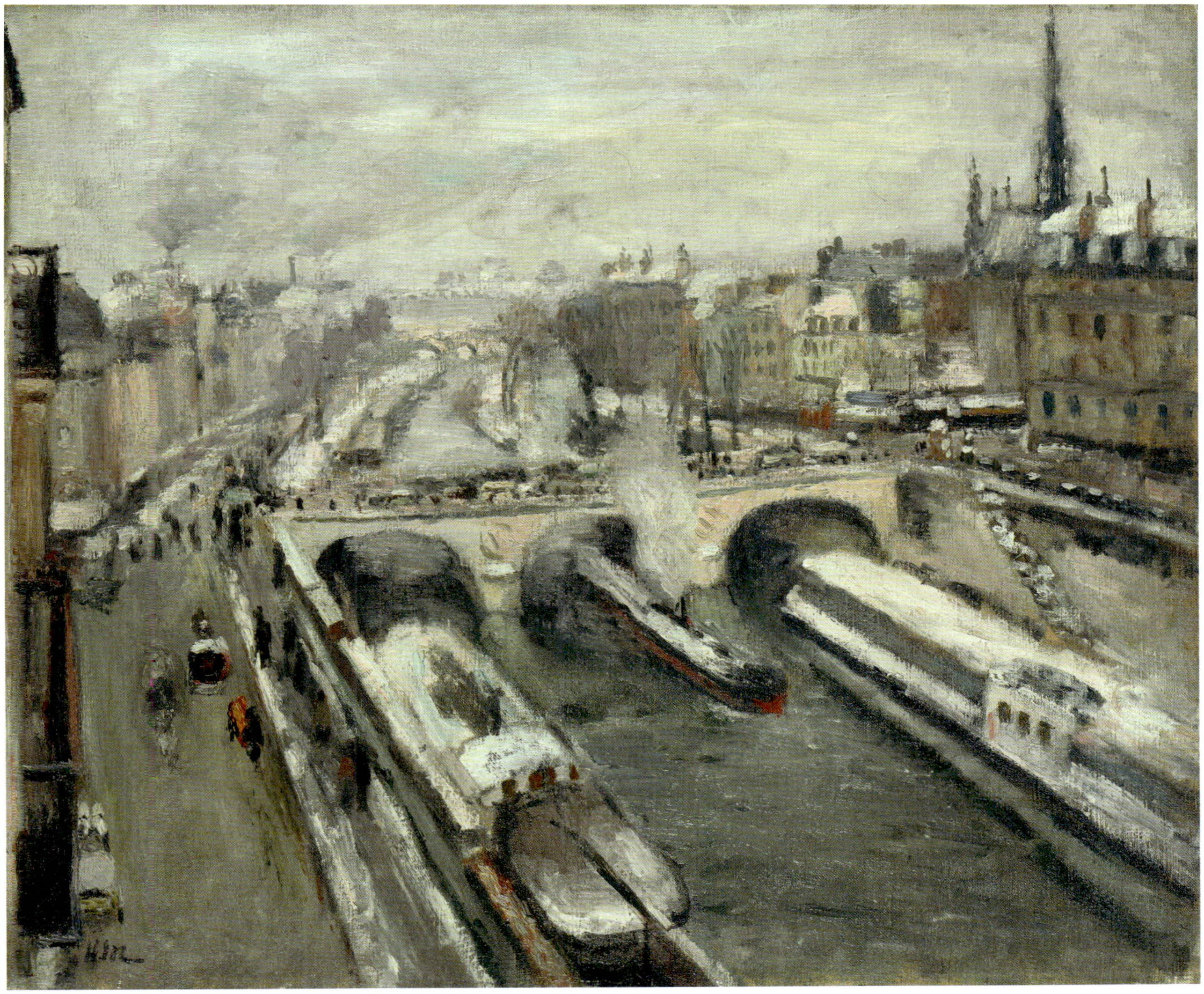

3 | *Pont Saint-Michel, Snow Effect*, ca. 1897

Oil on canvas, 23⅝ x 28¾ in. (60 x 73 cm). Fondation E. G. Bührle Collection, Zürich

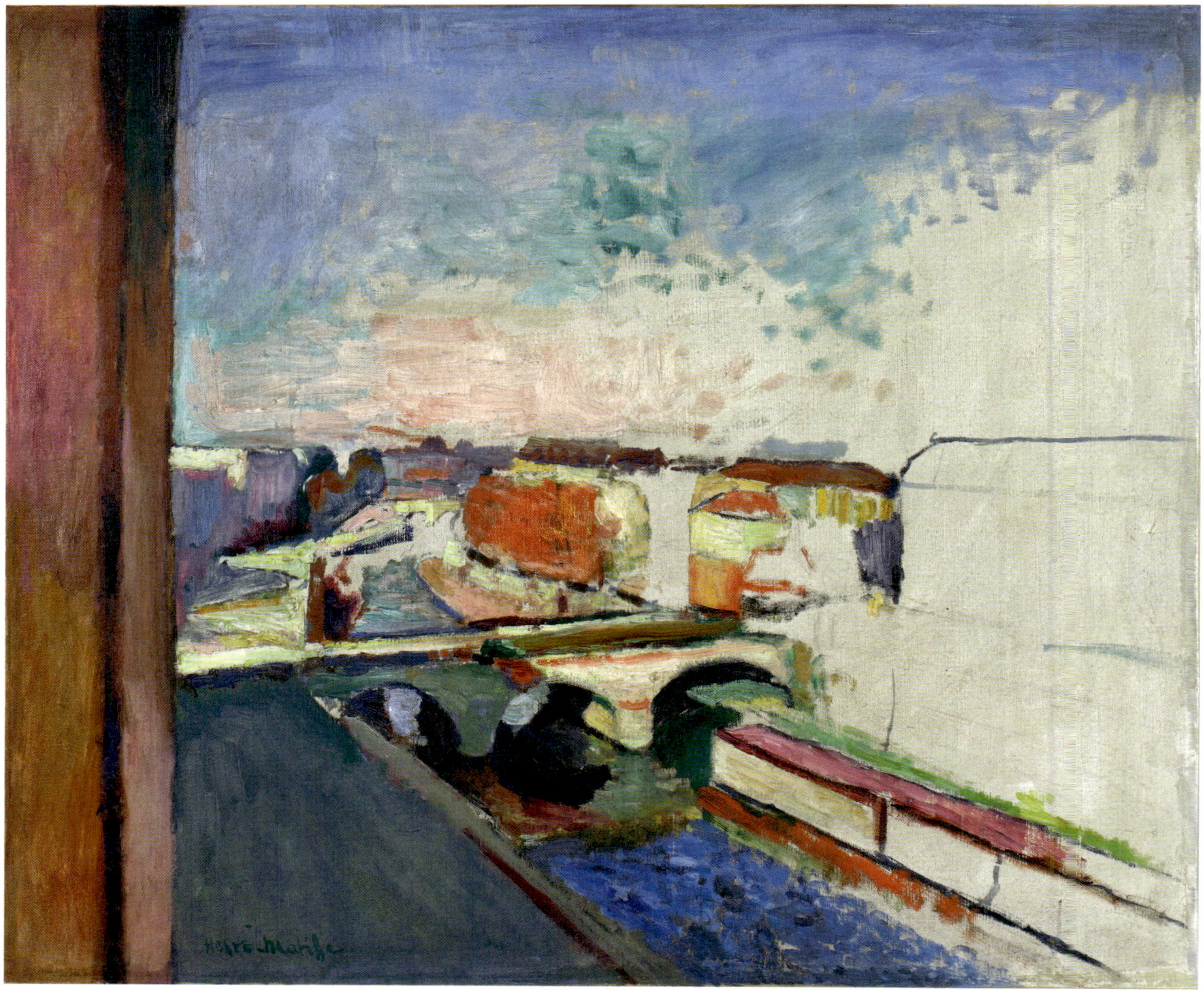

4 | *Pont Saint-Michel*, ca. 1900

Oil on canvas, 22⅞ x 28 in. (58 x 71 cm). Centre Pompidou, Musée National d'Art Moderne, Paris, Gift in lieu of estate taxes, 2001

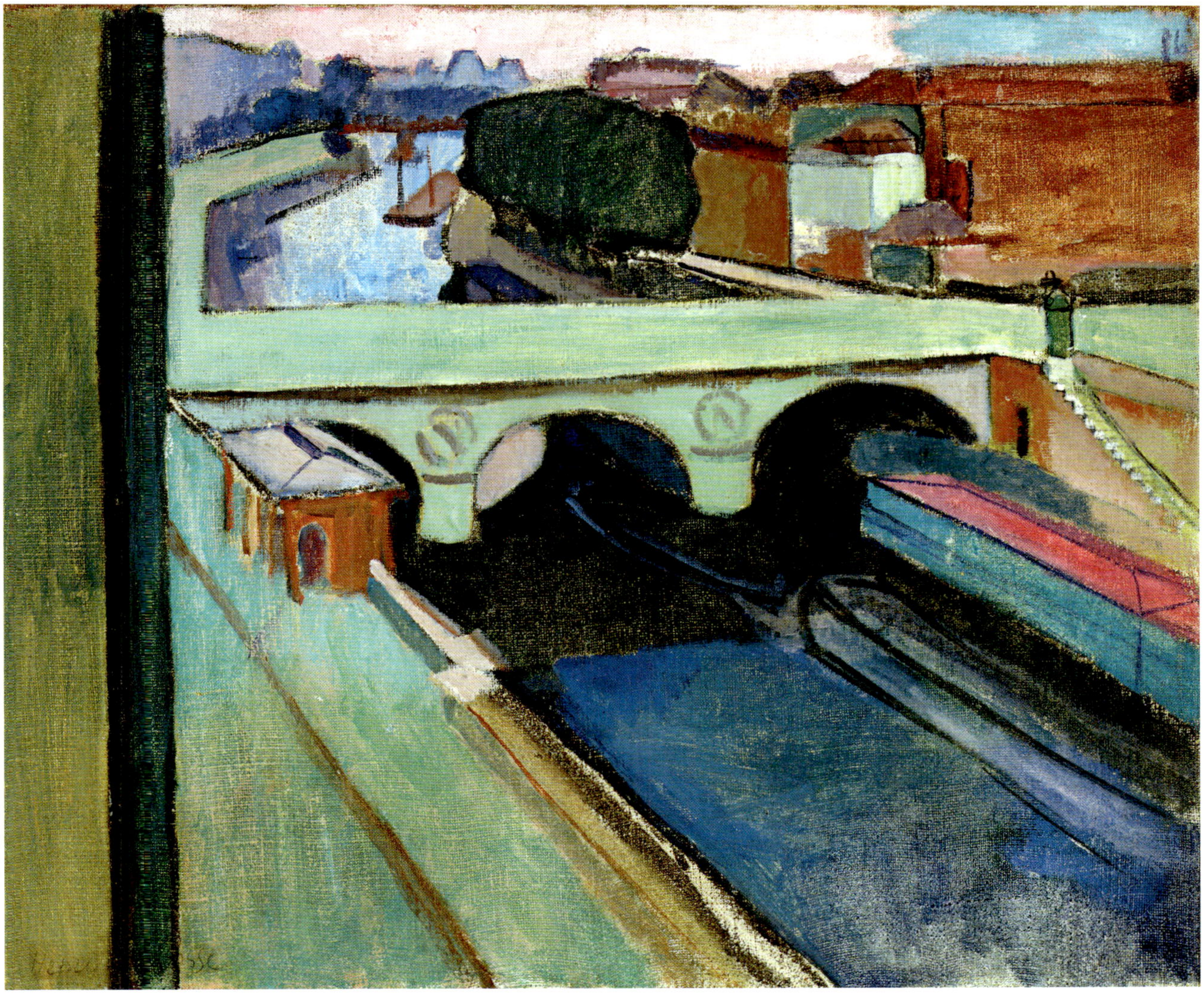

5 | *Pont Saint-Michel*, ca. 1901

Oil on canvas, 23⅝ x 28¾ in. (60 x 73 cm). Santa Barbara Museum of Art, Bequest of Wright S. Ludington

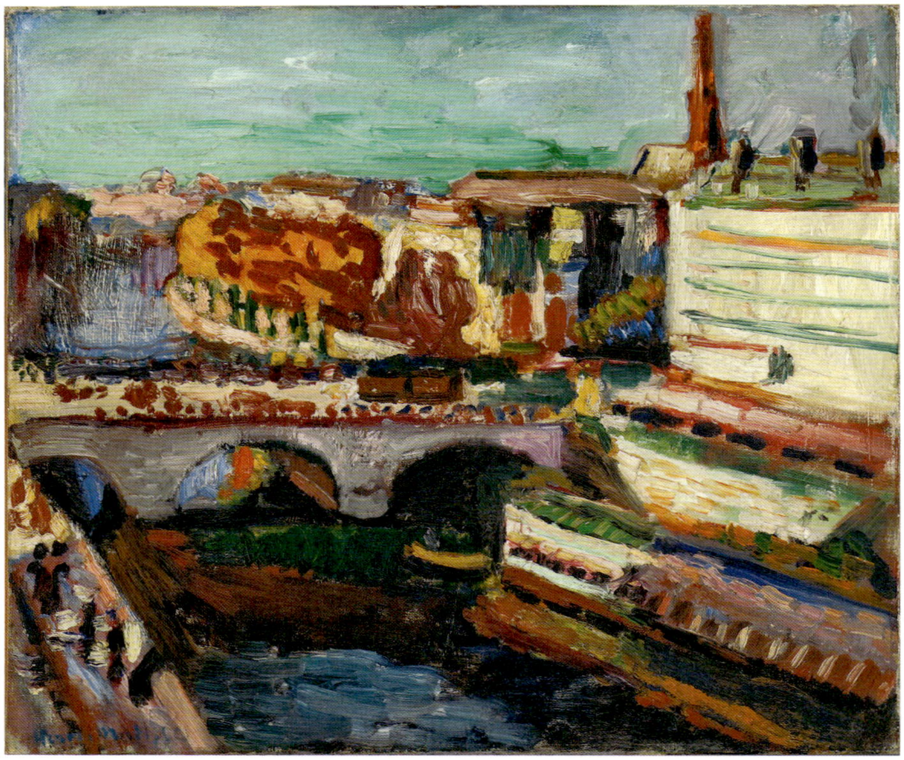

Fig. 14. *Pont Saint-Michel*, 1901–2. Oil on canvas, 18⅜ x 22 in. (46.7 x 55.9 cm). Isabelle and Scott Black Collection

unmixed. Two other versions, in Paris (cat. 4) and in Santa Barbara (cat. 5), are identical in size and form a pair, to which a third, slightly larger view can be added (fig. 15). Known to date from around 1900, and most likely to 1902–3, this homogeneous set contains more or less the same arrangement of elements, with only the horizon line raised in the Santa Barbara version. Matisse's search for stability in the construction is clearly most prominent here. The linear structure, elaborated from the plumb line established by the band along the left edge, has become the determining factor. A key element of stability for Matisse, the vertical is provided in all three versions by the edge of the open window and a section of shutter. In addition to serving as a fixed point for the various axes of the composition (primarily the bridge, quays, and laundry boats), the band orients the viewer's gaze, drawing it into the image through the shadowed plane in the foreground.[7] Already prominent in these early views is a pictorial space constructed from the arrangement of colored planes;[8] the views of Notre-Dame, painted at the same time, are equivalent but deploy along a different sight line (cat. 23, fig. 44). Hence the notion of space, which is very elastic and subjective for Matisse, expands through the complementary points of view. More metaphorically, the pair (or one should rather say the trio) reflects an enlargement of the possibilities for pictorial treatment.

Unlike Monet, who tends in his series to reproduce even the most subtle variations of atmosphere and light without varying the technical approach to the motif, Matisse tries out various modes of representation in his views of the quai Saint-Michel. In the Santa Barbara version, the diluted colors are applied

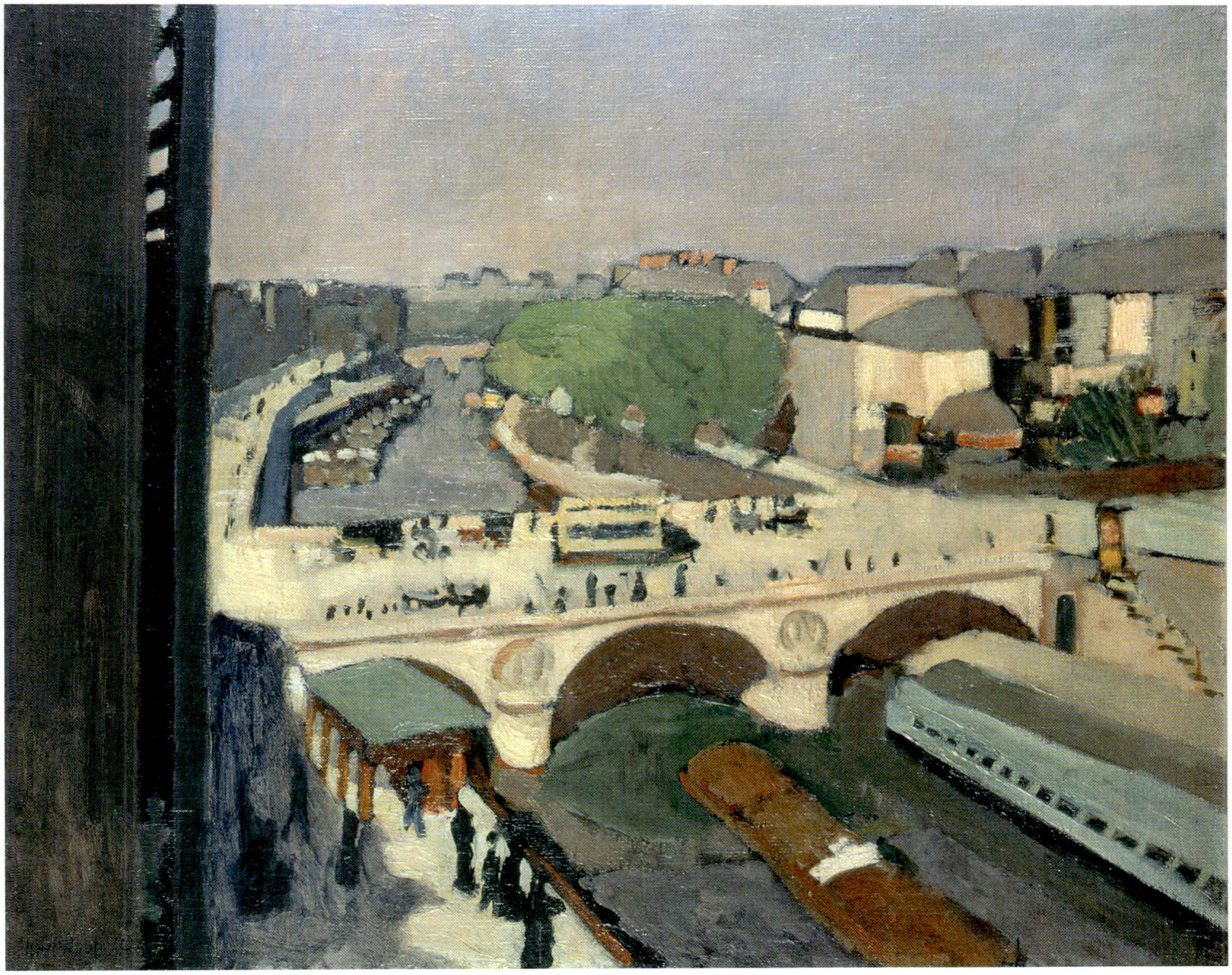

Fig. 15. *Pont Saint-Michel*, ca. 1900. Oil on canvas, 25½ x 31¾ in. (64.8 x 80.6 cm). Private collection

flat to accord with the basically linear arrangement. In the painting in Paris, which is quite Cézannesque, Matisse leaves areas uncovered at the right, a degree of incompleteness that reinforces the work's sketchy quality but does not prevent it from being extremely accomplished in its construction. The last version—also very synthetic but less radically so than that in Santa Barbara—is similar in color to views of the quays by Matisse's friend Albert Marquet. Yet Marquet's rigidly serial paintings display a repetitive sameness (except for nuances of the day and season), whereas Matisse's continually seek out difference. It is as if they are so many experiments that the artist could later study in order to better understand what distinguishes each.

BLINDED BY THE SUN

Alastair Wright

> *What [Matisse and his disciples] restore to us of the Sun is the retinal trouble, the optical trembling, the painful sensation of dazzling, the vertigo that a white wall or esplanade causes at high noon in the summer. Their aesthetic permits them to attempt to blind us.*
>
> —MAURICE DENIS

The Gulf of Saint-Tropez and *Luxe, calme, et volupté* are generally seen as the before and after of Matisse's renewed engagement with Neo-Impressionism in the autumn of 1904, following an earlier period of experimentation with the style in the late 1890s. *The Gulf of Saint-Tropez* (cat. 6), painted in late summer after Matisse had accepted Paul Signac's invitation to spend time with him in Saint-Tropez, belongs to the period when Matisse had only just begun once more to come under the sway of Pointillism. The tentative adoption of the trademark color complementaries of that technique—for example, in the blue outline given to the pale orange cloud—does little to diminish the appearance of sketchlike spontaneity that allies the painting to late Impressionism. *Luxe, calme, et volupté* (cat. 7) is very different, even though it shares the same vantage point, looking north across the beach as the sun dips below the low-slung mountains on the far side of the Gulf of Saint-Tropez. Four nudes now dominate the foreground, and a fifth can be seen beyond the artist's wife and son. But the most dramatic change is in technique. The image is composed of dabs and dashes of paint that show Matisse more fully embracing his friend Signac's Pointillism.

The two paintings, then, are very different in terms of style. Where they are similar is in what they do to the pictorial traditions with which they work. Each picks up an established style—Impressionism in the case of *The Gulf*, Neo-Impressionism for *Luxe, calme, et volupté*—but only in order to disrupt its rules. That this is true of *The Gulf* is clear when we compare it with Matisse's earlier, more submissively Impressionist effort, *Rocks at Belle-Île (Seascape)* (fig. 16). There the entire surface was treated with a consistency that allowed individual marks to be read as part of a coherent mimetic system: each area of loose brushwork stood as the signifier of a section of the artist's perceptual field, which is to say of his "impression." *The Gulf* lacks this consistent facture. Certain areas are conventionally Impressionist, including the staccato yellow strokes in the middle of the painting

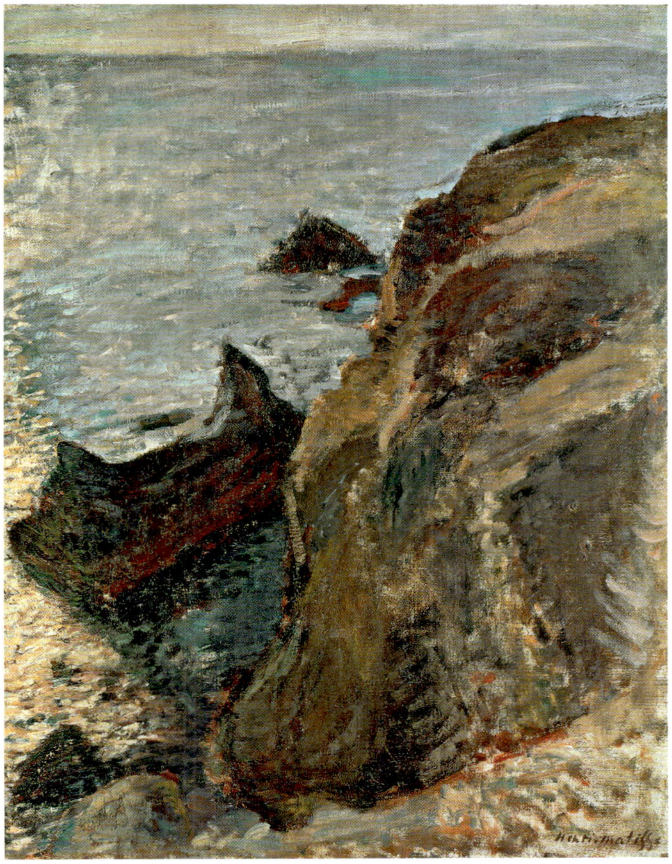

Fig. 16. *Rocks at Belle-Île (Seascape)*, 1897. Oil on canvas, 25⅝ x 21⅝ in. (65 x 55 cm). Private collection

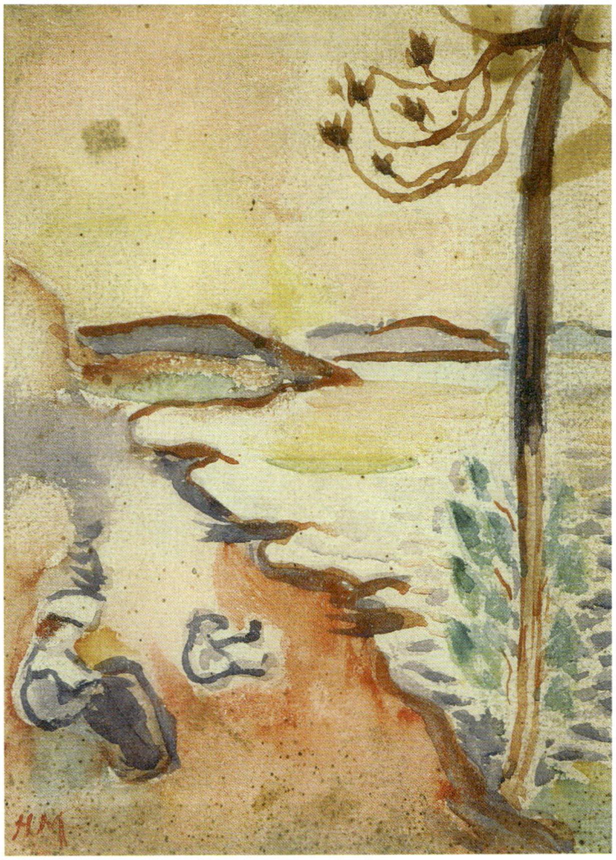

Fig. 17. *Study for "The Gulf of Saint-Tropez,"* 1904. Watercolor, 5¾ x 4⅛ in. (14.5 x 10.5 cm). Private collection, Paris

that successfully evoke the play of light across the undulating surface of the sea. Other aspects, however, undermine the painting's claim to be a record of the artist's vision. The thick contour given to the hills on the horizon, a direct contradiction of Impressionism's avoidance of the drawn line, fails to correspond to anything we imagine Matisse would have seen in nature. The visibility of pencil underdrawing, such as that found at the top of the pine tree, further distances the image from the direct, unmediated vision to which Impressionism conventionally laid claim. (The premeditated nature of the image is confirmed by the existence of a number of watercolor preparatory studies; fig. 17.) More than anything, it is the insistent presence of heavily worked pigment that counteracts the ability of the painting to be read as a direct transcription of the artist's impression. Witness the red and orange wall of color that constitutes the beach, or the dispersed strokes of pink in the upper left corner, disarticulated dabs of pigment that, in large part because of the emphatically visible areas of white ground between them, impress themselves

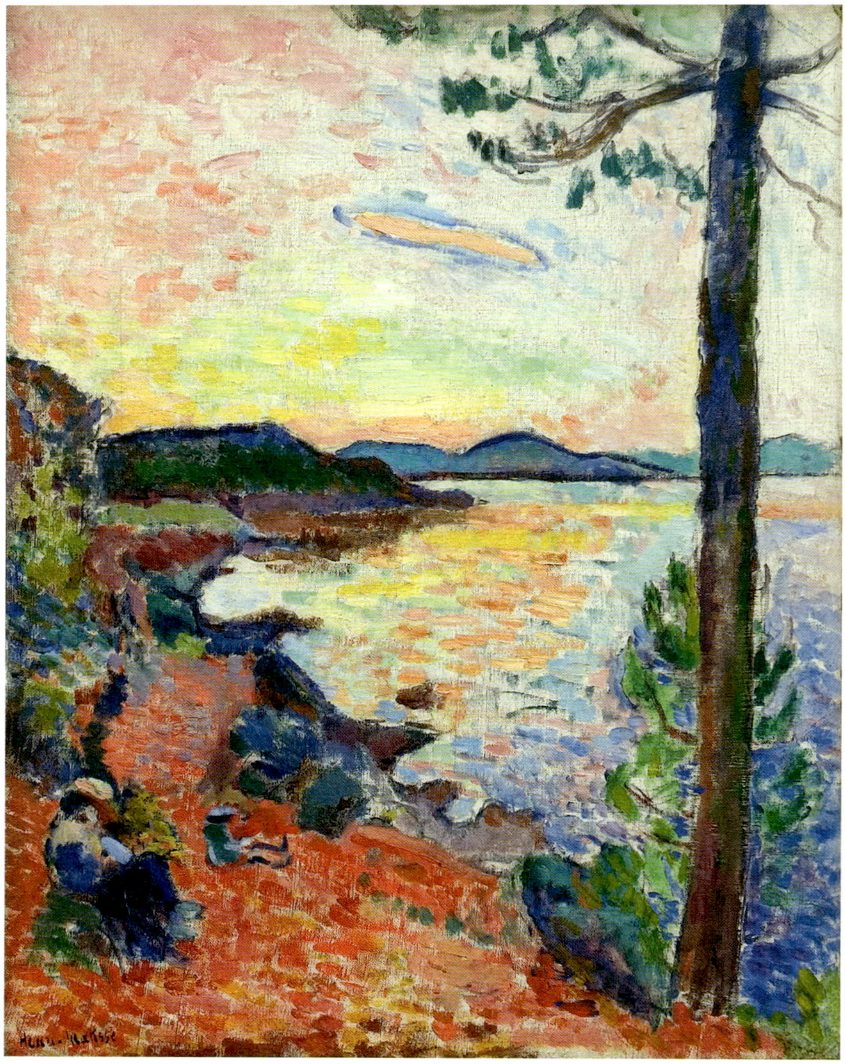

6 | *The Gulf of Saint-Tropez*, 1904

Oil on canvas, 25⅝ x 19⅞ in. (65 x 50.5 cm). Kunstsammlung Nordrhein-Westfalen, Düsseldorf

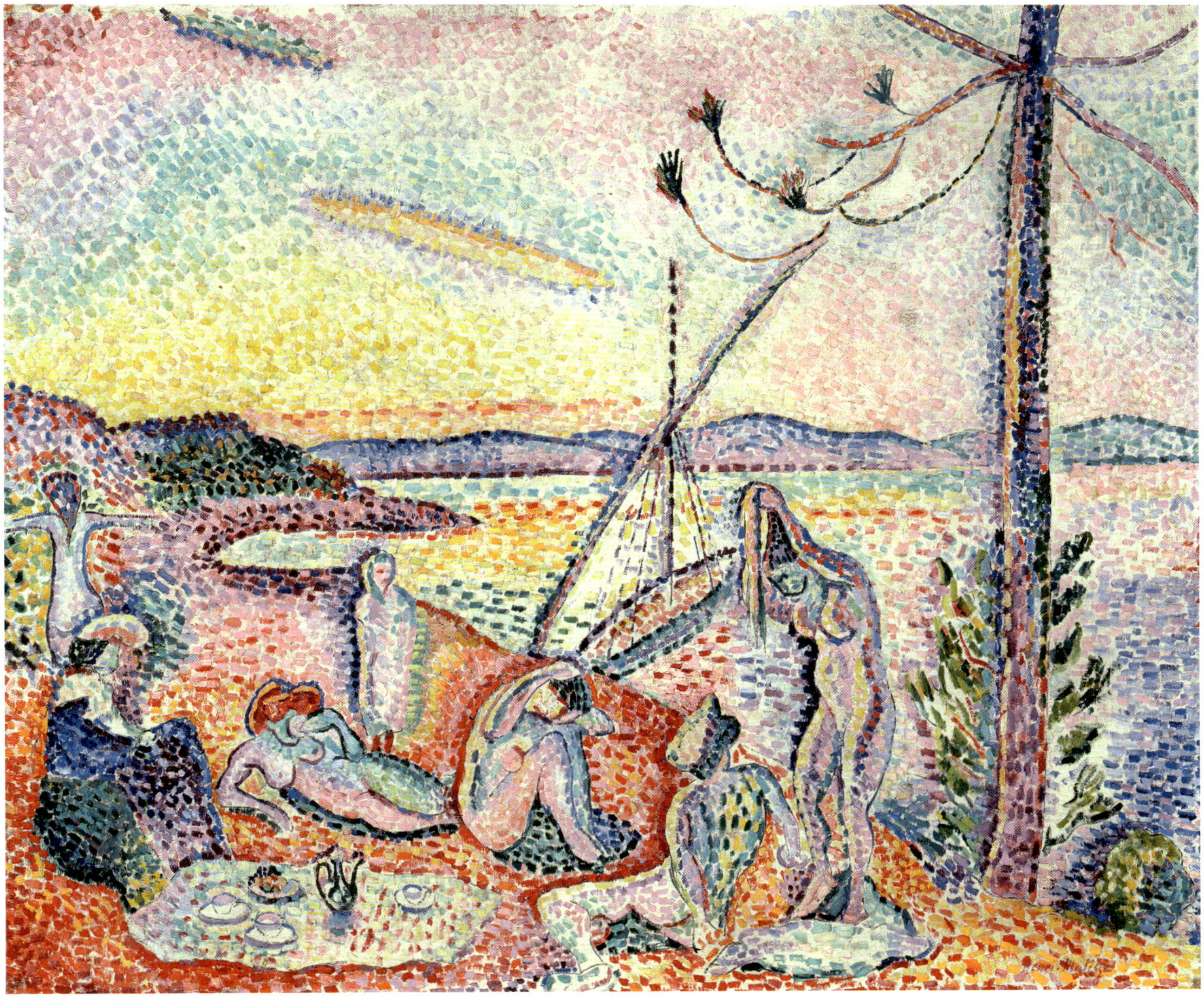

7 | *Luxe, calme, et volupté*, 1904

Oil on canvas, 38¾ x 46⅝ in. (98.5 x 118.5 cm). Centre Pompidou, Musée National d'Art Moderne, Paris, Gift in lieu of estate taxes, 1982. On extended loan to the Musée d'Orsay, Paris

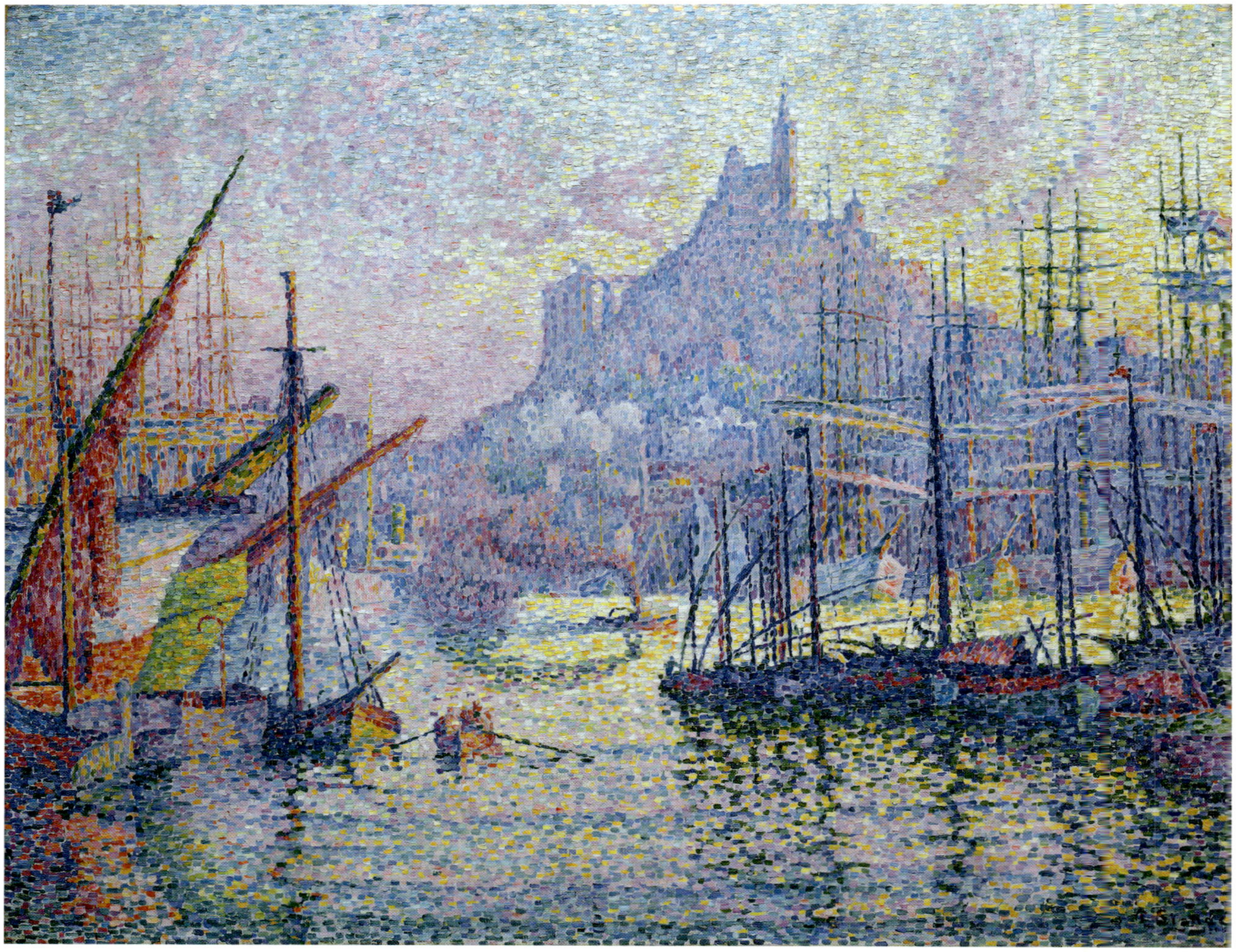

Fig. 18. Paul Signac. *Notre-Dame-de-la-Garde (La Bonne-Mère), Marseilles*, 1905–6. Oil on canvas, 35 x 45¾ in. (88.9 x 116.2 cm). The Metropolitan Museum of Art, New York, Gift of Robert Lehman, 1955

upon the viewer's eye first and foremost as brute painterly material and only secondarily as an image of the sun's afterglow.

The disruption of the painting's status as a record of the artist's vision is even more marked in *Luxe, calme, et volupté*. Although Signac seems to have been satisfied with the painting, purchasing it to install in the dining room of his villa at Saint-Tropez, *Luxe, calme, et volupté* is an exaggeration, even an undoing, of the Pointillist technique.[2] The controlled facture of Signac's contemporaneous view of the Mediterranean coast (fig. 18) cedes in Matisse's image to a heterogeneous array of irregular lines and dashes dispersed across a surface rent by areas of empty canvas. The painting coheres neither on the micro level, as each stroke fails to match its neighbor, nor on the macro, as Signac's systematic evocation of depth and atmosphere is rejected (note in particular the illegible orientation of the spar of the boat). As a consequence, individual brushstrokes register as fragments stranded on a surface that no longer obeys the overall logic of Neo-Impressionism. Pictorial signifiers that in Signac's work perform mimetic functions—for example, the use of blue and yellow complementaries to evoke light and shade—here become divorced from any stable relation to such signifieds.[3]

One way to make sense of this would be to think of it in terms of abstraction. Matisse, we might suggest, is becoming more interested in paint than in sight. Art historical accounts have often taken this view, discussing the artist's work in terms of a "liberation of color," of pigment freed from the demands of representation. But to see Matisse's work simply as a move toward formalism is to miss how he destabilizes Impressionism and Neo-Impressionism without abandoning their representational goals. *The Gulf of Saint-Tropez* and *Luxe, calme, et volupté* sit halfway between two kinds of vision: on the one hand, the eye of Impressionism or Neo-Impressionism, all eager regard, scanning the shifting surfaces of the world; on the other, the eye of modernist visuality, absorbed in the formal qualities of the painting surface itself. It is this suspension between two kinds of vision that explains the intensity of our experience as we stand before *The Gulf* and, in particular, before *Luxe, calme, et volupté*. The irradiated brightness of the latter arises not only from the concentrated color of the pigments but also from the way in which this color seems to erupt from a representational schema being torn apart from within.

As we look at these paintings, our experience is akin, I would suggest, to what the literary theorist Fredric Jameson has described as the schizophrenic experience of isolated signifiers bereft of stable sense, an experience that pushes the materiality of those signifiers more insistently and more intensely into view.[4] This aspect can be felt as privation, associated as it is with a loss of stable meaning. Many of Matisse's contemporaries experienced it that way (they would be even more disquieted when Fauvism went further in destabilizing the relation between pictorial signifiers and signifieds).[5] But it can also be celebrated, accompanied as it is by a sense of euphoric intensity—an intensity that was surely Matisse's goal, as the more perceptive critics sensed. Complaining the following year that Matisse's work was an attempt to blind the viewer, Maurice Denis intuited that the process of pushing representation to its limits, pushing it to the point at which it began to break down and the viewer's experience became one of disarticulated signifiers, allowed the artist to translate the intensity of his vision of the world into paint.

Matisse understood well that the blinding light and overpowering color of the Mediterranean shore could not be captured directly: no pigment could match their raw power. But the rupturing of painting's signifying chain and the consequent intensification of the viewer's own visual experience—an intensification that is one of Matisse's singular achievements—made his works from this period the most compelling of equivalents. Allowing the mimetic systems of his predecessors to fall to pieces, Matisse showed us representation, and even vision itself, breaking up in the face of the sun's overwhelming power.

CÉZANNE VERSUS SIGNAC

Claudine Grammont

In 1904 Matisse, invited to spend the summer with Paul Signac in Saint-Tropez, again tried his hand at Neo-Impressionism, which he had put aside in 1899. Instead of immediately doing so, however, he continued in the openly Cézannesque vein that had dominated his so-called dark period of 1900–1904.[1] Executed in Saint-Tropez in 1904, *The Terrace, Saint-Tropez* (Isabella Stewart Gardner Museum, Boston), *Place des Lices, Saint-Tropez* (Statens Museum for Kunst, Copenhagen), and *Still Life with Purro I* (cat. 8) are in fact considered the most exemplary paintings of that early style.[2] *Still Life with Purro I* is Cézannesque in both its organization and its palette, with the dominant blue-green set off by the red-and-white cloth, which reappears in a comparable Matisse still life most likely dating to the same time (fig. 19).

Still Life with Purro II (cat. 9) is a smaller, Divisionist adaptation of the same motif. The objects are positioned in exactly the same way and have similar proportions; the lighting is also the same. Although Matisse claimed that this work was painted that summer in Saint-Tropez,[3] opinions differ as to whether there might have been an interval between the two versions. In that case, the second one, like the large Divisionist painting *Luxe, calme, et volupté* (cat. 7), would have been done after the artist's return to Paris.[4]

When Matisse undertook *Luxe, calme, et volupté*, he was beginning to sense the antagonism between the systems of Cézanne and Signac, an issue that would preoccupy him until the summer of 1905.[5] His misgivings were motivated at least in part by his reading of Émile Bernard's article on Cézanne, which appeared in *L'Occident* in July 1904.[6] Furthermore, Signac's additive, dot-by-dot method ran counter to Matisse's understanding of Cézanne, particularly his belief in the need to be aware of the totality of the painting at every moment of its execution. That problem is, in fact, what Matisse was most likely seeking to test with this pair of still lifes, and the difficulty in integrating the parts into the whole is altogether palpable in them.[7]

Matisse's goal—making a Divisionist adaptation of Cézanne—was undoubtedly difficult. Although he had been singled out by critics for his "chameleon-like" abilities,[8] he would have had to possess the talents of an acrobat to succeed in such a transformative effort. The two paintings were conceived in radically different ways. In *Still Life with Purro I*, as

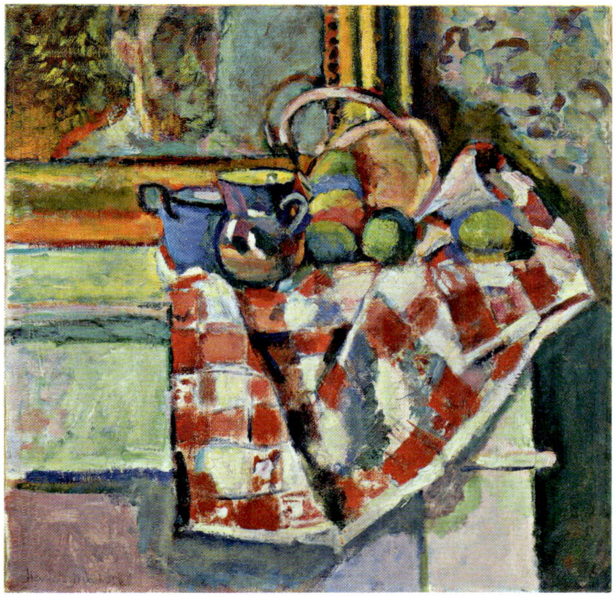

Fig. 19. *Still Life with a Checked Towel*, ca. 1903. Oil on canvas, 20⅝ x 21½ in. (52.4 x 54.6 cm). Private collection

in Cézanne (fig. 20), the space is constructed upon the basis of the objects and their relationships: each object has its own specific form and mass; the interaction between the objects and the axiality of the composition is very strong. In the second version, the pictorial logic stems largely from the effects of light and its transcription into color. The muted, cool spectrum of the first painting is converted into a brilliant range of pure colors, with red dominating. In addition, the difference in technique appreciably modifies the appearance of the objects (except for the checked napkin), along with their relationships and spatial integration. Lightweight and floating, the objects all seem diminished, especially the *purro*, the spouted glass drinking vessel at the center. To compensate, Matisse doubled the contour of the green jug at the far left, a solution comparable to the "superaddition of lines" that Henri-Edmond Cross mentioned in his criticism of *Luxe, calme, et volupté*.[9] Finding that, in Divisionism, "objects are differentiated only by the luminosity given them,"[10] Matisse needed to add this artificial contour, which unfortunately breaks up the continuous mosaic of colors.

When *Luxe, calme, et volupté* was displayed at the Salon des Indépendants in 1905, its indebtedness to both Cézanne and Signac was regarded not as an opposition but as a synthesis. Charles Morice asked, "Has not Matisse been delegated by the pure Cézannians to the Pointillists, to test their practice in order to provide a lesson to them both? In the Pointillists' efforts, less negligible than ever . . . do we not nonetheless find a few analogies with Cézanne's activity?"[11] *Still Life with Purro I* and *II* are the only two of Matisse's paired paintings that so radicalize the dual impact of Cézanne and Signac.

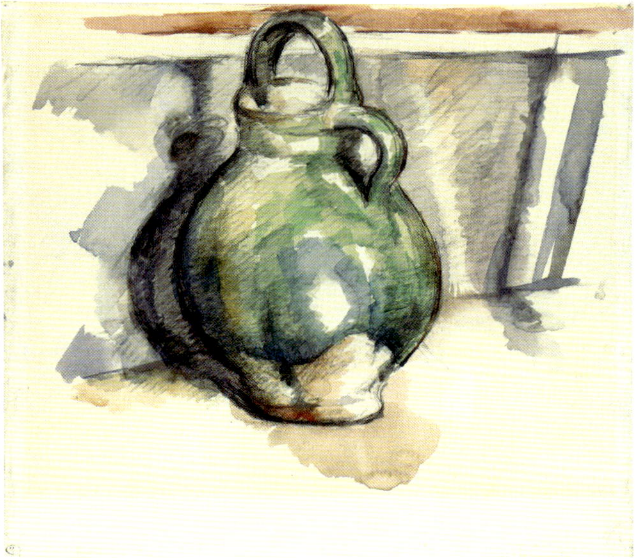

Fig. 20. Paul Cézanne. *The Green Jug*, 1885–87. Watercolor and graphite on paper, 8⅝ x 9¾ in. (22 x 24.7 cm). Département des Arts Graphiques, Musée du Louvre, Paris, Bequest of Count Isaac de Camondo, 1911

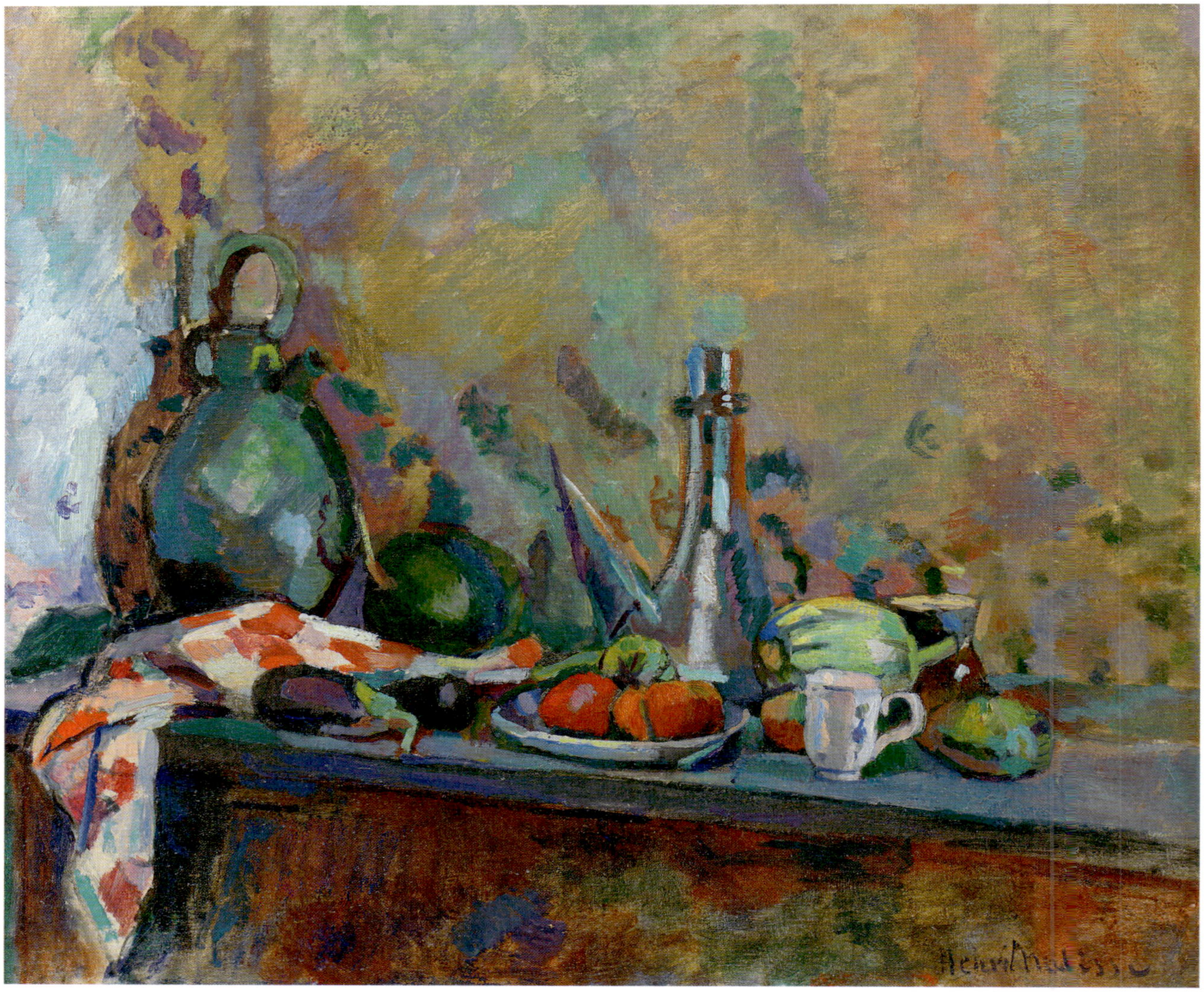

8 | *Still Life with Purro I*, 1904

Oil on canvas, 23¼ x 28½ in. (59 x 72.4 cm). The Phillips Family Collection

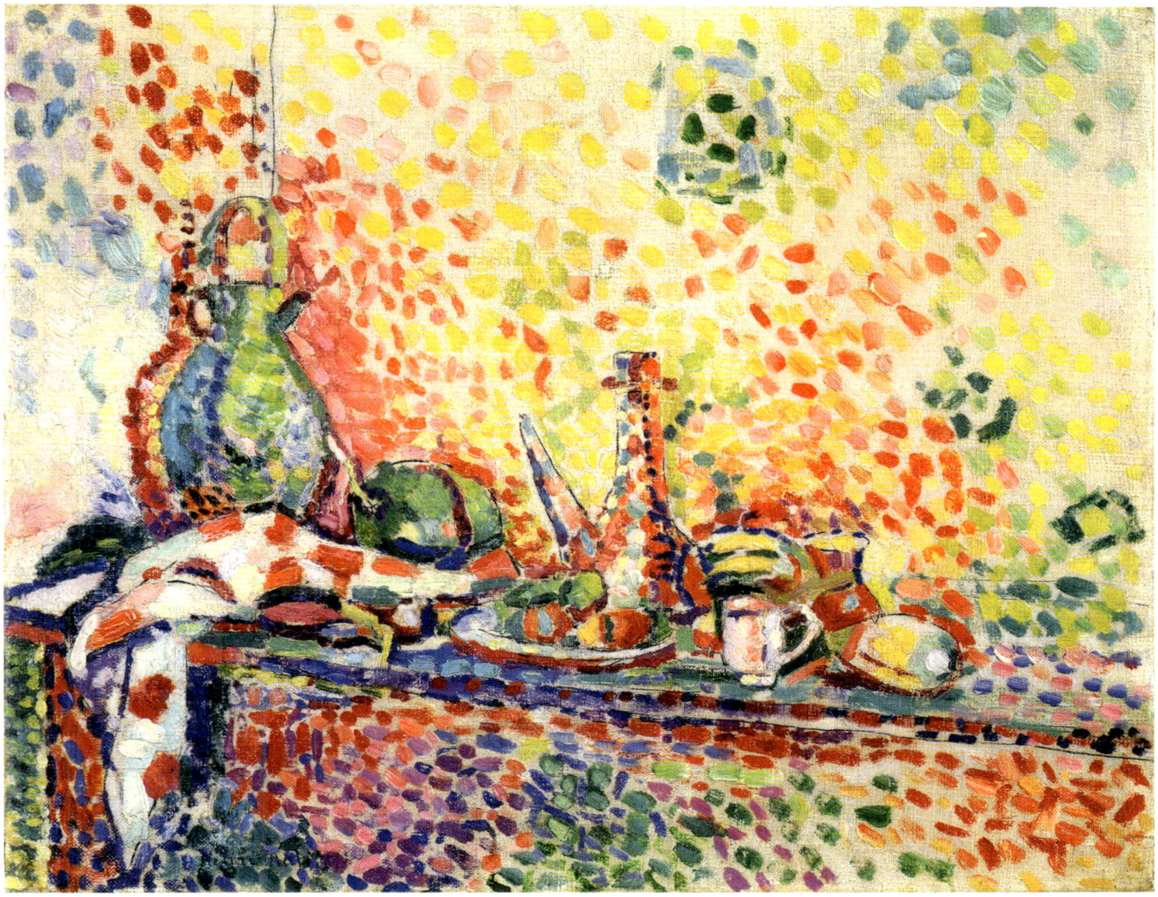

9 | *Still Life with Purro II*, 1904–5

Oil on canvas, 11 x 14 in. (27.9 x 35.6 cm). Private collection

AN EXPERIMENT IN DEFORMATION

Rebecca Rabinow and Isabelle Duvernois

In the middle of the first decade of the twentieth century, a small but growing group of critics and collectors recognized Matisse as "one of the most robustly gifted of today's painters."[1] He was especially commended for challenging preconceived notions of what painting should be. "[Matisse] could have obtained easy bravos: he prefers to drive himself to undertake passionate experiments," wrote the critic Louis Vauxcelles.[2] The paintings *Young Sailor I* and *II* (cats. 10, 11) are a case in point. The American collector Leo Stein distinctly remembered Matisse returning from the South of France with the two canvases. "One summer he brought back from the country a study of a young fisherman, and also a free copy of it with extreme deformations. At first he pretended that this had been made by the letter-carrier of Collioure, but finally admitted that it was an experiment of his own. It was the first thing he did with forced deformations."[3] While Matisse's supporters may have seen superior draftsmanship and color sense in *Young Sailor I*, many found the artist's burgeoning interest in "deformation," as exemplified by *Young Sailor II*, absolutely incomprehensible.

Matisse is thought to have created both versions of *Young Sailor* while at Collioure, an isolated fishing village near the Spanish border, about 17 miles (27 kilometers) southeast of his in-laws' residence in Perpignan. During the summer of 1906, the artist painted vibrantly colored landscapes and still lifes, but it was the human form that most inspired him. His wife and eleven-year-old daughter posed for him, as did a local teenager, Camille Calmon, who was the model for *Young Sailor I* and *II*.[4]

A technical examination of *Young Sailor I* supports the recollection of Matisse's elder son, Jean, that Calmon modeled for just one day.[5] Infrared reflectography reveals that Matisse used thin, repetitive pencil lines to block out the figure onto a prestretched canvas.[6] Once he began to paint, he made only minor changes: he moved the model's face slightly to the left and shortened the extension of Calmon's right arm along his thigh. Otherwise, he followed his pencil lines closely, outlining the figure's contours in black and then filling in the resulting fields with loose, multidirectional strokes of blue, green, purple, alizarin, pink, and orange. Before the work was finished, Matisse applied particularly thin paint

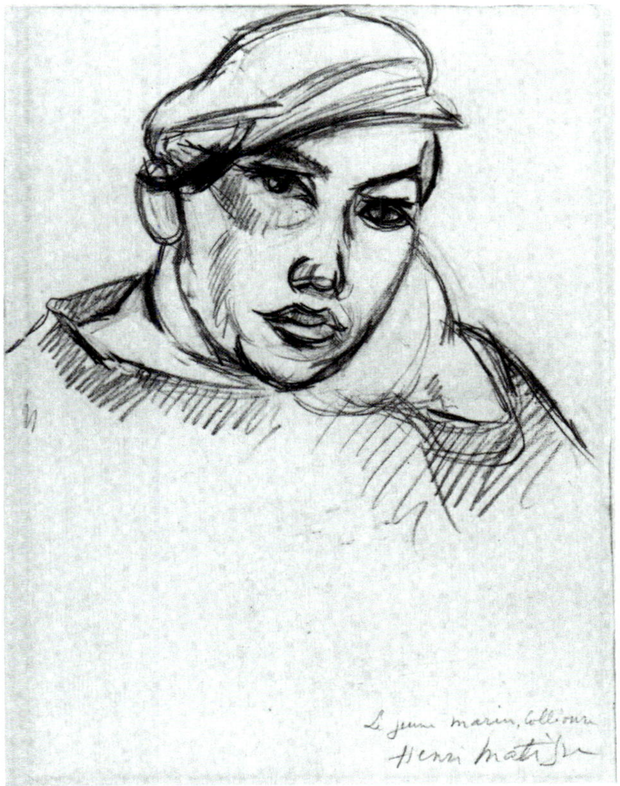

Fig. 21. *Study for "Young Sailor I,"* 1906. Graphite on paper, 10 x 7¼ in. (25.4 x 18.4 cm). Art Gallery of Ontario, Toronto, Gift of Sam and Ayala Zacks, 1970. On extended loan to the Israel Museum, Jerusalem

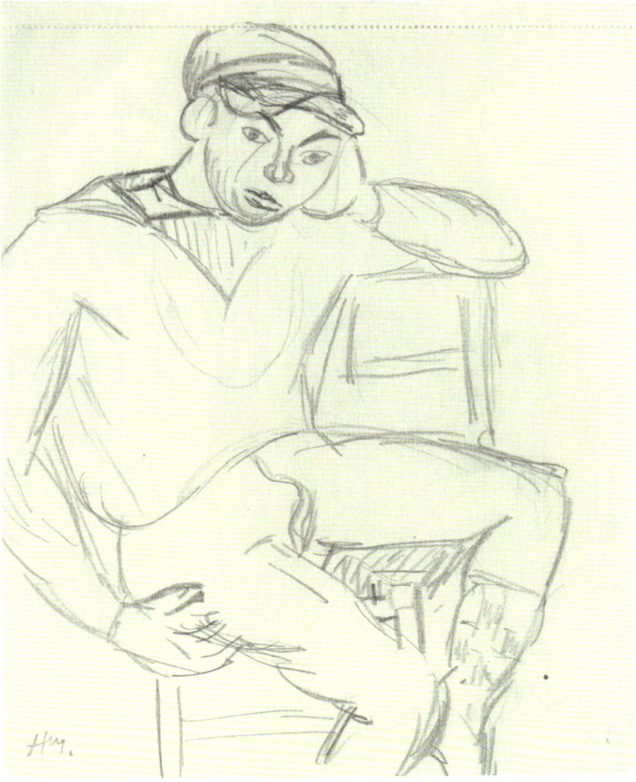

Fig. 22. *Study for "Young Sailor,"* 1906. Graphite on paper, 8¼ x 7¼ in. (21 x 18.4 cm). The Metropolitan Museum of Art, New York, Jacques and Natasha Gelman Collection, 1998

that ran down the thumb and both thighs, creating an effect that emphasizes both the painterly process and the two-dimensionality of the canvas. At some later point, he repainted areas around Calmon's left elbow, right arm, shoulder, and ear, as well as the chair seat, with pale matte pink and turquoise blue.[7]

Two known works on paper relate to the painted versions of *Young Sailor*. A drawing of Calmon's head annotated "Le jeune marin Collioure" (fig. 21) is probably a study for *Young Sailor I*. The placement of the oversized hand, the curved volumes of the face, and the standing collar of the jacket appear in both the drawing and painting. Another sketch (fig. 22), likely made after *Young Sailor I* was complete, anticipates changes that appear in the second canvas, including the exaggerated looping brim of the cap, the altered position of the hands, the striped shirt, the drape of the jacket, and the slightly shifted vantage point, which reveals more of the chair's rails and seat.[8]

Examination of *Young Sailor II* with infrared reflectography supports Leo Stein's assertion that it was a "free copy" of *Young Sailor I*. Using a canvas of the same size as the first version, Matisse drew the figure of the sailor in pencil before he began to paint.

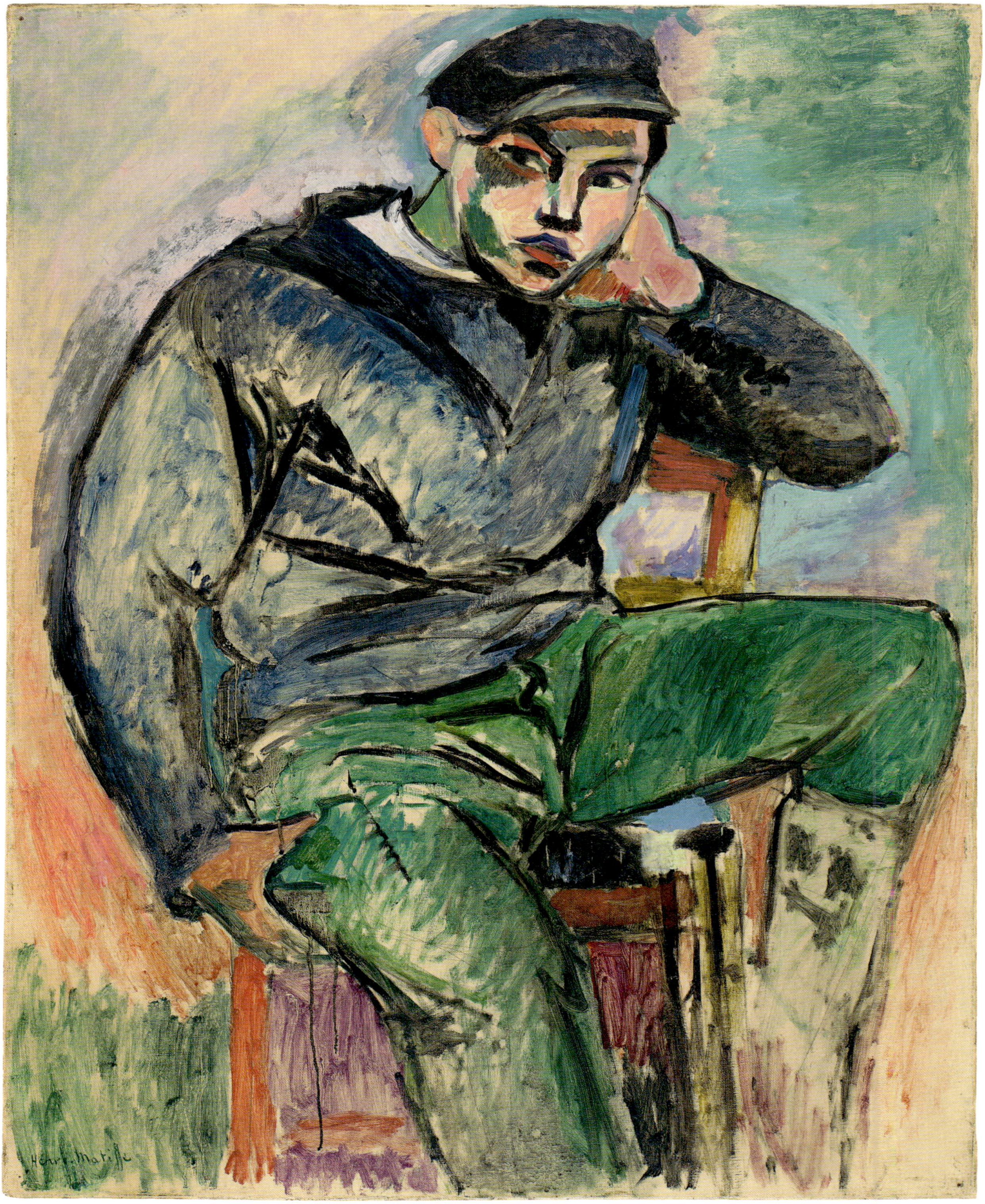

10 | *Young Sailor I*, 1906

Oil on canvas, 39¼ x 32 in. (99.7 x 81.3 cm). Collection of Sheldon H. Solow

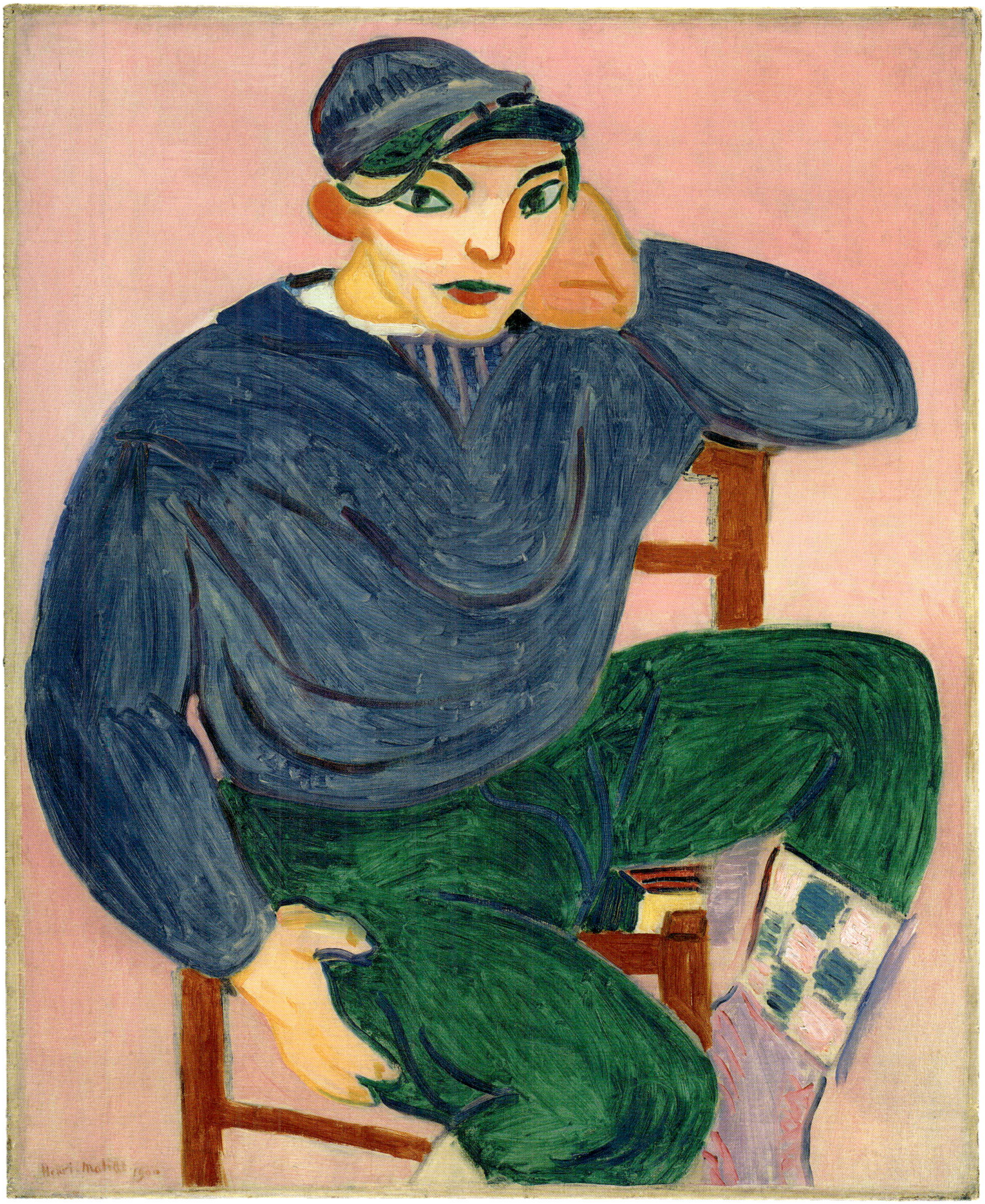

11 | *Young Sailor II*, 1906

Oil on canvas, 39⅞ x 32⅝ in. (101.3 x 82.9 cm). The Metropolitan Museum of Art, New York, Jacques and Natasha Gelman Collection, 1998

This time he used precise pencil lines that have none of the sketchiness and angularity seen in the first version. Here, all the outlines are rounded and gone over a few times as if to stabilize them. There is no sign of a grid or any registration marks that would indicate that the composition was traced.

Matisse could well have been referring to the *Young Sailor* pair when he explained his working methods in "Notes of a Painter" (1908). He often began painting a figure by recording "superficial sensations," he said, which he then reduced to the most essential lines—an approach that provided his figures with stability, even if it sometimes diminished their charm.[9] Simplification of form and the related concept of "deformation" intrigued increasing numbers of artists working in Paris during the early twentieth century. As Jack Flam has pointed out, Matisse's texts on his art bear marked similarities to the writings of the Polish-born anarchist philosopher Mécislas Golberg, an acquaintance of the artist. "In art deformation is the basis of all expression," Golberg stated. "The more the personality becomes intense, the clearer also deformation becomes."[10]

The same interests partially account for the enthusiasm with which many artists rediscovered non-Western art. In 1906 Matisse happened upon a curio shop on the rue de Rennes that sold African sculpture. "I was astonished to see how they were conceived from the point of view of sculptural language; how it was close to the Egyptians . . . ," he recalled in an interview. "Compared to European sculpture, which always took its point of departure from musculature and started from the description of the object, these Negro statues were made in terms of their material, according to invented planes and proportions."[11]

Similarly, there was an interest in naive art created by "Sunday painters" who lacked formal training. Henri Rousseau, a former toll officer, had long exhibited at the unjuried Salon des Indépendants, where his paintings were either ridiculed or ignored. However, at just the moment that Matisse's pictures started to attract critical attention, Rousseau's began to be lauded for their "childlike imagination" and "unpretentious naiveté."[12] The November 1905 issue of *L'Illustration*, in reproducing the twelve paintings that best summarized the recent Salon d'Automne, juxtaposed *The Hungry Lion Attacking an Antelope* by Rousseau (1905; Fondation Beyeler, Basel) with *Woman with a Hat* by Matisse (1905; San Francisco Museum of Modern Art). Four months later, the art dealer Ambroise Vollard purchased *The Hungry Lion*, a few weeks before buying twenty studies and paintings from Matisse. While these influences—from African art to Rousseau—are diverse, they were all part of the visual culture to which Matisse responded when he painted *Young Sailor II*.[13]

The simplification of form in *Young Sailor II* is underscored by Matisse's decision to forfeit all narrative context in favor of a monochromatic pink background. Did someone tell Matisse, who was still in Collioure, about the paintings Picasso had just brought back to Paris from Gósol, in particular *Nude with Joined Hands* (1906; The Museum of Modern Art, New York), which features a figure silhouetted against a pink background? But whereas Picasso's pink is indebted to Puvis de Chavannes, Matisse's bright bubble-gum shade—created from an organic cochineal lake pigment mixed with lead white[14]—recalls the fourteenth- and fifteenth-century Sienese and Florentine paintings he and Leo Stein so admired. That particular pink was making a comeback during the first years of the twentieth century, appearing in important exhibitions of the works of Paul Gauguin (1903, 1905) and Vincent van Gogh (1901, 1905) as well as in the paintings of Matisse's friends Maurice de Vlaminck and André Derain.[15] Indeed, in 1899, when the young

Matisse made his first purchases of contemporary art from Vollard, the painting he most wanted to acquire was a version of Van Gogh's *Arlésienne*, in which Madame Ginoux is shown against a pink background (fig. 23).[16]

Derain was a particularly significant sounding board for Matisse during this period. Sometime in the fall of 1906 or spring of 1907,[17] he saw *Young Sailor II* and shared his thoughts:

> *As for your sailor, you can see that I essentially like it, but it shocks me in terms of the relationship between the expression and the means. Your blue in the shirt, your green in the pants, and the pink in the background, the orange tone in the face strike me as different materials that do not relate to each other and are prone to merge with the objects of similar luminosity in the room, which would destroy the whole decorative impact. As a drawing it would be self-sufficient in terms of decorative pattern, and independently through the color it would be self-sufficient as a patch on the wall, but the merging of both aspects bestows upon the appearance something like an excess of good health that somewhat diminishes the impact of the whole composition.*[18]

While Matisse avidly solicited his friends' opinions of the *Young Sailor* pair, he never publicly exhibited the paintings together. The first version was purchased in late 1906 or 1907 by Leo Stein's eldest brother and sister-in-law, Michael and Sarah Stein. The more challenging *Young Sailor II* led a peripatetic existence, appearing at several major exhibitions of modern art: the 1908 Salon d'Automne in Paris,

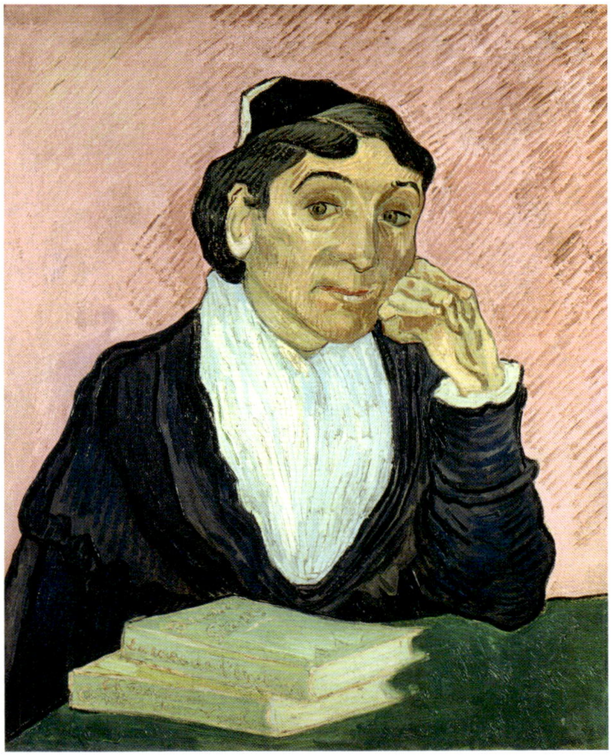

Fig. 23. Vincent van Gogh. *L'Arlésienne (Madame Ginoux)*, 1890. Oil on canvas, 25⅝ x 21¼ in. (65 x 54 cm). Museu de Arte de São Paulo Assis Chateaubriand–MASP

the 1909–10 Izdebsky Salon in various Russian cities, the 1912 "Second Post-Impressionist Exhibition" in London, and the 1913 Armory Shows in New York, Chicago, and Boston. Like the rest of Matisse's contributions, *Young Sailor II* was routinely mocked, but by this point, the public reaction was of secondary importance to him. Creating the *Young Sailor* canvases side by side had proved inspiring and educational. Matisse now fully grasped the possibilities of using canvases of identical size to explore the effects of his radically different stylistic experiments.

THE ACADEMIC TRADITION REVISED

Dorthe Aagesen and Kathrine Segel

A photograph from the summer of 1907 shows Matisse dressed in work clothes and standing next to his wife and daughter in his studio at Collioure, a small fishermen's village in the South of France (fig. 24). Behind them is the most prominent result of that summer's work, the large canvas *Le Luxe I*, reaching more than six and a half feet (2 meters) in height; the painting, resting on the floor and as yet unframed, is possibly unfinished. The photograph confirms that the first version of *Le Luxe* (cat. 12) was created in Collioure, where Matisse had spent his summers since 1905 and where he had painted the pair *Young Sailor I* and *II* (cats. 10, 11) the preceding year. On October 1, when the 1907 Salon d'Automne opened at the Grand Palais, *Le Luxe I* could be found on the wall as exhibit number 758 under the title *Le Luxe (esquisse)*.[1]

A second version of the painting exists (cat. 14), but its genesis and relationship to the first have long been uncertain.[2] After questioning the artist and his family about when and where both works were made, Alfred Barr concluded that while the first was certainly painted in Collioure in 1907, the second must have been done in the autumn or no later than the beginning of 1908 at Matisse's studio at Couvent des Oiseaux in Paris.[3]

Although Barr clarified the origins of the paintings, the relationship between them has taken longer to elicidate. In 2005 Yve-Alain Bois set out to examine this issue, asking why two almost identical versions of the painting exist and what purpose was served by such doubling.[4] While Bois's text offers one possible answer, recent technical studies have yielded new data that allow us to reconstruct Matisse's working process and add important elements to our understanding of his motives in creating this pair.[5]

Le Luxe I was likely executed without any prolonged preparation, and there were no significant changes to the composition as Matisse painted. Technical studies revealing thin layers of oil paint but only a few traces of pencil lines indicate that the artist merely outlined the motif loosely on the canvas before beginning to paint in broad, irregular brushstrokes. In certain places, he made small corrections to the figures, but these and all the paint layers are visible to the naked eye.

A large charcoal drawing, or cartoon (cat. 13), depicts the same motif and is in the same format as the painting.[6] Opinions vary as to the purpose of this drawing, but it is probable that Matisse—in a

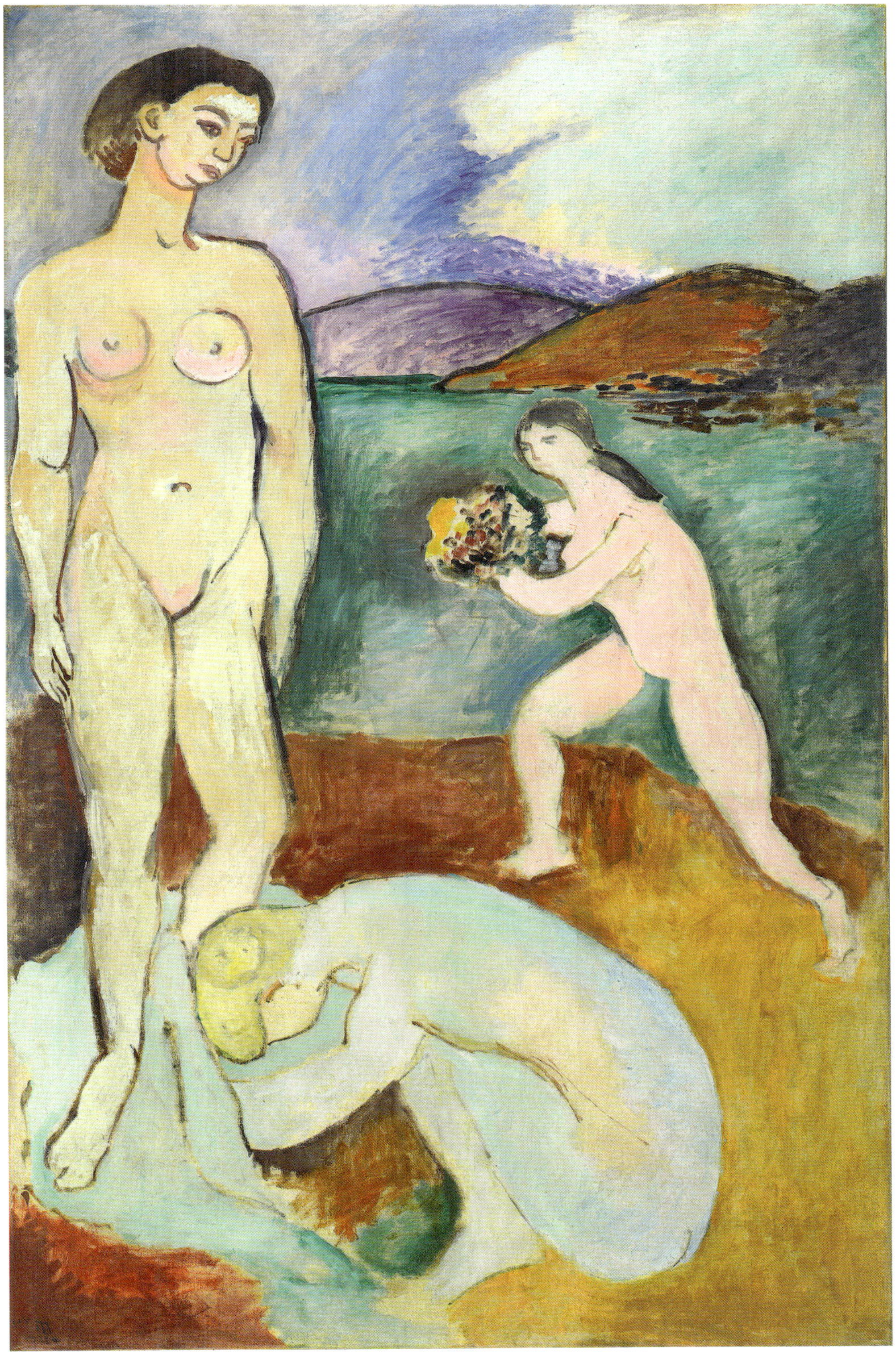

12 | *Le Luxe I*, 1907

Oil on canvas, 82⅝ x 54⅜ in. (210 x 138 cm). Centre Pompidou, Musée National d'Art Moderne, Paris, Purchase, 1945

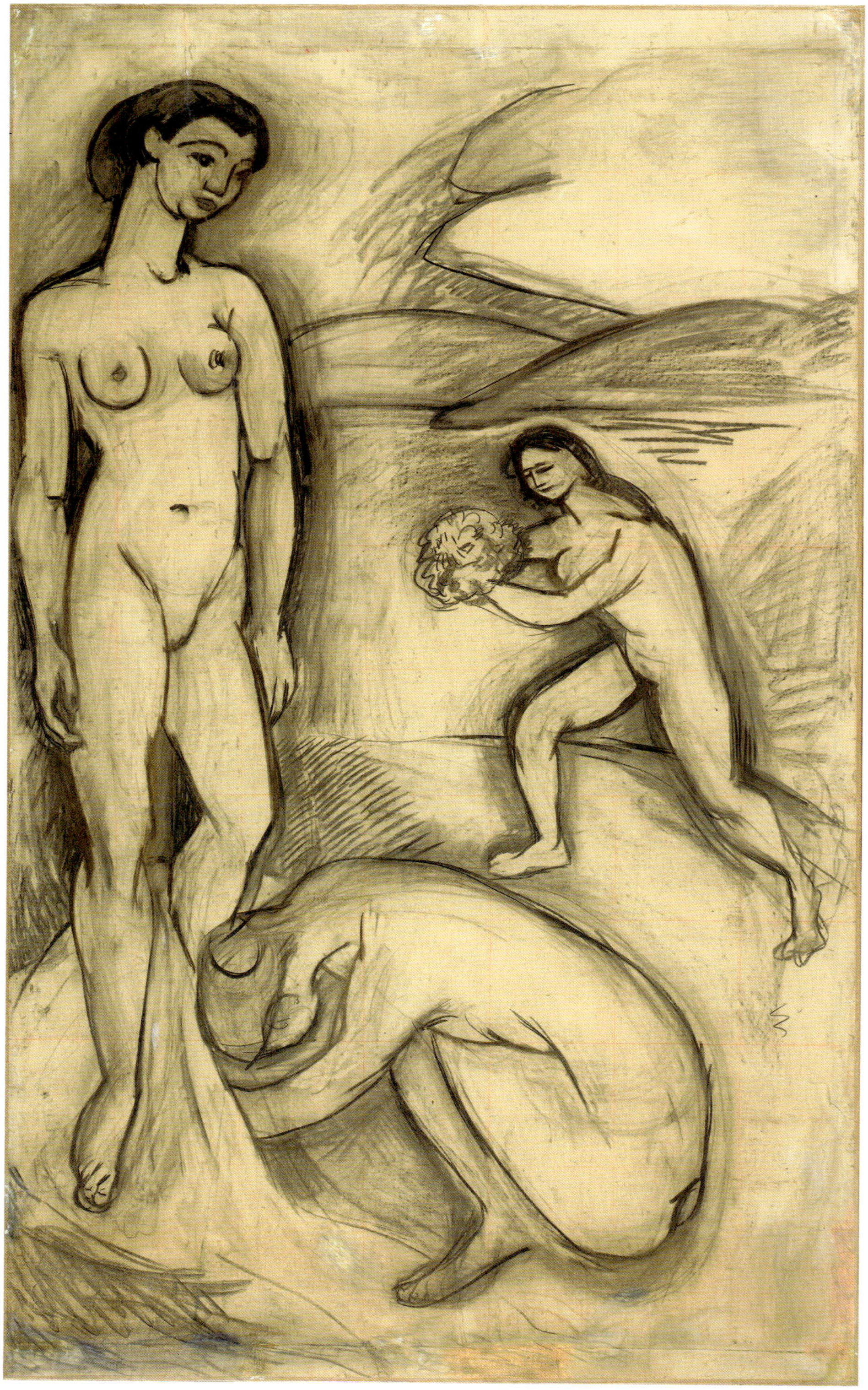

13 | *Drawing for "Le Luxe,"* 1907

Charcoal, squared for transfer, on paper mounted to canvas, 88⅝ x 54 in. (225 x 137 cm). Centre Pompidou, Musée National d'Art Moderne, Paris, Gift of Marguerite Duthuit, 1976

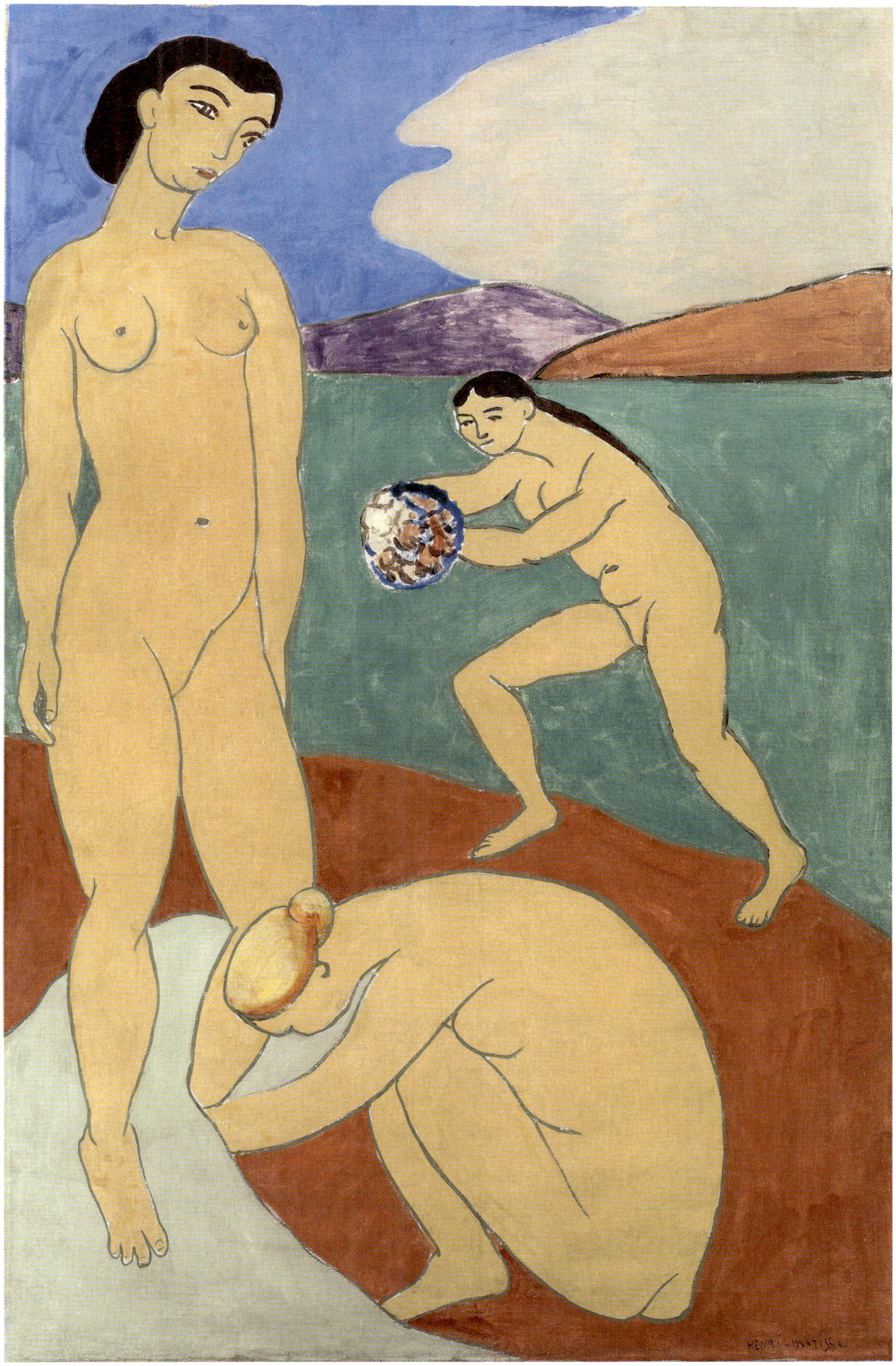

14 | *Le Luxe II*, 1907–8

Distemper on canvas, 82½ x 54⅜ in. (209.5 x 138 cm). Statens Museum for Kunst, Copenhagen, J. Rump Collection

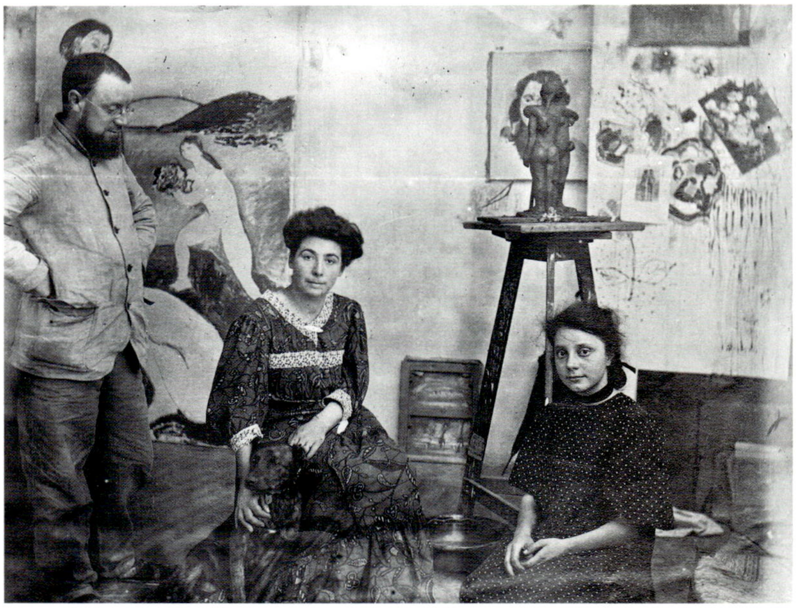

Fig. 24. Matisse's studio in Collioure with *Le Luxe I*, possibly unfinished, in the background, summer 1907. From left to right: the artist; his wife, Amélie; and his daughter, Marguerite. Archives Matisse, Paris

very unusual move—made it *after* he completed *Le Luxe I*, before the painting was submitted to the Salon d'Automne.[7] Having such a drawing on hand would facilitate his work on a second version of the motif while the first was unavailable to him.[8] At some point after the drawing was finished, it was subdivided by a grid of thin red-chalk lines measuring 7⅞ inches (20 centimeters) square.

Le Luxe II has exactly the same format as the first version and the drawing; with only a few modifications, it depicts an almost identical motif. Its greatest difference lies in the simplification of shapes into unmodulated planes of color. This may have been inspired to some degree by Matisse's trip to Italy in July–August 1907, during which he reacted enthusiastically to the Italian primitives and particularly to Giotto's frescoes in Padua. Filled with renewed faith in his attempt to develop a simplified, plane-oriented style, he set out to apply it to a large-scale canvas and also to experiment with a different medium.

Like the drawing, *Le Luxe II* bears traces of a grid. Pencil marks along all its edges (fig. 25) indicate where Matisse attached nails or needles to hold lines of string covered in red chalk, which he then snapped against the canvas to produce straight lines. The grid marked on the canvas exactly matched that on the drawing. Referring to the drawing, Matisse next outlined the motif with thin charcoal lines. Before he began to paint, however, he did make several changes: the cloud and the running figure were moved toward the left, across the central axis of the painting; the back of the crouching woman became more curved; and the cloth beneath the feet of the standing figure was extended to fill the entire left-hand corner. For this version, Matisse used a thin, water-soluble distemper,[9] which produced the same unmodulated, matte effect as found in frescoes. The chalk grid and underlying drawing were largely washed away as he painted; only fragments remain visible (fig. 26). Since distemper dries quickly and leaves no room for revisions, Matisse had to work

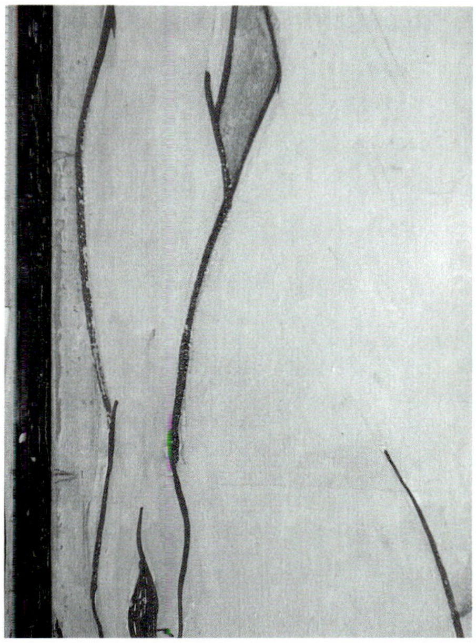

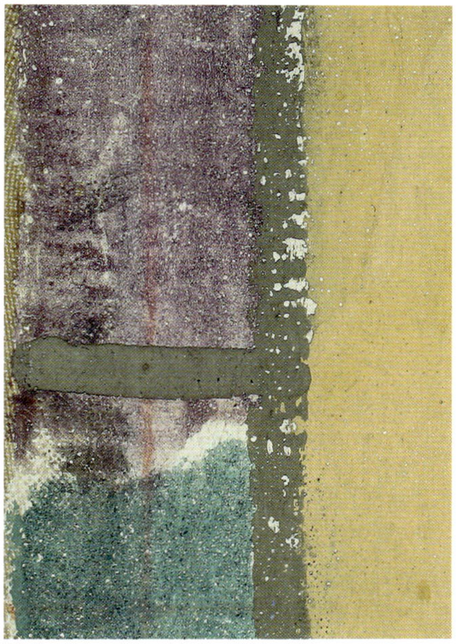

Fig. 25. Infrared photograph showing the pencil registration marks along the left edge of *Le Luxe II*

Fig. 26. Fragment of an original red-chalk vertical grid line visible through the paint layer of *Le Luxe II* (left of center)

swiftly and surely to preserve the flat, uniform color effect. Only the cloud, which was originally green (as in *Le Luxe I*), shows signs of scratching in the paint layer before he covered it in a pale pink. He finished by outlining the contours in gray.

Matisse had presumably been taught how to make tracings, grids, and cartoons during the course of his studies in the 1890s.[10] These classic methods for transferring a motif from one surface to another were central features of the educational approach at the art academies. It is certainly noteworthy that Matisse should return to such labor-intensive disciplines after his Fauvist paintings had received so much praise. Yet the crucial questions are why he employed these methods in creating *Le Luxe II*, and what purpose they served within the context of his artistic endeavor.

That the return to such procedures may indicate Matisse's ongoing dialogue with the academic tradition is reinforced by his choice of the title *Le Luxe (esquisse)* for the first version of the pair. As John Elderfield and others have pointed out, the *esquisse*, or sketch, was an established category in nineteenth-century academic practice.[11] Traditionally, it was regarded as expressing an immediate, almost spontaneous idea. Yet because the sketch was rapidly conceived, it also ran the risk of being imperfect; therefore, it had to be refined, tempered through reflection and discipline, until it took on the deeper, more ideal meaning that would transform it into the *tableau*, or final work. For the academic artist, the two states were not equal. Sketches, which revealed methods and mental processes, were to remain in the studio, while only finished paintings were worthy of being presented in public.[12]

The advent of Impressionism prompted a general reassessment of the sketch, which eventually came to be seen as an independent work in its own right. Viewed in this light, Matisse's two versions of *Le Luxe* can be regarded as a return to, and a reinterpretation of, the two basic categories established in the academic system. While *Le Luxe I* has the immediacy of a sketch, *Le Luxe II* has been infused with the control and reflection that belong to a definitive work. However, in a significant deviation from academic norms, Matisse exhibited and treated both images as equally valid takes on the same pictorial idea. The paintings simultaneously reinforce and reject the classic categories, thereby opening them up to new interpretations.[13]

Le Luxe I and *II* also deviate from standard academic practice by sharing the same format. While traditionally the sketch would be smaller than the finished work, Matisse thought it crucial that the motif be repeated in identical formats.[14] The year after he worked on *Le Luxe*, he wrote the following in his "Notes of a Painter": "An artist who wants to transpose a composition from one canvas to another larger one must conceive it anew in order to preserve its expression; he must alter its character and not just square it up onto the larger canvas."[15] It follows, then, that he considered "expression" as inextricably linked to the format of a painting and that it was important to him to preserve this aspect from one version to the next.[16]

In executing the same composition with two different approaches—spontaneous and carefully considered—Matisse must have been testing how each of them could convey this "expressive" dimension, which, to him, was the very essence of his art. In *Le Luxe II*, although he took great care to recreate his composition as accurately as possible, he nevertheless moved certain elements and adjusted their proportions, retaining the fundamental concept of the first version while condensing and honing its "expressive" qualities.

Besides *Le Luxe I*, three other paintings that Matisse exhibited at the 1907 Salon d'Automne had the designation *esquisse* in their titles.[17] Critics were not sure how to interpret the artist's intentions. Taking the term at face value, François Thiébault-Sisson expressed the hope that one day Matisse would overcome "this malady of the unfinished," which the critic saw as characteristic of his painting.[18] Michel Puy questioned the designation itself. His discussion of Matisse's painting reveals how the categories of "sketch" and "finished work" were being negotiated at the time:

> *Are these . . . canvases really sketches, as the catalogue would have it? One would prefer that Matisse give up putting into a painting forms that matter only for guidance and for the general understanding that they impart, but do not at all enter into the conception we have of a definitive work. . . .*
>
> *But if this determination to simplify, this disdain of accommodating himself to the spectator's imagination, is disturbing, one cannot, looking at these canvases together, keep from admiring their pictorial beauty. . . . [One] feels uplifted by the painterly qualities displayed in them, though they may appear less in conformity with the requirements that our most admired painters—to say nothing of Cézanne and Gauguin—have for interpreting the human form in a finished work.*[19]

Matisse never repeated the specific method involved in *Le Luxe I* and *II*, but he continued to use "*esquisse*" to distinguish between different categories of his paintings. He included it, for example, in the title of the first version of *Dance* (1909; The Museum of Modern Art, New York) when he exhibited the work, as well as in landscapes and still lifes from 1911 onward.[20] Ultimately, his use of the term in the title of *Le Luxe I* underscores the extent to which this particular pair was carried out in dialogue with traditional academic methods.

MODEL / BATHER / ODALISQUE

Kasper Monrad

At first glance, *Nude with a White Scarf* (cat. 16) appears to be a life study: the nude woman leans back, supporting her left arm on a table or console, just as a model would while posing for an artist. However, several aspects suggest that Matisse had greater ambitions for this motif. His very obvious changes indicate that he did not simply wish to depict the first pose selected for the model, but instead varied her position over the course of his work. Matisse also began another version of the motif, *Seated Nude* (cat. 15), that has almost exactly the same dimensions and shows the figure adopting an almost identical pose against a red background. While he left this work unfinished, he clearly wanted to continue working with the motif, trying out other approaches and devices, which he would not have done if the painting were only a life study.

In *Nude with a White Scarf*, which was presumably executed in the spring of 1909,[1] Matisse uses painted black lines and dark shadows to model the woman's body, giving it a distinct plasticity. Although he painted a few life studies around the same time (fig. 27),[2] this work diverges from them in that the artist's alterations transpose the figure from the milieu of a modeling session into an entirely different atmosphere. X-radiography reveals that Matisse brought her body forward, hiding the part he erased underneath the black paint at the right (fig. 28). His changes to the position of the legs are immediately visible to the naked eye. The left leg was originally more parallel with the torso; the right, first drawn up closer to the torso, is now more extended, as if the woman is about to stand. All these alterations increase the dynamism of the figure, who reclines in an otherwise restful, harmonious setting.

Matisse covered these changes with the black patch of paint and the red background color but did not hide them completely. There was, however, one radical change that is not immediately apparent. As Stephanie D'Alessandro has pointed out, Matisse at some point painted a blue background around the woman's feet; she has compellingly argued that he originally intended to depict a bathing woman with her feet in the water.[3] In D'Alessandro's view, the woman can be linked to the first draft of *Bathers by a River* (fig. 56) and may also have been intended as a pendant to another painting from the same period that shows a single bathing figure.[4]

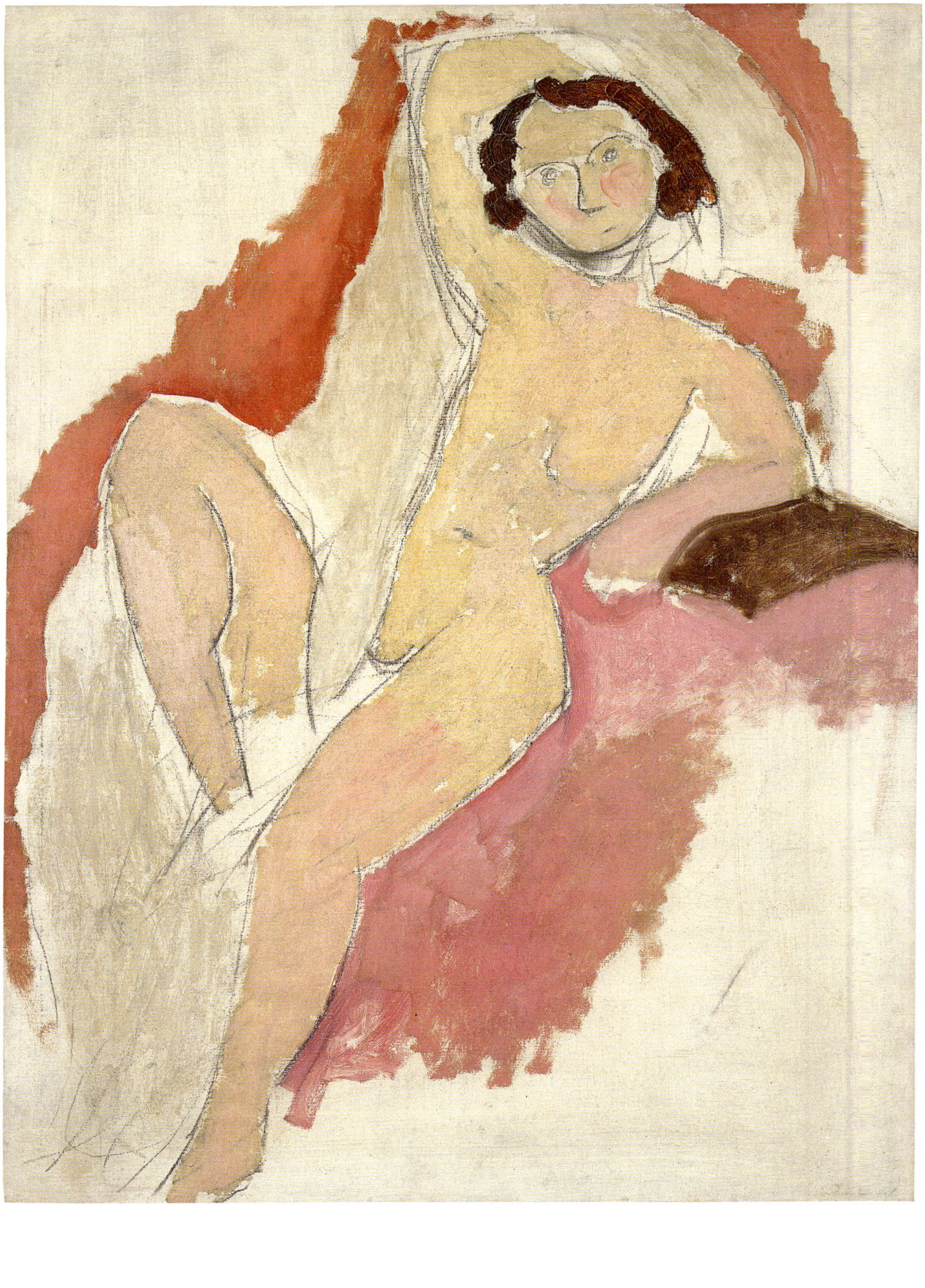

15 | *Seated Nude*, 1909

Oil on canvas, 45½ x 35 in. (115.5 x 89 cm). Pierre and Tana Matisse Foundation, New York

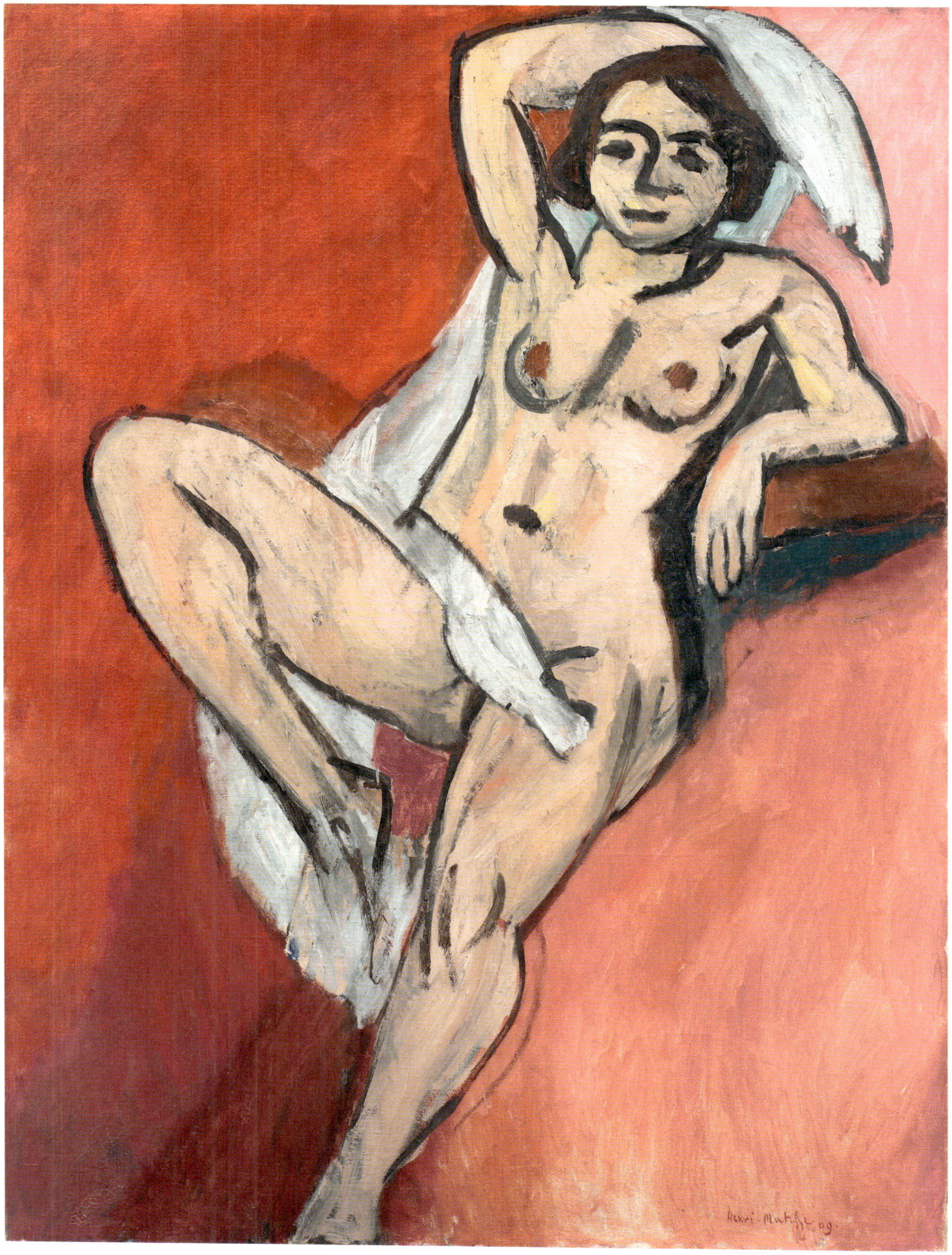

16 | *Nude with a White Scarf*, 1909

Oil on canvas, 45⅞ x 35 in. (116.5 x 89 cm). Statens Museum for Kunst, Copenhagen, J. Rump Collection

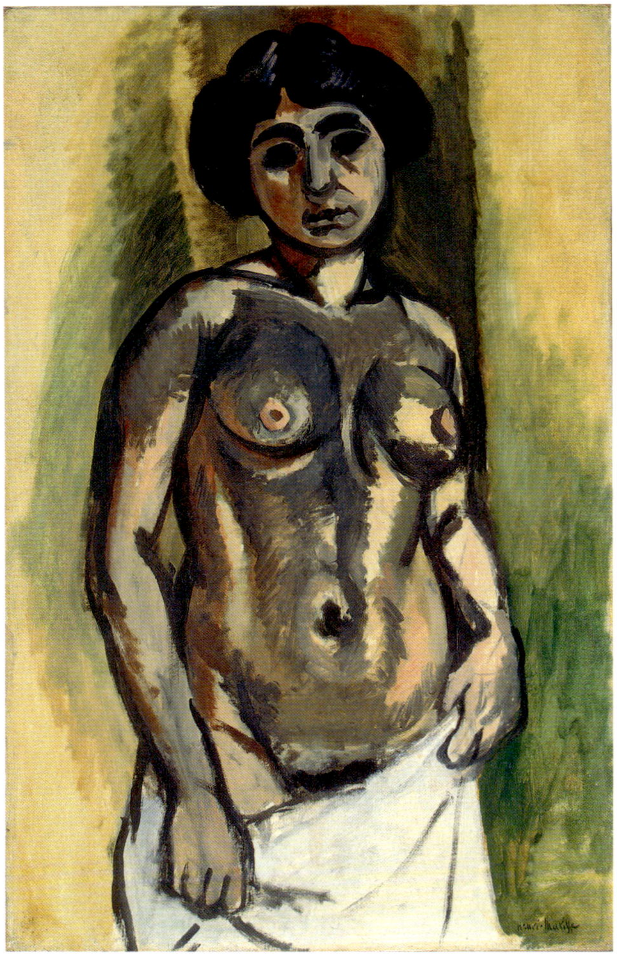

Fig. 27. *Nude, Black and Gold*, 1908. Oil on canvas, 39⅜ x 25⅝ in. (100 x 65 cm). The State Hermitage Museum, Saint Petersburg

This matter proves to be more complicated in light of Isabelle Duvernois's thorough study of *Seated Nude*, which compares the painting with the X-radiograph and two paint-layer cross sections of *Nude with a White Scarf*.[5] Duvernois's finding that the blue is actually on top of two other paint layers, one pink and the other red, indicates that blue was not the first color selected for this section of the work. The painting cannot therefore have been conceived as a bathing scene initially, but only at a later, transitional stage.[6] In either case, Matisse ultimately chose the red background that definitively removed the figure from such a context. She now occupies an indeterminate space in which she resembles a reclining odalisque more than a bather.

Duvernois's examination also raises questions concerning the sequence of the two paintings. *Seated Nude* may not be an unfinished variation of *Nude with a White Scarf*, as first thought, since Duvernois has determined that some outlines of the former work are visible in the X-radiograph of the latter. Most notably, the position of the left leg and hip, slightly bent and anchored higher up on the picture plane, was the same in both paintings before Matisse altered it in *Nude with a White Scarf*. Duvernois has therefore concluded that Matisse probably began *Seated Nude* first, then reprised the motif for the finished painting, which he then modified as he worked on it.

Nevertheless, the exact relationship between the two paintings remains uncertain. Everything suggests that in *Seated Nude* Matisse intended to experiment with a more surface-oriented, decorative version of the motif, much as he had in *Young Sailor II* and *Le Luxe II* (cats. 11, 14).[7] Perhaps he worked on the two paintings concurrently. We do not know how much progress Matisse had made on *Nude with a White Scarf* when he left *Seated Nude* unfinished. Nor do we know how he intended *Seated Nude* to turn out. We cannot, moreover, be sure that he actively decided to abandon the painting. He may have simply been interrupted in his work, put it aside, and did not subsequently have the opportunity to complete it. Whatever the case may be, the painting remained at his studio in Issy-les-Moulineaux for a long time.

Two versions of this motif appear on the wall in several paintings depicting Matisse's studio that date to 1911–12.[8] The unfinished *Seated Nude* is seen in

Fig. 28. X-radiograph of *Nude with a White Scarf* showing changes made by Matisse

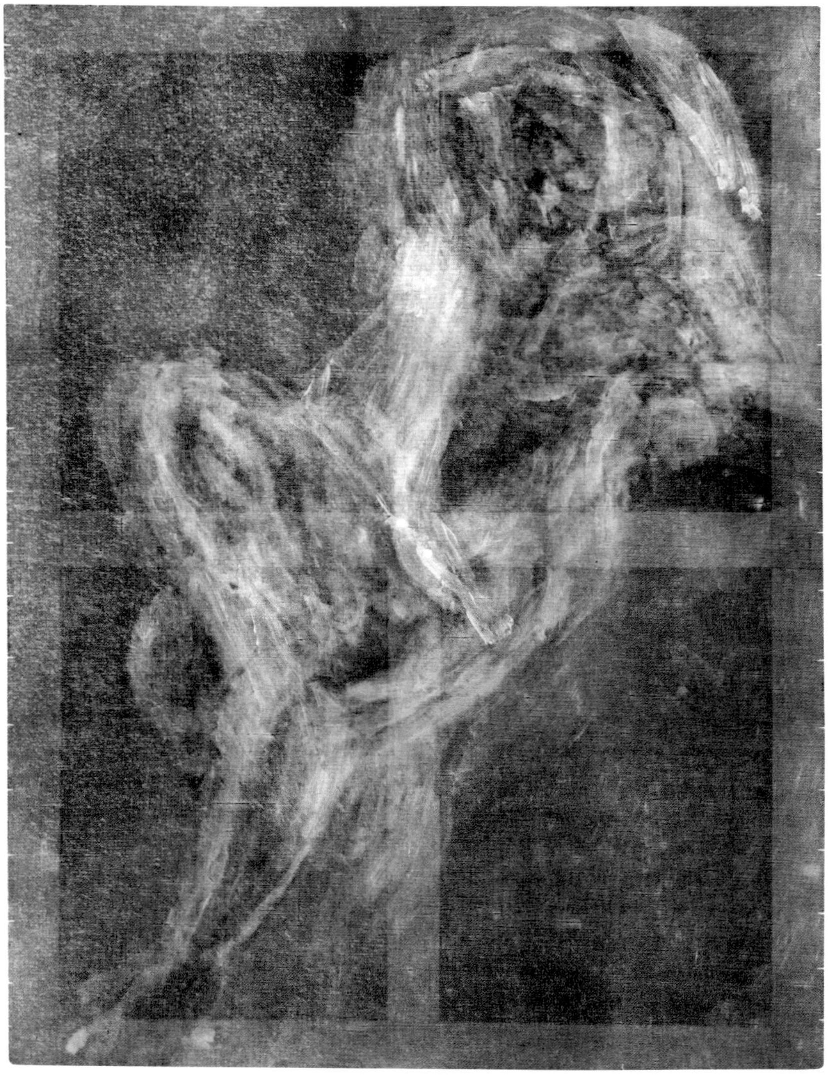

The Pink Studio (fig. 3) as well as in François Campaux's film, shot in the winter of 1945–46;[9] the completed version hangs on the wall in *The Red Studio* (fig. 4). Matisse probably kept the paintings at the Issy-les-Moulineaux studio until he departed for Nice in late 1917. In addition to the present works, a few others are featured in both paintings of the studio, *Le Luxe II* being the most prominent of these. If, indeed, the *Red Studio* and *Pink Studio* reflect the paintings and sculptures with which Matisse chose to surround himself during this period, both versions of this nude appear to have been on display, not far from each other, for some time. Matisse may have felt that he had not finished with the theme when he was interrupted in his work on *Seated Nude*. By keeping the paintings in plain view every day, he allowed himself the opportunity to continue thinking about the motif, its nature, and its potential.

INVENTING A DECORATIVE SPACE

Cécile Debray

Inspired by a major exhibition of Islamic art that he had visited in Munich in October, Matisse left for Spain on November 16, 1910, intending to see for himself the Moorish architecture of Andalusia and the Nasrid art of southern Spain.[1] Shortly before his departure, Sergei Shchukin had written him two letters, one confirming the purchase of the large panels *Dance II* and *Music* (both 1910; The State Hermitage Museum, Saint Petersburg), despite the scandal they had caused, and the other proposing a new commission:

> *Could you please now do two still lifes the same size as the Munich piece and somewhat in the same vein? Could you please set the price for each picture at 5,000 francs. . . .*
>
> *I shall have to endure a great struggle with the two large panels, and the two still lifes should help me to win greater acceptance for you. . . .*
>
> *Paintings of that sort are easy to understand. . . . I hope to receive confirmation that you are not only strong, but also charitable.*[2]

Eager to comply with his client's request, Matisse rented a temporary studio in Seville that he shared with his painter friend Francisco Iturrino, who at the same time executed a pair of works that were true duplicates of his friend's (figs. 29, 30). Matisse enjoyed painting in the company of his friends, as he did, for example, in the series of studio views he had done with Albert Marquet, Henri Manguin, and Charles Camoin in 1900–1901. Matisse envisioned for Shchukin two lighthearted, decorative, colorful paintings that recalled the floral themes in his still lifes of 1907–8, which were inspired in part by Odilon Redon.[3] To conform with the collector's request for works similar to his *Still Life with Geraniums* (fig. 31)—painted in the spring of 1910 for Hugo von Tschudi, director of Munich's Neue Pinakothek—Matisse placed a pot of geraniums at the center of both Seville compositions. He supplemented the furnishings of the bright, pink-walled studio with a few objects and fabrics he had unearthed at local antique shops, along with an assortment of peppers, pomegranates, and fruits.[4] Still quoting *Still Life with Geraniums*, he replaced its strip of toile de Jouy,[5] a central diagonal motif, with a white-and-blue nineteenth-century cloth from Las Alpujarras that was to become equally important in "his visual library."[6]

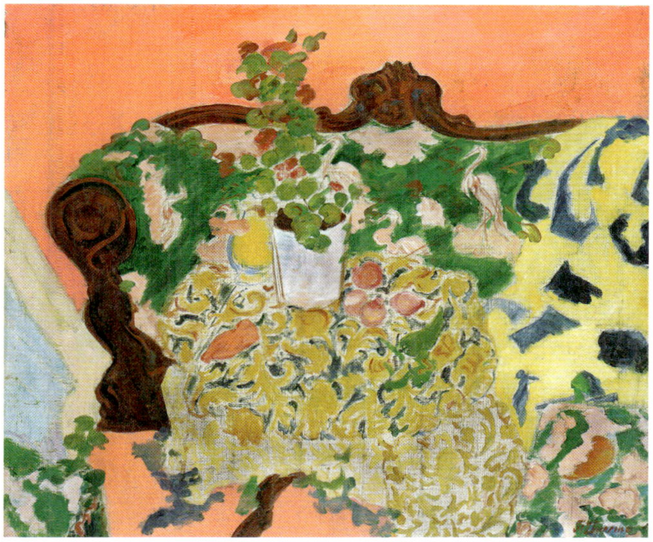

Fig. 29. Francisco Iturrino. *Still Life (Seville Interior)*, 1910–11. Oil on canvas, 32¼ x 38⅝ in. (82 x 98 cm). Museo de Bellas Artes de Bilbao, Deposit of Zorrilla-Lequerica Collection, 2005

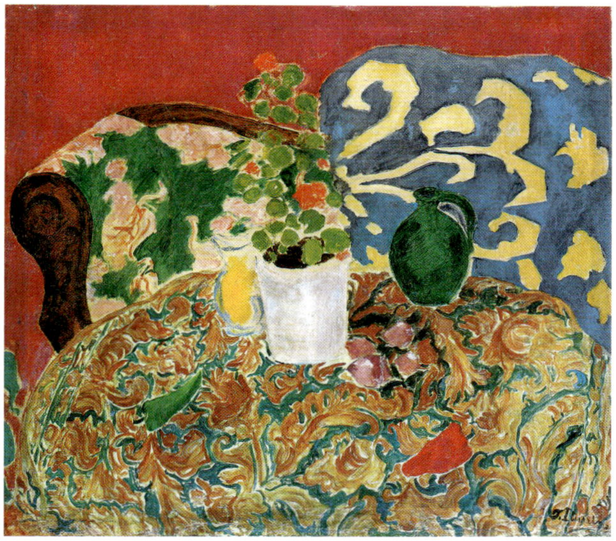

Fig. 30. Francisco Iturrino. *Still Life (Seville Interior)*, 1910–11. Oil on canvas, 34¼ x 39⅜ in. (87 x 100 cm). Museo de Bellas Artes de Bilbao, Deposit of Zorrilla-Lequerica Collection, 2005

Seville Still Life I (cat. 17) presents an interior composed of various decorative surfaces arranged in a three-dimensional, illusionistic space. The cloth, thrown over an armchair at the right, is enlivened by folds of fabric that form diagonal lines. As its pattern develops from right to left, the relationship between the colors of the ground and of the motifs is gradually inverted, the ground turning from white to blue. Curiously, it is the inverted version that reappears in the second still life and in later paintings, the transposition having been "solidified" or made permanent. Although the second version may appear to be simply a close-up view of the first, the differences between the two compositions cannot be reduced to mere framing. In *Seville Still Life I*, the objects and fabrics are arranged in a clearly defined space, so that it is possible for a viewer to understand each of them.[7] Its descriptive organization gives way in *Seville Still Life II* (cat. 18) to a "plastic space" inspired by Persian miniatures. The cloth, in close-up, is presented as a flat, seemingly vertical surface—a sort of "ceramic wall"—and the tabletop is flattened onto the picture plane; the couch, rendered in perspective, occupies the ground. This stacking of planes obscures the depiction of space, turning it into a surface animated by patches of decoration.

Rémi Labrusse has aptly shown how the use of fabrics allowed Matisse to impart tension to the pictorial space, either through rhythm (the repetition of the motif) or through folds (the partitioning effect). Two antithetical systems are at work, according to Labrusse:

> *The rhythmical repetition of pattern does not inhabit an unequivocal decorative universe; patterns are displayed in such a way that . . . the*

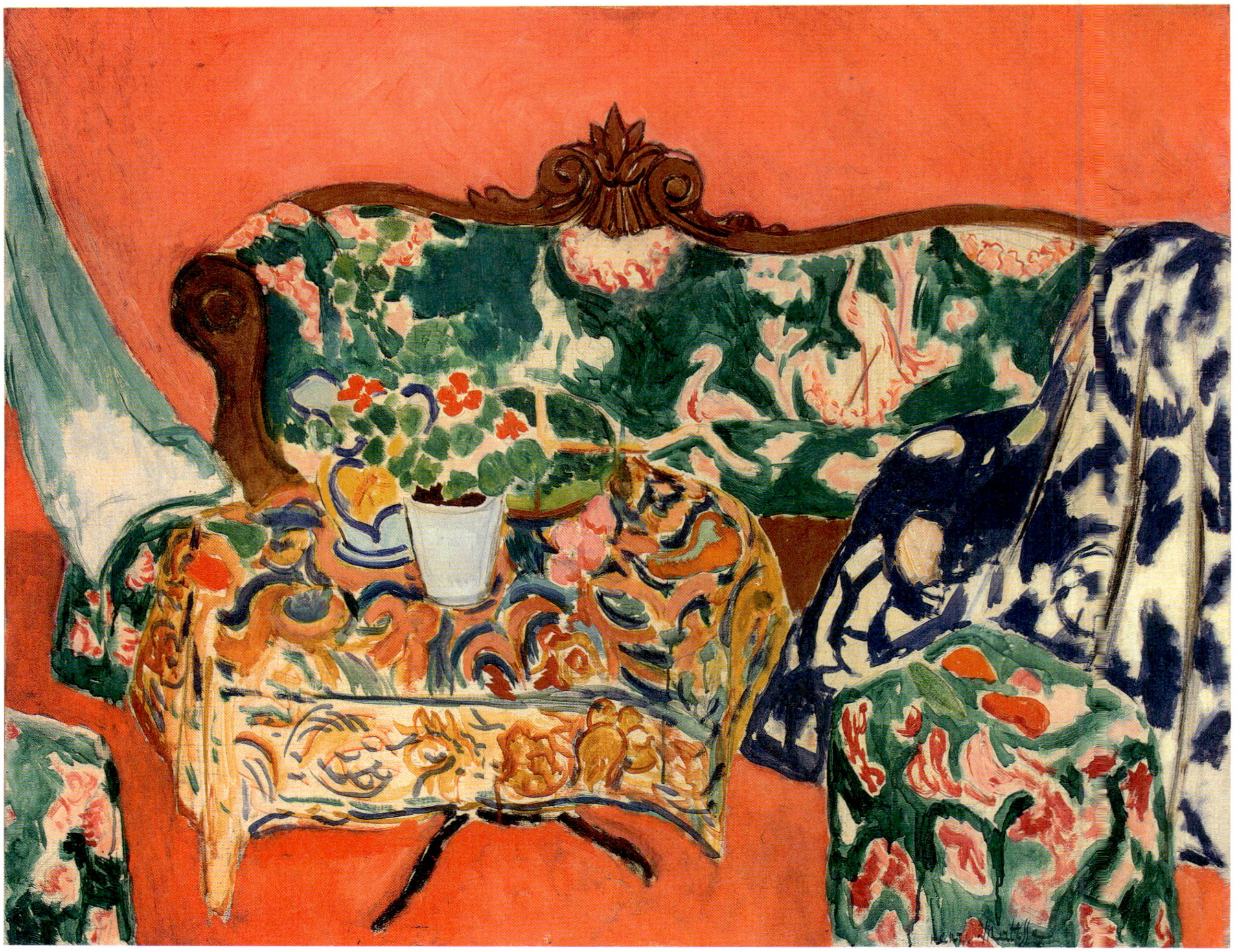

17 | *Seville Still Life I*, 1910–11

Oil on canvas, 35⅜ x 46⅛ in. (90 x 117 cm). The State Hermitage Museum, Saint Petersburg

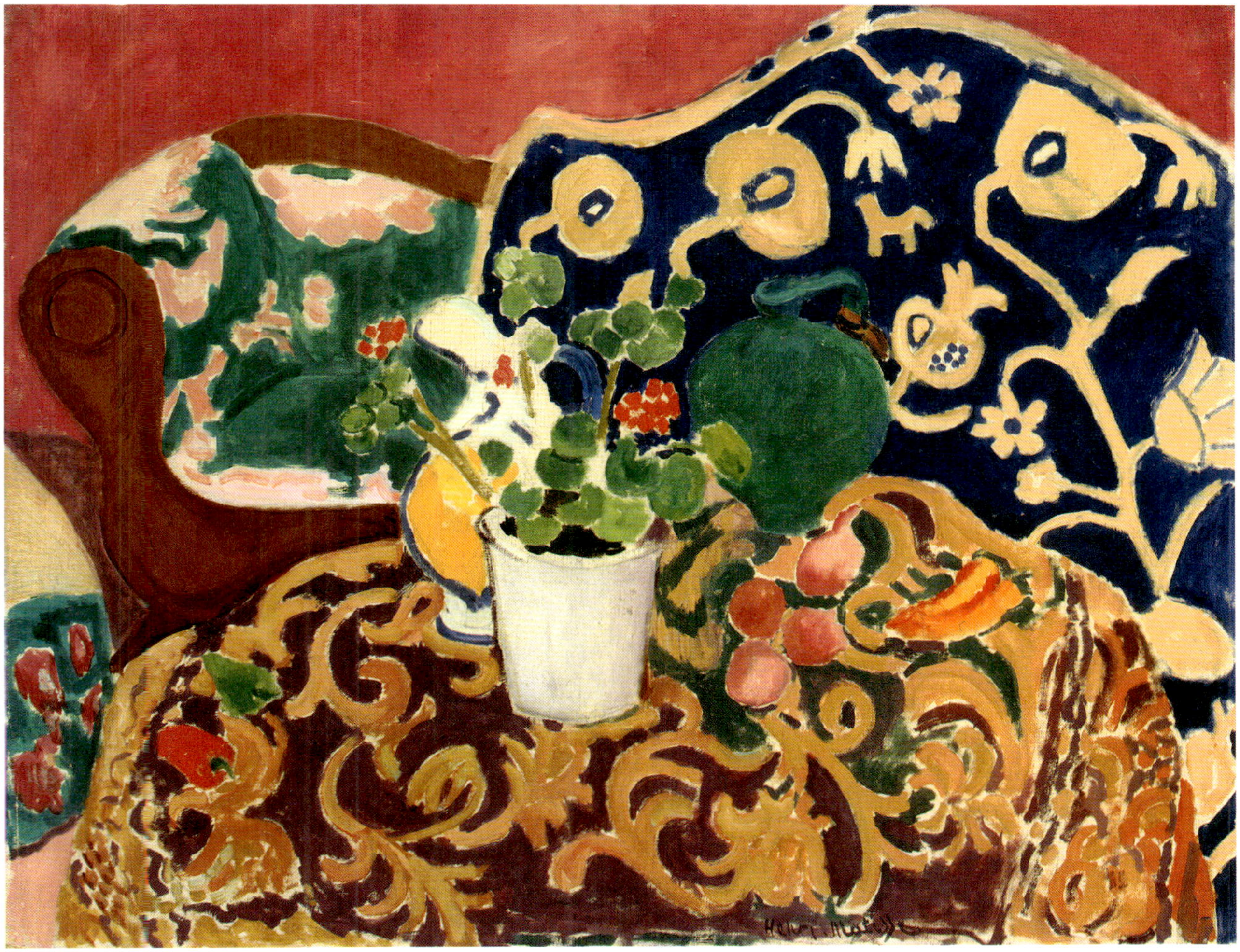

18 | *Seville Still Life II*, 1910–11

Oil on canvas, 35 ¼ x 45 ¾ in. (89.5 x 116.3 cm). The State Hermitage Museum, Saint Petersburg

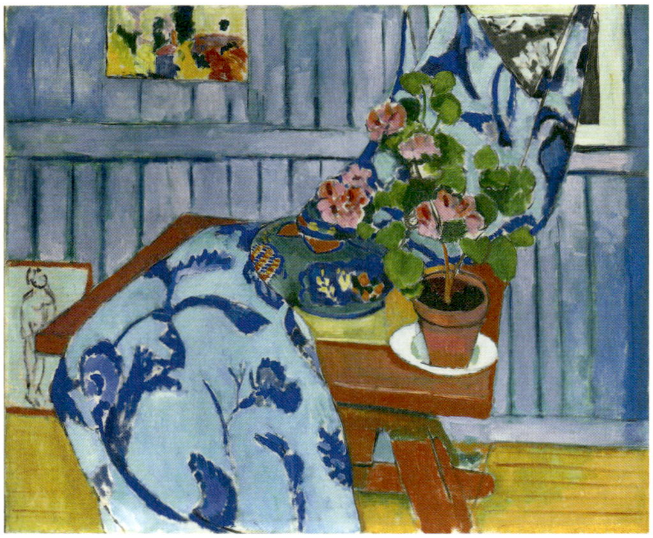

Fig. 31. *Still Life with Geraniums*, 1910. Oil on canvas, 36⅝ x 45¼ in. (93 x 115 cm). Pinakothek der Moderne, Bayerische Staatsgemäldesammlungen, Munich

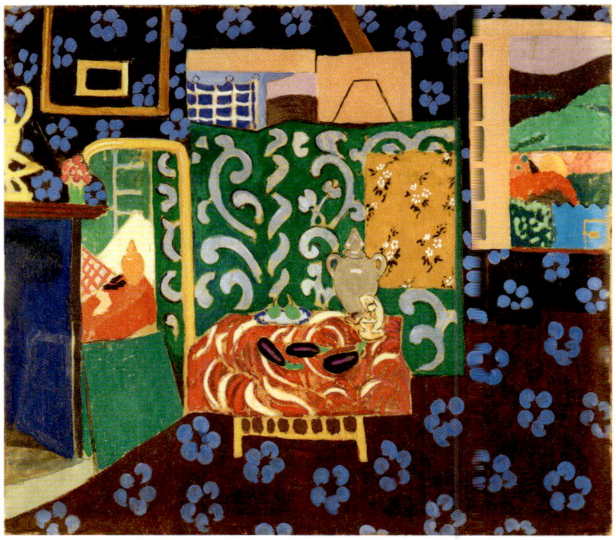

Fig. 32. *Interior with Eggplants*, 1911. Distemper on canvas, 83½ x 96⅞ in. (212 x 246 cm). Musée de Grenoble, Gift of Henri Matisse, 1922

> *ambiguous relationship between the referential value of the pattern as such and the pure rhythms that emerge from the spaces between the patterns is* deliberate. *The systematic intertwining of the plants and the textile designs based on plant forms is an excellent illustration of this ambiguity. The spectator is inevitably challenged on the nature of the figurative impulse and the way it is overstepped.*[8]

It has often been said that the two Seville still lifes anticipated the "great symphonic interiors" by Matisse, such as *Interior with Eggplants* of 1911 (fig. 32), with their invention of a decorative space.[9]

Several of Matisse's pairs or pendants did stem from Shchukin's commissioning of decorative works.[10] However, in the fall of 1911, when the artist hung the two Seville still lifes in the Trubetskoy Palace, he clearly indicated the autonomy of each by not placing them side by side.[11] The parallel (or successive) elaboration of these two paintings—as Matisse worked alongside Iturrino with the makeshift means available to traveling artists—very much coincided with the kind of "plastic" research that Matisse developed through variations, readjustments, and repetitions. In this case, he resolved the artistic challenge with ease, and possibly impatience, in view of the new avenues he had glimpsed.

A SLIGHT SHIFT IN PERSPECTIVE

Rebecca Rabinow and Isabelle Duvernois

Several of the commissions Matisse received in the early 1910s resulted in pairs of paintings.[1] Although he valued the first versions, which were thinly brushed onto full-size canvases, and routinely exhibited them, it was the second, more heavily worked versions that were sent to clients. The pairs of pictures he made in this manner usually have more or less identical compositions. *Nasturtiums with the Painting "Dance" I* and *II* (cats. 19, 20) stand apart because Matisse altered his vantage point in the second canvas. The catalyst for this unusual change was probably a visit in June or July 1912 from the Russian textile merchant Sergei Shchukin.

Shchukin had been an important patron of the artist since 1908. A pivotal moment in their relationship occurred in 1910, when two large works that Shchukin had commissioned for his grand staircase, *Dance II* and *Music* (both 1910; The State Hermitage Museum, Saint Petersburg), were exhibited at the Salon d'Automne. Critics were scathing in their assessment, and Shchukin hesitated briefly before accepting the canvases. Exhausted by his efforts to finish the pictures and emotionally drained by the negative response, Matisse departed for Spain.

Almost at once, Shchukin reaffirmed his support for Matisse, buying finished works and commissioning others. On December 20, he wrote the artist and asked him to create a trio of identically sized canvases: "The choice of subject . . . depends on you. What do you think of youth, maturity, and old age? Or spring, summer, and autumn?"[2] Just days later, Shchukin revised his request. He wanted Matisse to decorate an entire room, a grand space with a vaulted ceiling. He invited the artist to visit his Moscow residence, an eighteenth-century mansion known as the Trubetskoy Palace. When Matisse made the trip in November 1911, he was shown the room, with its colorful decorative ceiling and walls hung with deeply saturated Tahitian-period paintings by Paul Gauguin (fig. 39).

Immediately after his Russian trip, Matisse embarked on an extended stay in Morocco. When he finally returned to France in the late spring of 1912, he was revitalized and ready to paint. Matisse was particularly inspired by the interior of the studio he had constructed next to his house at Issy-les-Moulineaux, a suburb southwest of Paris. The white-walled structure boasted pine floors and large windows, but most important, at 1,076 square feet (100 square meters),

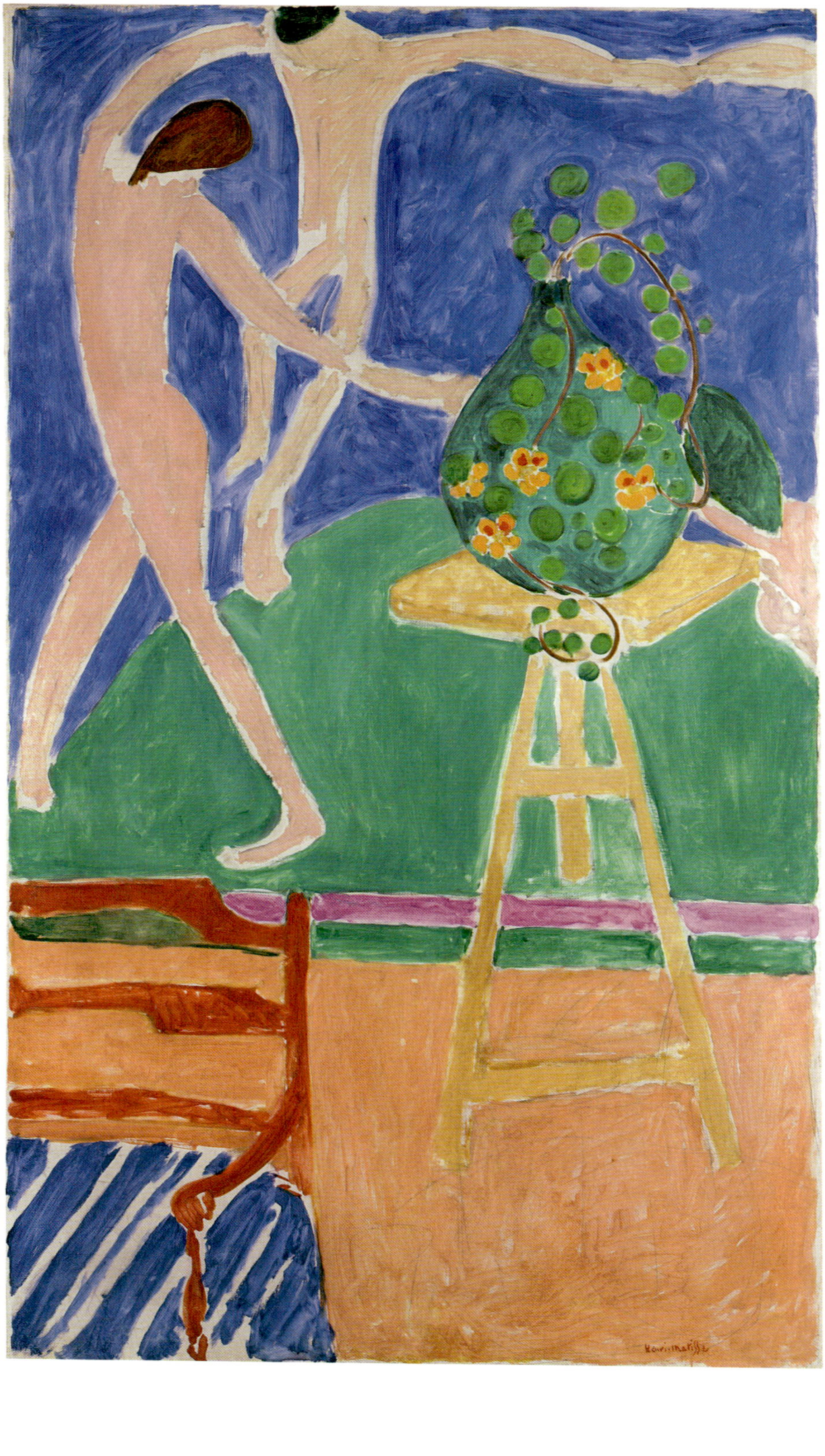

19 | *Nasturtiums with the Painting "Dance" I*, 1912

Oil on canvas, 75½ x 45⅜ in. (191.8 x 115.3 cm). The Metropolitan Museum of Art, New York, Bequest of Scofield Thayer, 1982

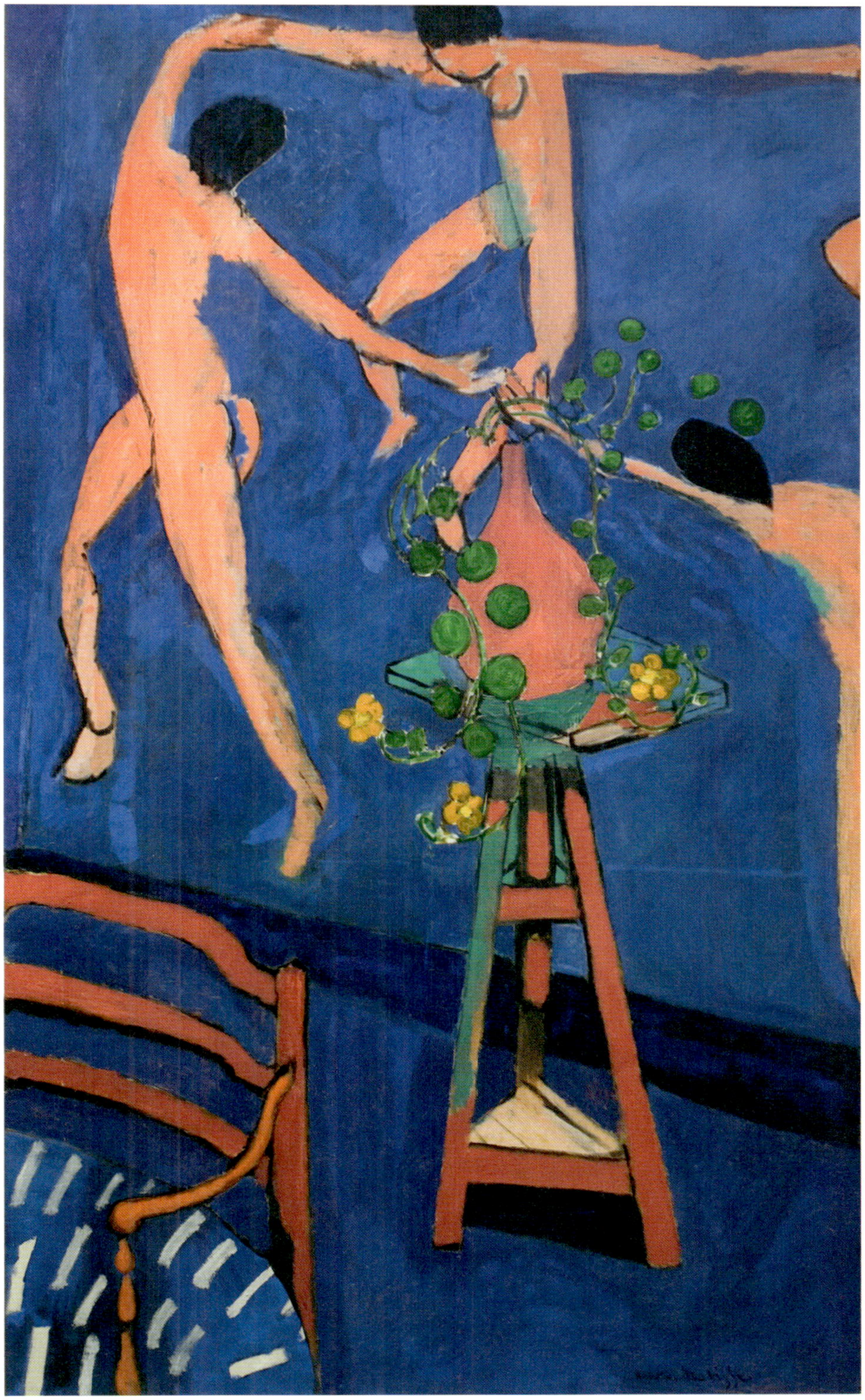

20 | *Nasturtiums with the Painting "Dance" II*, 1912

Oil on canvas, 76 x 44⅞ in. (193 x 114 cm). The State Pushkin Museum of Fine Arts, Moscow

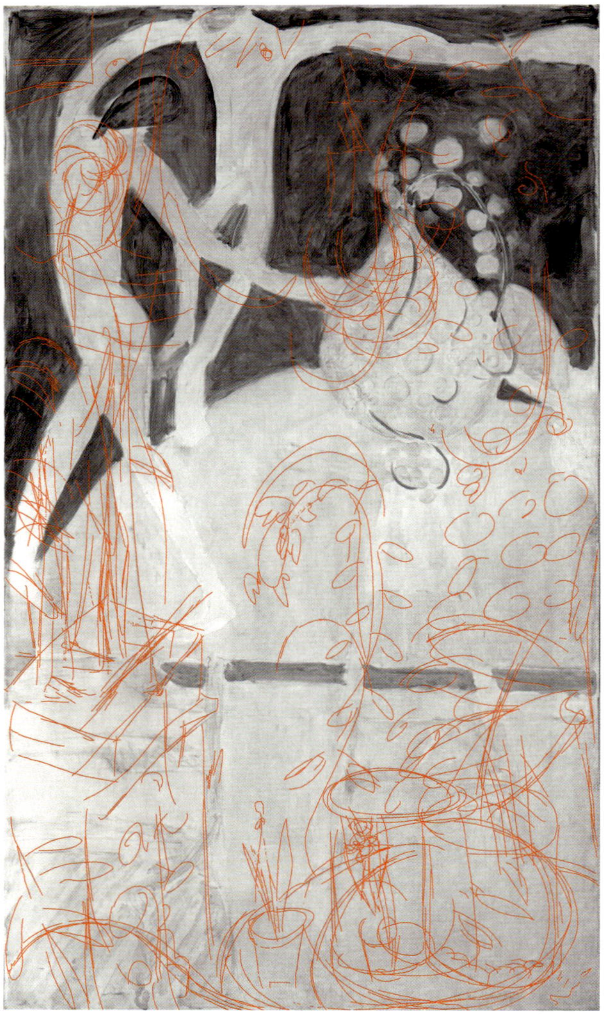

Fig. 33. Infrared reflectogram of *Nasturtiums with the Painting "Dance" I*, with drawing under the paint layer outlined in red

it was large enough to hold his supplies and artwork. *Dance I* (1909; The Museum of Modern Art, New York), the full-size preparatory study for the painting hanging on Shchukin's staircase, was propped against a wall. Glimpses of its vibrant blue, green, and pink tones appear in several canvases painted during the spring and summer of 1912, including both versions of *Nasturtiums with the Painting "Dance."*

The first painting (cat. 19) depicts two still-life elements—a wooden chair with a cloth cushion and a vase of nasturtiums on a tripod sculpture stand—positioned in front of the left side of *Dance I*, the painting within the painting. Matisse directly faced the motif as he worked. Infrared reflectography reveals that he used a canvas on which he had already sketched a different studio scene (fig. 33). While the pencil drawing as a whole does not correspond to any known painting by the artist, elements recall several compositions on which he was working in the spring and summer of 1912. The arrangement in the lower right quadrant, for instance—the cylindrical glass jar with small fish, the potted plants on a round tabletop, the nasturtium leaves and other flowers, all of which were shifted a number of times—is similar to that in the painting *Goldfish* (fig. 34). Additionally, the curvilinear elements depicted at the top center echo areas of *Corner of the Artist's Studio* (fig. 38). Other elements of the drawing do not feature in either painting: the cabinet or small dresser, surmounted by a boxy form that may be a pedestal, visible in the left foreground, as well as the fine lines rising vertically from it, which may represent a sculpture or a standing figure, with drapery folds above.

There are many playful moments in *Nasturtiums with the Painting "Dance" I*. The viridian green vase mimics the shape and color of the dancer's head just behind it. A missing portion of the back leg makes the sculpture stand appear to be propped on the grassy hill depicted in *Dance I*. The top rail of the wooden armchair is aligned with a horizontal pink stripe that continues across the canvas.[3] Matisse's interest in layering planes and flattening space seems particularly modern and explains why this picture was long considered the second of the pair.[4]

Matisse executed *Nasturtiums with the Painting "Dance" II* (cat. 20)—the picture now recognized as the second version—on a canvas the same size as the first.[5] He shifted himself a few feet to the right and turned to view his subject on a diagonal. Though subtle, this adjustment imbues the work with a dynamic energy and a more traditional sense of depth. Unlike the first version, which is painted so thinly that the ground and underlying pencil marks are clearly visible, the second is constructed in a complex manner that involved much reworking, scraping, overpainting, and incising.

Matisse explained his method to the American reporter Clara MacChesney, who visited him at Issy that June:

> *"Well, take that table, for example," [he said] pointing to one nearby, on which stood a jar of nasturtiums. "I do not literally paint that table, but the emotion it produces upon me."* . . .
>
> *"I always use a preliminary canvas the same size for a sketch as for a finished picture, and I always begin with color. With large canvases this is more fatiguing, but more logical. I may have the same sentiment I obtained in the first, but this lacks solidity, and decorative sense. I never retouch a sketch: I take a new canvas the same size, as I may change the composition somewhat. But I always strive to give the same feeling, while carrying it on further. A picture should, for me, always be decorative. While working I never try to think, only to feel."*[6]

Matisse had used the same process—full-size study, followed by a second, more heavily worked painting—in 1910 when he completed *Dance II* for Shchukin.

The brightly colored *Nasturtiums with the Painting "Dance" II* initially looked much more like the first version.[7] Deep drying cracks in the top layer of paint have exposed many of the same colors that were employed in *Nasturtiums with the Painting "Dance" I.* For instance, brown is visible underneath the deep pink rails of the armchair, dark green can be seen underneath the red vase, and the grassy hill of *Dance I* was covered with blue.[8]

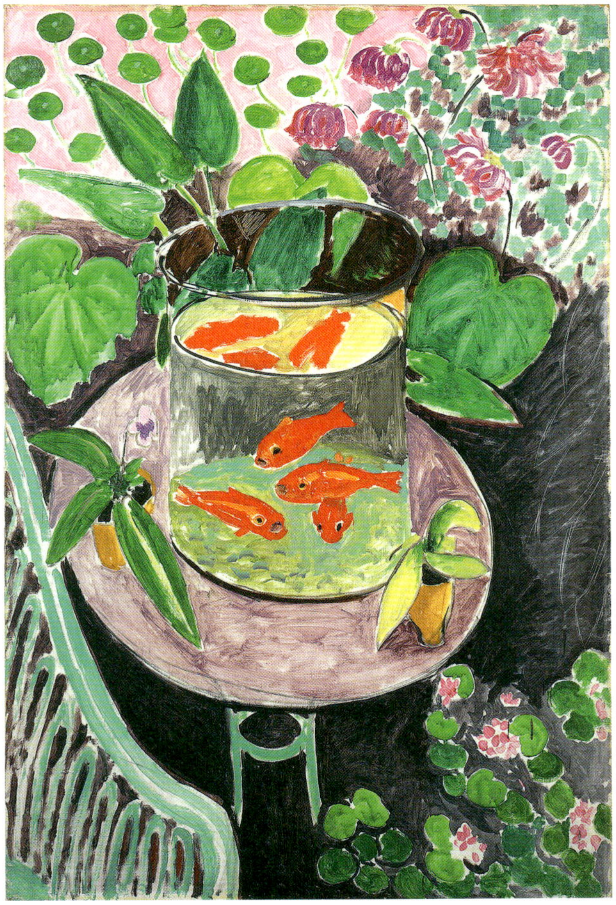

Fig. 34. *Goldfish*, 1912. Oil on canvas, 57½ x 38¼ in. (146 x 97 cm). The State Pushkin Museum of Fine Arts, Moscow

Matisse used various approaches to make changes in the second version. Sometimes he scraped away the oil paint layer before repainting: scrape marks

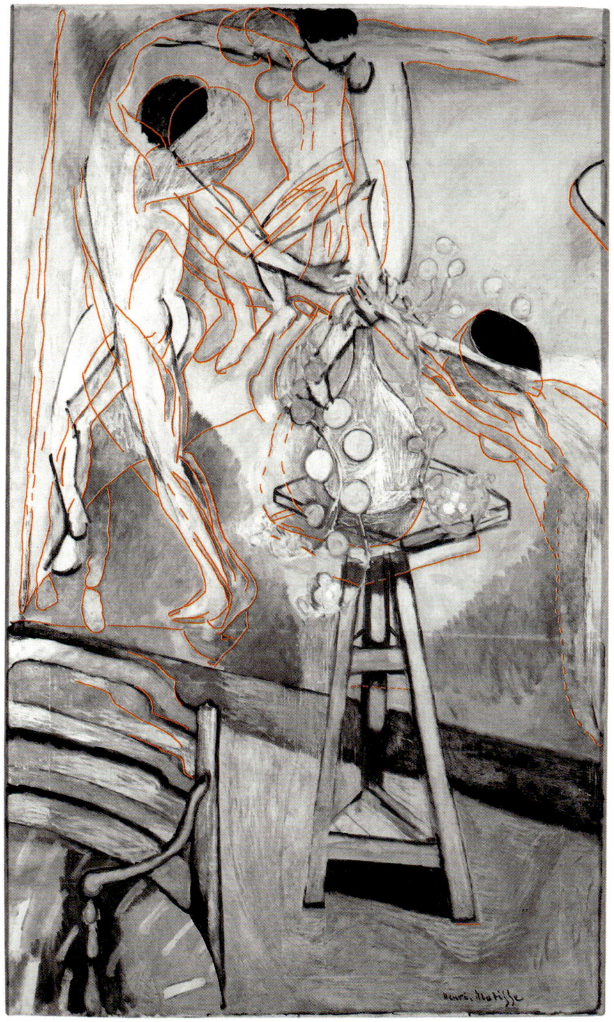

Fig. 35. Infrared reflectogram of *Nasturtiums with the Painting "Dance" II*, with compositional changes traced in red

are particularly apparent around the figure at the left, which he reworked multiple times. (These marks are distinct from the deep incisions that he made around some contours to add a subtle texture.) A second technique, revealed through X-radiography, involves the use of solvent to remove the underlying paint layer before reworking; this was employed along the left thigh of the central dancer. Matisse's third method was simply to work on top of the existing paint layer. Pink flesh tones show through the drying cracks of the blue paint that Matisse applied when he changed the positions and contours of the central figure. Another example of this approach can be seen in a detail of the raised foot of the figure at the left. After painting over the contour of a preexisting foot with a lighter shade of blue, the artist outlined the new foot with a thick black stroke and later added touches of dark ultramarine blue. Various shades and textures of blue, painted over an extended period of time, animate the background.[9]

Significantly, the composition of *Nasturtiums with the Painting "Dance" II* was not initially depicted on a diagonal.[10] Matisse originally painted the left and bottom edges of *Dance I* as if he were standing directly in front of the canvas. Infrared photography and X-radiography reveal that the dancers' outlines originally appeared much as they do in the first version. Once Matisse decided to present the painting from an angle, he reworked the dancers (fig. 35). He slimmed down the figure at the right; altered the central figure so that she is viewed from the right; and moved the figure at the left farther left, turning her head, narrowing and elongating her back, and shifting her legs. Additional changes were made elsewhere, including the base of the sculpture stand (raised and shifted to the right) and the vase (reduced in size).

The canvas may well have been reworked in July after the visit to Matisse's studio by Shchukin, who still hoped to receive a decorative ensemble from the artist. On this particular visit, Matisse showed him *The Conversation* (fig. 37), a large picture depicting an early morning scene in a ground-floor room of the house at Issy: Matisse stands in his pajamas to the left of a window overlooking the front lawn, while his

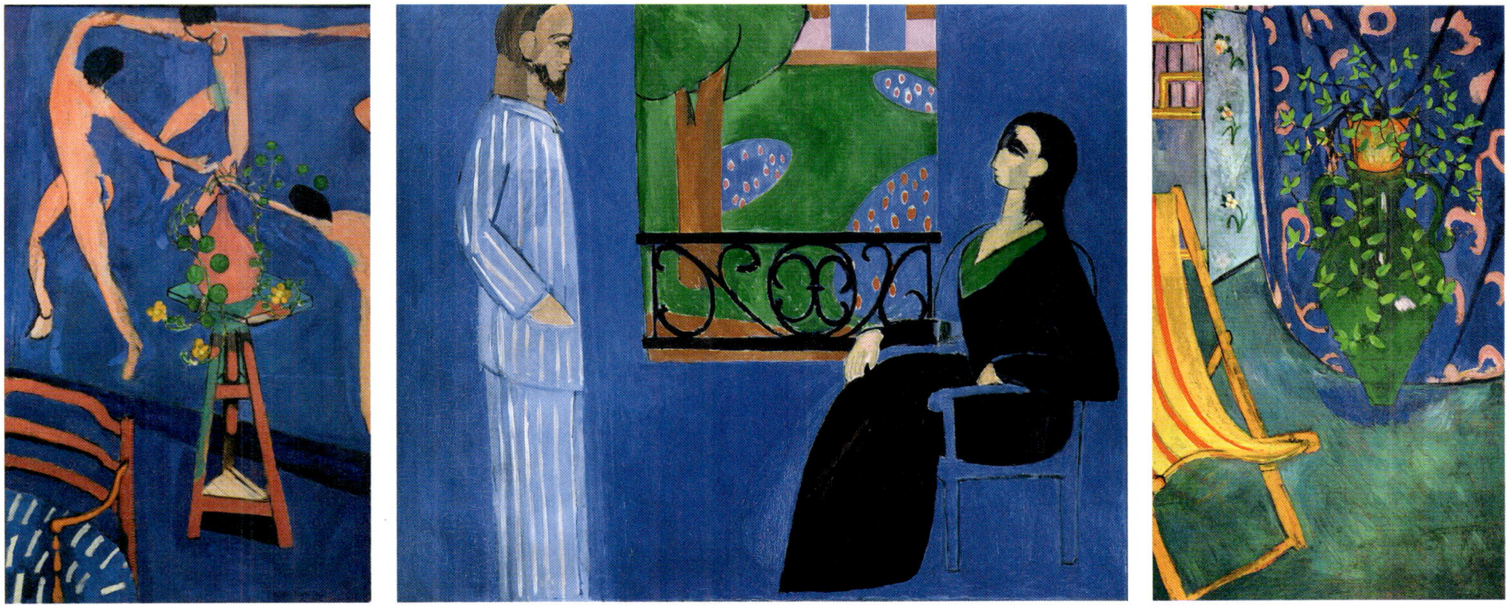

Figs. 36–38. Left: *Nasturtiums with the Painting "Dance" II* (cat. 20). Center: *The Conversation*, ca. 1908–12. Oil on canvas, 69⅝ x 85⅜ in. (177 x 217 cm). The State Hermitage Museum, Saint Petersburg. Right: *Corner of the Artist's Studio*, 1912. Oil on canvas, 75⅜ x 44⅞ in. (191.5 x 114 cm). The State Pushkin Museum of Fine Arts, Moscow

wife, in a dressing gown, sits at the right; the two figures are connected by a horizontal black balustrade. Shchukin immediately purchased the painting and asked Matisse to order a frame for it.

The Conversation ultimately was installed on the far wall of Shchukin's dining room as the central section of a triptych. The setting for all three panels is the property at Issy. *The Conversation* is flanked by two views of the studio's interior: at left, *Nasturtiums with the Painting "Dance" II*, and at right, *Corner of the Artist's Studio* (figs. 36–38). These two pendants have exactly the same unusual format. Although *The Conversation* is not as tall as the other two canvases, the frame Matisse ordered for it is so substantial that the tops and bottoms of the three paintings align when displayed together. If these three paintings evolved into a triptych (and it is worth noting that they exactly fit the available space on Shchukin's end wall), the reworking of *Nasturtiums with the Painting "Dance" II* may have been prompted by Matisse's desire to incorporate a diagonal that mirrors the one in *Corner of the Artist's Studio*.

The histories of the two versions of *Nasturtiums with the Painting "Dance"* have long been tangled because of an error in the 1912 Salon d'Automne catalogue, in which Matisse's submissions are listed as numbers "769, *Capucines à la danse*, [owned by] M. le Dr. G. . ." and "770, *Intérieur*, [owned by] M. S. . . , de Moscou." The owners' names were simply reversed. Shchukin permitted Matisse to exhibit *Nasturtiums with the Painting "Dance" II* in Paris before sending it to Moscow. Its inclusion in the exhibition is confirmed by a review that mentions "a red bottle entwined with nasturtium leaves and flowers."[11] (The vase in the earlier version of the painting

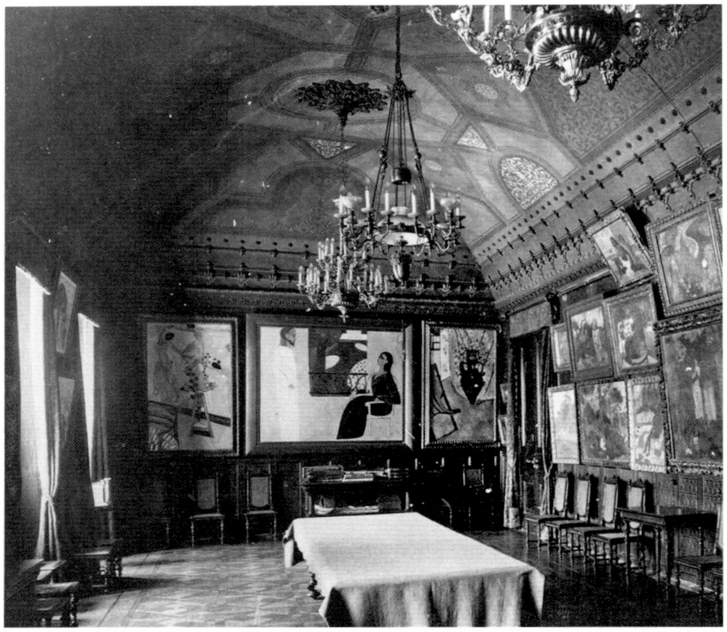

Fig. 39. Room in the Trubetskoy Palace, residence of Sergei Shchukin, Moscow, ca. 1914. Archives Matisse, Paris

is green.) During the summer of 1912, Matisse had painted another view of his studio for Hugo Kolker, the Portuguese consul to Breslau. Kolker's son-in-law, the art historian Curt Glaser (the "M. le Dr. G. . ." listed in the Salon catalogue), handled most of the correspondence pertaining to this commission.[12] Like Shchukin, Kolker permitted Matisse to exhibit his painting at the 1912 Salon d'Automne. Several reviews as well as congratulatory letters from Matisse's friends make clear that the subject of the "Intérieur" shown at this exhibition was a goldfish bowl.[13] Additional unpublished documentation confirms that Kolker's painting was *Interior with Goldfish* (The Barnes Foundation, Philadelphia).

Four days after the Salon d'Automne opened at the Grand Palais, Roger Fry's "Second Post-Impressionist Exhibition" debuted at the Grafton Galleries in London. The exhibition featured more than two hundred and fifty works by contemporary artists based in England, France, and Russia. Matisse was represented by some forty-two paintings, sculptures, and works on paper, including the first versions of both of the pictures simultaneously on view at the Salon d'Automne.[14] In December *Nasturtiums with the Painting "Dance" I* was sent from the Grafton Galleries to New York for display at the Armory Show. It was available for purchase for four thousand francs.[15]

Meanwhile, back in Russia, Shchukin anxiously worried about the fate of both *Nasturtiums with the Painting "Dance" II* and *The Conversation*. Shipping delays postponed the arrival of the former by several months, and of the latter by almost a year.[16] It was not until the end of 1913 that the ensemble was installed, but it was clearly worth the wait (fig. 39). Upon seeing the room, a Russian critic remarked:

> *[Matisse] would have done well to have been born in the age of stained glass, shining enamels and faience ovens. It becomes especially clear when, from the threshold of Shchukin's parlor you see his* Nasturtiums with the Dance *and* Conversation: *the orange-rose bodies of the former blaze on the dark blue background, like arabesques of glass. Glance at Gauguin's paintings and once more at Matisse's* Nasturtiums: *the former will appear to you to be matte fresco, the second—a colorful window.*[17]

Collectors in France may still have struggled to appreciate Matisse's art, but for some Russians, acceptance and admiration came sooner. Shchukin's mansion was now the site of Matisse's most spectacular decorative ensembles; yet within the year, political developments would render them virtually inaccessible.

A GARDEN "REDONE THREE TIMES"

Cécile Debray

Many of the works Matisse painted in Tangier are closely associated with the emergence in his art of pendants, triptychs, and triads.[1] While in Morocco, he fulfilled the commission for a triptych from the Russian collector Ivan Morosov,[2] and after he returned to France, most of the Tangier paintings were hung together in threes at the Galerie Bernheim-Jeune in April 1913.[3] Morosov's triptych was exhibited there, as was *Seated Riffian* (1912–13; The Barnes Foundation, Philadelphia), flanked by *Calla Lilies* and *Calla Lilies, Irises, and Mimosas* (figs. 40, 41). In light of this fact, there has been much discussion concerning a possible link among the three views of the Englishman Jack Brooks's garden in Tangier, made during Matisse's first visit, between January 30 and April 14, 1912 (fig. 42, cats. 21, 22).[4]

Immediately after his arrival in Morocco, Matisse, faced with almost four weeks of incessant rain, painted still lifes and views from his window. Finally, the appearance of the sun over the irrigated lands produced a magical spring awakening. He wrote to a friend about the "molten light . . . and the Norman vegetation like blazing heat, but how decorative!!! How brand new it is as well and how difficult to do with blue, red, yellow, and green."[5] Years later, he remembered that "wondrous bulbous flowers and greenery emerged from the earth, and all the hills surrounding Tangier went from the lion skin color they had been to a fresh green."[6] For the entire month of March, Matisse painted on the grounds of the Brooks villa, attempting to capture the subtle colors, the "wood sorrel blossoming yellow, pink, or white as far as the eye could see. My spirit was stirred by the trees, very high in the sky, the green and sumptuous mass of the acanthus and the luminous space that united these two forces."[7]

His three views of the garden are all the same size and painted from almost the same point of view. Composed with a fluid, light technique, *Periwinkles/Moroccan Garden* (fig. 42) displays patterns of concave and convex curves, with bright tones and more intense notes of green and brownish pink, reminiscent of the Edenic landscape of *Le Bonheur de vivre* (1905–6; The Barnes Foundation). The picture was quickly painted, and carefully copied, from an underlying preliminary drawing.[8] *Palm Leaf, Tangier* (cat. 21), also rapidly executed, employs a cooler palette and more rectilinear shapes, as dictated by

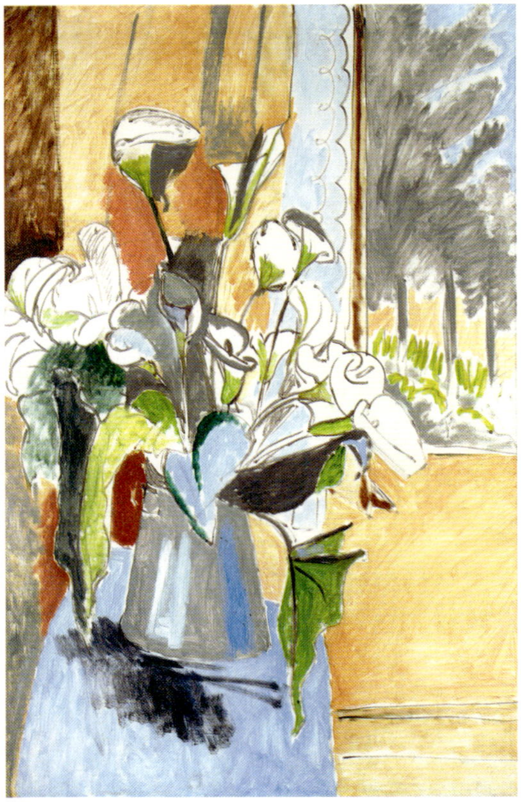

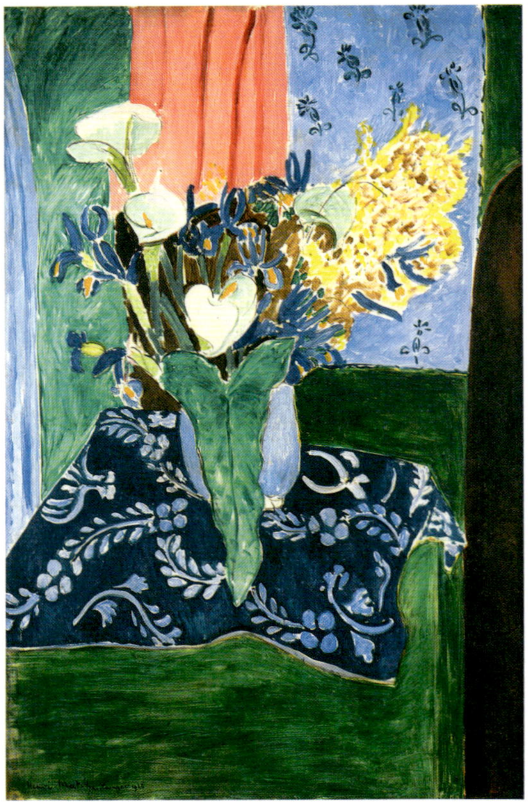

Fig. 40. *Calla Lilies*, ca. 1912. Oil on canvas, 57½ x 38¼ in. (146 x 97 cm). The State Hermitage Museum, Saint Petersburg

Fig. 41. *Calla Lilies, Irises, and Mimosas*, 1913. Oil on canvas, 57⅞ x 38⅝ in. (147 x 98 cm). The State Pushkin Museum of Fine Arts, Moscow

the subject.[9] Matisse deviated from his preliminary drawing here, recalling that the work burst forth as a "spontaneous creation, like a flame—in a fervor."[10] The third painting, *Acanthus (Moroccan Landscape)* (cat. 22), is much more complex: its erased and thinly painted areas, layers of flat, superimposed colors, heavily worked motifs, and barely sketched forms attest to a lengthy and difficult elaboration.[11] Matisse seems to have struggled with the painting for the entire month; he eventually brought it back with him on his second visit to Morocco, although in the end he made no changes at all.[12] The intensity of the labor involved and its singular harmonies of violets, blues, and pinks make *Acanthus* a strongly enigmatic work.

John Elderfield, in discussing the meaning of the word "sketch" (*esquisse*) for Matisse, has established a typology for these three paintings, based on their different ways of depicting a landscape: "[*Acanthus*] through long improvisation; [*Periwinkles*] through careful planning; [*Palm Leaf, Tangier*] through spontaneous expression."[13] What these categories reveal, above all, is the unique status of *Acanthus*. The work crystallized Matisse's anxiety about painting at a time when the Paris scene was reverberating with Cubist and Futurist triumphs and when he himself was assimilating all he had seen in Russia. While in Tangier, he continually put off fulfilling Morosov's request for two landscapes and a still life. Matisse would always associate the memory of Morocco with the fear of "expressing my feelings in paint. I was obliged to split myself in two; to let go of a panic-stricken man filled with self-doubt in order to achieve a few moments of calm that allowed me to work."[14] He had come to dread the landscape genre, which he had rarely practiced after his Fauve period, because he found the mutability of nature incompatible with his attempts to simplify and stabilize his compositions.

The three landscapes here can be regarded as one path Matisse considered in response to the Morosov commission, based as they are on Pierre Bonnard's triptych *Mediterranean* (1911; The State Hermitage Museum, Saint Petersburg), garden views produced the previous year for the same collector. Prompted by Bonnard's example—or, more generally, by that of the Nabis—and encouraged by Morosov's and Sergei Shchukin's commissions for decors, Matisse seems to have wanted to combine the paintings into a set from the beginning of the project. In a letter of April 1, 1912, he was already using the term "triptych" for certain (as yet unidentified) works: "I wrote a nicely phrased letter to Shchukin this morning. I added a sketch representing Morosov's still life and two landscapes, the blue one and the periwinkles, they made up a nice sketch-triptych."[15] Some believe that the "blue" landscape was *Landscape Viewed from a Window* from the final triptych, others that it was *Acanthus*, which, with *Periwinkles*, framed a work also painted during the first visit, *Basket of Oranges* (1912; Musée National Picasso, Paris), which has color harmonies and a complex genesis similar to those of the garden paintings.[16]

When Matisse returned to Tangier in the fall of 1912, drought had greatly transformed the landscape, and he most likely abandoned the idea of the garden views for the Morosov triptych. Never exhibited together as a set, *Periwinkles*, *Palm Leaf, Tangier*, and *Acanthus* were eventually dispersed among various collections. They nonetheless remain linked by that extraordinary, evanescent Moroccan spring of 1912.

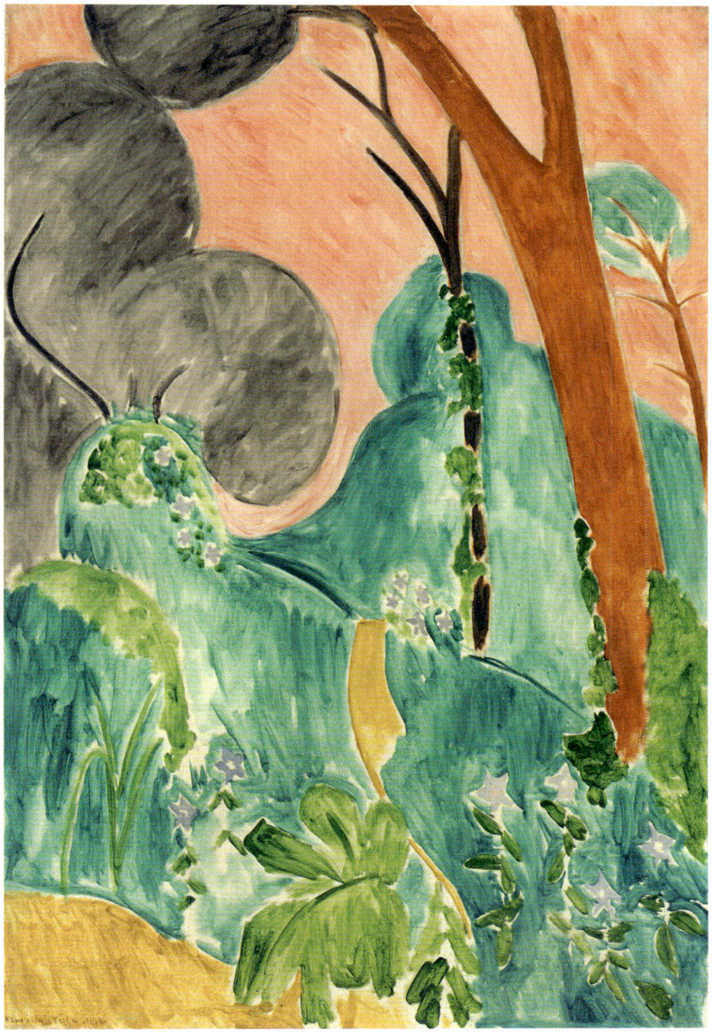

Fig. 42. *Periwinkles / Moroccan Garden*, 1912. Oil, pencil, and charcoal on canvas, 46 x 32½ in. (116.8 x 82.5 cm). The Museum of Modern Art, New York, Gift of Florene M. Schoenborn

A few years later, in 1920, the writer Marcel Sembat pointed to the paradisiacal perfume of that season: "But the gardens especially were revelatory. I know of one, redone three times, and each time elevated toward decoration, toward calm, toward abstract simplicity."[17]

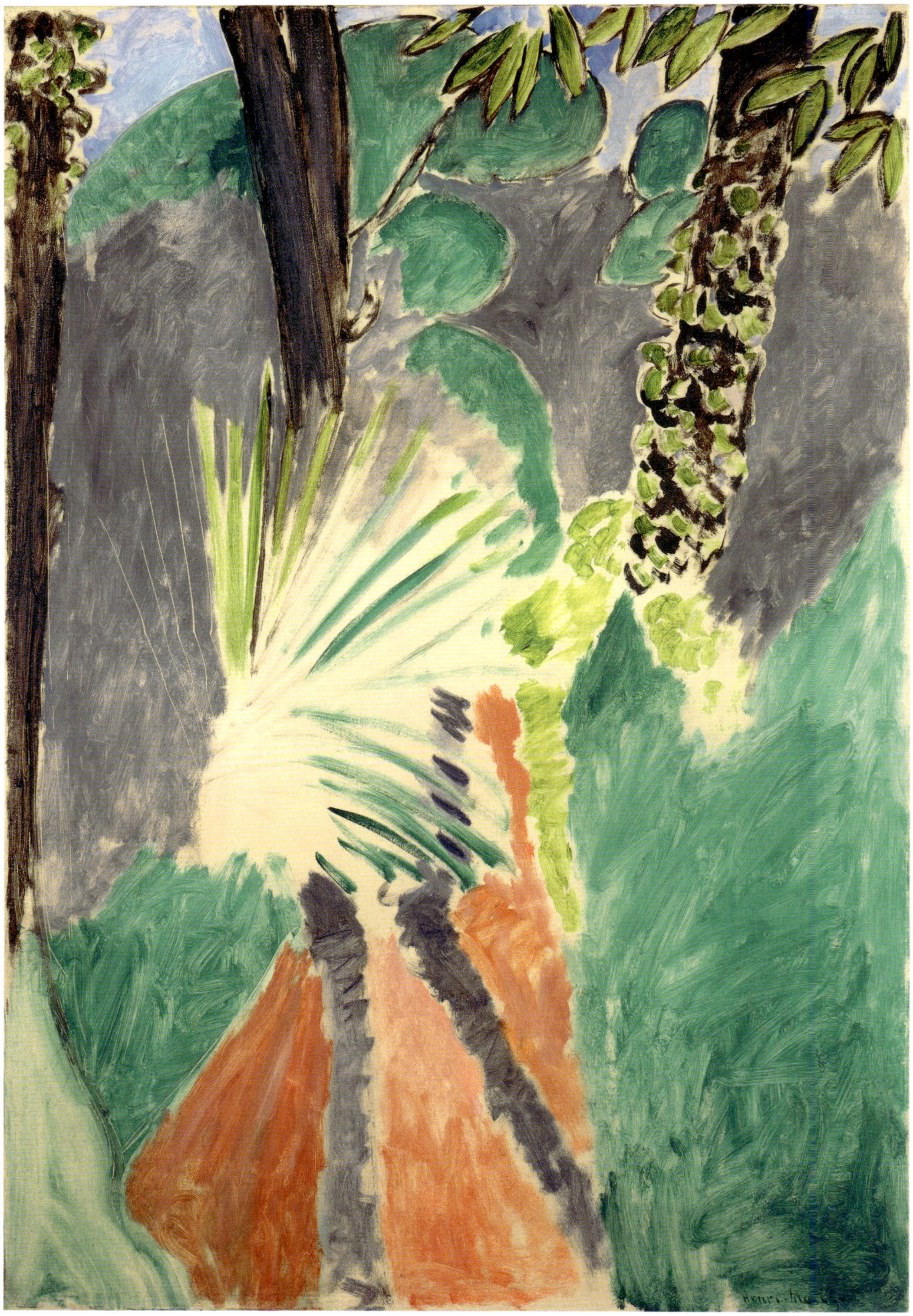

21 | *Palm Leaf, Tangier*, 1912

Oil on canvas, 46¼ x 32¼ in. (117.5 x 81.9 cm). National Gallery of Art, Washington, Chester Dale Fund

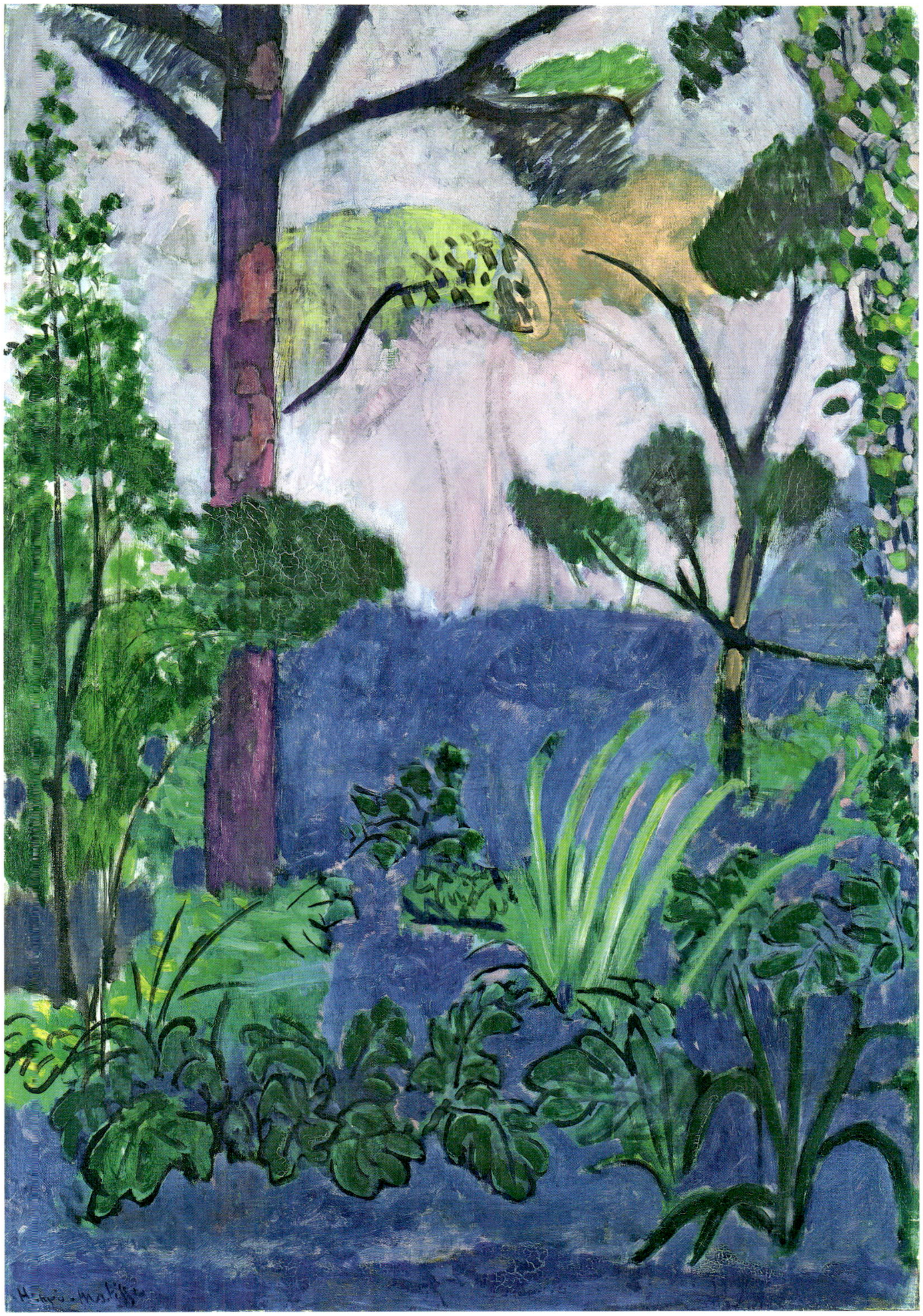

22 | *Acanthus (Moroccan Landscape)*, 1912

O l on canvas, 45¼ x 31½ in. (115 x 80 cm). Moderna Museet, Stockholm, Gift of Walther Halvorsen, 1917

NOTRE-DAME BETWEEN HEAVEN AND EARTH

Rémi Labrusse

At first glance, order reigns. One work (cat. 24) is a descriptive, earthly version in a familiar world. There is something of Albert Marquet (fig. 43) in this lighthearted and joyful canvas, embracing—in a lilting, almost leaping manner—the movement of urban life along the river. It is as if Matisse were paying homage to his lifelong friend, recalling the verve of their early years in that very spot (cat. 23, fig. 44) and giving new life to the solid construction of masses.[1] No nostalgia attached Matisse to a cityscape laden with recollections; rather, the present incessantly brims forth, as if the burden of memory borne by the act of painting were being swept away by immediate sensation.

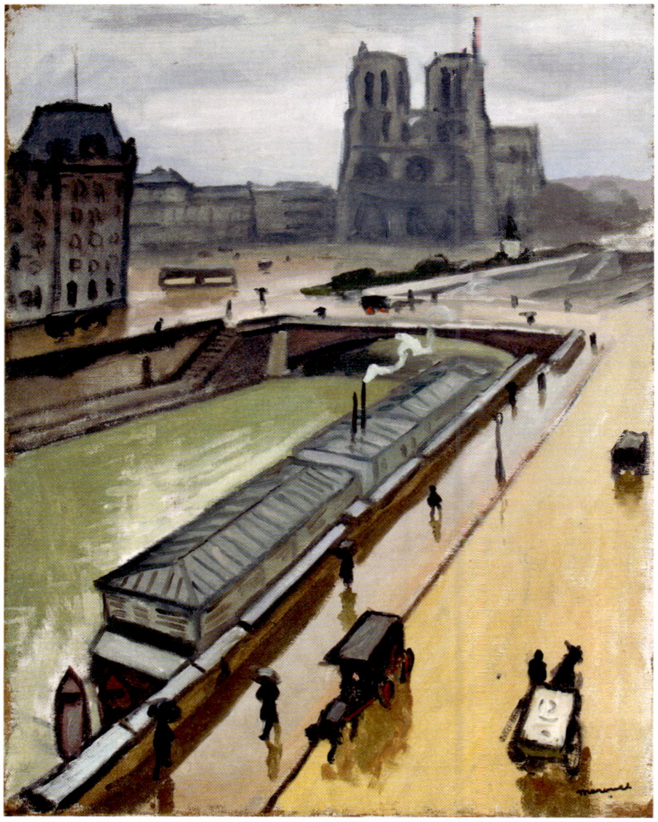

Fig. 43. Albert Marquet. *Rainy Day, Notre-Dame*, 1910. Oil on canvas, 31 ⅞ x 26 in. (81 x 66 cm). The State Hermitage Museum, Saint Petersburg

The other work (cat. 25) is a schematic, heavenly version of the same scene, but emptied of nearly everything except for a simplified tree, bridge, and cathedral. An end to anecdotes, people in motion, passing clouds, shifting shadows, reflections in the water: an end, therefore, to the representation of time. Everything that in the descriptive canvas designates the temporal flow of daily life is distilled here into a crystalline atemporality, the ethereal nature of which is emblemized by a vast expanse of blue. The

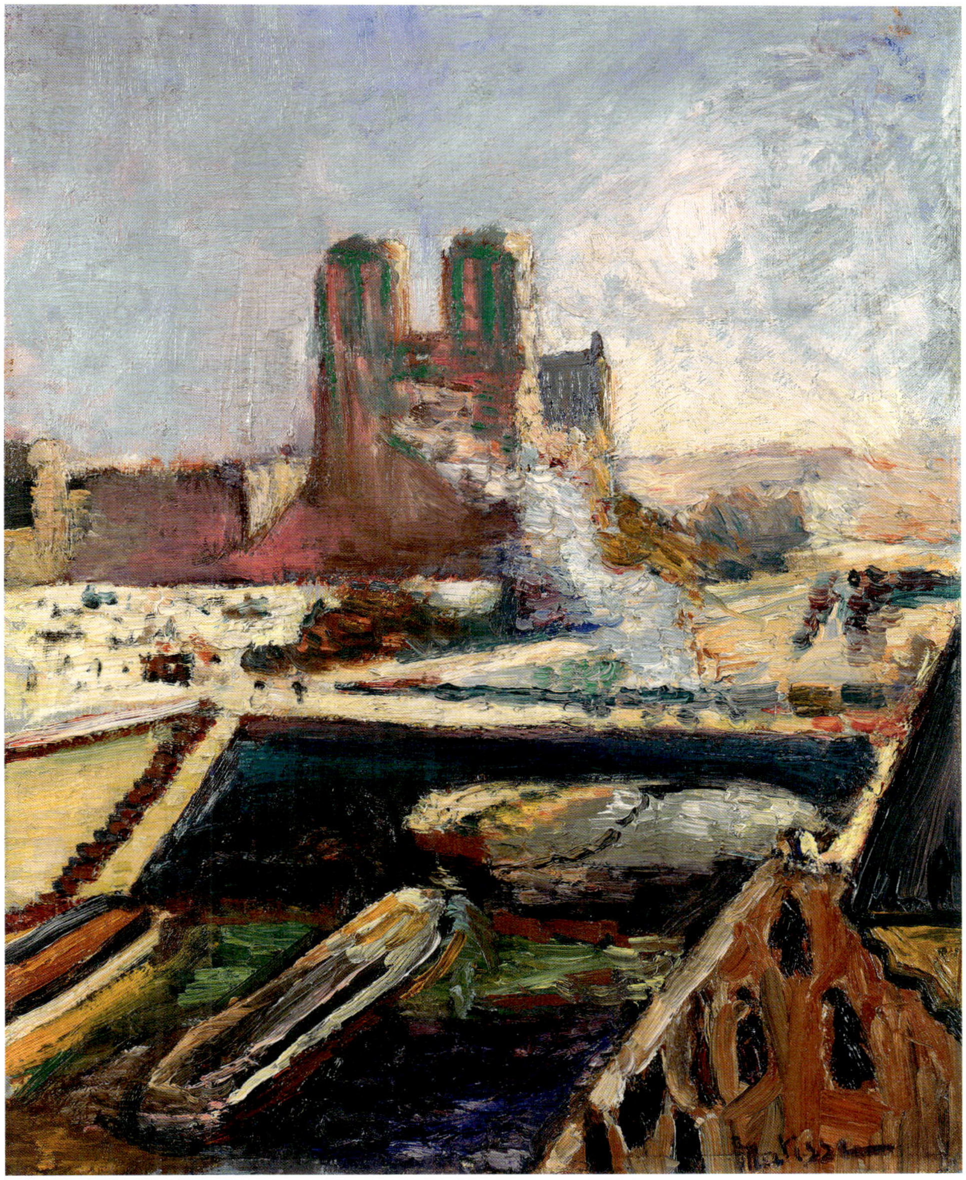

23 | *Notre-Dame*, ca. 1900

Oil on canvas, 18⅛ x 14¾ in. (46 x 37.5 cm). Tate: Purchased 1949

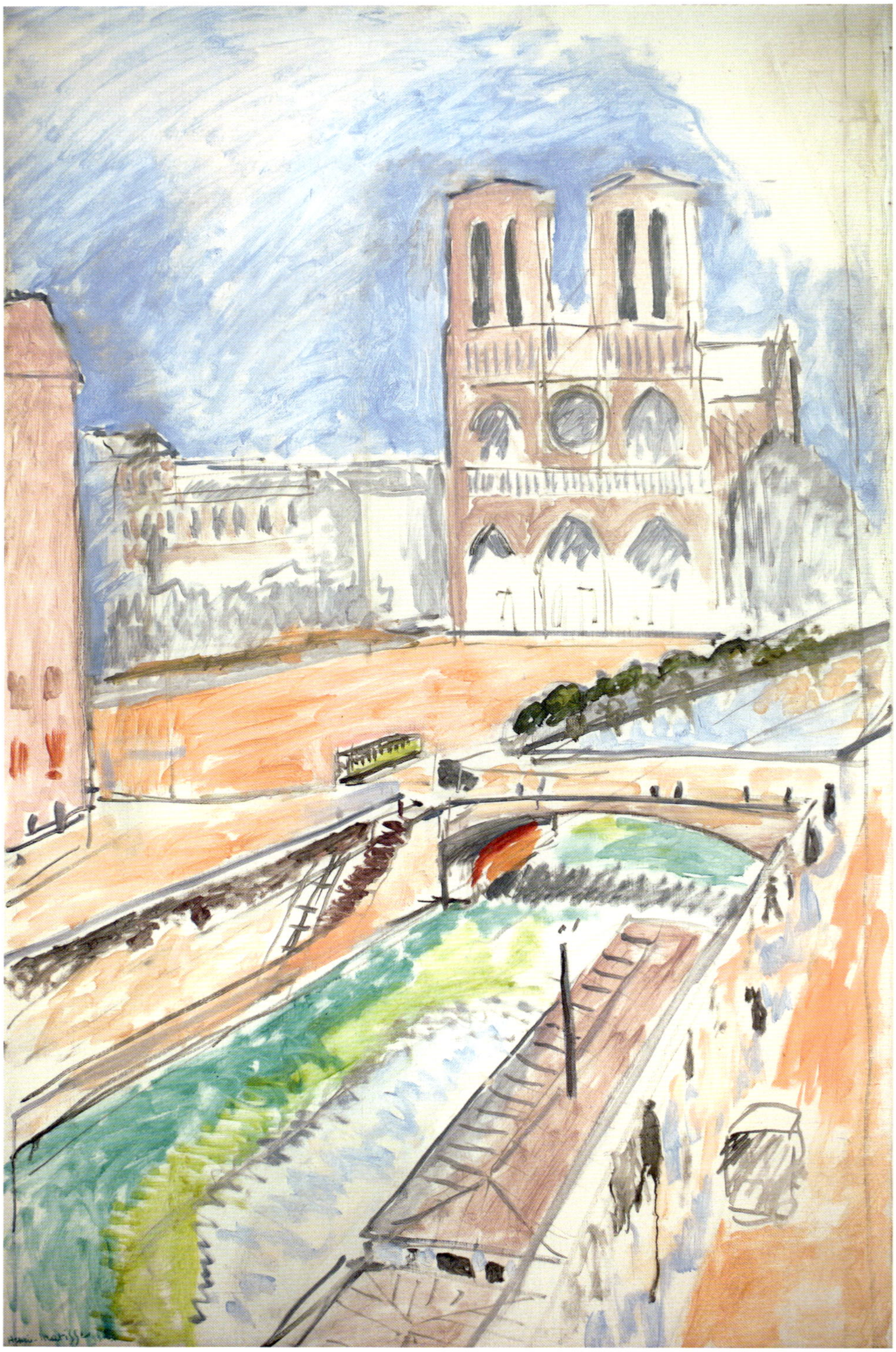

24 | *Notre-Dame*, 1914

Oil on canvas, 57⅞ x 38⅝ in. (147 x 98 cm). Kunstmuseum Solothurn, Dübi-Müller-Stiftung, Switzerland

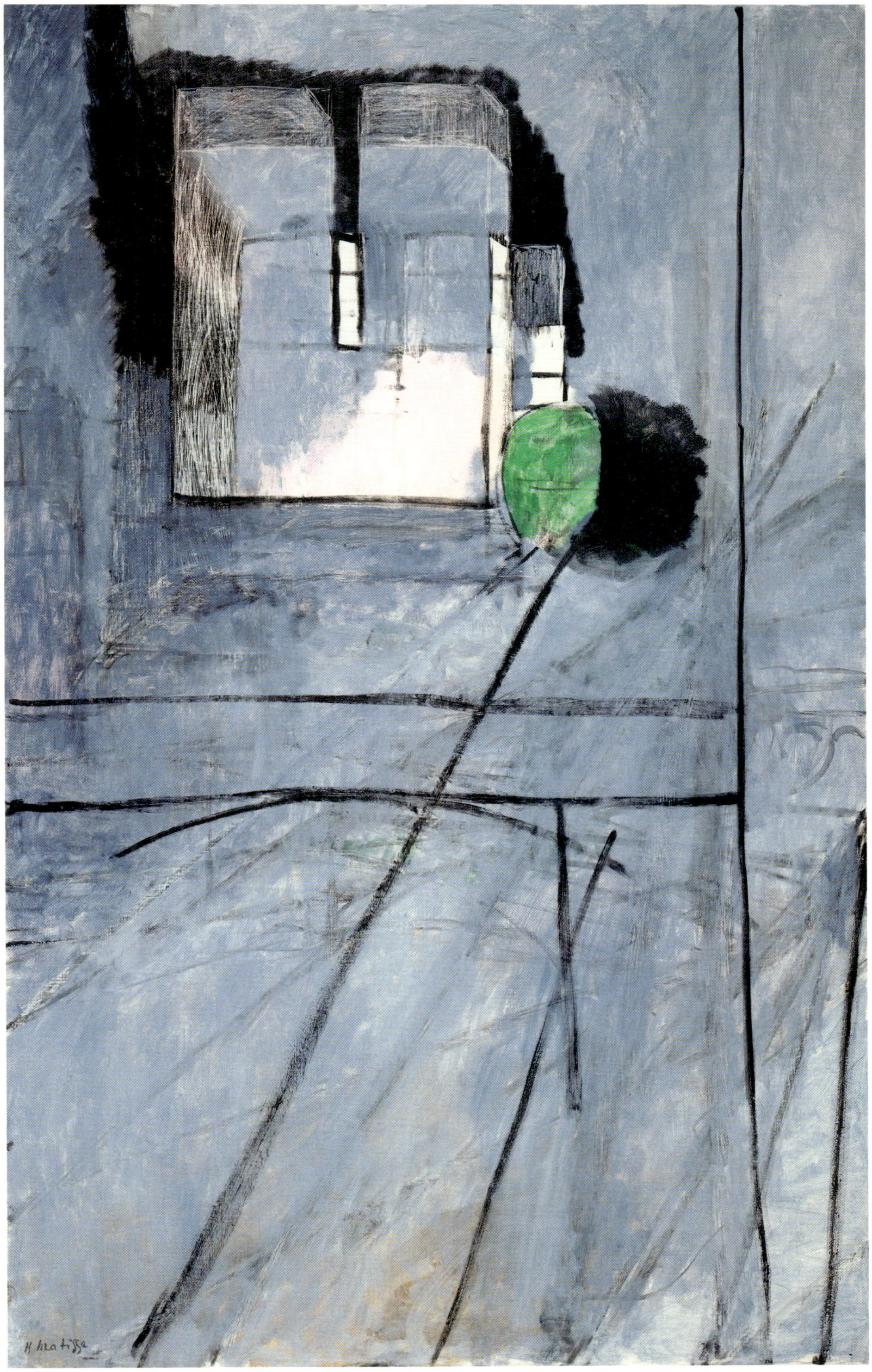

25 | *Notre-Dame*, 1914

Oil on canvas, 58 x 37⅛ in. (147.3 x 94.3 cm). The Museum of Modern Art, New York, Acquired through the Lillie P. Bliss Bequest, and the Henry Ittleson, A. Conger Goodyear, Mr. and Mrs. Robert Sinclair Funds, and the Anna Erickson Levene Bequest given in memory of her husband, Dr. Phoebus Aaron Theodor Levene, 1975

familiarity of the known world and the ceaseless web of insignificant events give way to the uncanniness of the absolute, the labile contingency of phenomena, the sharp edge of essences—qualities that have been linked to the aesthetic of Russian icons, which Matisse saw in Russia in 1911.[2] Without prior knowledge of the subject, it would be difficult to recognize in the second work the motifs that inspired its juxtaposition of geometric forms and irregular blots of pigment. Actual forms have been literally effaced to give free rein to an epiphany of being. It is as if, paradoxically, our everyday world turns out to be rooted in something like heaven, with an idea of form underlying it that musically rises up and lifts matter from within, consumes it, returning it to its noumenal truth.

In their 1912 manifesto *Du "cubisme"* (*On "Cubism"*), the artists Albert Gleizes and Jean Metzinger included a clearly anti-Matissian charge, denouncing "decorative" painting in the name of an idealistic conception of the image, "essentially independent, necessarily total, [whose] task is not to satisfy the spirit immediately but on the contrary to lead it gradually toward the fictive depths where an organizing light shines forth."[3] The imposing presence of the cathedral's towers at the top of the second composition suggests that the cubical—if not Cubist—*Notre-Dame* was a response to criticism of the decorative in painting, allowing Matisse to confirm, for himself and his disciples,[4] that the new "neo-Platonic academies" at the crossroads of Orphism, Cubism, and Futurism did not have a monopoly on the reign of essences in painting.[5]

However, what is at issue is not the choice of one style of representation over another; it is, more fundamentally, the way painting *rubs* against time, which finally occurs in and through disorder, first in one canvas and then in the other. In both works, disorder rises to the surface like a tide, obstinately thwarting

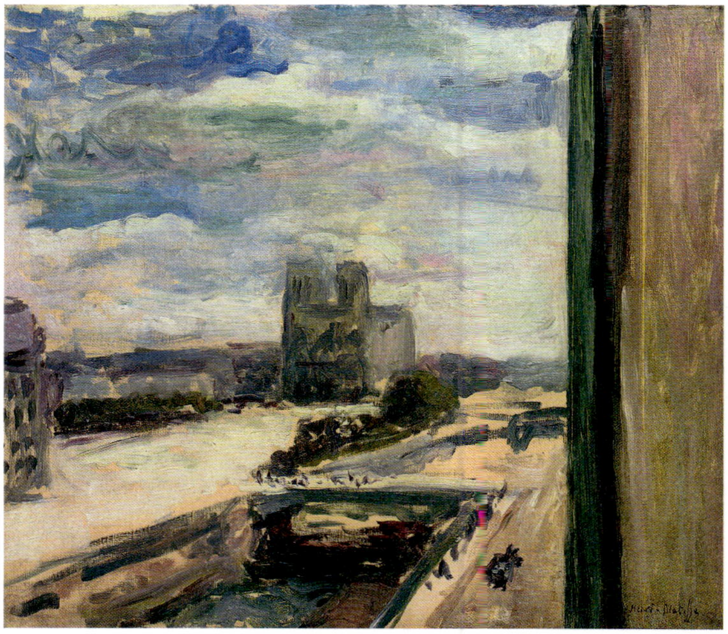

Fig. 44. *Notre-Dame*, 1902. Oil on canvas, 18½ x 22 in. (46.5 x 56 cm). Private collection

any chance of becoming fixed within a stable composition. The first version already manifests this, in the roughly daubed color, entire zones left unfinished, human figures and carriages barely sketched out. In the second, the strategy of disordering reaches a level of self-consciousness and becomes systematic.

The crystalline structure of being, a notion that haunts the blue canvas, is shaken from every direction. The effects of transparency allow pentimenti to show through, creating an intentionally failed palimpsest in which one version never completely obscures the previous one.[6] All the forms seem carried upward, the shifted traces following the forms like so many wakes. The cathedral ends up embodying an opposition between gravity and levitation. There is nothing heavier than this Notre-Dame, an enormous system of blocks with an orthogonality that ought to embed it like a rock in the ground. And there is nothing lighter than this Notre-Dame, a translucent emanation of ether, surprisingly propelled to the top of the blue field by oblique construction lines. The black above the towers acts as a restraint, preventing a definitive drift and conferring a strange, airy gravity of sorts on this celestial castle. In other words, the setting in motion of a *decorative* gaze ceaselessly unweaves the fabric of a *contemplative* gaze, which, however, ceaselessly re-forms itself. In the blue canvas, everything would like to be pure and univocal: the luminous unity of that heavenly color; the merging of depth perception and the flat surface; the fusion of exterior and interior (with, on the right side, the vertical line of the window frame). But everything is actually impure: the insistent strokes that soil the blue with black and that produce glistening, indefinable layers of ocher at the bottom and of pinkish mauve at the top; the lines that like blades pierce the motif or are suddenly interrupted; and above all the scratches that physically assault the picture plane along the perimeter of the cathedral. The imperious splendor of the structure deploys, only to immediately turn against itself.

Rare are the paintings in which disorder asserts itself with such productive energy, with such intrinsic life force (what the philosopher Henri Bergson called élan vital), as in the levitating *Notre-Dame* of spring 1914.[7] There is something profoundly Bergsonian in the work's preference for the future, that is, for the unpredictable. There is something profoundly Cubist in it as well, in the form developed by Braque and Picasso (fig. 45) rather than that of Gleizes and Metzinger: a rise of *chaos*, which assaults the iconic geometry of forms, apart from any dogmatic program, in a dizzying, experimental undermining of the ideal of completeness.[8] An ethics and an aesthetics of disorder linked Braque, Picasso, and Matisse in these years. Although irreducibly heterogeneous, their works bequeath to the beholder the notion that the image has value, has *life*, only through that which, in it, incessantly undoes what it is.

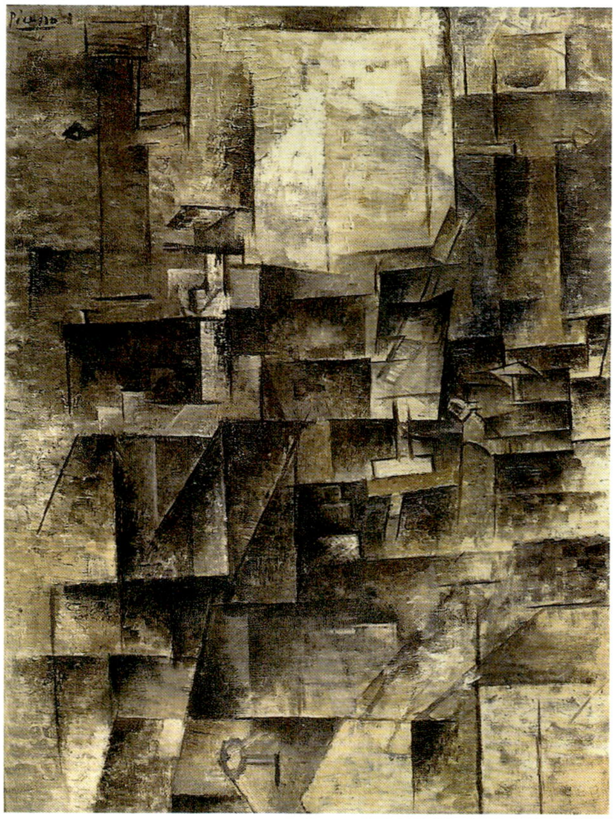

Fig. 45. Pablo Picasso. *The Dressing Table*, 1910. Oil on canvas, 24 x 18⅛ in. (61 x 46 cm). Private collection

TIME EMBODIED

Jack Flam

Time is an implicit theme in all of Matisse's paired paintings, and nowhere more so than in *Interior with Goldfish* and *Goldfish and Palette*. The first depicts a particular atmosphere and moment in time, while the second addresses the elusive relationships between time, space, and identity as well as the complex ways in which we experience them. These two pictures also embody different attitudes toward pictorial stability. In the first, the objects are fairly fixed; in the second, they and their surrounding spaces seem to be in constant flux.

Interior with Goldfish (cat. 26) was painted in the spring of 1914, a few months after Matisse rented a studio at 19, quai Saint-Michel, where he had lived and worked from the early 1890s until 1907. Happy to be back in this place that meant so much to him, he wrote to Simon Bussy that it was "a great pleasure for us to have new sensations in a familiar environment."[1] To create a fresh balance between the familiar and the new, Matisse took as his subject a bowl of goldfish similar to those he had painted at Issy-les-Moulineaux in 1912 (cat. 30). As in those earlier paintings, he put the goldfish in a cylindrical glass jar instead of the traditional bowl.[2] The fundamental geometry of this jar provided him with a stable form around which to anchor the composition: its curved forms served as a perfect foil to the cubic volumes of the furniture and the room itself.

Interior with Goldfish lovingly evokes the late afternoon light on a clear day in early spring as it falls on the Préfecture de Police and the Petit Pont below it. The impression of a specific moment in time is conveyed throughout by the way the light plays across the buildings, glances through the goldfish bowl, and casts shadows within the room. Matisse also explores the relationships between the interior of the room and the world outside, along with the time-bound transparencies through which our perceptions are filtered. The glass bowl, for example, is a confined space from which the fish peer out at a world whose complexity is unimaginable to them; similarly, the glass window allows us, too, to gaze out beyond the confines of the room.

The goldfish bowl is pivotal to the painting. Transparent and placed near the window, it mediates the transition from the room to the view of the city. But at the same time, it extends some of the opacity of the colors within the room over to the window and out into the city; the opaque blues from the bowl are echoed in the lower part of the window and block our view of what is most immediately below us. Across the quay, the afternoon traffic is silhouetted against the shaded street, and the world is in motion, as men and women go about their daily tasks. Through the transparency of the window, we see that world from aloft, from an isolated place no outside eye can penetrate. The fish, two floating flashes of crimson surrounded by stillness, are the only animated creatures in the silent room.

The relationships between the transparencies of the bowl and the window are accentuated by the early spring shoots growing from the small clay pot, which connect in curving lines with the arch of the Petit Pont and the steps leading down to the (invisible) river. Below those arcing lines, the blues within the bowl also leap across the windowpane and are thrust under the arch of the bridge. While the transitional passages between the interior and the window are pictorially quite complicated, both the room and the far quay are rather straightforwardly rendered.

Inside the room, the crimson goldfish stir in the water amid flashes of light. Near as they are to us physically, we are psychologically as removed from them as we are from the street outside, most especially because of the chair and table in the foreground that literally block our access to the room. The interior of the room sets limits, cuts off, encloses. In the waning hours of daylight, as we contemplate these two goldfish so clearly contained within their bowl, we are forced to consider the self-contained world of the room itself: the artist's studio, from which the outside world is seen from a distance. And in doing so we are impelled to contemplate the self that hesitates at the threshold of this silent room: our own physical presence as we stand before the picture and, by extension, the presence of the artist who once stood there—now invisible but felt everywhere in the image he has left for us to ponder.

When Matisse returned to the goldfish theme again that fall, he started out with a reprise of the earlier picture but with one important difference: he purposely added a depiction of himself. A postcard he sent Charles Camoin at the time includes a small sketch of the new composition in which he is seated with a palette next to the still life (fig. 46).[3] In the sketch, the details of the still life and the figure of

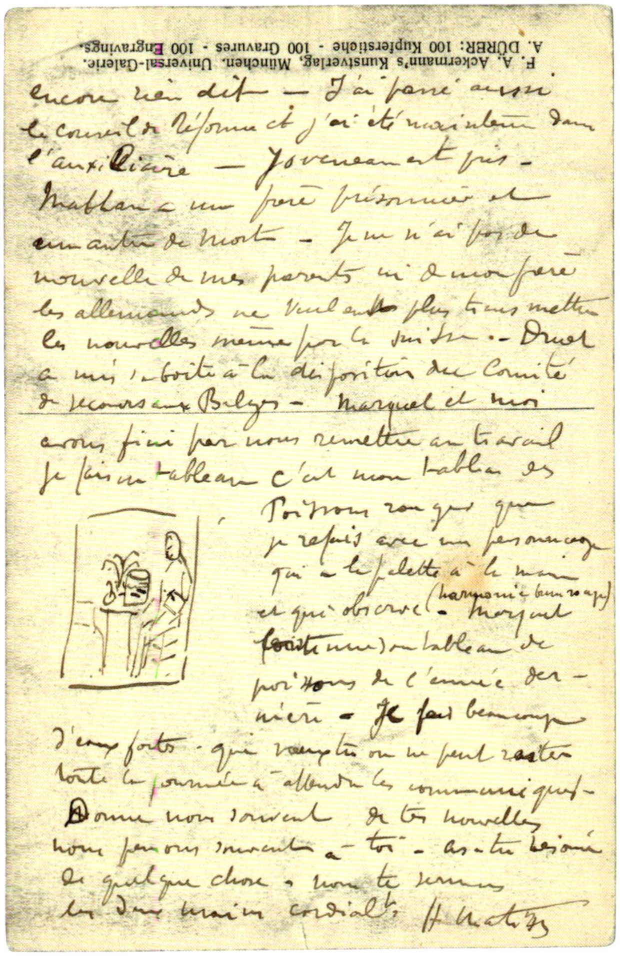
A. DÜRER: 100 Kupferstiche - 100 Gravures - 100 Engravings.
F. A. Ackermann's Kunstverlag, München. Universal-Galerie.

encore rien dit — J'ai passé aussi
le conseil de réforme et j'ai été maintenu dans
l'auxiliaire — Jovenneau est pris —
[illegible] a un frère prisonnier et
un autre de mort — Je n'ai pas de
nouvelles de mes parents ni de mon frère
les allemands ne veulent plus transmettre
les nouvelles même par la Suisse. — Druet
a mis sa boutique à la disposition du Comité
de secours aux Belges — Marquet et moi
avons fini par nous remettre au travail
je fais un tableau c'est mon tableau des
poissons rouges que
je reprends avec un personnage
qui a la palette à la main
et qui observe (harmonie brun rouge) — Marquet
continue son tableau de
poissons de l'année der-
nière — Je fais beaucoup
d'eaux fortes — [illegible] on ne peut rester
toute la journée à attendre les communiqués —
Donne nous souvent de tes nouvelles
nous pensons souvent à toi — as-tu besoin
de quelque chose — nous te serrons
les deux mains cordialt. H Matisse

Fig. 46. Postcard from Matisse to Charles Camoin, autumn 1914. Archives Camoin, Paris

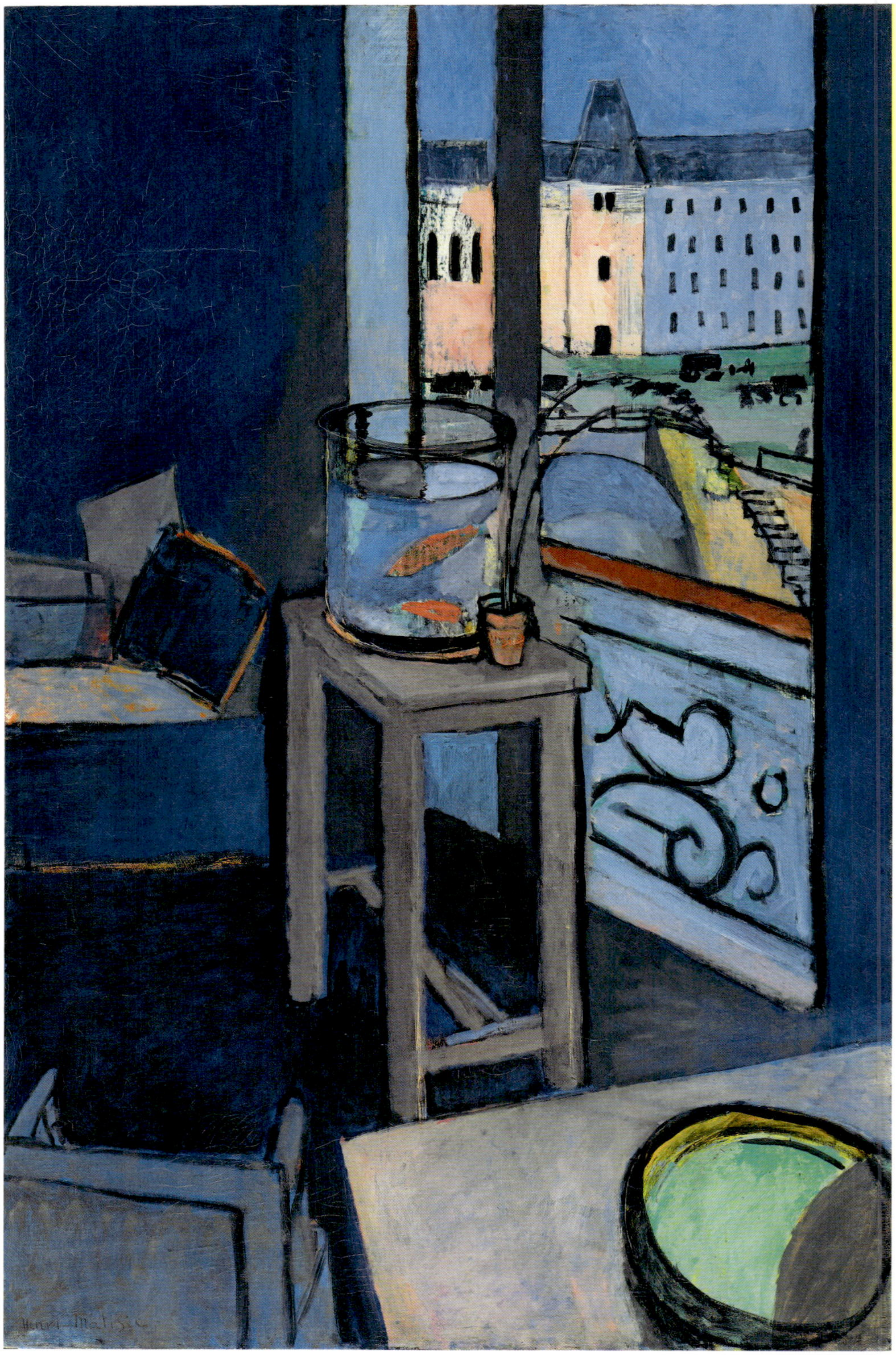

26 | *Interior with Goldfish*, 1914

Oil on canvas, 57⅞ x 38¼ in. (147 x 97 cm). Centre Pompidou, Musée National d'Art Moderne, Paris, Bequest of Baronne Eva Gourgaud, 1965

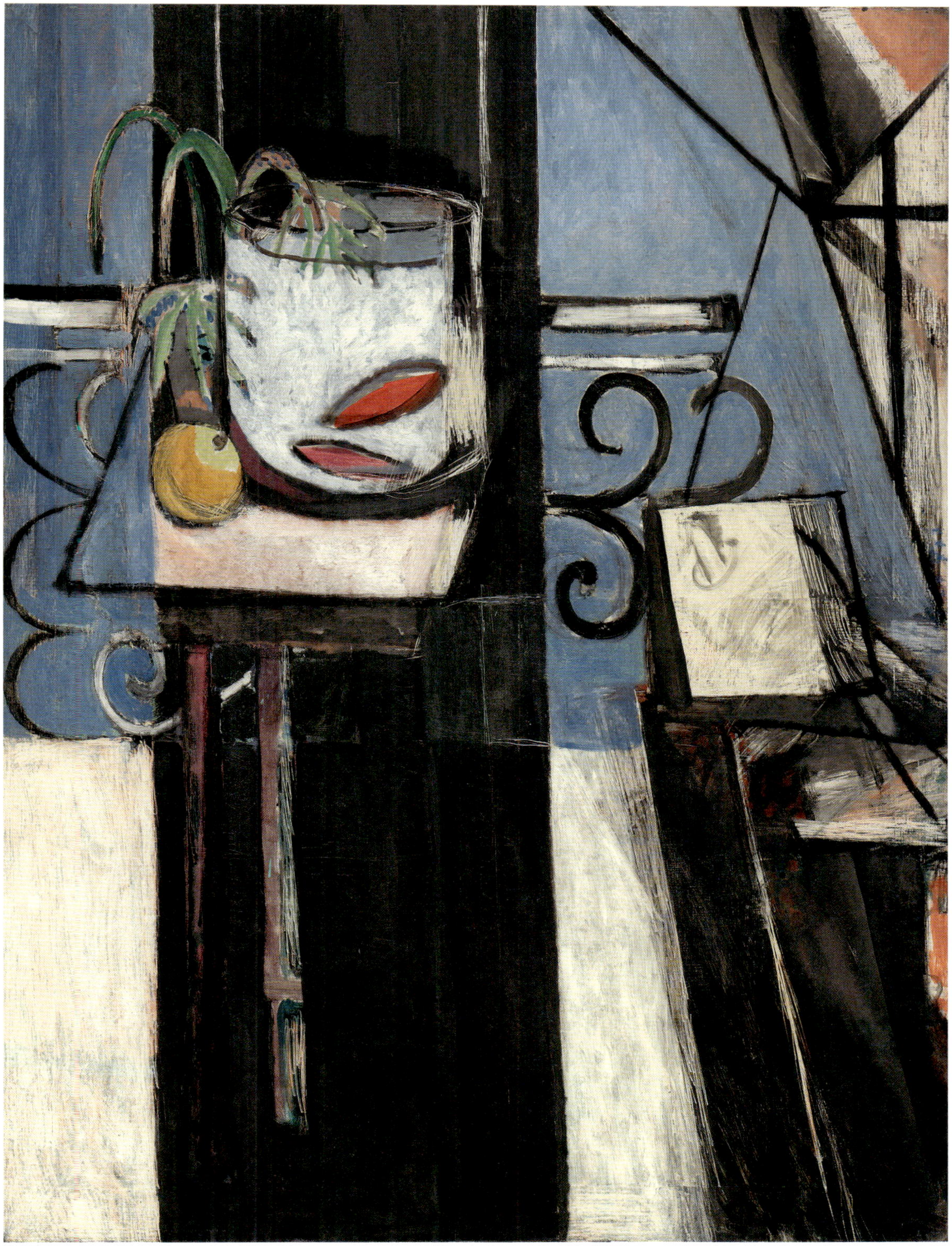

27 | *Goldfish and Palette*, 1914

Oil on canvas, 57⅞ x 44¼ in. (146.5 x 112.4 cm). The Museum of Modern Art, New York, Gift and bequest of Florene M. Schoenborn and Samuel A. Marx, 1964

the artist are depicted very clearly, but almost no attention is given to the setting. In the final painting (cat. 27), by contrast, the setting fairly overwhelms everything except the goldfish bowl, and the artist in particular remains only as a fragmentary, translucent presence. In fact, the rendering of his body ultimately became so abstracted that many commentators have doubted whether anything more of him than his palette is physically present.[4] But Matisse did indeed leave more of himself: the right side of the picture contains clear indications of his legs and left arm and an abstracted rendering of his upper body and head, translated into architectonic forms similar to those in a contemporaneous portrait of his daughter, *White and Pink Head* (cat. 29).[5] In this dispersal of the forms of the figure into an almost unreadable architectural scaffolding, *Goldfish and Palette* is one of Matisse's strongest responses to Cubism.

The ambiguous form of the artist is an essential element in the drama of the painting, for it most explicitly embodies the tension between internalized and externalized versions of what we see before us. Matisse is in effect representing his state of mind as well as his physical being.[6] In his previous paintings of people, the integral quality of the body and face had always been of paramount importance. Here, the intermittent legibility of the representation of the artist is emblematic of the difficult legibility of the entire picture, as is the constant readjustment of the forms in relation to one another. We are continually cognizant of the evidence, all over the surface, of the intensive process of painting, scraping out, and repainting. This heightens our awareness of two somewhat different but coterminous aspects of time. The heavily worked surface quite literally contains the physical evidence of how long it took for the artist to produce the image. Simultaneously, the imagery seems not only to suggest but also to contain the passage of time; the shifting forms are all charged with an ambiguity and translucence that make it hard to say exactly where they begin and end. They are *there*, before our eyes, but it is hard to say *where* there is.

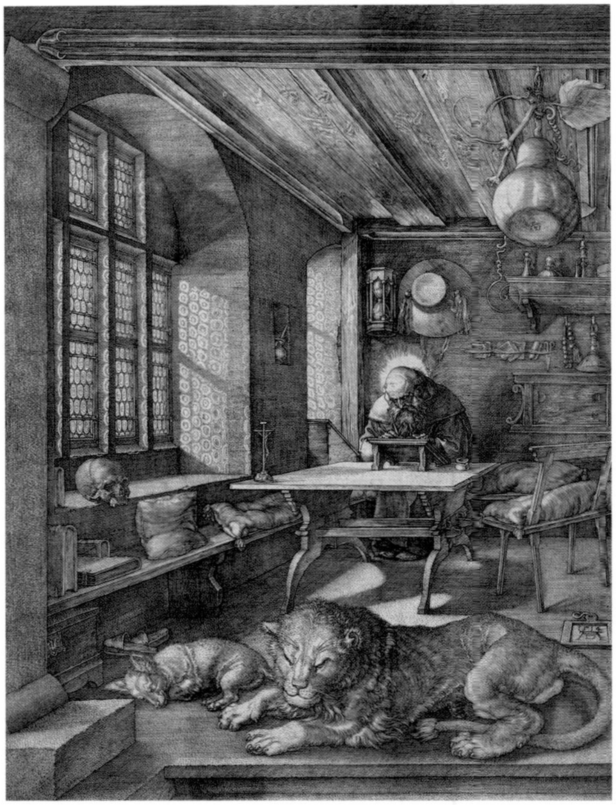

Fig. 47. Albrecht Dürer. *Saint Jerome in His Study*, 1514. Engraving, 9¾ x 7½ in. (24.6 x 18.9 cm). The Metropolitan Museum of Art, New York, Fletcher Fund, 1919

This sense of seeing the forms primarily within a temporal continuum rather than in a specific place is reinforced by the fact that nothing is depicted outside the studio except the sky. The whole of reality appears to be compressed within this mysteriously shifting space. The window offers only a stark blueness that calls to mind Stéphane Mallarmé's *azur*—the all-encompassing emptiness that underlies all the struggles of art and life. Within this sealed room, the still life represents not so much a kind of miniaturized nature but an ensemble of signs for things. The bowl, water, fish, plant, and fruit are rendered as compressed distillations of the things they represent. Moreover, these condensed images contain a surprising élan vital—in no small measure because of the tightly sprung curves of the window grillwork, radiating out from the still life like abstract signs for the inner force of the objects.

It is not only objects that are translated into signs. The light itself is similarly transformed. The roles of black and white, the polarities of darkness and light, are intermittently reversed. The vertical black strip that dominates the painting functions as a band of light as well as of darkness, and the whites that flank it also act uncannily as signs for shadow as well as for light. Hermetic and introverted, this painting is perceived primarily as a projection of a state of mind. The fluctuant articulation of the forms acts as a metaphor for thought: the scratching, scumbling, and repeated repainting are like visual equivalents for the contradictions, tensions, and digressions inherent in the process of contemplation that guided the creation of the painting. Surely it is no coincidence that the postcard to Camoin bore a reproduction of Albrecht Dürer's engraving *Saint Jerome in His Study* (fig. 47), in which the reclusive saint sits writing by a window, rendered in terms of vertical bars of light and shadow, through which nothing of the outside world can be seen.

Goldfish and Palette is one of Matisse's most resonant and most somber works—and also one of his most introspective. In it we see the artist quite literally as he "sees" himself in the act of painting. The room and goldfish are more clearly focused in his mind's eye than is his own being, which he represents as a complexly skewed network of lines, violently intersecting planes, and roughly scraped and scumbled afterthoughts. The image as a whole—its subject, its tensely worked surface, and its provisionally placed forms—is like a projection of Matisse's inner state of being, laid down coterminously over a description of the external world. The two are not exactly the same, but neither are they entirely separate. In fact, one could say that the image of the artist here adjusts itself to the picture, even more than the rest of the picture adjusts itself to him. It is an active image, presented as if still in progress. In *Interior with Goldfish*, the image remains constant, and we in effect adjust ourselves to our expanding awareness of its implications. Here, it is the picture that keeps adjusting itself.

The culmination of Matisse's early use of the goldfish theme, *Goldfish and Palette* is a key image in the development of his lifelong preoccupation with time and with the pictorial and psychological implications of beholding and being beheld.[7]

BLACK RIBBON AND BLUE STRIPES

Isabelle Monod-Fontaine

Over a period of two decades, Matisse made at least twenty painted portraits of Marguerite, his eldest child, as well as a greater number of drawings and engravings. The five paintings discussed here were produced in 1914 and 1915, in a sequence that is by no means self-evident. In each, the twenty-year-old Marguerite wears a blouse or jacket with a V-neck and her customary black ribbon, which calls to mind one of Manet's models.[1] These canvases might at first seem to be merely exercises in style—brilliant variations on the simple, appealing theme of a woman in a hat—but one of them clearly stands out. *White and Pink Head* (cat. 29) belongs to an entirely different pictorial world. It is as if Manet had lapsed into Cubism, as if the splashes of color had been intentionally imprisoned behind the bars of a grid, and as if black were now demanding pride of place.

On the basis of information currently available, the following sequence may be proposed for the portraits. The first was *The Rose Hat* (fig. 48), which depicts the sitter in a hat with a fairly high crown and a solid-color blouse with the collar knotted into a scarf. This canvas was photographed in March 1914 for the Galerie Bernheim-Jeune, which then acquired it on May 8.[2] After this point, the chronological evidence becomes less precise. Did Matisse undertake several other similar portraits in the spring of 1914, including *Marguerite in a Leather Hat* (fig. 49), which the Bernheim-Jeune records also date to 1914,[3] but which was not acquired until May 21, 191[illegible]? Although Marguerite wears a smaller hat in this painting, her hair and ribbon are arranged the same way as in the earlier work, and the blouse appears just as simple.

Should this canvas be linked in turn to the other, undated *Marguerite in a Leather Hat* (cat. 28), which was to remain unknown, and perhaps incomplete, in the artist's studio? The only early evidence of that canvas (discovered by Pierre Schneider in the 1980s and first exhibited then) is an often-reproduced archival photograph, probably dating to late 1916,[4] that shows it, in the same condition as today, hanging on the wall of the studio on the quai Saint-Michel.[5] Marguerite sports the same little leather hat, but here the cool blue and green of her hat and blouse are applied as juxtaposed patches, allowing the white of the canvas to come into play, as if this were a first draft that was never realized. There is another new detail: a gold pendant hangs from the black ribbon and transforms it into a necklace. Photographs of Marguerite from this period attest to the new care she was taking in her appearance and to the inventiveness she displayed in making her sad little choker a true ornament.

Next would come—but when precisely?—two canvases that have often been paired: *Marguerite in a Striped Jacket* (fig. 50) and *White and Pink Head* (cat. 29).[6] What connects them, aside from a perhaps somewhat later date (the Bernheim-Jeune records place them both in 1915), is that they apparently depict the very same motif, down to the detail of the stripes on the bodice and the gold pendant. They might thus fall within Matisse's well-known system of "pairs," in which a first, "soft" version, relatively legible and fluidly rendered in bright colors (*Striped Jacket*), is followed by a "hard" version—geometric, more opaque and hermetic—that is worked to the point of veering toward abstraction (*White and Pink Head*). That reading, proposed by Alfred Barr in 1951,[7] must be reexamined in light of subsequent research.

In the first place, there is no evidence as to which canvas came first. Was one (or were both) undertaken at the very start of the summer of 1914?[8] Might *Striped Jacket* actually be a second, more marketable version of an obviously more difficult picture that had been reworked several times? Judging from certain of Matisse's other pairs,[9] it is possible that *Striped Jacket* was painted quickly during the elaboration of *White and Pink Head*. The work on the latter would then have been resumed and taken in a radically different direction in November 1914, after Matisse's return from several weeks at Collioure, and would have continued throughout the winter of 1914–15.

This was a time when Matisse's exposure to Cubism, particularly through his friendship with Juan Gris, became intense and almost all-consuming. In Collioure, between September 10 and October 22,

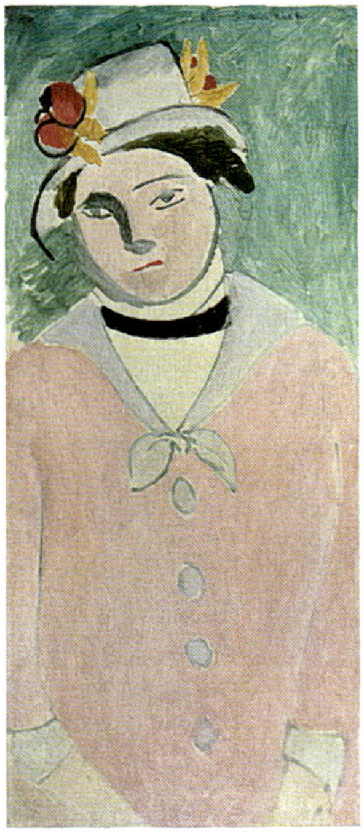

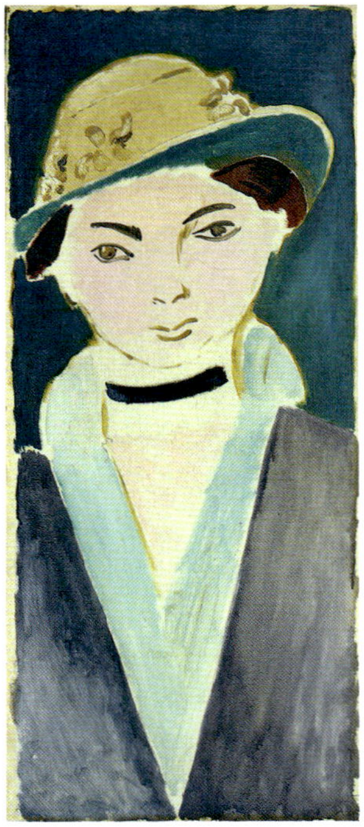

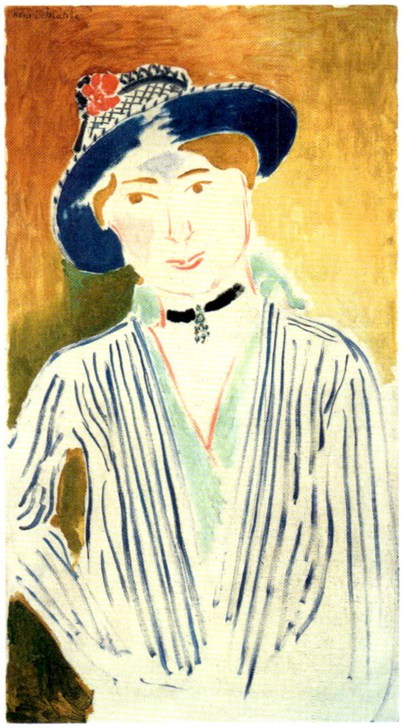

Fig. 48. *The Rose Hat*, 1914. Oil on canvas, 44⅛ x 19¼ in. (112 x 49 cm). Private collection

Fig. 49. *Marguerite in a Leather Hat*, 1914. Oil on canvas, 38¼ x 17⅛ in. (97.2 x 43.5 cm). Private collection

Fig. 50. *Marguerite in a Striped Jacket*, 1914. Oil on canvas, 48⅝ x 26⅞ in. (123.6 x 68.4 cm). Bridgestone Museum of Art, Ishibashi Foundation, Tokyo

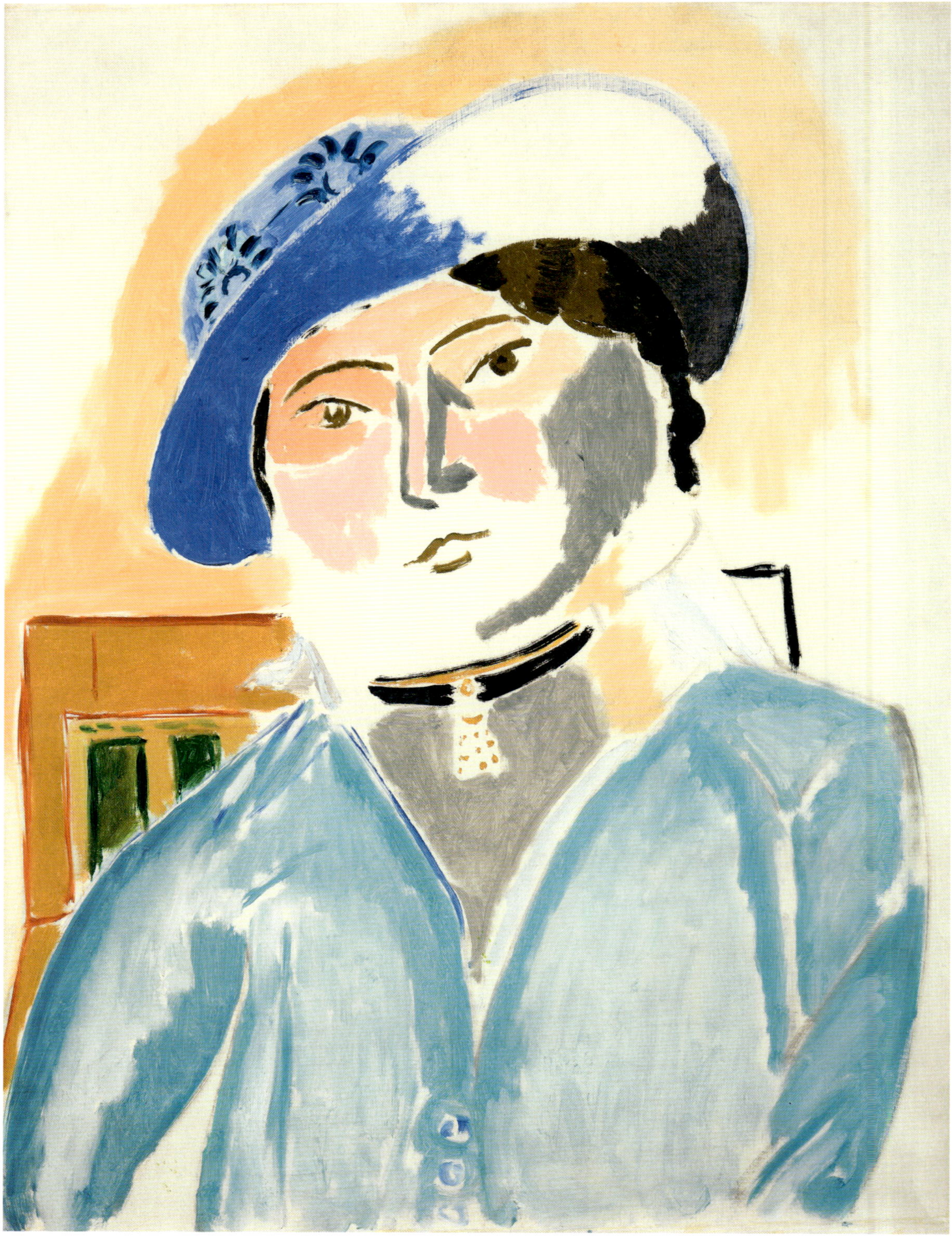

28 | *Marguerite in a Leather Hat*, 1914

Oil on canvas, 32¼ x 25⅝ in. (82 x 65 cm). Musée Matisse, Le Cateau-Cambrésis, Gift of Marie Matisse

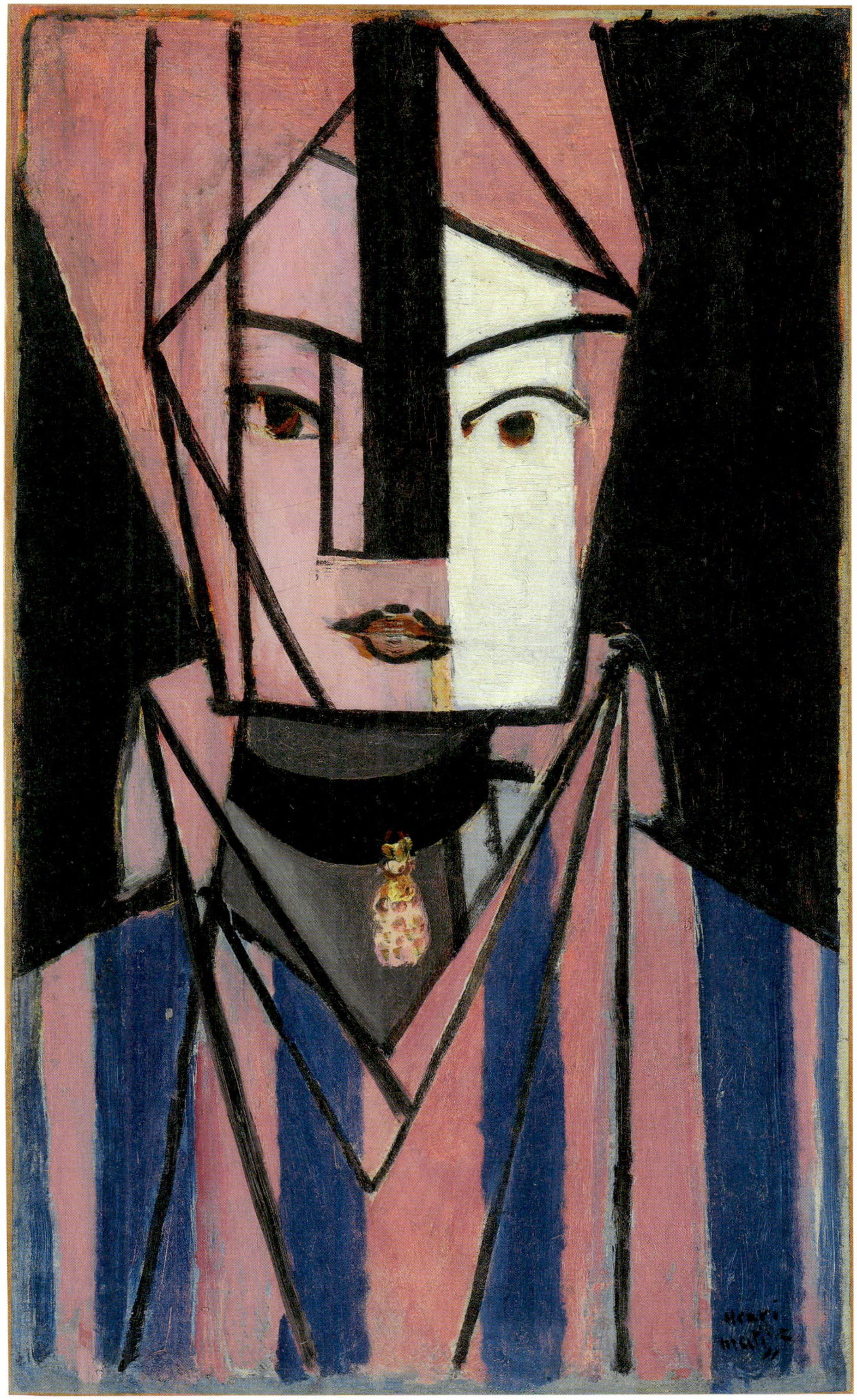

29 | *White and Pink Head*, 1914–15

Oil on canvas, 29½ x 18½ in. (75 x 47 cm). Centre Pompidou, Musée National d'Art Moderne, Paris, Purchase, 1976

the two artists established a solid intellectual and personal relationship that they later continued in long conversations in Paris. Since Matisse had trouble returning to work in that sinister autumn of 1914,[10] he was undoubtedly all the more receptive to Gris, who encouraged him to question his work and seek out new directions. Writing of a critical juncture for *White and Pink Head*, Jack Flam reported, "[It] started out to be fairly naturalistic, but after a time Matisse said to his daughter . . . , 'This painting wants to take me somewhere else. Do you feel up to it?' She agreed, and he began to rework the painting."[11]

In fact, the task of elaboration and concentration that Matisse had set for himself in *White and Pink Head* is evident in the actual handling of the paint. A few traces of the "fairly naturalistic" first state, including the pendant and the modeling of the mouth, are still visible beneath the striking orthogonal grid that the artist imposed.[12] The device that structures most of Gris's paintings and papiers collés from 1913–14 is reflected here in the way the face is divided into flat, contrasting parallel bands as well as in the correspondence established between these bands and the original motif of alternating stripes on the bodice.[13]

Nevertheless, though Gris's and Matisse's grids are similar, they serve different ends. Gris used them to examine his subject from different angles and to weave the slender shapes together in a way that would reconstitute the architectonic unity of the picture plane. Matisse, conversely, sought a method of composition that would correspond with his simplified, condensed formal vocabulary while also conveying his perceptions of shadow and light. In the end, Matisse actually used this grid very little, believing that its bands artificially carved up a living reality that he regarded as all of a piece, especially since, in this case, it was his beloved daughter at issue. However, *White and Pink Head* does attest to the artist's advance deep into Cubist, or Cubistic, territory, as does *French Window at Collioure* (1914; Centre Pompidou, Musée National d'Art Moderne, Paris), another "banded" painting, which had been left incomplete in Collioure a few weeks earlier, in October 1914, before he returned to Paris.

Disconcerting, tense, and dark, this strange portrait increased interest in Matisse but remained unconvincing to collectors. It was purchased by Bernheim-Jeune in December 1915, and from November of that year to April 1917, Léonce Rosenberg,[14] Alphonse Kann,[15] and Marchesa Luisa Casati[16] each in turn considered acquiring the work but then almost immediately backed out. Finally, on March 21, 1919, by means of a diplomatic letter from Félix Fénéon, the gallery very politely asked Matisse to take back his canvas, which the artist did four days later.[17]

White and Pink Head ultimately ended up in the collection of Matisse's elder son, Jean, along with the portrait of Marguerite that had remained in his father's studio. For a long time, then, *Marguerite in a Leather Hat* (cat. 28) and *White and Pink Head* hung side by side on the walls of the house in Pontoise.[18] These two views of the same model, different in every respect, display the complexity and subtlety of Matisse's approach to the portrait. In the first picture, bright, lively splashes of color are freely spattered over the white canvas, with almost no lines defining or intersecting them. In the second, the black ground (one of the first times Matisse used this as a major device) acts as the backdrop for a rigid system of verticals and obliques, underscored with black, that severely constrains the dense, opaque pinks, grays, and blues. In both canvases, however, Marguerite's gaze pierces through—resistant, intact, and fresh.

SUPERNATURAL INTERIORS

Cécile Debray

Matisse often placed his sculptures in his compositions, where they acted as miniature evocations of earlier formal solutions and reflected his own obsessive repetitiveness: "I discovered myself by considering at first my earliest works. They rarely deceive. There I found something that was always the same. . . . It was the manifestation of my personality, which appeared the same no matter what different states of mind I passed through."[1] Two still lifes titled *Sculpture and Vase of Ivy* (cats. 31, 32), painted in Issy-les-Moulineaux during the war, feature Matisse's *Reclining Nude I* (1906–7) posed with a potbellied glass vase and a scattering of winter fruit. Matisse apparently borrowed the central motif from an earlier painting of a vase holding an ivy branch, a subject that seems to have given him much delight.[2]

In these paintings, Matisse's subtle rendering of the transparent glass, the glossy ivy leaves, and the matte plaster recalls the very Flemish interplay of materials found in his early paintings, from *The Dinner Table* (1897; private collection) to *Still Life with Oranges* (1899; Centre Pompidou, Musée National d'Art Moderne, Paris). However, the present works belong to a series painted between 1908 and 1924 that frequently combines this particular sculpture with the motif of floral stems or vines, including *Sculpture and Persian Vase* (1908; National Museum of Art, Architecture, and Design, Oslo), the first in the series; *Still Life with a Pewter Jug and Statuette* (fig. 51); and *Goldfish* (cat. 30).[3] After Matisse's model for the sculpture, entitled *Aurora*, was accidentally destroyed, he memorialized it in *Blue Nude, Memory of Biskra* (1907; The Baltimore Museum of Art), a work emblematic of the relationship between sculpture and painting. Reversing that order here, Matisse begins by representing *Reclining Nude* in paint as he delves further into the problem of volumetric versus planar surfaces.

The constructed nature of the sculpture is an explicit subject in *Goldfish*, painted in 1912. While the sculpture was originally painted in a pink that was close to the actual color of the terracotta (and the model's flesh), Matisse redid it in a remarkable ghostlike gray that underlines the inanimate quality of the reclining nude. At the same time, he elongated the body of the woman and stretched it out in space so that it loses its three-dimensionality. This change combines with the dramatic dark tones of the

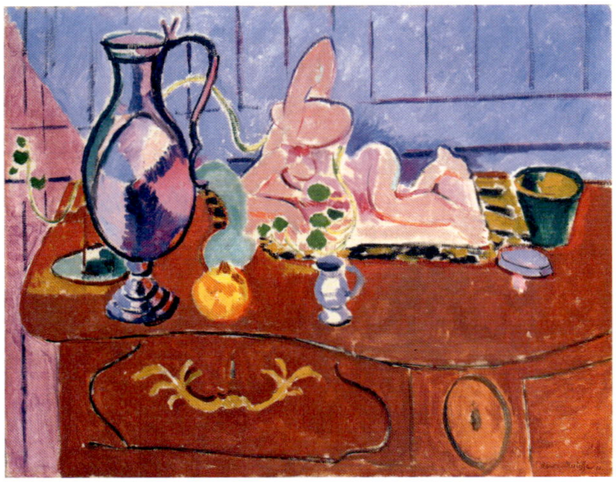

Fig. 51. *Still Life with a Pewter Jug and Statuette*, 1910. Oil on canvas, 35⅜ x 46⅛ in. (90 x 117 cm). The State Hermitage Museum, Saint Petersburg

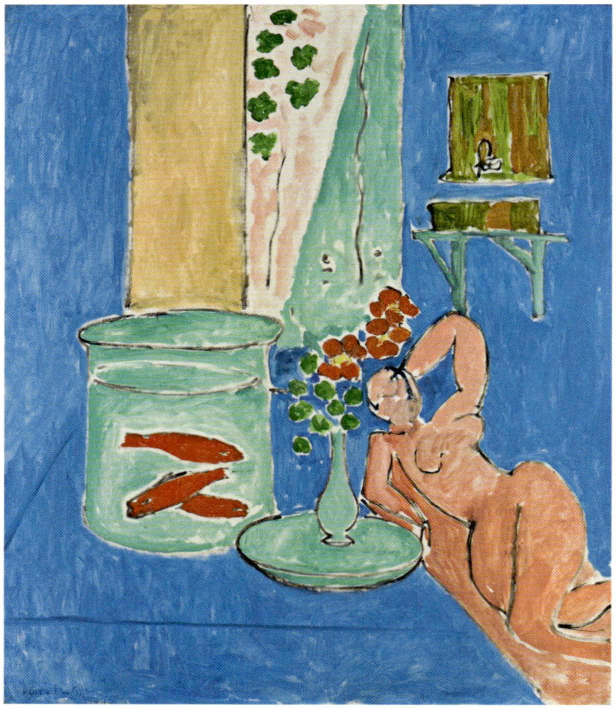

Fig. 52. *Goldfish and Sculpture*, 1912. Oil on canvas, 46 x 39⅝ in. (116.2 x 100.5 cm). The Museum of Modern Art, New York, Gift of Mr. and Mrs. John Hay Whitney

surroundings, which reduce the sense of spatiality, to stress the symbolic character of the arrangement. Although Matisse would revisit the subject again twice the same year, he did not retain this method of representing the sculpture. In later versions, including *Goldfish and Sculpture* (fig. 52), as well as in the two compositions discussed below, he reintroduced the pink flesh color in his depiction of the sculpture and found other means to explore issues of representation and construction.

Cézanne had examined the same issue in several canvases, such as *Still Life with Plaster Cast* of about 1895 (fig. 53), with regard to a small copy of a putto attributed to Pierre Puget.[4] Joachim Gasquet has noted certain remarks Cézanne made about this painting that strongly echo Matisse's preoccupations.

> *Here, look at that hair, this cheek, it is drawn, it's skillful; there, those eyes, that nose, it's painted. . . . And in a good painting, such as I dream of, there is unity. Drawing and color are not distinct from one another. Little by little as one paints, one draws, and the more harmonious the colors, the more precise the drawing will be. . . . When color is at its richest, form is at its fullest. Contrast and harmony between tones, that's the secret of drawing and modeling.*[5]

In his Bathers series, Cézanne sought to attain a well-balanced and complete plastic insertion (and even integration) of his figures into the landscape. Similarly, Matisse aims here for a "deindividualization" of his figures through a gradual process of construction and simplification, one that Rémi Labrusse has read as literal "eviction proceedings" against the live model.[6] In effect, the recourse to sculpture allows for three-dimensionality without the model's destabilizing presence. In 1942 Matisse was to clearly

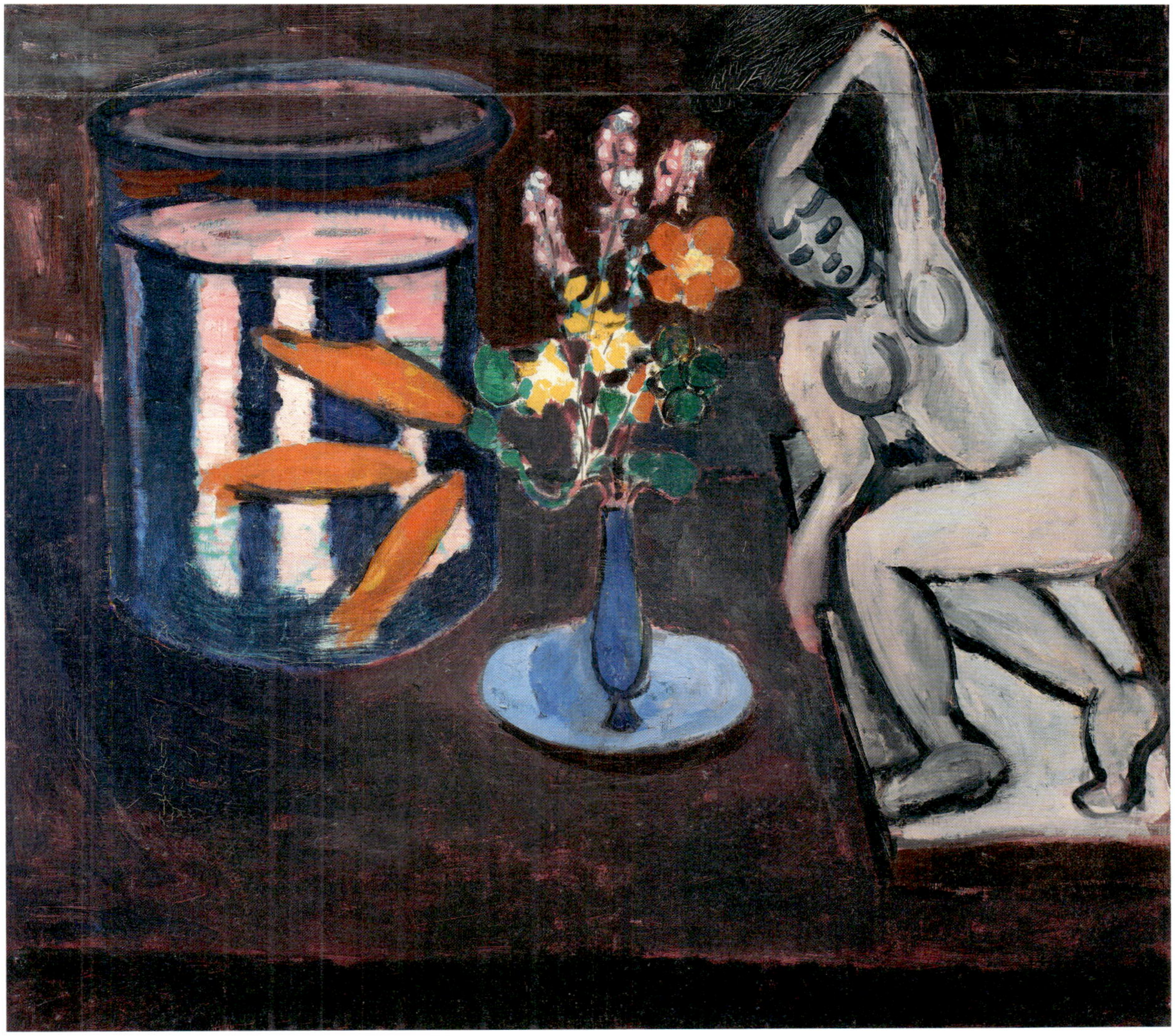

30 | *Goldfish*, 1912

Oil on canvas, 32¼ x 36¾ in. (82 x 93.5 cm). Statens Museum for Kunst, Copenhagen, J. Rump Collection

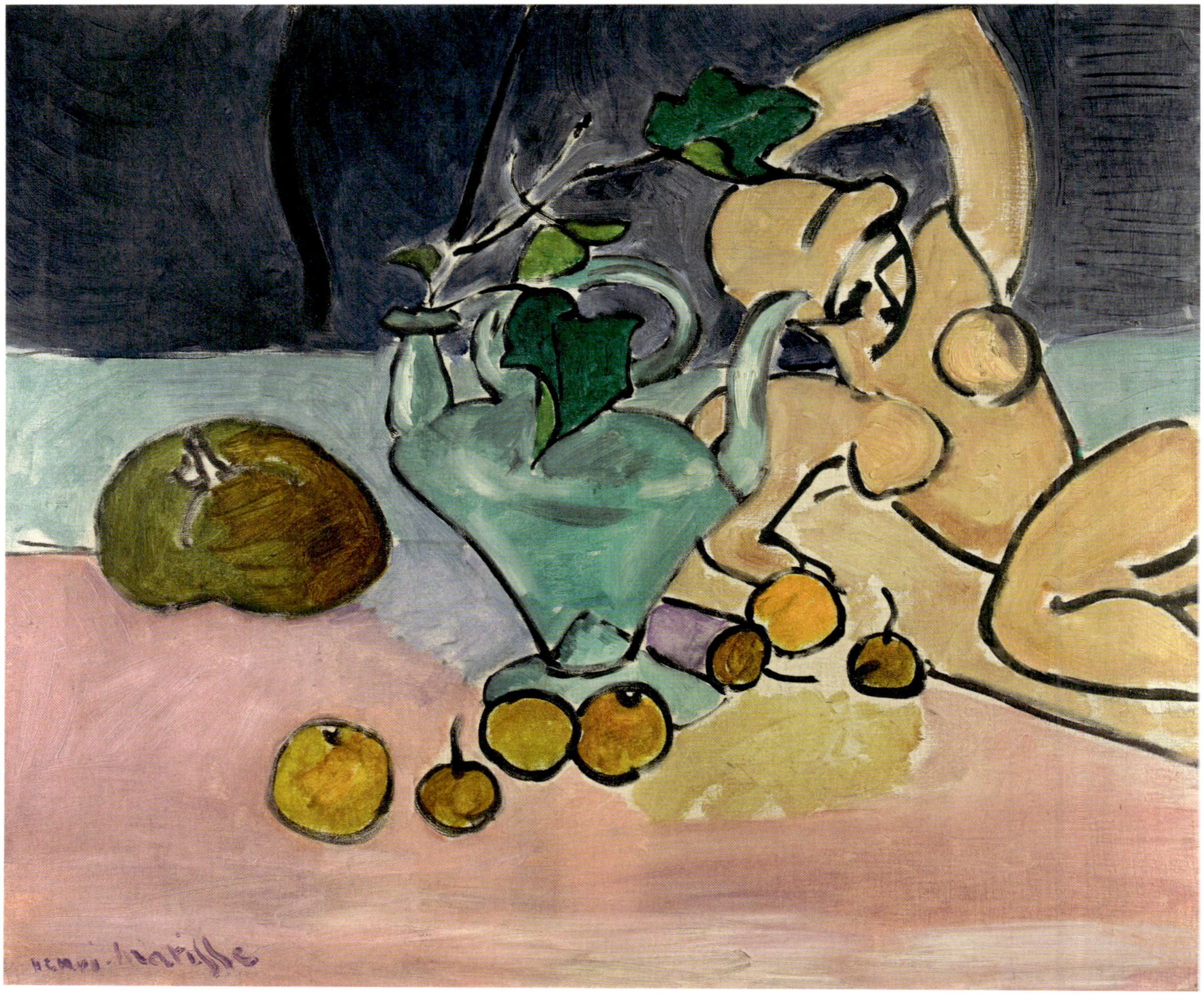

31 | *Sculpture and Vase of Ivy*, 1916

Oil on canvas, 23⅝ x 28¾ in. (60 x 73 cm). Centre Pompidou, Musée National d'Art Moderne, Paris, Gift of Adèle and George Besson, 1963. On extended loan to the Musée des Beaux-Arts et d'Archéologie, Besançon

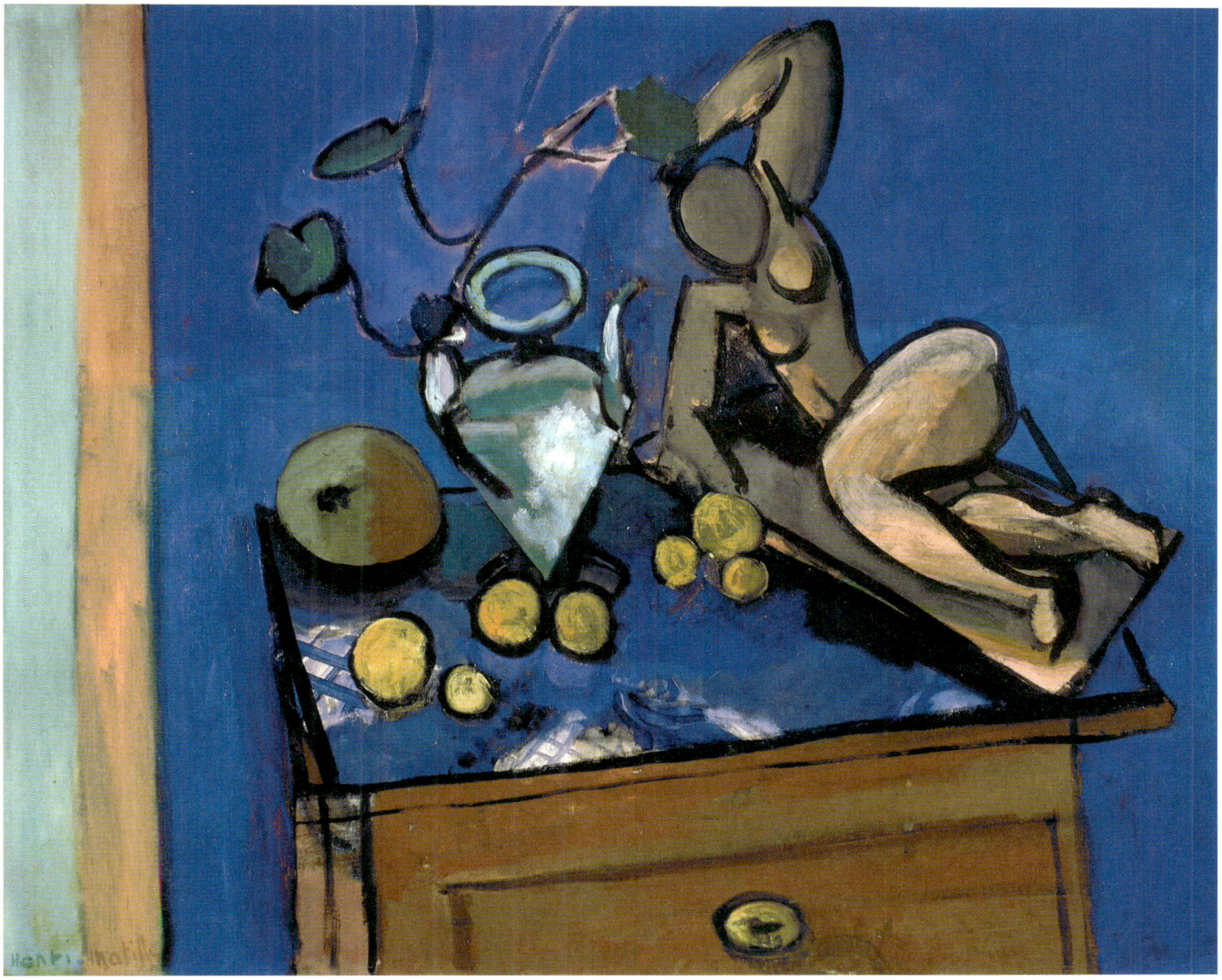

32 | *Sculpture and Vase of Ivy*, 1916–17

Oil on canvas, 28¾ x 36¼ in. (73 x 92 cm). Tikanoja Art Museum, Vaasa, Finland

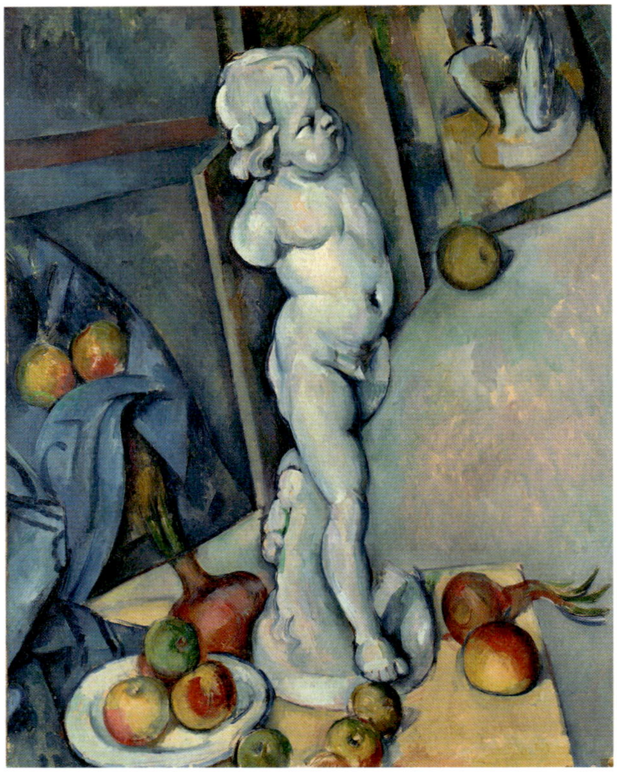

Fig. 53. Paul Cézanne, *Still Life with Plaster Cast*, ca. 1895. Oil on paper mounted on panel, 27¾ x 22½ in. (70.6 x 57.3 cm). The Samuel Courtauld Trust, The Courtauld Gallery, London

spell out this ambivalent relationship: "My progress, I consider I have made some progress when I note in my work an increasingly evident independence from the support of the model. . . . The model is a springboard for me—it's a door which I must break down to reach the garden in which I am alone and so happy—even the model exists only for the use I can make of it."[7]

These two still lifes are often considered equally austere, stylized compositions influenced by Cubism and the work of Matisse's friend Juan Gris. Axel Salto, a Danish artist who visited Matisse in the spring of 1916, mentioned seeing "supernatural interiors . . . in touch with Cubist theories," a vague reference that could indicate these works, among others.[8] But the two paintings actually display different approaches to the same motifs. In one (cat. 31), the composition stands out against an abstract, colored ground composed of three horizontal bands recalling Matisse's large Arcadian compositions of the 1910s. In the other (cat. 32), the composition is anchored in a space defined by the plane of the quadrangular buffet tray and is clearly characterized as a studio still life. Theodore Reff has pointed out that the sculpture's sensual reclining figure, which appears many times in Matisse's Arcadian scenes—for example, *Luxe, calme, et volupté* (cat. 7) and *Le Bonheur de vivre* (1905–6; The Barnes Foundation, Philadelphia)—is regularly linked to ivy, an attribute of Bacchus, classical symbol of intoxication and indolence.[9]

Through the first still life, Matisse once again summons a vision of the Golden Age, capturing the polarity between the natural and the artificial, the vegetal elements and the sculpture. The statuette is depicted faithfully and vibrantly; the expressive facial features and movement of the limbs lend it an ambiguous vitality. The indefinite context of the representation allows us to see it as a sort of little theater, an Arcadian chamber scene. In the second, more clear-cut and stylized, painting, the sculpture is reduced to an object firmly attached to its base, a still life presenting itself as such. Simplified volumes and forms echo one another—the accentuated mass of the thigh mimics the belly of the vase; the circles of the breasts, those of the fruit—in a space crisscrossed by black rectilinear axes suggestive of Gris's famous grid. The pair thus externalizes in two versions the polarity between nature and artifice, the tension between the decorative and the expressive.

SURFACE AND DEPTH

Stephanie D'Alessandro

Bowl of Apples on a Table and *Apples* (cats. 33, 34), as they are known today, were purchased together by Matisse's dealer, Galerie Bernheim-Jeune, on November 13, 1916, and subsequently photographed during that month. Considered one of Matisse's painted pairs from the 1913–17 period, they are close in size and subject and were once even more similarly titled: the dealer's stock book records them as "Nature morte aux pommes sur fond vert" (no. 20775) and "Nature morte aux pommes sur fond noir et jaune" (no. 20776).[1] Over the years and in translation, however, the titles have changed, perhaps reflecting the generally held assumption regarding the order of their production and the fact that the artist progressively engaged in a process of greater simplification and radical abstraction.[2]

Indeed, the dramatic shift represented by these works parallels that seen in certain earlier painted pairs by Matisse, such as the two 1914 views of Notre-Dame (cats. 24, 25) in which the composition of one is more detailed and naturalistically rendered, while the other is more summary and abstract. The two related still lifes here recall the nineteenth-century academic tradition of first executing an *esquisse* (a freely painted, preparatory sketch) of a subject, which was then used as the basis of a *tableau* (a more finished painting). Although Matisse would challenge this traditional approach early in his career, devising various other relationships between pairs of painted pictures, he would also return to the *esquisse-tableau* concept. He likely did so in the case of *Bowl of Apples on a Table* and *Apples*, for the stock-book numbers, while not exact confirmation of the sequence of production, may reflect the order in which the artist presented the works to his dealer. However, without further historical documentation to confirm the precise chronology and relationship of the works, we must look instead to the context of Matisse's studio to better understand his process in producing this particular pair.[3] In doing so, the canvases reveal significant technical differences that underscore Matisse's continued struggle in these years to find painted equivalents for the effects of light on atmosphere, mass, and matter and that perhaps even challenge our assumptions about the order of production.

Though often seen as a pair, *Bowl of Apples on a Table* and *Apples* also belong to a group of still-life and interior scenes that Matisse took up in the late spring and summer of 1916. In April or May of that year, the

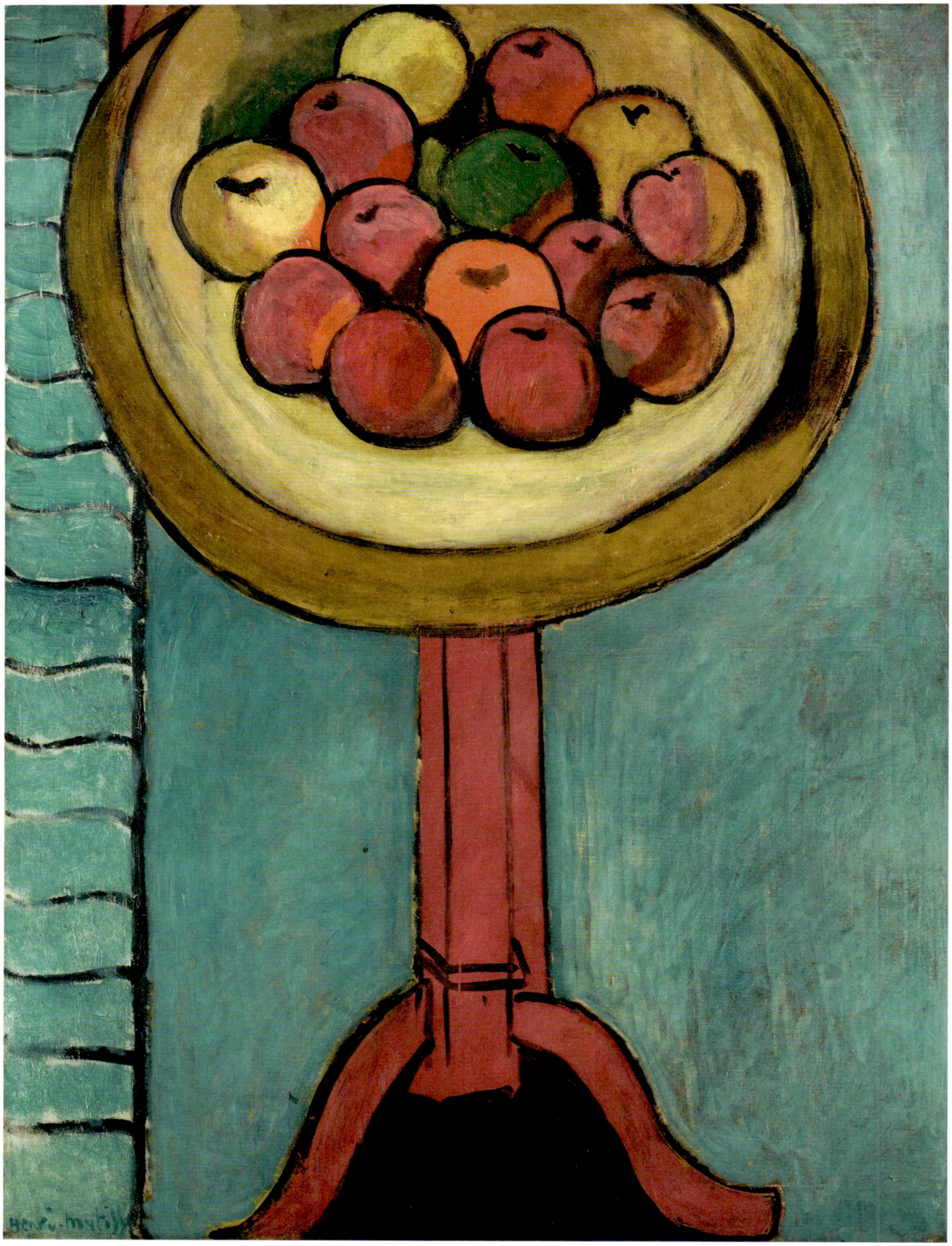

33 | *Bowl of Apples on a Table*, 1916

Oil on canvas, 45 ¼ x 35 ¼ in. (114.9 x 89.5 cm). Chrysler Museum of Art, Norfolk, Virginia, Gift of Walter P. Chrysler, Jr.

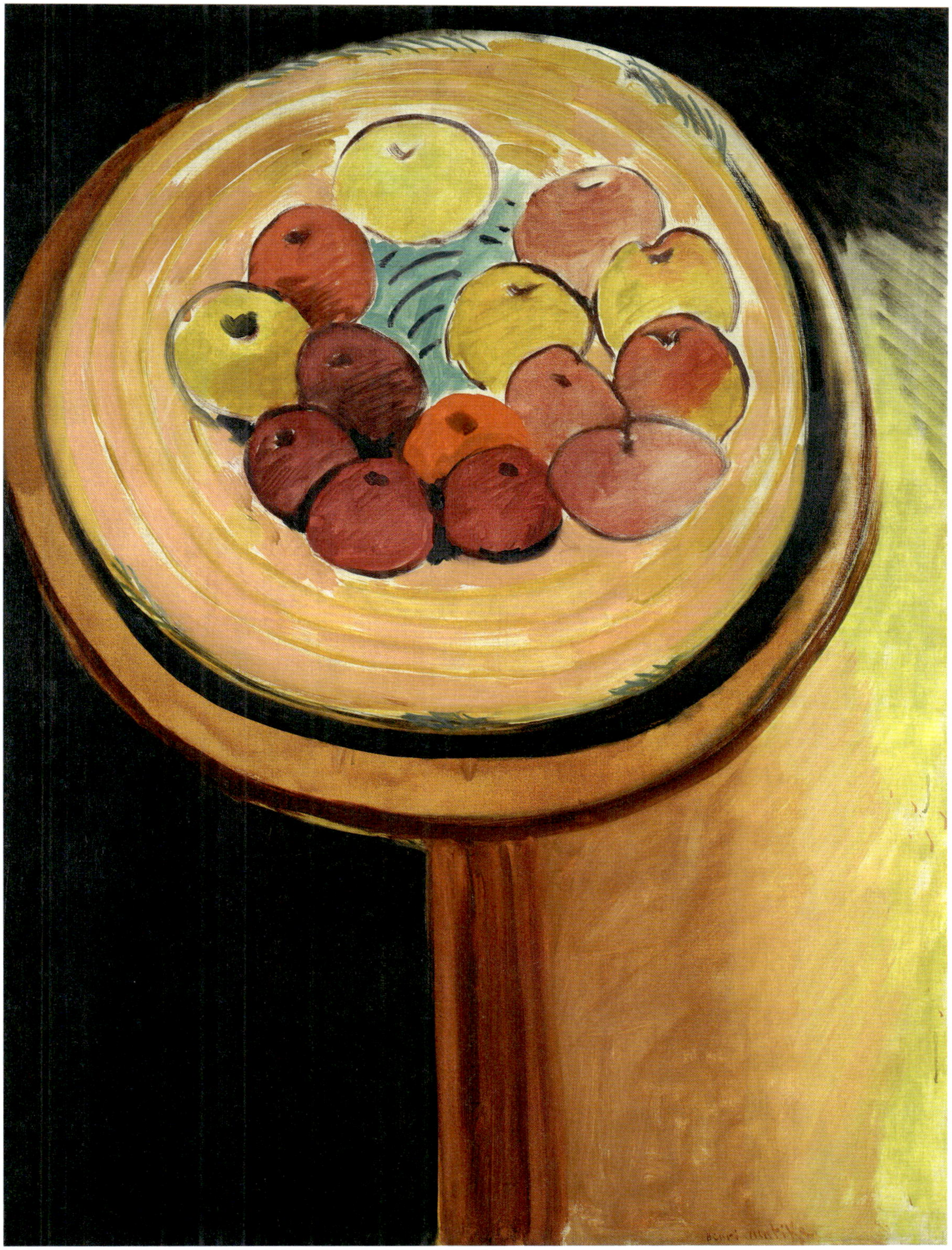

34 | *Apples*, 1916

Oil on canvas, 46 x 35 in. (116.8 x 88.9 cm). The Art Institute of Chicago, Gift of Florene May Schoenborn and Samuel A. Marx

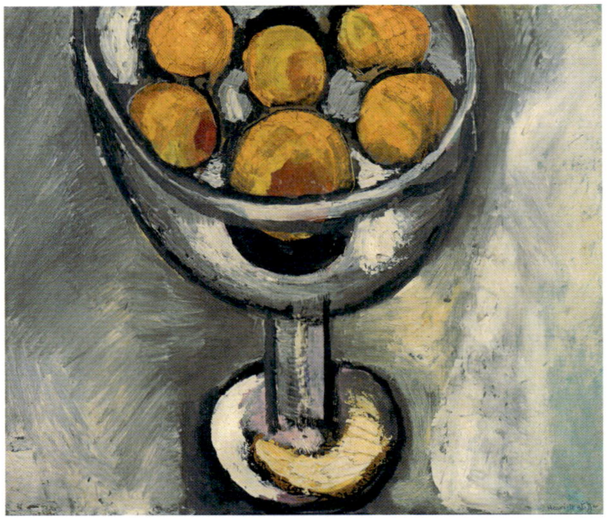

Fig. 54. *Bowl of Oranges*, 1916. Oil on canvas, 21¼ x 25⅝ in. (54 x 65 cm). Private collection

Danish painter and critic Axel Salto visited the artist's studio and not only witnessed *The Moroccans* (November 1915–November 1916; The Museum of Modern Art, New York) under way, but also saw "some supernatural interiors. Stronger, more pure in style and in touch with Cubist theories . . . larger and larger 'displays of force.'"[4] Three of these interiors can be identified from Matisse's letter of June 1 to the dealer Léonce Rosenberg in which he announced the completion of *The Window* (late April–May 1916; Detroit Institute of Arts) and *Bowl of Oranges* (fig. 54) as well as *The Ivy Branch* (May 1916; Kunsthaus Zürich), a composition he planned "to work again on another canvas."[5] Likewise, in late July, the Galerie Bernheim-Jeune confirmed the purchase of another interior that Salto likely saw in process, *Still Life with Plaster Bust* (July 1916; The Barnes Foundation, Philadelphia). *Bowl of Apples on a Table* and *Apples* were surely part of this group, for toward the end of July the painter Albert Huyot visited Matisse's studio and later asked about the progress of one of them, writing that "the still life of apples impressed me with its beauty."[6]

In each of these works, Matisse explored the material effects of light and space by translating optical depth into built-up layers of paint on canvas. Such effects were markedly different from those found in his contemporaneous monotypes, images of shallow black ink in which Matisse suggested illumination by removing medium from the plate and leaving lines of unprinted white paper in the final print composition (fig. 55). Conversely, in such paintings as *The Window*, he rendered the areas of most brilliant light, translucency, and atmosphere with a thick band of white paint. In *Bowl of Oranges*, Matisse similarly investigated the dematerializing nature of light, describing the space around the fruit bowl and glass and the areas between each orange with white paint that was applied heavily with a palette knife. These canvases demonstrate a change in the artist's

Fig. 55. *Fruits on a Moroccan Plate*, 1914–15. Monotype, image: 2¼ x 6⅛ in. (5.7 x 15.7 cm). The Museum of Modern Art, New York, Abby Aldrich Rockefeller Fund

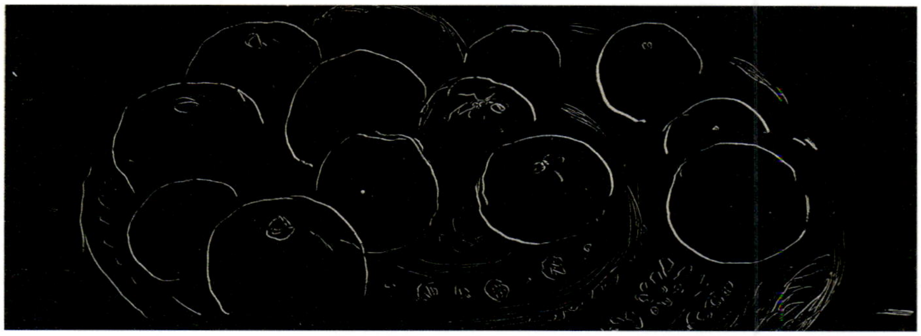

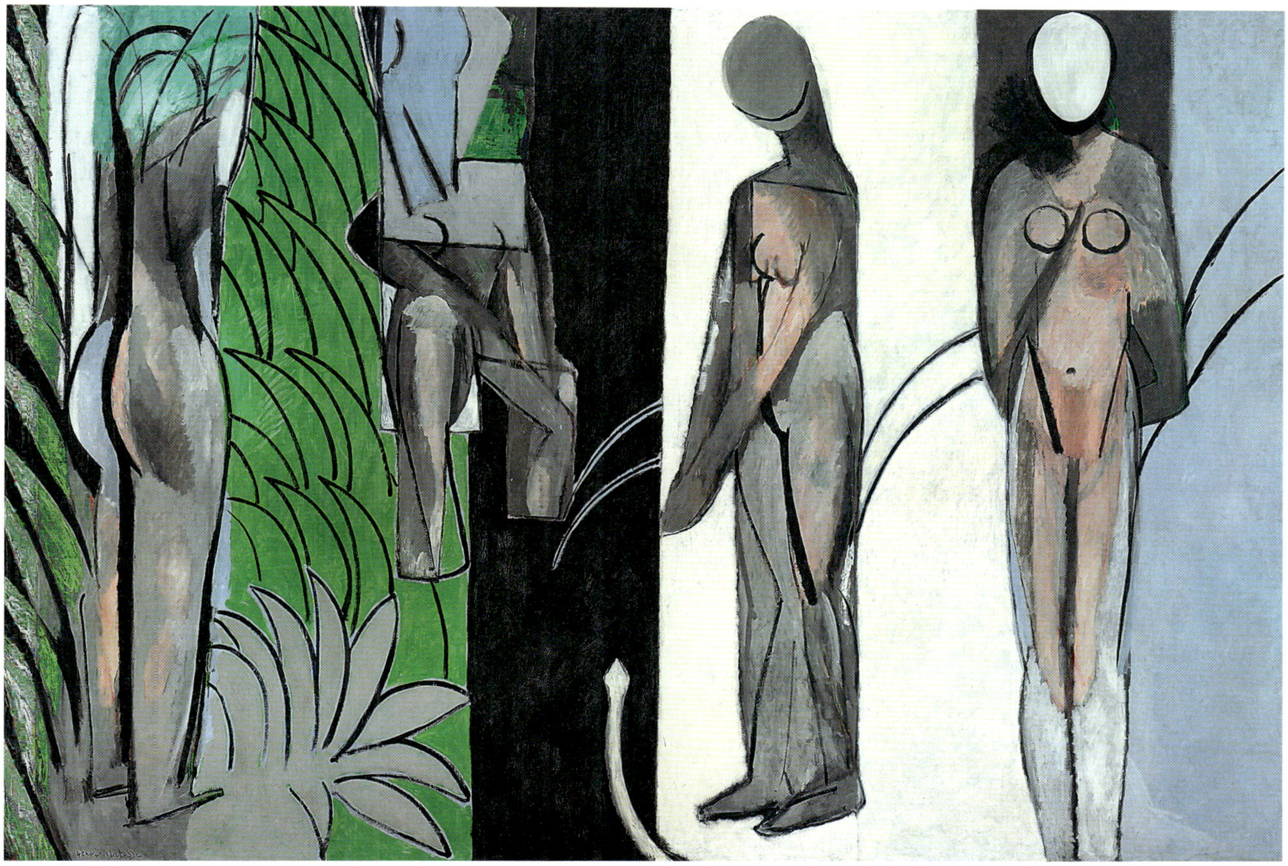

Fig. 56. *Bathers by a River*, 1909–17. Oil on canvas, 8 ft. 6½ in. x 12 ft. 10⅜ in. (260 x 392 cm). The Art Institute of Chicago, Charles H. and Mary F. S. Worcester Collection

approach and his interest in bringing an almost sculptural quality to paint application, a quality that is inherently reversed. In *Bowl of Oranges* the areas of illumination—those that embody the greatest physical immateriality—are the thickest passages on the canvas, while in contrast, the shady depths of the composition are described in the thinnest layers of dark black paint.

A similar dichotomy can be seen in the two apple compositions: *Bowl of Apples on a Table* (cat. 33) is thickly painted with broad passages that cover earlier colors and, in their materiality, stand in for the atmosphere of the room. But it is at the left edge of the canvas that Matisse's greatest invention appears. Here, he described the source of illumination by building up the surface with a heavy impasto of white paint over which he added green and black; using a heavy-bristled brush, he then scraped at the green surface to reveal some of the white below. The effect is one of dematerialized, intense light, produced through the matter of paint itself.

In contrast, *Apples* (cat. 34) is a thinly, quickly painted work, one in which the overwhelming black of the composition serves to elide and compress the space. It is also about light, like its companion, but instead recalls the artist's comments on the far smaller *Gourds* (summer–fall 1916; The Museum of Modern Art, New York), a painting that uses "pure black as a color of light and not as a color of darkness."[7] Yet, while *Apples* describes the effect of light, its shallow surface recalls the many monotypes of related images. The painting seems a surprising return at a moment when Matisse was exploring the connections between optical and constructed depth in both small-scale interiors and monumental works, such as *The Piano Lesson* and *Bathers by a River* (figs. 5, 56).[8] In this regard, it is worth considering whether *Apples* may have preceded *Bowl of Apples on a Table*. This possibility might better reflect the artist's move to greater explorations of constructed depth, his transformation of shallow black surfaces into ones of greater nuance, and his increasing experimentation with the left edge of a number of canvases (*Bathers by a River* being the most extreme example), in which he incised into paint and layered or banded colors to suggest not only a potential source of light but also a transition from the viewer's space into that of the painted composition.

While this idea may be tempting, however, it is without historical documentation. Perhaps far more relevant is Matisse's stated interest in what he would term "hygiene," a desire after having explored possible variations of a theme to go on to "something new."[9] His adoption of the more traditional *esquisse-tableau* model for *Bowl of Apples on a Table* and *Apples* would thus be less a compositional device than a vehicle for a different approach, construction, and sensory effect. In returning to an earlier painting mode, he might explore something he had previously overlooked. And as all his painted pairs attest, that approach held the promise for Matisse of refreshing and reviving his work.

LAURETTE: LINE AND COLOR

Hilary Spurling

The Italian woman called Laurette (the French form of Loreta) was one of the most important, and remains one of the most mysterious, figures in Matisse's life and work. He painted her obsessively for six or seven months at the height of World War I. No other model ever absorbed him so exclusively and at this degree of intensity either before or afterward.

Laurette came to Matisse's studio looking for work sometime in November 1916.[1] From then on, he painted no one and nothing else, producing one or two canvases a week—an astonishing production rate for an artist who habitually spent months, sometimes years, on a single painting. Laurette liberated him, recharging him as a painter and laying down patterns he retained to the end. His fifty or so pivotal portraits of her play with the theme in variations so inventive, energetic, and concentrated they might be said to constitute multiple parts of a single work.

Laurette was the first professional model Matisse employed on anything like a regular basis,[2] and she transformed his working method by importing for the first time into his studio the standard paraphernalia, as well as the tricks, of her trade: the costumes and props, the ability to assume different characters at

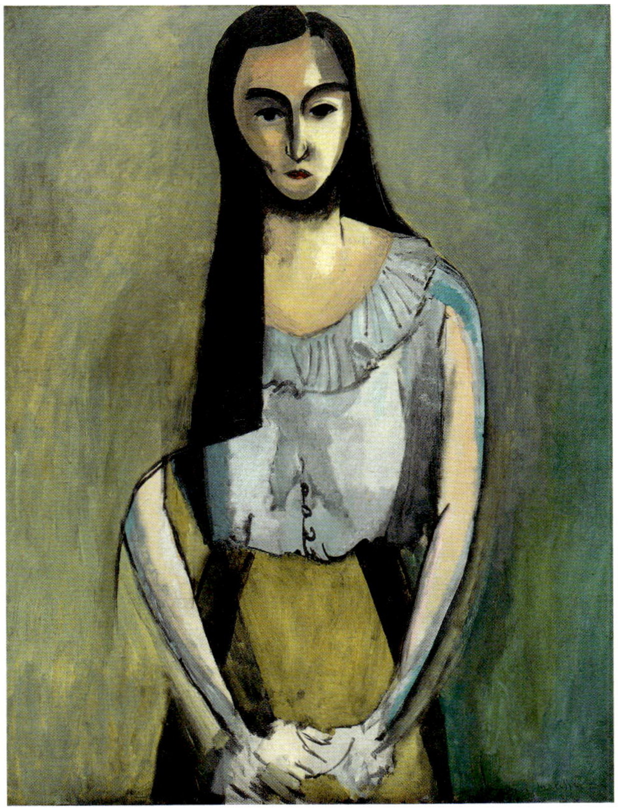

Fig. 57. *The Italian Woman (L'Italienne)*, 1916. Oil on canvas, 46 x 35¼ in. (116.7 x 89.5 cm). Solomon R. Guggenheim Museum, New York, by exchange

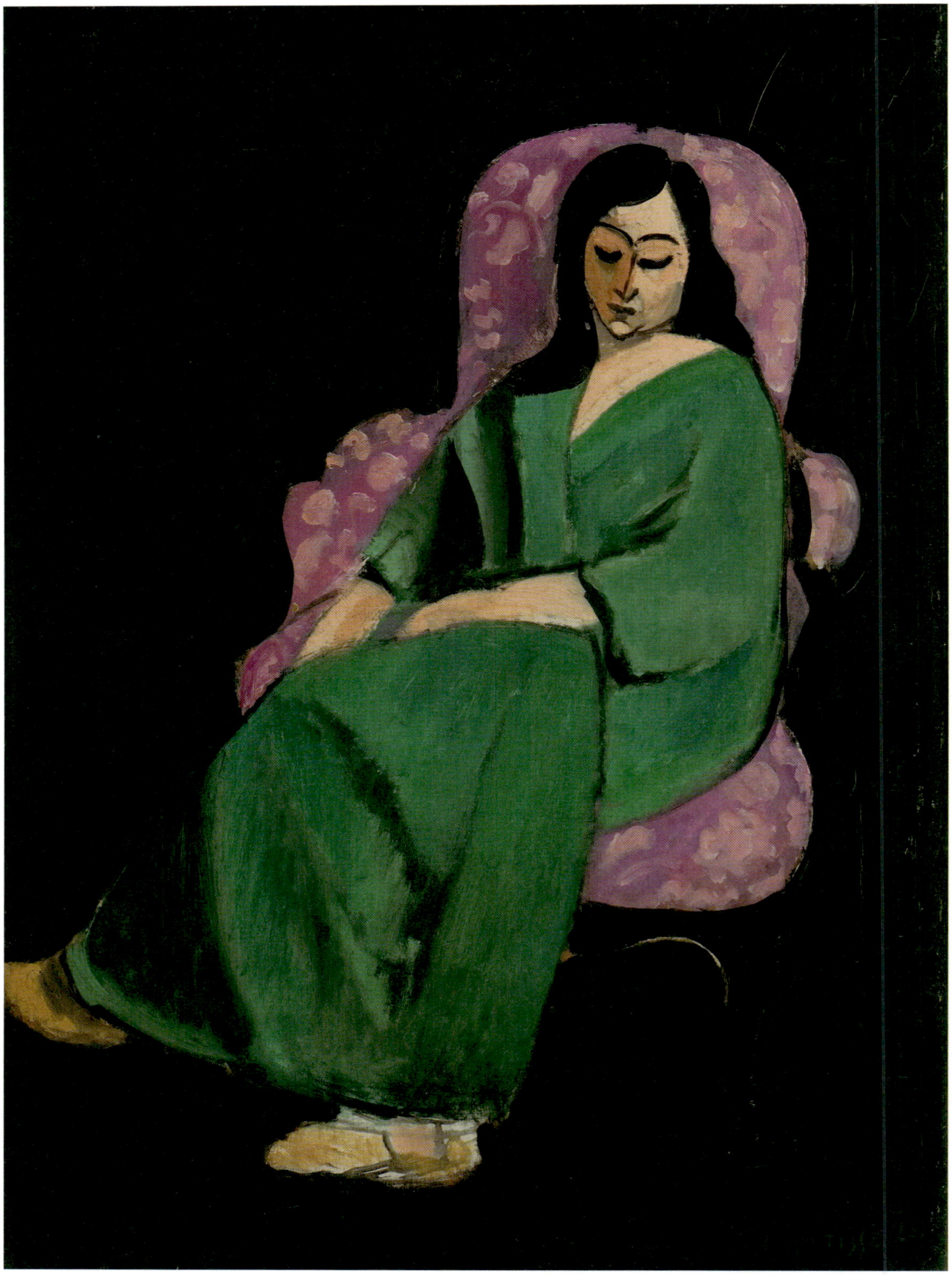

35 | *Laurette in a Green Robe, Black Background*, 1916

Oil on canvas, 28¾ x 21⅜ in. (73 x 54.3 cm). The Metropolitan Museum of Art, New York, Jacques and Natasha Gelman Collection, 1998

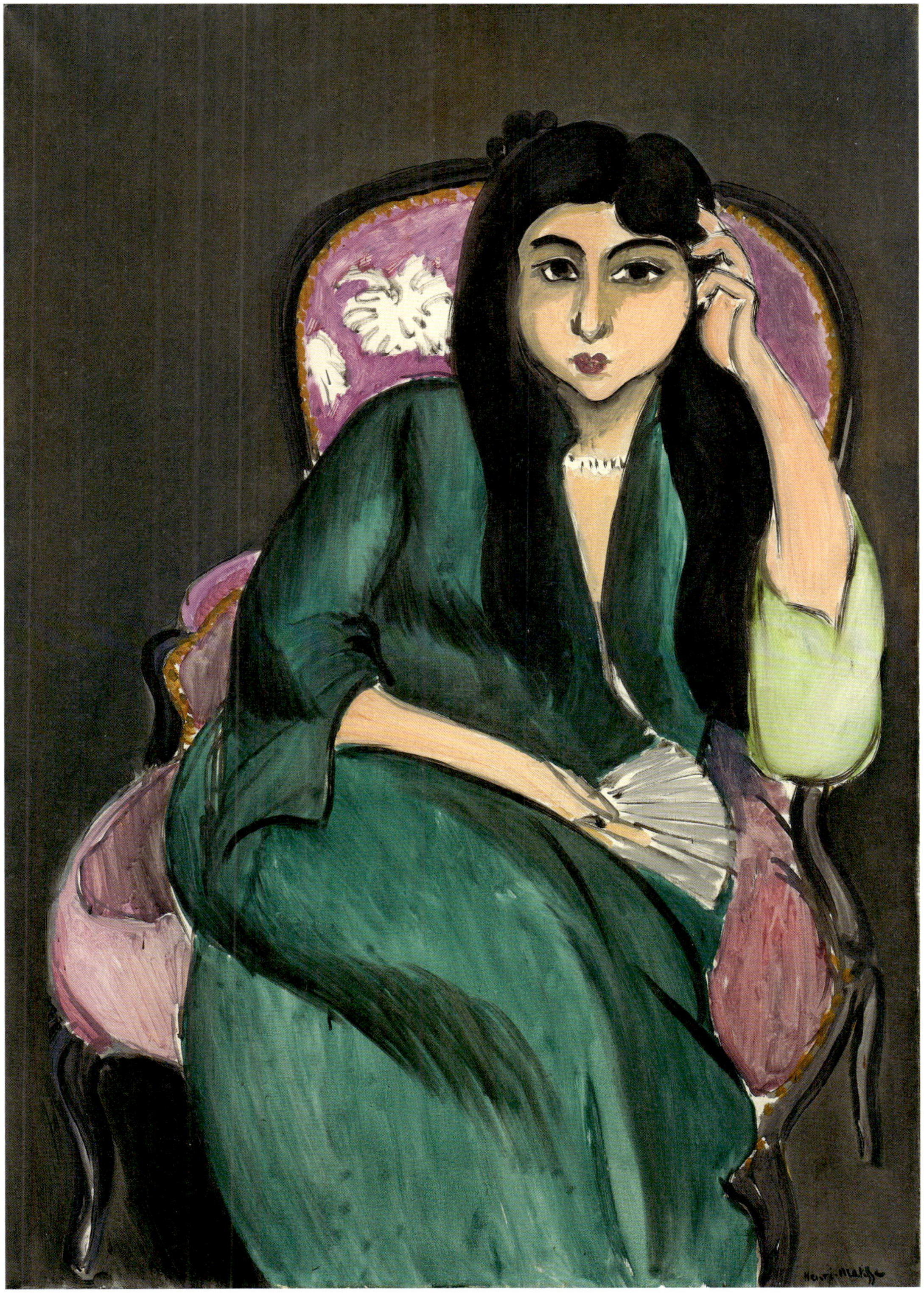

36 | *Laurette Seated on a Pink Armchair*, 1916–17

Oil on canvas, 39⅜ x 28¾ in. (100 x 73 cm). Private collection

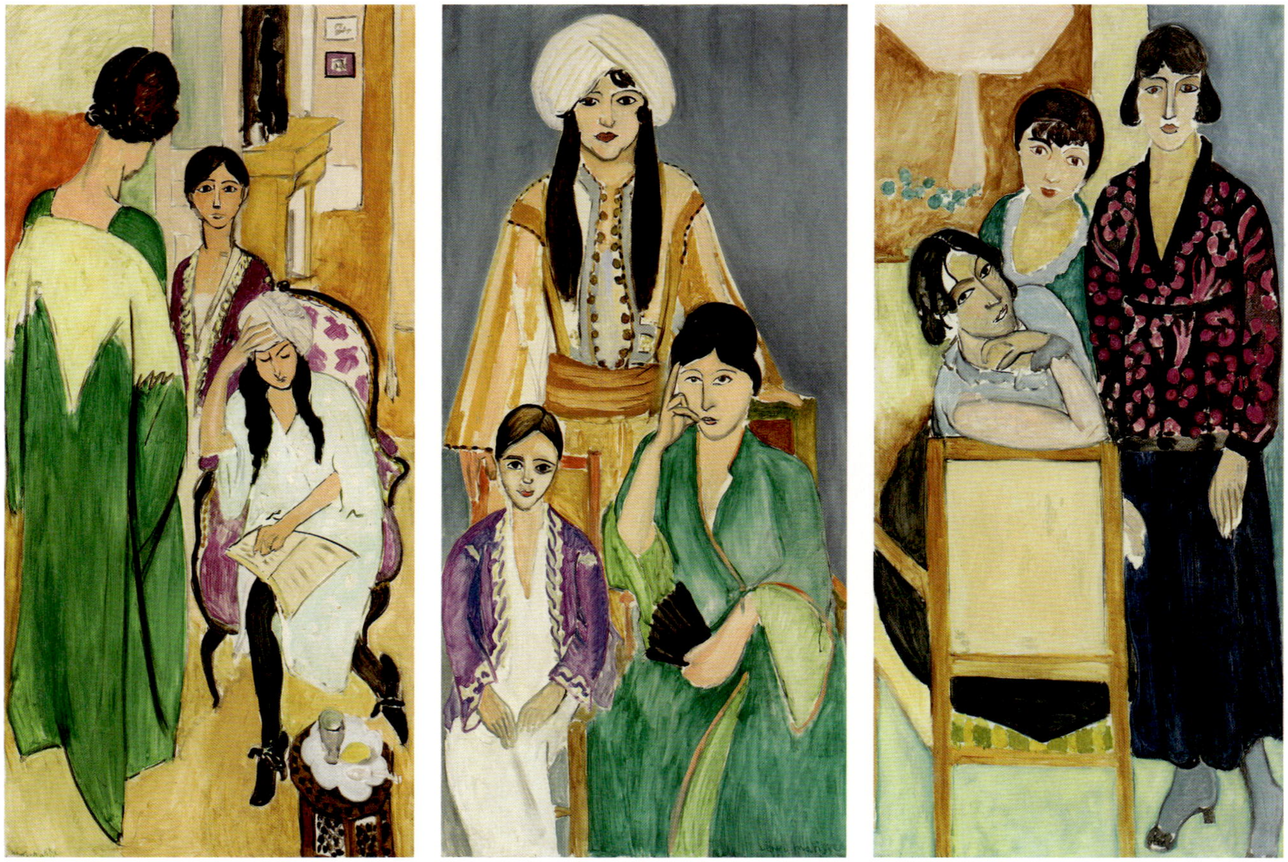

Fig. 58. *Three Sisters Triptych*, 1917. Oil on canvas. From left to right: *Three Sisters with an African Sculpture*, 77⅛ x 38¼ in. (195.9 x 97.2 cm); *Three Sisters with Gray Background*, 77 x 38 in. (195.6 x 96.5 cm); *Three Sisters and "The Rose Marble Table,"* 76½ x 37⅞ in. (194.3 x 96.2 cm). The Barnes Foundation, Philadelphia

will, the sheer theatricality of the professional model. For more than a hundred years, a specialized Italian community based in and around Montparnasse had supplied the academic painters of Paris with a cheap, plentiful, constantly replenished stream of models. They came from the harsh region known as the Ciociaria, in the mountains south of Rome, driven by poverty, hardship, and political unrest. World War I, which dried up the supply of male models altogether, left women with husbands away at the front, small children to feed, and little or no prospect of bringing in an income except through the traditional occupation of modeling.[3]

The Italian Woman (fig. 57), Matisse's first portrait of Laurette, is the least naturalistic of them all, and at the same time the one that most vividly suggests the actuality of an economic migrant. It shows a thin, gaunt, sad-faced figure with a closed expression wearing a cheap blouse and skirt. Lively gray-brown brushstrokes invade and dehumanize one side of her body in the somber, expressive, semiabstract style Matisse had perfected earlier the same year in majestic canvases such as *The Piano Lesson*, *Bathers by a*

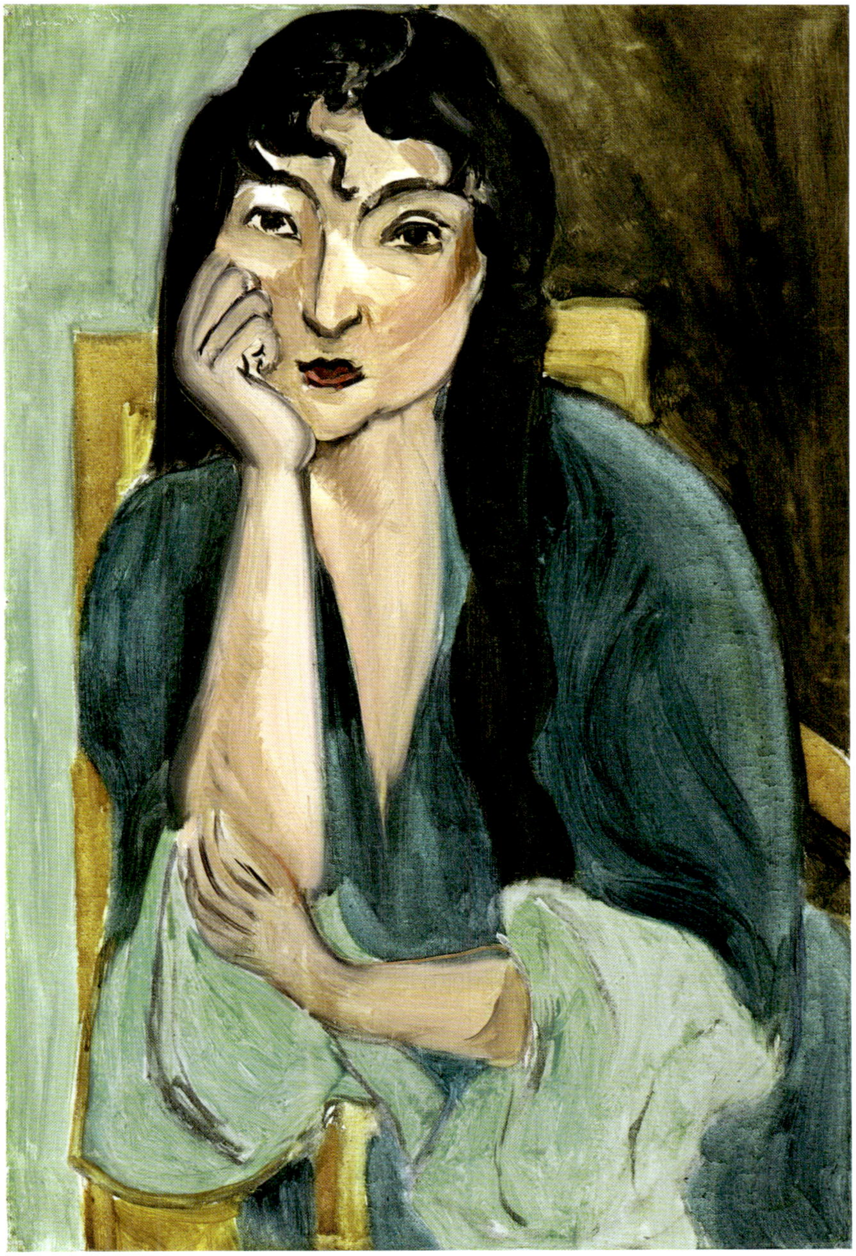

37 | *Meditation (Portrait of Laurette)*, 1916–17

Oil on canvas, 19½ x 13½ in. (49.5 x 34.3 cm). The Museum of Fine Arts, Houston, Gift of Miss Ima Hogg

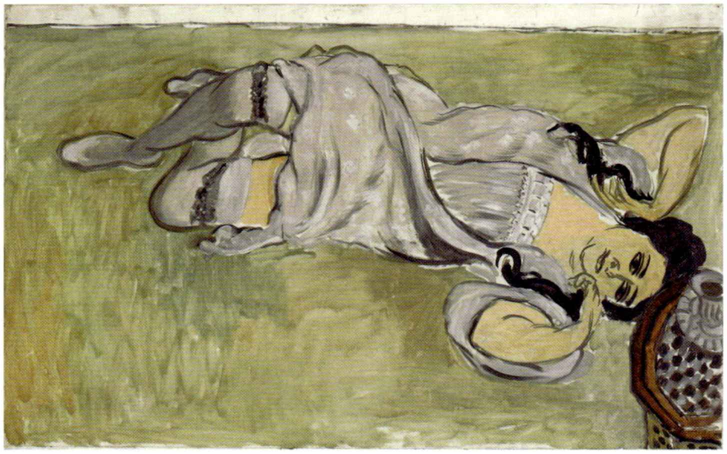

Fig. 59. *Laurette with Coffee Cup*, 1917. Oil on canvas, 35⅞ x 58¼ in. (91 x 148 cm). Centre Pompidou, Musée National d'Art Moderne, Paris

River (figs. 5, 56), and *The Moroccans* (The Museum of Modern Art, New York). The speed and alacrity with which he changed course in subsequent paintings of Laurette suggest that, by the beginning of 1917, he had gone as far as he could in that particular direction. His new model's professionalism supplied an essential impetus. She dressed up for him in assorted outfits, mostly Oriental, shifting her mood through the gamut from the hieratic gravity of the *Three Sisters Triptych* (fig. 58) to the flirtatious playfulness of *Laurette with Coffee Cup* (fig. 59), showing a flash of bare thigh above white stockings and frilly garters, or *Reclining Laurette* (private collection), all plump curves and pink flesh tightly bound in a transparent black lace mantilla.

But more often than not Matisse returned to the same simple formula seen in *Laurette in a Green Robe, Black Background; Laurette Seated on a Pink Armchair*; and *Meditation (Portrait of Laurette)* (cats. 35–37). He posed his model in a green gandoura and yellow Moroccan slippers, facing the viewer on one of the few available chairs—a hard wooden upright, a high-sided basket chair, or the shabby, pink-and-white padded bergère that was apparently the only comfortable seat in his cramped studio. In each case, the overall design is patterned by the black lines of Laurette's arched eyebrows, the two dark ropes of her hair, her long, slim arms, and the curved or rectangular wooden rim of the chair. These loosely brushed, lightly painted canvases adopt a straightforward naturalism rarely seen in Matisse's work before, although in *Laurette Seated* a fan sprouts like fringed palm fronds from the straight trunk formed by a barely delineated arm and hand.

The impact of this unique series is easily grasped by comparing a pair of paintings produced immediately before and afterward, *The Piano Lesson* of 1916 and *The Music Lesson* of 1917 (figs. 5, 6). Both show Matisse's son Pierre practicing the piano in the family salon, with a glimpse of the garden beyond, but that is as far as the resemblance goes. The formal severity and emotional depth of the first have been replaced in the second by a new and assured graphic fluidity that weaves everything in sight—the human figures, the garden plants, the living-room furniture, even the radiator and the decorative iron window grille that echoes the piano's elaborate music stand—into a swirling, rhythmic whole. In the Laurette paintings, Matisse achieved the marriage of line and color he would pursue in one form or another for the rest of his life.

PAINTING THE LIGHT

Dorthe Aagesen

On Christmas Day 1917, Matisse checked into the modest Hôtel Beau-Rivage in Nice, where he would live and work until early April 1918.[1] The period 1917–18 and his relocation to Nice are universally regarded as watershed moments in the artist's development. Matisse had recently turned away from an experimental mode that had resulted in some of the most austere and innovative compositions of his career.[2] Moreover, Nice offered him a much-needed respite from his life in Paris and from the demands imposed by the art world there. The change of scene and lifestyle afforded him the opportunity to reflect on his intense artistic efforts over the past few years, as well as a chance to test a new course. A closely linked series of interiors dating from his first months in Nice became a vehicle for this new outlook and direction.

Shortly after his arrival, Matisse began his first painting, an interior depicting his simply furnished hotel room with a window facing the sea (cat. 38). Significantly, it was the appearance of the sun that prompted him to begin the painting. In a letter to his wife, Amélie, dated December 31, 1917, he remarked, "The weather . . . was very beautiful this morning, so I quickly ran to my '15' canvas and did a view from my open window. I am not too displeased with it."[3] The letter included a hastily executed illustration outlining the fundamental features of the composition (fig. 60).

Matisse would return to the motif twice in the following months. In an almost identical version, executed on a slightly larger canvas and showing more of the ceiling and floor (cat. 39), the rapid, fluid brushstrokes of the first interior give way to greater detail and a more nuanced rendition of the decorative motifs on the textiles, wallpaper, and ceiling.[4] Whereas the earlier work is dominated by cool blues, greens, and whites, contrasting with deep reds, the second employs warm, golden colors applied in thin, translucent layers. In a letter to Amélie from March 1918, Matisse refers to the work as "the sunny interior."[5]

As far back as February, the artist was well under way on a third version of the subject, *Interior with a Violin* (cat. 40), this time on a significantly larger canvas and with yet another cropping, in which the ceiling and top of the window were omitted. At first, Matisse retained central elements of the previous versions, such as the pink floor, the yellow

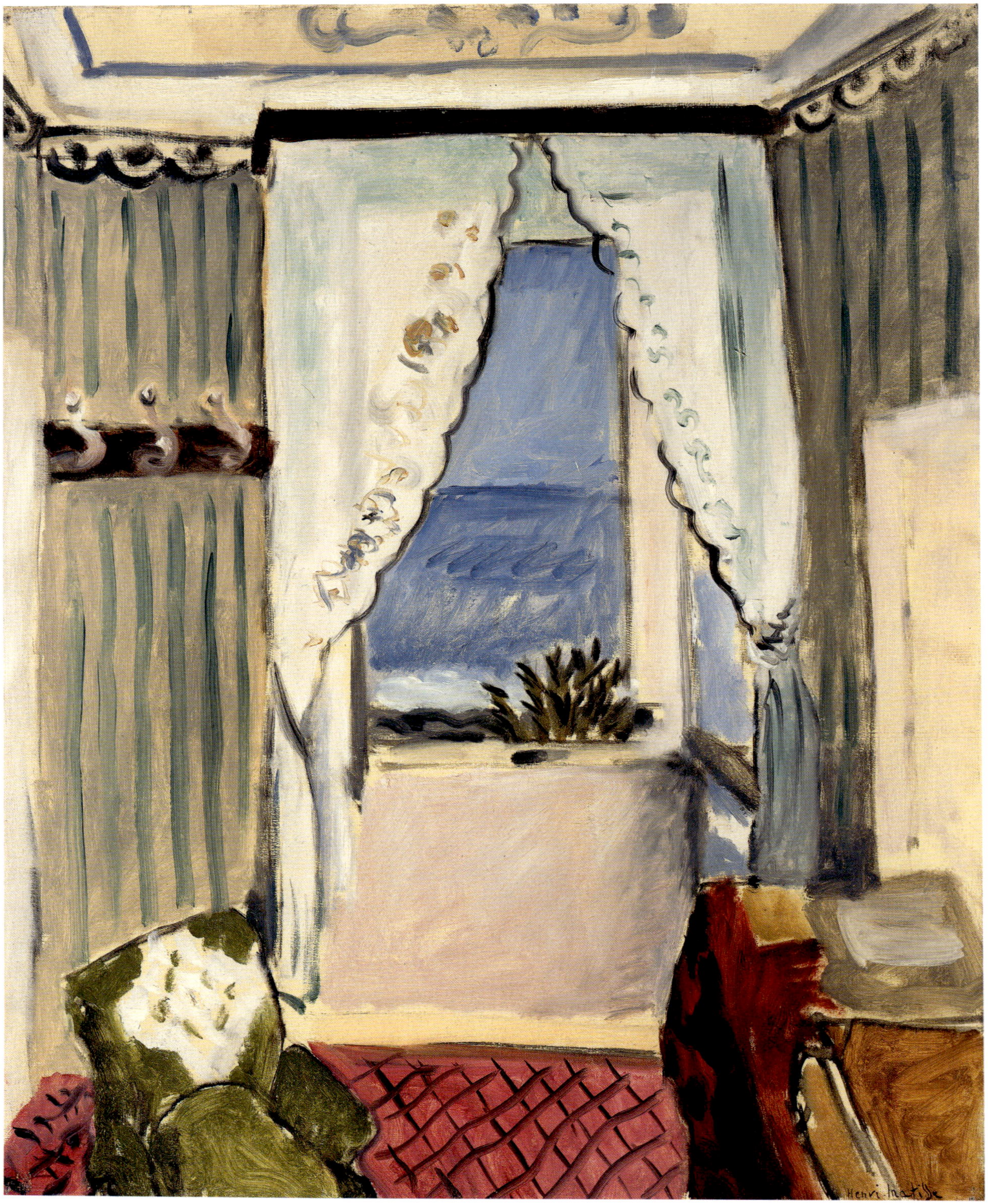

38 | *The Open Window (Room at the Hôtel Beau-Rivage)*, 1917–18

Oil on canvas, 25¾ x 21½ in. (65.5 x 54.5 cm). Private collection

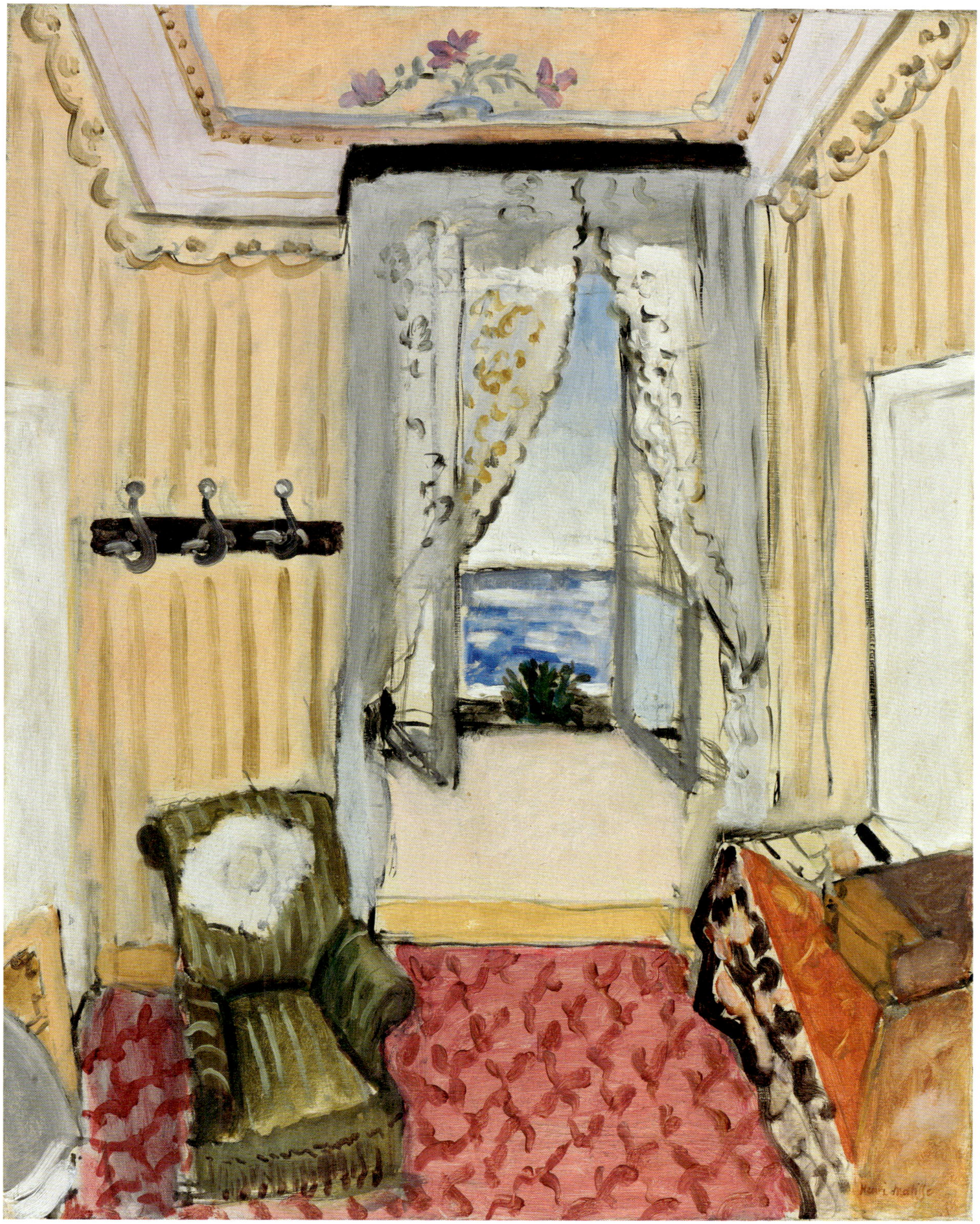

39 | *Interior at Nice (Room at the Hôtel Beau-Rivage)*, 1918

Oil on canvas, 29 x 23¾ in. (73.7 x 60.3 cm). Philadelphia Museum of Art, A. E. Gallatin Collection, 1952

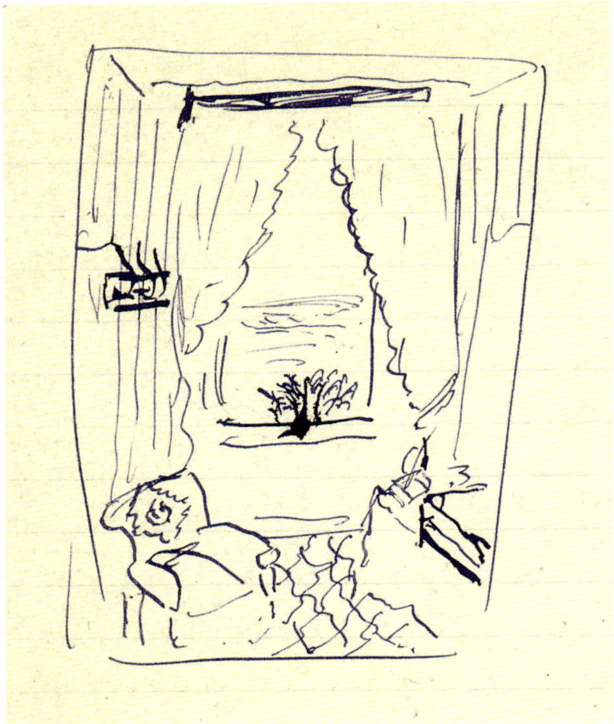

Fig. 60. Sketch in a letter from Matisse to his wife, Amélie, December 31, 1917. Archives Matisse, Paris

baseboard, and the armchair with green upholstery. However, he continued to work on this version longer than on the others. While the two first paintings were presumably painted in rapid succession, the third was nearing completion only in early April.[6] At that point, the painting had been completely transformed. The soft curves of the chair were replaced by angular, schematic forms, and an open violin case was prominently placed on the chair.[7] Even more radically, large areas of the surface were painted over in black. Light was pushed out of the room, which now harbored a darkness that contrasted with the brightness outside. At the same time, the light seemed to penetrate the room precisely because of the black color. "In that painting I painted light in black," Matisse said on a later occasion.[8]

The distinctive light in Nice was the thing that impressed Matisse most during his first stay there. Over and over, he would speak of it, "soft and tender despite its brilliance."[9] Looking back, he believed that, ultimately, the light was what made him stay in Nice: "the richness and the silver clarity of the light of Nice . . . seem to me unique and indispensable to the mind of the plastic artist."[10] Each in its own way, the three interiors he painted on his first visit are about this very light. In the first, light simply floods through the curtains, giving them their blinding whiteness and contrasting with the blue sky and sea. In the second, the focus shifts to the decor, and light seems to penetrate the entire space by means of translucent layers of paint. The third version took Matisse back to the bright light spilling in, and thus to the theme that originally sparked the series. Quite paradoxically, the black proved to be the strongest means for expressing the brightness and clarity of the light.

The experience of bright light and the ways to convey it were of keen interest to Matisse at critical stages of his career.[11] In such moments, he was prompted to question his system of representation, and each time, in response, he reconsidered whether the naturalistic ideology of Impressionism, from which he had distanced himself at an early point in his career, might offer a solution. Upon his arrival in Nice, it was clear that this was again the path to be tested. Whereas Paul Cézanne had arguably been Matisse's most important inspiration until then, Auguste Renoir now came to play a crucial part in his artistic reorientation. During his very first week in Nice, Matisse sought out the elderly painter, whom he had never met, at his home in Cagnes-sur-Mer. In late January, he returned with some of his most recent canvases, among them the first version of the Hôtel Beau-Rivage interior. Despite reservations about certain works, Renoir was enthusiastic about the

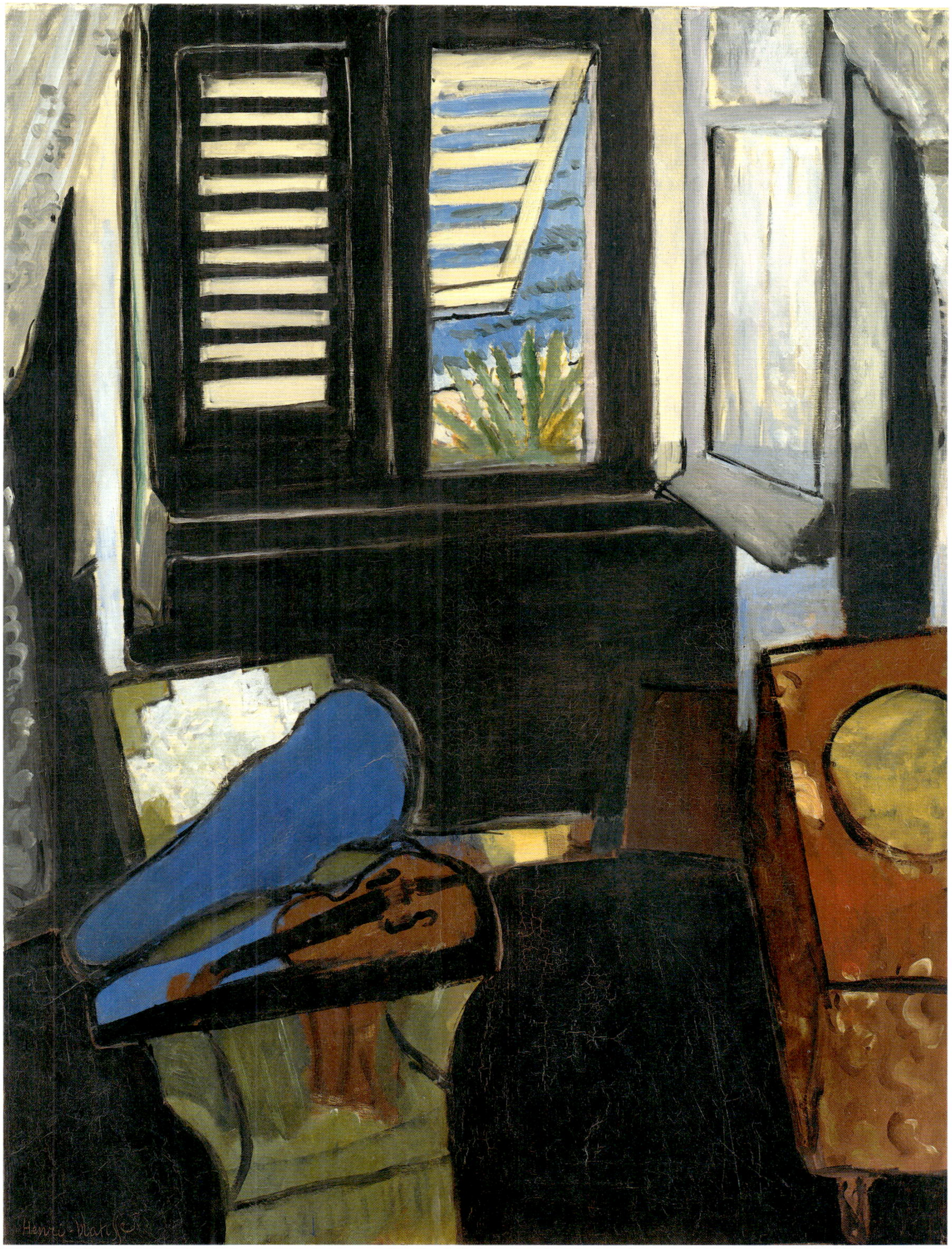

40 | *Interior with a Violin (Room at the Hôtel Beau-Rivage)*, 1918

Oil on canvas, $45\frac{5}{8}$ x 35 in. (116 x 89 cm). Statens Museum for Kunst, Copenhagen, J. Rump Collection

interior, praising its "stability, the overall harmony without anything extraneous."[12] Later describing the scene to Pierre Courthion, Matisse noted that Renoir

> *was surprised to see that the [black bar above the window] didn't leap out, but stayed at the distance indicated by its position in the room. . . . "How do you do that? If I used a black like that in a painting, it would jump out at you." I couldn't come up with an explanation straight away, and yet the explanation is very simple: it comes from a combination of forces in the canvas, which is what my generation has contributed. . . . It is constructed with an ensemble of forces that has nothing to do with a direct copy of nature.*[13]

The visits with Renoir helped Matisse establish a link to the nineteenth-century French tradition at a time when he was ready to respond to its influence.[14] In 1918 he was to write, "After Cézanne, who immediately became highly influential among artists, Renoir saved us from the dryness of pure abstraction."[15] Matisse would later realize, as his explanation to Courthion indicates, that he and his generation were not required to choose between Cézanne and Renoir, between abstract and realist modes of representation: they could accept both. This became even more obvious as he continued to work on the interiors from the Hôtel Beau-Rivage. If the first two paintings of the series addressed the question of whether the naturalistic tradition of Impressionism could help Matisse achieve the greater immediacy he yearned for, the third, *Interior with a Violin*, can be said to supply the answer: Impressionism's system of representation could not do it alone. In hindsight, he realized that even the "Impressionistic" first version, which had so intrigued Renoir, was an image "constructed with an ensemble of forces"[16] he had experienced in the past rather than from pure observations of nature—and that this was indeed the painting's preeminent quality.

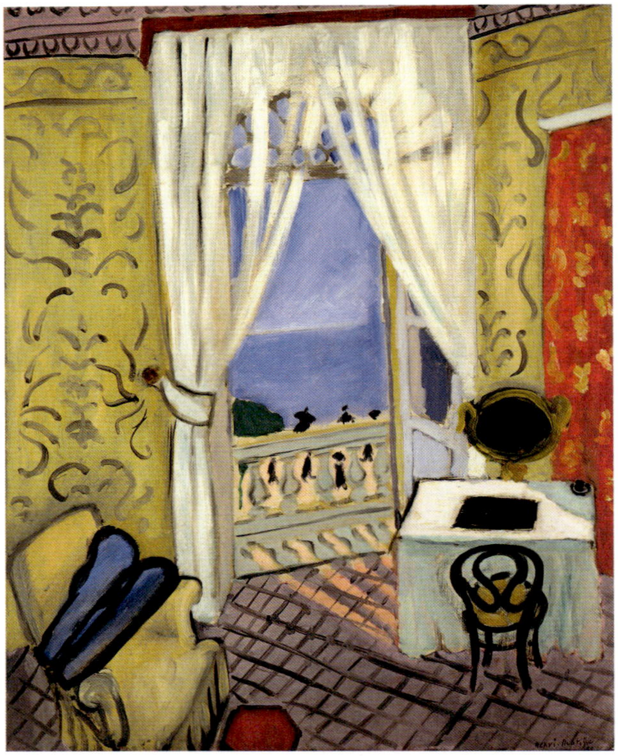

Fig. 61. *Interior with a Violin Case*, 1918–19. Oil on canvas, 28¾ x 23⅝ in. (73 x 60 cm). The Museum of Modern Art, New York, Lillie P. Bliss Collection

Matisse himself regarded *Interior with a Violin* as an important work that summed up where he stood at that particular moment: "[In it] I have combined all that I've gained recently with what I knew and could do before," he told the Swedish art historian Ragnar Hoppe in 1919.[17] He would later explain, "A will to rhythmic abstraction was battling with my natural innate desire for rich, warm, generous colors and forms. . . . From this duality issued works that, overcoming my inner constraints, were realized in the union of poles."[18] Representing a reconciliation of the opposing urges driving Matisse, this "programmatic" painting skillfully and eloquently links his previous work on simplifying forms with the immediacy of sensation that was part of the Impressionist legacy.

When Matisse returned to Nice in November 1918, he secured a room at the Hôtel Méditerranée et de la Côte d'Azur that was somewhat less modest than the one at the Hôtel Beau-Rivage but that again overlooked the sea. He would spend the winter seasons there for the next three years as he resumed his examination of the subject of the hotel interior. The rooms at the Méditerranée were decorated in an old-fashioned rococo style, with heavily ornamented wallpaper, ceiling moldings, and tiled floors. Looking back, Matisse enthusiastically described the decor as "fake, absurd, amazing, delicious."[19] This new ambience is apparent in *Interior with a Violin Case* (fig. 61), a fourth variant of the Hôtel Beau-Rivage motif that retains certain formal and stylistic features of the earlier versions while introducing a stronger decorative dimension that would hold Matisse's interest into the 1920s.

The three Beau-Rivage interiors inspired other experiments that more subtly tested the lessons Matisse had learned. Another sequence of three paintings—*Interior at Nice* (cat. 41), *Interior at Nice, Seated Woman with a Book* (fig. 62), and *Woman on a Divan* (cat. 42), all painted at the Hôtel Méditerranée—once again addressed the experience of light in Nice, as well as the question of how to balance immediate sensations with simplified forms. The organization of the pictures is comparable to that of the previous series. An opening to the outside world is still the center of the composition, with a table situated at the right and a seat at the left. In contrast to the earlier series, however, the painter now places a model in the seat; hand supporting her cheek, she is lost in thought, passively integrated among the furnishings.[20] While the motif is almost the same in all

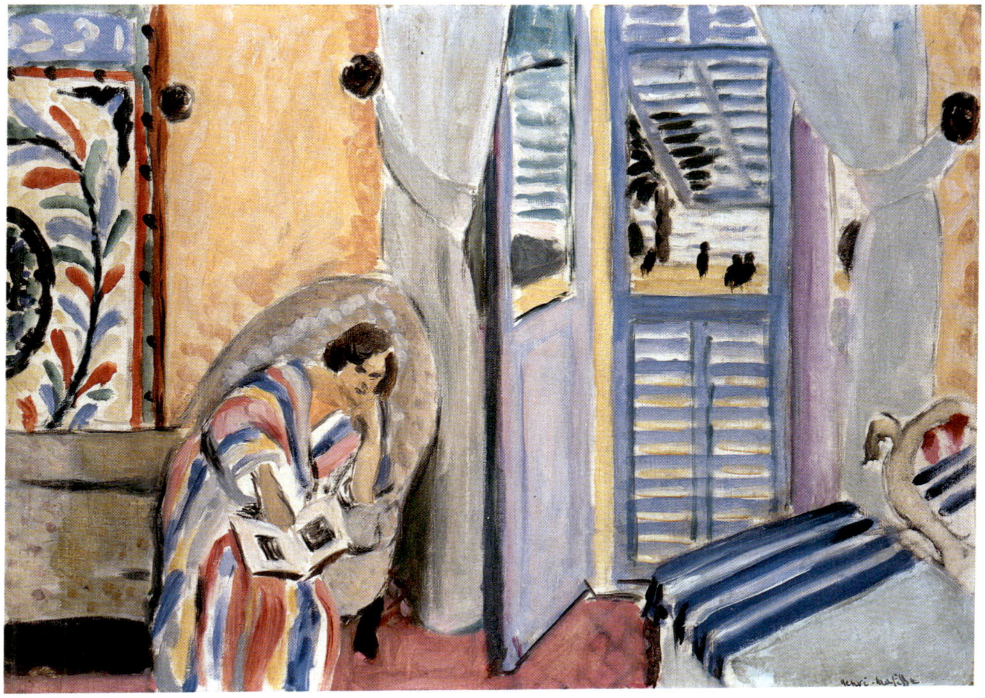

Fig. 62. *Interior at Nice, Seated Woman with a Book*, 1920. Oil on canvas, 18½ x 26 in. (47 x 66 cm). Private collection, Courtesy of Acquavella Galleries

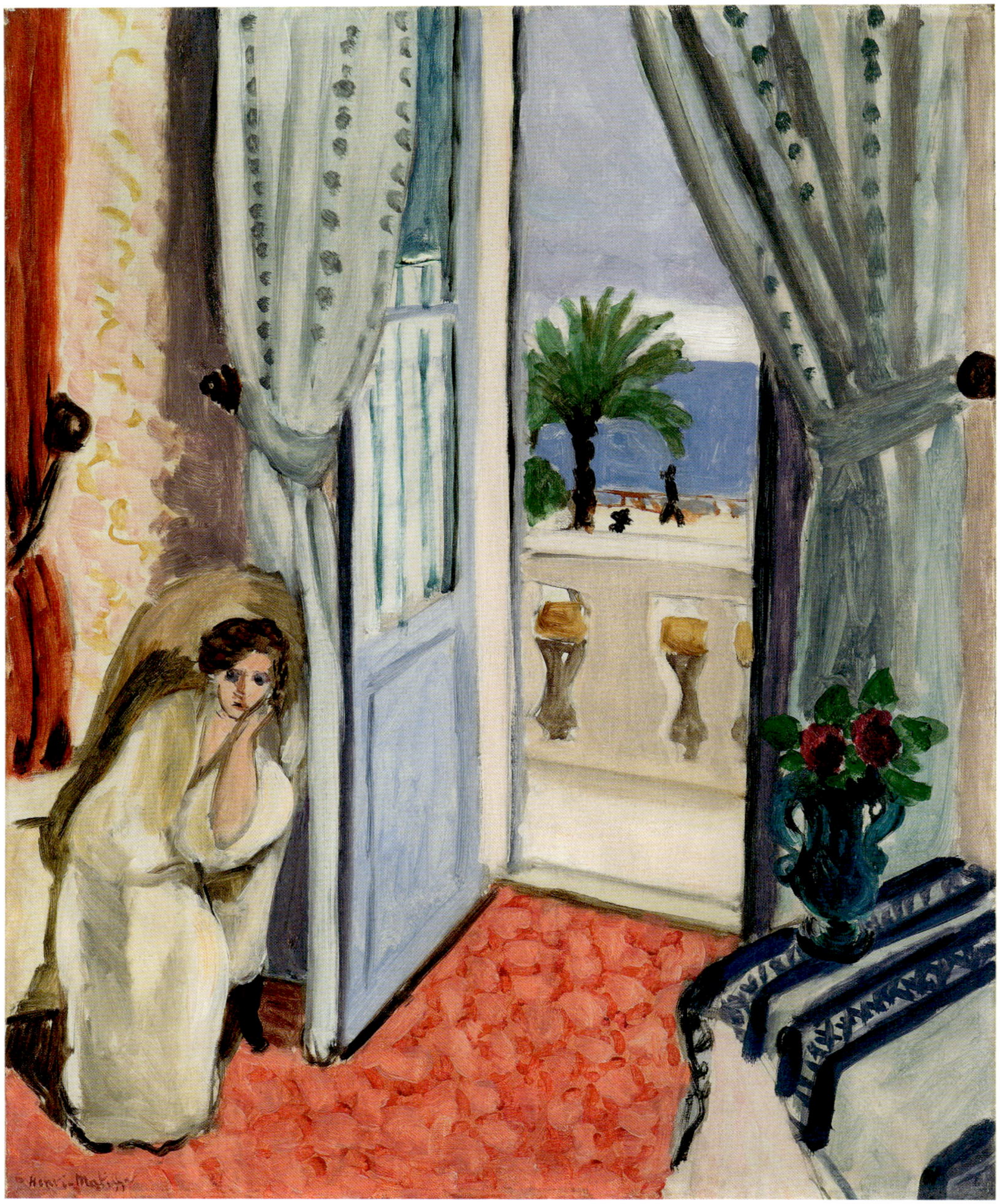

41 | *Interior at Nice (Room at the Hôtel Méditerranée)*, ca. 1919

Oil on canvas, 26¼ x 21⅝ in. (66.7 x 54.9 cm). Saint Louis Art Museum, Museum Purchase

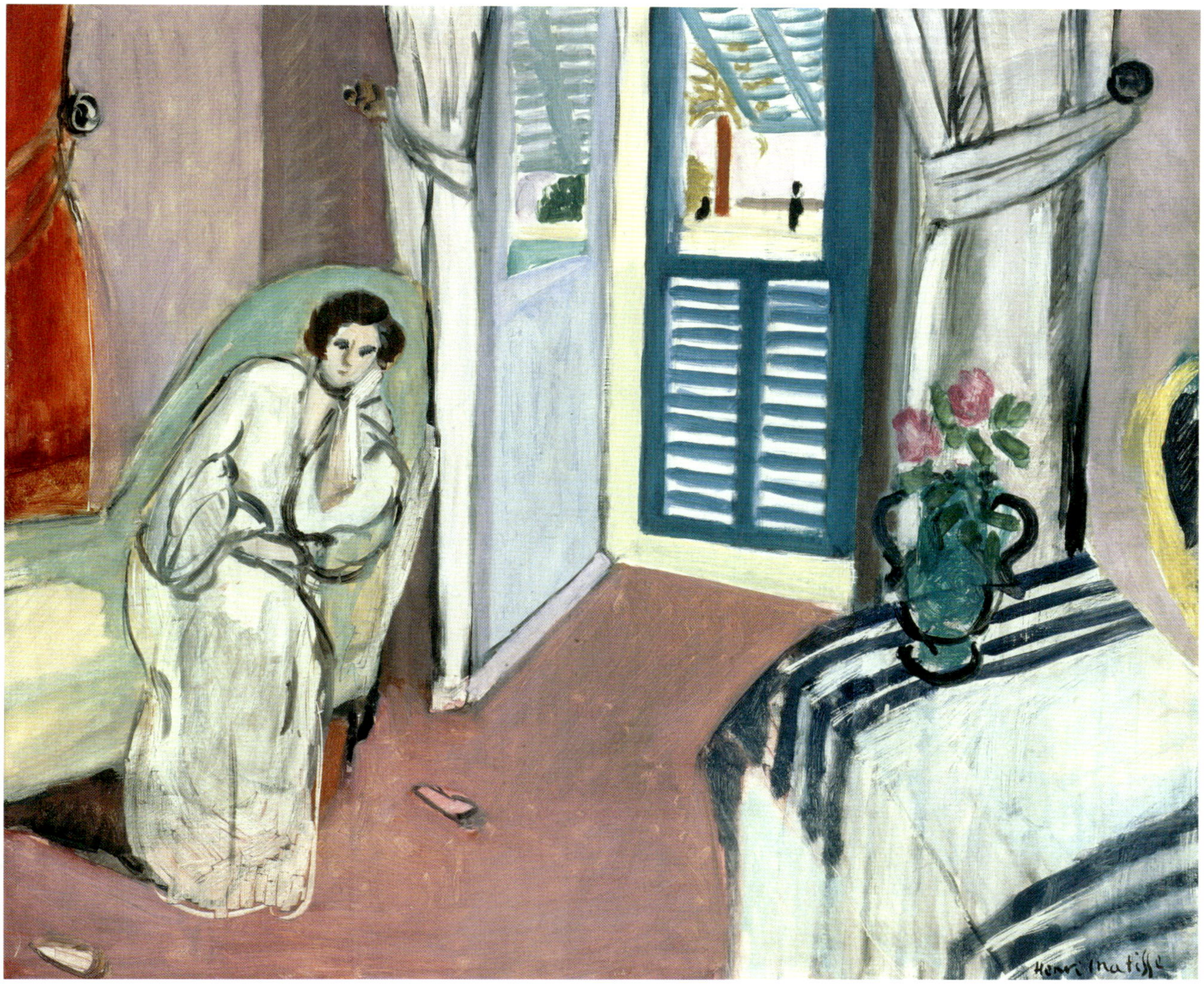

42 | *Woman on a Divan (Room at the Hôtel Méditerranée)*, 1920–21

Oil on canvas, 23¾ x 28⅞ in. (60.2 x 73.4 cm). Kunstmuseum Basel, Bequest of Dr. h.c. Richard Doetsch-Benzinger, Basel, 1960

three canvases, once again Matisse would vary format, stylistic expression, and palette.

In *Interior at Nice* (cat. 41), which is probably the earliest of the three, Matisse maintains the vertical format, emphasizing the role of the outside world and the view of the sea and sky. The color scheme of this painting is closely related to that of the second Beau-Rivage interior (cat. 39), and light is conveyed with similar means as it radiates from various thinly painted areas of the canvas, including the balustrade, the door frame, the model's dress, and the strip of wallpaper at the left. The depiction of observed reality seems to have been the main objective of this version.

The format of the two later versions (fig. 62, cat. 42), probably painted the following year, has been changed from vertical to horizontal, and the blinds are closed except for one section that offers merely a glimpse of the beach. Emphasis shifts to the interior and to the relationship between its parts, which, in addition, are given new weight by the repetition of a striking pattern. In *Interior at Nice, Seated Woman with a Book*, the striped dress of the model is mirrored in the pattern of the wall hanging behind her; in both paintings, the stripes in the tablecloth at the lower right echo the rhythmical lines of the tall blue blinds. Much later, Matisse would speak of a "great tension brewing" in his paintings from the early years in Nice, "a tension of a specifically pictorial order . . . that comes from the interplay and interrelationship of elements."[21] Here, the underlying, nearly abstract geometric structure lends rigor to the composition and emphasizes its construction, an element that was still fundamental to Matisse's work, although it was balanced by the representational nature of the image.[22]

In the two later versions, tension also arises from the color scheme, which has been transformed into a palette of primary colors that intensify the impression of light. Although the bright light of Nice is again the

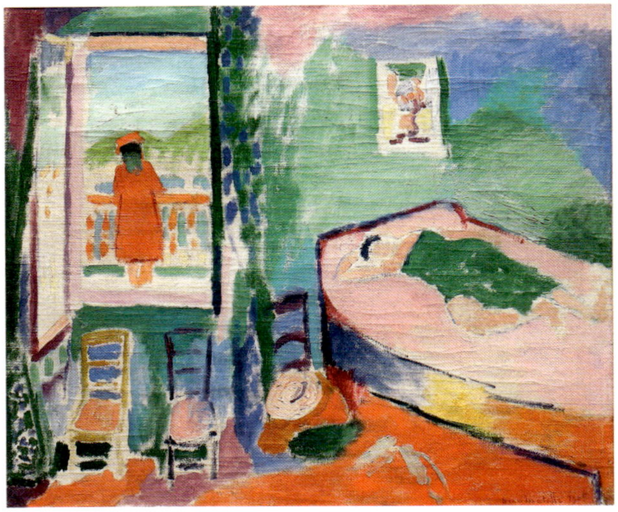

Fig. 63. *Interior at Collioure: The Siesta*, 1905. Oil on canvas, 23¼ x 28⅜ in. (59 x 72 cm). Private collection

subject of the canvases, it is now conveyed by different pictorial means. The strongest effect can be found in *Woman on a Divan*, in which all superfluous details are eliminated, the composition is boiled down to its most essential elements, and the colors are reduced to contrasting red/green and blue/orange tones. In this respect, the painting recalls Matisse's much earlier depictions of windows and hotel rooms, including *Interior at Collioure: The Siesta* (fig. 63), which similarly depicts a woman resting in a sun-filled, simply furnished room with a window facing the Mediterranean. Back then, experiments with complementary colors were a primary focus for Matisse, along with the related attempt to develop a method to represent bright light. Indeed, *Woman on a Divan* would be unthinkable without the artist's previous investigation of color contrasts and simplification of forms in the first decade of the century. In effect, the paintings of the Nice hotel rooms from the late 1910s and early 1920s represent not only a new direction in Matisse's art but also a reconsideration of a long-familiar motif.

THE BEACH AT ÉTRETAT

Rebecca Rabinow

Matisse's visit to the resort town of Étretat on the Normandy coast in the summer of 1920 resulted in scores of modestly scaled paintings. Of these, three vertical "size 30" canvases stand apart. They are hybrids—part still life, part landscape—arranged in a format typically used for figure painting. Matisse divided the composition of each so that the lower half features the glistening catch of the day arranged atop a nest of seaweed; the upper section is a distant view of two of Étretat's most distinctive rock formations, the Porte d'Aval and the Aiguille (Needle). These iconic cliffs had been depicted by a succession of nineteenth-century French artists, and Matisse was now presenting himself as an heir to that tradition.

The artist's decision to spend the summer on the Channel Coast was surely born out of concern for his daughter, Marguerite, who for the previous two years had undergone a series of procedures to repair her damaged larynx. Once her health began to improve, it was decided that she should convalesce in the fresh sea air.[1] Matisse preceded his family to Étretat and, on June 17, 1920, sent his wife, Amélie, a postcard noting that the town reminded him of a cleaned-up version of Collioure, the Mediterranean port near the Spanish border where they had often spent their summers.[2] Delighted with his surroundings, he remarked on the "green-topped white cliffs beside a tender blue and turquoise green sea from which I can see emerging superb creamy-white turbots, iron-grey dogfish, lesser spotted dogfish and skate, skate all over the harbour."[3]

Matisse painted many small landscapes that summer as well as still lifes of his meals and images of Marguerite resting in her hotel room. A view out the window toward a fishing boat decorated with French flags commemorated the second Bastille Day celebration since the end of World War I.

Although the Matisse family left Étretat at the height of the tourist season, the artist returned shortly before Saturday, September 11, when he wrote Amélie to say that he had established a routine of two painting sessions per day. Working primarily on small, easily transportable "size 8" canvases, he had begun a view of his hotel room, which he intended to complete during periods of inclement weather. His immediate plan was to paint still lifes of fish arranged next to the water, but unfortunately there were no fish to be had at that time. "There are only rays and eels. There are no more . . . Red Mullet nor St. Pierre."[4]

Fig. 64. Gustave Courbet. *The Étretat Cliffs after the Storm*, 1870. Oil on canvas, 52⅜ x 63¾ in. (133 x 162 cm). Musée d'Orsay, Paris

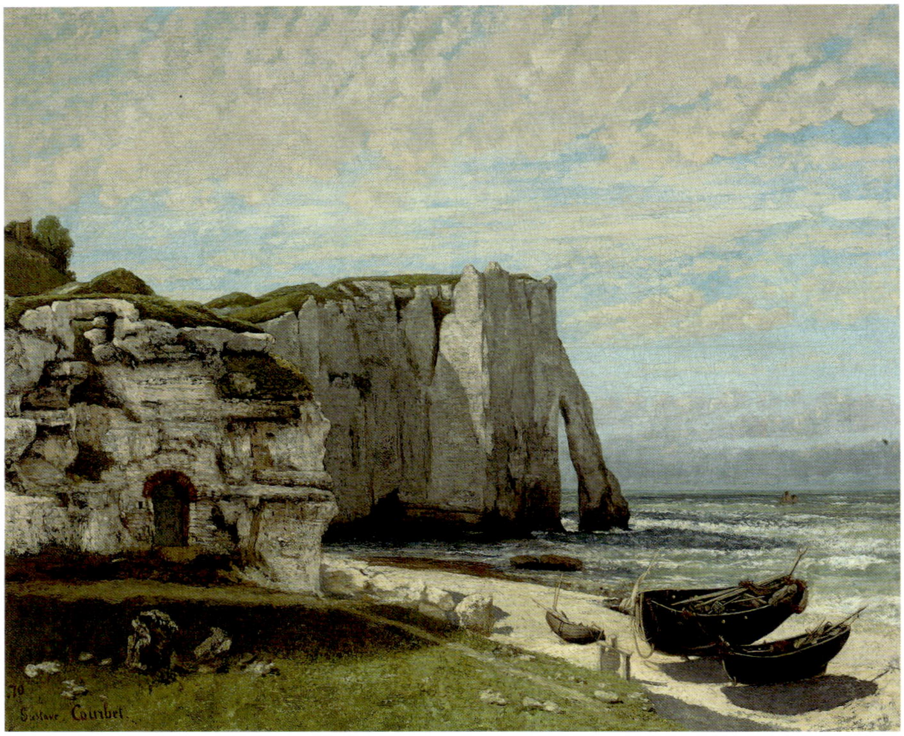

Half a century earlier, when the forty-two-year-old Claude Monet had arrived at Étretat, he admitted that it was audacious to attempt a view of the cliffs "after Courbet who did it admirably [fig. 64], but I will try to do it differently."[5] In the summer of 1920, Matisse found himself in a similar predicament. He was drawn to the work of Eugène Delacroix and Gustave Courbet, both of whom had spent time at Étretat, and was also familiar with Monet's paintings of the cliffs. His Russian patron, Sergei Shchukin, whom Matisse had visited in 1911, owned Monet's *Fishing Boats Leaving Étretat* (fig. 65), and his dealer, Galerie Bernheim-Jeune, owned several others, including a close-up of the Porte d'Aval and the Needle that the gallery acquired in May 1920.[6] Matisse's relation to Monet is likely to have been somewhat ambivalent. At the turn of the century, Matisse had experimented with Monet's Impressionist style before resolutely rejecting it. A few years later, at the time of his first solo exhibition, he had watched as throngs of visitors flocked to Monet's "Views of the Thames" exhibition at Durand-Ruel's gallery, while Matisse's own show just up the street at Ambroise Vollard's remained empty. In May 1917, thanks to an introduction from Bernheim-Jeune, Matisse finally met the illustrious artist at his home in Giverny.

By all accounts, Matisse's visit with Monet was not particularly revelatory; however, Matisse soon arranged an introduction to another esteemed French artist of the previous generation, Auguste Renoir. Their initial meeting took place on December 31, 1917, Matisse's forty-eighth birthday, and soon Matisse was regularly spending time with Renoir at Cagnes-sur-Mer. After Renoir died, in December 1919, Matisse was permitted access to the master's studio. He stopped by several times during the winter and

Fig. 65. Claude Monet. *Fishing Boats Leaving Étretat*, 1886. Oil on canvas, 26 x 31⅞ in. (66 x 81 cm). The State Pushkin Museum of Fine Arts, Moscow

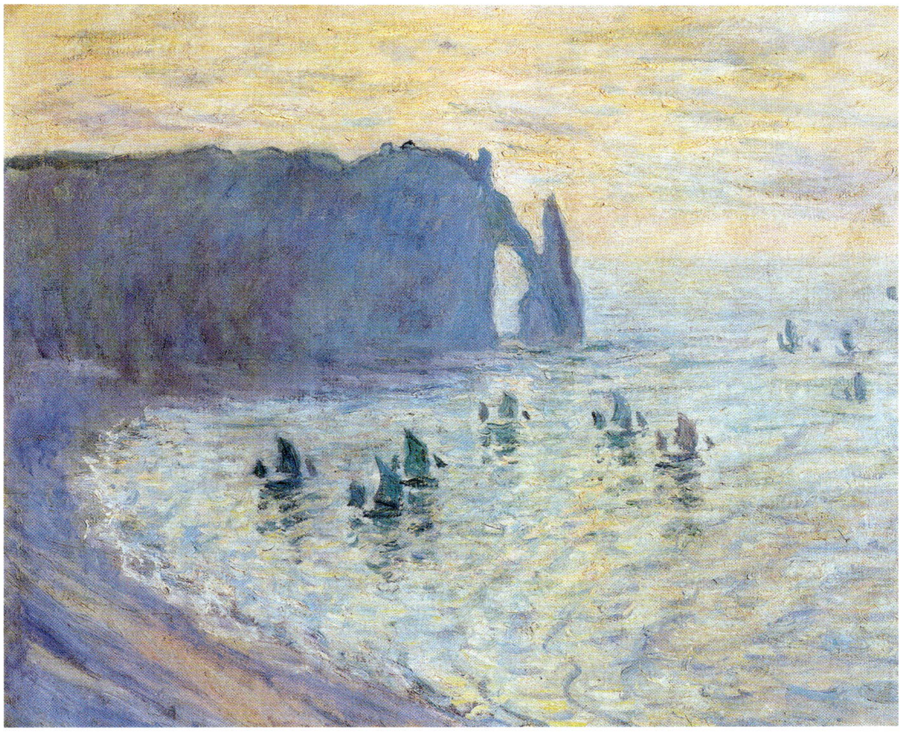

spring of 1920. On March 7 he wrote Amélie, "The visit I made to Renoir's last week, where I leisurely looked at his paintings, helped me greatly."[7] It surely is no coincidence that Matisse began painting still lifes of fish just a few months after seeing a score of paintings of the same subject in Renoir's studio (fig. 66).[8]

In the three Étretat pictures discussed here, Matisse edited out all activity on the busy beach as well as any sign of the town. In order to see the landscape as he presents it, with the cliff in the left midground and the Needle to the right of the Porte d'Aval, one must be positioned at the extreme northeast end of the beach, in the shadows of another arch, the Porte d'Amont. It is unlikely that Matisse transported his three "size 30" canvases to that location.

Matisse seems to have been interested in using these works to compare painterly effects. *Large Cliff—Two Rays* and *Large Cliff—Eel* exhibit a particularly strong visual rapport. *Large Cliff—Two Rays* (cat. 43) is more traditional. The convex cliffs at the left and the brownish tide line emphasize the curve of the beach, which leads the viewer's eye farther back to the dark brown sail of the fishing boat and to the rock formations beyond. Curved lines are deliberately employed to emphasize textural details, such as pebbles, waves, and clouds. By comparison, *Large Cliff—Eel* (cat. 44) seems flat. Instead of traditional perspective bringing the viewer's eye into the distance, Matisse uses a few strokes of salmon pink at the end of the beach to achieve the same result. Certain elements of the two paintings mirror one another: the tail of the ray in the foreground curves down, that of the eel curves up; the cliff face in the midground in one work appears convex, in the other, concave; one beach is full of calligraphic pebbles, the other smooth (although animated with visible brushstrokes

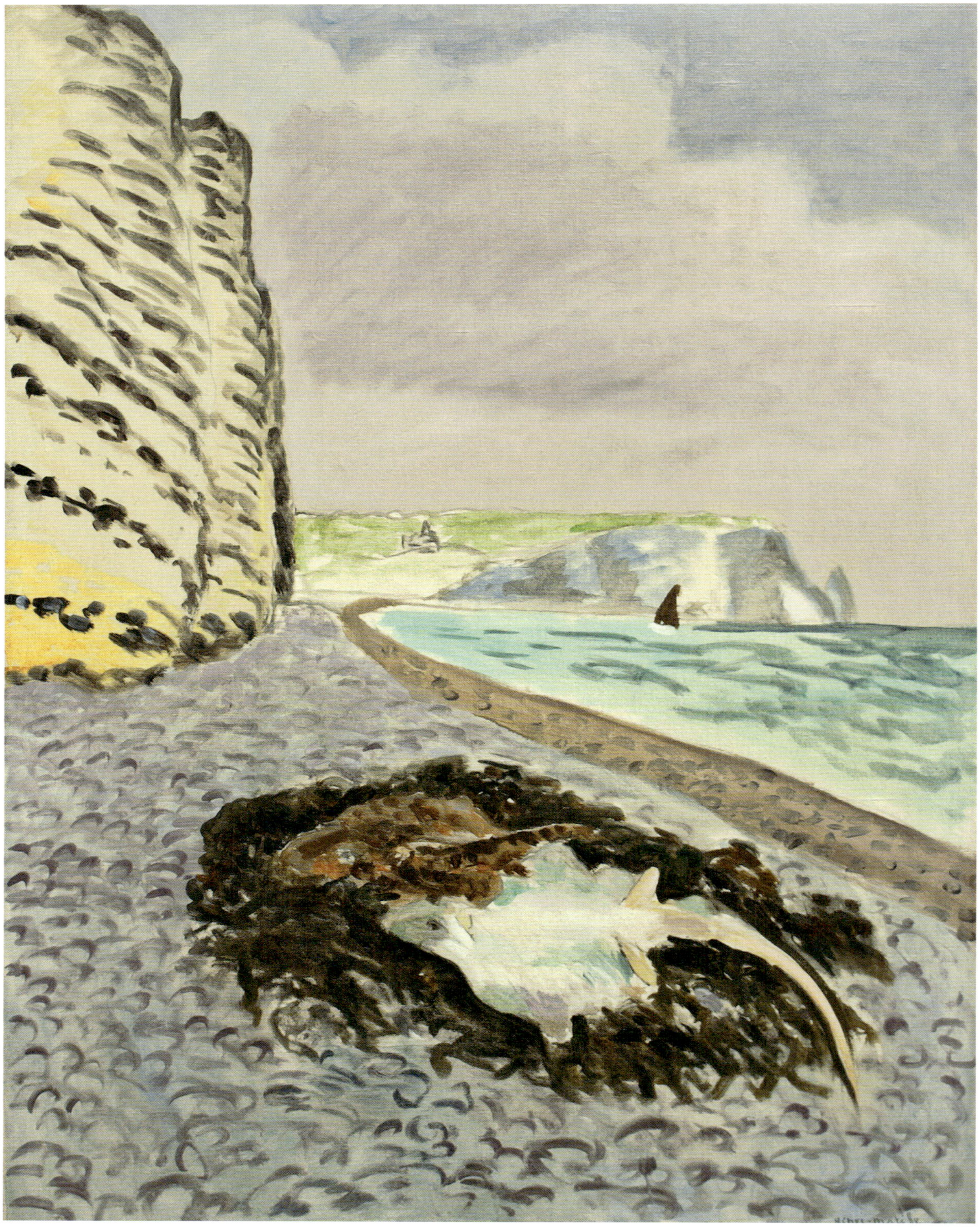

43 | *Large Cliff—Two Rays*, 1920

Oil on canvas, 36⅝ x 29 in. (93 x 73.7 cm). Norton Museum of Art, West Palm Beach, Florida, Bequest of R. H. Norton

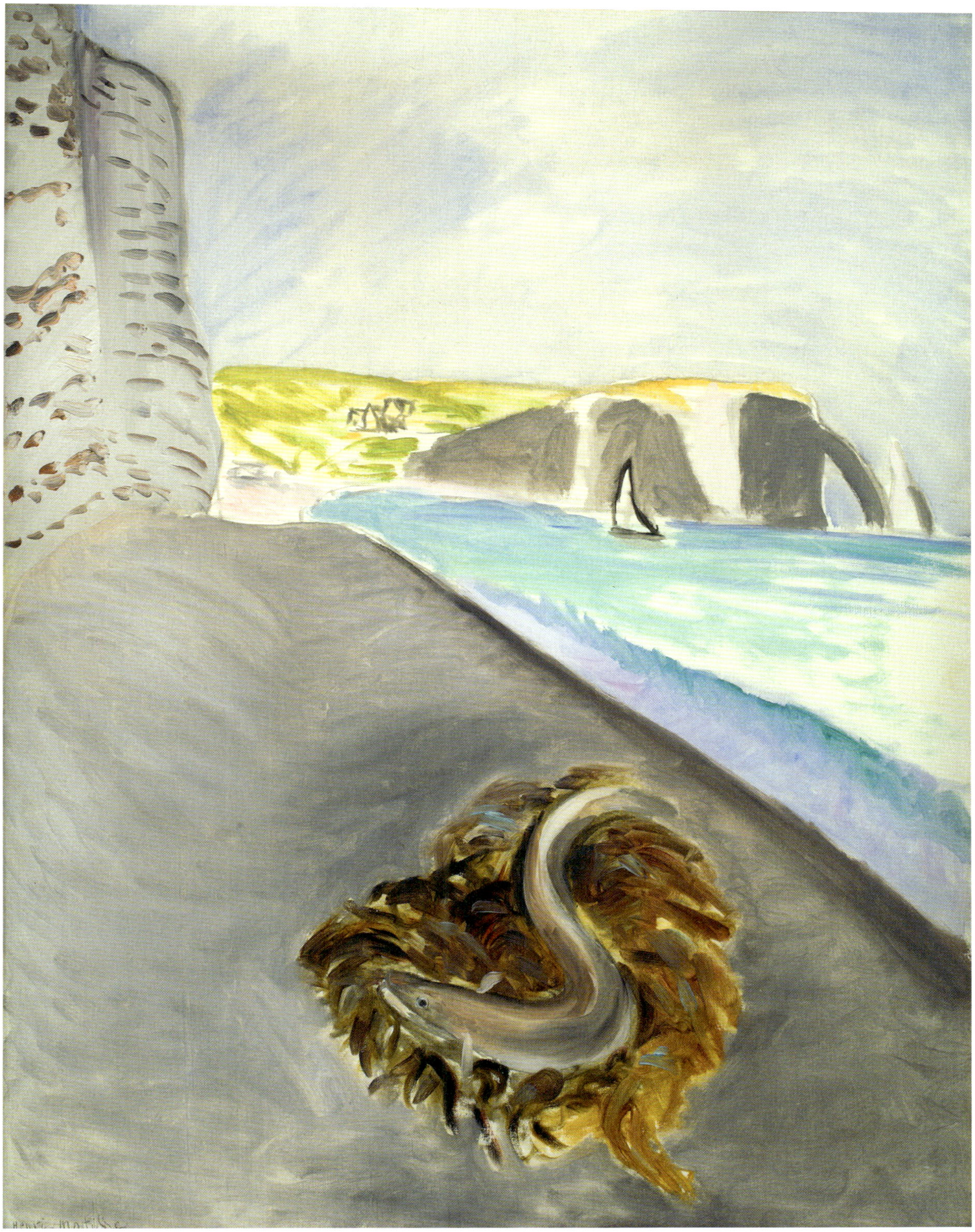

44 | *Large Cliff—Eel*, 1920

Oil on canvas, 35⅞ x 28⅜ in. (91 x 72 cm). Columbus Museum of Art, Ohio, Gift of Ferdinand Howald

of turquoise paint); one sailboat is dark brown, the other white and outlined in purplish black. In both paintings, the scale and shape of the sails mirror the negative spaces in the rock arches behind them.

Matisse's approach in *Large Cliff—Fish* (cat. 45) is much freer. This canvas, most likely the first of the three to be created, is thinly painted, with no pencil drawing underneath and copious areas of exposed primed ground.[9] Contemporary photographs of Étretat show that the beach was often littered with clumps of seaweed and other vegetation, which Matisse represents in this painting but has edited out of the other two. The jumble of fish, an eel, rays, lobster, and oysters contrasts with the still lifes in the other two works, which feature only one or two items carefully arranged in an arabesque. Similarly, the boat is presented here as an indistinct, almost incidental form, with no relation to the nearby arch, and the villa on the cliff is practically indiscernible.

When Bernheim-Jeune opened an exhibition of Matisse's recent work on October 15, 1920, it was heralded as one of the most important art events of the season.[10] Most of the thirty-one Étretat paintings sold within a few weeks. The New York lawyer John Quinn, for example, purchased *Large Cliff—Eel* on October 21.[11] The following year, Quinn lent the canvas to the "Exhibition of Impressionist and Post-Impressionist Paintings" at The Metropolitan Museum of Art, where it was displayed in the same room as *The Manneporte near Étretat* by Monet (1886; The Metropolitan Museum of Art, New York). While Monet's canvas did not cause a stir, *Large Cliff—Eel* was found so offensive that one New York resident cited it as the reason he chose to stay away from the city during the run of the show.[12] Clearly, Matisse had achieved his goal of presenting a traditional French subject in a thoroughly modern and thought-provoking way.

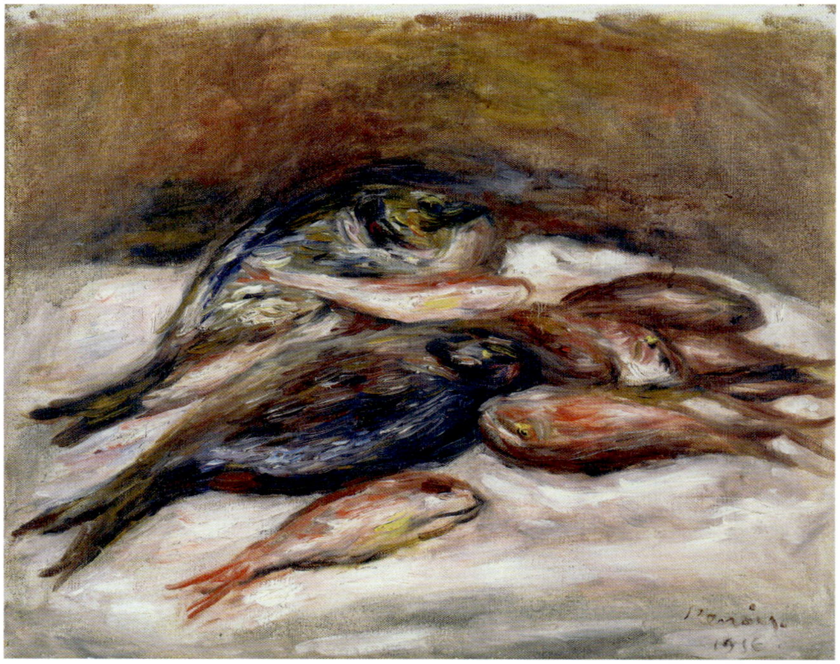

Fig. 66. Auguste Renoir. *Still Life with Fish*, 1916. Oil on canvas, 15¾ x 19¾ in. (40 x 50 cm). Musée National Picasso, Paris

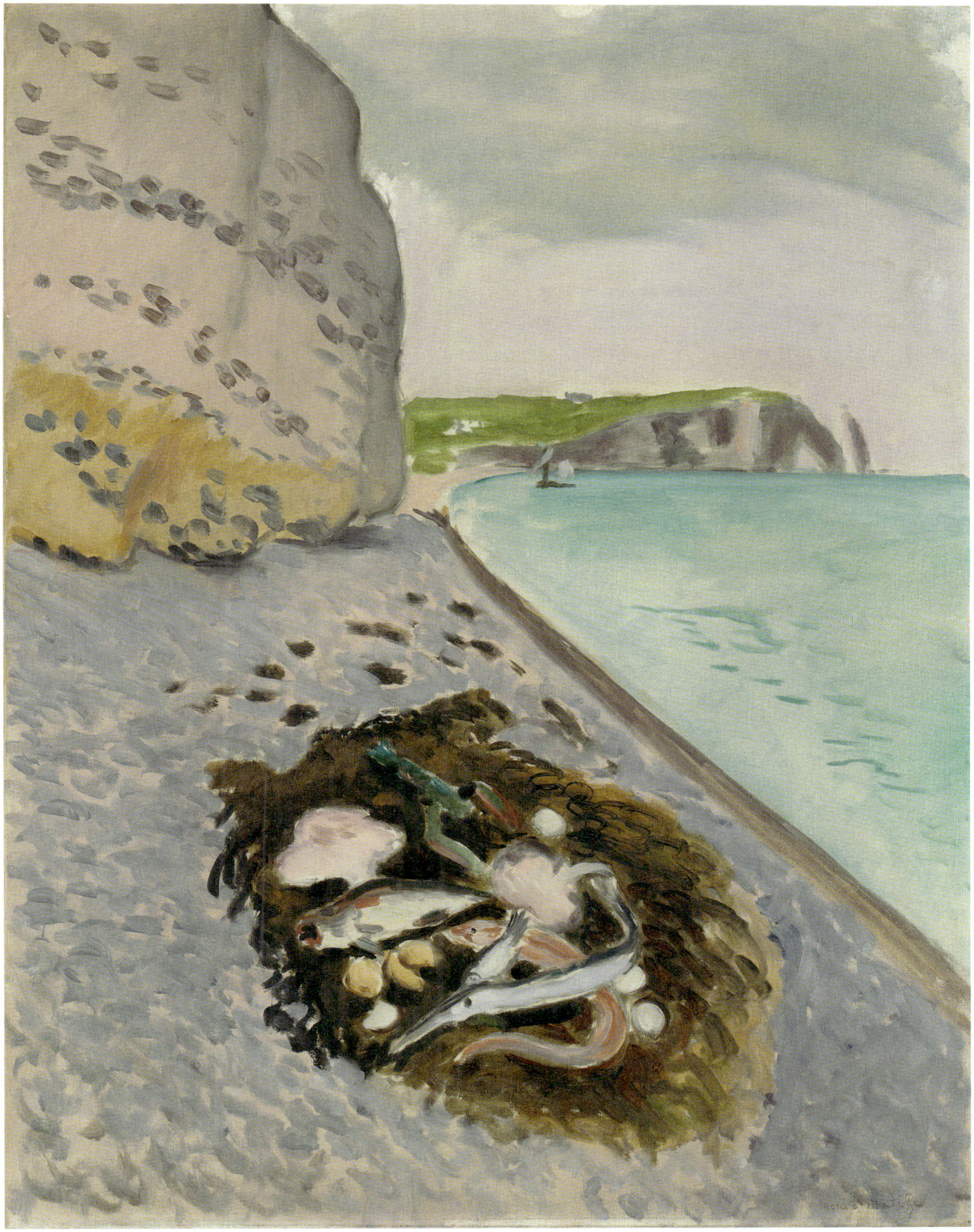

45 | *Large Cliff—Fish*, 1920

Oil on canvas, 36½ x 29 in. (92.7 x 73.7 cm). The Baltimore Museum of Art, The Cone Collection, formed by Dr. Claribel Cone and Miss Etta Cone of Baltimore, Maryland

ANEMONISM: "A DREAMY TREATMENT OF COLOR"

Cécile Debray

Although Matisse considered his early years in Nice (1917–30) an integral part of his artistic career, that period has often been regarded as something of a parenthesis, marked by a different kind of naturalism than that found in his works from 1907 to 1914. In 1919 the painter spoke of his desire to subsume all his artistic experiences into a whole: "I first worked as an impressionist, directly from nature; I later sought concentration and more intense expression, both in line and color, and then, of course, I had to sacrifice other values to a certain degree, corporeality and spatial depth, the richness of detail. Now I want to combine it all."[1]

The still lifes with bouquets of anemones from 1924–25 (cats. 46–48) stem not only from Matisse's reexamination of his earlier works, such as the paintings of flowers from 1905–8, but also from Impressionism and its avatars. Accompanying these influences was the artist's synthesis of an abstract (decorative) space and a realist (illusionist) one, what Pierre Schneider has termed a "*simulated realism* through abstraction."[2] In 1925, in his studio on the place Charles-Félix in Nice, Matisse painted a series of compositions depicting a table covered with a pink tablecloth, on which are arranged a candied pineapple in a wicker basket, a bouquet of anemones, a fruit bowl, and lemons. In addition to the examples discussed here, the series included *Pink Tablecloth, Lemons, and Candied Pineapple* (fig. 67) and *The Pink Tablecloth* (fig. 68), both also dating to 1925. In these paintings, Matisse was seeking to transcribe "corporeality and spatial depth, the richness of detail" by combining a perspectivist rendering of the table, expressed as sharp obliques, and a precise, colorful description of the many objects and decorative elements that structure—or perhaps annihilate—the space. That decorative overabundance, characteristic of the artist's works of the 1920s (especially the theatricalized representations of odalisques), strongly evokes the interplay of surfaces in Édouard Vuillard's Nabi paintings and in those of Matisse's friend and neighbor Pierre Bonnard.

During this period, Matisse had set up a veritable staging area in his studio, which Hans R. Hahnloser describes as follows:

> *As we were waiting for Matisse, we visited his studio, with Bonnard as our guide. That visit*

took place in 1929: [a] photograph shows the large wooden easel where Matisse liked to hang draperies of various colors, depending on the color scheme he needed for his paintings. In the foreground, the blue-green cloth with jeweled diamond shapes and, in the background, the arcades of Persian embroidery. . . . That way of hanging the multicolored fabrics explains why the colored grounds so typical of Matisse are not at all part of the wall and, as a result, do not correspond to the structure of the room they decorate. Their function is merely that of a multicolored screen that can be placed anywhere.[3]

Ornate surfaces, erected like the movable parts of a stage set, were no longer integrated as decorative, flat zones, as in *Harmony in Red (The Red Room)* (1908; The State Hermitage Museum, Saint Petersburg) and *Interior with Eggplants* (fig. 32). Rather than relying on a unified plastic resolution, a "harmony," Matisse constructed his paintings on the basis of discreet contrasts, an understated heterogeneity: "In that ambiance of languid relaxation, and under the sunlit torpor washing over things and beings, a great tension is brewing, which is on the specifically pictorial order, a tension that comes from the interplay of the elements, their relationships with one another."[4]

Of these elements, the textile or wallpaper patterns tend to become indistinguishable from the flowers, with a concerted ambivalence as the result. Flowers are a basic motif in Matisse's painting: as living entities, they incarnate pure color and very often suggest the color scheme of the compositions. The anemone, in fact, confers a languid note on a number of paintings from the Nice period, including *Still Life with "Histoire Juive"* (cat. 48), a tone that Schneider has aptly termed "anemonism," a "dreamy treatment of color."[5] The corolla of the

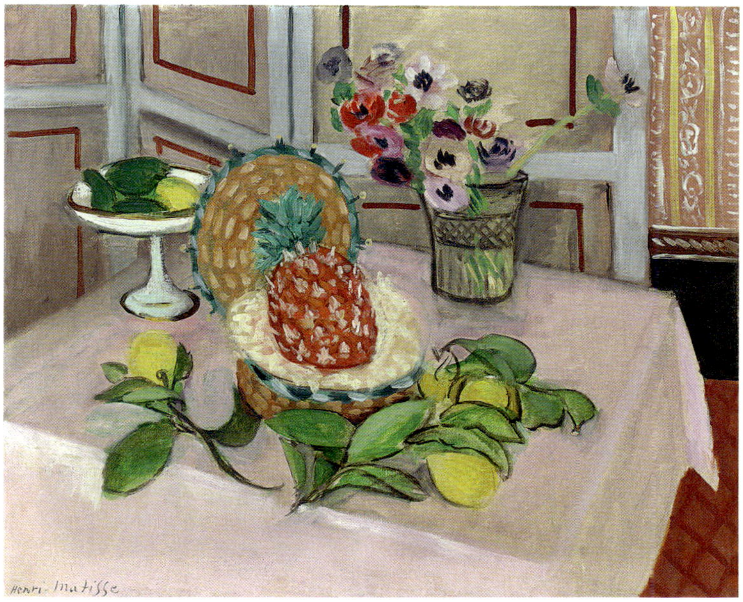

Fig. 67. *Pink Tablecloth, Lemons, and Candied Pineapple*, 1925. Oil on canvas, 25⅝ x 32⅛ in. (65 x 81.5 cm). Private collection

Fig. 68. *The Pink Tablecloth*, ca. 1925. Oil on canvas, 23¾ x 31⅞ in. (60.3 x 81 cm). Kelvingrove Art Gallery and Museum, Glasgow, Bequest of William McInnes, 1944

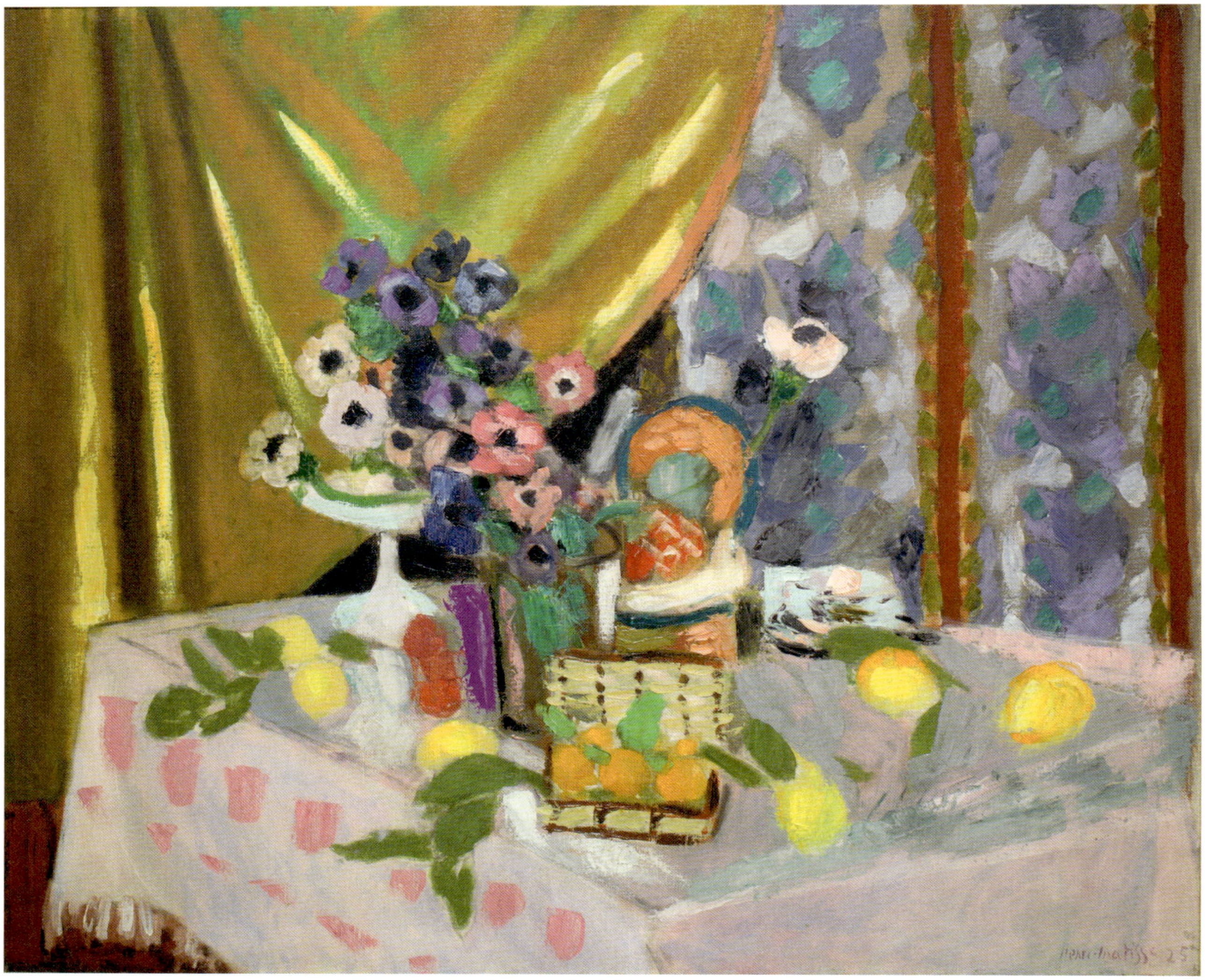

46 | *Still Life with Yellow Curtain, Anemones, and Fruit*, 1925

Oil on canvas, 31½ x 39⅜ in. (80 x 100 cm). Private collection

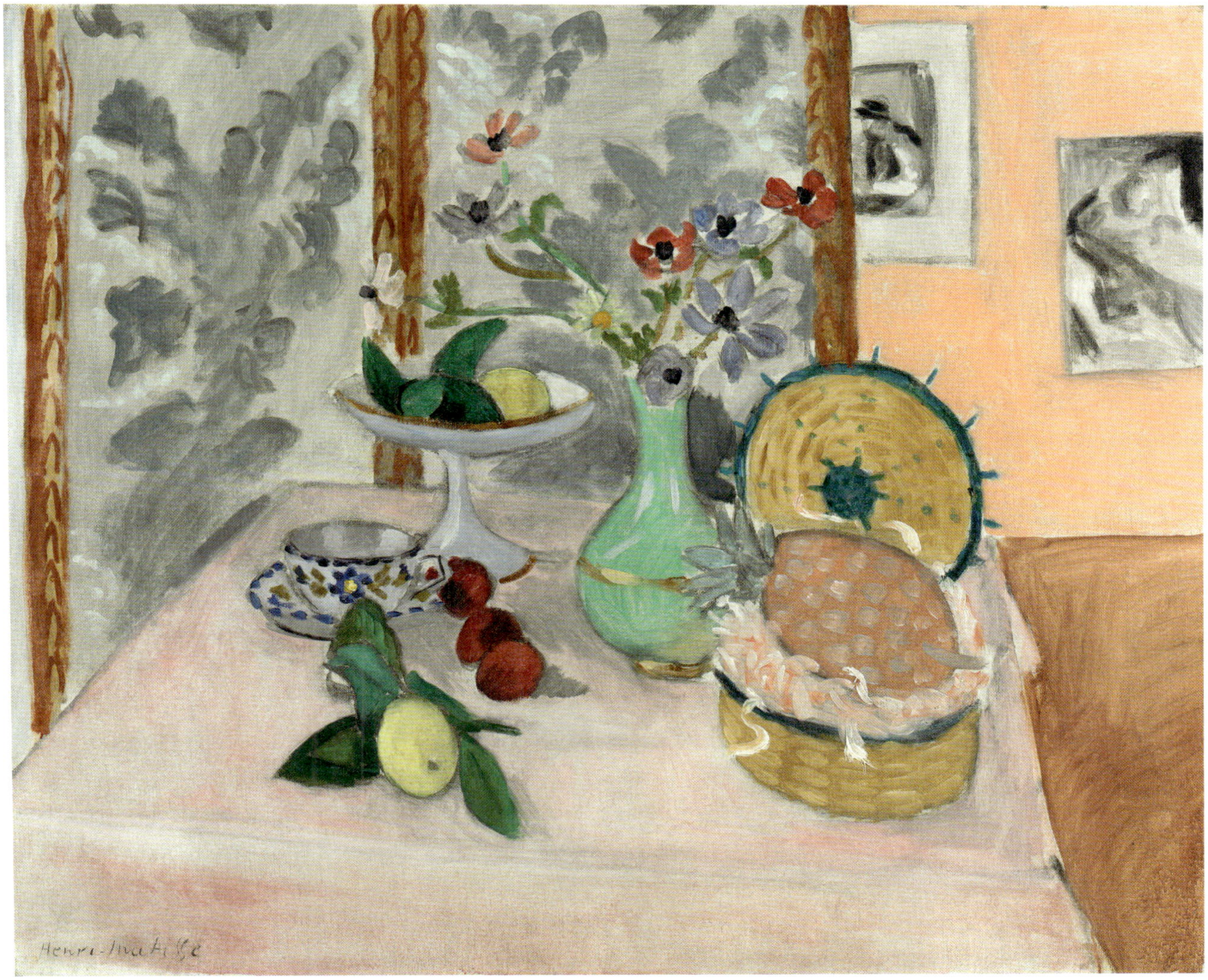

47 | *Still Life with Candied Pineapple, Anemones, and Fruit*, 1925

Oil on canvas, 31¾ x 39¼ in. (80.6 x 99.7 cm). Philadelphia Museum of Art, Gift of Henry P. McIlhenny, 1964

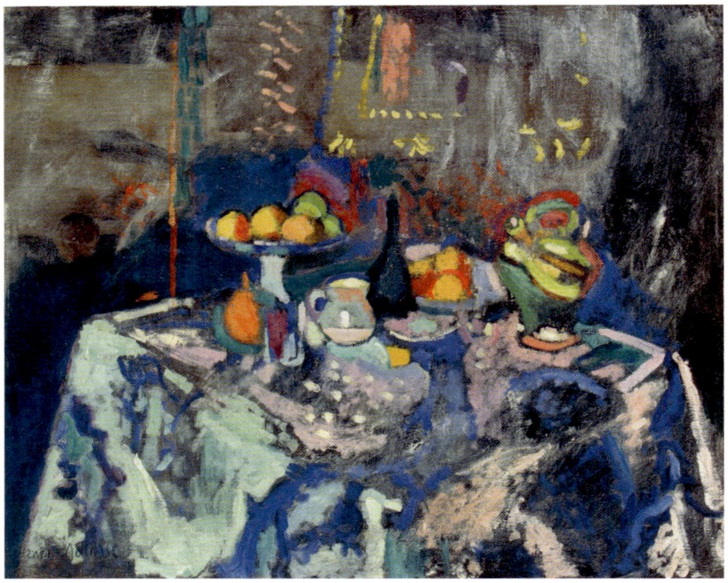

Fig. 69. *Still Life with Blue Tablecloth*, ca. 1906. Oil on canvas, 28¾ x 36¼ in. (73 x 92 cm). The State Hermitage Museum, Saint Petersburg

flower, anchored to a black core, initiates a circular movement that is amplified and reflected back through the deployment of multicolored notes. That brilliance of color, exaggerated in the two paintings from the Philadelphia Museum of Art (cats. 47, 48), alludes to the still lifes of 1905–8, especially *Still Life with Blue Tablecloth* (fig. 69). The refined, dispersed treatment of color owes a great deal to Odilon Redon's bouquets and, above all, to his decorative panels with floral motifs.[6]

Matisse seemed to be evoking the example of his elders—Monet, Manet, Renoir, and Redon—as he reflected on the course of his artistic pursuits and on his attempt to reconcile opposites.[7] In some sense, he revisited the still lifes of 1905–6 through the 1924–25 series, which proposes a less lyrical reformulation, a more calculated and destabilizing intimism. Like *The Painter's Family* (State Hermitage Museum), his large painting from 1911, and its reprise from 1924, *Pianist and Checker Players* (National Gallery of Art, Washington, D.C.), the Philadelphia still lifes at first appear as three-dimensional, illusionist constructions. This impression is gradually undermined, however, by an ornamental impulse orchestrated by the concentrated colors in the wall hangings, screen, flowers, and fruit. As Schneider notes, "Soon all that remains of the representation is a veil stretched over the construction of the picture."[8] That "veil" stiffens the composition, and therein lies the entire difference between these paintings and *Still Life with Blue Tablecloth*, which is animated by a more artless energy.

Matisse would continue his obsessive reworkings and restatements of the anemone motif, producing in February 1940 a last version, *Pineapple and Anemones* (private collection). An extremely detailed, brightly colored composition with flat zones of color and black rings, it achieves the harmony the artist had so ardently sought between line drawing and color but abandons the luminous plane that, according to Dominique Fourcade, characterized his most beautiful paintings of the 1920s: "A kind of supreme plane of light pervades and unifies the otherwise implausible diversity of colors (diametrically opposed to the spectrums of realism or naturalism). This unique luminous plane, an architecture without pillars, is so strong that it achieves the annihilation of the third dimension of space."[9]

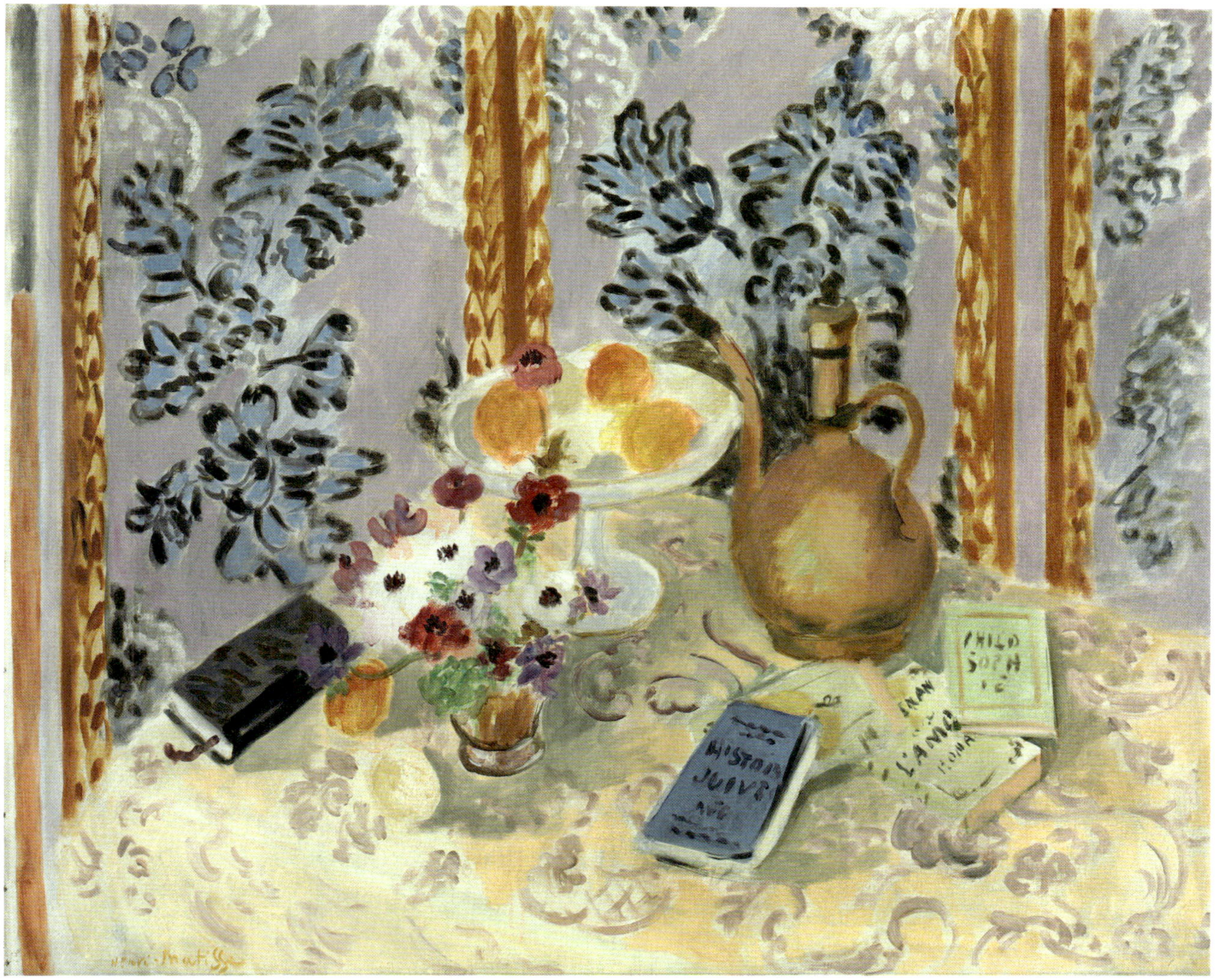

48 | *Still Life with "Histoire Juive,"* 1924

Oil on canvas, 32⅛ x 39½ in. (81.6 x 100.3 cm). Philadelphia Museum of Art, The Samuel S. White 3rd and Vera White Collection, 1967

VARIATIONS ON THE ODALISQUE

Isabelle Monod-Fontaine

All the odalisques that Matisse painted in Nice between 1921 and 1928 can be considered explorations of a theme and its variations. This process was not yet established with the conceptual clarity that he later attained—in drawings, with the *Themes and Variations* album (published 1943; cats. 57, 58), and in paintings, with the series of Vence interiors (1946–48; cats. 59–64). The artist's move to Nice was less a way to repudiate the abstract austerity of the years 1910–17 than a response to a set of impulses: to find the means to "do nudes" more systematically than previously;[1] to return to intimate painting; to make the volume of a body and the flat elements of a decor hold together compositionally. Frequently reproduced archival photographs indicate that these elements were literally flat, since Matisse situated his models within fragile, unstable, and shallow stages, composed of fabric panels, screens, thin mattresses, and rugs, punctuated by a few objects.

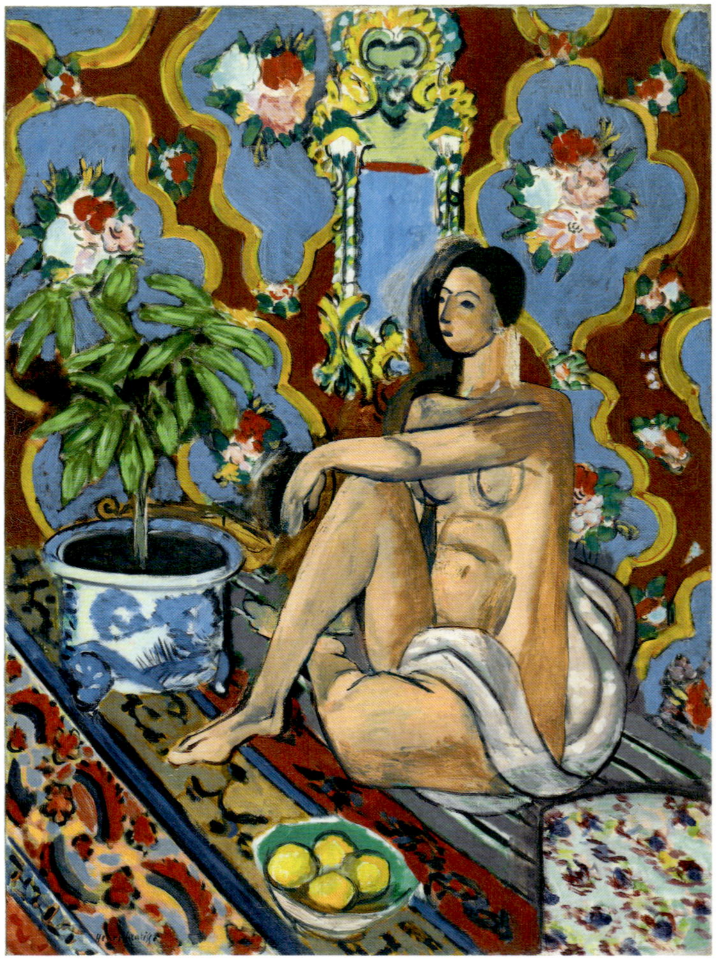

Fig. 70. *Decorative Figure on an Ornamental Ground*, 1925–26. Oil on canvas, 51 ⅛ x 38 ⅝ in. (130 x 98 cm). Centre Pompidou, Musée National d'Art Moderne, Paris

Fig. 71. *Two Odalisques*, 1928. Oil on canvas, 21¼ x 25⅝ in. (54 x 65 cm). Moderna Museet, Stockholm

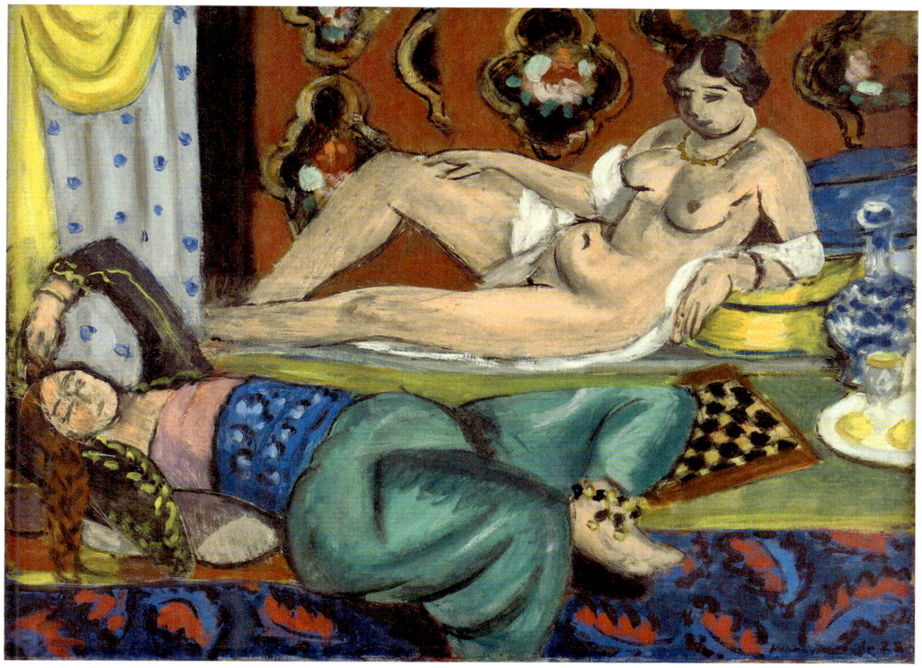

During these seven years, the central motif of Matisse's paintings, as well as his drawings, engravings, and sculptures, was a nude, or scantily clad, light-skinned, brown-haired young woman (from the beginning until near the end of the series, Matisse used a single model, Henriette Darricarrère). The figure usually lies in what resembles a bedroom—a space without windows, doors, air, or light other than that produced (in profusion) by the color.[2]

On that theme, repeated to the point of obsession, Matisse produced several variations. Three pivotal moments in the evolution of the series can be distinguished. Between 1921 and 1925, he depicted the odalisque as a living sculpture in an enveloping space or niche that had a perceptible depth. The closely related *Odalisque with Red Harem Pants* (1921; Centre Pompidou, Musée National d'Art Moderne, Paris) and *Odalisque with Magnolias* (1923–24; private collection) mark the beginning and end of this sequence. The "climax" of the entire sequence is *Decorative Figure on an Ornamental Ground* (fig. 70), in which a sculptural figure is embedded in a background of swirling motifs that appear to push her away. After this canvas, Matisse continued to play with the opposition between body and decor but in a different, less insistent manner.

In a second series of canvases, dating to 1926–27, the body gradually sinks into the plane of the "wall," which is defined by interchangeable, repetitive decorative elements, both similar and different in each work. At least five variations, including catalogue numbers 49 and 50, can be linked to that series.[3] Each time, Matisse made himself use identical components—two or three background fabrics (one with large motifs inscribed in diamonds, a striped cloth, and one of the embroidered Moorish arches he so admired), a thin green mattress, a blue-and-white-striped garment rolled into a cushion on which the

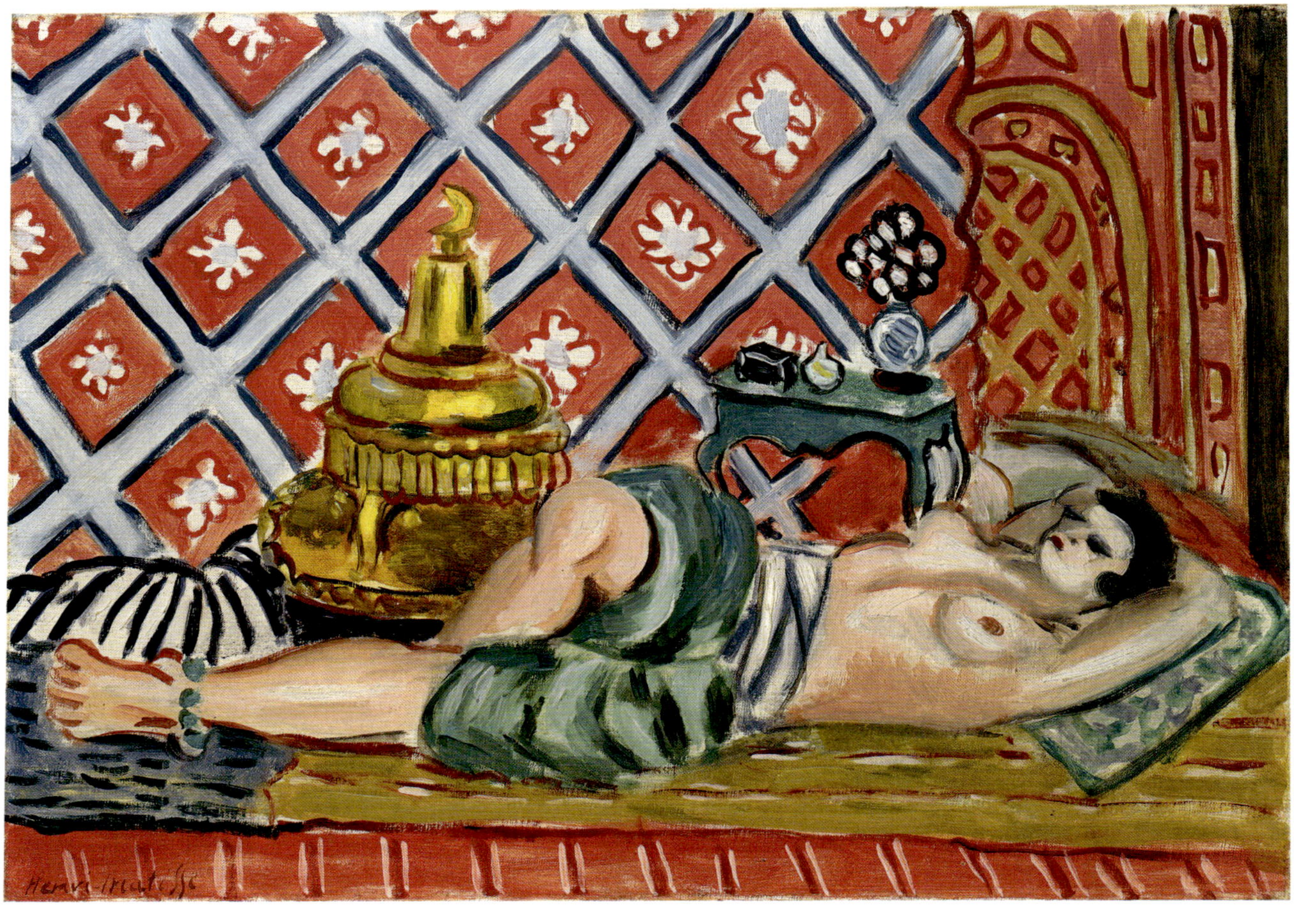

49 | *Reclining Odalisque*, 1926

Oil on canvas, 15 ⅛ x 21 ⅝ in. (38.4 x 54.9 cm). The Metropolitan Museum of Art, New York, Bequest of Miss Adelaide Milton de Groot (1876–1967), 1967

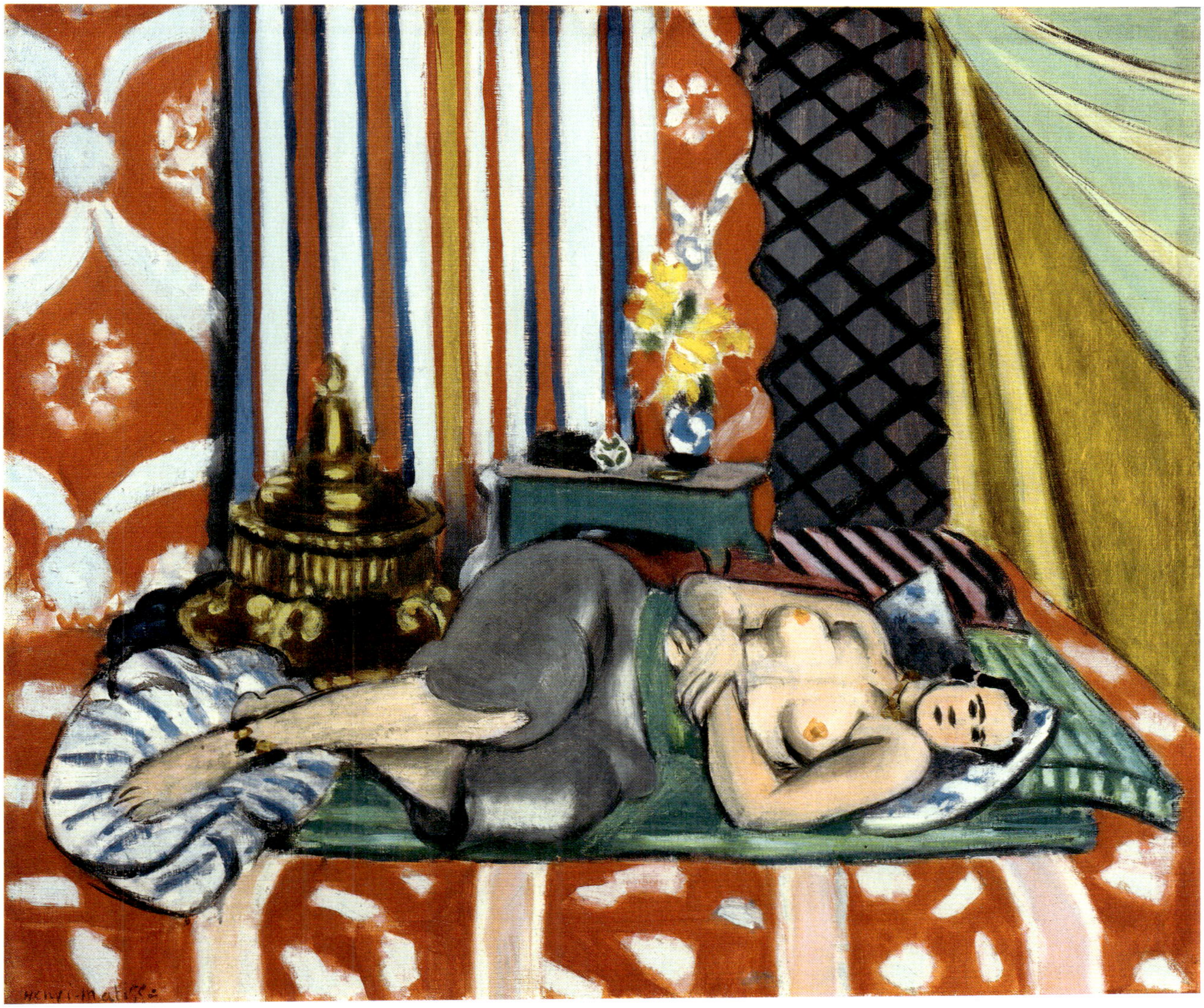

50 | *Odalisque in Gray Harem Pants*, 1926–27

Oil on canvas, 21 ¼ x 25 ⅝ in. (54 x 65 cm). Musée de l'Orangerie, Paris, Collection Jean Walter and Paul Guillaume

Fig. 72. *Two Models Resting*, 1928. Oil on canvas, 18 ½ x 28 ⅞ in. (47 x 73.3 cm). Philadelphia Museum of Art, Gift of Mrs. Frank Abercrombie Elliott, 1964

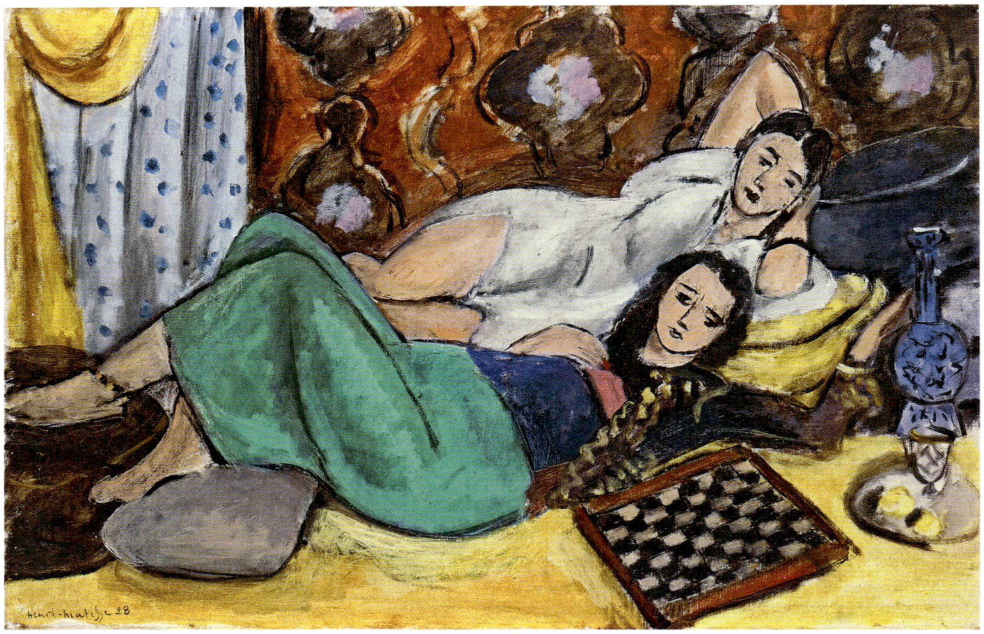

model rests her feet, a copper brazier, and a small green table—but he emphasized different ones. The figure is always recumbent and viewed in profile; only the color harmonies differ.

Odalisque in Gray Harem Pants (cat. 50) is the most accomplished of these variations. Beyond its large, shimmering motifs and the heaviness of the striking, sensual red (a red note is present in the other canvases but is less bright), its greatest impact lies in the forcefulness of the geometric organization: vertical bands and strongly marked stripes that structure and flatten the space from top to bottom. On her green mattress, the little odalisque seems to float as if on a flying carpet, liberated from the force of gravity. It is as if Matisse, only a few months after finishing *Decorative Figure on an Ornamental Ground*, had wanted to invert the elements: the swirling decor in the first work becomes geometric in the second; the ponderous seated figure in the earlier canvas is replaced in the later one by a horizontal body in profile, a silhouette without volume; her small, ghostly face turns tentatively toward the beholder. Here the background plane begins to absorb the odalisque. She is merely a piece (albeit a central one) of a powerful abstract geometric pattern whose rhythm she barely interrupts.

When Henriette Darricarrère stopped working for Matisse in 1927, he replaced her with several other models. In the third and last series of variations, which includes *Two Odalisques* and *Two Models Resting* (figs. 71, 72), he sometimes had more than one pose for him.[4] In this way, he duplicated the motif in order to experiment with symmetry and pose reversals, as well as with the complementary nature of colors. Multiplied, the odalisque loses her identity and becomes one element among many. Each canvas of this last series shows a checkerboard, which not only signals the matrix at the core of any decorative grid but also serves as a metaphor for the game of painting, which begins over and over again.

THE ETERNAL FEMININE

Jack Flam

As early as 1908, Matisse had written about his ambition to render the essential aspect of his subjects, an ambition particularly notable in his paired works. "Underlying this succession of moments which constitutes the superficial existence of beings and things," he wrote, "and which is continually modifying and transforming them, one can search for a truer, more essential character, which the artist will seize so that he may give to reality a more lasting interpretation."[1] Of all the themes whose essential character preoccupied him, that of Woman was the most significant and most persistent. Matisse sought not only to depict the appearance of specific women but also to express an ideal akin to that of the Eternal Feminine, in which the power of Woman is associated with creativity, fecundity, and even a state of grace. The four paintings here provide an excellent example of the artist's search for the essential character of Woman in the depiction of an individual figure. Because they were done within a short time, they clearly reveal how he reconceived their basic theme, distilling and flattening the forms in an evolutionary process similar to that recorded in his photographs of the development of a single painting.[2]

These works (cats. 51, 52, figs. 73, 74), painted in 1936, came at an especially critical time for Matisse. During the 1920s, he had worked in a somewhat naturalistic way, depicting things from a specific point of view and emphasizing transitory effects of light, shadow, and mood. Then, between 1931 and 1933, in his work on a mural for the Barnes Foundation, he had employed bold, flat planes of color set against a highly abstracted ground to render the bodies of dancing women. By 1935, in paintings of his muse and companion, Lydia Delectorskaya, including *Large Reclining Nude* (1935; The Baltimore Museum of Art) and *The Dream* (1935; Centre Pompidou, Musée National d'Art Moderne, Paris), Matisse had become increasingly involved with the evocation of objects in a flattened, abstracted space. As he continued to emphasize flat areas of bright color and the rhythmic patterning of the spaces between the things represented, his paintings were eventually transformed into ensembles of distilled pictorial signs that asserted a certain independence from their surroundings.

One of Matisse's major preoccupations during the 1930s was the dichotomy between design and color, between drawing and painting. In moving away

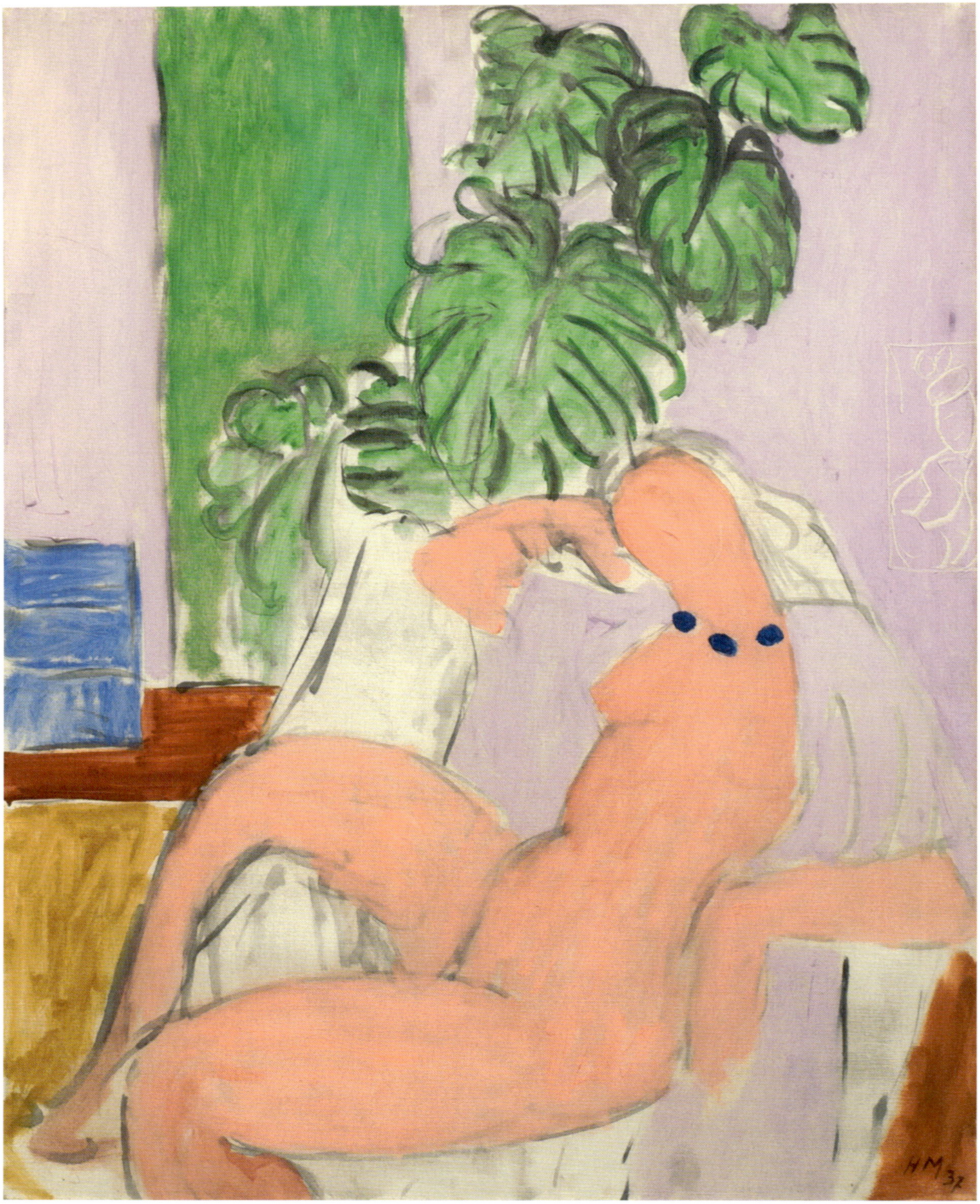

51 | *Seated Nude with Foliage, Sketch*, 1936

Oil on canvas, 28½ x 23⅞ in. (72.5 x 60.5 cm). Musée Matisse, Nice, Gift of the Estate of Mrs. Henri Matisse, 1960

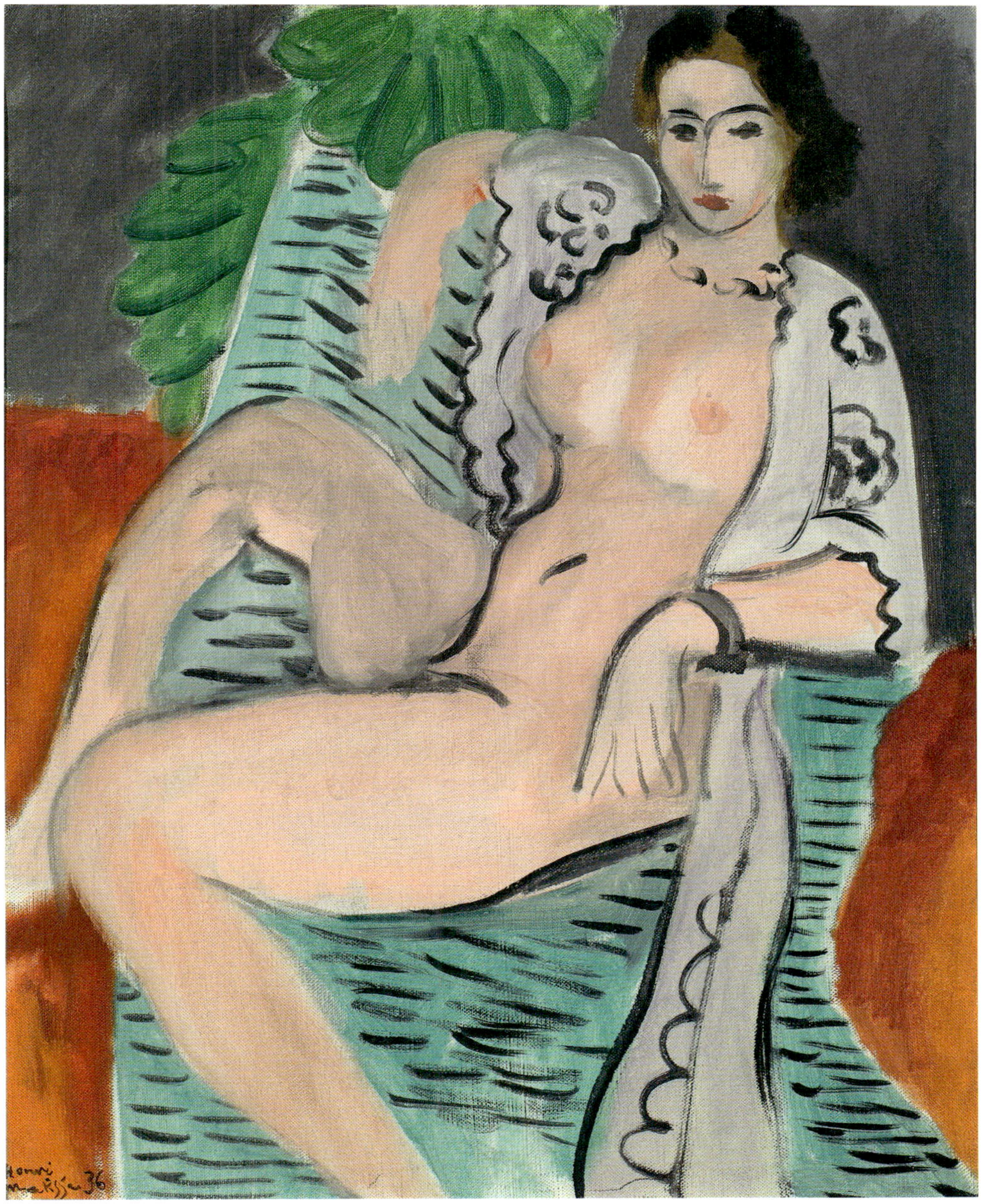

52 | *Draped Nude*, 1936

Oil on canvas, 18 x 14¾ in. (45.7 x 37.5 cm). Tate: Purchased 1959

from an overt dialogue between the two, he indicated an important change in his notion of how pictorial space could be made to signify both the physical world and states of mind. His numerous erotically charged pen-and-ink drawings, made between 1935 and 1937, stressed spontaneity and barely arrested motion. By contrast, his paintings at this time were often quite calculated and distilled, imbued with a sense of timelessness. Design and color were kept somewhat separate: the linear definition of the composition often seems to precede its chromatic aspects, which could be subsequently varied without substantially modifying the drawn elements.[3] Matisse was no longer thinking in terms of his Fauvist paintings, in which the violent interaction of color and drawing had been paramount, but of a flatter, more static space in which color and drawing were set against each other in measured counterpoint. Although he continued to work directly from life, he was already moving toward the kind of imagery that would characterize his cutouts. He was turning away from the description of objects in their surrounding space to the evocation of objects by signs; from a modeled space to a suggested one; from images based on what is directly seen and felt to those based on what is recollected and thought; from the individual to the typical.

Of the four paintings described here, *Seated Nude with Foliage, Sketch* (cat. 51), done between November 3 and 5, contains the most relaxed representation of the woman. Its thinly painted surface and spontaneous appearance alone suggest a certain casualness. The woman and her immediate surroundings are pale, the contours of her body generalized and rendered in gentle, curving forms. Her facelessness and barely indicated hands further emphasize the decorative, depersonalized aspect of the composition.[4] The luxuriant leaves of the plant provide an elaborate decorative motif, juxtaposed against the woman's soft body. The way the plant grows up behind her, just tangent to her arm and head, creates an electric moment of interaction. Because the picture is so lightly painted, the pictorial space is understood as a force field, and the brush marks as modifications of that field. This allows Matisse to depict the exchanges of energy between beings and things, to suggest how they can interact with each other conceptually, physically, and spiritually. Here, as in many of his other paintings, plants and decorative motifs express the inner vitality of the woman in a way that transcends her individuality. The two areas of bright reddish paint reinforce that vitality, as does the repetition of blue in the necklace and the box. Such interactions create a symbiotic effect: the woman's body simultaneously draws energy from, and radiates out into, her surroundings.

Draped Nude (cat. 52) was done only a couple of days later, on November 6 and 7. Here the woman fills more of the picture, and the rendering is more specific. She is seen from a particular viewpoint, and her face, though not very detailed, is fairly portraitlike. The floral patterns on the cloth draped over her shoulders are set against the unevenly spaced horizontal lines of the upholstery and create a lyrical counterpoint to their rhythmic ground. These floral motifs, bringing forward the now somewhat muted plant, transpose some of its decorative vigor to her body. This is one of Matisse's most persistent visual conceits. When he paints women next to plants or flowers, both are often animated by the transfer of linear energy. Keeping the viewer's eye in continual motion, this transfer was part of Matisse's strategy for dispersing the individuality of the women in his pictures. Such constant displacement has important psychological implications, for while we are invited to look at one thing, we are simultaneously drawn away to look at another. Thus, the main subject of the picture is diffused over the entire surface of the canvas.

Fig. 73. *Nude in an Armchair with Gray Scarf*, 1936. Oil on canvas, 18⅛ x 15 in. (46 x 38 cm). Private collection

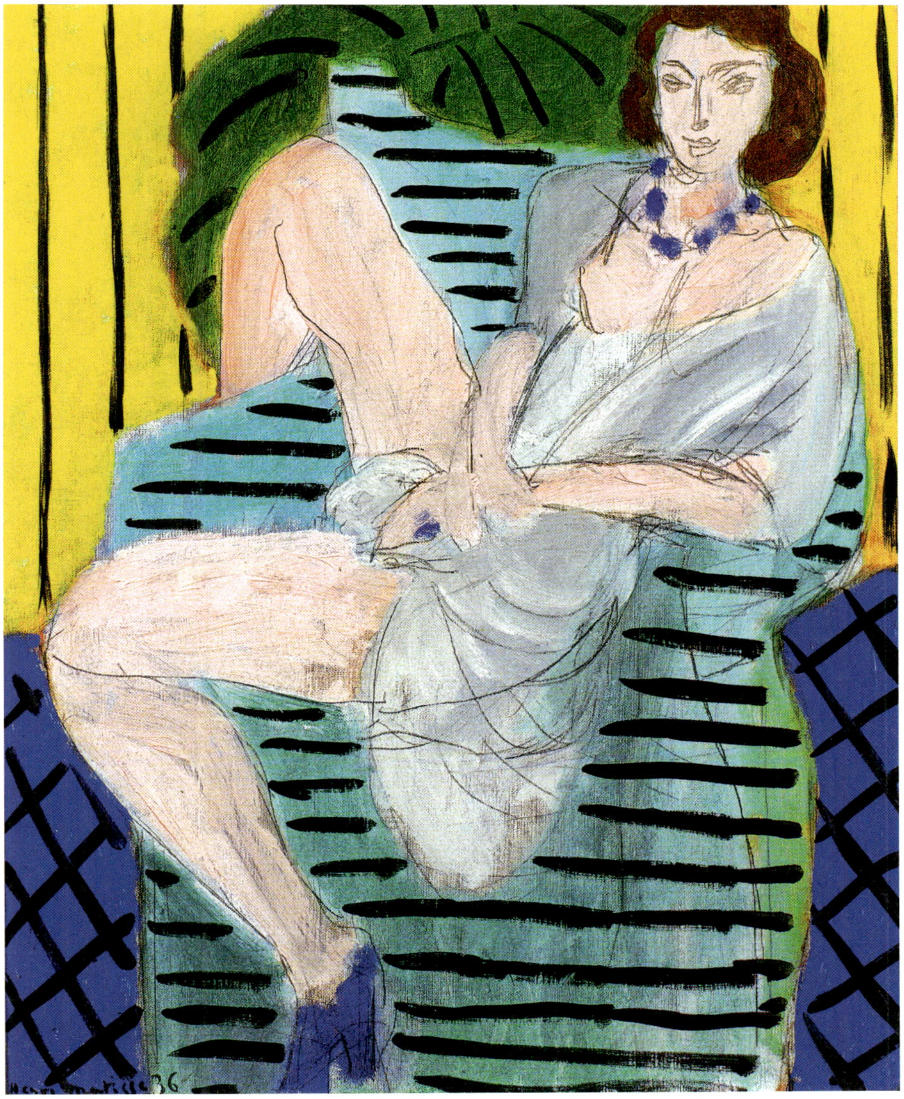

Nude in an Armchair with Gray Scarf (fig. 73), painted on November 9 and 10, reflects a distinct shift in style. The woman's pose is less casual and less natural, the forms more severely flattened. The horizontal stripes on the cloth are bold, near-parallel black lines that are set against the crisscrossed pattern on the floor. Besides helping to flatten out the space, these decorative motifs create a musical effect, with areas of different rhythmic inflection serving as orchestration for the main subject. Most strikingly, the woman's body is both more abstracted and more sensual. Her legs are widely spread and her hands converge at her crotch, where a spot of blue paint picks up the rhythm of the dots of her necklace and echoes the color of her high-heeled shoe. The plant seems almost to caress the top of her chair, and the fluidly material way the pencil lines describing her body were incised into the wet paint enhances the aura of

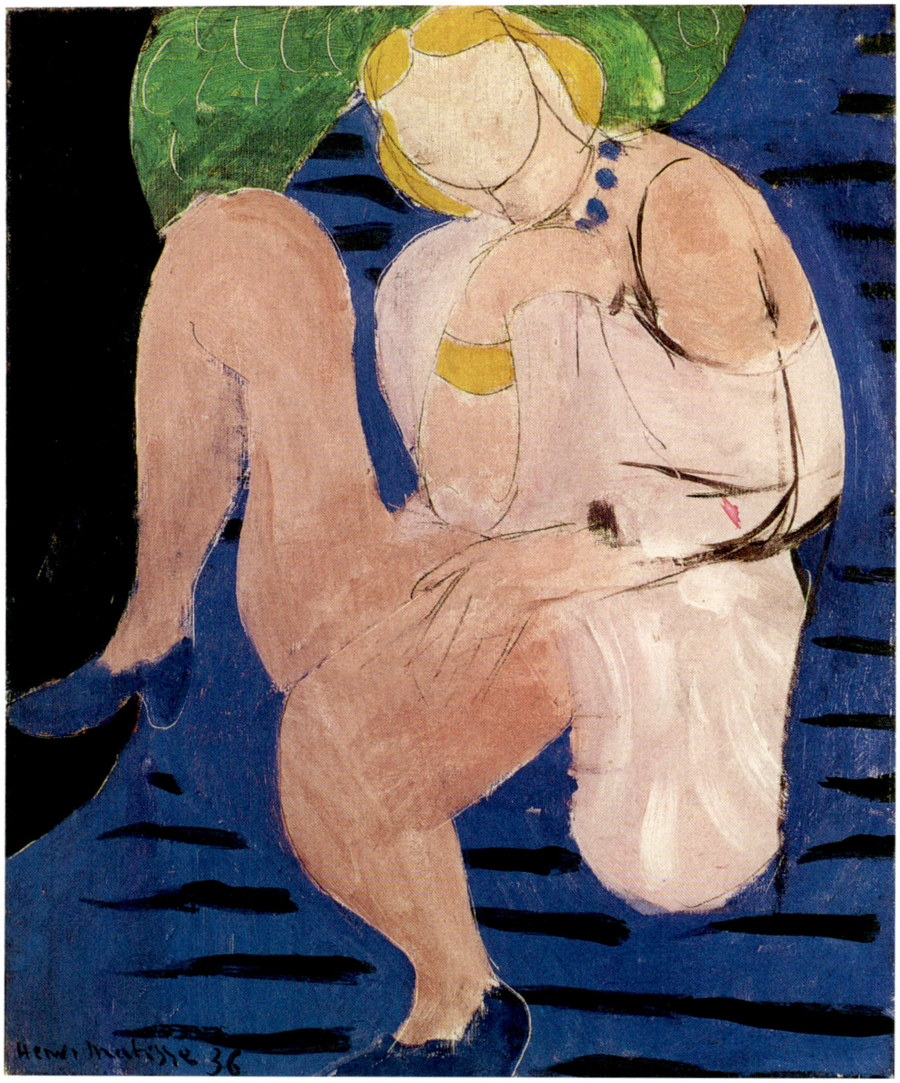

Fig. 74. *Nude in Armchair, Blue Ground*, 1936. Oil on canvas, 18⅛ x 15 in. (46 x 38 cm). Private collection

OPPOSITE
Fig. 75. *Large Nude*, 1911. Distemper on canvas, dimensions unknown. Destroyed

Fig. 76. *Blue Nude IV*, 1952. Gouache on cut and pasted paper, and charcoal on white paper, 40½ x 30¼ in. (102.9 x 76.8 cm). Musée Matisse, Nice

lyrical sensuousness. Matisse has struck an especially fine balance in the woman's face between portraiture and the somewhat depersonalized conception of the whole. The flattening of the forms in this painting and the way the drawn lines both define and radiate out from the woman recall earlier works by Matisse, such as *Nude with a White Scarf* of 1909 (cat. 16). In fact, the flattened, rather disembodied figure seems to realize Matisse's great preoccupation, around 1910, with creating images that represent women as free from the constraints of normal space and time, as he did notably in the *Large Nude* of 1911 (fig. 75).

The progression toward "placeless" representations of women is taken even further in *Nude in Armchair, Blue Ground* (fig. 74), which Matisse struggled with from November 16 until December 6. Although the most intensely reworked of these four paintings, it appears to be the most spontaneous because the forms

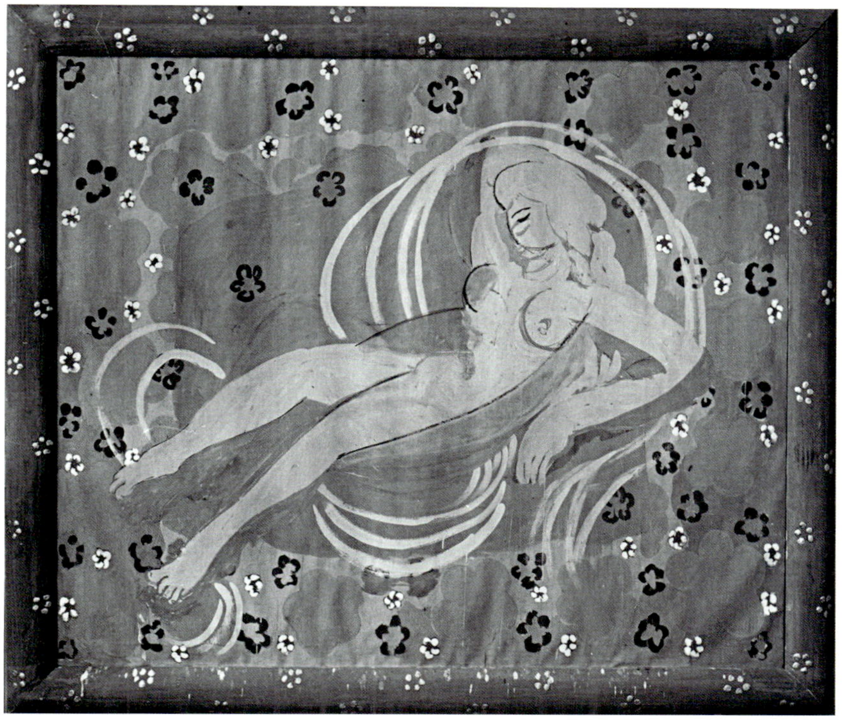

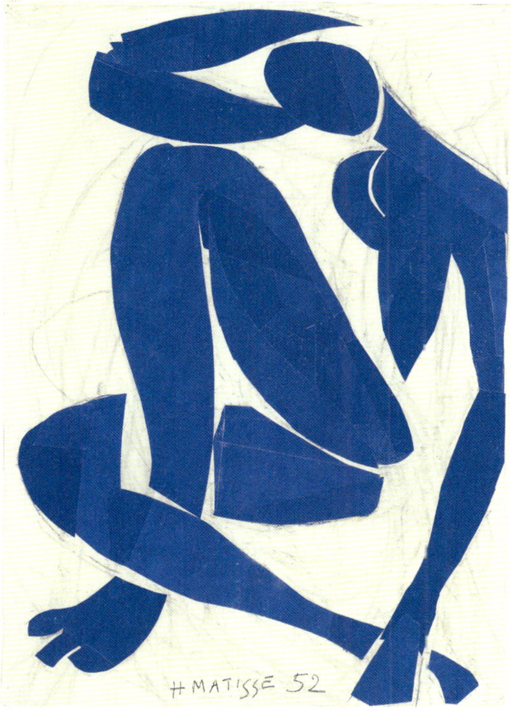

are so simplified. The woman's body and her surroundings have been so drastically distilled that they function more as signs than as representations. The blue area with black stripes is no longer recognizable as upholstery or even as a piece of cloth; rather, it functions as an abstract "blue ground." Similarly, the plant has been condensed into a curving green form, with only the most delicate suggestion of leaves. The woman's body, in particular, is seen from a much less specific viewpoint than in the other three paintings; it is flatter and set in a more generalized kind of space.

For all the abstraction of the forms, however, this woman projects the strongest erotic presence of the four. Her lower body is exposed and her legs provocatively splayed. Intriguingly, the gesture of abandon implied by her lower body contrasts with the rather modest gesture of her arms and shoulders. Once again, the figure is faceless, removed from the realm of the everyday and transformed into part of a decorative ensemble. And, in a touching simile, Matisse makes a clear connection between her gold bracelet and the gold of her hair. With its increasing emphasis on decorative patterning, abstracted figures, and bold chromatic harmonies, this painting clearly anticipates the direction Matisse's art would take during the next few years. It even foreshadows the most transcendent and abstracted of all his seated nudes—those in the blue cutouts of 1952. In works such as *Blue Nude IV* (fig. 76), the woman's surroundings are entirely eliminated, along with the logical arrangement of the parts of her body. These powerful, timeless symbols of Woman well reflect the artist's stated goal of making images that transcended the literal subject of the painting and allowed him to create a space that he described as being beyond him, "beyond any motif . . . a cosmic space."[5]

THE WOMAN IN BLUE

Rebecca Rabinow

In the 1930s Matisse hired an Armenian photographer named Matossian to record the progress of his paintings.[1] Between February 26 and April 3, 1937, Matossian took at least ten photographs of *The Large Blue Dress* (cat. 53).[2] At times the canvas was photographed daily; on two occasions, more than a week passed between sessions.[3] Viewed in chronological order, the images produce an effect akin to that of time-lapse photography, revealing Matisse's progression from a more naturalistic painted sketch to a flatter, stylized image (fig. 79a–j). The photographs raise as many questions as they answer. Did Matisse consult them as he painted? Did any serve as points of departure for related canvases? Clearly he valued these photographs, and once he had finished the painting, he shared these testaments to its creation with his public.

The model for *The Large Blue Dress* was Lydia Delectorskaya, a Russian émigré who had begun working as a studio aide for Matisse in October 1932.[4] In January 1936 she posed for the artist in a theatrical costume of her own creation: a blue gown with leg-of-mutton sleeves, embellished with white organza cuffs and ruffles along the edges of the

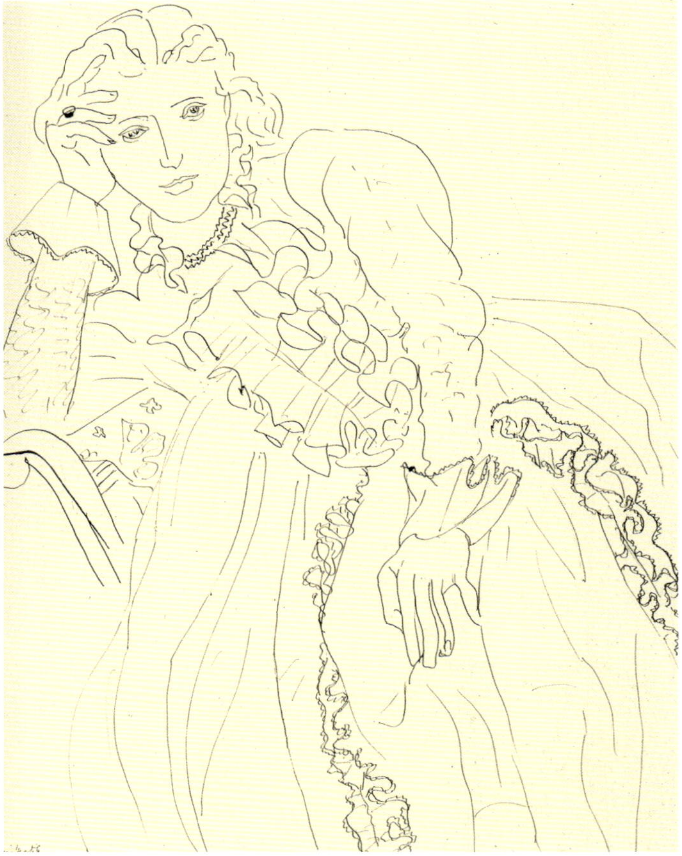

Fig. 77. *Young Woman*, 1936. Ink on paper, 22⅞ x 18½ in. (58 x 47 cm). Private collection

overskirt, neckline, and bodice. Several drawings and at least one painting of Lydia in the blue dress are dated to 1936.[5] In one of these, she is shown seated, leaning against the rolled arm of a settee with her head propped on her hand (fig. 77). On February 21, 1937, Matisse sketched Lydia in the same pose, albeit in reverse, on a "size 30" canvas.[6] The earliest known photographs of the painting are dated Friday, February 26, and Wednesday, March 3, 1937 (fig. 79a, b). By the time Matossian returned to Matisse's studio nine days later, the artist had rubbed out some of his work and straightened Lydia's posture (fig. 79c). Her head was moved directly in front of a vase of flowers on the mantelpiece. Matisse evidently wanted to keep Lydia's left elbow on the settee, so he exaggerated the dimensions of her hand, stretching it to fill the extra space.[7]

The painting evolved dramatically over the following ten days. The sense of depth diminished, and the composition became more rhythmic. The arabesques of the settee's arms gained prominence and echoed the newly defined trim on Lydia's skirt. The mantelpiece disappeared, but the identity of the setting—Matisse's fourth-floor studio in his apartment at 1, place Charles-Félix, Nice—was preserved thanks to the addition of a background grid that indicates the room's faux-tile wall covering (fig. 78).[8] The black paint, representing the floor, wide baseboards, and possibly shadows, crept up the canvas, higher on the left side, where it covered part of the settee and was rounded at the top to mirror the exaggerated curve of Lydia's shoulder. The empty rectangles in the background metamorphosed into framed artwork, and a necklace-cum-rosary was wound around Lydia's hand.[9]

Beginning on Monday, March 22, Matossian returned to Matisse's studio for four days in a row. His photographs reveal the artist's continued reworking

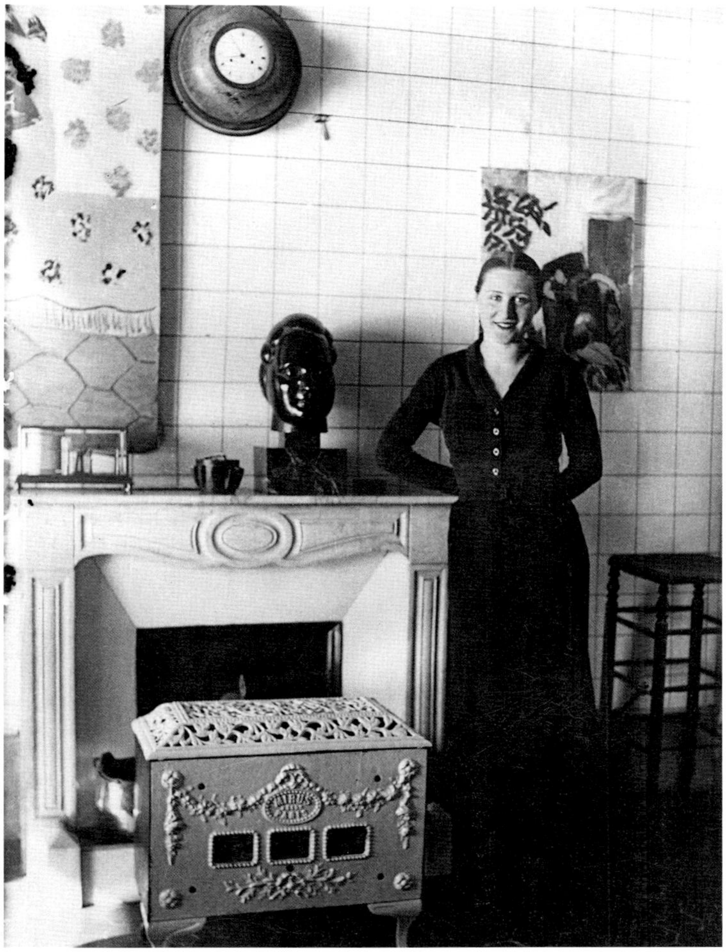

Fig. 78. Lydia Delectorskaya standing next to the fireplace in Matisse's studio at 1, place Charles-Félix, Nice, ca. 1935. Archives Matisse, Paris

of the contours of Lydia's skirt, the black floor, and the background wall, which was repainted and inscribed with thinner, more delicate grid lines (fig. 79e–h). Matossian's final photograph of the painting is dated Saturday, April 3, although Matisse still continued to work on the canvas.

At least two more paintings of Lydia in the blue dress were completed by Matisse during the late winter and early spring of 1937: *Blue Dress Reflected in a*

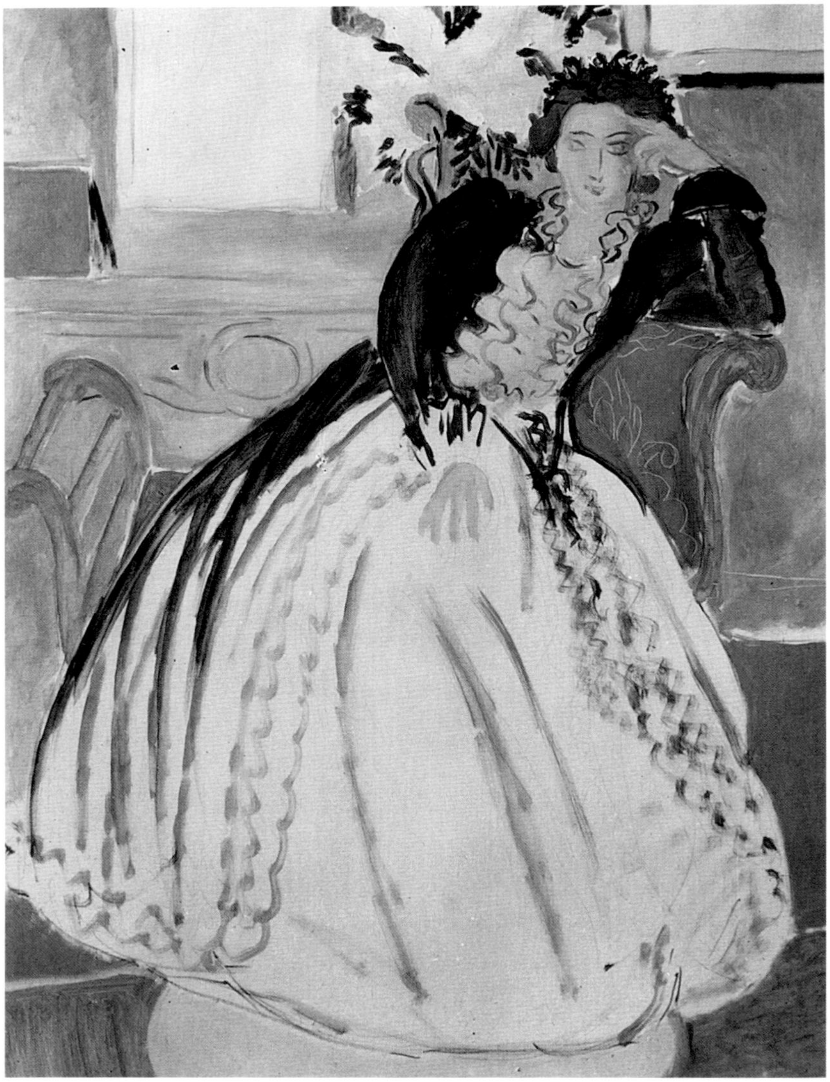

a

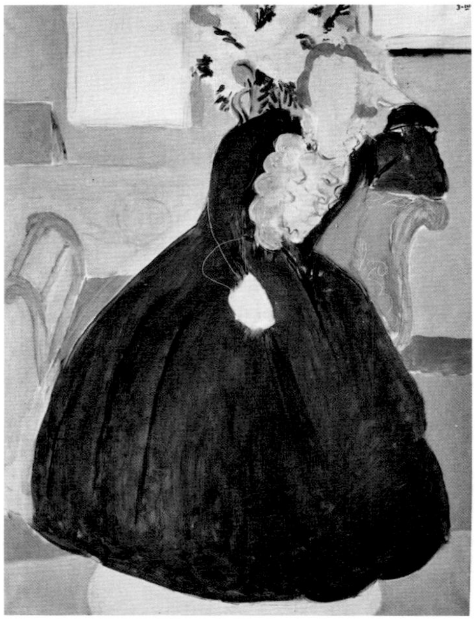

b

Fig. 79a–j. Matossian. Series of photographs showing the development of *The Large Blue Dress* in 1937: a. February 26, b. March 3, c. March 12, d. March 13, e. March 22, f. March 23, g. March 24, h. March 25, i. April 2, j. April 3. Archives Matisse, Paris

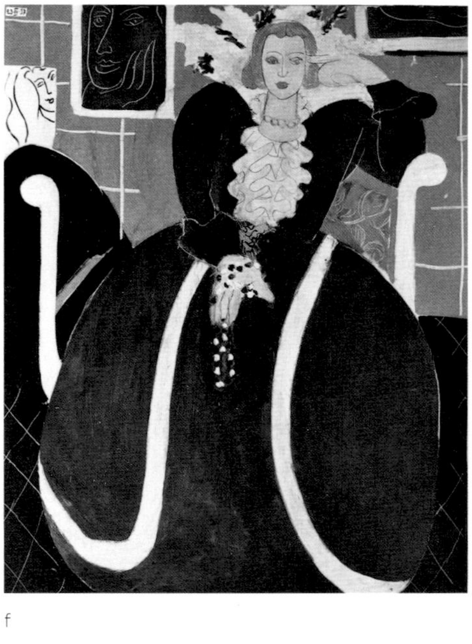

f

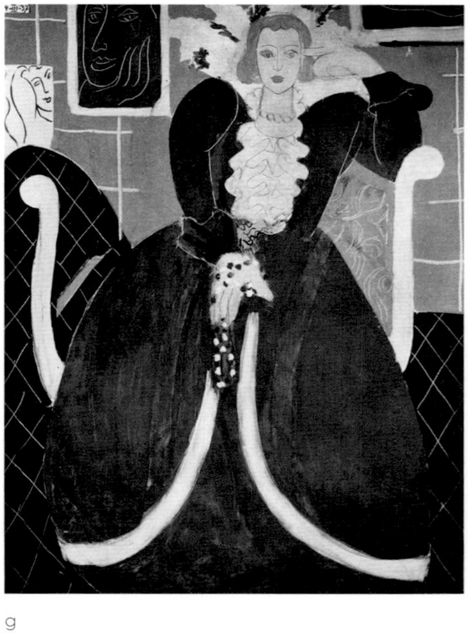

g

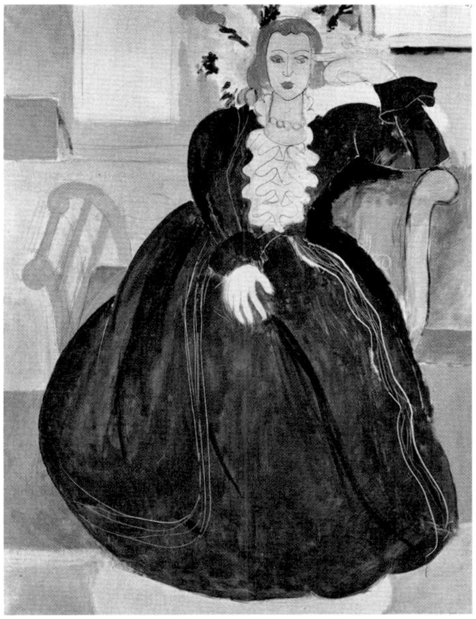
c

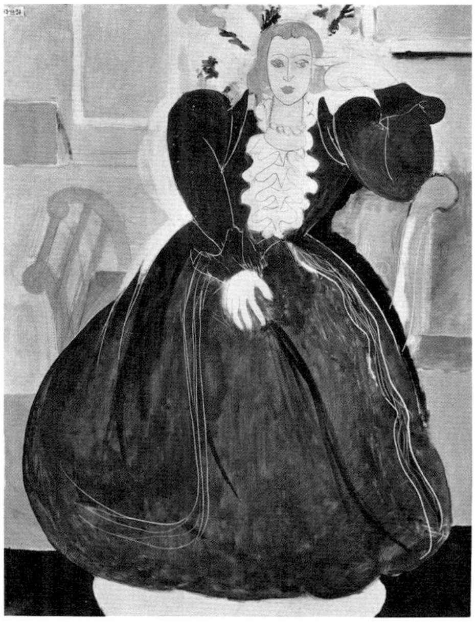
d

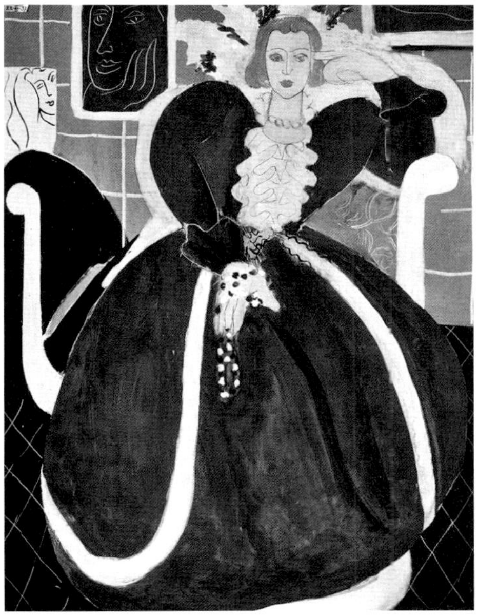
e

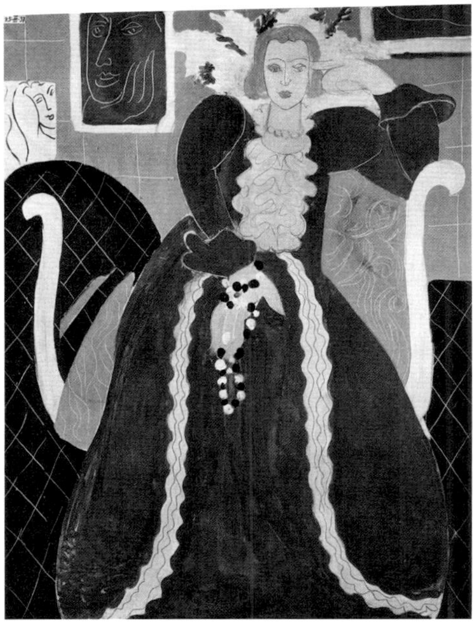
h

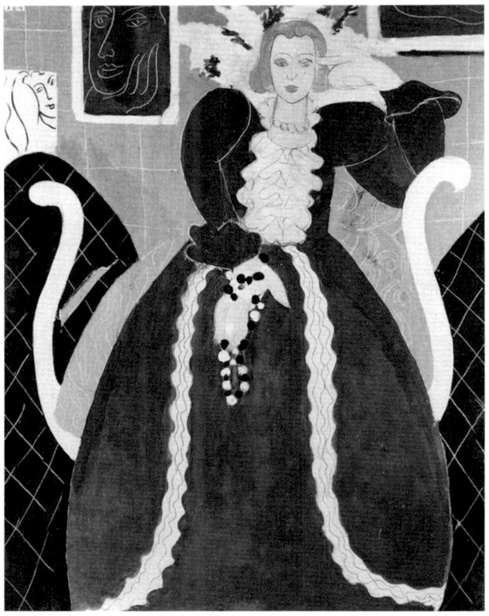
i

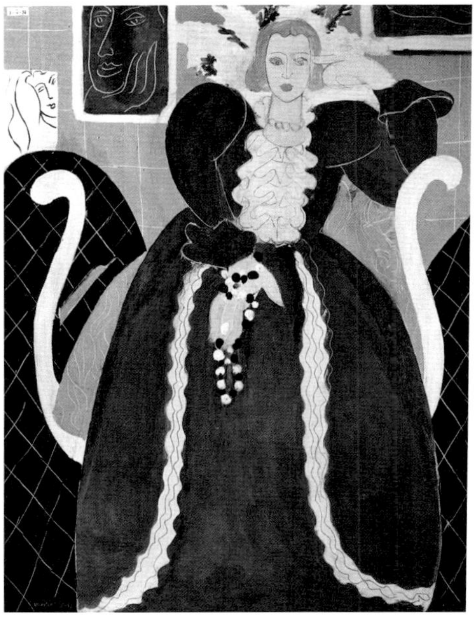
j

Mirror (The National Museum of Modern Art, Kyoto) and a profile view of Lydia seated in front of the studio mantelpiece (Henie-Onstad Art Center, Høvikodden, Norway). However, it was *The Large Blue Dress* that held the greatest significance for him.[10] As with earlier pairs such as *Nasturtiums with the Painting "Dance" I* and *II* (cats. 19, 20), Matisse substantially reworked only one of the compositions, and when he did, he made little effort to hide the revisions. Even the most cursory glance at *The Large Blue Dress* reveals the repeatedly modified contours of the dress and the altered position of Lydia's head. Matisse used a pointed object (possibly the end of his paintbrush) to remove lines of wet paint. The underlying colors are clearly visible in places, including the areas of red and blue underneath the black floor and the traces of red under the blue dress. (A striking example is in the line indicating Lydia's left underarm.)

Matisse had etched into his paint for decades, but the technique is particularly prominent in *The Large Blue Dress*. It speaks to his interest in the relationship between positive and negative space and to the possibilities of unifying color and line. It also reflects Matisse's substantial experience as a printmaker. Just a few years earlier, he had created scores of etchings for an elegant edition of Stéphane Mallarmé's *Poésies* (published by Albert Skira in 1932). Matisse may have used his photographed states the way a printmaker works with etchings. Proofs are pulled whenever an artist reaches a moment of interest, and based on the result, additional changes are made. It is no accident that Matisse referred to Matossian's photographs of his works in progress as "states," a term derived from printmaking.

It is unlikely that Matisse methodically consulted each of Matossian's photographs while revising *The Large Blue Dress*. In some instances, Matossian may not even have had time to develop a picture and return it to the artist before the canvas was reworked. Lydia recalled that Matisse generally used the photographs to rethink his compositions—perhaps they even provided some distance for him—but it is likely that at certain points during the creation of *The Large Blue Dress*, the knowledge that the photographs existed was sufficient to provide him with the sense of freedom necessary to wipe down areas of his canvas and rework them, without having to overanalyze his changes.[11]

Less than a decade earlier, Matisse had been criticized for creating art that was too facile. He believed that the photographs were evidence to the contrary, and so he shared them. He sent copies of the photographed states of *The Large Blue Dress* to Henry McIlhenny in Philadelphia, just as he had sent photographed states of charcoal drawings and canvases to Etta Cone in Baltimore a year or two earlier.[12] In July 1939 all ten photographs of *The Large Blue Dress* were published in the *Magazine of Art*. The editors grumbled that they would have preferred "a similar record of a painting from Matisse's revolutionary youth," but they had to admit that the "photographic indication of [the] painter's working method . . . [shows] that he remains adept at picture making."[13] Matisse would likely have argued that the finished painting was proof enough.

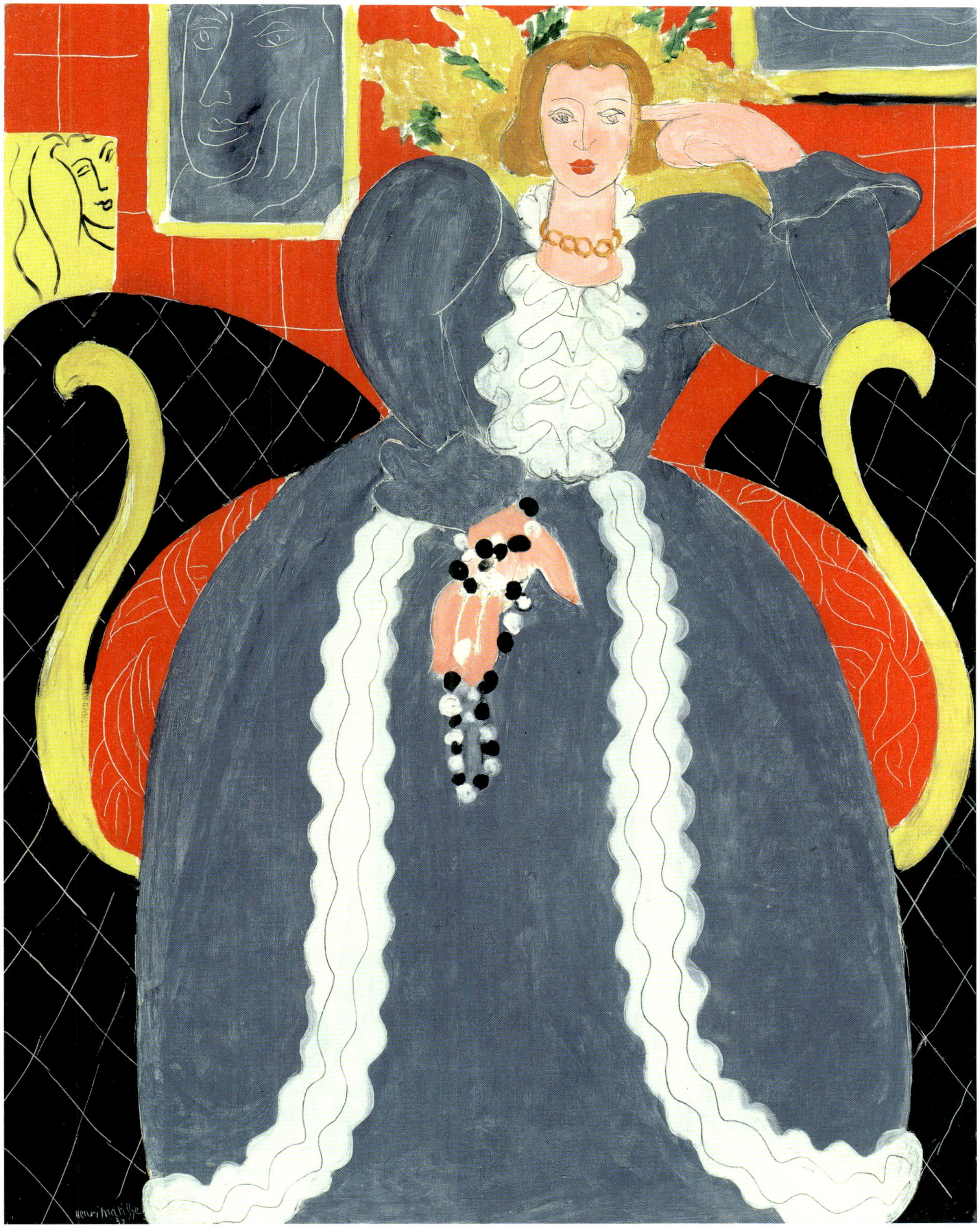

53 | *The Large Blue Dress*, 1937

Oil on canvas, 36½ x 29 in. (92.7 x 73.7 cm). Philadelphia Museum of Art, Gift of Mrs. John Wintersteen, 1956

THE METAPHYSICS OF DECORATION

Doïna Lemny

Matisse clearly believed that decoration was not a subordinate element in a pictorial composition: "Expression and decoration are one and the same thing, the second term being condensed in the first."[1] Long interested in fabrics of all sorts, the artist collected rugs, remnants of material, and decorated objects, using them as a sort of "work library."[2] According to Lydia Delectorskaya, Matisse developed a penchant for embroidered shirts during his visits in 1935–36 to Nice, where "all the shops . . . were overflowing at the time with lightweight blouses in white batiste, embroidered with bright-colored fleurettes."[3] During the same period, he also became intrigued with several Romanian blouses that he rediscovered among his possessions. He was particularly taken with their sober geometric motif, inspired by the oak leaf.[4] Several examples of this native folk costume were sent to Matisse by the Romanian painter Theodor Pallady, who also conducted a lively correspondence with his friend relating to the decorative aspects of painting.[5]

After first photographing Hélène Galitzine wearing a Romanian blouse in 1937, Matisse went on to analyze the motif in studies with several other models. He paid no heed to the actual color of the various garments, painting a *Green Romanian Blouse* (ca. 1939; private collection, Geneva), for example. He focused instead on the perfect harmony between the cut of the blouse—its ample body with two rows of embroidery and its puffy sleeves with grouped decoration—and the geometrical organization of the motifs. Preoccupied at the time with "liberating" his paintings from perspective, Matisse treated the embroidered areas on the blouse almost as découpage. Gradually, the features of the individual women in these studies became less important than the blouse, as he worked to synthesize the embroidery motif and to purify the composition.

Photographs of various stages of these paintings commissioned by Matisse allowed him to reflect on the "découpage" of the image. These were part of the December 1945 exhibition at the Galerie Maeght in Paris, which included thirteen photographs of *The Romanian Blouse* and fourteen of *The Dream*, or *Sleeping Woman* (cat. 54, fig. 80a–o).[6] The presentation attracted the attention of critics:

> *At issue are successive states, to borrow the engraver's vocabulary. We witness a birth in slow motion and see the rhythm and values shifting*

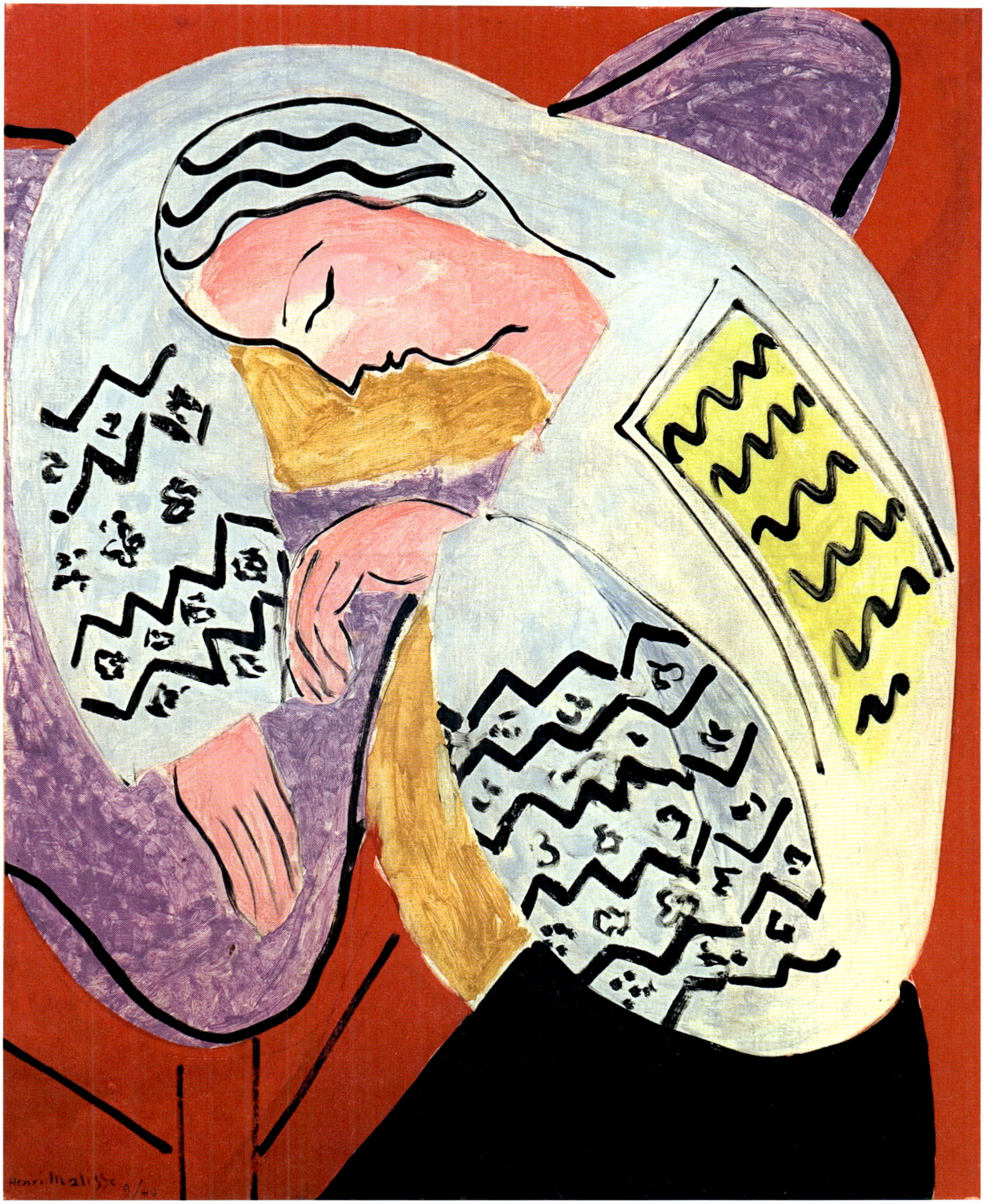

54 | *The Dream*, 1940

Oil on canvas, 31⅞ x 25⅝ in. (81 x 65 cm). Private collection

Fig. 80a–o. Series of photographs showing the development of *The Dream* in 1940: a. January 7, b. January 8, c. January 9, d. January 11, e. January 13, f. January 17, g. January 18, h. February 13, i. March 7, j. March 8, k. March 9, l. September 16, m. September 17, n. September 19, o. final (September 1940). Archives Matisse, Paris

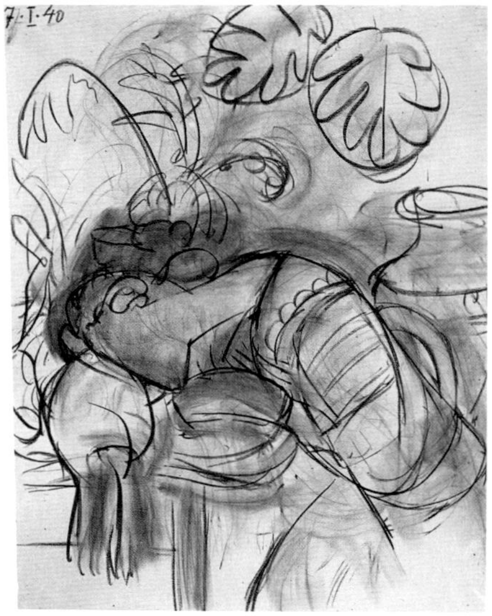

a

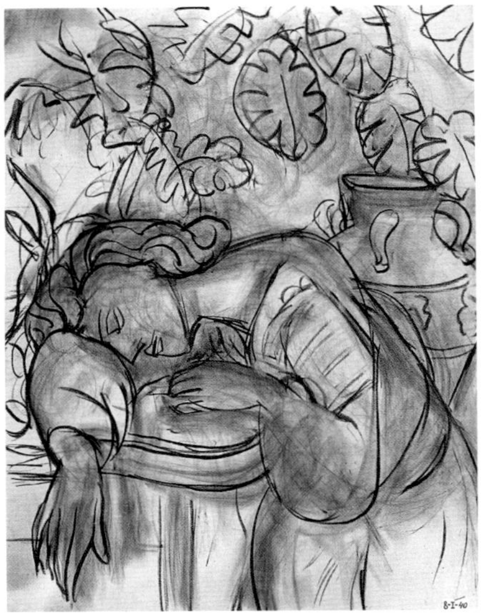

b

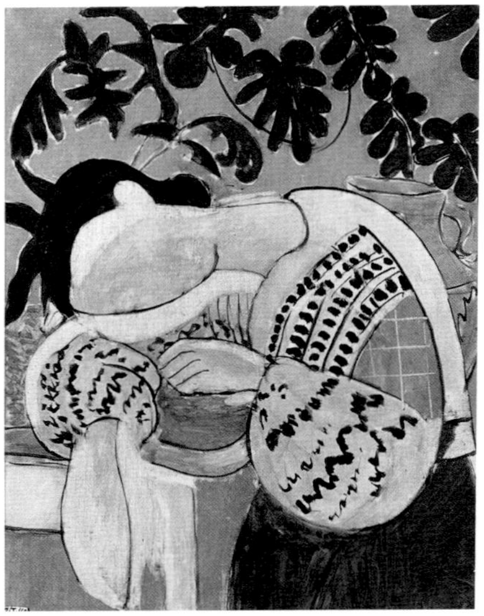

f

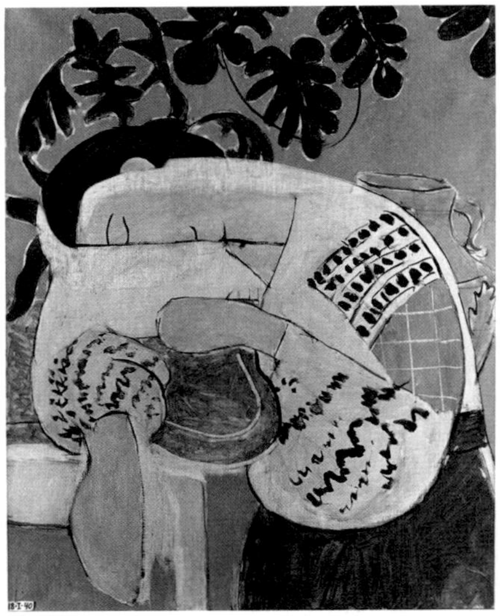

g

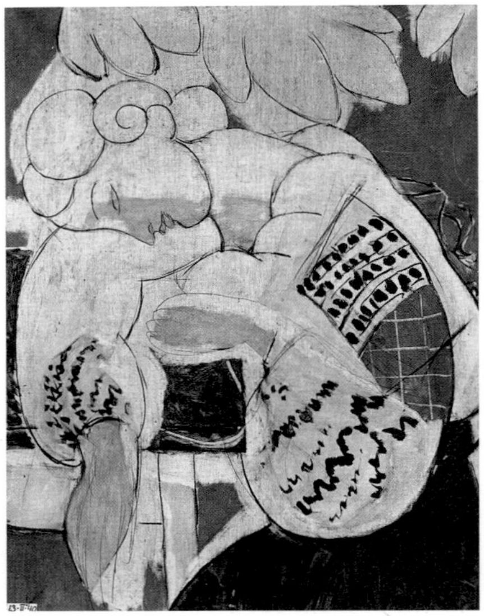

h

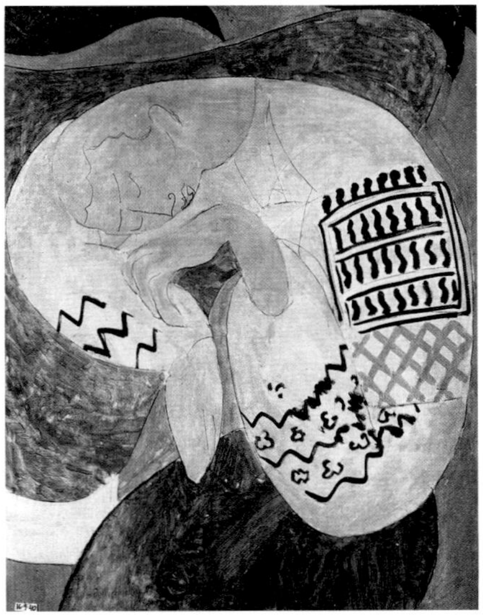

l

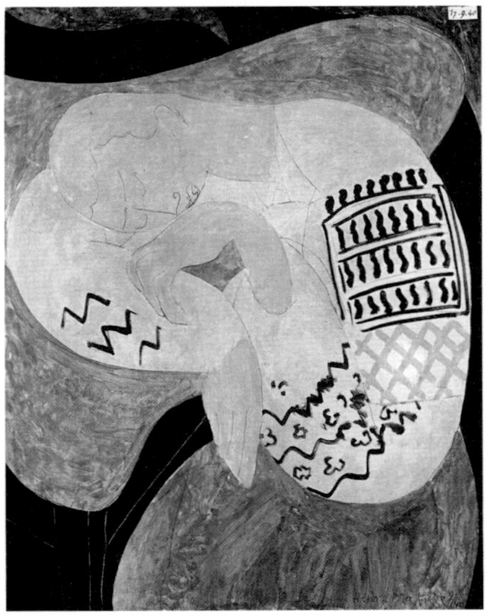

m

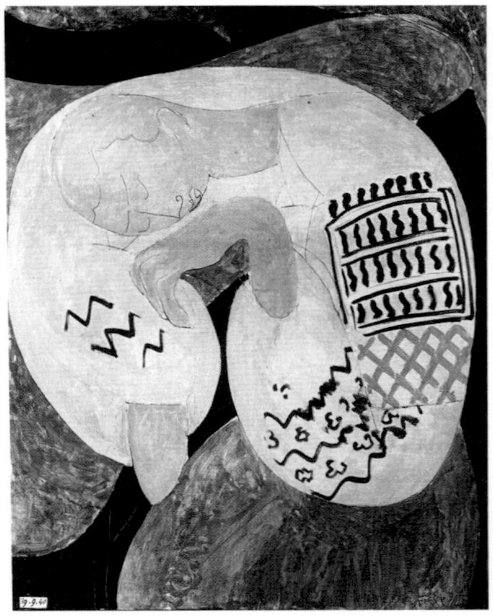

n

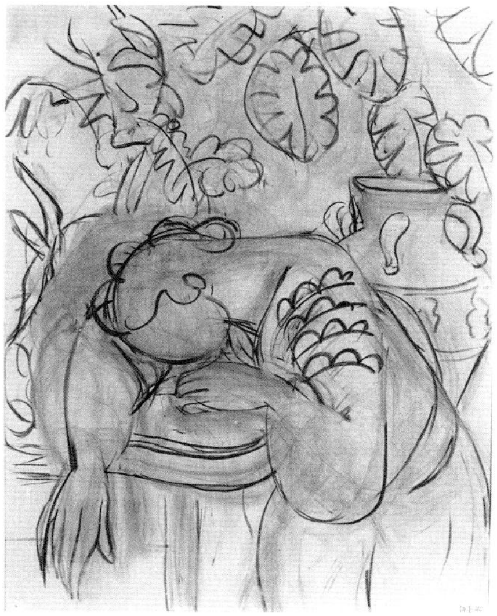

c

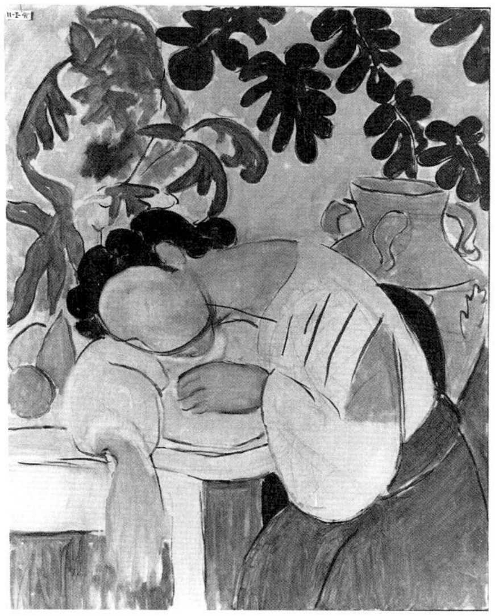

d

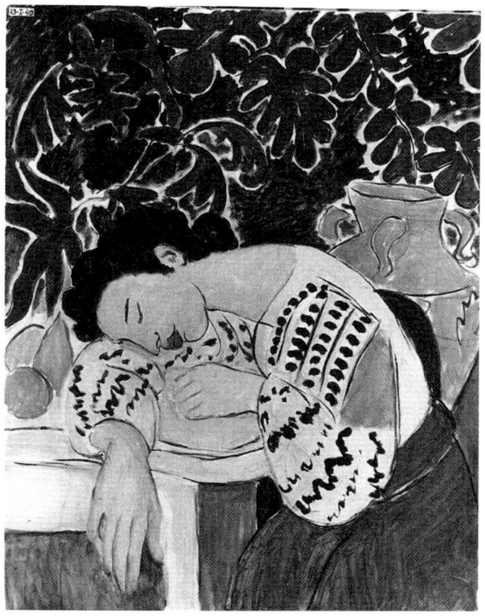

e

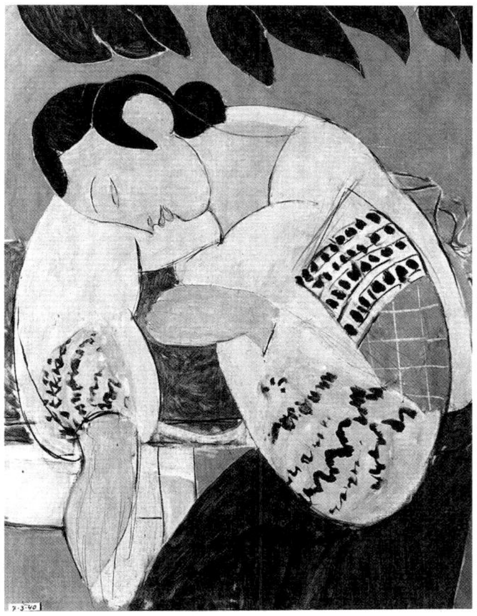

i

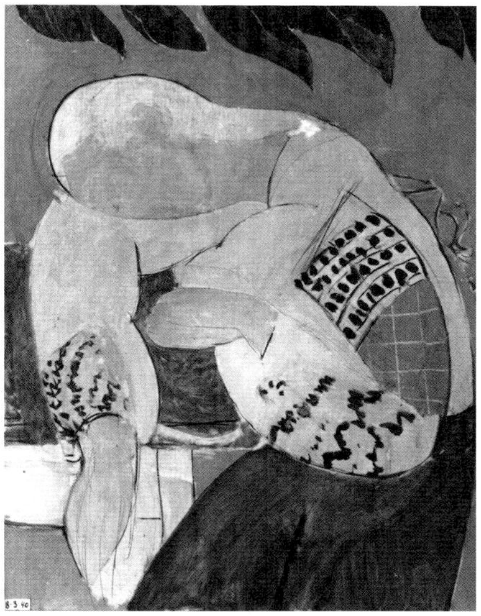

j

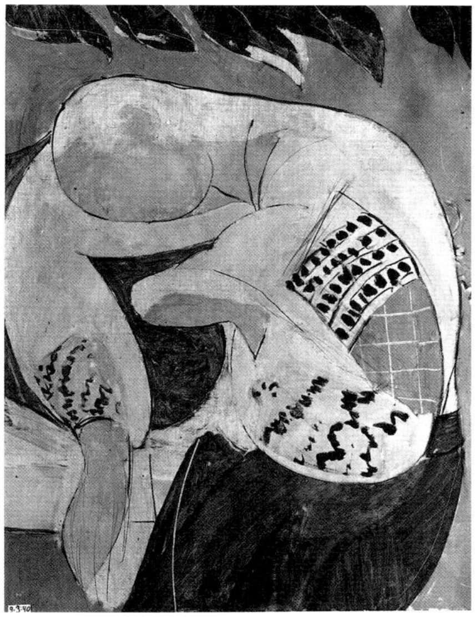

k

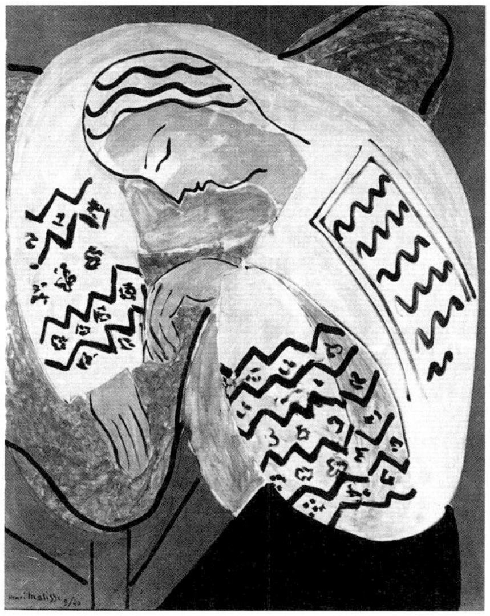

o

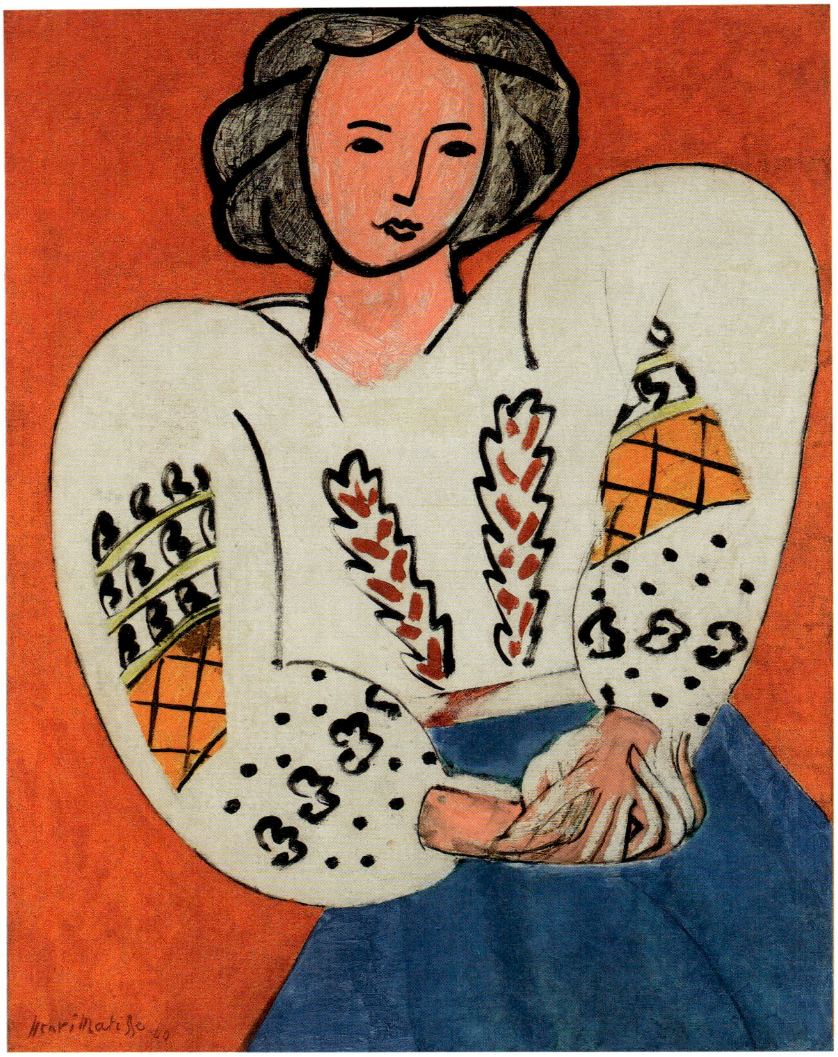

Fig. 81. *The Romanian Blouse*, 1939–40. Oil on canvas, 36¼ x 28¾ in. (92 x 73 cm). Centre Pompidou, Musée National d'Art Moderne, Paris

slightly before our eyes, the distribution of solids and voids changing, a single space assuming a different density, volumes being reduced or amplified, one ornament or another becoming sharper or disappearing, a ground filling with objects or becoming unified, a dominant color singing louder or falling silent.[7]

While working on *The Romanian Blouse* (fig. 81) from October 5, 1939, to April 9, 1940, Matisse also examined the motif in several other paintings, most notably *The Dream*. Like *The Romanian Blouse*, this painting was at first endowed with abundant ornamentation, precise decorative elements, and a human figure with recognizable features. The photographs of the intermediate versions indicate that Matisse simplified the motif to a mere sign, turning his attention away from the blouse and concentrating on the figure, which became the subject of the work. The final version, with its perfect orchestration based on the balance of colors, fully satisfied him, as he noted in a letter to his son Pierre:

> *Fortunately I have just nearly, or perhaps altogether, finished a picture begun 1 year ago and which I pursued as the fancy took me. . . . Hence this painting, which started out very realistic with a beautiful woman sleeping on a marble table amid fruit, has become an angel sleeping on a violet surface—the most beautiful violet I've seen; her flesh is the pink of fleshy hot flowers and her dress and blouse a periwinkle blue, pale very very soft and the skirt an emerald green (with a little white in it) quite tender sustaining all this with a luminous jet black. The visible sleeve is embroidered, it's the Romanian blouse.*[8]

In a letter to Pallady, probably dating to September 1940, Matisse included a drawing of the work, indicating the color used for each part (fig. 82). And he concluded, "Here's a painting that went on for a year—those who see only how I represented the hair and the embroidery on the shoulder will think I'm joking. But you . . . you know!"[9]

Having completed *The Dream*, Matisse believed his experiments with the subject had come to an end. He wrote Pierre, "All in all, nearly every one of my pictures is an adventure, therein lies its interest, and since I don't offer it until the adventure is over and successful, the risk is with me alone."[10] Nevertheless, he did use the motif in other compositions, including a charcoal from October 1939, *Dancer Resting* (Centre Pompidou, Musée National d'Art Moderne, Paris), in which the sleeves of the blouse unfurl like wings. In the 1940 painting *Dancer Resting* (Toledo Museum of Art), the motif is barely indicated, while the multiple

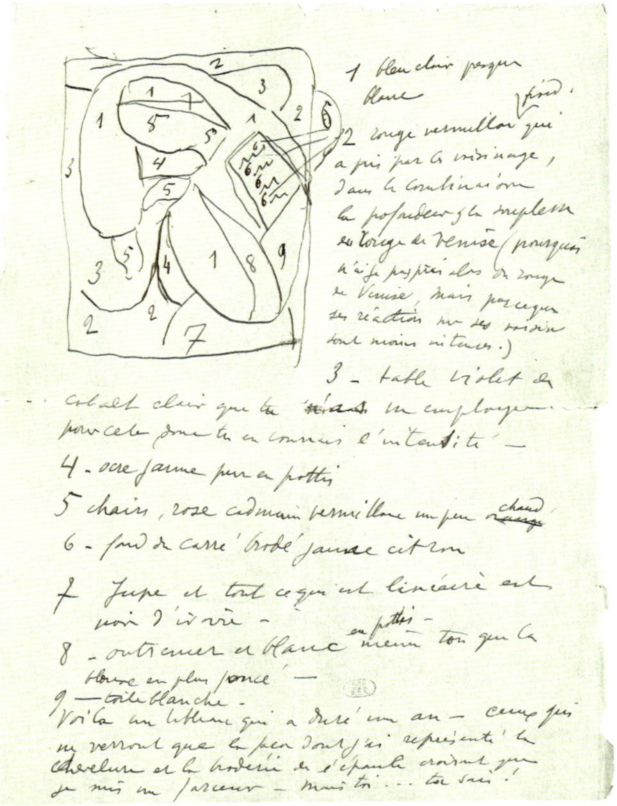

Fig. 82. Matisse's drawing of *The Dream*, indicating the color used for each part, ca. September 1940. National Library of Romania, Bucharest

curves of the body are highlighted. Later, the embroidered oak leaves invade the ground of the 1948 painting *Plum Blossoms, Green Background* (Pinacoteca Giovanni e Marella Agnelli, Turin), where they compete with fruit blossoms. This systematic reprise confirms the motif as a subtle tool in Matisse's pictorial arsenal, one that allowed the artist, as Jack Flam has noted, "to extend the energy within individual things beyond their physical boundaries and to create, in effect, a kind of metaphysics of decoration."[11]

TOWARD A STATE OF PURE ESSENCE

Dorthe Aagesen

Still Life with Seashell on Black Marble (cat. 55) occupied Matisse throughout the autumn of 1940, during a time of anxiety and deprivation. In the summer of that year, German troops had invaded Paris and France had capitulated. Among the Parisians who fled the city were several of the artist's family members and friends, some of whom went abroad for safety. Matisse, who was himself in Paris during the invasion in June, was determined to stay in France and arrived in Nice in August after a long and strenuous journey. The division of France into a northern, occupied zone and a southeastern, nominally free zone (Vichy) meant that Matisse was cut off from anything other than sporadic contact with Paris. In Nice, he also faced the threat of an invasion by Mussolini's troops. In the autumn of 1940, then, Matisse lived a life of isolation, in the shadow of war. At the same time, he was beset by a serious illness, which worsened toward the end of the year and led to his hospitalization in December and an operation in January.[1]

As was the case during World War I, Matisse responded by immersing himself in his painting.[2] In a letter of December 7, 1940, to the Romanian painter Theodor Pallady, a friend from their student days under Gustave Moreau, he wrote:

> *As for me, I have continued despite the fact that working is rather difficult, because the artist possesses his mind only when he is standing in front of his easel. At the moment, one must no longer count on the unconscious labor that used to occur between two sessions; it has been replaced by a vague collective anxiety composed of the misfortune of every kind that is assailing everyone without exception, I think. We, fortunately, have our old idea of painting, which has already led us to banish so many things to which others cling above all.*[3]

A few weeks later Pallady wrote back: "Your letter . . . moved me. I told myself: 'Like me, he's withdrawing into art, which has remained our raison d'être.'"[4] In the spring of 1940, Pallady had gone to Bucharest in order to prepare an exhibition and had ended up stranded there because of the war.[5] "My life here is reduced to this hotel room, where I came for 24 hours, and where I have now been for . . . 9 months!"

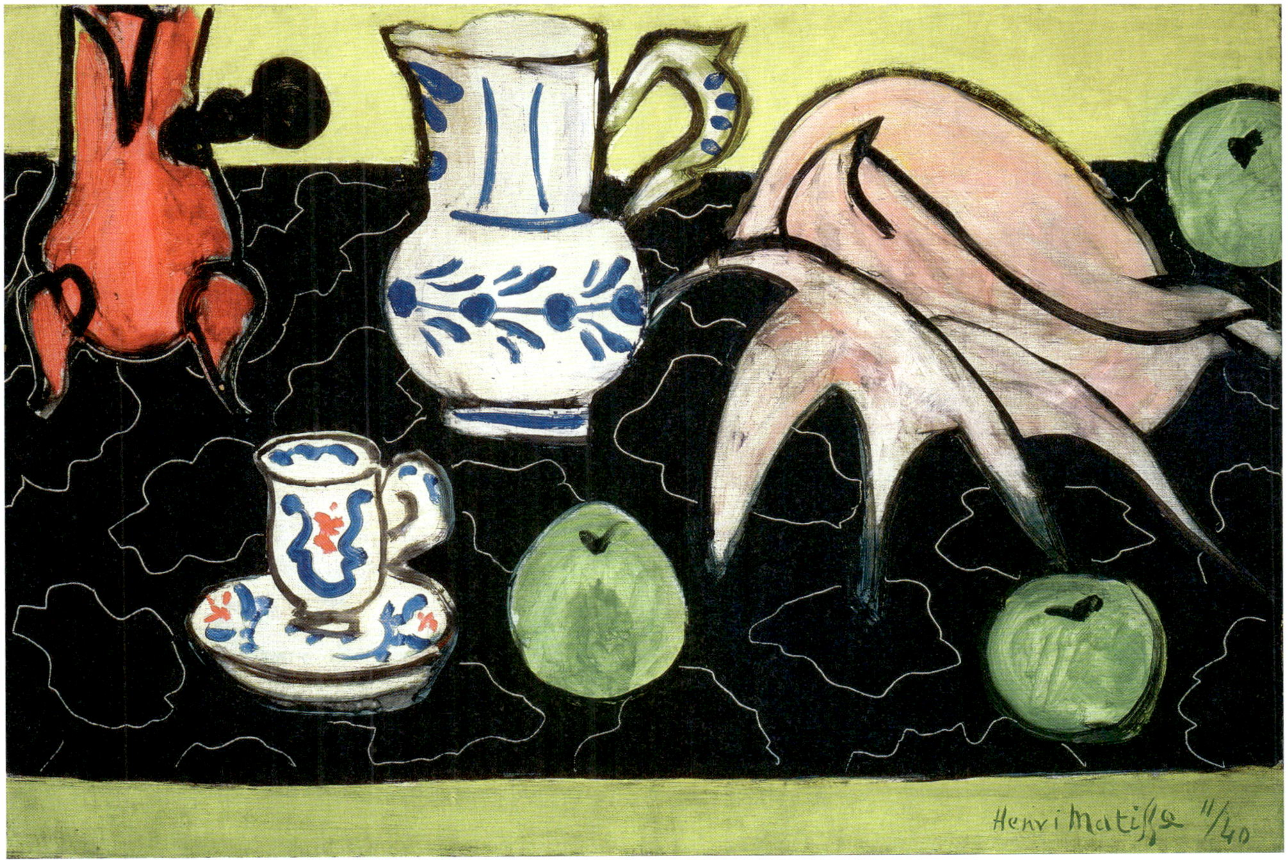

55 | *Still Life with Seashell on Black Marble*, 1940

Oil on canvas, 21 ¼ x 31 ⅞ in. (54 x 81 cm). The State Pushkin Museum of Fine Arts, Moscow

Fig. 83a–e. Series of photographs showing the development of *Still Life with Seashell on Black Marble* in 1940: a. October 20, b. October 26, c. November 16, d. November 21, e. final (December 1940). Archives Matisse, Paris

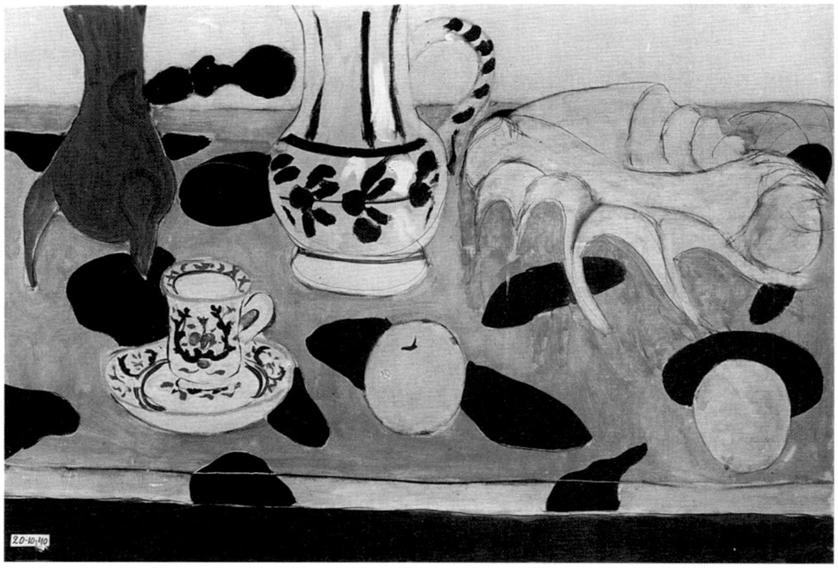

a

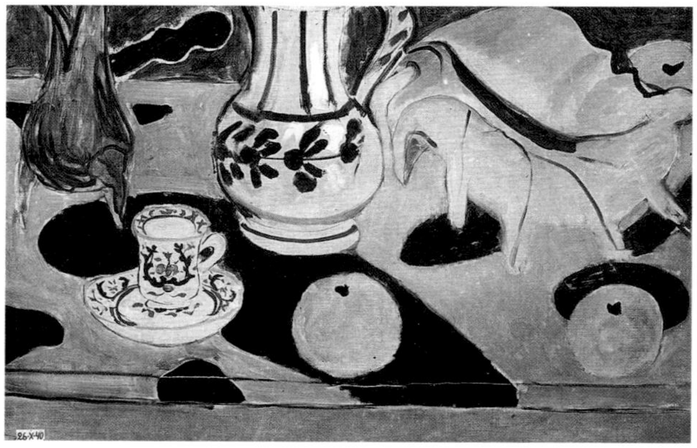

b

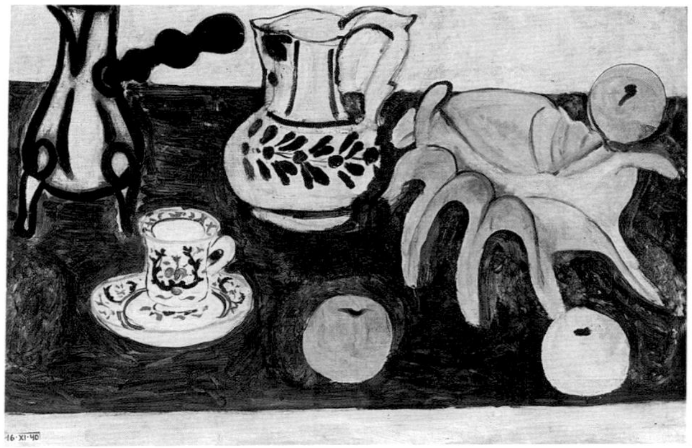

c

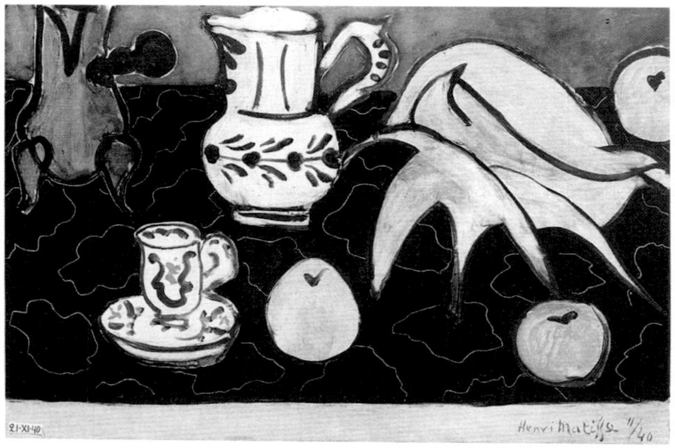

d

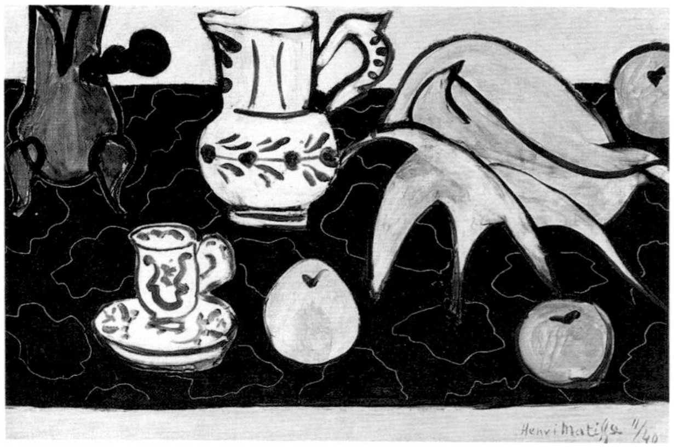

e

he lamented in his letter to Matisse. From their isolated positions, the two aging painters corresponded about life in wartime and, especially, about their art. The letters they exchanged are notable both for their historical context and for their privileged insights into Matisse's thoughts and working processes during this period.

Still Life with Seashell on Black Marble was created between September 25 and December 4, 1940. Five photographs (fig. 83a–e) reveal the main stages of its genesis and the development of each element toward its final expression. When the painting was completed, the artist considered it a radical creation, a high point in his attempts to achieve a new pictorial stringency. (The work would be among the six paintings selected for the 1945 exhibition at the Galerie Maeght, where it would be accompanied by three of the photographs.)[6] Writing to Pallady that December, Matisse described the recently finished painting:

> *with a still life composed of a shell, a blue flower-pot, a coffee cup, a coffee pot, and 3 green apples on a black and green marble table—and which I have worked on (transformed) over 30 sessions—I think I have reached the end of what I can do in that abstract sense, through contemplation, testing various levels of elevation, analysis. I hope you understand me or rather that I make myself understood—for the moment I can go no further, cannot even repeat myself, that's out of the question.*[7]

Matisse had also enclosed an annotated drawing of the still life that showed two stages of its development (fig. 84) and, presumably, photographs of the painting taken at corresponding stages.[8] The drawings explained what the black-and-white photographs did not show: how the colors in the composition had been changed over the course of the creative process. The

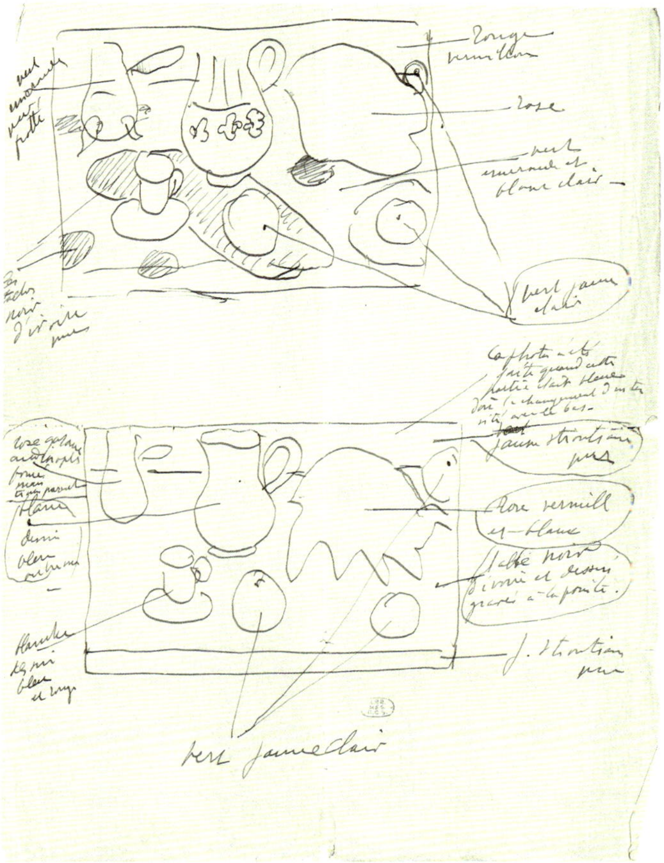

Fig. 84. Matisse's drawings of the painting *Still Life with Seashell on Black Marble*, attached to his letter to Theodor Pallady, probably December 7, 1940. National Library of Romania, Bucharest

drawing of the earliest stage indicates that the background at the top of the painting was originally red (*rouge vermillon*). Below, on the drawing of the later stage, Matisse noted, "The photo was taken when that part was blue," a fact that supports the presumption that he sent at least one photograph of a stage; this color was subsequently changed to one that resembled the yellow at the bottom. The coffee jug at the left was green and somewhat rubbed (*vert émeraude pur frotté*) in the early version, not red as in the final

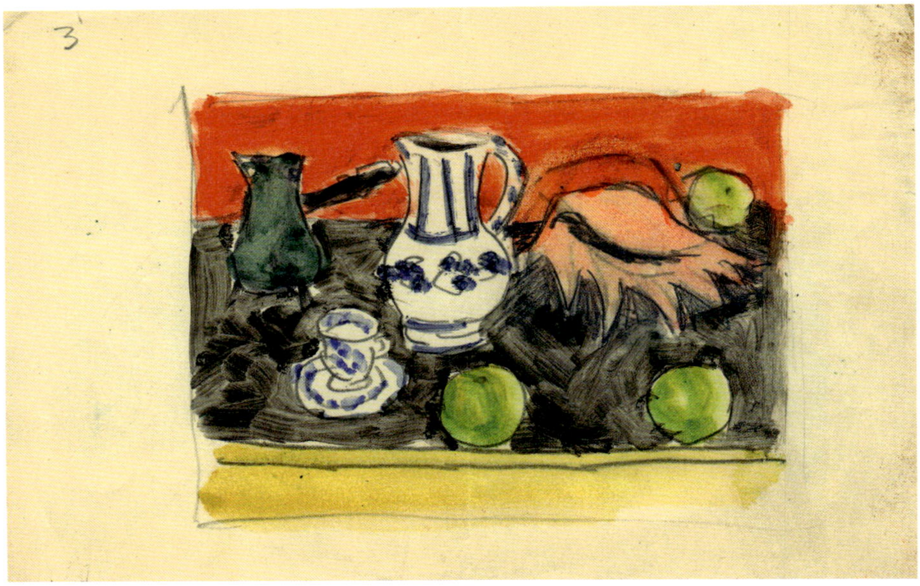

Fig. 85. Pallady's sketch of *Still Life with Seashell on Black Marble* in his letter to Matisse, December 22, 1940. Archives Matisse, Paris

painting, whereas the table was green (*vert émeraude*) and light blue, with areas of pure ivory black (*les taches noir d'ivoire pur*), before it was painted over entirely in black and decorated with a pattern scratched with the end of the paintbrush. The drawing testifies that Matisse needed more than the photographs in order to describe his intentions and that the changes in color were as important to him as the transformations of forms.[9]

Shortly after receiving Matisse's letter, Pallady embarked on a drawn reconstruction of *Still Life with Seashell on Black Marble* (fig. 85): "Thank you for having added, to the news that you gave me, the images of your most recent works and the annotations that accompany them. I am attaching one of the ones that were colored following your instructions; I hope it does not deviate too much from the original?"[10] Although Pallady confused the colors from the two stages, he had understood Matisse's basic intention, identifying it in his letter as to "strip Painting of all inessentials," creating instead a state of pure "essence." Matisse's own explanation makes it apparent that to him, the painting represented a "spiritual perception," which contrasted greatly with the still lifes of oysters that he painted during the same autumn months.[11] Just as, twenty years before, he had weighed the tension between abstraction and realism, he now used the oyster motif to examine "the true matter of things," as reflected in sensuous enjoyment, and to counter the abstract, spiritual aspirations and approach expressed in this still life. In 1940 Matisse felt that he could go no further in the direction of abstraction than *Still Life with Seashell on Black Marble*, but the next autumn he returned to the theme and continued his endeavors with the closely related *Still Life with Magnolia* (cat. 56).

PAINTING AS FILM

Dorthe Aagesen

François Campaux's remarkable film about Matisse, shot in the winter of 1945–46, documents the painstaking effort that lay behind such seemingly simple paintings as *Still Life with Magnolia* (cat. 56).[1] The film shows a series of early stages of two selected paintings: five of *Still Life with Magnolia* and fourteen of *The Romanian Blouse* (fig. 81). Matisse himself had requested that each "state" (*état*), as he called them, be documented as he worked. Together, the succession of photographs would capture a process that took place over time, in much the same way as the frames of a film do. In fact, there is much to suggest that Matisse regarded *Still Life with Magnolia* as a "filmic" painting—an image whose contents were governed by its genesis.

The five photographed states of *Still Life with Magnolia* date from September 7 to November 18, 1941; the painting was not completed until December. The work actually took shape through a complex interplay between these photographs and numerous drawings made by the artist. Preliminary studies from August 1941 show an arrangement on a table in Matisse's studio that included all the elements featured in the painted composition (fig. 86). In September the motif was treated in a suite of six drawings, later published as Series G in the *Themes and Variations* album. On September 12 and 13, after work on the painting had commenced, Matisse executed drawings exploring individual elements of the painting and the relationships between them.[2]

Lydia Delectorskaya, the artist's assistant, model, and secretary from the mid-1930s until his death, supplied an informative description of his working methods in which she distinguished between paintings created in a few sessions and those, such as *Still Life with Magnolia*, that developed slowly. Speaking of the latter, she explained, "It is not that Matisse failed at it. Very much to the contrary: he sensed the possibility in such a canvas of taking a step forward in his pictorial research, and he constantly reworked it for weeks on end: the desired solution took on magnitude and drove him further and further."[3]

The photographs of *Still Life with Magnolia* (fig. 87a–f) reveal how the painting gradually fell into place. Viewed as a whole, they may seem at first to describe a linear progress toward a specific end, a movement toward simplification and clarity as superfluous details are culled away, elements are rendered

Fig. 86. *Still Life*, 1941. India ink on paper, 16 x 20½ in. (40.6 x 52.2 cm). Centre Pompidou, Musée National d'Art Moderne, Paris

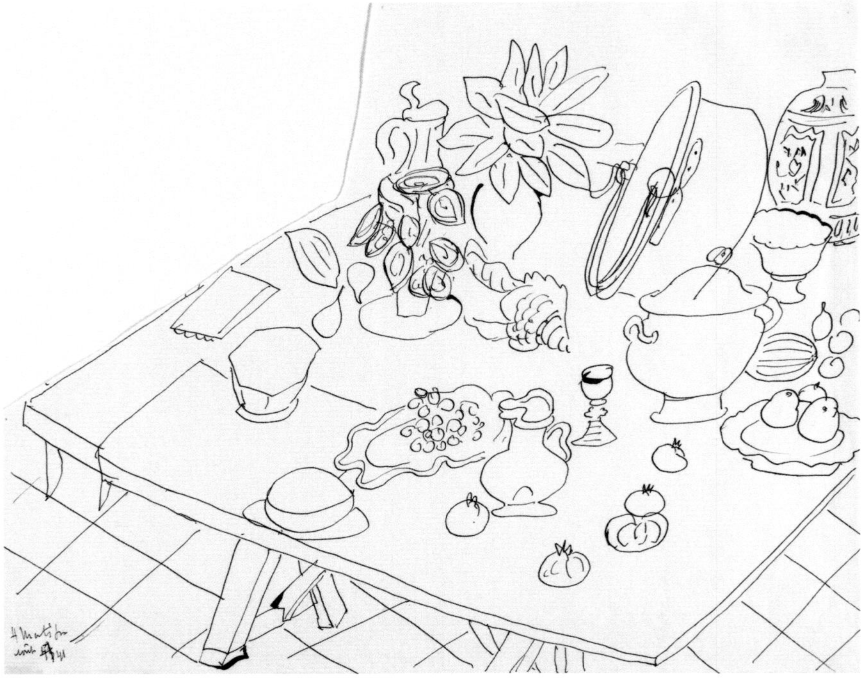

more distinctly, and differences are accentuated so that each element becomes a sign.[4] Yet, upon close inspection, they may also be viewed as a sequence of different—and, in principle, equally valid—"takes" on how the final painting might have looked.[5] According to Marguerite Duthuit, her father had his works photographed only when he felt they had reached a certain stage of completion.[6] This suggests that in addition to capturing stages of the creative process, the photographs were also intended to catalogue different versions of a given motif that had proved productive for that process. They may therefore be regarded as analogous to the multiple canvases that Matisse employed as he worked out various versions of a painting. Here, however, each version is painted on a single canvas, which is repeatedly scraped and painted over. Since the states represented by the photographs no longer exist, the photographs act as both documents and replacements.

Matisse's interest in such photographs during the 1940s is evident from the fact that he put them at Campaux's disposal for his film. However, the most remarkable proof of their importance is the exhibition presented in 1945 at the Galerie Maeght in Paris, in which they played a major part.[7] One of the main walls of the exhibition featured *Still Life with Magnolia* accompanied by the five photographed states (fig. 88). The exhibition was described as "didactic" in letters exchanged between Aimé Maeght and Matisse. Lydia Delectorskaya has pointed out a similar dimension in Matisse's Themes and Variations series (cats. 57, 58), which belongs to the same period,[8] and there is also a certain structural resemblance between Matisse's display of these drawings on the wall of his studio in Nice and the positioning of the paintings and photographs at the Galerie Maeght. Both were intended to provide insight into the creative process, to demonstrate how each individual picture was related

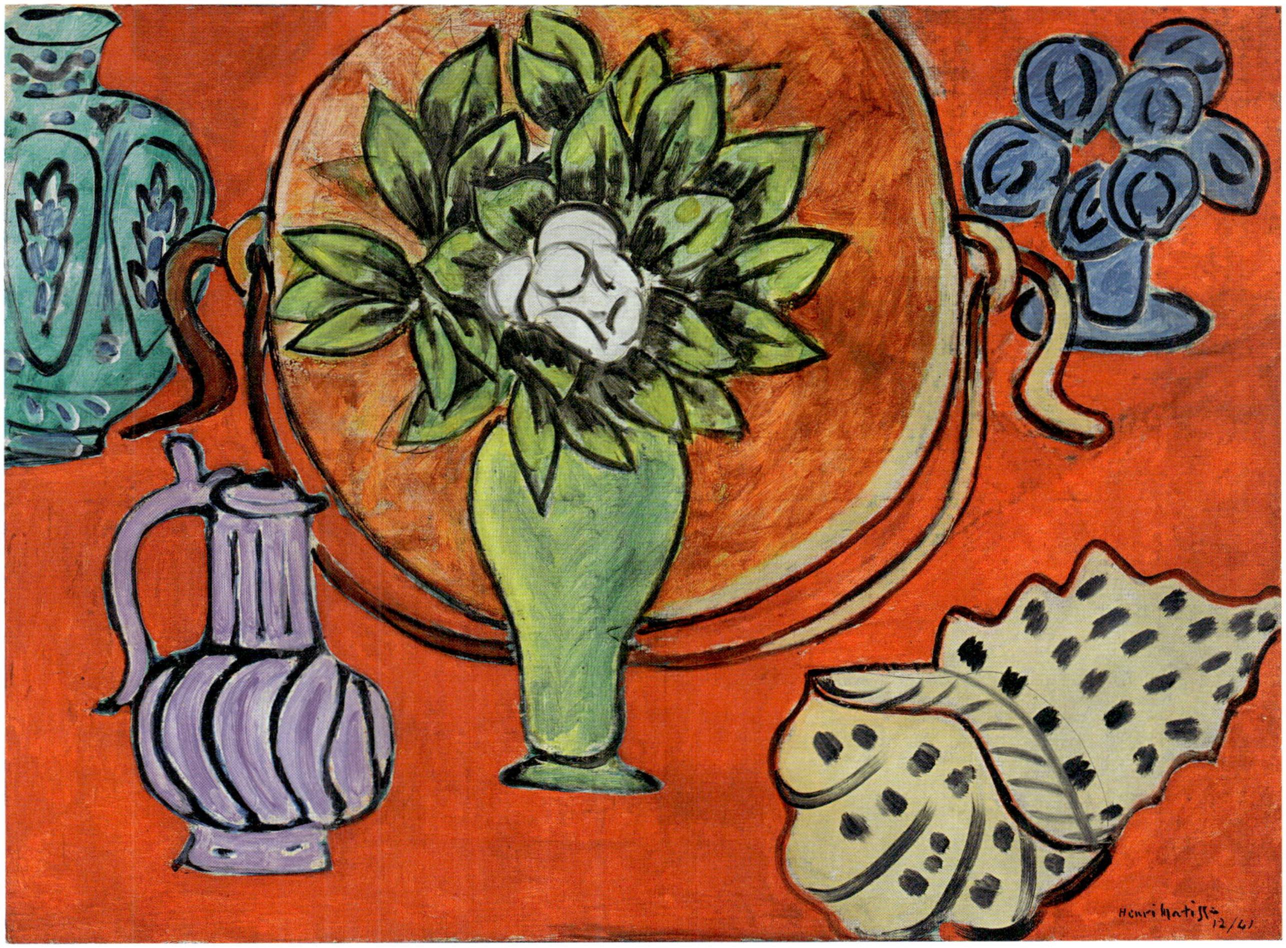

56 | *Still Life with Magnolia*, 1941

Oil on canvas, 29⅛ x 39¾ in. (74 x 101 cm). Centre Pompidou, Musée National d'Art Moderne, Paris, Purchase, 1945

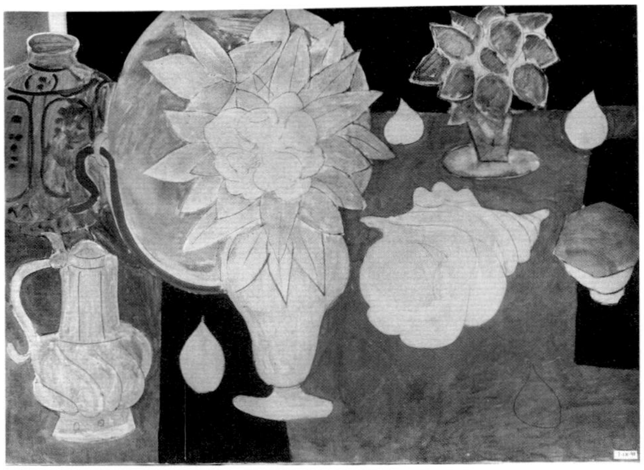

a

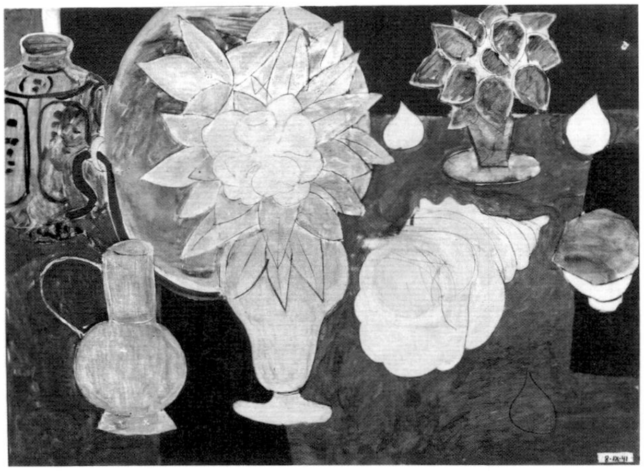

b

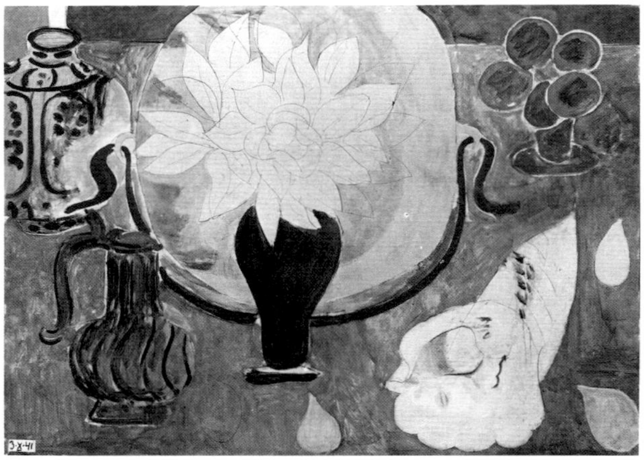

c

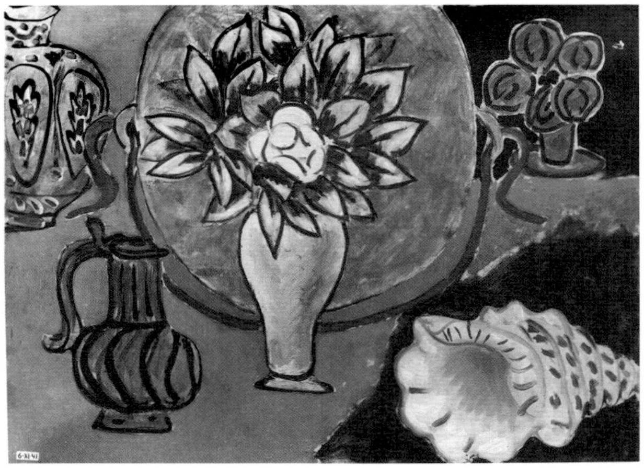

d

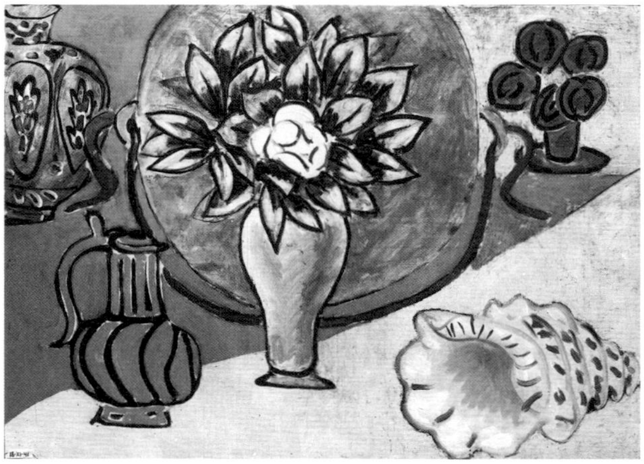

e

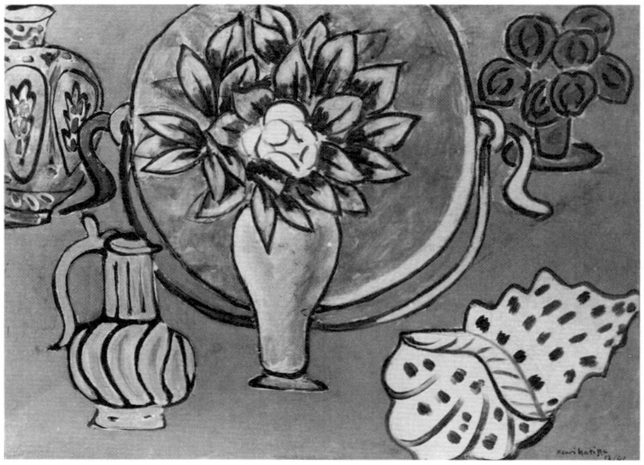

f

OPPOSITE
Fig. 87a–f. Series of photographs showing the development of *Still Life with Magnolia* in 1941: a. September 7, b. September 8, c. October 3, d. November 6, e. November 18, f. final (December 1941). Archives Matisse, Paris

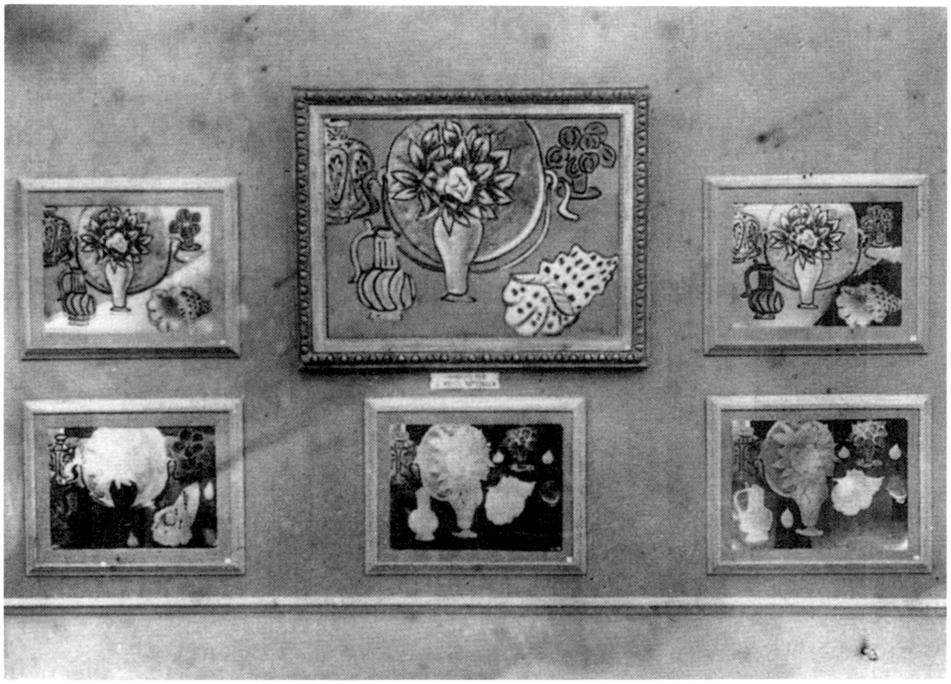

Fig. 88. Marc Vaux. Installation view of *Still Life with Magnolia* accompanied by five photographed states, Galerie Maeght, Paris, December 1945. Archives Matisse, Paris

to the ones preceding it. The rows of drawings in Themes and Variations traced the ineffable "series of visions" that descended upon the artist as he made his drawings;[9] the Maeght exhibition illustrated one vision repeatedly reformulated in the course of the painting process.[10]

But why did Matisse attach such importance to showing the genesis of his works? The sequences of photographs served as obvious testaments to the fact that even the simplest of his paintings was the result of a long, complex process, and Matisse wished to make this clear.[11] The Maeght presentation also demonstrated that the inception of a work was as important as its end result and that the final painting took on richer significance when viewed in relation to the other formulations that had preceded it. Although the ultimate objective of all the effort Matisse expended on the painting was undoubtedly to reach a definitive conclusion, the Maeght exhibition suggested that he had realized such a goal was unattainable.

In the autumn of 1945, Matisse received a visit from the young poet Jacques Kober, who was to write a text for the Maeght catalogue. As the two spoke, the artist referred to a painting on the wall in front of them, which may very well have been *Still Life with Magnolia*.[12] "The film of a picture is the picture," he said. "As for this one, I didn't think it would be easy to finish, and then the picture threw me out. Every time I've done something successfully, I say to myself, 'that's it, I've got it, I understand'; but no, nothing has been learned. The conclusion of a picture is another picture."[13]

THEMES AND VARIATIONS

Samantha Rippner

In the early spring of 1942, a little more than a year after being treated for intestinal cancer, Matisse wrote to his daughter, Marguerite, about a significant breakthrough in his work: "I have made a very important exertion, one of the most important of my life. I have perfected my drawing making surprising progress in ease, expressing emotion freely with a large variety of feeling and a minimum of means. This is one of the things for which I wished to continue to live. I have made a profusion of completely astonishing drawings."[1] One hundred and fifty eight of these drawings—divided into seventeen distinct series (marked A–P),[2] each containing a preliminary theme drawing and several variations—would become the basis of the book *Dessins: Thèmes et variations* (*Drawings: Themes and Variations*), which Martin Fabiani published in 1943 with an insightful preface by the Surrealist poet Louis Aragon. While Matisse did not make the drawings with publication in mind, he surely recognized the importance of preserving them as a comprehensive body of work, for they openly revealed and documented his rigorous working method for the first time.

The Themes and Variations drawings were made mostly from Matisse's bed during late 1941 and early 1942 as he recuperated from surgery. With his ability to paint large-scale, ambitious canvases curtailed, he focused intensely on drawing, producing what he called a "flowering after fifty years of effort."[3] The works summarize the serial nature of Matisse's artistic method—a principal characteristic of this period and one that had its roots in his earliest paintings. Their subjects, the female figure and the still life, were also pervasive throughout his career. Each series begins with a theme drawing, usually a study in charcoal and stumping. When working with a model, Matisse considered her "character . . . , her human expression, the quality of surrounding light, the atmosphere and all that can only be expressed by drawing."[4] Over the course of several sessions, he freely worked out his composition using the tonal quality of charcoal. These sheets often contain extensive pentimenti that provide insights into the artist's thought processes.

The variations, by contrast, were drawn with the utmost economy of line in pen and ink, black chalk, or graphite and contain no corrections. Springing from the initial theme drawing, these number from three to nineteen depending on Matisse's mental engagement with the particular model or subject. The theme drawings are reflections of his diligent exploration and study, the variations incisive, one-shot expressions of his emotional state. "My line drawing is the purest and most direct translation of my emotion," he had declared in his 1939 treatise "Notes of a Painter on His Drawing."[5]

Matisse rendered the variations spontaneously one after the other in rapid succession "like a medium in a trance."[6] Although his subject remained in sight during this period of focused concentration, he rarely consulted it. He worked almost unconsciously, with one variation sparking the next, creating a continuous sequence of interrelated drawings that he called "the cinema of my sensibility."[7] The serial nature of this practice was certainly not new to Matisse, but it is especially distilled in the Themes and Variations drawings. The method derived, he admitted, from an "[inability] to improvise. In order for things to click I must recover the idea I had the previous day."[8] Earlier work stimulated new work and allowed the artist to play out his interest in a subject until he had completely exhausted it. Yet the emotional and technical effort that went into the drawings remains unseen: their curving arabesques and gracefully undulating rhythms appear effortless. "This effect of ease," remarked Aragon, "is the greatest illusion about the whole thing. Matisse is a difficult artist."[9]

As Jack Flam has noted, the Themes and Variations drawings elucidate Matisse's "refusal to fix a single image as the single truth of a person or thing," a belief the artist held throughout his career but one that finds its most direct expression here.[10] Each series not only captures the "multiple truths" inherent in the subject but also records the passage of time as experienced by the artist. Reality for Matisse is neither absolute nor fixed but, as Flam has eloquently stated, a "perpetual state of becoming."[11] This is apparent in the two sets of drawings from the series that are shown here. In B1 of the first set (cat. 57), Matisse established the theme drawing: a languorous woman reclining in an armchair lost in thought, her head turned and her gaze diverted from the viewer. In the following six variations, Matisse freely captured the ever-changing character of his model's face, which in one sheet (B2) is specific and individualized, with deep-set eyes and a strong jaw, and in another (B3) vague and ethereal, with a knowing smile and downward gaze offering not a likeness but merely a hint of her personality. In the second set (cat. 58), he was similarly adept at depicting the changing nature of a still life by using shifting points of view to convey the liveliness of a single leaf in a vase of flowers.

Matisse's interest in producing a publication to showcase the entire suite of Themes and Variations drawings surely says something about their significance. While the original drawings would eventually be disseminated to various public and private collections, the book would preserve them intact for a larger audience.[12] Unlike Matisse's many *livres d'artiste*, which were conceived as independent works of art, this volume served a didactic function, for the drawings themselves elucidated the central role that seriality and repetition played in his artistic practice. Matisse's dedication to every detail of the book's development, from the printing and layout to the writing of the preface,[13] only reinforces the singular importance he gave to these drawings, which defined himself as much as his work.

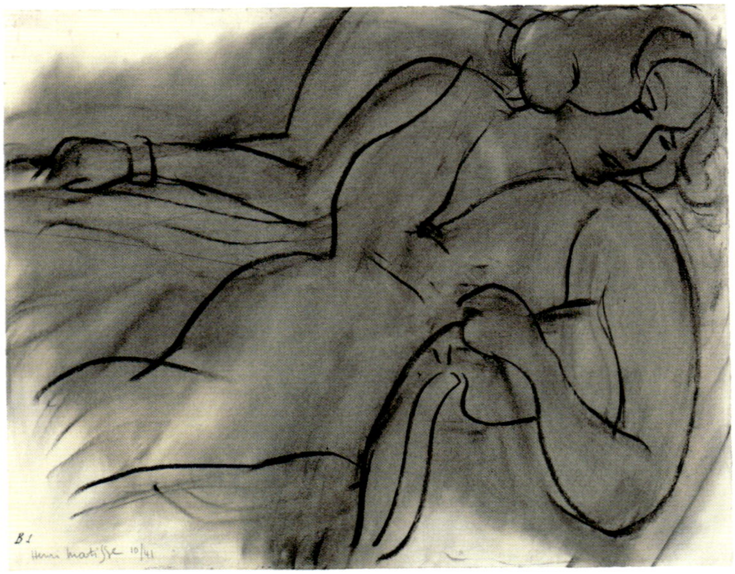

B1

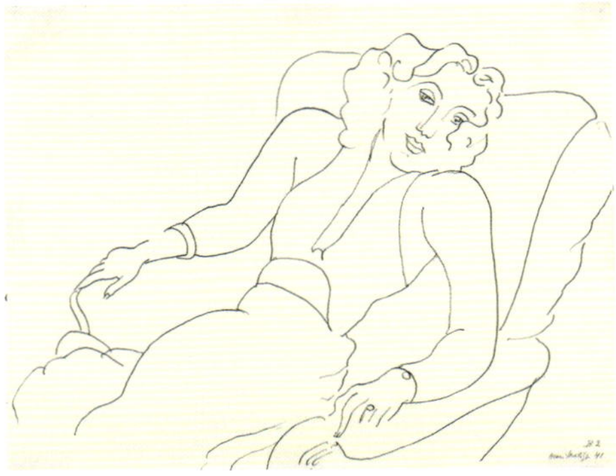

B2

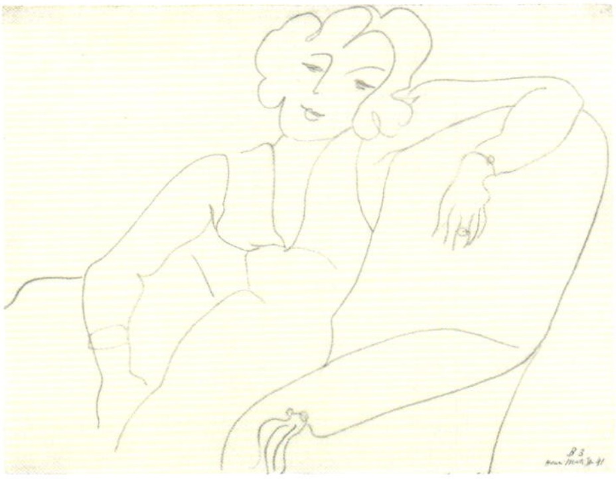

B3

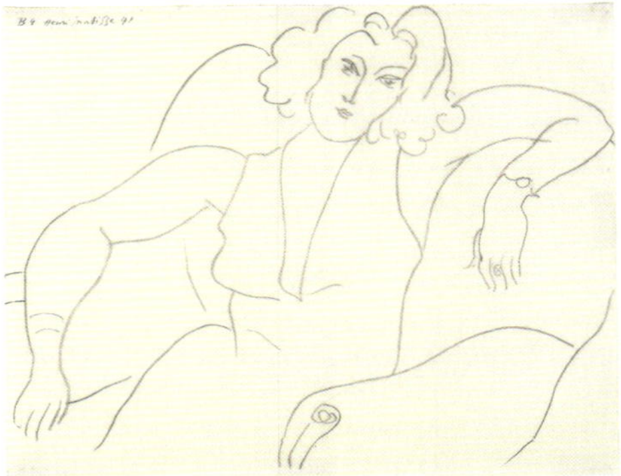

B4

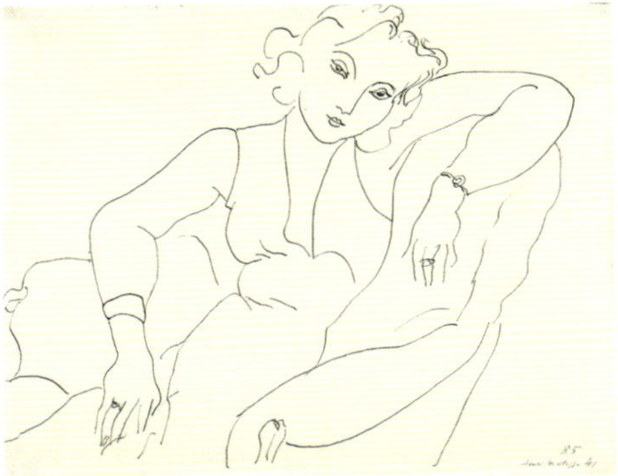

B5

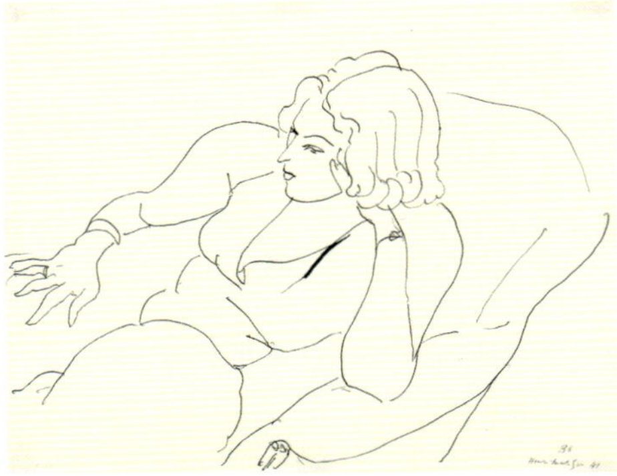

B6

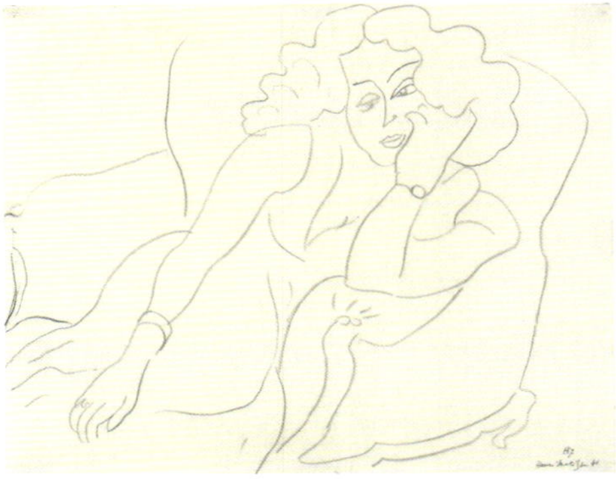

B7

57 | Themes and Variations, Series B, 1–7, 1941

B1. Charcoal on Vélin d'Arches paper. B2. Ink on Vélin d'Arches paper. B3, 4. Black chalk on Vélin d'Arches paper. B5, 6. Ink on Vélin d'Arches paper. B7. Black chalk on Vélin d'Arches paper. Each 16⅛ x 20½ in. (41 x 52 cm). Musée Fabre, Montpellier

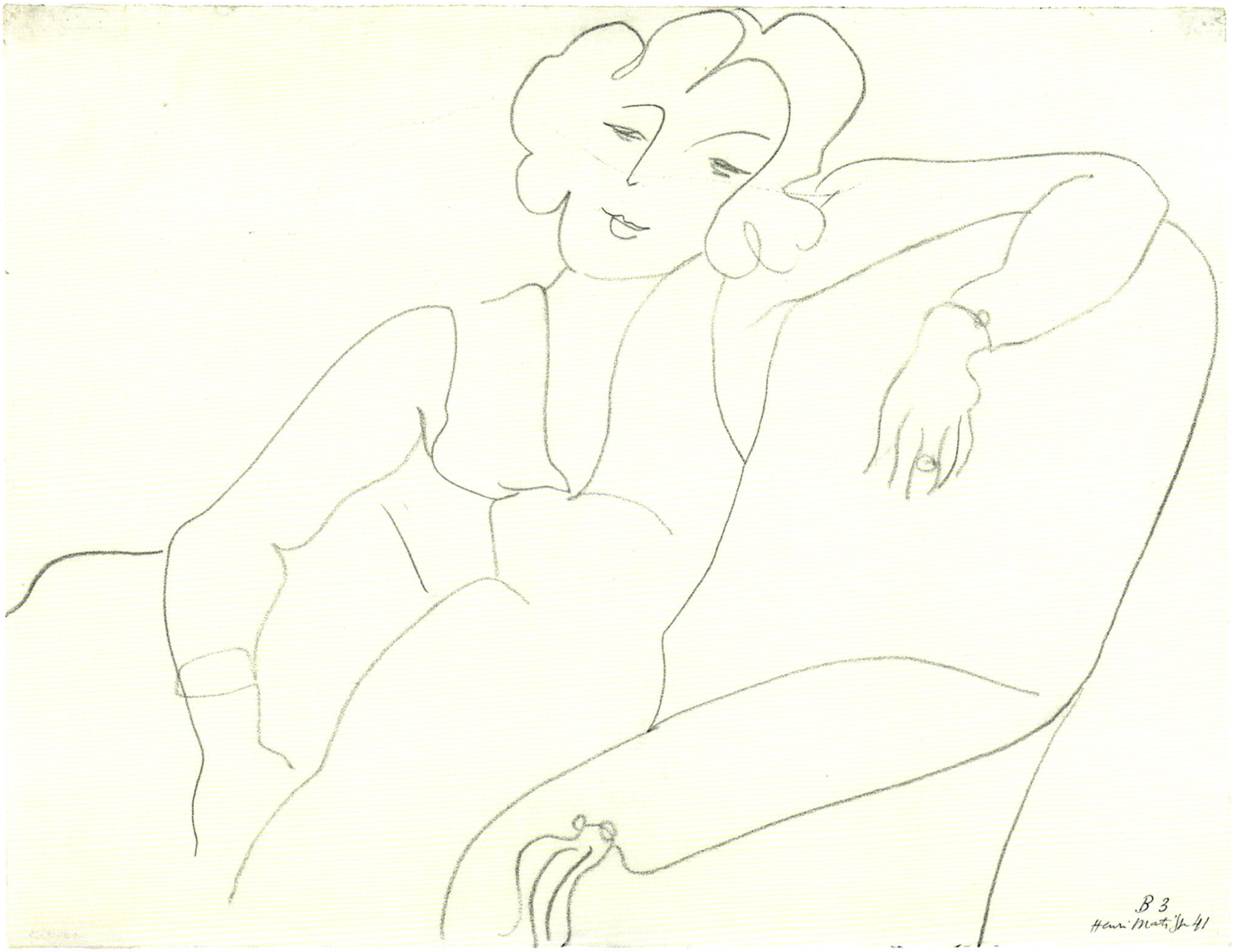

B3

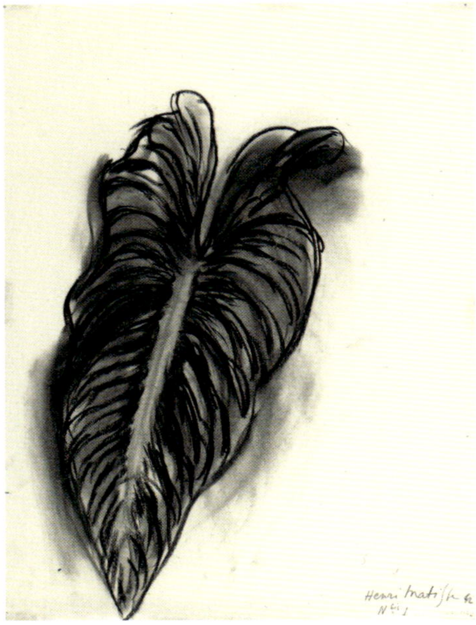

Nbis 1

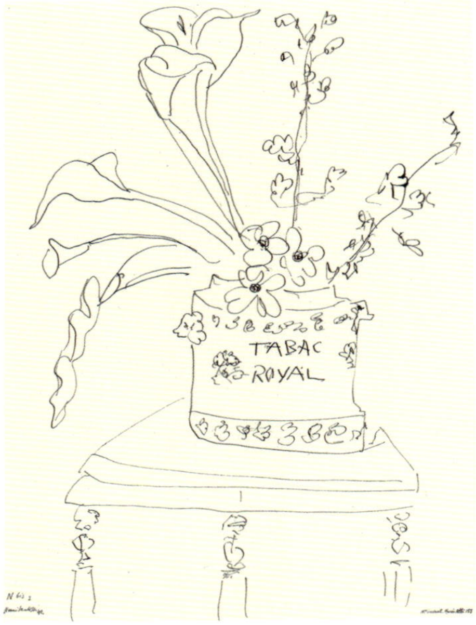

Nbis 2

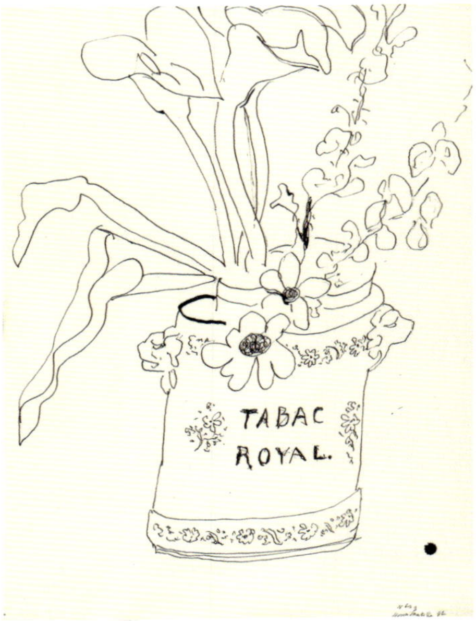

Nbis 3

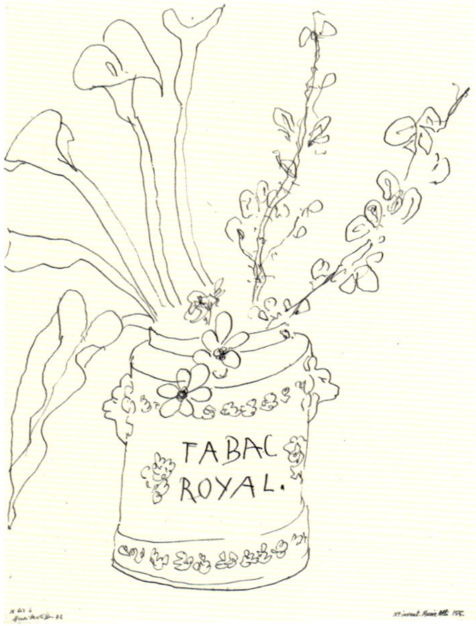

Nbis 4

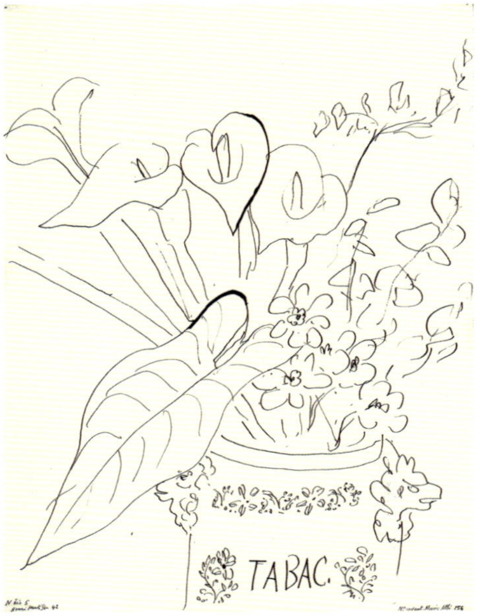

Nbis 5

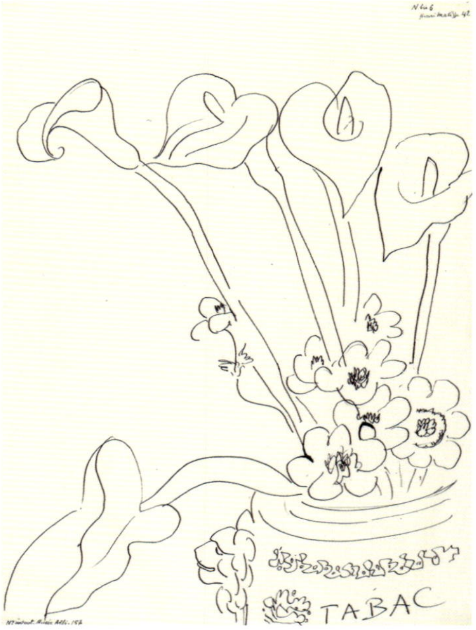

Nbis 6

58 | Themes and Variations, Series Nbis, 1–6, 1942

Nbis 1. Charcoal on Vélin d'Arches paper. Nbis 2–6. Ink on Vélin d'Arches paper. Each 20⅞ x 16 in. (53 x 40.5 cm). Musée Toulouse-Lautrec, Albi, France

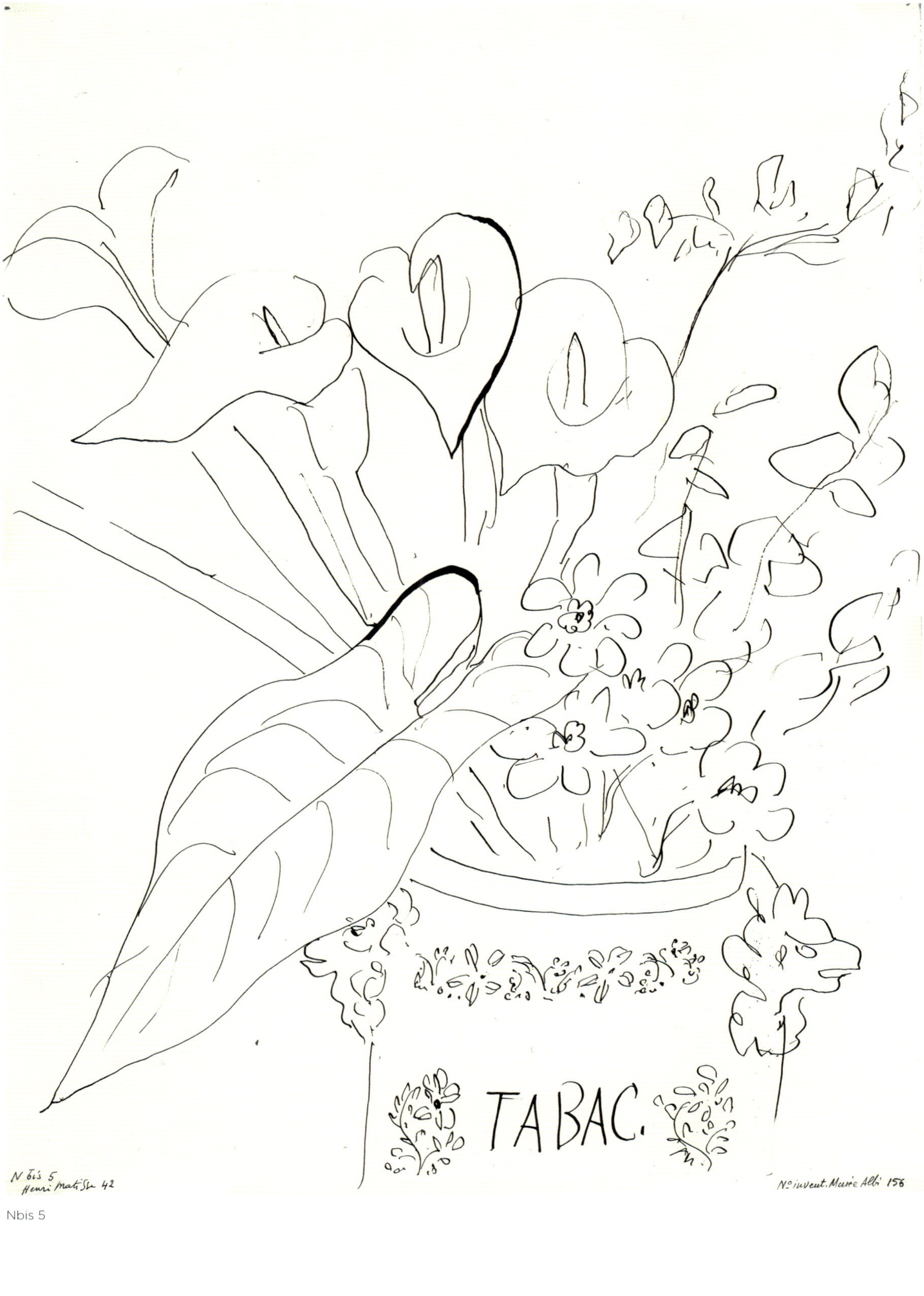

Nbis 5

FRONT VIEWS

Cécile Debray

In 1943, when Matisse moved into the Villa Le Rêve at Vence, he gradually—and with some difficulty—returned to painting after his experiments with drawing, which had produced the Themes and Variations series (cats. 57, 58).[1] After creating three works focusing on the motif of lemons,[2] he placed his still lifes within the broader framework of the studio and also adopted the frontal, outlined motifs of his paintings from 1940, especially *Still Life with Magnolia* (cat. 56). Termed "masterpieces illustrating a new fauvism" by Pierre Schneider,[3] the series of Vence interiors (1946–48) began with the two small paintings discussed here, which hung side by side in Matisse's studio (fig. 89). Although less lyrical than the works that would follow, this pair established Matisse's vocabulary for representing the Vence studio, a vocabulary conceived in terms of thematic and plastic oppositions: interior/exterior, still life/landscape, straight lines/curves, and, especially, drawing/color. In a letter to his old friend and neighbor André Rouveyre, the painter very precisely described how he aimed in these paintings to reconcile heightened, unmodulated color (what he terms "local color") with simplified drawing.

> *Wishing to make a kind of painting that is related to my drawings, those that come to me directly from the heart and are traced with the greatest simplicity, I have set out on a very hard road that seems troublesome to me because of the little time that my age will grant me. And yet, to be at peace with myself, I cannot do otherwise. With the sort of color relations that I am led to use to render what I feel, freed from the accidental, I find myself representing the objects without the vanishing lines. I mean* FRONT VIEWS, *one almost next to the other, linked to one another by my feeling, in an atmosphere created by the magical relations of color. To be logical why not use only local tones, without reflections? Human figures on the same plane as in a game of Aunt Sally[;] on these elements of simplified representation, put a color coming from the exalted local tone, or even invented altogether in accordance with my feeling, warmed by the presence of nature itself—a kind of poem.*[4]

The two interiors both show a corner of a room in the villa furnished with a marble table holding a Fez vase, a stemmed glass, and watermelons and, behind

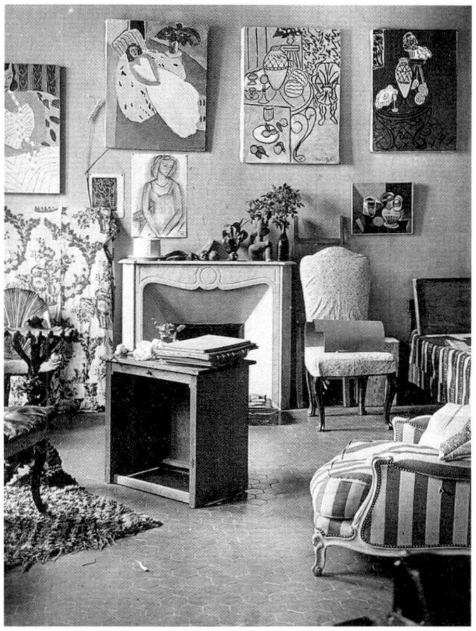

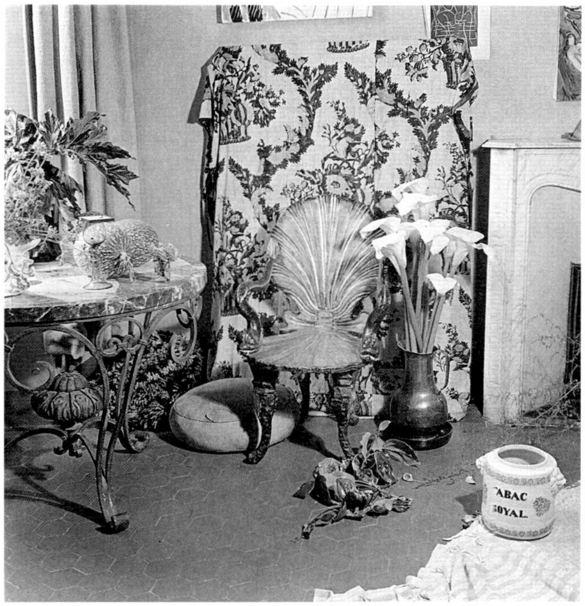

Fig. 89. Brassaï. *Matisse's Studio at the Villa Le Rêve, Vence*, 1946. Private collection

Fig. 90. Hélène Adant. *The Rocaille Armchair, Villa Le Rêve, Vence*, 1946. Bibliothèque Kandinsky, Centre Pompidou, Musée National d'Art Moderne, Paris

it, a stand with flowers (fig. 90). The point of view shifts completely from one painting to the other: the window located on the left in the red version appears on the right in the yellow one. Everything is described in a fluid, sharp drawing that is equal in importance to the color. In *Interior in Yellow and Blue* (cat. 59), the drawing seems to be superimposed upon the flat zones of ocher and blue that structure the space. These segmented colored planes, which appeared in Matisse's paintings from 1939 on, were probably influenced by his paper cutouts, in this case those in the collection *Jazz* (1943–47). A few motifs, including the vase and the fruit, are meticulously "filled in" with color, for the most part on the blue rectangular plane. Two opposing systems are thus set in motion: the free lines in the color field versus the outlined motifs. Hence, the rectangle at the bottom of the composition—a reference to the canvases from 1940—can be read here as a picture within the picture.

This opposition is emphasized by the contrast between the two *Interiors*. In *Interior in Venetian Red* (cat. 60), the drawing seems similarly rapid and fluid, but the dominant color is applied almost haphazardly, with rough reserve spaces left around the vase, flowers, and watermelons. The opacity and power of the Venetian red recall Matisse's emblematic *Still Life in Venetian Red* of 1908 (The State Pushkin Museum of Fine Arts, Moscow) and *The Red Studio* of 1911 (fig. 4). Against that ground, the drawing is transformed into calligraphy with Oriental arabesques, while the space, now mysterious and "painterly," is expanded. As in the symphonic interior of 1911 or in *Large Red Interior* of 1948 (cat. 64), the missing corner of the room creates a floating space of poetic indecisiveness—an effect reinforced by the ambiguous window, a white rectangle enlivened by a thick black motif that could be either a depiction of the external world or one of Matisse's contemporaneous India ink drawings.

Interior in Yellow and Blue was reproduced in an issue of the review *Verve* devoted to the Vence interiors, where it appeared as the first in the series.[5]

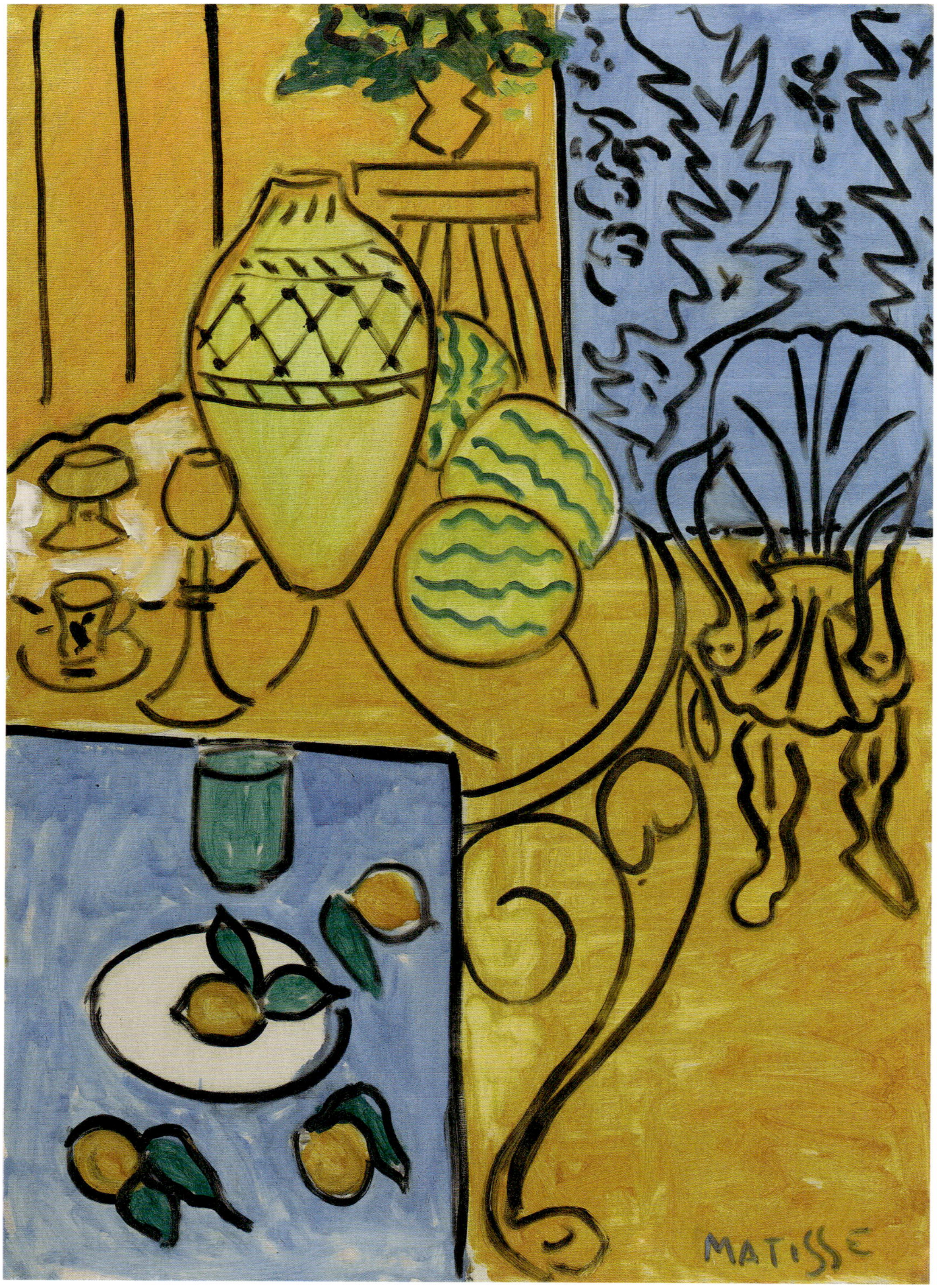

59 | *Interior in Yellow and Blue*, 1946

Oil on canvas, 45⅝ x 31⅞ in. (116 x 81 cm). Centre Pompidou, Musée National d'Art Moderne, Paris, State purchase, 1947

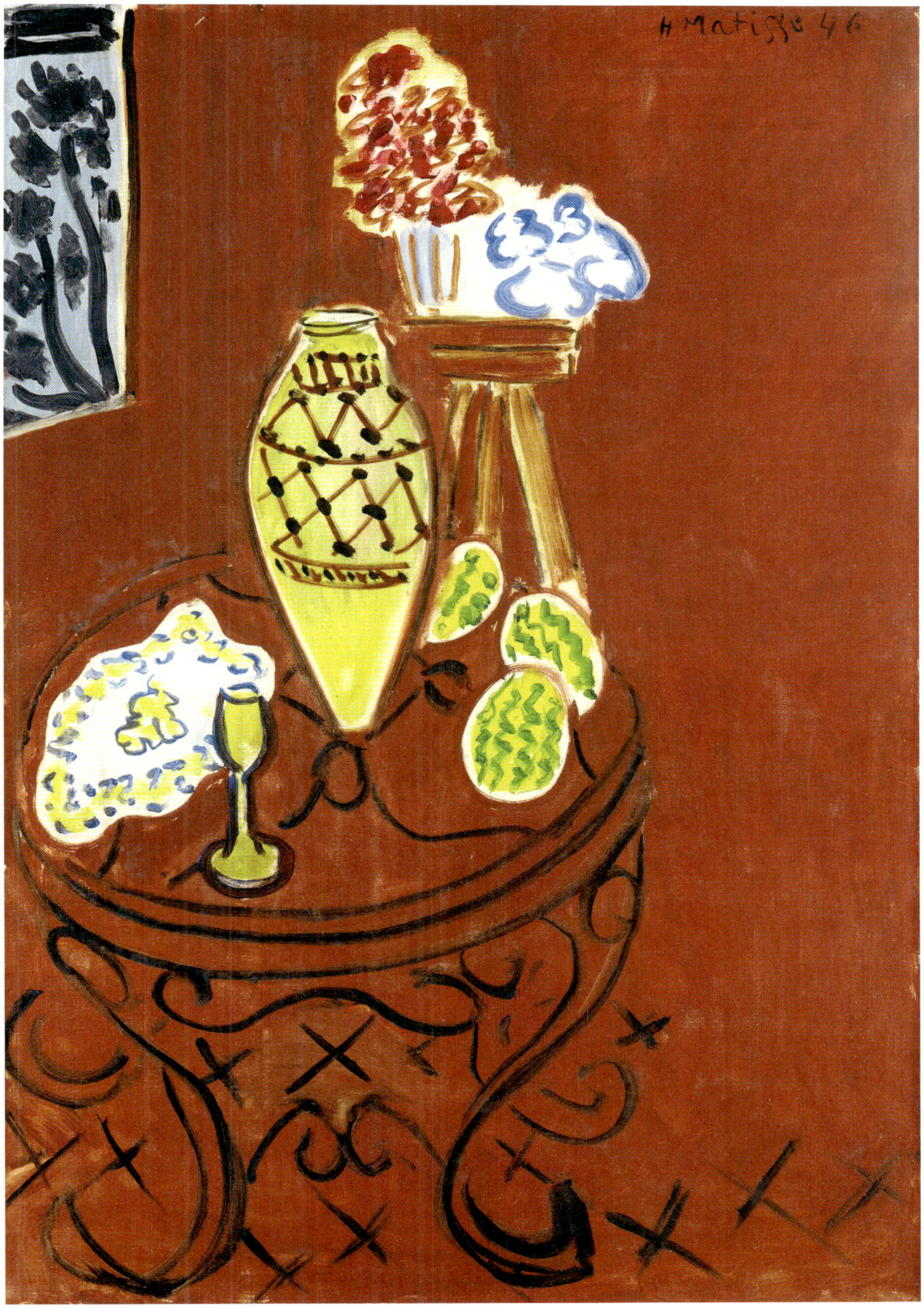

60 | *Interior in Venetian Red*, 1946

Oil on canvas, 36¼ x 25⅝ in. (92 x 65 cm). Royal Museums of Fine Arts of Belgium, Brussels

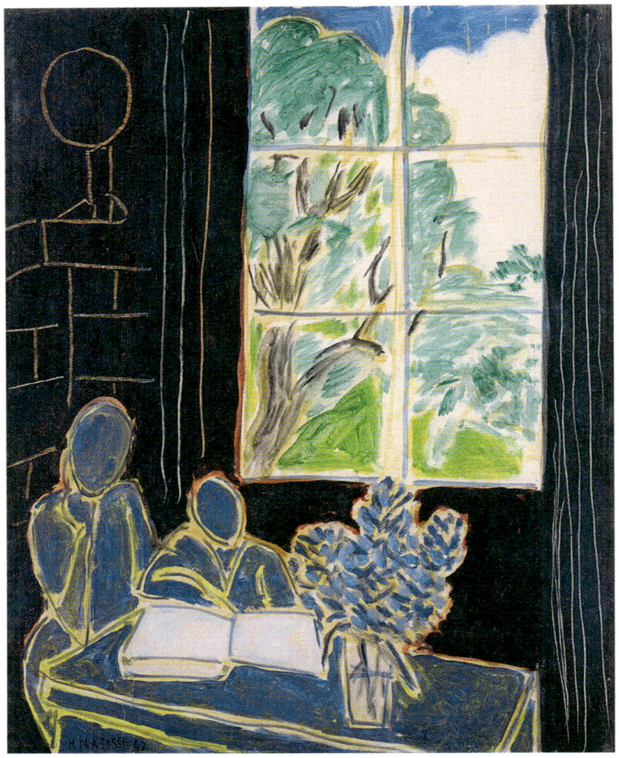

Fig. 91. *The Silence Living in Houses*, 1947. Oil on canvas, 24 x 19¾ in. (61 x 50 cm). Private collection

Matisse, who designed the maquette for the volume, interleaved the paintings with line drawings; the former, reproduced in color, represented interiors, while the latter were conceived as coming from the garden outside. Several of the alternating works appear successively as tonal variations. Strikingly, the Two Girls series is elaborated in eight paintings with shifting chromatic chords, the ground by turns chestnut, blue, yellow, red, mauve, gray-black, blue with red window, and coral. The most astonishing of these paintings, to which Louis Aragon gave the evocative title *The Silence Living in Houses* (fig. 91), shows the figures as rigid, faceless blue silhouettes on a black ground, the window frame and colored landscape breaking through behind them. That intensification of the contre-jour effect evokes a sort of photographic negative that accentuates the play of color contrasts within the group.[6]

All the Vence interiors are marked by a decidedly flexible relationship between line and color, a relationship that the artist articulated ever more loosely and quickly.[7] Beginning with the rigorous dialectic of this pair from 1946, Matisse was drawn into a series of poetic variations that expressed a relaxation and a liberation that completed his journey as a painter:

> *What I experienced after the operation was a liberation. I told myself that life was gratis from now on. Up until then I had felt overwhelmed by Courbet's saying that "one always had to be capable of doing a picture over again, to be sure that one was not just being played on by one's nerves and chance." So I would do my pictures over again to try and find the law that governed my work, and I destroyed them so as to be able to begin again.*
>
> *It came to me like a ray of sunlight on my house, a kind of liberation.*
>
> *Before, between my studio and the world outside, there was no complete continuity. Before, I would change the spirit somewhat, there was always a slight gap between nature and what I did: for example, I would look at the sea, and in what I did, the breath one finds in the sea would be missing. Now I no longer understand everything I am doing. I don't know why.*[8]

RADIANT COLOR

Rebecca Rabinow

Matisse created his final, fully realized easel paintings in his second-floor studio at the Villa Le Rêve[1] during the late winter of 1947 and early spring of 1948 (fig. 92). The seventy-nine-year-old artist was regarded as one of the greatest French colorists of his generation, but few admirers were prepared for these "profuse, luxuriant, exuberant" pictures.[2] "[The paintings] are strong!" Matisse wrote to his son Pierre from Vence. "They impress everyone who has seen them because they are vivid and rich."[3] Matisse had claimed that during the first decade of the twentieth century his palette had been inspired by "the revelation of light in nature;"[4] now, decades later, he was once again conjuring light out of color.

Shortly after World War II, French critics began commenting on the increased role of color in contemporary art. Some cited Matisse's influence,[5] although the artist himself worried about the effect of the public's indiscriminate taste for ever brighter, more extreme color combinations: "We are living at a time when collectors, fascinated by pure color, will swallow anything. But color for color's sake signifies nothing. It is a snobbery that will simply be replaced by the next snobbery."[6] Matisse felt that "it is only after years of preparation that the young artist should touch color—not color as description, that is, but as a means of intimate expression. . . . One must go through a severe preparation to be worthy of [color]. But first of all, it is clear that one must have a gift for color as a singer must have a voice."[7]

Matisse had nurtured his own gift for decades, and his virtuosity dazzles in *Interior with an Egyptian Curtain* (cat. 61), painted in February 1948.[8] Light is introduced into the composition in a traditional manner. The leaves of a palm tree appear drenched in sunlight, which streams inside the studio through a window, deconstructs the bowl of pomegranates in the foreground, and casts an intense black shadow on the table. The thick white paint in the large medallion on the curtain mimics the white cotton appliqués of the actual textile. The tactility of the paint creates a trompe l'oeil effect, appearing to catch the light, in marked contrast with other unpainted (and thus also white) passages.[9]

In March 1948, Matisse informed his friend the poet André Rouveyre that he was taking advantage of the springlike weather in Vence to paint three "size 50" canvases.[10] The artist had already used this format,

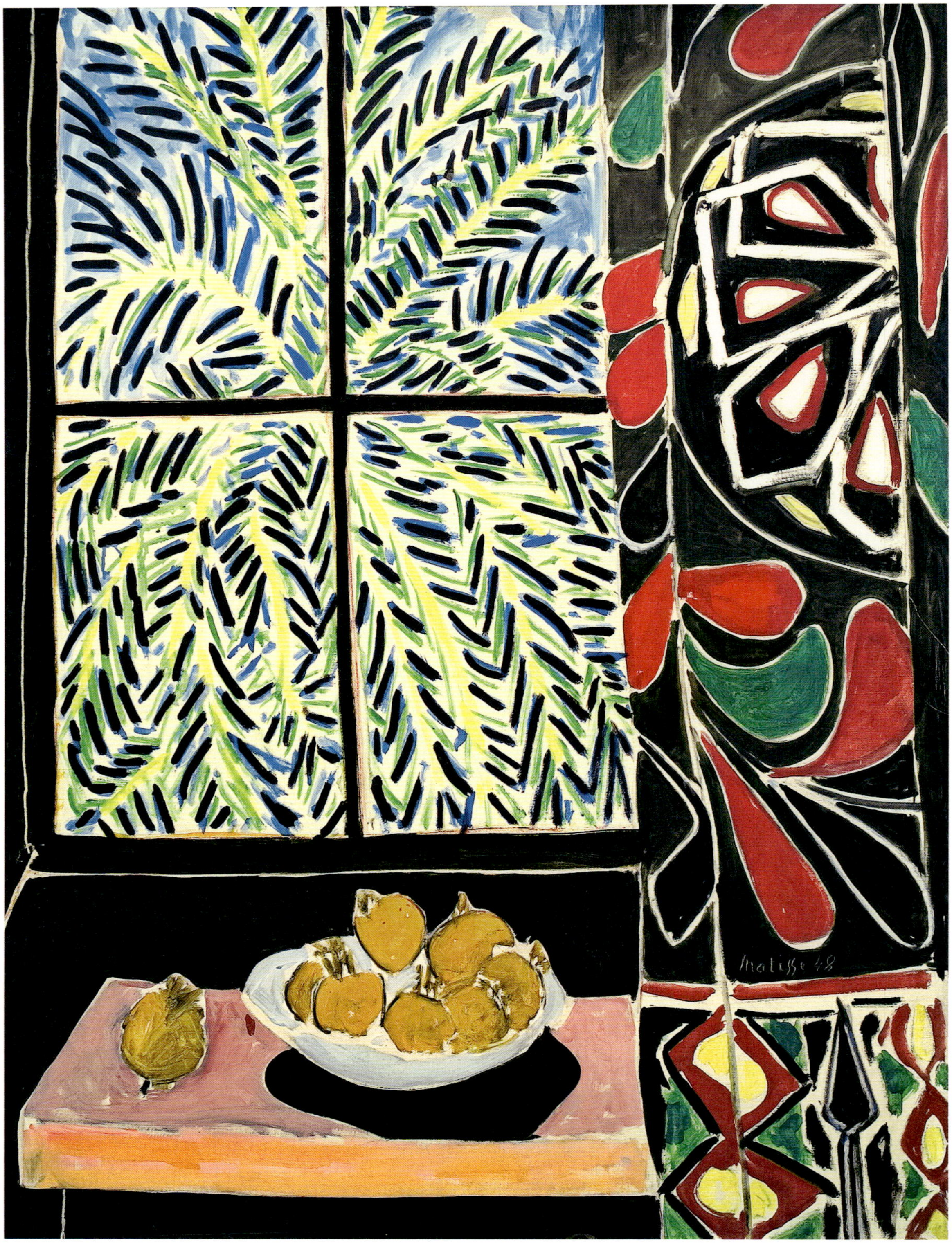

61 | *Interior with an Egyptian Curtain*, 1948

Oil on canvas, 45¾ x 35⅛ in. (116.2 x 89.2 cm). The Phillips Collection, Washington, D.C.

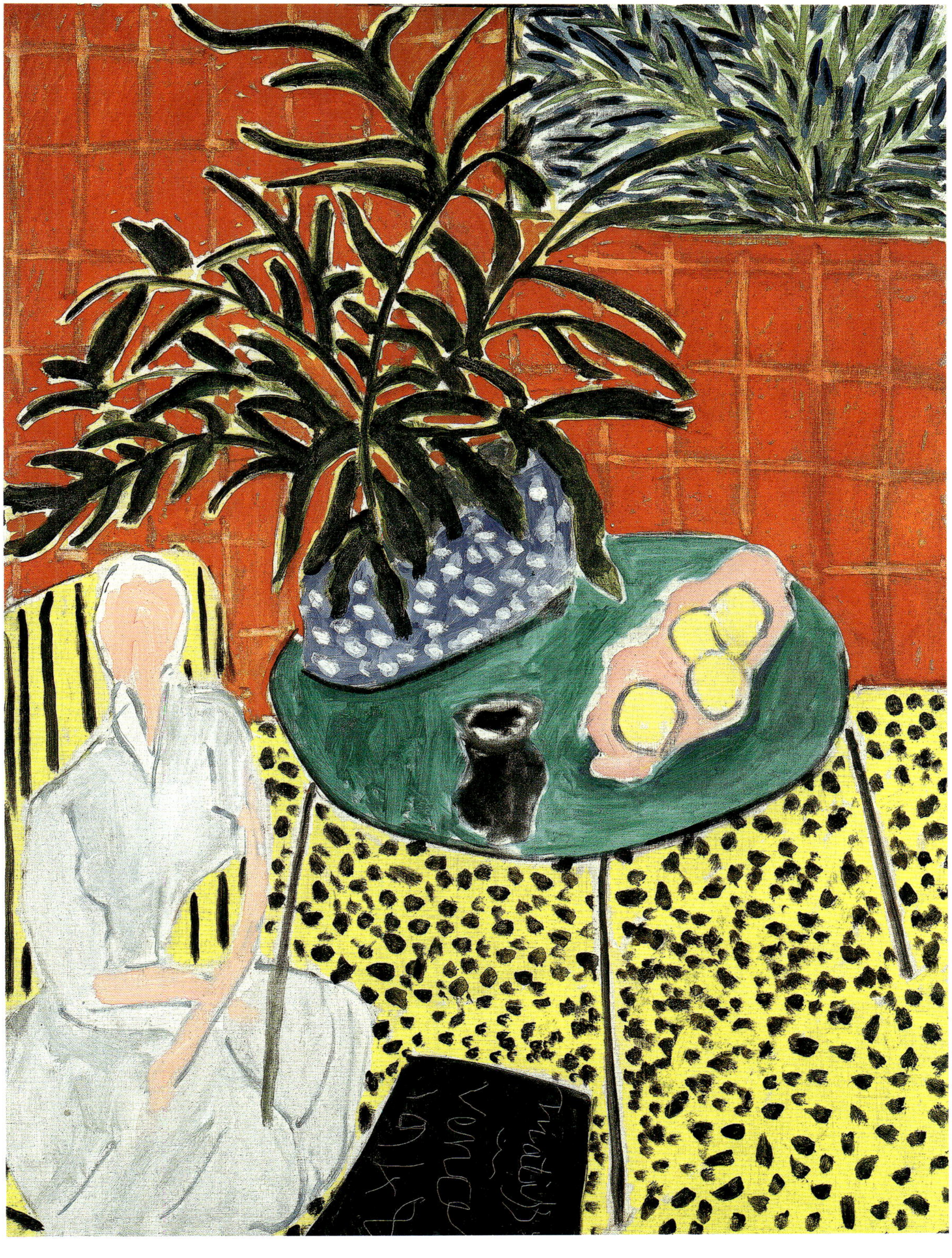

62 | *Interior with Black Fern*, 1948

Oil on canvas, 45⅝ x 35 in. (116 x 89 cm). Fondation Beyeler, Basel

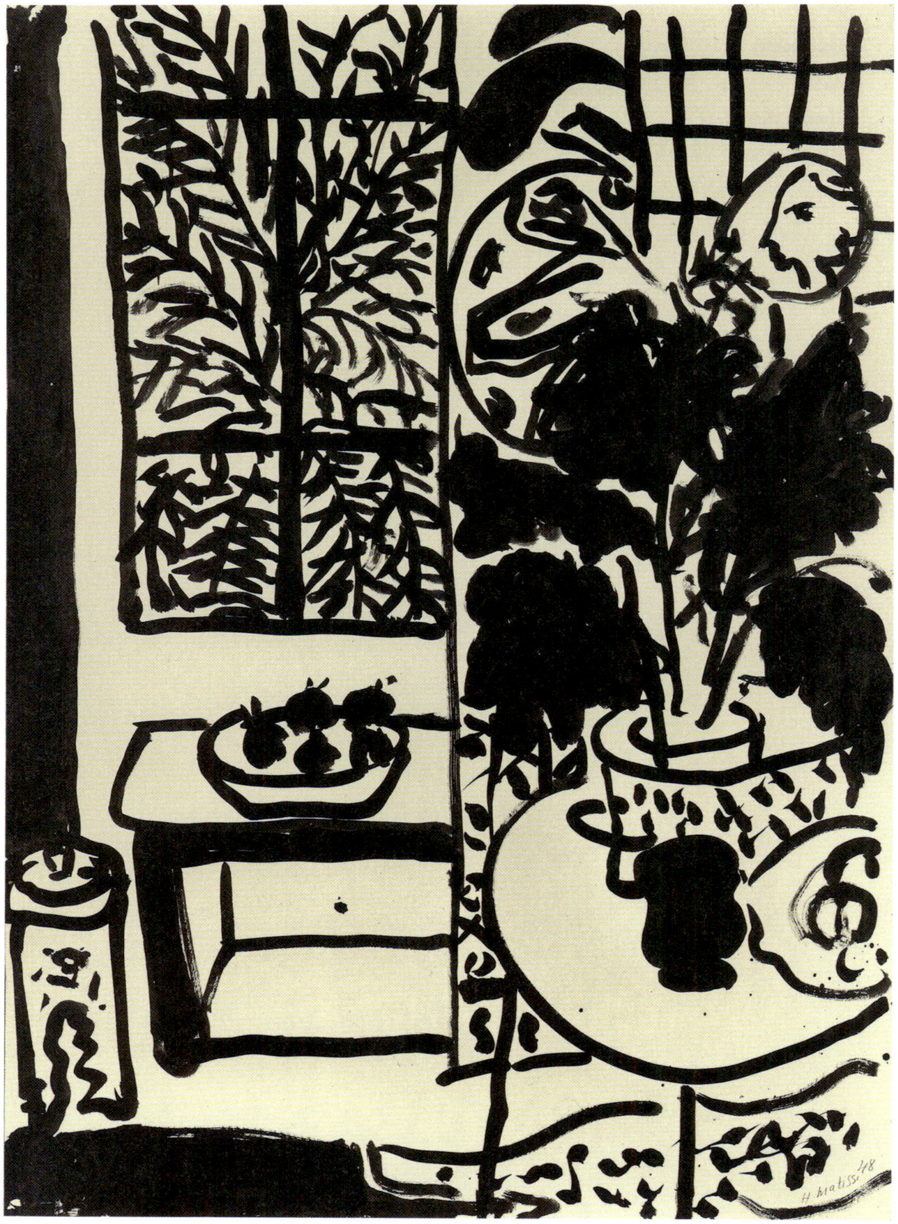

63 | *Interior with View of a Palm Tree*, 1948

Ink on paper, 41⅜ x 29½ in. (105 x 75 cm). Private collection

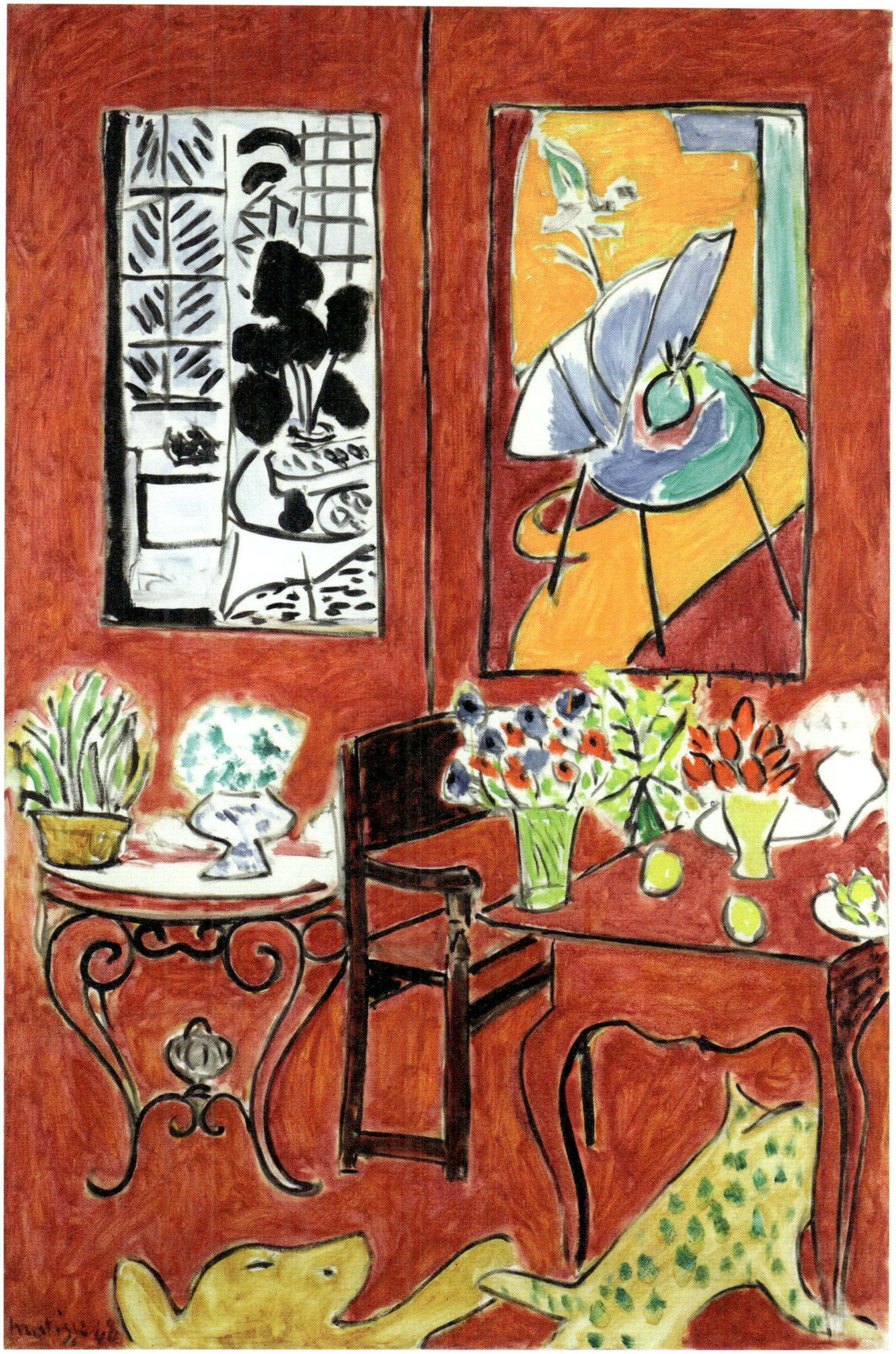

64 | *Large Red Interior*, 1948

Oil on canvas, 57½ x 38¼ in. (146 x 97 cm). Centre Pompidou, Musée National d'Art Moderne, Paris, State purchase, 1950

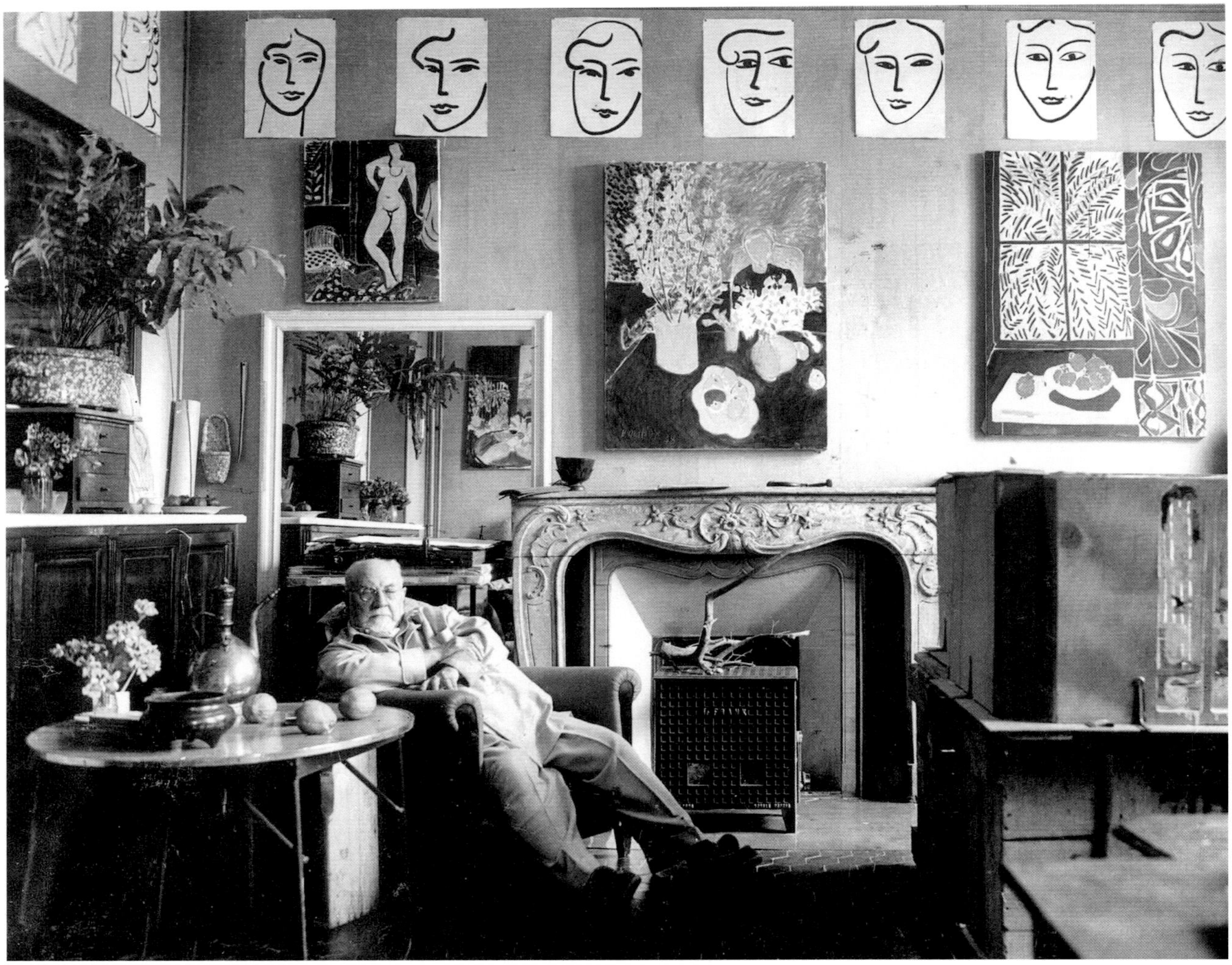

Fig. 92. Michel Sima. Matisse in his studio at the Villa Le Rêve, Vence, 1948

measuring 45⅝ by 35 inches (116 by 89 centimeters), that winter: in late 1947 for *Red Interior with Blue Table* (Kunstsammlung Nordrhein-Westfalen, Düsseldorf), in mid-January 1948 for *The Pineapple* (private collection),[11] and in February for *Interior with an Egyptian Curtain*. Now he chose it for *Plum Blossoms, Green Background* (Pinacoteca Giovanni e Marella Agnelli, Turin), *Plum Blossoms, Ocher Background* (The Museum of Modern Art, New York, Promised gift of Marie-Josée and Henry R. Kravis), and *Interior with Black Fern* (cat. 62).

Interior with Black Fern is among the most disquieting of Matisse's late paintings. A diminutive, faceless woman dressed in gray is simultaneously menaced by a writhing black fern hovering over her and impaled by the stiletto-like leg of a card table. Matisse's decision to etch his name, the location, and the date into a black plaque in front of the woman does nothing to diminish the sense of unease. However, a counterbalance is provided by the decorative patterns and bright colors, as well as by the sensation of light that emanates not from the window at the upper right but from the bright red wall and dotted yellow floor covering—the artist's own leopard-skin rug,[12] stretched to the scale of a wall-to-wall carpet. Matisse fervently believed that "color helps to express light, not the physical phenomenon, but the only light that really exists, that in the artist's brain."[13]

By early April, Matisse had almost completed *Large Red Interior* (cat. 64), one of the last and the largest of his late Vence studio views.[14] The composition clearly developed out of *Interior in Venetian Red* of 1946 (cat. 60), but in the later painting, Matisse presents a wider view of the studio. He arranges symmetrical still lifes—two tables, two rugs, two artworks—on either side of the central vertical line that indicates the corner of the room. A photograph (fig. 11) clarifies that, in this painting, the black-and-white rectangle at left represents an India ink drawing (cat. 63), but again Matisse plays with the ambiguity. The drawing is in the shape of a window, contains the depiction of a window, and as presented in *Large Red Interior*, seems to emanate light as a window might, obliterating the color from the top of the round table underneath, as if bright sunshine were washing over it. Matisse struggled to find the words to explain to Pierre the precise importance of these India ink drawings. "The work is not terribly practical in terms of selling it but [it is] quite helpful for my ~~training~~ ~~development~~ conclusion."[15] The juxtaposition of a brightly colored composition with a black-and-white drawing as seen in *Large Red Interior* represents a significant dichotomy in Matisse's late work. For him, these two means of expression were not only compatible but complementary.[16]

Matisse's late Vence paintings made their public debut in February 1949 at Pierre Matisse's New York gallery, where they were displayed unframed so that visitors would feel embraced and then transported by the color.[17] Clement Greenberg declared that "Matisse is at the present moment painting as well as he ever has painted before, and, in some respects perhaps, even better."[18] The critic considered *Large Red Interior* "the best picture on hand . . . as completely [considered] in design as in color."[19] The paintings were widely seen as a tour de force, an example of "Matisse's incredible ability to make things stay in place, to create space with color alone."[20] Unbeknownst to many of his admirers, Matisse's interests were already evolving. Possibly he felt he had achieved all that he could with his easel painting. The rest of his life would be devoted to book illustrations, paper cutouts, and designs for a chapel at Vence, a project his friend Tériade described as the "supreme endeavor by a painter who has always been involved with the problems of radiant color and light."[21]

NOTES

DORTHE AAGESEN AND
REBECCA RABINOW
Introduction

1. We thank Jack Flam for sharing his thoughts on this topic, which shaped our understanding of Matisse's pairs in the broader context of the artist's work.
2. Letter from Matisse to his wife, Amélie, January 9, 1919, in Hilary Spurling, *Matisse the Master: A Life of Henri Matisse; the Conquest of Colour, 1909–1954* (New York, 2005), p. 223.
3. Albert Boime, *The Academy and French Painting in the Nineteenth Century* (London, 1971), pp. 122–27.
4. "Interview with Clara T. MacChesney, 1912," in Jack Flam, *Matisse on Art*, rev. ed. (Berkeley and Los Angeles, 1995), p. 67. See also Xavier-Philippe Guiochon, "Quand Henri Matisse copiait les Maîtres," November 15, 2011, Centre National des Arts Plastiques, www.cnap.fr/quand-henri-matisse-copiait-les-maîtres, and Roger Benjamin, "Recovering Authors: The Modern Copy, Copy Exhibitions, and Matisse," *Art History* 12 (June 1989), pp. 176–201.
5. Matisse was impressed by the purity of Japanese woodcuts and inspired by early French and Italian primitivism as well as by the art of the Islamic world and Africa; see his "Interview with Jacques Guenne, 1925," in Flam, *Matisse on Art*, p. 80.
6. See, for example, Charles Morice, "Le XXe Salon des Indépendants," *Mercure de France* 51, no. 173 (May 1904), pp. 405–8.
7. *Exposition des oeuvres du peintre Henri Matisse*, exh. cat. (Paris, 1904), copy annotated by Carl V. Petersen, The Geertsen Archive, Statens Museum for Kunst, Copenhagen.
8. Charles Morice, "Art moderne: Exposition Henri Matisse," *Mercure de France* 51, no. 176 (August 1904), pp. 533–34.
9. Marius-Ary Leblond, "La peinture nouvelle: À propos des 'Indépendants,'" *Les Arts de la vie* 3, no. 16 (April 1905), p. 235.
10. "Interview with Guillaume Apollinaire, 1907," in Flam, *Matisse on Art*, p. 29.
11. Ibid., p. 28.
12. Stephanie D'Alessandro and John Elderfield, *Matisse: Radical Invention 1913–1917*, exh. cat. (Chicago, 2010), pp. 236–39.
13. John Elderfield, "Un nouveau départ," in *Matisse, paires et séries*, exh. cat. (Paris, 2012), pp. 119–24.
14. This aspect of Matisse's art was one of the subjects of the exhibition "Matisse: Radical Invention 1913–1917," held at The Art Institute of Chicago, March 20–June 20, 2010, and The Museum of Modern Art, New York, July 18–October 11, 2010.
15. Flam, *Matisse on Art*, p. 272, text 10, n. 4.
16. Jack Flam, *Matisse in Transition: Around Laurette*, exh. cat. (West Palm Beach, 2006), p. 19.
17. Jeffrey Weiss, "The Matisse Grid," in *The Repeating Image: Multiples in French Painting from David to Matisse*, ed. Eik Kahng, exh. cat. (Baltimore, 2007), p. 178.
18. Anon., "Art in Paris; The Henri Matisse Exhibition," *The Times* (London), June 18, 1931, p. 12.
19. Virginia Nirdlinger, "The Matisse Way: Forty Years in the Evolution of an Individualist," *Parnassus* 3, no. 7 (November 1931), p. 6.
20. "Interview with Jacques Guenne," in Flam, *Matisse on Art*, p. 80.
21. Henri Matisse, "Letters to Alexander Romm, 1934," in Flam, *Matisse on Art*, pp. 113–15.
22. Lydia Delectorskaya: *With Apparent Ease . . . Henri Matisse: Paintings from 1935–1939* (Paris, 1988), p. 23.
23. See D'Alessandro in D'Alessandro and Elderfield, *Matisse: Radical Invention*, pp. 80–83.
24. For more on this subject, see ibid., particularly pp. 80ff. and 175, 177. Photographic documentation was crucial to the analysis of the long and complicated genesis of *Bathers by a River*, which served as the pivotal point for the above-mentioned exhibition and accompanying catalogue.
25. "Statement on Photography, 1908," in Flam, *Matisse on Art*, p. 44.
26. "Interview with Léon Degand, 1945," in Flam, *Matisse on Art*, p. 161.
27. "Interview with J. Sacs, 1910," in Flam, *Matisse on Art*, p. 60.
28. Serial photographed states of Matisse's paintings first appeared in Roger Fry, *Henri-Matisse* (Paris, 1935), pl. 57, and E. Tériade, "Constance du fauvisme," *Minotaure*, ser. 2, no. 9 (October 15, 1936), pp. 6–8.
29. Aimé Maeght's initial idea, as he outlined it in a letter to Matisse, was to present an exhibition for the benefit of the French Resistance that would feature decorative painting by several prominent artists working in France. In addition to Matisse, he hoped to include pictures by Pierre Bonnard, Georges Rouault, Georges Braque, and Pablo Picasso as well as some younger talents such as André Marchand and Roger Chastel. When that exhibition proved impossible to organize, the exhibition was devoted to Matisse.
30. Letter from Matisse to Maeght, January 3, 1946, Archives Matisse, Paris.
31. Undated telegram from Matisse to Maeght, Archives Fondation Maeght, courtesy Archives Matisse.
32. Matisse's exact words were, "Je marche selon ma logique personnelle d'état en état vers résultats concluants et définitives." Second undated

telegram from Matisse to Maeght, Archives Fondation Maeght, courtesy Archives Matisse.

33. Our thanks to Jeff Rosenheim, Curator, Department of Photographs, The Metropolitan Museum of Art, for a engaging conversation about twentieth-century painters' use of photography.
34. Letter from the Galerie Maeght to Lydia Delectorskaya, March 23, 1945, Archives Fondation Maeght, courtesy Archives Matisse.
35. Letter from Maeght to Matisse, December 22, 1945, Archives Matisse.
36. For example, in "Matisse, Picasso" (Palais des Beaux-Arts, Brussels, May 1946) and in an exhibition of Matisse's sculpture and three paintings with photographic studies that opened at the Tate Gallery, London (January 9–February 22, 1953), and traveled to several other venues, including the Ny Carlsberg Glyptotek, Copenhagen (November 6–December 6, 1953), and the Kunstnernes Hus, Oslo (February 20–March 7, 1954).
37. Yve-Alain Bois, *Matisse and Picasso*, exh. cat. (New York, 1998), p. 204.
38. Alfred H. Barr Jr., *Matisse: His Art and His Public* (New York, 1951), p. 277. Barr tried in vain to purchase the painting for the Museum of Modern Art, New York; see the Pierre Matisse Gallery Archives, The Morgan Library & Museum, New York.
39. Isabelle Monod-Fontaine, "Vence 1943–1948," in *Matisse: A Second Life*, ed. Hanne Finsen, exh. cat. (Paris, 2005), pp. 47–48.

CLAUDINE GRAMMONT
"A Picture Is like a Game of Cards"

1. Matisse first used this method in landscapes painted at Belle-Île-en-Mer in the summer of 1897. Later, in Corsica and Toulouse (where he stayed between August 1898 and February–March 1899, and again in May), he persisted in this vein, experimenting with color but also adopting the Impressionist practice of elaborating a single motif in several versions. The interlude in Toulouse was dominated by work on still lifes rather than landscapes, however.
2. Jack Flam, *Matisse: The Man and His Art, 1869–1918* (Ithaca, N.Y., and London, 1986), p. 66.
3. Ibid.
4. Ibid.
5. Only an examination of the underpainting would allow us to confirm or invalidate that hypothesis.
6. Paul Signac, "D'Eugène Delacroix au néo-impressionnisme," *La Revue blanche* 16 (May–August 1898), pp. 13–35, 115–33, 357–69, published in 1899 and repr. Paul Signac, *D'Eugène Delacroix au néo-impressionnisme* (Paris, 1964).
7. Signac, *D'Eugène Delacroix au néo-impressionnisme*, p. 40.
8. Ibid., p. 103.
9. On the sketch and academic theory, see Philippe Grunchec, *Les concours d'esquisses peintes, 1816–1863*, exh. cat. (Paris, 1986).
10. Matisse saw Cézanne's *Three Bathers* (fig. 13) at Vollard's when he came through Paris in spring 1899. He thought of it again during his stay in Toulouse, probably in May (see his statement in Pierre Courthion, "Bavardages," manuscript, 1941, Archives Matisse, Paris), and acquired it when he returned.
11. "Interview with Clara T. MacChesney, 1912," in Jack Flam, *Matisse on Art*, rev. ed. (Berkeley and Los Angeles, 1995), pp. 65–69.
12. Hans Purrmann, "From the Workshop of Henri Matisse," *The Dial* 73 (July 1922), p. 36; English trans. of Hans Purrmann, "Aus der Werkstatt Henri Matisses," *Kunst und Künstler* 20 (1922), p. 172.
13. Flam, *Matisse on Art*, p. 40.

CLAUDINE GRAMMONT
Impressionism in Question

1. In addition to those cited here, there is a painting in a vertical format: *Pont Saint-Michel*, 1901, repr. Pierre Schneider, ed., *Matisse: Exposition du centenaire*, exh. cat. (Paris, 1970), no. 402, and two other views that omit almost all the elements at the left of the composition: one, sold at Christie's, London, April 4, 1978, no. 22, and the other, *Pont Saint-Michel*, former collection Pierre Matisse, repr. Guy-Patrice Dauberville and Michel Dauberville, *Matisse: Henri Matisse chez Bernheim-Jeune* (Paris, 1995), vol. 1, pp. 354–55, no. 42.
2. *Pont Saint-Michel*, about 1895, sale, Christie's, London, June 21, 2006, no. 215.
3. Matisse himself linked his discovery of Impressionism to the Caillebotte Bequest, exhibited in an annex to the Luxembourg Museum in February 1897, while he was still a student in Gustave Moreau's studio. See "Interview with Jacques Guenne, 1925," trans. Jack Flam, *Matisse on Art*, rev. ed. (Berkeley and Los Angeles, 1995), pp. 78–82.
4. Henri Evenepoel, *Lettres à mon père, 1892–1899*, ed. Danielle Derrey-Capon (Brussels, 1994), vol. 2, pp. 264–65.
5. The painting appears in one of Ambroise Vollard's inventory books, which can be dated to 1904 (no. 3410, "Vue de Paris, effet de neige"). See Rebecca Rabinow, "Vollard and Matisse," in *Ambroise Vollard, Patron of the Avant-Garde*, exh. cat. (New York, 2006), p. 141, n. 24. It was exhibited at Vollard's in June 1904 under the title "Effet de neige, vue du Pont Saint-Michel."
6. Although Matisse painted mountain landscapes again in 1902, in his views of snowy peaks at Villars-sur-Ollon, the particular treatment of snow seen in *Pont Saint-Michel, Snow Effect* does not appear elsewhere in his oeuvre.
7. The same shadow is indicated at the edge of the left border of *Pont Saint-Michel, Snow Effect*, but there it does not really constitute a plane.
8. Regarding one of the three versions of *Pont Saint-Michel* (probably the one in Paris), Matisse confided to Georges Duthuit that it corresponded to the "beginning of color . . . he wanted to assure the quality of his blues." Quoted in Georges Duthuit, *Écrits sur Matisse*, ed. Rémi Labrusse (Paris, 1992), p. 281.

ALASTAIR WRIGHT
Blinded by the Sun

Epigraph: Maurice Denis, "Le soleil," *L'Ermitage*, December 15, 1906, n.p.; my translation.

1. *Luxe, calme, et volupté* was regarded by Matisse's contemporaries as a sharp change of direction, even as a loss of the artist's own identity. See Alastair Wright, *Matisse and the Subject of Modernism* (Princeton, 2004), pp. 17–53.
2. This should not surprise us, for Matisse spoke often of his inability to stick to the rules of Pointillism. See, for example, his comments to Gaston Diehl, quoted in *Henri Matisse, 1904–1917*, exh. cat. (Paris, 1993), p. 63.
3. One result is that Matisse's work could less easily be seen as transcribing the facts of vision. Hence Édouard Sarradin's rather odd description of the painting as a "blue and gold effect of rain on the sea" (Édouard Sarradin, "Le Salon des Indépendants," *Journal des débats*, March 26, 1905, p. 3; my translation). Unable to read the marks as part of the Neo-Impressionist system, the critic was brought to a halt at the surface of the work, mistakenly taking the divided blue and yellow tones for crude iconic signs mimicking the appearance of falling rain.
4. Fredric Jameson, "Postmodernism, or the Cultural Logic of Late Capitalism," *New Left Review* 146 (1984), pp. 68–72. Tzvetan Todorov's analysis of modernist literature is an equally useful model. Todorov describes Symbolist literature (to which we might add Symbolist painting) as "paranoid" because it replaces the world of external "reality" with an imaginary substitute, a coherent parallel universe linked to our own by a series of legible, stable correspondences. Literature produced after the Symbolist period, he argues, is conversely best characterized as a kind of schizophrenic malfunctioning. Rather than creating a consistent picture of an imagined world, it is internally contradictory. The reader is thus unable to organize the elements into a coherent narrative, and all is experienced as fragments—as in schizophrenia, a condition in which the subject loses his or her ability to synthesize sensation and thought. See Tzvetan Todorov, *Les genres du discours* (Paris, 1978), especially pp. 78–85.

5. On the hostile reaction to Fauvism's destabilization of pictorial meaning, see Wright, *Matisse and the Subject of Modernism*, pp. 55–90.

CLAUDINE GRAMMONT
Cézanne versus Signac

1. See Jack Flam, *Matisse: The Man and His Art, 1869–1918* (Ithaca, N.Y., and London, 1986), especially chap. 3, "Years of Struggle, 1900–1903," pp. 78–107.
2. Ibid., pp. 110–11. Yve-Alain Bois has suggested that it is precisely for that reason that they are the least interesting of Matisse's Cézannesque paintings. See Y.-A. Bois, "Cézanne and Matisse: From Apprenticeship to Creative Misreading," in *Cézanne and Beyond*, exh. cat. (Philadelphia, 2009), pp. 103–35.
3. In 1950 John Rewald, adviser to the Whitneys, who owned the painting at the time, told Matisse they had purchased it. The artist confirmed that it had been painted in Saint-Tropez in 1904 (letter from Rewald to John Hay Whitney, February 26, 1951, cited in *Impressionist and Modern Art*, sale cat., Sotheby's, New York, May 5, 2004, p. 117). However, in late August 1904, Matisse had written Henri Manguin that he had painted only one "canvas of 15 done at sunset" (the work mentioned is *The Gulf of Saint-Tropez* [cat. 6]; letter from Matisse to Manguin, late August 1904, Archives Jean-Pierre Manguin, Avignon). He therefore would have done the other six, larger works known from this period within a fairly short time, after he returned to Paris in mid-September.
4. Jack Flam and Hilary Spurling are inclined to adopt that hypothesis (Flam, *Matisse: The Man and His Art*, p. 120; Spurling, *The Unknown Matisse: A Life of Henri Matisse; the Early Years, 1869–1908* [New York, 1998], p. 293), but Alfred H. Barr Jr. and John Elderfield are not (Barr, *Matisse: His Art and His Public* [New York, 1951], p. 315; Elderfield, *Henri Matisse: A Retrospective*, exh. cat. [New York, 1992], no. 48).
5. According to Yve-Alain Bois, the principal problem raised by Divisionism is the discordance between the two plastic arts—line and color—which was solved in 1906 by Matisse's *Bonheur de vivre* (1905–6; The Barnes Foundation, Philadelphia); see "Matisse and Arche-Drawing," in Yve-Alain Bois, *Painting as Model* (Cambridge, Mass., 1990), pp. 3–63. See also Catherine C. Bock, *Henri Matisse and Neo-Impressionism, 1898–1908* (Ann Arbor, Mich., 1981), pp. 76–77.
6. Bernard writes, "Paul Cézanne believes that there are two 'plastiques,' or methods of giving aesthetic form to things, one sculptural or linear, the other decorative or coloristic." Émile Bernard, "Paul Cézanne," *L'Occident*, July 1904, trans. *Conversations with Cézanne,* ed. Michael Doran (Berkeley, 2001), p. 38. In September 1904, Matisse, who was still in Saint-Tropez, asked Albert Marquet to buy the review and send it to him, which Marquet did on the 11th (letter from Matisse to Marquet, early September 1904, and letter from Marquet to Matisse bearing a September 11 postmark, quoted in Claudine Grammont, ed., *Matisse–Marquet: Correspondance* [Lausanne, 2008], pp. 36–37). Matisse regarded Bernard's article as important enough that he asked Signac for excerpts the following summer, which implies that they must have previously spoken about it (letter from Matisse to Signac, July 14, 1905, quoted in Rémi Labrusse and Jacqueline Munck, *Matisse, Derain: La vérité du fauvisme* [Paris, 2005], p. 231).
7. Henri-Edmond Cross believed that Matisse had not managed to integrate his figures in *Luxe, calme, et volupté*. Letter from Cross to Matisse, July 18, 1905, quoted in Labrusse and Munck, *Matisse, Derain*, p. 232.
8. Marius-Ary Leblond, "La peinture nouvelle: À propos des Indépendants," *Les Arts de la vie*, no. 16 (April 1905), p. 235.
9. Letter from Cross to Matisse, July 18, 1905, quoted in Labrusse and Munck, *Matisse, Derain*, p. 232.
10. "Statement to Tériade: On Fauvism and Color, 1929," in Jack Flam, *Matisse on Art*, rev. ed. (Berkeley and Los Angeles, 1995), p. 84.
11. Charles Morice, "À propos du Salon des Indépendants de 1905," *Le Mercure de France*, no. 188 (April 15, 1905), p. 552.

REBECCA RABINOW AND
ISABELLE DUVERNOIS
An Experiment in Deformation

1. Louis Vauxcelles in *Gil Blas*, suppl. October 17, 1905, quoted in Jack Flam, *Matisse: The Man and His Art, 1869–1918* (Ithaca, N.Y., and London, 1986), p. 143.
2. Ibid.
3. Leo Stein, *Appreciation: Painting, Prose, Poetry* (1947; repr. Lincoln, Neb., and London, 1996), p. 192.
4. For more information about the model, see Joséphine Matamoros in *Matisse–Derain: Collioure 1905, un été fauve*, exh. cat. (Paris, 2005), pp. 22–23.
5. Sabine Rewald in Sabine Rewald et al., *Twentieth-Century Modern Masters: The Jacques and Natasha Gelman Collection*, exh. cat. (New York, 1989), p. 91, n. 1.
6. The verso of the canvas is stamped with its size, "40F[igure]." The stretcher bears the stenciled logo of the art store Lefranc & Cie, an anchor crossed by a caduceus within a small coin.
7. When viewed under ultraviolet illumination, the pink overpainting fluoresces bright yellow-green, which indicates a high level of zinc and differentiates it from the salmon pink paint applied earlier. It is possible that Matisse added more pink to the background of *Young Sailor I* after completing *Young Sailor II*.
8. Rachel Mustalish, paper conservator at The Metropolitan Museum of Art, discovered the impression of an unrelated drawing of two standing female nudes while examining the sheet under raking light. One appears above the sailor's right elbow. She faces left and her arms terminate in oval shapes just under her shoulder, as those of a damaged classical sculpture might. Her elongated neck, hair pulled back into a bun, and almond-shaped eyes may relate to the standing female figure in *Le Luxe I* and *II* (cats. 12, 14). The impression of a second nude standing on her tiptoes is visible in the sailor's face and chest. These nudes were drawn in a sketchbook (the page's perforations are visible at the top of the sheet), presumably on the page or two before the *Young Sailor* drawing. They likely were made in conjunction with a group of small sculptures of female nudes that Matisse created at Collioure in 1906. See, for example, the terracotta torso reproduced in Claude Duthuit, *Henri Matisse: Catalogue raisonné de l'oeuvre sculpté* (Paris, 1997), p. 52, no. 21.
9. Henri Matisse, "Notes of a Painter," in Jack Flam, *Matisse on Art*, rev. ed. (Berkeley and Los Angeles, 1995), pp. 38–39.
10. Flam, introduction to ibid., p. 34.
11. Henri Matisse, "First Encounter with African Art, 1906," in *Primitivism and Twentieth-Century Art*, ed. Jack Flam and Miriam Deutch (Berkeley and Los Angeles, 2003), p. 31.
12. Félicien Fagus [Georges-Eugène Faillet], "Au Salon d'Automne," *L'Occident* 8 (November 1905), p. 257.
13. Years later, when discussing the Barnes Collection, the artist spoke about the benefits of juxtaposing art from different cultures and time periods: "The old master paintings are put beside the modern ones, a Douanier Rousseau next to a Primitive, and this bringing together helps students understand a lot of things that the academies don't teach." Henri Matisse, "Statement to Tériade: On Travel," 1930, in Flam, *Matisse on Art*, p. 92.
14. Pigment analysis conducted in 2011 by Marco Leona, Silvia Centeno, and Mark Wypyski, Department of Scientific Research, The Metropolitan Museum of Art.
15. In 1929, when Matisse reflected on this period, he particularly acknowledged the influence of Gauguin and Van Gogh: "Here are the ideas of that time: Construction by colored surfaces. Search for intensity of color." Matisse, "Statement to Tériade: On Fauvism and Color, 1929," in Flam, *Matisse on Art*, p. 84.

16. For further information, see Rebecca A. Rabinow, "Vollard and Matisse," in *Ambroise Vollard, Patron of the Avant-Garde*, exh. cat. (New York, 2006), pp. 131, 139, n. 2.
17. *Matisse–Derain: Collioure*, p. 345, n. 113.
18. Ibid., pp. 343–44. Translation by Christel Hollevoet-Force.

DORTHE AAGESEN AND KATHRINE SEGEL

The Academic Tradition Revised

Special thanks are owed to conservators Anne-Catherine Proudhom, and Véronique Sorano-Stedman, Centre Pompidou, Musée National d'Art Moderne, Paris, for their contributions to this essay.

1. Five paintings by Matisse were accepted by the Salon committee. In addition to *Le Luxe I*, these were no. 757, *Tête d'expression* (*The Red Madras Headdress*, 1907; The Barnes Foundation, Philadelphia); no. 757 bis, *La musique (esquisse)* (*Music [Sketch]*, 1907; The Museum of Modern Art, New York); and two unidentified landscapes, nos. 759 and 759 bis, both designated as *Paysage (esquisse)*. The artist also exhibited two untitled drawings, nos. 760 and 760 bis, as well as several painted ceramics. *Salon d'Automne, 5ᵉ exposition: Catalogue* (Paris, 1907).
2. Over the years, Matisse's family and even the artist himself became increasingly unsure as to the dating of the canvases. In addition, as time went by, the two canvases had erroneously come to be called *Luxe, calme, et volupté*, presumably because the painting of that name (cat. 7), which was bought soon after its completion by Paul Signac, was kept at his Saint-Tropez residence until 1950. See Alfred H. Barr Jr., *Matisse: His Art and His Public* (New York, 1951), p. 95.
3. Ibid. As source materials for his conclusions, Barr referred to his questionnaires III (answered in writing by Mme Georges Duthuit [Marguerite Matisse], April 1950) and IV (answered in writing and conversation by Matisse and Mme Matisse July–September 1950 through Pierre Matisse). The questionnaires, now housed in the archives of the Museum of Modern Art, New York, are described in Barr, *Matisse: His Art and His Public*, p. 529.
4. Bois views the two versions of *Le Luxe* as reflecting a "theoretical experiment" that Matisse was conducting to provide definitive corroboration for his theory that the quality of a color is related to the size of the area it covers—a relationship he had posited in 1906 and first tested in *Le Bonheur de vivre* (1905–6; Barnes Foundation). Yve-Alain Bois, "A De Luxe Experiment," in Dorthe Aagesen et al., *Matisse: Masterpieces at Statens Museum for Kunst* (Copenhagen, 2005), pp. 109–30. A revised version of this text appears in *Matisse: Paires et séries*, ed. Cécile Debray, exh. cat. (Paris, 2012), pp. 45–55
5. The studies were carried out by conservators at the Statens Museum for Kunst, Copenhagen, and the Centre Pompidou, Musée National d'Art Moderne, Paris. Their findings appear in a report published as an appendix in *Matisse: Paires et séries*, pp. 255–61.
6. New measurements reveal that the drawing measures 82⅝ by 54 inches (210 x 137 centimeters) when the bent edges are not included; this corresponds exactly to the size of the two paintings. Ibid., p. 260. It is not known how Matisse transferred the motif from *Le Luxe I* to the large sheet of paper. He may have drawn it by hand, since the contours seem tentative in places, but may also have used a transfer technique such as tracing. This did not, however, deter him from adjusting the motif once it had been transferred. The similarities and differences between the two compositions are clearly demonstrated by digitally overlapping the drawing and painting; see Stephanie D'Alessandro and John Elderfield, *Matisse. Radical Invention 1913–1917*, exh. cat. (Chicago, 2010), p. 64, fig. 2g. The grid is instantly visible in the drawing, but, contrary to D'Alessandro's claim, no traces of a similar grid have been discovered on *Le Luxe I*.
7. D'Alessandro believes that the large drawing was made first and was the basis for both *Le Luxe I* and *II* (ibid., p. 63). Several factors argue against this scenario. If the drawing was created as a preliminary study for *Le Luxe I*, traces left behind by the transfer process, such as a grid or a coherent sketch, would most likely be found underneath the paint. Our technical studies document with absolute certainty that no such traces exist. In addition, the painting bears no traces of charcoal, and the drawing no sign that a stylus was used. If they had, it might have indicated that Matisse had applied charcoal to the back of the drawing and then used a stylus to trace its main lines, thereby transferring the motif to the canvas—a technique he had used on other occasions. Finally, since certain areas of the drawing are more confidently executed than corresponding areas of *Le Luxe I*—including the floral bouquet and the profile of the mountains in the background, both of which have been corrected on the canvas—we conclude that the drawing was done after *Le Luxe I* had been completed.
8. For a detailed discussion of the circumstances surrounding the genesis of the paintings, see Bois, "De Luxe Experiment," pp. 119–21.
9. Until 2009, scholars disagreed on what medium was employed for *Le Luxe II*. An analysis carried out that year revealed that the pigment contains collagen and traces of keratin, which indicates that Matisse used a bone-based glue such as that of distemper rather than casein, as had been claimed. See Kathrine Segel and Ole Nørregaard Jensen, "*Le Luxe II* by Henri Matisse," *SMK Art Journal 2010–11* (Copenhagen), forthcoming 2012.
10. William Bouguereau, one of the most influential academic painters of the period, taught Matisse at the Académie Julian. Matisse also studied under the more liberal Gustave Moreau for six years, during which he spent much of his time copying old masters. For more details about the artist's early education, see Roger Benjamin, *Matisse's "Notes of a Painter": Criticism, Theory, and Context, 1891–1908* (Ann Arbor, Mich., 1987), pp. 9–40.
11. John Elderfield, "Matisse in Morocco: An Interpretive Guide," in Jack Cowart et al., *Matisse in Morocco*, exh. cat. (Washington, D.C., 1990), p. 212.
12. For more on the relationship between the *esquisse* and the *tableau*, see Albert Boime, *The Academy and French Painting in the Nineteenth Century* (London, 1971), pp. 79–89.
13. The same applies to the choice and form of the subject matter. Bringing tradition into play while also subverting its norms, Matisse opted for a large-scale figure painting of nude women in a rural landscape, a theme that evoked memories of the long pastoral tradition within European art, but he did not clearly indicate who and what the paintings represent. For analyses of Matisse's reinterpretation of the classic pastoral motif and his destabilization of established categories, see Margaret Werth, *The Joy of Life: The Idyllic in French Art, circa 1900* (Berkeley and Los Angeles, 2002), and Alastair Wright, *Matisse and the Subject of Modernism* (Princeton, 2004).
14. Bouguereau would first work out his composition in a small oil study, enlarge it by means of a grid, and then carry out a detailed, full-sized cartoon, which in turn he would transfer to the final canvas, also by means of a grid. Matisse's alternative method may have been inspired by Signac, with whom he was frequently in touch during 1904. In contrast to academic practice, Signac explored his basic idea in a sketch but did not develop the composition until he drew the cartoon, which shared the same format as the finished painting. He reasoned that the composition would not make sense if enlarged. See Benjamin, *Matisse's "Notes of a Painter,"* p. 202.
15. "Notes of a Painter, 1908," in Jack Flam, *Matisse on Art*, rev. ed. (Berkeley and Los Angeles, 1995), p. 38.
16. For a discussion of Matisse's use of the word "expression," see Benjamin, *Matisse's "Notes of a Painter,"* pp. 203–9.
17. See note 1 above. The retrospective presentation of Cézanne's paintings (notorious for their sketchy, unfinished quality) at the very same Salon

might have prompted Matisse to explore the category of the "sketch" and to present himself nearly exclusively by means of sketches that year.

18. Quoted in *Henri Matisse 1904–1917*, exh. cat. (Paris, 1993), p. 442.
19. Michel Puy, "Les Fauves," *La Phalange*, November 15, 1907, trans. Jack Flam, ed., *Matisse: A Retrospective* (New York, 1990), pp. 69–70.
20. Elderfield, "Matisse in Morocco," pp. 211ff.

KASPER MONRAD
Model / Bather / Odalisque

1. The painting was sold to the Galerie Bernheim-Jeune on June 2, 1909; see Kasper Monrad, *Henri Matisse: Four Great Collectors*, exh. cat. (Copenhagen, 1999), pp. 290–91, no. 69. Stephanie D'Alessandro and John Elderfield have estimated that Matisse began work on it in mid-March of that year; see *Matisse: Radical Invention 1913–1917*, exh. cat. (Chicago, 2010), p. 41.
2. See, in addition to *Nude, Black and Gold* (fig. 27), his *Seated Nude* (1908; The State Hermitage Museum, Saint Petersburg) in Monrad, *Henri Matisse: Four Great Collectors*, no. 43.
3. See D'Alessandro and Elderfield, *Radical Invention,* pp. 93, 95 n. 4, fig. 6h.
4. See ibid., pp. 98–101, no. 8.
5. E-mail message to the author from Isabelle Duvernois, Associate Conservator at The Metropolitan Museum of Art, February 29, 2012.
6. There are no traces of blue pigment in the background of *Seated Nude*.
7. Stephanie D'Alessandro has suggested that the unfinished version might be a preliminary study for the finished work; see D'Alessandro and Elderfield, *Matisse: Radical Invention*, p. 95 n. 6. I myself proposed the opposite sequence; see Monrad, *Henri Matisse: Four Great Collectors*, no. 69. For a similar view, see Margaret Werth, "Nude with a White Scarf: A Thick and Full Material," in Dorthe Aagesen et al., *Matisse: Masterpieces at Statens Museum for Kunst* (Copenhagen, 2005), p. 147.
8. See Werth, "Nude with a White Scarf," pp. 147–50.
9. *Un grand peintre français: Henri Matisse* (n.p.: La Compagnie Générale Cinématographique, 1946), 16-mm, black-and-white film, 25 min.

CÉCILE DEBRAY
Inventing a Decorative Space

1. See Francisco Jarauta Marión et al., *Matisse and the Alhambra, 1910–2010*, exh. cat. (Madrid, 2010).
2. Letter from Shchukin to Matisse, November 14–27, 1910, in Albert Kostenevich and Natalia Semyonova, *Collecting Matisse* (Paris, 1993), pp. 167–68, letter XXIV.
3. If we are to believe the correspondence with Shchukin, the paintings were completed before the end of December; in a letter of December 23, 1910, Shchukin asked Matisse to send them to Russia and announced he was paying for them. See ibid., p. 169, letter XXVII.
4. Jarauta Marión et al., *Matisse and the Alhambra*, pp. 88, 90.
5. In 1903, while riding a bus in Paris, Matisse noticed a length of blue-and-white fabric in the window of a used clothing shop. The textile is commonly referred to in the Matisse literature as a "toile de Jouy." For more information, see Ann Dumas, "A Balance of Forces," in *Matisse, His Art and His Textiles: The Fabric of Dreams*, ed. Ann Dumas, exh. cat. (London, 2004), pp. 81–82.
6. Matisse foresaw the importance of the new textile in a letter to his wife: "In Madrid I bought a very pretty white cloth with blue designs, not in very good condition, but I will work with it a lot, I think." Letter to Amélie Matisse, December 11, 1910, Archives Matisse, Paris. It would appear in such later works as *The Pink Studio* and *Corner of the Artist's Studio* (figs. 3, 38). The toile de Jouy had been elaborated in several paintings, including *Harmony in Red (The Red Room)* (1908; The State Hermitage Museum, Saint Petersburg), *Still Life with a Blue Tablecloth* (1908–9; State Hermitage Museum), and *Portrait of Greta Moll* (1908; The National Gallery, London).
7. Matisse referred to his desire to capture all he had seen of the city in a letter to his friend Jean Biette, in which he remarked that "since I could not store up Seville in my head, I did two still lifes that I believe are interesting." Letter to Biette, January 9, 1911, Archives Matisse.
8. Rémi Labrusse, "'What Remains Belongs to God': Henri Matisse, Alois Riegl, and the Arts of Islam," in *Matisse, His Art and His Textiles*, p. 57
9. Pierre Schneider, "Figure et décoration," in *Le Maroc de Matisse*, exh. cat. (Paris, 1999), p. 170.
10. In addition to *Dance II* and *Music*, Matisse painted pendants such as *Calla Lilies* and *Calla Lilies, Irises, and Mimosas* (figs. 40, 41) for Shchukin and also gathered works together in triptychs (see Rebecca Rabinow and Isabelle Duvernois's essay "A Slight Shift in Perspective," in this volume).
11. Matisse's installation of these paintings attracted a great deal of notice, especially with respect to the harmony of the colors. A letter from Véra Chamchina to Boris Ternovets states, "Matisse . . . decided to hang his works in the beautiful pink eighteenth-century drawing room, which had previously provided such a lovely setting for Cézanne and Degas. . . . To be sure, certain still lifes, as objects—blue porcelain pieces and others in pink and green tones—are a very good match for the pink sofas; some paintings practically repeat the tones of the material." Quoted in Kostenevich and Semyonova, *Collecting Matisse*, p. 34.

REBECCA RABINOW AND ISABELLE DUVERNOIS
A Slight Shift in Perspective

1. Examples from 1909–10 include *Dance I* (The Museum of Modern Art, New York) and *Dance II* (The State Hermitage Museum, Saint Petersburg), both related to a commission from Shchukin. See also note 14 below.
2. Letter from Shchukin to Matisse, December 20, 1910, in Albert Kostenevich and Natalia Semyonova, *Collecting Matisse* (Paris, 1993), p. 169, letter XXVI.
3. Both visual examination and X-radiography reveal that Matisse made one significant change to this painting. He painted over the salmon-pink foreground color under the upper rail of the chair at the lower left with green in order to continue the green border along the bottom of *Dance I*.
4. See, for example, Alfred H. Barr Jr., *Matisse: His Art and His Public* (New York, 1951), pp. 156–57.
5. Both compositions were painted on a canvas commercially prepared with a white ground. The narrow vertical format does not correspond to any prestretched standard size available for purchase at the time. Over the years the recorded size of *Nasturtiums with the Painting "Dance" I* has varied slightly because, more than once, it was taken off its original stretcher, mounted on a new one, and restretched.
6. "Interview with Clara T. MacChesney, 1912," in Jack Flam, *Matisse on Art*, rev. ed. (Berkeley and Los Angeles, 1995), pp. 66, 67.
7. Infrared reflectography reveals no signs of pencil or charcoal drawing, grid, or registration marks under the paint layer.
8. Shchukin was particularly fond of these saturated tones. In a letter postmarked March 26, 1911, he wrote Matisse, "I like your light blue and green with dark pink tremendously." Kostenevich and Semyonova, *Collecting Matisse*, p. 170, letter XXIX.
9. John Elderfield has suggested that Matisse created false pentimenti around the figures, thus connecting the temporal movement of the figures to the painting process. See John Elderfield, "Construction by Means of Color," in Stephanie D'Alessandro and John Elderfield, *Matisse: Radical Invention 1913–1917*, exh. cat. (Chicago, 2010), p. 116.
10. We are indebted to Igor Borodin, Chief Conservator of the State Pushkin Museum of Fine Arts, for generously providing access to the infrared photography, the X-radiography, and various digital photographs of *Nasturtiums with the Painting "Dance" II*.
11. James Huneker, "Decade of the New Art Movement Shows Big Changes," *New York Times*, November 10, 1912, p. SM12.

12. Like Shchukin's commission of *Nasturtiums with the Painting "Dance,"* Kolker's commission resulted in two paintings. When the second, more heavily worked canvas was shipped to Kolker in November 1912, Matisse wrote Curt Glaser, "I think it will surprise you a little because it has much improved since your visit, I must say that I have worked on it a great deal." Matisse to Glaser, November 16, 1912, Archives Matisse. The first version of the painting is *Goldfish and Sculpture* (fig. 52); the second is *Interior with Goldfish* (The Barnes Foundation, Philadelphia).
13. "A pail of blue water in which swim gold fish is decorative." Huneker, "Decade of the New Art Movement," p. SM12. Also see letters to Matisse from Jean Puy (January 20, 1913) and André Rouveyre ("Friday" [1912]), Courtesy Wanda de Guébriant, Archives Matisse, Paris. Thanks to Mary Clare McKinley, who located the following mention: Léon Plée, "La vie artistique: Le futuro-cubisme et le Salon d'Automne," *Les Annales politiques et littéraires*, no. 1529 (October 13, 1912), pp. 320–21.
14. While Kolker's *Intérieur* was on display at the Salon d'Automne, the other version of the painting, *Goldfish and Sculpture* (fig. 52), was exhibited at the "Second Post-Impressionist Exhibition" at the Grafton Galleries, London. Flavia Frigeri, Assistant Curator, Tate Modern, kindly confirmed that an archival copy of the Grafton Galleries catalogue in the collection of the Tate is annotated with a watercolor sketch of the MoMA painting.
15. The Grafton Galleries exhibition was so popular that it was extended; however, a number of Matisse's pictures were removed at the original closing date so they could be shipped to New York in time for the opening of the Armory Show. Letter from Matisse to Walter Pach, December 6, 1912, Archives of American Art. Available in facsimile at: http://www.aaa.si.edu/collections/viewer/henri-matisse-tangiers-morocco-letter-to-walter-pac-new-york-ny-9964/ 26206. A photograph of the Armory Show installation in Chicago confirms that *Nasturtiums with the Painting "Dance" I* was included. See Samuel Sachs II, "Reconstructing the 'Whirlwind of 26th Street,'" *Artnews* 61, no. 10 (February 1963), p. 26.
16. While awaiting the arrival of *The Conversation* and *Nasturtiums with the Painting "Dance" II*, Shchukin installed *Corner of the Artist's Studio* at the right end of his wall, with *Harmony in Red (The Red Room)* (1908; The State Hermitage Museum, Saint Petersburg) in the center and a double hang of two unidentified canvases at the left. A photograph of this display appears in Kostenevich and Semyonova, *Collecting Matisse*, p. 32.
17. Ia[kov] Tugenkhol'd, "Frantsuzskoe sobranie S.I. Shchukina," *Apollon* 5 (January–February 1914), pp. 27–28. Translated by Margaret Samu.

CÉCILE DEBRAY
A Garden "Redone Three Times"

1. Pierre Schneider, "The Moroccan Hinge," in Jack Cowart et al., *Matisse in Morocco*, exh. cat. (Washington, D.C., 1990), pp. 17–56.
2. Matisse stayed in Tangier for almost seven months, arriving on January 30, 1912, and returning to Paris on April 14, then coming back on October 8, 1912, and remaining until mid-February 1913. See *Le Maroc de Matisse*, exh. cat. (Paris, 1999).
3. The group painted for Morosov consisted of *Zorah on the Terrace*, surrounded by two landscapes, *Landscape Viewed from a Window* and *The Casbah Gate* (all 1912–13; The State Pushkin Museum of Fine Arts, Moscow). Also exhibited were *The Standing Riffian*, framed by two full-length portraits, *Zorah Standing* (both 1912; The State Hermitage Museum, Saint Petersburg) and *Fatma the Mulatto Woman* (1912; private collection). See the photographs from the "Exposition Henri-Matisse: Tableaux du Maroc et sculpture," April 14–19, 1913, Paris, Galerie Bernheim-Jeune, repr. Cowart et al., *Matisse in Morocco*, pp. 8, 12, and 15, fig. 4.
4. Information about the genesis of these paintings can be found in Matisse's correspondence and interviews. See Claudine Grammont, "Matisse aux portes de l'Orient: Une chronique," in *Le Maroc de Matisse*, pp. 228–35.
5. Letter of March 1 to Henri Manguin, quoted in ibid., p. 228.
6. Interview with Pierre Courthion, 1941, quoted in ibid., p. 228.
7. Ibid.
8. For an X-radiograph revealing the underdrawing, see *Le Maroc de Matisse*, p. 261, fig. 140.
9. Technical examination of the work reveals that it was painted in two or three sessions. Ibid., p. 60.
10. Matisse in response to Barr's questionnaire and in conversation with John Rewald, in "Questionnaire V," August 1950, archives, The Museum of Modern Art, New York; Alfred H. Barr Jr., *Matisse: His Art and His Public* (New York, 1951), pp. 156, 540 n. 1.
11. See Rémi Labrusse, "L'épreuve de Tanger," in *Le Maroc de Matisse*, pp. 28–53. Two sketches for the canvas are known; see ibid., pp. 102 (fig. 41), 143, no. 27.
12. "I stood before the landscape with the idea of retouching my work. Everything appeared to me much smaller than I had seen it the first time, and I said to myself: 'Now then, what I believed was not on my canvas is really there and is not in the landscape!' Then I came back without having retouched my canvas." Interview with Pierre Courthion, 1941, quoted in Labrusse, "L'épreuve de Tanger," p. 42.
13. John Elderfield, "Matisse in Morocco: An Interpretive Guide," in Cowart et al., *Matisse in Morocco*, p. 214.
14. Quoted in Labrusse, "L'épreuve de Tanger," p. 40.
15. Quoted in Schneider, "Moroccan Hinge," p. 42.
16. Elderfield supports the first hypothesis, whereas Schneider prefers the second, which also seems more accurate to me, solely from an aesthetic standpoint. See Elderfield, "Matisse in Morocco," pp. 201–39.
17. Marcel Sembat, *Henri Matisse* (Paris, 1920), p. 10.

RÉMI LABRUSSE
Notre-Dame between Heaven and Earth

1. Marquet was responsible for Matisse's return in 1914 to 19, quai Saint-Michel. In 1891 Matisse had lived there briefly, in the attic; he resided there at length between 1894 and 1907 on the sixth floor (Hilary Spurling, *The Unknown Matisse: A Life of Henri Matisse; the Early Years, 1869–1908* [New York, 1998], pp. 102–4), looking out on a cityscape he had already painted many times (Jeanne Siegel, "Henri Matisse's *View of Notre-Dame*, Spring 1914," *Arts Magazine* 54, no. 5 [January 1980], pp. 158–61). In late 1907, he left the apartment to Marquet (Spurling, *Unknown Matisse*, pp. 423–24). After paying his friend a visit on December 25, 1913, Matisse decided to return to the same address. He moved to the fifth floor one week later (Hilary Spurling, *Matisse, the Master: A Life of Henri Matisse; the Conquest of Colour, 1909–1954* [New York, 2005], p. 161).
2. Dora Vallier, "Matisse et la Russie en 1911: Influences textuelles et influences contextuelles," in *Matisse aujourd'hui* (Nice, 1992), p. 67.
3. Albert Gleizes and Jean Metzinger, *Du "cubisme"* (Paris, 1912), p. 11.
4. The schematic version (cat. 25) was most likely not exhibited before 1964, when it was shown at the Baltimore Museum of Art. Wanda de Guébriant of the Archives Matisse, Paris, pointed out to the organizers of the 2010 "Radical Invention" exhibition that the signature on that work had been stamped on the canvas after Matisse's death, a fact later confirmed by conservators. John Elderfield concluded, but too late for it to be acknowledged in the catalogue, that the artist considered the painting unfinished and probably did not exhibit it in his lifetime (personal communication from Elderfield to Christel Hollevoet-Force). However, it seems that in Matisse's opinion and that of his friends, it nonetheless superseded the realist version. Marcel Sembat, writing in his journal on February 17, 1914, considered the blue version "the more beautiful of the two, the more ingenious, the one in which Matisse is the more personal," but stated that, if he were to exhibit it, "no one would understand immediately" (Marcel Sembat, *Les Cahiers noirs* 5 [February 17, 1914]); see Stephanie D'Alessandro and John

Elderfield, *Matisse: Radical Invention 1913–1917*, exh. cat. (Chicago, 2010), pp. 193, 195; Dominique Fourcade and Isabelle Monod-Fontaine, eds., *Henri Matisse, 1904–1917*, exh. cat. (Paris, 1993), p. 498. Matthew Stewart Prichard announced to his friend Isabella Stewart Gardner in March 1914 that the later canvas truly looked like "a classical work, in the sense that it typifies a new formula" (Jack Flam, *Matisse: The Man and His Art, 1869–1918* [Ithaca, N.Y., and London, 1986], p. 380; Fourcade and Monod-Fontaine, *Henri Matisse*, p. 113).

5. For "neo-Platonic academies," see Georges Duthuit, *Les Fauves* (Geneva, 1949), p. 3. Between 1908 and 1911, Matisse expressed to the students of his "academy" his own obsession with the internal logic of forms, so much so that the schematic view of Notre-Dame seems designed to illustrate one or another of his lessons, collected in 1908 by Sarah Stein: "It was in the decadent periods of art that the artist's chief interest lay in developing the small forms and details. In all great periods the essentials of form, the big masses and their relations, occupied him above all other considerations" ("Sarah Stein's Notes, 1908," in Jack Flam, *Matisse on Art*, rev. ed. [Berkeley and Los Angeles, 1995], p. 47).
6. D'Alessandro and Elderfield, *Matisse: Radical Invention*, p. 195.
7. Obviously, that élan is not an illustration of Bergson's philosophy. Marguerite Matisse recalled that in 1914 her father had been "shocked" to learn that "Metzinger was working on a painting based on a page from Bergson" (handwritten note, Archives Matisse, Paris). Nonetheless, there are connections between the art and thinking of Matisse and the philosopher; for a general discussion of this question, see D'Alessandro and Elderfield, *Matisse: Radical Invention*, pp. 110–11.
8. Charles Palermo, "A Project for Wholeness," in *Picasso and Braque: The Cubist Experiment, 1910–1912*, exh. cat. (Santa Barbara, 2011), pp. 15–37.

JACK FLAM
Time Embodied

1. Letter from Matisse to Bussy, Monday, January 26, 1914. Matisse and the painter Simon Bussy met as students and remained lifelong friends. A copy of Bussy's correspondence with Matisse was kindly given to me by Lawrence Gowing, who also gave a copy to the Center for Advanced Study in the Visual Arts, National Gallery of Art, Washington, D.C.
2. This type of jar was used in chemical laboratories, and Matisse had obtained his from a supplier of scientific equipment. Since Matisse had contemplated returning to Morocco during the spring of 1914, his reprise of the goldfish motif may have been a way of evoking the place that had inspired his first paintings of goldfish, which appear in *Zorah on the Terrace* and most notably in *Goldfish* (both 1912; The State Pushkin Museum of Fine Arts, Moscow) and the three pictures of the Goldfish and Sculpture theme painted during the summer of 1912 (cat. 30), shortly after he returned from his first trip to Morocco. For details, see Jack Flam, "Goldfish," in Dorthe Aagesen et al., *Matisse: Masterpieces at Statens Museum for Kunst* (Copenhagen, 2005), pp. 160–83.
3. That Matisse intended from the start to include a depiction of himself is clear from his words on the postcard: "I made a painting—it's my painting of *Goldfish*, which I'm redoing with a figure who has the palette in his hand and who is observing (red-brown harmony)." Matisse to Camoin, October 1914, as cited in Claudine Grammont, ed., *Correspondance entre Charles Camoin et Henri Matisse* (Lausanne, 1997), p. 67.
4. See, for example, Grammont (in ibid.), who writes, "In the final version, the self-portrait has practically disappeared; only the finger slipped into the palette can be discerned." See also Kirk Varnedoe, in Elizabeth Cowling et al., *Matisse, Picasso*, exh. cat. (Paris, 2002), p. 135, who is doubtful about the presence of the head and legs.
5. When *Goldfish and Palette* was purchased from Matisse by the Galerie Bernheim-Jeune on May 25, 1915, the title was given as "Poissons rouges, harmonie en bleu, noir et blanc." (When it was reproduced in *Cahiers d'art* in 1931, it was titled "Poissons Rouges et Personnage." Roger Fry, "Henri-Matisse," *Cahiers d'art* 6 [1931], p. 285, fig. 53.) The unusual mixture of abstraction and figuration in this painting has generally made people uncomfortable, and to this day most who write about it resist fully acknowledging the presence of the figure, preferring instead to make exaggerated claims about the abstract character of the image or to consider that area of the painting as part of a somewhat imperfect formal ensemble, what Alfred Barr called "the rather unresolved upper right-hand corner." See Alfred H. Barr Jr., *Matisse: His Art and His Public* (New York, 1951), p. 168.
6. One of the first paintings Matisse did after the outbreak of World War I, this work may well reflect the atmosphere in Paris during that trying time. But even more, it expresses Matisse's own troubled state of mind as well as his ambivalent feelings about the direction that his work was taking and about his entire relationship to the world around him. See, for example, the letter he wrote to Camoin the following year, at two o'clock in the morning, in which he voices his disquiet and his reevaluation of his artistic accomplishments as compared with those of Delacroix, Seurat, and Cézanne. Grammont, *Correspondance entre Camoin et Matisse*, pp. 77–80.
7. It should also be noted that goldfish have been associated with Matisse himself. The artist's friend Jean Puy memorably likened him to "a brave goldfish rejoicing intensely in the iridescence of the colors and shapes through the distorting globe of its bowl, and which, if it could paint, would show them without concern for what they represent materially: nude women, landscapes, still lifes, devoid of their substance and their real meanings and no longer anything but cheerful phantoms for its wonderstruck eye." Jean Puy, "Souvenirs," in "Matisse," *Le Point*, no. 21 (July 1939), p. 24; my translation.

ISABELLE MONOD-FONTAINE
Black Ribbon and Blue Stripes

1. At the age of six, Marguerite underwent a tracheotomy after a bout of diphtheria. Subsequent operations, cauterizations, and painful treatments obliged her to always wear a dark choker or ribbon concealing the raw scar on her throat.
2. Guy-Patrice Dauberville and Michel Dauberville, *Matisse: Henri Matisse chez Bernheim-Jeune* (Paris, 1995), no. 143 (BJ 20280).
3. Ibid., no. 150 (BJ 20468), purchased on May 21, 1915, for 1,071 francs.
4. John Elderfield, *Henri Matisse: A Retrospective*, exh. cat. (New York, 1992), p. 241.
5. Set on the floor in the same photograph are several other major canvases (portraits of Michael and Sarah Stein, Greta Prozor, and the "Italian Woman"), in various stages of completion.
6. *Marguerite in a Striped Jacket* (initially called *Young Woman in Boater Hat*), no. BJ 20466, purchased on May 21, 1915, for 1,704 francs; *White and Pink Head*, no. BJ 20513, purchased on December 20, 1915, for 885 francs. Dauberville and Dauberville, *Matisse chez Bernheim-Jeune*, nos. 149 and 151, respectively.
7. Alfred Barr did not like this canvas, which he called "the earliest and least successful of Matisse's cubistic experiments." Alfred H. Barr Jr., *Matisse: His Art and His Public* (New York, 1951), p. 188; see also pp. 181 and 194; and Isabelle Monod-Fontaine, *Matisse: Oeuvres de Henri Matisse, 1869–1954* (Paris, 1979), pp. 38–41.
8. Pierre Schneider claimed that work on *White and Pink Head* was begun even before the declaration of World War I in July 1914; see Pierre Schneider, *Matisse: Exposition du centenaire*, exh. cat. (Paris, 1970), p. 81.
9. For example, the 1916 and 1917 portraits of Auguste Pellerin or the strange pair comprising the austere, admirable *Piano Lesson* (completed in autumn 1916; fig. 5) and the more easygoing, "lifelike" *Music Lesson* (summer 1917; fig. 6).
10. Sinister in every respect for Matisse: the persistent war, the deadly battles, nearly all his companions gone, his family trapped in the Nord on

the German side, and finally, major financial difficulties; see Hilary Spurling, *Matisse, the Master: A Life of Henri Matisse; the Conquest of Colour, 1909–1954* (New York, 2005), pp. 161–72.

11. Jack Flam, *Matisse: The Man and His Art, 1869–1918* (Ithaca, N.Y., and London, 1986), p. 403. Flam interviewed Marguerite Duthuit on November 26, 1979.
12. An X-radiograph of *White and Pink Head*, published in 1979 (see Monod-Fontaine, *Matisse: Oeuvres*, p. 40), for the first time revealed these elements, which Matisse had painted over. The recent catalogue by Stephanie D'Alessandro and John Elderfield, *Matisse: Radical Invention 1913–1917*, exh. cat. (Chicago, 2010), pursues and broadens the scientific inquiry (see pp. 236–39).
13. Two blurry photographs in the Archives Matisse, Paris, contemporary with the portrait series of 1914–15, show a playful Marguerite posing in pajamas with broad stripes and a turned-up collar, as in *White and Pink Head*, her black ribbon and pendant presenting a marked contrast to that masculine attire. This is undoubtedly mere coincidence, just odd enough to catch the eye.
14. "Léonce Rosenberg tells me of a portrait of your daughter, for which he asked you the price," wrote Félix Fénéon on November 17, 1915. Then, on November 25: "After seeing the recent portrait at your home, M. Léonce Rosenberg wrote me that he withdraws his offer, though he also declared that 'it's a very beautiful thing.'" Fénéon to Matisse, both Archives Matisse.
15. Fénéon wrote Matisse on December 27, 1915 (Archives Matisse), "Dear Sir, disregard what I told you on the phone today about the sale to M. Alphonse Kann of the picture (*White and Pink Head,* no. 20513) that we purchased from you on December 21 for 885 francs, plus the right to a quarter of the profits. The buyer changed his mind, the transaction is thus canceled, and he will bring back the picture tomorrow. It is therefore at the shop that you will sign it. We are waiting for that to be done before we give it to the photographer." He added as a postscript, "Again, all my compliments for this admirable work."
16. On March 30, 1917, Fénéon made note of the purchase in progress. On April 25, however, he wrote to Matisse: "Marchese Viteleschi telegraphed us yesterday from Italy: 'Marchesa Casati has made you an offer of 2000 for the pink and white Matisse. She counts on your accepting.' We replied with this dispatch: '2000 offer unacceptable. Regrets. Matisse *White and Pink Head* is 4000 very moderate price.'" Archives Matisse.
17. Fénéon wrote, "If you were to agree to exchange, for different paintings, *White and Pink Head,* 75 x 46, no. 20513, and the *Lemons* in the 'Tapis' catalogue, 70 x 54, no. 20516, we would readily return them to you, having the sense that, with the help of your authority, you would make a better profit than we could on these two excellent but difficult pictures." Letter from Fénéon to Matisse, Archives Matisse. The receipt is dated March 25, 1919.
18. *White and Pink Head* was purchased from Jean Matisse by the Centre Pompidou, Musée National d'Art Moderne, in 1976; *Marguerite in a Leather Hat,* bequeathed by his widow, Marie Matisse, went to the Musée Matisse, Le Cateau-Cambrésis, in 2002.

CÉCILE DEBRAY

Supernatural Interiors

1. "Interview with Guillaume Apollinaire, 1907," trans. Jack Flam, *Matisse on Art*, rev. ed. (Berkeley and Los Angeles, 1995), p. 28.
2. *The Ivy Branch*, 1916; Kunsthaus Zürich. "Another event . . . a canvas representing a Spanish water jug in glass, in which I immersed a branch of ivy, [was purchased] by Alphonse Kann. It is a painting subject that I like a great deal. . . . I have an ivy branch that is contorting itself in a harmonious fashion." Letter from Matisse to Léonce Rosenberg of June 1, 1916 (Bibliothèque Kandinsky, Centre Pompidou, Musée National d'Art Moderne, Paris), quoted in *Henri Matisse, 1904–1917*, exh. cat. (Paris, 1993), p. 506.
3. *Still Life with Tin Pot* (1910; The State Hermitage Museum, Saint Petersburg), *Goldfish and Sculpture* (fig. 52), *The Music Lesson* (fig. 6), and *The Three-o-Clock Sitting* (1924; private collection) are among the others in the series.
4. Matisse was probably familiar with this work, which at the time belonged to his dealer, Bernheim-Jeune.
5. Joachim Gasquet, "What He Told Me," excerpted from *Cézanne* (Paris, 1921), trans. *Conversations with Cézanne*, ed. Michael Doran (Berkeley, 2001), pp. 157–58.
6. Rémi Labrusse, *Matisse: La condition de l'image* (Paris, 1999), p. 230.
7. Letter from Matisse to Aragon, March 1942, in Louis Aragon, *Henri Matisse, a Novel*, trans. Jean Stewart (New York, 1972), vol. 1, p. 235. See also Dominique Fourcade, ed., *Henri Matisse: Écrits et propos sur l'art* (Paris, 1972), p. 162.
8. Axel Salto, "Henri Matisse," *Klingen* 1, no. 7 (April 1918), n.p., quoted in Stephanie D'Alessandro, "The Challenge of Painting," in Stephanie D'Alessandro and John Elderfield, *Matisse: Radical Invention 1913–1917*, exh. cat. (Chicago, 2010), p. 264. Among the other possibilities are *Still Life with a Plaster Bust* (1916; The Barnes Foundation, Philadelphia) and even the large panel *Bathers by a River* (fig. 56).
9. Theodore Reff, "Matisse: Meditations on a Statuette and Goldfish," *Arts Magazine* 51, no. 3 (November 1976), pp. 109–15.

STEPHANIE D'ALESSANDRO

Surface and Depth

1. Bernheim-Jeune's photographs also follow this order: "Nature morte aux pommes sur fond vert" was assigned no. 1531 and "Nature morte aux pommes sur fond noir et jaune," no. 1532. See Guy-Patrice Dauberville and Michel Dauberville, *Matisse: Henri Matisse chez Bernheim-Jeune* (Paris, 1995), nos. 159, 160.
2. By 1919, for its New York debut, "Nature morte aux pommes sur fond noir et jaune" had already changed to "Apples." For more information on the 1913–17 period, see Stephanie D'Alessandro and John Elderfield, *Matisse: Radical Invention 1913–1917*, exh. cat. (Chicago, 2010).
3. There are, for example, no references to the paintings in Alfred Barr's questionnaires to Matisse or in Pierre Courthion's interviews with him. While the artist occasionally used numbers to record the order of his experimentation with a theme, Barr is the source of many of the numbered pairs known today; see Alfred H. Barr Jr., *Matisse: His Art and His Public* (New York, 1951). In the case of the present paintings, Barr did not number them, but wrote that *Bowl of Apples on a Table* was the second of the pair (ibid., pp. 189–90).
4. Axel Salto, "Henri Matisse," *Klingen* 1, no. 7 (April 1918), n.p.
5. Letter from Matisse to Rosenberg, June 1, 1916, Bibliothèque Kandinsky, Centre Pompidou, Musée National d'Art Moderne, Paris.
6. Letters from Fénéon to Matisse, July 26, 1916, and Huyot to Matisse, undated (probably late July), Archives Matisse, Paris. Thanks to Wanda de Guébriant for sharing these materials with the author.
7. Matisse in response to Barr's questionnaire and in conversation with Mrs. Bertha Slattery Lieberman, in "Questionnaire I," 1945, archives, Museum of Modern Art, New York.
8. D'Alessandro and Elderfield, *Matisse: Radical Invention*, pp. 290–99, 304–9, 347–49.
9. Ragnar Hoppe, "På visit hos Matisse" (1919), in *Städer och konstnärer* (Stockholm, 1931), trans. D'Alessandro and Elderfield, *Matisse: Radical Invention*, p. 350. For the full interview, trans. Desirée Koslin, see Jack Flam, *Matisse on Art*, rev. ed. (Berkeley and Los Angeles, 1995), pp. 73–77.

HILARY SPURLING

Laurette: Line and Color

1. She was recommended to Matisse by a fellow artist at a time when models were as scarce as all other necessities in wartime Paris. For an authoritative assessment of her importance, see Jack Flam, *Matisse in Transition: Around Laurette*, exh. cat. (West Palm Beach, 2006).
2. Her only known predecessors, Rosa Arpino in 1907 and Loulou Brouty in 1909, posed comparatively

briefly and intermittently; see respectively Hilary Spurling, *The Unknown Matisse: A Life of Henri Matisse; the Early Years, 1869–1908* (New York, 1998), pp. 362–63, and Hilary Spurling, *Matisse the Master: A Life of Henri Matisse; the Conquest of Colour, 1909–1954* (New York, 2005), pp. 27–30.

3. My information about the models from the Ciociaria comes from Michele Santulli, *Modelle e modelli Ciociari nell'arte Europea a Roma, Parigi, Londra nel 1800–1900* (Arpino, 2011). Santulli tentatively identifies Laurette as Loreta Arpino, the older sister of Matisse's earlier model Rosa (Loreta Arpino's husband was away, and Rosa's was killed at the front in 1915), a hypothesis with strong evidence both for and against it. Whether or not her name was Arpino, Matisse's Laurette was clearly someone very similar from the same background. See Hilary Spurling, "Matisse's Italian Models," in Ann Dumas, *Matisse and the Model*, exh. cat. (New York, 2011), pp. 70–74.

DORTHE AAGESEN

Painting the Light

1. This arrival date is given in Matisse's letter to André Rouveyre, December 23, 1917 (Hanne Finsen, ed., *Matisse, Rouveyre Correspondance* [Paris, 2001], p. 29). Most sources state that Matisse stayed at the hotel until February or March and then went on to rent an apartment next door. However, letters to his wife, Amélie, reveal that their children Marguerite and Pierre arrived in Nice on April 7 and helped their father move on that occasion. See Hilary Spurling, *Matisse, the Master: A Life of Henri Matisse; the Conquest of Colour, 1909–1954* (New York, 2005), p. 209.
2. For the most comprehensive treatment of Matisse's art in the period immediately preceding his relocation to Nice, see Stephanie D'Alessandro and John Elderfield, *Matisse: Radical Invention 1913–1917*, exh. cat. (Chicago, 2010).
3. Letter from Matisse to Amélie, December 31, 1917, Archives Matisse, Paris. I wish to thank Wanda de Guébriant for making available this passage and other documentation concerning the three early interiors from Nice.
4. Sources disagree on which of the two versions was painted first. However, Matisse's description of the canvas format ("15," or 65 x 54 cm) in his letter to his wife helps establish that the smaller canvas must have been the first. X-radiographs and infrared photography of the second version indicate that the motif had largely been settled, for only a few changes to the compositional sketch and layers of paint are apparent. I wish to thank Suzanne Penn, Conservator of Paintings at the Philadelphia Museum of Art, for sharing her observations and documentation.
5. Letter from Matisse to Amélie, March 18, 1918, Archives Matisse.
6. Writing to her father in 1943, Marguerite refers to *Interior with a Violin* as she saw it in its first state during a visit to Nice. Spurling's assessment (*Matisse, the Master*, p. 207) is that Marguerite is referring to her own and Amélie's arrival in Nice in February 1918. In a letter to his wife dated April 8, 1918, Matisse related how the children had praised the way in which the painting had grown: "The children found I had worked hard and that my interior was really good, that's what I think" (Archives Matisse). From this it follows that the most likely scenario is that Marguerite saw the painting twice: first, in its early stage in February, and subsequently in April around the time of its completion.
7. X-radiographs also show that the position of the chair and table was originally much closer to that in the first version. The violin was incorporated at this stage—first as a closed violin case stretching all the way to the left-hand edge, then lying in an open case and painted on a smaller scale. I wish to thank Conservator Troels Filtenborg from the Statens Museum for Kunst, Copenhagen, for his analysis of the underlying layers revealed in the X-radiograph.
8. Quoted in Erik Zahle, *Fransk maleri efter 1900* (Copenhagen, 1938), p. 10. See also Kasper Monrad, *Henri Matisse: Four Great Collectors*, exh. cat. (Copenhagen, 1999), pp. 300–301, and Isabelle Monod-Fontaine, "A Question of Windows," in Dorthe Aagesen et al., *Matisse: Masterpieces at Statens Museum for Kunst* (Copenhagen, 2005), p. 200.
9. Letter from Matisse to Charles Camoin, May 23, 1918, trans. Jack Flam, *Matisse on Art*, rev. ed. (Berkeley and Los Angeles, 1995), p. 288 n. 4; see also Dominique Fourcade, ed., *Henri Matisse: Écrits et propos sur l'art* (Paris, 1972), p. 109.
10. Matisse radio interviews, 1942, second broadcast, trans. Flam, *Matisse on Art*, p. 147.
11. Yve-Alain Bois, "On Matisse: The Blinding," *October 68* (Spring 1994), pp. 84–85.
12. Georges Besson, "Arrivée de Matisse à Nice," in "Matisse," special issue of *Le Point* (Colmar), no. 21 (July 1939), pp. 41–42.
13. Interview with Pierre Courthion in "Autres propos de Matisse," ed. Dominique Fourcade, *Macula* 1 (1976), p. 102, trans. Bois, "On Matisse: The Blinding," p. 70.
14. See Jack Flam, *Matisse: The Man and His Art, 1869–1918* (Ithaca, N.Y., and London, 1986), p. 473.
15. Preface to *Den Franske utstilling*, exh. cat. (Oslo, 1918), p. 12.
16. See note 13 above.
17. Ragnar Hoppe, "På visit hos Matisse" (1919), in *Städer och konstnärer* (Stockholm, 1931), trans. Desirée Koslin in Flam, *Matisse on Art*, p. 75.
18. André Verdet, *Entretiens, notes et écrits sur la peinture: Braque, Léger, Matisse, Picasso* (Paris, 1978), p. 124; trans. D'Alessandro and Elderfield, *Matisse: Radical Invention*, p. 310.
19. Francis Carco, *L'ami des peintres* (Paris, 1953), pp. 262–63, trans. Jack Cowart, "The Place of Silvered Light: An Expanded, Illustrated Chronology of Matisse in the South of France, 1916–1932," in Jack Cowart and Dominique Fourcade, *Henri Matisse: The Early Years in Nice, 1916–1930*, exh. cat. (Washington, D.C., 1986), p. 24.
20. Dominique Fourcade has observed that "in the end, all of Matisse's research during these first years in Nice arrives at a new unity of the surface: human beings and objects are not treated differently than floors or walls on the painting's surface. Matisse progressively abolishes all pictorial distinction between the apparent subject of his paintings (a woman reading, or a bouquet of anemones) and the background of these same paintings." Fourcade, "An Uninterrupted Story," in Cowart and Fourcade, *Henri Matisse: Early Years in Nice*, p. 55.
21. Verdet, *Entretiens*, p. 125.
22. Pierre Schneider draws a more radical conclusion concerning Matisse's paintings from the early period in Nice: "It was no longer a question of skillfully combining realism with abstraction, but of getting abstraction to simulate realism. . . . The two registers on which the forms in Matisse's work of the twenties play are not, therefore, of equal importance. It is only at first glance—when the spectator's conservative vision falls for the feint—that the painting is seen as three-dimensional. Almost immediately, the decorative image filters in and begins to swallow the realistic representation. Soon all that remains of the representation is a veil stretched over the construction of the picture" (Pierre Schneider, *Matisse* [New York, 1984], p. 508).

REBECCA RABINOW

The Beach at Étretat

1. For more information, see Hilary Spurling, *Matisse, the Master: A Life of Henri Matisse; the Conquest of Color, 1909–1954* (New York, 2005), pp. 227–28, 236.
2. Postcard from Matisse to Amélie, June 17, 1920, Archives Matisse, Paris. Courtesy of Wanda de Guébriant, who also notes that there is no evidence in Matisse's correspondence that he returned to Étretat in 1921, as has sometimes been suggested.
3. Spurling, *Matisse the Master*, p. 236.
4. Letter from Matisse to Amélie, September 11, 1920, Archives Matisse, courtesy of Wanda de Guébriant.
5. Robert L. Herbert, *Monet on the Normandy Coast: Tourism and Painting, 1867–1886* (New Haven, 1994), p. 71.

6. The work, acquired in partnership with Durand-Ruel, was *The Rock Needle Seen through the Porte d'Aval*, ca. 1886; oil on canvas, 28¾ x 36¼ in. (73 x 92 cm); private collection. See Daniel Wildenstein, *Monet: Catalogue raisonné*, vol. 3 (Cologne, 1996), pp. 397–98, no. 1050.
7. Augustin de Butler, "Matisse aux Collettes," in *Renoir et les familiers des Collettes*, exh. cat. (Cagnes-sur-Mer, 2008), p. 114.
8. Renoir's paintings of fish are reproduced in *L'atelier de Renoir*, vol. 2, introduction by Marc Elder (Paris, 1931), pls. 161, 178, 189, 197, 199, 217, figs. 512–15, 561, 562, 604, 605, 630, 638, 686.
9. My thanks to Metropolitan Museum paintings conservator Isabelle Duvernois for examining the painting with infrared reflectography.
10. "Exposition Henri-Matisse," MM. Bernheim-Jeune & Cie, Paris, October 15–November 6, 1920.
11. The provenance information in Guy-Patrice Dauberville and Michel Dauberville, *Matisse: Henri Matisse chez Bernheim-Jeune* (Paris, 1995), vol. 2, p. 898, no. 407, is contradicted by the more complete entry for Quinn's acquisition of the painting in John Quinn Papers, 1901–1926, Ledger, vol. 2, p. 34, Manuscripts and Archives Division, The New York Public Library.
12. James W. Barney, letter to the editor, Hamilton Easter Field, dated September 19, 1921, *The Arts* 2 (October 1921), p. 60.

CÉCILE DEBRAY
Anemonism: "A Dreamy Treatment of Color"

1. Remarks reported by Ragnar Hoppe, "På visit hos Matisse" (1919), in *Städer och konstnärer* (Stockholm, 1931), trans. Desirée Koslin in Jack Flam, *Matisse on Art*, rev. ed. (Berkeley and Los Angeles, 1995), pp. 75–76.
2. Pierre Schneider, *Matisse* (Paris, 1984), p. 508.
3. Hans R. Hahnloser, "En visite chez Henri Matisse," in *Henri Matisse: Gravures et lithographies de 1900 à 1929*, ed. Margrit Hahnloser-Ingold, exh. cat. (Pully, Switzerland, 1970), pp. 8–9.
4. Interview with A. Verdet, quoted in Schneider, *Matisse*, p. 506.
5. Schneider, *Matisse*, p. 513.
6. On this question, see Cécile Debray, "Fleurs et capucines," in *Odilon Redon. Prince du rêve, 1840–1916*, exh. cat. (Paris, 2011), pp. 268–350.
7. Speaking of his paintings of the Étretat cliffs, Matisse recalled an interior dialogue not only with Courbet and Monet but also with Manet. See Louis Aragon, *Henri Matisse, a Novel*, trans. Jean Stewart (Paris, 1972), vol. 1, p. 95.
8. Pierre Schneider, *Matisse* (New York, 1984), p. 508.
9. Dominique Fourcade, "An Interrupted Story," in Jack Cowart and Dominique Fourcade, *Henri Matisse: The Early Years in Nice, 1916–1930*, exh. cat. (Washington, D.C., 1986), p. 52.

ISABELLE MONOD-FONTAINE
Variations on the Odalisque

1. "I do odalisques in order to do nudes," Matisse explained in his "Statement to Tériade: On Fauvism and Color, 1929," trans. Jack Flam, *Matisse on Art*, rev. ed. (Berkeley and Los Angeles, 1995), p. 86.
2. The term "odalisque" (from the Turkish *odalik*) derives from *oda* (Turkish for "bedroom") and refers to "what belongs in the bedroom." The meaning of the word was extended to refer to a female slave engaged in domestic service.
3. In addition to catalogue numbers 49 and 50, these are *Odalisque with Green Sash* (1926; The Baltimore Museum of Art); *Reclining Odalisque, Green Harem Pants, Blue Sash* (1927; Henry Ford II Collection); and *Reclining Nude Seen from the Back* (1927; private collection).
4. The other paintings in this group are *Odalisque with a Turkish Chair* (1927–28; Musée d'Art Moderne de la Ville de Paris) and *Seated Odalisque, Left Knee Bent* (1928; The Baltimore Museum of Art).

JACK FLAM
The Eternal Feminine

1. Henri Matisse, "Notes d'un peintre," *La Grande Revue* 2, 24 (December 25, 1908), pp. 731–45, trans. Jack Flam, *Matisse on Art*, rev. ed. (Berkeley and Los Angeles, 1995), p. 39.
2. Lydia Delectorskaya, Matisse's muse and companion until the end of his life, kept notebooks and photographic albums of the artist's work at this time that contained photographs of finished works and of works in progress. It is from her that we know the precise dates and names of the models of the four paintings under discussion. See Lydia Delectorskaya, *With Apparent Ease . . . Henri Matisse: Paintings from 1935–1939* (Paris, 1988), pp. 201–4.
3. In 1936 Matisse spoke of the motivation that underlay his recent change of style. "When the means have become so refined, so attenuated that their power of expression wears thin," he told Tériade, "it is necessary to return to the essential principles that made human language. These are, after all, the principles that 'go back,' that restore life, that give us life. Pictures . . . call for beautiful blues, beautiful reds, beautiful yellows—materials to stir the sensual depths in men. This is the starting point of Fauvism: the courage to return to the purity of the means." E. Tériade, "Constance du fauvisme," *Minotaure* 2, no. 9 (October 15, 1936), p. 3, trans. Flam, *Matisse on Art*, pp. 122–23.
4. As Matisse would tell Louis Aragon only a few years later, the rendering of details such as hands, and especially faces, could undermine the sweep and grandeur of a composition. According to him, Delacroix painted hands in such a generalized way because "he had to finish off, at a certain place, the movement, the line, the curve, the arabesque that ran through his picture. . . . The painter who composes on the grand scale, carried away by the movement of his picture, cannot stop over details, paint each detail *as if it were a portrait*." Louis Aragon, "Matisse-en-France," in Henri Matisse, *Dessins: Thèmes et variations* (Paris, 1943); repr. Louis Aragon, *Henri Matisse, roman* (Paris, 1971), vol. 1, p. 111. As translated in Flam, *Matisse on Art*, p. 150.
5. Matisse, note to Aragon, ca. 1942; in Aragon, *Matisse, roman*, vol. 1, p. 208.

REBECCA RABINOW
The Woman in Blue

1. Wanda de Guébriant in Dominique Szymusiak et al., *Lydia D.: Lydia Delectorskaya, muse et modèle de Matisse*, exh. cat. (Paris, 2010), p. 204. See also Lydia Delectorskaya, *With Apparent Ease . . . Henri Matisse: Paintings from 1935–1939* (Paris, 1988), p. 23. According to de Guébriant, Matisse lost touch with Matossian during World War II.
2. This painting was usually cited by Matisse in his diary as *The Large Blue Dress*, although on two occasions (February 25 and March 10) he added the word "mimosas" to the title. Information courtesy Archives Matisse, Paris.
3. Matisse's diary for the year notes certain days that he worked on the painting (February 21, 25, 26, March 3, 5, 10, 11, 12, 16, 17, 20, 22, 23, 25, and April 2). He evidently did so on other days as well. These sessions do not specifically conform to Matossian's known visits (February 26, March 3, 12, 13, 22, 23, 24, 25, and April 2, 3). Information courtesy Archives Matisse.
4. For an excellent chronology of Lydia's years with Matisse, see Wanda de Guébriant in Szymusiak et al., *Lydia D.*, pp. 202–13.
5. Two charcoal drawings dated January 1936 are reproduced in Delectorskaya, *With Apparent Ease*, pp. 90–91. These drawings of Lydia seated in a hard-backed armchair relate to a painting of the same year, *The Blue Blouse* (Kunstmuseum, Bern).
6. Matisse's diary entry for February 21, 1937, reads: "dessiné sur toile 30F[igure] robe bleu." Information courtesy Wanda de Guébriant, Archives Matisse.
7. The prominent position of Lydia's hand has led art historians to compare *The Large Blue Dress* to Ingres's portrait of *Madame Moitessier* (1856; The National Gallery, London); see, for example, Nicholas Watkins, *Matisse* (Oxford, 1984), p. 183.
8. For more information on this room, see Jack Cowart's chronology, "The Place of Silvered

Light," in Jack Cowart and Dominique Fourcade, *Henri Matisse, The Early Years in Nice, 1916–1930*, exh. cat. (Washington, D.C., 1986), pp. 36–37.

9. A number of ink drawings dated 1937 show Lydia holding a necklace while modeling the blue dress; for reproductions, see Christie's, New York, May 9, 2000, no. 360, and Sotheby's, London, June 20, 2005, no. 29. While some Matisse scholars refer to the necklace as a rosary, the composition also recalls Italian Renaissance portraits that depict a woman posing in a long gown while clutching the end of her jeweled girdle (or belt). An example is Veronese's sixteenth-century *Portrait of a Woman* (Musée de la Chartreuse, Douai), which Matisse saw when he visited the "Exposition de l'art italien de Cimabue à Tiepolo" at the Petit Palais, Paris, in June 1935.
10. When the Philadelphia collector Henry P. McIlhenny asked Matisse to recommend a figure painting available for purchase, the artist noted that *The Large Blue Dress* was his most important of the year. Joseph J. Rishel, *The Henry P. McIlhenny Collection: An Illustrated History* (Philadelphia, 1987), p. 68.
11. The photographs of *The Large Blue Dress* clearly show areas of paint that were wiped off during the course of its creation. Lydia served as his studio assistant once her modeling session had concluded for the day; see de Guébriant in Szymusiak et al., *Lydia D.*, p. 204. For Lydia's description of how Matisse used Matossian's photographs, see Delectorskaya, *With Apparent Ease*, pp. 23–24.
12. For information on the many photographed states of drawings and paintings that Matisse sent Etta Cone in the mid-1930s, see Brenda Richardson, *Dr. Claribel & Miss Etta: The Cone Collection of the Baltimore Museum of Art* (Baltimore, 1985), pp. 121–40.
13. "Evolution of a Painting," *Magazine of Art* 32, no. 7 (July 1939), p. 415.

DOÏNA LEMNY

The Metaphysics of Decoration

1. Letter from Matisse to his daughter, Marguerite Duthuit, dated November 29, 1943 (Archives Matisse, Paris).
2. Dominique Fourcade, ed., *Henri Matisse: Écrits et propos sur l'art* (Paris, 1972), p. 308, n. 31.
3. Lydia Delectorskaya, *Henri Matisse: Contre vents et marées; peinture et livres illustrés de 1939 à 1943* (Paris, 1996), p. 229.
4. The geometrical form of the vegetal embroidery on these blouses is particularly characteristic of Moldavia, the native region of Theodor Pallady, Matisse's friend and fellow painter.
5. Twenty-six letters from Theodor Pallady to Matisse (from 1939 to 1945) are conserved in the Archives Matisse; in several of these, dating from about January or February 1940, Pallady mentions sending blouses to Matisse. Matisse's responses were probably dispersed among various Romanian libraries and private collections. Three are currently at the National Library of Romania, Bucharest.
6. In the 16-mm black-and-white film *Un grand peintre français: Henri Matisse* (n.p.: Compagnie Générale Cinématographique, 1946, 25 min.), François Campaux filmed fourteen states of *The Romanian Blouse*, of the sixteen recorded in the Galerie Maeght catalogue (*Henri Matisse*, exh. cat. [Paris, 1945]). The same catalogue published twelve of the fourteen photographs of *The Dream* that were exhibited.
7. Claude Roger-Marx, "À propos de la présentation de quelques toiles d'Henri Matisse," *Arts et spectacles*, December 5–20, 1945, p. 1.
8. Letter from Henri Matisse to his son Pierre, September 18, 1940, Pierre Matisse collection, The Morgan Library & Museum, New York.
9. Fragment of an undated letter, National Library of Romania, Bucharest, private collections.
10. Letter from Matisse to his son Pierre, September 18, 1940, Pierre Matisse collection, The Morgan Library & Museum, New York.
11. Jack Flam, "Matisse and the Metaphysics of Decoration," in *Matisse, His Art and His Textiles: The Fabric of Dreams*, ed. Ann Dumas, exh. cat. (London, 2004), p. 34.

DORTHE AAGESEN

Toward a State of Pure Essence

1. Hilary Spurling, *Matisse, the Master: A Life of Henri Matisse; the Conquest of Colour, 1909–1954* (New York, 2005), pp. 393ff.
2. For Matisse's response to World War I, see Stephanie D'Alessandro, "The Challenge of Painting," in Stephanie D'Alessandro and John Elderfield, *Matisse: Radical Invention 1913–1917*, exh. cat. (Chicago, 2010), pp. 262–69. For comments by the French writer Francis Carco on Matisse's devotion to his art in 1941, see "Interview with Francis Carco, 1941," in Jack Flam, *Matisse on Art*, rev. ed. (Berkeley and Los Angeles, 1995), p. 133.
3. Letter from Matisse to Pallady, December 7, 1940, National Library of Romania, Bucharest. Doïna Lemny at the Centre Pompidou, Musée National d'Art Moderne, Paris, has studied Matisse's letters to Pallady in Romania and is planning to publish the entire correspondence between the two artists. I owe her a great debt of gratitude for placing the letters at my disposal for this essay.
4. Letter from Pallady to Matisse, December 22, 1940. Archives Matisse, Paris.
5. See Doïna Lemny, "La manche visible est brodée, c'est la blouse roumaine," in *Matisse: Paires et séries*, ed. Cécile Debray, exh. cat. (Paris, 2012), p. 185.
6. A traveling exhibition that opened at the Tate Gallery in London in January 1953 and subsequently toured throughout Europe, Canada, and the United States until 1955 presented a comprehensive selection of Matisse's sculpture and three examples of his painting: *Still Life with Seashell on Black Marble, The Dream,* and *Still Life with Magnolia* (cats. 54–56). All three paintings were accompanied by photographs showing their earlier stages—*Still Life with Seashell on Black Marble* by only two photographs, *The Dream* by thirteen, and *Still Life with Magnolia* by all five.
7. Letter from Matisse to Pallady, December 7, 1940, National Library of Romania, Bucharest (see note 3 above).
8. In the letter, Matisse states that he has enclosed "two photos of the painting that you saw [I had] worked on so much and which ultimately came to be something you will judge imperfectly from the photograph." Since Pallady visited Matisse in March 1940, before going to Romania, the painting referred to must be *The Dream* (cat. 54). Matisse continues, "But in my opinion it is the most significant thing I've done in the way of colored expression." We know that a photograph and a drawing of *The Dream* were sent to Pallady; they are now housed at the National Library of Romania (see fig. 82). However, we do not conclusively know whether these pictures were sent to Pallady in September or with the letter of December 7. Matisse's notes on his drawings of the two states of *Still Life with Seashell on Black Marble* refer to one photograph (and possibly two) that was presumably enclosed with the letter of December 7.
9. While working on the composition, Matisse also made use of a collage of colored paper cutouts, entitled *Still Life with Shell (Still Life with Coffee Pot)* (1940; private collection) that represented all the elements of the painting and allowed him to test the relationship between these elements in another medium. On this subject, see Éric de Chassey, "Une cohabitation instable" in *Matisse: Paires et séries*, pp. 195–200.
10. Letter from Pallady to Matisse, December 22, 1940, Archives Matisse, Paris.
11. For example, *Interior with Oysters, Blue and Red Table* (1940; Kunstmuseum Basel) and *Oysters, Green Table* (1940; private collection, Zürich); see Lydia Delectorskaya, *Henri Matisse: Contre vents et marées; peinture et livres illustrés de 1939 à 1943* (Paris, 1996), pp. 125, 126.

DORTHE AAGESEN

Painting as Film

1. *Un grand peintre français: Henri Matisse* (n.p.: Compagnie Générale Cinématographique, 1946), 16 mm, black-and-white film, 25 min. For selected

scenes from the film, see www.artic.edu/aic/exhibitions/matisse/matissevideo.html.

2. For reproductions of several of these drawn studies, see Lydia Delectorskaya, *Henri Matisse: Contre vents et marées; peinture et livres illustrés de 1939 à 1943* (Paris, 1996), pp. 166, 170–77.
3. Lydia Delectorskaya, *With Apparent Ease . . . Henri Matisse: Paintings from 1935–1939* (Paris, 1988), p. 25. André Rouveyre, who saw Matisse frequently in the autumn of 1941, noted the following about the genesis of the painting: "For an entire winter, the painter struggled to reach the point of being satisfied with respect to the definitive attainment seen here. I saw this canvas on a particular day, in progress, a quarter of it ruined, demolished by what the painter denounced as a mistake. Then he managed to get hold of his coalescing creation once again, to finally fix in place these subtle and delightful relationships." André Rouveyre, "Henri Matisse," in "De la couleur," special issue of *Verve* 4, no. 13 (1945), p. 52.
4. See Isabelle Monod-Fontaine: "Nature morte au magnolia," in Isabelle Monod-Fontaine, Anne Baldassari, and Claude Laugier, *Oeuvres de Henri Matisse*, Collections du Musée National d'Art Moderne, Centre Pompidou (Paris, 1989), p. 106. In 1945, Matisse spoke of such "signs": "Some artists . . . have readymade signs. I never know in advance which sign is to be made and which one I will make. I do not use signs readymade; rather, I find them" (Jacques Kober, text for an exhibition brochure issued on the occasion of "L'exposition inaugurale de peintures et dessins de Henri Matisse," Galerie Maeght, Paris, 1945, unpaginated). For a fuller explanation, see "Conversations with Louis Aragon: On Signs" (1943), in Jack Flam, *Matisse on Art*, rev. ed. (Berkeley and Los Angeles, 1995), pp. 149–54.
5. As noted, for example, by Jeffrey Weiss, "The Matisse Grid," in *The Repeating Image: Multiples in French Painting from David to Matisse*, ed. Eik Kahng, exh. cat. (Baltimore, 2007), p. 178.
6. John Elderfield, *Matisse in the Collection of The Museum of Modern Art* (New York, 1978), p. 72, n. 6. This accords well with Delectorskaya's statement that Matisse had his works photographed "each time when, at the end of a session, it seemed to Matisse he had come to the end of his work or he decided he had arrived at a significant stage." Delectorskaya, *With Apparent Ease*, p. 23.
7. The exhibition was shown at the Galerie Maeght, 13, rue de Téhéran, Paris, from December 7 to 29. For further information, see the introduction to this volume, pp. 11–13.
8. See Lydia Delectorskaya, "'Thèmes et variations': Album didactique de Henri Matisse," in *Henri Matisse: Zeichnungen und Gouaches découpées*, exh. cat. (Stuttgart, 1993), pp. 135–36.
9. In a 1942 letter to his son Pierre, Matisse described the Themes and Variations series as "a motion picture film of the feelings of an artist." Quoted in Alfred H. Barr Jr., *Matisse: His Art and His Public* (New York, 1951), p. 268.
10. Yve-Alain Bois has noted that there are also significant differences between the drawings of the Themes and Variations series and the photographs of the painted states. While the photographs show a painting in progress, the drawings are indisputably complete and finite works and do not relate to each other as a gradual process of trial and error. Yve-Alain Bois, *Matisse and Picasso*, exh. cat. (New York, 1998), p. 161.
11. The objective would be to counteract the belief—among the younger generation of artists, for example—that his art was rapidly and easily executed. For more on this, see ibid., p. 184, and Chika Amano, "L'exposition Henri Matisse à la galerie Maeght," in *Matisse: Processus / Variation*, exh. cat. (Tokyo, 2004), appendix (in French), p. 27.
12. The text refers to the painting as "still life with tin pot."
13. Kober, text for an exhibition brochure (see note 4 above). A note from Matisse in 1949 confirms that he continued to be intrigued by the picture: "This shell, which I was obliged to depict in a certain way, always seemed incomplete to me, now in October 1949, I suspect that within the expressive form of this painting, I cannot draw a very organic shell, just in order not to distract the attention of the viewer from the general expression of the painting." Archives Matisse, Paris. I wish to thank Barbara Duthuit for kindly sharing this material with the author.

SAMANTHA RIPPNER
Themes and Variations

1. Letter from Matisse to Marguerite Duthuit, April 7, 1942, cited in Claude Duthuit, *Henri Matisse: Catalogue raisonné des ouvrages illustrés* (Paris, 1988), p. 48. Translated in Hanne Finsen, ed., *Matisse: A Second Life*, exh. cat. (Paris, 2005), pp. 97, 102.
2. Although the sets are labeled A to P, there are two marked N, one of which, Nbis, is illustrated here.
3. Letter from Matisse to Pierre Matisse, April 3, 1942, cited in Jack Flam, "Matisse's *Dessins Thèmes et variations*: A Book and a Method," in *Henri Matisse: Zeichnungen und Gouaches découpées*, exh. cat. (Stuttgart, 1993), p. 121. Flam's essay is the authoritative study of *Dessins: Thèmes et variations* and has been freely consulted here.
4. Henri Matisse, "Notes of a Painter on His Drawing," July 21, 1939, trans. Jack Flam, *Matisse on Art*, rev. ed. (Berkeley and Los Angeles, 1995), p. 131.
5. Ibid., p. 130.
6. Lydia Delectorskaya quoted in Flam, "Matisse's *Dessins Thèmes et variations*," p. 127.
7. Matisse quoted in "Conversation avec Matisse," in Francis Carco, *L'ami des peintres* (Paris 1953). The interview dates from 1941; "Interview with Francis Carco, 1941," trans. Flam, *Matisse on Art*, p. 135. For a discussion on the role of the unconscious in Matisse's drawings, see Yve-Alain Bois, *Matisse and Picasso* (New York, 1998).
8. "Interview with Carco," in Flam, *Matisse on Art*, p. 136.
9. "Matisse-en-France," in Louis Aragon, *Henri Matisse, a Novel*, trans. Jean Stewart (New York, 1972), vol. 1, p. 70.
10. Flam, "Matisse's *Dessins Thèmes et variations*," p. 125.
11. Ibid., p. 121.
12. The book was printed in an edition of 950 with numbers 1–10 printed on Japon Impérial paper and 11–30 printed on Vélin d'Arches. These "deluxe" editions were signed by the artist. The entire volume, including Aragon's preface, was unbound and housed in a portfolio, which allowed the viewer to look at the drawings side by side.
13. Matisse so freely presented his opinions and comments that Aragon wryly claimed, "I was no longer *the author*." Quoted in "Matisse, or Greatness," in Aragon, *Henri Matisse: A Novel*, vol. 1, p. 49. For Matisse's involvement with the production of the book, see correspondence with Roger Lacourière, Mlle Fequet, and Martin Fabiani dated February 20, 1943, March 5, 1943, March 11, 1943, March 12, 1943, March 15, 1943 March 18, 1943, Archives Matisse, Paris.

CÉCILE DEBRAY
Front Views

1. See Lydia Delectorskaya's statement, quoted in Xavier Girard, *Matisse: Le grand atelier, 1935–1948*, exh. cat. (Nice, 1994), pp. 16–25.
2. These first paintings of 1943 were *Lemons and Saxifrage* (Museum Sammlung Rosengart, Lucerne), *Lemons and Mimosas on a Black Background*, and *Lemons, Fleur-de-Lis Background* (both, private collection).
3. Pierre Schneider, *Matisse* (New York, 1984), p. 652.
4. Dominique Fourcade, ed., *Henri Matisse: Écrits et propos sur l'art* (Paris, 1972), pp. 193–94. Aunt Sally was an old carnival game in which players attempted to knock down wooden silhouettes by throwing balls at them.
5. "Vence, 1944–48," *Verve* 6, nos. 21–22 (1948).
6. For the Two Girls series, which includes *The Silence Living in Houses*, see Girard, *Matisse: Le grand atelier*, pp. 16–25.
7. John Golding sees Matisse's method at the time as stemming from the way he had worked on the Themes and Variations series: he made a study on canvas in color, with several simultaneous attempts at composition; his assistant then erased the canvas using turpentine while the

paint was still wet; after that, the final painting was executed as quickly and freely as possible. See Golding in Elizabeth Cowling et al., *Matisse, Picasso*, exh. cat. (London, 2002), p. 298.

8. Interview with Brother Rayssiguier, Nice, June 14, 1949, quoted in Schneider, *Matisse*, p. 650. The "operation" Matisse mentions was the serious surgery for cancer that he underwent in 1941.

REBECCA RABINOW

Radiant Color

1. A series of nine photographs taken that year by Michel Sima allows for an almost complete reconstruction of the studio, which consisted of two contiguous rooms with fireplaces overlooking the front garden. At some point, a portion of the wall separating the rooms had been demolished, creating a larger space.
2. Dorothy Adlow, "High Lights [*sic*] of Art Scene in New York," *Christian Science Monitor*, February 19, 1949, p. 10.
3. Letter from Matisse to Pierre Matisse, begun on March 9 and finished on April 5, 1948, Pierre Matisse Gallery Archives, MA5020: Box 205, letter 637, Department of Literary and Historical Manuscripts, The Morgan Library & Museum, New York. Unless otherwise noted, all letters cited in the notes below can be found in Box 205 at the Archives.
4. E. Tériade, "Matisse Speaks," *Art News Annual* 21 (1952), p. 42; also repr. "Statements to Tériade: Matisse Speaks, 1951," in Jack Flam, *Matisse on Art*, rev. ed. (Berkeley and Los Angeles, 1995), p. 201.
5. André Warnod, "Le Salon d'Automne 1945 marque le triomphe de la couleur," *Le Figaro*, September 27, 1945, pp. 1–2. See also Adlow, "High Lights of Art Scene," p. 10.
6. Letter from Matisse to Tériade, August 13, 1946, in Rebecca A. Rabinow, "The Legacy of la rue Férou: *Livres d'artistes* created for Tériade by Rouault, Bonnard, Matisse, Léger, Le Corbusier, Chagall, Giacometti, and Miró" (PhD diss., Institute of Fine Arts, New York University, 1995), p. 107.
7. Letter from Matisse to Henry Clifford, trans. *Henri Matisse: Retrospective Exhibition of Paintings, Drawings, and Sculpture Organized in Collaboration with the Artist*, exh. cat. (Philadelphia, 1948), p. 16.
8. A chronology of the paintings is provided by Isabelle Monod-Fontaine, "Grenades et palmiers," in *Henri Matisse; Vence: L'espace d'un atelier*, exh. cat. (Paris, 2007), p. 32. On February 22, 1948, Matisse informed Pierre that he had completed two 50-format canvases, one of which was presumably *Interior with an Egyptian Curtain*; Pierre Matisse Gallery Archives, letter 634. The painting is related to several compositions from the previous year, including a pair of identically sized canvases, both titled *Still Life with Pomegranates* (1947; private collection and Musée Matisse, Nice), that hung side by side on the walls of Matisse's two-room studio.
9. A detail of this nineteenth-century Egyptian cotton hanging is reproduced in Ann Dumas et al., *Matisse, His Art and His Textiles: The Fabric of Dreams*, exh. cat. (London, 2004), p. 198.
10. Letter from Matisse to André Rouveyre, March 13, 1948, in Hanne Finsen, ed., *Matisse, Rouveyre Correspondance* (Paris, 2001), p. 490.
11. Matisse wrote Pierre on January 18, 1948, "I have begun a canvas of 40 or 50 with a pineapple and its wrapping paper. The pineapple alone cost me 1,000 francs." Pierre Matisse Gallery Archives, letter 631.
12. Rouveyre saw the rug, "leopard or jaguar, I don't know which," in an antique shop in Vence and wrote Matisse on January 10, 1943, to see if he was interested in acquiring it. Matisse, who was at that time living in Nice, received it four days later. Finsen, *Matisse, Rouveyre Correspondance*, pp. 158–59.
13. Matisse, quoted by Gaston Diehl in "The Role and Modalities of Color, 1945," in Flam, *Matisse on Art*, p. 156.
14. In the letter cited in note 3 above, Matisse informed Pierre that he had recently finished three paintings of a "size 50" format and almost completed one of a "size 80" format (*Large Red Studio*). Pierre Matisse Gallery Archives, letter 637.
15. Matisse uses the words "~~formation developpement~~ conclusion" in a letter to Pierre, January 18, 1948. Pierre Matisse Gallery Archives, letter 631.
16. This duality was very much on Matisse's mind in the mid-1940s and early 1950s. As early as 1944, for example, he had decided to separate the brightly colored plates of *Jazz*, his *livre d'artiste*, with pages of black-and-white calligraphed text in order to rest the viewer's eyes; see Rabinow, "Legacy of la rue Férou," pp. 126–28. Matisse repeated the same idea several years later in an issue of *Verve* devoted to his Vence paintings (autumn 1948) in which the vibrant paintings were interleaved with pages of floral motifs executed in black India ink on white pages. He further developed the concept in the chapel at Vence, where colorful stained glass is juxtaposed with graphic black-and-white ceramic tiles.
17. On a more practical note, the removal of the frames ensured that all the paintings would fit in the available space. Pierre Matisse, letter to his father, February 9, 1949. See also Matisse's reply, February 15, 1949. Both, Pierre Matisse Gallery Archives, MA 5020: Box 186, Folder 40.
18. Clement Greenberg, *The Nation*, March 5, 1949; repr. *Clement Greenberg: The Collected Essays and Criticism*, ed. John O'Brian, vol. 2 (Chicago, 1986), p. 293.
19. Ibid.
20. B. K., "Reviews and Previews: Henri Matisse," *Art News* 47, no. 10 (February 1949), p. 45.
21. E. Tériade, "Statements to Tériade: Matisse Speaks," in Flam, *Matisse on Art*, p. 207.

WORKS IN THE EXHIBITION

Compiled by Christel Hollevoet-Force and Mary Chan

All works were exhibited in both New York and Copenhagen unless otherwise stated.

1

***Still Life with Compote and Fruit*, 1899**

Oil on canvas, 18⅛ x 21⅞ in. (46 x 55.6 cm)
Mildred Lane Kemper Art Museum, Washington University in Saint Louis, Gift of Mr. and Mrs. Sydney M. Shoenberg, Jr., 1962 (WU 4044)
Signed (on verso, upper left): Henri Matisse

Provenance: Eugène Boch, Monthyon, Seine-et-Marne (until d. 1941); Boch estate in care of his great-nephew Luitwin von Boch-Galhan (until sale, Hôtel Drouot, Paris, February 16, 1951, no. 41, as *Sur une table, une tasse, un compotier, des oranges, un pichet vert*, for 1,060,000 francs to Schempp); [Theodore Schempp, Paris and New York, 1951]; Mr. and Mrs. Sydney M. Shoenberg Jr., Saint Louis, Missouri (1951–62; their gift to Washington University Gallery of Art, later Mildred Lane Kemper Art Museum, 1962)

Exhibitions: Possibly *Matisse* (Berlin 1930), no. 10; *St. Louis Collects* (Saint Louis 1952), no. 54; "Washington University Collection" (Kansas City 1966), no cat.; *Matisse: Retrospective* (London 1968), no. 11; "Cubist, Expressionist, and Surrealist Paintings and Sculptures" (Saint Louis 1980), no cat.; "Centennial Exhibition" (Saint Louis 1981), unnumbered cat., pp. 54, 55 (ill.); "Capsule of Modern Art" (Saint Louis 1983a), no cat.; "Cubists, Surrealists, and Expressionists" (Saint Louis 1983b), no cat.; *Matisse Retrospective* (New York 1992–93), no. 20; *Matisse* (Brisbane–Canberra–Melbourne 1995), no. 5; "Early Modern European and American Art" (Saint Louis 1998), no cat.; *Modern Art at Washington University* (New York–Saint Louis 2002), no. 13; "Picasso to Pollock" (San Antonio 2004), no cat.; *Exil und Moderne* (Rüsselsheim and other cities 2004–6), no. 16

References: Barr, *Matisse: His Art and His Public* (1951), pp. 48, 67 (ill.); Spar, *Annuaire du collectionneur* (1951), pp. 248, 249 (ill.); Diehl and Humbert, *Matisse* (1958), p. 13; *Washington University Magazine*, "University Collections" (1963), p. 25 (ill.); Eisendrath, "Washington University Collections" (1964), p. 294 (fig. 12); Faider-Thomas, *Anna Boch und Eugène Boch* (1971), pp. 39, 79 n. 83; Wadley, *Cézanne* (1975), p. 86 (pl. 78); Watkins, *Matisse* (1977), pp. 6, 16, pl. 46; Izerghina, *Matisse in Soviet Museums* (1978), p. 117 (ill.); Gowing, *Matisse* (1979), pp. 24, 25 (fig. 14), 26–27, 33–34, 62, 99, 205; *Washington University Magazine*, "Centennial" (1981), pp. 1 (ill.), 3, cover ill.; Watkins, *Matisse* (1984), pp. 37 (pl. 19), 38; Flam, *Matisse: The Man and His Art* (1986), pp. 64, 67 (fig. 48), 497 n. 2; Mousseigne, "Toulouse . . . la couleur" (1986), pp. 78, 80 (fig. 5); Flam, *Matisse: A Retrospective* (1988), p. 35 (pl. 3); Bois, *Painting as Model* (1990), p. 12; Izerghina, *Matisse in Soviet Museums* (1990), p. 121 (ill.); Wilson, *Matisse* (1992), pp. 9, 40 (fig. 12), 126; Flam in Neidhardt, *Gallery of Modern Art at Washington University* (1994), pp. 74, 75 (ill.), 195 nn. 2, 3, p. 196, nn. 5, 7, no. 29; Milner, *Matisse* (1994), pp. 34–35 (ill.); Benjamin, "Vital Sign" (1995), p. 22; Néret, *Matisse* (1996), p. 13 (ill.); Flam, *Matisse in the Cone Collection* (2001), pp. 27, 29 (pl. 6), 30–31; Monod-Fontaine in Cowling et al., *Matisse, Picasso* (2002), p. 207; Otten, "Bold, Modern Collection" (2002), p. 18 (ill.); Monery, *Matisse: Émerveillement pour le sud* (2004), p. 24 (fig. 13); Alliez and Bonne, *La pensée-Matisse* (2005), vol. 1, pp. 134–35, vol. 2, fig. 15; Bois, "Cézanne and Matisse" (2009), pp. 106 (fig. 4.1), 107, 110; D'Alessandro and Elderfield, *Matisse: Radical Invention* (2010), pp. 46–47 (fig. 6); Klein, "Matisse, Still Life with Oranges" (2011)

2

***Still Life with Compote, Apples, and Oranges*, 1899**

Oil on canvas, 18¼ x 21⅞ in. (46.4 x 55.6 cm)
The Baltimore Museum of Art, The Cone Collection, formed by Dr. Claribel Cone and Miss Etta Cone of Baltimore, Maryland (BMA 1950.224)
Signed (lower right): Henri Matisse

Provenance: André Level, Paris, and associates (acquired ca. 1906 or 1910–until 1914; sale, "Collection de la 'Peau de l'Ours,'" Hôtel Drouot, Paris, March 2, 1914, no. 40, as *Compotier de pommes et oranges*, for 5,000 francs to Affolter); Monsieur Affolter (1914–); Jules Chavasse, Paris (his sale, Hôtel Drouot, Paris, June 22, 1922, no. 19, as *Compotier, pommes et oranges*, for 4,600 francs to Bernheim-Jeune); [Galerie Bernheim-Jeune, Paris, 1922–23, sold to Cone]; Dr. Claribel Cone and Miss Etta Cone, Baltimore (1923–49; their bequest to the Baltimore Museum of Art, 1949)

Exhibitions: *Cone Collection* (Baltimore 1930), no. 25 or 42; *Cone Collection* (Baltimore 1934), no. 29; "Selections from the Cone Collection" (Baltimore 1949), no cat., checklist, p. 12, no. 28; *From Ingres to Gauguin* (Baltimore 1951), no. 171; *Cone Collection* (New York 1974), no. 14; "Matisse and Master Drawings from the Baltimore Museum of Art" (New York 1979), no cat.; "Van Gogh to Matisse" (Houston 1993–94), no cat.; *Matisse and Modern Masters* (Tokyo–Osaka 1996–97), no. 4; "Matisse from the Baltimore Museum" (Denver–Birmingham–Toronto 2000–2001), no cat.

References: *Gazette de l'Hôtel Drouot* (1914), n.p.; "La vente de la Peau de l'Ours" (1914), n.p. (ill.); *Gazette de l'Hôtel Drouot* (1922), n.p.; Barr,

Matisse: His Art and His Public (1951), pp. 48, 67 (ill.), 531 (n. 4 under p. 48), 557, 575; Bell, *Modern French Painting: Cone Collection* (1951), pp. 3–4, 11; *Vogue*, "Matisse: A Rare Collection Record" (1955), pp. 132, 134 (ill.); Salmon, *Souvenirs sans fin* (1956), p. 259; Diehl and Humbert, *Matisse* (1958), p. 13; Rosenthal, *Paintings, Sculpture and Drawings in the Cone Collection* (1967), pp. 31 (ill.), 66, no. 36; Gowing, *Matisse* (1979), p. 24; Gee, *Dealers, Critics, and Collectors* (1981), p. 165 (no. 37); Richardson, *Dr. Claribel & Miss Etta* (1985), pp. 173, 197; Flam, *Matisse: The Man and His Art* (1986), pp. 64, 67 (fig. 47), 497 n. 12; Mousseigne, "Toulouse . . . la couleur" (1986), p. 78; Flam, in Neidhardt, *Gallery of Modern Art at Washington University* (1994), pp. 74 (ill.), 195 nn. 2, 3; FitzGerald, *Making Modernism* (1995), pp. 40, 273 n. 20; Cauman, "Matisse and America" (2000), vol. 1, p. 416 n. 17; Flam, *Matisse in the Cone Collection* (2001), pp. 20, 27, 28 (pl. 5), 30–31; Schneider, *Matisse* (2002), p. 38

3

***Pont Saint-Michel, Snow Effect*, ca. 1897**

Oil on canvas, 23⅝ x 28¾ in. (60 x 73 cm)
Fondation E. G. Bührle Collection, Zürich (1960.67)
Copenhagen only
Monogrammed (lower left): HM

Provenance: [Ambroise Vollard, Paris, possibly purchased from the artist in 1904 for 150 francs, or accepted on consignment; stock book B, no. 3410]; [Marlborough Fine Art Ltd., London, by 1954; sold on May 17, 1954, for 75,000 Swiss francs to Bührle]; Emil G. Bührle, Zürich (1954–d. 1956); his heirs (1956–60; their gift to the Fondation Bührle, 1960)

Exhibitions: Probably *Matisse* (Paris 1904), no. 4; *Sammlung Emil G. Bührle* (Zürich 1958), no. 293; *Französische Malerei aus der Sammlung Bührle* (Berlin 1958), no. 65; *Hauptwerke der Sammlung Bührle* (Munich 1958–59), no. 103; *Französische Malerei von Delacroix bis Picasso* (Munich 1961), no. 94; *Die Ile de France und ihre Maler* (Berlin 1963), no. 58; *Matisse* (Zürich 1971), no. 1; *Passionate Eye* (Washington and other cities 1990–91b), no. 74; *Paris sous le ciel de la peinture* (Paris 2000b), unnumbered cat., p. 157 (ill.); *Matisse e Bonnard* (Rome 2006–7), no. 73; "Van Gogh, Cézanne, Monet" (Zürich 2010), no cat.

References: Kauffmann, *Stiftung Sammlung Emil G. Bührle* (1971), no. 67; Gowing, *Matisse* (1979), p. 27; Flam, *Matisse: The Man and His Art* (1986), pp. 94, 98 (fig. 80); Reidemeister et al., *Stiftung Sammlung Emil G. Bührle* (1986), pp. 256, 257 (ill.), no. 109; Maurer, *Stiftung Sammlung E. G. Bührle* (1992), pp. 32, 34; Gloor and Goldin, *Foundation E. G. Bührle Collection* (Eng. and Ger. eds., 2003–5), no. 136, Ital. ed.: vol. 3, pp. 110 (ill.), 163 (ill.); Rabinow, "Vollard and Matisse" (2006), pp. 141 n. 24, 382 (under no. 132)

4

***Pont Saint-Michel*, ca. 1900**

Oil on canvas, 22⅞ x 28 in. (58 x 71 cm)
Centre Pompidou, Musée National d'Art Moderne, Paris, Gift in lieu of estate taxes, 2001 (AM 2001-213)
Copenhagen only
Signed in green paint (lower left): Henri Matisse

Provenance: The artist (1900–d. 1954; his estate; to his son); Jean Matisse, Pontoise (until d. 1976; to his widow); Marie Matisse, Pontoise (until d. 1999; her estate, 1999–2001; payment in kind to the French State in lieu of estate taxes [*dation*]; assigned to the Centre Pompidou, Musée National d'Art Moderne, Paris, 2001)

Exhibitions: Possibly *Matisse* (Berlin 1930), no. 6; *Salon d'automne* (Paris 1945a), no. VIII; *Picasso and Matisse* (London 1945), no. 4; *Picasso, Matisse* (Glasgow–Birmingham 1946), no. 4; *Picasso, Matisse* (Amsterdam 1946), no. 4; *Matisse, Picasso* (Brussels 1946), no. 4; *Matisse Retrospective* (Philadelphia 1948), no. 7; *Matisse* (Lucerne 1949), no. 20; *Les Fauves* (Bern 1950), no. 90; *XXV*^{e} *Biennale* (Venice 1950), "Fauves" section, no. 39; *Triumph der Farbe* (Schaffhausen–Berlin 1959), no. 10; *Matisse* (Aix-en-Provence 1960), no. 5; *Matisse* (Albi 1961), no. 3; *Les Fauves* (Paris 1962), no. 90; *La cage aux fauves du Salon d'automne 1905* (Paris 1965), no. 18; *Le fauvisme français* (Paris–Munich 1966), no. 88; *Matisse und seine Freunde* (Hamburg 1966), no. 69; *Matisse: Retrospective* (London 1968), no. 15; *Matisse centenaire* (Paris 1970), no. 36; *Matisse* (Stockholm 1984–85), hors cat.; "Matisse" (Humlebaek 1985), checklist no. 15; *Matisse et l'Italie* (Venice 1987), no. P10; *Matisse Retrospective* (New York 1992–93), no. 39; *Matisse* (London 1998), no. 1; *Roger Marx* (Nancy 2006), no. 188; *Rouault, Matisse: Correspondances* (Paris–Le Cateau-Cambrésis 2006–7), unnumbered cat. (for Le Cateau), p. 6; *Matisse hoje* (São Paulo 2009), unnumbered cat., pp. 26, 27 (ill.); *L'Impressionnisme au fil de la Seine* (Giverny 2010), no. 50

References: Diehl and Humbert, *Matisse* (1958), p. 14; Leymarie, "Il Fauvismo" (1967), p. 240 (ill.); Gowing, *Matisse* (1979), pp. 27, 28 (fig. 15), 205; Bock, *Matisse and Neo-Impressionism* (1981), pp. ix, 46, 130 n. 51, pl. 20; Girard, *Matisse: "Une splendeur inouïe"* (1993), p. 33 (ill.); Monod-Fontaine, "La dation Marie Matisse" (2002), pp. 16 (ill.), 17 (fig. 1); Monod-Fontaine, "Variations autour d'un sujet" (2004), p. 46 (fig. 6); Blum, *Matisse: Rooms with a View* (2010), pp. 30, 32 (pl. 17)

5

***Pont Saint-Michel*, ca. 1901**

Oil on canvas, 23⅝ x 28¾ in. (60 x 73 cm)
Santa Barbara Museum of Art, Bequest of Wright S. Ludington (1993.1.5)
Copenhagen only
Signed (lower left): Henri Matisse

Provenance: [Possibly Ambroise Vollard, Paris, ca. 1904; "Pont Saint-Michel" sold on July 12, 1937, for 5,000 francs to Reid & Lefevre]; [likely co-share between Reid & Lefevre, London; Étienne Bignou (Georges Keller), Paris and New York; and M. Knoedler & Co., New York, 1937–40; sold on January 31, 1940, to Ludington]; Wright Saltus Ludington, Santa Barbara (1940–d. 1992; his bequest to the Santa Barbara Museum of Art, 1993)

Exhibitions: Likely *Matisse* (Paris 1904), no. 26; *Modern Painting Isms* (Baltimore 1940), unnumbered cat.; *From the Ludington Collection* (Los Angeles 1964), no. 26; *Matisse Retrospective* (Los Angeles–Chicago–Boston 1966), no. 11; *Matisse: Retrospective* (London 1968), no. 19; *Matisse centenaire* (Paris 1970), no. 41; *Matisse Retrospective* (New York 1992–93), hors cat.; *Matisse* (Brisbane–Canberra–Melbourne 1995), no. 12

References: Seldis, "Magic of Matisse" (1966), pp. 246 (pl. II), 250; Gowing, *Matisse* (1979), pp. 27, 28 (fig. 16), 30, 205; Bock, *Matisse and Neo-Impressionism* (1981), pp. ix, 46, 130 n. 51; Flam, *Matisse: The Man and His Art* (1986), pp. 94, 99 (fig. 81); Monod-Fontaine, Baldassari, and Laugier, *Oeuvres de Matisse* (1989), pp. 138 (fig. d), 139, under no. 43; Hahnloser in *Passionate Eye* (1990), p. 243 n. 1, under no. 74; Monod-Fontaine, "La dation Marie Matisse" (2002), p. 16; Schneider, *Matisse* (2002), pp. 114, 116; Monod-Fontaine, "Variations autour d'un sujet" (2004), p. 46 (fig. 7); Rabinow, "Vollard and Matisse" (2006), p. 139; Bois, "Cézanne and Matisse" (2009), pp. 106 (fig. 4.2), 107, 110; Blum, *Matisse: Rooms with a View* (2010), pp. 30, 33 (pl. 18)

6

***The Gulf of Saint-Tropez*, 1904**

Oil on canvas, 25⅝ x 19⅞ in. (65 x 50.5 cm)
Kunstsammlung Nordrhein-Westfalen, Düsseldorf (0233)
Signed (lower left): Henri Matisse

Provenance: Marcel Bernheim, Paris (sold to Bernheim-Jeune, April 21, 1926); [Galerie Bernheim-Jeune, Paris, April 21, 1926; no. 24632, sold to Lucerne branch, September 13, 1926]; [Galerie Bernheim-Jeune, Lucerne]; [Galerie Paul Vallotton, Lausanne]; Colonel Robert R. McCormick, Chicago (until his d. 1955;

Collection Contigny Trust, Wheaton, Illinois); The Robert McCormick Charitable Trust, Chicago, known today as the Robert R. McCormick Foundation (1955–86; Robert R. McCormick Museum, Cantigny; extended loan to the Art Institute of Chicago, 1974–86; sale, "Impressionist and Modern Paintings and Sculpture," part 1, Sotheby's, New York, May 13, 1986, no. 28); Marina Picasso, Geneva; [Galerie Jan Krugier, Geneva, sold to Kunstsammlung Nordrhein-Westfalen for 2,5 million German marks in 1986]; Kunstsammlung Nordrhein-Westfalen, Düsseldorf (1986–)

Exhibitions: *Places of Delight* (Washington 1988–89a), no. 123; *Fauve Landscape* (Los Angeles–New York–London 1990–91), unnumbered cat., p. 157 (pl. 163); *Matisse Retrospective* (New York 1992–93), no. 46; *Matisse* (Paris 1993), no. 2; *Farben des Lichts* (Münster–Grenoble–Weimar 1996–97), no. 54; "Unser 20. Jahrhundert" (Düsseldorf 2000), no cat.; *Méditerranée* (Paris 2000–2001), no. 40; *Matisse* (Saint-Tropez 2004), no. 10; *Masterpieces of Kunstsammlung Nordrhein-Westfalen* (Nagoya–Tokyo–Kobe 2008–9), no. 1; *Die Kunstsammlung Nordrhein-Westfalen* (Schleswig 2009), unnumbered cat., pp. 90, 91

References: Courthion, *Matisse* (1934), p. 55, pl. 8; Barr, *Matisse: His Art and His Public* (1951), pp. 59, 60, 316 (ill.); Besson, *Matisse* (1954), pl. 17; Diehl and Humbert, *Matisse* (1958), pp. 22, 120; Leymarie, "Il Fauvismo" (1967), p. 273 (ill.); Elderfield, *Matisse in the Museum of Modern Art* (1978), pp. 36, 37, 38, 177 (fig. 12); Bock, *Matisse and Neo-Impressionism* (1981), pp. 139–40 n. 9; Carrà and Deryng, *Tout l'oeuvre peint de Matisse* (1982), pp. 7, 86 (ill.), no. 26; Mezzatesta, *Matisse, Sculptor/Painter* (1984), pp. 49, 51 n. 6; Watkins, *Matisse* (1984), pp. 53 (pl. 34), 54, 55; Flam, *Matisse: The Man and His Art* (1986), pp. 114, 115 (fig. 99), 116; Schmalenbach, *Bilder des 20. Jahrhunderts* (1986), erratum, ill.; Monod-Fontaine, *Matisse ou la couleur découpée* (1989), pp. 30–31 (ill.); Monod-Fontaine, Baldassari, and Laugier, *Matisse: Oeuvres* (1989), pp. 26, 28 (fig. a); Whitfield, *Fauvism* (1991), pp. 46, 48–49, 51 (fig. 32); Ferrier, *Les Fauves* (1992), p. 35 (ill.); Herbert, *Fauve Painting* (1992), pp. 84, 85 (fig. 38), 86, 104–5, 108, 112, 115–16, 124; Wilson, *Matisse* (1992), p. 11 (ill.); Benjamin, "Decorative Landscape" (1993), pp. 307, 308 (fig. 9); Fourcade and de Chassey, "Anthologie" (1993), p. 419, no. 2 (1904 letter to Manguin); Herrera, *Matisse: A Portrait* (1993), pp. 48, 49 (ill.), 50; Robinson and Bréda, *Matisse au Centre Pompidou* (1993), p. 39; Bois, "On Matisse: The Blinding" (1994), pp. 85, 86 (ill.), 87, 90–91; Monneret, *Matisse* (1994), p. 88 (ill.), no. 34; Dauberville and Dauberville, *Matisse chez Bernheim-Jeune* (1995), vol. 1, pp. 380–81 (ill.), no. 55; Zürcher, *Les Fauves* (1995), pp. 44, 48 (ill.), 73–74, 76, 111; de Chassey, "Signac und di 'Fauves'" (1996), pp. 146, 147 (ill.), no. 54; Néret, *Matisse* (1996), p. 26 (ill.); Schmalenbach, *Die Lust auf das Bild* (1996), pp. 171 (ill.), 172–73; Herbert, "Matisse and Derain" (1998), pp. 175, 176 (fig. 55), 177, 191; Spurling, *Unknown Matisse* (1998), pp. 284–85, 293, fig. 16; Essers et al., *Einblicke das 20. Jahrhundert* (2000), pp. 18 (ill.), 585–87; Green, *Art in France* (2000), pp. 191 (fig. 226), 192–93; Kruszynski, "Die Malerei der Fauves" (2000), p. 6 (ill.); Klein, *Matisse Portraits* (2001), p. 72; Schneider, *Matisse* (2002), pp. 193, 196 (ill.), 251–52, 314, 324; Werth, *Joy of Life* (2002), p. 199; Essers et al., *K20, K21* (2003), p. 101 (ill.); Nonne and Elliott in Goldin, *L'oro e l'azzurro* (2003), pp. 154 (ill.), 223 (ill.); Wright, *Matisse and the Subject of Modernism* (2004), pp. 39, 40 (pl. 18), 52, 94; Alliez and Bonne, *La Pensée-Matisse* (2005), vol. 1, pp. 135–36, 144, 161, vol. 2, fig. 16; Cachin, "Néo-impressionnisme et fauvism" (2005), pp. 82 (fig. 1), 86; Labrusse and Munck, *Matisse-Derain* (2005), pp. 213 (fig. 163), 214–15, 217; Lobstein, *Les Salons au XIXe siècle* (2006), p. 290; Girard, *Matisse: Une splendeur inouïe* (2008), p. 24 (ill.)

7

***Luxe, calme, et volupté*, 1904**

Oil on canvas, 38¾ x 46⅝ in. (98.5 x 118.5 cm)
Centre Pompidou, Musée National d'Art Moderne, Paris, Gift in lieu of estate taxes, 1982 (AM 1982 96). On extended loan to the Musée d'Orsay, Paris (DO 1985 1)
Signed (lower right): Henri Matisse

Provenance: Paul Signac, Saint-Tropez (1905–34; purchased from the artist in September 1905 for 500 francs; to his daughter); Ginette Cachin-Signac, Saint-Tropez and Paris (1934–82; payment in kind to the French State in lieu of estate taxes [*dation*] in 1982; assigned to the Musée National d'Art Moderne, Paris, 1982–85; on extended loan to the Musée d'Orsay, Paris, March 25, 1985, to date)

Exhibitions: *Salon des Indépendants* (Paris 1905), no. 2771; *Matisse* (Paris 1950), no. 39; *Le Fauvisme* (Paris 1951), no. 94; *Matisse* (New York and other cities 1951–52), no. 11; *Salon des Indépendants* (Paris 1955a), no. 46; *Rétrospective Matisse* (Paris 1956), no. 13; *Cent chefs-d'oeuvre de l'art français* (Paris 1957), no. 52; *Les sources du XXème siècle* (Paris 1960–61), no. 430; *Les Fauves* (Paris 1962), no. 94; *Le Fauvisme français* (Paris–Munich 1966), no. 89; *Matisse und seine Freunde* (Hamburg 1966), no. 70; *Neo-Impressionism* (New York 1968), no. 159; *Baudelaire* (Paris 1968–69), no. 777; *Matisse centenaire* (Paris 1970), no. 55; *Matisse* (Zürich–Düsseldorf 1982–83), no. 11; *De Manet à Matisse* (Paris 1990–91), unnumbered cat., pp. 232, 233 (ill.); *Matisse* (Paris 1993), no. 6; *Le Fauvisme* (Paris 1999–2000b), no. 1; *1900* (Paris 2000a), no. 357; *Méditerranée* (Paris 2000–2001), no. 41; *Le Néo-impressionnisme* (Paris 2005), unnumbered cat., pp. 306, 307 (ill.)

References: Denis, "La réaction nationaliste" (1905), pp. 196–97; Girieud, "Au Salon des Indépendants" (1905), p. 1; Morice, "Le XXIe Salon des Indépendants" (1905), pp. 542–43; Sarradin, "Le Salon des Indépendants" (1905), p. 3; Vauxcelles, "Le Salon des Indépendants" (1905), n.p.; Sembat, *Matisse* (1920), p. 6; Sembat, "Matisse und sein Werk" (1920), p. 192; Escholier, *Matisse* (1937), p. 52; Romm, *Matisse* (1937), p. 22; Barr, *Matisse: His Art and His Public* (1951), pp. 53–54, 59–61, 63–64, 81–82, 88–89, 94–96, 126, 132, 218, 262, 317 (ill.), 531 (n. 9 under p. 54); Barr, "Matisse, Picasso and the Crisis of 1907" (1951), p. 164; Naesgaard, "Matisse's Luxe" (1952), p. 68; Tériade, "Matisse Speaks" (1952), p. 42; Escholier, *Matisse, ce vivant* (1956), pp. 37, 114, 156; Diehl and Humbert, *Matisse* (1958), pp. 23, 26–27, 97, 102–3, 120–21, pl. 30; Lassaigne, *Matisse* (1959), pp. 42 (ill.), 43, 46, 48; Leymarie, *Fauvism* (1959), pp. 23, 60, 61 (ill.), 64–66, 86; Crespelle, *Les Fauves* (1962), p. 353, pl. 3; Aragon, "Matisse ou le peintre français" (1963), p. 11 (ill.); Gowing, *Matisse* (1966), pp. 7, 25 (ill.), no. 8; Werner, "Earthly Paradise of Matisse" (1966), p. 35; Brill, *Matisse* (1967), pp. 10, 13, 23, 34, pl. 8; Guichard-Meili, *Matisse* (1967), pp. 45–46, 49 (fig. 32), 55, 246; Levêque, "Matisse 1" (1967), p. 25 (ill.); Leymarie, "Il fauvismo" (1967), pp. 243–44, 246 (ill.), 273, 282; Marchiori, *Matisse* (1967), pp. 13, 17 (fig. 12), 34, 133; Müller, *Fauvism* (1967), pp. 38, 40 (pl. 25), 44, 212; Lévêque, *Matisse* (1968), pp. 9 (ill.), 10; Russell, *World of Matisse* (1969), pp. 46–47 (ill.); Diehl, *Matisse* (1970), pp. 10, 51, 57, under pl. 7 (ill.); Taillandier, "Préhistoire du Bonheur" (1970), pp. 86 (ill.), 88; Aragon, *Matisse, roman* (1971), vol. 1, pp. 291 (pl. 37), 349; Cachin, *Paul Signac* (1971), pp. 79, 82 (fig. 72), 83, 140; Jacobus, *Matisse* (1972), pp. 21, 26, 36, 38, 106–7 (pl. 11); Orienti, *Matisse* (1972), pp. 14–15, 16 (ill.), 22–23; Milhau, "Matisse, Picasso et Braque" (1974), pp. 125, 127; Diehl, *The Fauves* (1975), pp. 21, 78, 79 (ill.); Fourcade and Monod-Fontaine, *Matisse* (1975), pp. 19, 25, 80, under no. 30; Elderfield, *"Wild Beasts* (1976), pp. 19, 25 (ill.), 31–32, 35–36, 49, 54, 69, 87, 97–99, 102, 104–5, 133; Oppler, *Fauvism Reexamined* (1976), pp. 102–3, pl. 26; Watkins, *Matisse* (1977), pp. 6–7, 15, pl. 11; Elderfield, *Matisse in the Museum of Modern Art* (1978), pp. 36, 37 (ill.), 38–40, 52, 107, 167, 176 (fig. 10), 177; Flam, *Matisse on Art* (1978), pp. 4, 11, 25, 132, fig. 13; Gosling, *Paris, 1904–1914* (1978), pp. 85, 104; Gowing, *Matisse* (1979), pp. 44 (fig. 31), 47, 49, 55–56, 64, 67, 70, 199, 206; House, "Legacy of Impressionism in France" (1979), pp. 15–16 (fig. 3); Monod-Fontaine, *Oeuvres de Matisse* (1979), p. 107; Bock, *Matisse and Neo-Impressionism* (1981), pp. ix, 28, 47, 65, 67–82, 89–90, 93, 139 n. 9, 141 nn. 23, 24, pl. 23; Carrà and Deryng, *Tout l'oeuvre peint de Matisse* (1982), pp. 6–7, 9–10, 12, 86 (ill.), no. 23, and pl. 1; Giry, *Fauvism* (1982), pp. 27, 59 (pl. 18), 68, 70, 79, 91, 112, 132, 135, 180; Elderfield, "Drawings of Henri Matisse" (1984), pp. 48–49 (ill.); Mezzatesta, *Matisse, Sculptor/Painter* (1984), pp. 7, 10, 16, 49, 50 (fig. 26), 51–52, 61, 73; Monod-Fontaine, *Sculpture of Matisse* (1984), p. 11 (fig. 3); Watkins, *Matisse* (1984), pp. 51, 53–55, 56 (pl. 36), 57–59, 70, 72, 211, 224; Flam, *Matisse: The Man and His Art* (1986), pp. 114–16 (figs. 100–102), 117 (fig. 103), 118–21, 123, 140,

151, 153, 156, 161, 196, 203, 207, 209, 254, 488 nn. 16, 27, 490 n. 33, 493 n. 40; Frèches-Thory, "After 1900" (1986), pp. 148, 154 (ill.); Guichard-Meili, *Matisse* (1986), pp. 17 (ill.), 18–19, 28, 134, 141; Benjamin, *Matisse's "Notes of a Painter* (1987), pp. 59, 86, 92, 94, 103, 116, 124, 166, 186, 192–93, 202, 320 n. 139; Crow, "Modernisme et culture de masse" (1987), p.43 (ill.); Guillaud and Guillaud, *Matisse: Rhythm and Line* (1987), pp. 17, 22 (pl. 14), 638; Noël, *Matisse* (1987), pp. 22, 24–25 (ill.), 35, 105; Flam, *Matisse: A Retrospective* (1988), pp. 45–46 (repr. Vauxcelles 1905), 51, 52, 61 (pl. 13), 77; Gowing, "Modern Vision" (1988), pp. 240 (fig. 226), 241, 243, cover ill.; Monod-Fontaine, *Matisse ou la couleur découpée* (1989), pp. 8, 11, 12 (ill.), 24, 30–31, slide no. 2; Monod-Fontaine, Baldassari, and Laugier, *Oeuvres de Matisse* (1989), pp. 26, 27 (ill.), 28–29, 318, no. 5; Bois, *Painting as Model* (1990), pp. 14, 15 (fig. 4), 17–18, 62–63; Freeman et al., *Fauve Landscape* (1990), pp. 32, 63–64, 67–68, 73, 79, 83, 167, 168 (pl. 175), 170–71, 178, 242, 245 (pl. 260), 246; Néret, *Matisse* (1991), pp. 24, 25 (fig. 43), 27, 30, 42, 46; Whitfield, *Fauvism* (1991), pp. 49, 50 (fig. 31), 52–53, 58–61, 82, 130, 139, 147, 149, 152; Elderfield, *Matisse Retrospective* (1992), pp. 32, 33 (fig. 9), 34–37, 41, 50, 52, 54–55, 57, 67, 81, 87, 131 (pl. 50), 419; Ferrier, *Les Fauves* (1992), pp. 23, 30, 36 (ill.), 42, 213; Herbert, *Fauve Painting* (1992), pp. 14, 78, 87–88, 112, 113 (fig. 55), 115–16, 118–20, 122, 124, 129, 131–33, 135, 137, 141–42, 146; Monod-Fontaine, "Matisse: Les années fauves" (1992), pp. 22 (fig. 1), 264–66; Szymusiak, *Matisse et Baudelaire* (1992), pp. 8 (ill.), 35; Wilson, *Matisse* (1992), pp. 11–12, 42 (ill.); Benjamin, "Decorative Landscape" (1993), pp. 303, 307, 308 (fig. 8); Flam, "Matisse" (1993), pp. 228 (fig. 1), 229–30; Fourcade and de Chassey, "Anthologie" (1993), pp. 419–22, no. 6; Girard, *Matisse: Une splendeur inouïe* (1993), pp. 24 (ill.), 38, 40–41 (ill.), 42, 47; Herrera, *Matisse: A Portrait* (1993), pp. 49–51, 65, 145, pl. 3; Kostenevich and Semyonova, *Collecting Matisse* (1993), pp. 109, 111; Robinson and Bréda, *Matisse au Centre Pompidou* (1993), pp. 37 (ill.), 38–41, 43, 113; Bois, "On Matisse: The Blinding" (1994), pp. 85, 87 (ill.), 92 n. 98; Frontisi, "L'Estaque" (1994), pp. 90 (fig. 70), 92; Monneret, *Matisse* (1994), pp. 10, 28 (ill.), 29 (ill.), 38, 88 (ill.), no. 38; Benjamin, "Vital Sign" (1995), pp. 15, 24 (fig. 6), 25, 163; Bernier, "Matisse, el conservador inspirado" (1995), pp. 14, 16 (ill.), 17; Flam, *Matisse on Art* (1995), pp. 4, 11, 25, 132, fig. 13; Freeman, *Fauves* (1995), pp. 16, 17 (fig. 3), 19, 187; Zürcher, *Les Fauves* (1995), pp. 44, 50 (ill.), 73, 76, 111, 152, 198–99, 208 n. 31; de Chassey, "Signac und die 'Fauves'" (1996), p. 148; Franz, "Paul Signac und die Befreiung der Farbe" (1996), pp. 37 (fig. 5), 38; Néret, *Matisse* (1996), pp. 23–24, 27 (ill.), 42, 54; Benjamin, "Expression, Disfiguration" (1997), pp. 83, 101; Bouillon and Herbert in Thomson, *Framing France* (1998), pp. ix, 133, 183, 184 (fig. 60), 185, 191; Elderfield, "Moving Aphrodite" (1998), pp. 23, 24 (fig. 2.5), 25–28; Monod-Fontaine in *Matisse: La collection du Centre Pompidou* (1998), pp. 7–8, 14–15, 109; Spurling, *Unknown Matisse* (1998), pp. 285, 293–94, 297, 315, 321, 323, 329, 337, fig. 17; Schneider, Cowart, and Elderfield, *Matisse au Maroc* (1999), pp. 34, 188 (fig. 94), 198; Cauman, "Matisse and America" (2000), vol. 1, p. 8; Green, *Art in France* (2000), pp. 15, 17, 72, 85 (fig. 86), 86–87, 193–94; Salé, "Le mythe de l'âge d'or" (2000), pp. 315 (ill.), 319, no. 357; Klein, *Matisse Portraits* (2001), pp. 71–72, 261 n. 50, 262 n. 18, 265 n. 3; Silver, *Making Paradise* (2001), pp. 39, 40 (fig. 7), 42, 44, 52, 181 n. 34; Essers, *Matisse* (2002), pp. 10 (ill.), 12, 14, 93; Schneider, *Matisse* (2002), pp. 97–98, 101, 104–6, 140, 183, 188, 193, 197, 198–99 (ill.), 201 n. 65, 221, 242, 244, 251–52, 262–64, 266, 268, 275 n. 93, 279, 302, 314, 324–25, 348, 427, 490, 519, 541, 590–91, 598, 706, 728; Werth, *Joy of Life* (2002), pp. 6, 119, 185, 192, 199- 201, 204, 224–26, 229, 237, 243 n. 14, 289 n. 63, 300 nn. 3, 4, pl. 2; Nonne and Elliott in Goldin, *L'oro e l'azzurro* (2003), pp. 155 (ill.), 223 (ill.); Lemoine, *Musée d'Orsay* (2004), pp. 747 (ill.), 748, 762; Monery, *Matisse: Émerveillement pour le sud* (2004), pp. 13, 16, 17 (fig. 10), 18, 37, 40, 42; Wright, *Matisse and the Subject of Modernism* (2004), pp. 16 (ill.), 21, 22 (pl. 7), 23–24, 27, 39–53, 55, 68, 81, 94, 112, 117–20, 121 (ill.), 125, 169, 212, 217, 234 n. 107, 235 n. 110; Alliez and Bonne, *La Pensée-Matisse* (2005), vol. 1, pp. 135–36, 142–46, 148, 174, vol. 2, fig. 18; Benjamin, "Landscape near Collioure" (2005), pp. 30, 32; Bois, "De luxe Experiment" (2005), pp. 109, 116, 117 (fig. 3); Coret, *Fauvisme* (2005), pp. 23, 90, 93 (ill.); Flam, "Matisse à Collioure" (2005), pp. 30 (fig. 28), 32–33, 37, 43, 45; Labrusse and Munck, *Matisse–Derain* (2005), pp. 20, 24, 30 (fig. 28), 32–33, 37, 43, 45, 68, 83, 105, 110, 114, 121, 132, 134, 182, 214, 217, 221–26, 227 (ill. 172), 230–32, 235–38, 248–50, 282, 299, 333 n. 11; Jeancolas, *L'art fauve* (2006), pp. 11, 48, 49 (ill.), 56, 74, 78, 80, 98, 186; Lobstein, *Les Salons au XIX*e *siècle* (2006), pp. 289 (fig. 200), 290; Monod-Fontaine in Léal, *Collection art moderne* (2006), pp. 438, 440 (ill.), 441; Bois, "Cézanne and Matisse" (2009), pp. 108 (fig. 4.4), 109; Jarauta Marión et al., *Matisse and the Alhambra* (2010), pp. 37, 38 (fig. 18); Fagioli, "Matisse, pittore e scultore" (2011), pp. 47–48, 51–52, 55 (ill.); Kropmanns, "Matisse au fil de l'eau" (2011), pp. 15 (fig. 7), 16

8

***Still Life with Purro I*, 1904**

Oil on canvas, 23¼ x 28½ in. (59 x 72.4 cm)
The Phillips Family Collection
New York only
Signed (lower right): Henri Matisse

Provenance: [Galerie Druet, Paris, until 1906; sold on October 4, 1906, to Fayet]; Gustave Fayet, Paris (1906–8; sold on December 18, 1908, to Bernheim-Jeune); [Galerie Bernheim-Jeune, Paris, 1908; stock no. 16883, sold on December 29, 1908, for 2,500 francs to Kann]; Alphonse Kann, Saint-Germain-en-Laye (1908–at least 1910); Jean Laroche, Paris (until 1928; his sale, "Tableaux modernes provenant de la villa 'Sauge pourprée' à Deauville," Hôtel Drouot, Paris, December 8, 1928, no. 59, as *Nature morte*, for 55,100 francs to Bignou); [Galerie Bignou, Paris, from 1928]; Mr. and Mrs. J. B. A. Kessler, London (1929–58; sold through Reid & Lefevre); [Lefevre Gallery, London, sold on April 14, 1958, to Lazarus Phillips]; The Phillips Family Collection (from 1958)

Exhibitions: *Matisse* (Paris 1906), possibly one of nos. 45–55; *Matisse* (Paris 1910), no. 34; *Matisse* (Paris 1931), no. 8; *French Paintings from Kessler Collection* (York 1948), no. 7; *Kessler Collection* (London 1948), no. 18; *XX Century French Masters* (London 1958), no. 11; *Matisse: 64 Paintings* (New York 1966), no. 9; *Matisse Retrospective* (New York 1992–93), no. 45; *Matisse* (Paris 1993), no. 1

References: Zervos, *Matisse* (1931), p. 30 (fig. 20); Barr, *Matisse: His Art and His Public* (1951), pp. 59, 86, 314 (ill.); Diehl and Humbert, *Matisse* (1958), pp. 22–23; Leymarie, "Il Fauvismo" (1967), pp. 243, 275 (ill.); Flam, *Matisse on Art* (1973), pp. 11, 24, fig. 12; Izerghina, *Matisse in Soviet Museums* (1978), p. 129 (ill.), under no. 13; Bock, *Matisse and Neo-Impressionism* (1981), pp. 38, 63; Carrà and Deryng, *Tout l'oeuvre peint de Matisse* (1982), p. 86 (ill.), no. 31; Rewald, *John Hay Whitney Collection* (1983), p. 119, under no. 49; Flam, *Matisse: The Man and His Art* (1986), pp. 110 (fig. 92), 120; Rewald, *Studies in Post-Impressionism* (1986), pp. 261, 262 (fig. 60), 289; Monneret, *Matisse* (1994), p. 88 (ill.), no. 33; Dauberville and Dauberville, *Matisse chez Bernheim-Jeune* (1995), vol. 1, pp. 378, 379 (ill.), no. 54; Spurling, *Unknown Matisse* (1998), pp. 283–84, 454 n. 57, 460 n. 11; Ferretti Bocquillon, "Matisse et le néo-impressionnisme" (2004), pp. 34, 37; Greentree Foundation Sale (2004), pp. 116 (fig. 1), 117, under no. 25; Korn, "Collecting Paintings by Matisse and by Picasso" (2004), p. 123; Labrusse and Munck, *Matisse–Derain* (2005), pp. 18 (pl. 10), 92, 200, 323

9

***Still Life with Purro II*, 1904–5**

Oil on canvas, 11 x 14 in. (27.9 x 35.6 cm)
Private collection
New York only
Signed (lower left): Henri Matisse

Provenance: [Possibly Galerie Druet, Paris, 1906]; André Level, Paris, and associates (acquired ca. 1906 or 1910–until 1914; sale, "Collection de la 'Peau de l'Ours,'" Hôtel Drouot, Paris, March 2, 1914, no. 39, as *La Nature morte à la serviette*, for 625 francs to Level); André Level, Paris (1914–27; his sale, Hôtel Drouot, Paris, March 3, 1927, no. 104, as *La desserte*, for 12,000 francs); private collection, Paris (sold to Janis); [Sidney Janis Gallery, New York, until 1950; sold on November 17, 1950, to Whitney]; Mr. and Mrs.

John Hay Whitney, New York (1950–his d. 1982); Mrs. John Hay Whitney, New York (1982–her d. 1998; her bequest to the Greentree Foundation); Greentree Foundation, New York (1998–2004; its sale, "Property of the Greentree Foundation from the Collection of Mr. & Mrs. John Hay Whitney, Impressionist & Modern Art," Sotheby's, New York, May 5, 2004, no. 25, for 1,856,000 dollars to private collection); private collection (from 2004)

Exhibitions: *Matisse* (Paris 1906), possibly one of nos. 45–55; *Les Fauves* (New York 1950), no. 27; *Selections from Five New York Private Collections* (New York 1951), unnumbered cat. (under Mr. and Mrs. John Hay Whitney); *Les Fauves* (New York and other cities 1952–53), no. 92; *5th Anniversary Exhibition* (New York 1953a), no. 30; *Seurat and His Friends* (New York 1953b), no. 109; *Rétrospective Matisse* (Paris 1956), no. 11; *Whitney Collection* (Washington 1983), no. 49; *Henri Matisse Retrospective* (New York 1992–93), no. 48; *Matisse* (Paris 1993), no. 7; *Matisse* (Düsseldorf 2005–6), no. 25

References: Barr, *Matisse: His Art and His Public* (1951), pp. 59, 315 (ill.); Diehl and Humbert, *Matisse* (1958), pp. 23, 120; Leymarie, *Fauvism* (1959), p. 64; Leymarie, "Il Fauvismo" (1967), pp. 243, 275 (ill.); Diehl, *Matisse* (1970), p. 51; Flam, *Matisse on Art* (1973), p. 11; Izerghina, *Matisse in Soviet Museums* (1978), p. 129 (ill.), under no. 13; Bock, *Matisse and Neo-Impressionism* (1981), pp. 78, 145 n. 56; Gee, *Dealers, Critics, and Collectors* (1981), p. 163; Carrà and Deryng, *Tout l'oeuvre peint de Matisse* (1982), p. 86 (ill.), no. 32; Flam, *Matisse: The Man and His Art* (1986), pp. 120, 121 (fig. 107); Rewald, *Studies in Post-Impressionism* (1986), pp. 261, 263 (fig. 61), 290; Guillaud and Guillaud, *Matisse: Rhythm and Line* (1987), pp. 17, 20 (pl. 12); Monneret, *Matisse* (1994), p. 88 (ill.), no. 39; FitzGerald, *Making Modernism* (1995), p. 273 n. 20; Spurling, *Unknown Matisse* (1998), pp. 283–84, 454 n. 57; Monery, *Matisse: Émerveillement pour le Sud* (2004), pp. 14 (fig. 5), 34, 37; Labrusse and Munck, *Matisse–Derain* (2005), pp. 19 (pl. 11), 92, 200

10

***Young Sailor I*, 1906**

Oil on canvas, 39¼ x 32 in. (99.7 x 81.3 cm)
Collection of Sheldon H. Solow
New York only
Signed (lower left): Henri-Matisse

Provenance: Sarah and Michael Stein, Paris (purchased from the artist, late 1906 or early 1907; one of 19 works from the M. Stein collection lent to Berlin dealer Fritz Gurlitt in July 1914 for an exhibition, shut down due to WWI; works possibly left in safekeeping with Greta and Oskar Moll, Berlin, 1914–17; to avoid confiscation as enemy property when the United States entered the war in 1917, allegedly bought by Gurlitt in a fictitious auction in December 1917; works claimed in 1919 by Hans Purrmann on behalf of and restituted to the Steins; sold to Christian Tetzen-Lund of Copenhagen [11 works], and Tryggve Sagen of Oslo [8 works]; arrived and exhibited in Copenhagen, October 1920, before the division of the collection); Tryggve Sagen, Christiania [Oslo] (by 1920–ca. 1922); Peter Krag, Consul General of Norway in Paris, and Oslo (ca. 1922–his d. 1939); Krag's widow, née Sigri Welhaven (who became Mrs. Schou in 1940), Oslo (1939–79; sale, "Impressionist and Modern Paintings," Christie, Manson & Woods Ltd., London, July 3, 1979, no. 99, for 720,000 pounds to Solow); Sheldon H. Solow

Exhibitions: *Matisse* (Berlin 1914), no. 12; *Den franske udstilling* (Oslo 1916), no. 31 (for sale, 6,000 kr.); *Utställning af fransk konst* (Stockholm 1918), no. 56; *Udstilling of fransk kunst* (Copenhagen 1919), no. 42; "Matisse in the Tetzen-Lund and Sagen Collections" (Copenhagen 1920), no cat.; *Matisse* (Copenhagen–Stockholm–Oslo 1924), hors cat. (shown only in Oslo, lent by Peter Krag); possibly *Matisse* (Berlin 1930), no. 18 (either this or *Young Sailor II*); *Matisse* (Paris 1931), no. 14; *Matisse* (Zürich 1971), no. 3; *Paris–New York* (Paris 1977b), unnumbered cat., pp. 183, 188 (photo), 202 (ill.); *Post-impressionism* (London 1979–80), no. 132; *Matisse Retrospective* (New York 1992–93), no. 89; *Matisse* (Paris 1993), no. 45; *Steins Collect* (San Francisco–Paris–New York 2011–12), unnumbered cat. (English ed.), pp. 200 (pl. 157), 414–15 (no. 133), 461, and no. 23 (French ed.)

References: Petersen, "Matisse: Den Stein'ske Samling" (1920); Schacht, *Matisse* (1922), p. 30 (ill.); Barnes and de Mazia, *Art of Matisse* (1933), pp. 132, 179, 434, no. 28; Tetzen-Lund, *Samling af moderne fransk malerkunst* (1934), ill., n.p. (photo); Grünewald, *Matisse och Expressionismen* (1944), p. 24 (ill.); Swane et al., *Matisse* (1944), pp. 60–61; Stein, *Appreciation* (1947), p. 192; Cassou, *Matisse* (1948), pl. 3; Besson, *Peinture française* (1949), cover ill.; Barr, *Matisse: His Art and His Public* (1951), pp. 20 (photo), 58, 82, 93, 96–97, 177–78, 194, 199, 334 (ill.), 540–41 (n. 4 under p. 178); Barr, "Matisse, Picasso, and the Crisis of 1907" (1951), p. 166; Diehl and Humbert, *Matisse* (1958), pp. 37, 41, 101 (under no. 26), 121; Lassaigne, *Matisse* (1959), p. 60; Leymarie, *Fauvism* (1959), pp. 92–93; Selz, *Matisse* (1964), p. 64; Leymarie, "Evoluzione di Matisse" (1967), p. 42; Leymarie, "Il Fauvismo" (1967), p. 317 (ill.); Marchiori, *Matisse* (1967), pp. 13, 34; Muller, *Fauvism* (1967), p. 46; Diehl, *Matisse* (1970), p. 57, under pls. 12 and 15; Golson, "The Michael Steins of San Francisco" (1970), p. 43; Carlson, *Matisse as a Draughtsman* (1971), p. 44, under no. 12; Fourcade and Monod-Fontaine, *Matisse* (1975), p. 77, under no. 26; Milhau, "Matisse, Picasso et Braque" (1975), p. 125; Elderfield, *"Wild Beasts"* (1976), p. 81 (ill.); Oppler, *Fauvism Reexamined* (1976), p. 309; Seckel, "Les Stein à Paris" (1977), pp. 183, 188 (photo), 202 (ill.); Gowing, *Matisse* (1979), pp. 59 (fig. 41), 206; Bock, *Matisse and Neo-impressionism* (1981), p. 112; Carrà and Deryng, *Tout l'oeuvre peint de Matisse* (1982), p. 88 (ill.), no. 85; Giry, *Fauvism* (1982), pp. 149, 197; Kean, *All the Empty Palaces* (1983), p. 163; Flam, "Matisse and the Fauves" (1984), pp. 221 (ill.), 223; Gottlieb, "Tetzen-Lund samling" (1984), p. 25; Flam, *Matisse: The Man and His Art* (1986), pp. 19, 148, 175, 176 (fig. 166), 187, 234, 296, 347, 355, 394, 502 n. 9; Guichard-Meili, *Matisse* (1986), pp. 24 (ill.), 141; Benjamin, *Matisse's "Notes of a Painter"* (1987), pp. 112, 165; Monod-Fontaine, *Matisse ou la couleur découpée* (1989), p. 33 (ill.); Rewald, "Gelman Collection" (1989), pp. 86 (fig. 1), 89–91; Bois, *Painting as Model* (1990), p. 266 n. 46; Néret, *Matisse* (1991), pp. 43 (fig. 66), 44 (inst. photo), 49, 51, 97; Flam, "Matisse" (1993), pp. 236, 246, 249 (fig. 3); Girard, *Matisse: Une splendeur inouïe* (1993), p. 50; Bois, "On Matisse: The Blinding" (1994), p. 105; Monneret, *Matisse* (1994), p. 92 (ill.), no. 101; Dauberville and Dauberville, *Matisse* (1995), vol. 1, p. 207; Zürcher, *Les Fauves* (1995), p. 189; Néret, *Matisse* (1996), pp. 44 (ill.), 45, 54–55, 92; Spurling, *Unknown Matisse* (1998), p. 378; Monrad, *Matisse: Four Great Collectors* (1999), pp. 142 (fig. 32), 146 (fig. 40); Persuy, "'Les sources du XXe siècle'" (1999), p. 63; Rewald, "Sailor's Yarn" (1999), pp. 119–22, 123 (ill.); Cauman, "Matisse and America," (2000), vol. 1, pp. 27–28, 251, 258, vol. 2, fig. 1.11; Klein, *Matisse Portraits* (2001), pp. 13, 256 n. 28; Schneider, *Matisse* (2002), pp. 235 (ill.), 281, 370, 410; Wright, *Matisse and the Subject of Modernism* (2004), pp. 150, 256 n. 80; Bois, "De luxe Experiment" (2005), p. 113; Flam, "Matisse à Collioure" (2005), pp. 39, 40 (ill.), 41, 43, 291 n. 48, no. 175; Labrusse and Munck, *Matisse–Derain* (2005), pp. 92, 100, 105, 106 (pl. 86), 200, 276, 345 n. 113; Matamoros, "L'Incidence du site de Collioure" (2005), pp. 22–23, 289 n. 68; Jeancolas, *L'art fauve* (2006), pp. 131 (ill.), 137, 144; Kropmanns, "Women's Painter and Men" (2008), pp. 59–60, 61 (fig. 4), 91 (fig. 1)

11

***Young Sailor II*, 1906**

Oil on canvas, 39⅞ x 32⅝ in. (101.3 x 82.9 cm)
The Metropolitan Museum of Art, New York,
Jacques and Natasha Gelman Collection, 1998
(1999.363.41)
Signed and dated (lower left): Henri-Matisse 1906

Provenance: The artist (1906–13; sold on October 9, 1913, to Bernheim-Jeune); [Galerie Bernheim-Jeune, Paris, 1913–22; stock no. 20027]; [Leopold Zborowski, Paris, 1922]; [J. B. Neumann, New York]; Hans Seligman-Schürch, Berlin and Basel (1923–52; sold on February 4, 1952, for 25,000 dollars to Matisse); [Pierre Matisse Gallery, New York; stock no. SP3, sold on March 22, 1952, partly by exchange, for 35,000 dollars to Block]; Mr. and Mrs. Leigh B. Block, Chicago (1952–69); [Marlborough Gallery, New York, 1969; sold to Gelman]; Jacques and Natasha

Gelman, Mexico City and New York (1969–his d. 1986); Natasha Gelman, Mexico City and New York (1986–d. 1998; her bequest to the Metropolitan Museum)

Exhibitions: *Salon d'automne* (Paris 1908), no. 902; *Izdebsky Salon* (Odessa and other cities 1909–10), no. 396; *Second Post Impressionist Exhibition* (London 1912), no. 36; *International Exhibition of Modern Art* [The Armory Show] (New York–Chicago–Boston 1913), no. 405 (New York; price: $1,350), no. 241 (Chicago), no. 122 (Boston); *Matisse* (New York 1915), no. 63; *Exposició d'art francès d'avant-guarda* (Barcelona 1920), no. 51; probably *Matisse* (Berlin 1930), no. 18 (either this or *Young Sailor I*); *Henri-Matisse* (Basel 1931), no. 14; *Henri-Matisse: Retrospective* (New York 1931), no. 14; *Matisse Retrospective* (Philadelphia 1948), no. 10; *Matisse* (Lucerne 1949), no. 34; *Les Fauves* (Bern 1950), no. 97; *XXVe Biennale* (Venice 1950), "Fauves" section, no. 45; *Mostra di Matisse* (Milan 1950), no. 16; *Matisse* (New York and other cities 1951–52), no. 15; *Matisse Retrospective* (Los Angeles–Chicago–Boston 1966), no. 24; *Matisse: 64 Paintings* (New York 1966), no. 12; *100 European Paintings & Drawings* (Washington–Los Angeles 1967), no. 31; *Matisse centenaire* (Paris 1970), no. 82; *Matisse* (New York 1973), no. 5; *Modern Masters* (Sydney–Melbourne–New York 1975), no. 64; *"Wild Beasts"* (New York–San Francisco–Fort Worth 1976), unnumbered cat., pp. 81, 96 (ill.); *Gelman Collection* (New York–London 1989–90), unnumbered cat., pp. 86–88 (ill.), 89–91, 304 (ill.); *Henri Matisse Retrospective* (New York 1992–93), no. 90; *Matisse* (Paris 1993), no. 45bis; *De Matisse à Picasso* (Martigny 1994), unnumbered cat., p. 113; *Painters in Paris* (New York 2000–2001), unnumbered cat., p. 64; *Picasso and the School of Paris* (Kyoto–Tokyo 2002–3), no. 9; *The Philippe de Montebello Years* (New York 2008–9), online cat.

References: Benois, "The 'Salon' and Bakst's School" (1910); Breshko-Breshkovskii, "The Salon," *Birzhevye vedomosti* (1910); [Caffin], "But Matisse and Picabia?" (1913), p. 8; Dorr, "Cubists and Futurists Have Reached America" (1913), sec. 2, p. 2; MacColl, "International Exhibition of Modern Art" (1913), p. 34; Caffin, "Matisse's Career Is Shown " (1915), p. 8; Pach, "Why Matisse?" (1915), pp. 633–36 (ill.); Sembat, *Matisse* (1920), p. 31 (ill.); Nirdlinger, "The Matisse Way" (1931), p. 6; Zervos, *Matisse* (1931), ill.; Scheiwiller, *Matisse* (1933), pl. 2; Fry, *Henri-Matisse* (1935), pl. 7; Swane et al., *Matisse* (1944), pp. 60–61, fig. 11; Stein, *Appreciation* (1947), p. 192; Caspers, "Philadelphia Honors Matisse with Retrospective" (1948), p. 9 (ill.); Frankfurter, "International Report" (1950), p. 5 (ill.), and cover ill.; Georges-Michel, "Tra Fauves e Cubisti" (1950), p. 10 (ill.); Sutton, "Aspects of the Venice Biennale" (1950), p. 265; Barr, *Matisse: His Art and His Public* (1951), pp. 82, 93–94, 97, 128–29, 149–50, 157, 163, 179, 194, 246, 335 (ill.); Myers, "Matisse and the Fauves" (1951), pp. 71 (ill.), 86; Trapp, "Paintings of Matisse" (1951), pp. 118–19 (fig. 88); Matisse, *Portraits* (1954), p. 91 (ill.); Duthuit, *Matisse: Période fauve* (1956), p. 15, pl. 5, Eng. ed.: no. 5, ill.; Diehl and Humbert, *Matisse* (1958), pp. 37, 41, 101, 106, 121, pl. 26; Lassaigne, *Matisse* (1959), p. 60; Leymarie, *Fauvism* (1959), pp. 92–93; Sachs, "Reconstructing the 'Whirlwind of 26th Street'" (1963), p. 26 (photo); Trovato, *1913 Armory Show: 50th Anniversary Exhibition* (1963), p. 197, no. 405; Selz, *Matisse* (1964), p. 64; Kay, "Matisse: Triumphant Exhibition" (1966), p. 6; Seldis, "Magic of Matisse" (1966), p. 250; *Time Magazine*, "Distiller of Sunshine" (1966), p. 78 (photo of 1966 exh.); Marchiori, *Matisse* (1967), p. 34; Muller, *Fauvism* (1967), pp. 46, 52 (pl. 36); Gowing, *Matisse: Retrospective* (1968), p. 18; Negri, *Matisse e i Fauves* (1969), p. 64 (pl. 38); Cassou, *Figaro Littéraire* (1970), p. B2 (ill.); Dittière, "Matisse ou le bonheur de vivre" (1970), p. 16; Ferrier, "1907: Painter of 'Immensité intime'" (1970), p. 40 (ill.); Aragon, *Matisse, roman* (1971 and Eng. ed. 1972), vol. 1, pp. 301, 311 (pl. 46), 350; Gordon, *Modern Art Exhibitions* (1974), vol. 2, p. 863; Milhau, "Matisse, Picasso et Braque" (1975), p. 125; Russell, "Birth of a Wild Beast" (1976), pp. 8–9 (ill.); Gowing, *Matisse* (1979), pp. 59 (fig. 42), 60, 206; Bock, *Matisse and Neo-Impressionism* (1981), p. 112; Carrà and Deryng, *Tout l'oeuvre peint de Matisse* (1982), p. 88 (ill.), no. 86, and pl. XIV; Giry, *Fauvism* (1982), pp. 141 (pl. 61), 149, 197; Dabrowski in Elderfield, *Drawings of Matisse* (1984), pp. 255–56, under no. 19; Flam, "Matisse and the Fauves" (1984), vol. 1, pp. 221 (ill.), 223, 238 n. 79; Watkins, *Matisse* (1984), pp. 110, 119, 122 (pl. 103); Klein, "Book Reviews" (1985), pp. 360, 367 n. 3; Flam, *Matisse: The Man and His Art* (1986), pp. 19, 148, 175, 177 (fig. 167), 178, 187, 190, 234, 296, 301, 321, 347, 396; Benjamin, *Matisse's "Notes of a Painter"* (1987), pp. 112, 165; Noël, *Matisse* (1987), pp. 23, 29 (ill.), 105; Brown, *Story of the Armory Show* (1988), pp. 127, 292, no. 405; Flam, *Matisse: A Retrospective* (1988), p. 86 (pl. 22); Monod-Fontaine, *Matisse ou la couleur découpée* (1989), pp. 32, 40, slide no. 3; Bois, *Painting as Model* (1990), p. 266 n. 46; Cauman, " Matisse's Letters to Pach" (1991), pp. 3, 5 (1912 letter), 9 (ill.); Néret, *Matisse* (1991), pp. 42 (fig. 65), 44, 49, 51–52, 97; Wilson, *Matisse* (1992), p. 55 (fig. 43); Girard, *Matisse: Une splendeur inouïe* (1993), p. 50; Bois, "On Matisse: The Blinding" (1994), p. 105; Monneret, *Matisse* (1994), pp. 54, 92 (ill.), no. 102; Benjamin, "Vital Sign" (1995), p. 25; Dauberville and Dauberville, *Matisse chez Bernheim-Jeune* (1995), vol. 1, pp. 416, 417 (ill.), no. 73; Fineberg, "Innocent Eye" (1995), pp. 118 (ill.), 121; Zürcher, *Les Fauves* (1995), pp. 189, 190 (ill.); Néret, *Matisse* (1996), pp. 44, 45 (ill), 54–55, 92; Fineberg, *Innocent Eye* (1997), pp. 13 (fig. 1.10), 15–16, 18, 228; Bois, *Matisse and Picasso* (1998), p. 72; Spurling, *Unknown Matisse* (1998), pp. 373, 378, fig. 30; Rewald, "Sailor's Yarn" (1999), pp. 118 (ill.), 119–22; Cauman, "Matisse and America" (2000), vol. 1, pp. 27–28, 191, 193, 201, 204, 229, 258, 262, 271, 276–77, 494, vol. 2, fig. 1.12; Green, *Art in France* (2000), pp. 237 (fig. 281), 238; Klein, *Matisse Portraits* (2001), pp. 13, 256 n. 28; Schnell, *"Das rote Atelier"* (2001), pp. 33, 70, 75, 156 (fig. 10); Baldassari in Cowling et al., *Matisse, Picasso* (2002), p. 125, French ed.: p. 127; Schneider, *Matisse* (2002), pp. 237 (ill.), 281, 372, 393, 410, 414, 591; Amano, "La peinture en procès" (2004), p. 12; Monod-Fontaine, "Variations autour d'un sujet" (2004), p. 46 (fig. 11); Wright, *Matisse and the Subject of Modernism* (2004), pp. 150–52, 256 n. 80; Bois, "De luxe Experiment" (2005), p. 113; Flam, "Matisse à Collioure" (2005), pp. 39, 40 (ill.), 41, 43, 291 n. 48, no. 177; Labrusse, "Das Ende des Bilderkultes" (2005), p. 302; Labrusse and Munck, *Matisse–Derain* (2005), pp. 100, 105, 107 (pl. 87), 108, 110, 133, 200, 276, 278, 280, 282, 284–85, 316, 343–45 n. 113 (1907 letter from Derain); Matamoros, "L'incidence du site de Collioure et du paysage" (2005), pp. 22–23, 289 n. 68; Werth, "Nude with a White Scarf" (2005), pp. 150, 153–54; Jeancolas, *L'Art fauve* (2006), pp. 131 (ill.), 137, 144; Kropmanns, "Women's Painter and Men" (2008), pp. 59–60, 61 (fig. 5), 69 n. 9; D'Alessandro, "Interruptions and Returns" (2010), p. 224; Grammont, "Matisse as Religion" (2011), p. 200 (pl. 157)

12

Le Luxe I, 1907

Oil on canvas, 82⅝ x 54⅜ in. (210 x 138 cm)
Centre Pompidou, Musée National d'Art Moderne, Paris, Purchase, 1945 (AM 2586 P)
Monogrammed (lower left): H.M.

Provenance: The artist (sold to the Steins, by December 6, 1907); Michael and Sarah Stein, Paris (end 1907–possibly 1917); the artist (bought back from the Steins, possibly in 1917, until 1945; sold to the Réunion des Musées Nationaux, Paris, 1945; assigned to the Musée National d'Art Moderne; at the Centre Pompidou since 1977)

Exhibitions: *Salon d'automne* (Paris 1907), no. 758; *Trente ans d'art indépendant* (Paris 1926), no. 1185; *Origines et développement de l'art international indépendant* (Paris 1937b), no. 37; *Paintings by Picasso and Matisse* (London 1945), no. 16; *Picasso, Matisse* (Glasgow–Birmingham 1946), no. 16; *Le Fauvisme* (Paris 1951), no. 99; *Rétrospective Matisse* (Paris 1956), no. 21; *Les sources du XXème siècle* (Paris 1960–61), no. 436; *Le Fauvisme français* (Paris–Munich 1966), no. 97; *Painting in France, 1900–1967* (Washington and other cities 1968), no. 25; *Matisse centenaire* (Paris 1970), no. 85; *Matisse* (Copenhagen 1970), no. 23; *"Wild Beasts"* (New York–San Francisco–Fort Worth 1976), unnumbered cat., pp. 97, 113 (ill.), 133, 136–37, 159 n. 137; *Paris–New York* (Paris 1977b), unnumbered cat., pp. 183, 204 (ill.), 205; *Matisse* (Tokyo–Kyoto 1981), no. 23; "L'art en France" (Moscow–Saint Petersburg 1989), no cat.; *Matisse et Baudelaire* (Le Cateau-Cambrésis 1992), no. 9; *Matisse Retrospective* (New York 1992–93), no. 102; *Matisse* (Paris 1993), no. 53; *Anri Matiss* (Moscow–

Saint Petersburg 1993), no. 18; *Matisse* (Lyon 1998), unnumbered cat., pp. 6, 15 (ill.), 20, 21 (ill.), 110, 115; *Rendezvous* (New York 1998–99), no. 11; *Le Fauvisme* (Paris 1999–2000b), no. 123; *Matisse, Picasso* (London–Paris–New York 2002–3), no. 6; *Matisse: Processus/Variation* (Tokyo 2004), no. 3; *Cézanne and Beyond* (Philadelphia 2009), unnumbered cat., pp. 116, 122 (pl. 9), 534; *Steins Collect* (San Francisco–Paris–New York 2011–12), no. 81 (French ed., shown only in Paris)

References: Apollinaire, "Matisse" (1907), ill.; Jean-Aubry, "La peinture au Salon d'automne" (1907); Malpel, "Le Salon d'automne à Paris" (1907); Puy, "Les Fauves" (1907); Vallotton, "Au Salon d'automne" (1907), p. 920; Duthuit, "Le Fauvisme" (1929), p. 431 (ill.); Courthion, *Matisse* (1934), p. 56, pl. 19; Escholier, *Matisse* (1937), p. 19 (ill); Zervos, *L'art contemporain* (1938), pp. 116, 117 (ill.); Cassou, *Matisse* (1939), pl. 4; Grünewald, *Matisse och Expressionismen* (1944), frontis. (photo); Dorival, "Musée d'Art Moderne" (1946), p. 15, cover ill.; Scheiwiller, *Matisse* (1947), p. 7 (photo); Cassou, *Matisse* (1948), pp. 6–7 (pl. 2); Dorival, "Musée d'Art Moderne (1948)" (1949), p. 156; Lejard, Matisse (1948), pl. 2; Duthuit, *Les Fauves* (1949), p. 224; Cassou, Dorival, and Homolle, *Catalogue-Guide* (1950), p. 88; Barr, *Matisse: His Art and His Public* (1951), pp. 54, 78, 83, 95–96, 132, 194, 260, 340 (ill.); Lejard, Matisse (1952), pl. 2; Naesgaard, "Matisse's Luxe" (1952), p. 68; Besson, *Matisse* (1954), pl. 19; Roger-Marx, "Le Nu et la mer" (1955), p. 663 (ill.); Chastel, "Le grand été de Matisse" (1956), p. 7; Cassou, *Matisse* (1958), pp. 6–7 (pl. 2); Diehl and Humbert, *Matisse* (1958), pp. 27, 37, 41, 101, 103, 122, pl. 33; Lassaigne, *Matisse* (1959), pp. 49, 50 (ill.); Escholier, *Matisse: Portrait* (1960), p. 12, pl. C; Dorival, *L'École de Paris* (1961), pp. 30, 125 (ill.); Jedlicka, *Der Fauvismus* (1961), pp. 25–26, pl. 9; Finsen, *J. Rumps samling etc.* (1964), p. 54, under no. R76; Leymarie, *Matisse* (1964), pl. IV; Jedlicka, *Matisse: La Coiffure* (1965), pl. 6; Brill, *Matisse* (1967), pp. 15, 24, 35; Leymarie, "Evoluzione di Matisse" (1967), pp. 41–42; Leymarie, "Il Fauvismo" (1967), p. 303 (ill.); Marchiori, *Matisse* (1967), pp. 24 (fig. 19), 34–35; Müller, *Fauvism* (1967), pp. 46, 50 (pl. 34); Lévêque, *Matisse* (1968), p. 56 (ill.); Moulin, *Matisse: Dessins* (1968), p. 11; Diehl, *Matisse* (1970), pp. 14–15, 35, 57, under pl. 9, pl. 15; Dittière, "Matisse ou le bonheur de vivre" (1970), p. 16 (photo); Ferrier, "1907: 'Immensité intime'" (1970), pp. 42, 43 (ill.); Roger-Marx, "Les dualités de Matisse" (1970), p. 32; Taillandier, "Préhistoire du Bonheur" (1970), pp. 87–88; Elsen, *Sculpture of Matisse* (1972), pp. 64, 108, 176; Jacobus, *Matisse* (1972), pp. 23–26, 29, 116–17 (pl. 16), 128; Orienti, *Matisse* (1972), pp. 26, 27 (ill.); Alpatov, *Matisse* (1973), p. 66; Diehl, *Fauves* (1975), pp. 34 (fig. 35), 84; Fourcade and Monod-Fontaine, *Matisse: Dessins et sculpture* (1975), pp. 25, 80, under no. 30; Milhau, "Matisse, Picasso et Braque" (1975), pp. 98, 106, 108, 133; Baldwin, "The Fauves" (1976), p. 99; Oppler, *Fauvism Reexamined* (1976), p. 310; Seckel, "Les Stein à Paris" (1977), pp. 183, 204 (ill.), 205; Elderfield, *Matisse in the Collection of the Museum of Modern Art* (1978), pp. 49, 52, 54; Gosling, *Paris, 1904–1914* (1978), pp. 96 (ill.), 97; Gowing, *Matisse* (1979), pp. 60 (fig. 43), 68, 206; Monod-Fontaine, *Matisse* (1979) pp. 14 (ill.), 30, 31 (ill.), 32–33, 107, no. 6; Bock, *Matisse and Neo-Impressionism* (1981), pp. xii, 93, 99, 151 n. 11, pl. 60; Carrà and Deryng, *Tout l'oeuvre peint de Matisse* (1982), pp. 7, 89 (ill.), 90, no. 89, pl. XIII; Giry, *Fauvism* (1982), pp. 197–98, 199 (pl. 99); Mezzatesta, *Matisse, Sculptor/Painter* (1984), pp. 65, 69–70 (fig. 40), 73; Watkins, *Matisse* (1984), pp. 77 (pl. 57), 79, 82, 210, 225; Flam, *Matisse: The Man and His Art* (1986), pp. 19, 148, 207, 209, 210 (fig. 209), 212, 216, 254, 296, 347, 491 n. 21, 492 nn. 37, 38; Frèches-Thory, "After 1900" (1986), p. 148; Guichard-Meili, *Matisse* (1986), pp. 24–25, 28, 134; Monod-Fontaine, "Matisse" (1986), p. 409 (ill.); Benjamin, *Matisse's "Notes of a Painter"* (1987), pp. 110, 129, 144–45, 166, 180, 202, 288 n. 182; Guillaud and Guillaud, *Matisse: Rhythm and Line* (1987), pp. 23, 48 (pl. 37); Noël, *Matisse* (1987), pp. 32, 33 (ill.), 105; Flam, *Matisse: A Retrospective* (1988), pp. 69–70, 77, 88 (pl. 24); Monod-Fontaine, *Matisse ou la couleur découpée* (1989), pp. 12, 34 (ill.); Monod-Fontaine, Baldassari, and Laugier, *Oeuvres de Matisse* (1989), pp. 32, 33 (ill.), 34 (figs. c, d), 35, 46, 154, 158, no. 7; Bois, *Painting as Model* (1990), pp. 20–21, 266 n. 46, 269 n. 68; Néret, *Matisse* (1991), pp. 48 (fig. 72), 51–53, 97; Whitfield, *Fauvism* (1991), p. 202, 203 (fig. 169); Asano, "Fauvism and Modern Japanese Painting" (1992), pp. 27 (ill.), 267–68; Ferrier, *Les Fauves* (1992), pp. 30, 31 (ill.), 32, 213 (ill.); Wilson, *Matisse* (1992), p. 50 (fig. 31); Girard, *Matisse* (1993), p. 55; Robinson and Bréda, *Matisse au Centre Pompidou* (1993), pp. 42 (ill.), 43, 113; Bois, "On Matisse: The Blinding" (1994), pp. 89 n. 90, 105–6, 112 n. 148; Lebovici and Peltier, "Lithophanies de Matisse" (1994), p. 11; Milner, *Matisse* (1994), p. 55 (ill.); Monneret, *Matisse* (1994), pp. 9 (photo), 11, 38 (ill.), 39 (ill.), 92 (ill.), no. 109; Freeman, *Fauves* (1995), p. 23; Turner and Benjamin, *Matisse* (1995), pp. 15, 26 (fig. 9), 163, 167; Zürcher, *Les Fauves* (1995), pp. 131, 140 (ill.), 189, 206; Néret, *Matisse* (1996), pp. 48 (ill.), 54–56, 92; Raaschou-Nielsen, *Fransk modernisme* (1996), pp. 101 (fig. 27), 102, under no. 33; Benjamin, "Expression, Disfiguration" (1997), pp. 75, 103, 104 (fig. 3.12), 105; Kostenevich, "Un dialogo lungo" (1997), pp. 33–34; Bois, *Matisse and Picasso* (1998), pp. 111, 180, 245 n. 101; Bois, "Matisse's 'Bathers with a Turtle'" (1998), pp. 9 (fig. 1.1), 15, French ed.: pp. 23, 31 (ill.), 32; Elderfield, "Moving Aphrodite" (1998), pp. 21, 22 (fig. 2.2), 23, 26–29, 32–33, 35–36, 43 n. 7; Monod-Fontaine et al., *Matisse: La collection du Centre Pompidou* (1998), pp. 6, 15 (photo), 20, 21 (ill.), 110, 115; Spurling, *Unknown Matisse* (1998), pp. 306, 395–96, 401 n. 76; Monrad, *Matisse: Four Great Collectors* (1999), pp. 168 (fig. 47), 170, 298–99, under no. 75; Cauman, Matisse and America" (2000), vol. 1, pp. 46, 85, 92, vol. 2, fig. 1.22; Monod-Fontaine, "Paysages avec ou sans figures" (2000), pp. 138–39; Klein, *Matisse Portraits* (2001), p. 152; Cowling et al., *Matisse, Picasso* (2002), pp. 34 (ill.), 35–37, 39 (pl. 6), 125, French ed.: pp. 38 (ill.), 39-41, 43 (pl. 6), 127; Essers, *Matisse* (2002), pp. 24, 25 (ill.), 93; Marin-David, "Matisse, Picasso" (2002), pp. 22 (ill.), 23–24; Percheron and Brouder, *Matisse* (2002), pp. 336, 337 (fig. 365), 342; Schneider, *Matisse* (2002), pp. 94 (ill.), 97–98, 106, 242, 266, 275 n. 93, 280, 284, 345, 372, 542; Werth, *Joy of Life* (2002), pp. 18, 204, 223, 225–26, 229–31, 234, 287 n. 40, 295 n. 113, 299 n. 1, pl. 13; Elliott, "Il Fauvismo e il Midi" (2003), p. 229 (ill.); Chalumeau, *Fauvisme* (2004), pl. 13; Wright, *Matisse and Modernism* (2004), pp. 131, 150 (pl. 76), 151–52, 180–82, 184–88; Aagesen in Anderberg et al., *SMK Highlights* (2005), p. 127; Bois, "De luxe Experiment" (2005), pp. 111, 112 (fig. 1), 113, 119, 121, 123, 127; Coret, *Fauvisme* (2005), pp. 148 (ill.), 158; Flam, "Matisse à Collioure" (2005), pp. 45–46, 47 (ill.), no. 206; Grammont, "'L'attitude lyrique contemporaine'" (2005), p. 36; Grammont, "Chronologie: L'atelier du sud" (2005), pp. 278, 283–84; Labrusse and Munck, *Matisse–Derain* (2005), pp. 20, 46, 68, 83, 114, 132, 135, 146, 166, 200, 295–97, 299–300, 301 (fig. 251), 302–3, 348 n. 143; Werth, "Nude with a White Scarf" (2005), pp. 141, 154; Benedetti, "Colore e luce" (2006), p. 94; Jeancolas, *L'art fauve* (2006), pp. 146–47, 150; Monod-Fontaine in Léal, *Collection art moderne* (2006), pp. 440, 441 (ill.); Bois, "Cézanne and Matisse" (2009), pp. 116, 122 (pl. 9), 534; D'Alessandro and Elderfield, *Matisse: Radical Invention* (2010), pp. 60 (pl. 2.1), 61, 63–65; Munier, *100 Chefs-d'oeuvre du Centre Pompidou* (2010), pp. 14 (ill.), 15; Kropmanns, "Matisse au fil de l'eau" (2011), p. 20 n. 5; Rabinow, Bishop, and Debray, *Steins Collect* (2011), pp. 150 (pl. 101), 380 (pl. 365), 416–17, no. 142; Séligny, "Matisse" (2011), pp. 27, 36 n. 22

13

***Drawing for "Le Luxe,"* 1907**

Charcoal, squared for transfer, on paper mounted to canvas, 88⅝ x 54 in. (225 x 137 cm)
Centre Pompidou, Musée National d'Art Moderne, Paris, Gift of Marguerite Duthuit, 1976 (AM 1976-279)
Not signed

Provenance: The artist (1907–d. 1954; his estate; to his daughter); Marguerite Duthuit, Paris (her gift to the Musée National d'Art Moderne, Paris, 1976)

Exhibitions: *130 dessins de Matisse* (Marseille 1974), no. 11; *Matisse: Dessins, sculpture* (Paris 1975), no. 30; *Matisse: Dessins, sculpture* (Brussels 1975), no. 28; *Acquisitions du Cabinet d'Art Graphique* (Paris 1977a), no. 212; *Cinq années* (Paris 1980–81), no. 252; *Matisse* (Tokyo–Kyoto 1981), no. 109; *Matisse* (Lyon 1998), unnumbered cat., pp. 7, 20 (ill.); *Rendezvous* (New York 1998–99), no. 10; *Le nu au XXe siècle* (Saint-Paul-de-Vence 2000), no. 88; *Forma* (Madrid 2001–2), no. 14

References: Barr, *Matisse: His Art and His Public* (1951), pp. 95–97; Matisse, "Notes d'un peintre" (1972 ed.), p. 43 (on transfer drawing); Bois, "Matisse: Dessins" (1975), p. 19; Carlson, *Matisse Drawings* (1975), ill.; Fourcade and Monod-Fontaine, *Matisse: Dessins et sculpture* (1975), pp. 19, 79 (ill.), 80, no. 30; Schneider, "Matisse's Lifelong Conflict" (1975), p. 126 (ill.); Elderfield, *"Wild Beasts"* (1976), pp. 136 (ill.), 159 n. 137; Musée National d'Art Moderne, *100 oeuvres nouvelles* (1977), p. 92 (ill.); Monod-Fontaine, *Matisse* (1979), pp. 14 (ill.), 32 (fig. a), 106 (ill.), 107, no. 30; Elderfield, *Drawings of Matisse* (1984), p. 53 (ill.); Flam, *Matisse: The Man and His Art* (1986), pp. 207, 213 (fig. 213); Guichard-Meili, *Matisse* (1986), p. 74; Monod-Fontaine, Baldassari, and Laugier, *Oeuvres de Matisse* (1989), pp. 32 (fig. a), 34, 154, 155 (ill.), 156–57 (ills., related drawings), 158, no. 50; Girard, *Matisse: Une splendeur inouïe* (1993), p. 55 (ill.); Flam, *Matisse on Art* (1995), p. 38 (on transfer drawing); Raaschou-Nielsen, *Fransk modernisme* (1996), p. 102 (fig. 28), under no. 33; Monnier, *Master Drawings* (1997), pp. 38, 39 (ill.), no. 13; Monod-Fontaine et al., *Matisse: La collection du Centre Pompidou* (1998), pp. 7, 20 (ill.); Schneider, *Matisse* (2002), p. 100 (ill.); Bois, "De luxe Experiment" (2005), pp. 114 (fig. 2), 116, 123, 130 n. 20; Labrusse and Munck, *Matisse–Derain* (2005), pp. 47, 83, 116 (ill. 94), 255 (ill.), no. 205, under nos. 206, 207; Beaumelle, *Collection art graphique* (2008), pp. 31 (ill.), 32; Bois, "Cézanne and Matisse" (2009), p. 122 (pl. 8); D'Alessandro and Elderfield, *Matisse: Radical Invention* (2010), pp. 61 (pl. 2.3), 63, 64 (fig. 2f), 65 n. 12

14

***Le Luxe II*, 1907–8**

Distemper on canvas, 82½ x 54⅜ in. (209.5 x 138 cm)
Statens Museum for Kunst, Copenhagen, J. Rump Collection (KMSr76)
Signed (lower right): HENRI-MATISSE

Provenance: The artist (1908–17; sold to Rump though Vildrac); [Galerie Charles Vildrac, Paris, acting as agent for Rump, 1917–20]; Johannes Rump, Copenhagen (1917–28; purchased from the artist through Vildrac, though not reaching Copenhagen until 1920; his gift to the Statens Museum for Kunst, Copenhagen, January 19, 1928)

Exhibitions: *Second Post-Impressionist Exhibition* (London 1912), no. 32; *International Exhibition of Modern Art* [The Armory Show] (New York–Chicago–Boston 1913), no. 407 (New York; price: $1,350), no. 244 (Chicago), no. 125 (Boston); *Grønningens udstilling* (Copenhagen 1924), no. 179; *Matisse* (Copenhagen–Stockholm–Oslo 1924), no. 32 (shown only in Copenhagen); *Matisse* (Copenhagen 1970), no. 24; *Matisse Retrospective* (New York 1992–93), no. 103; *Johannes Rump* (Copenhagen 1994–95), no. 166; *Franske mesterværker* (Aarhus 1996–97), no. 32; *Die Epocher der Moderne* (Berlin 1997), no. 5; *Anri Matiss* (Saint Petersburg 1998), no. 27; *Matisse: Four Great Collectors* (Copenhagen 1999), no. 75; *Le Fauvisme* (Paris 1999–2000b), no. 124; *Matisse &* (Copenhagen 2005), no. 15; *Matisse: Radical Invention* (Chicago–New York 2010), no. 2.2

References: Basler, "Matisse" (1921), p. 18 (ill.); Wanscher, "Grønningen" (1924); Kiersmeier, "La peinture française à Copenhague" (1929), p. 163 (ill.); Swane, *J. Rumps Samling* (1929), p. 45, no. 76, pl. 6; Swane, "J. Rumps Samling af moderne fransk Kunst i Kunstmuseet" (1929–31), p. 64; Huyghe, *Histoire de l'art contemporain* (1935), pp. 104 (fig. 119), 111; Zahle, *Fransk maleri efter 1900* (1938), pp. 8–9, pl. 15; Swane et al., *Matisse* (1944), pp. 49–50, 64, 66, fig. 7; Josephson, "Kvinnorna från Collioure och kvinnorna från Avignon" (1947), pp. 19–22 (ill.); Scheiwiller, *Matisse* (1947), p. 7 (ill.); Swane, *J. Rumps Samling* (1948), pp. 80, 82, 83 (ill.), no. 100; Barr, *Matisse: His Art and His Public* (1951), pp. 54, 87, 95–96, 123, 125, 132, 135–36, 149–50, 157, 163, 194, 201, 341 (ill.), 539 (n. 5 under p. 152); Barr, "Matisse, Picasso and the Crisis of 1907" (1951), p. 170 (ill.); Naesgaard, "Matisse's Luxe" (1952), pp. 65–66, 67 (ill.), 68; Lécuyer-Corthis, "Peintres et naïades" (1956), p. 603 (ill.); Diehl and Humbert, *Matisse* (1958), pp. 27, 41, 101, 103, 105–6; Lassaigne, *Matisse* (1959), pp. 49, 51–52; Trovato, *1913 Armory Show* (1963), p. 197, no. 407; Finsen, *J. Rumps samling etc.* (1964), pp. 54–55, no. R76, pl. R76; Selz, *Matisse* (1964), p. 33; Haftmann, *Malerei im 20. Jahrhundert* (1965), pp. 41 (fig. 53), 411; Brill, *Matisse* (1967), pp. 15, 35, pl. 14; Guichard-Meili, *Matisse* (1967), pp. 57 (fig. 38), 60, 210, 246; Leymarie, "Evoluzione di Matisse" (1967), p. 42; Marchiori, *Matisse* (1967), p. 35; Müller, *Fauvism* (1967), pp. 46–47, 51 (pl. 35); Bowness, *Matisse and the Nude* (1968), pl. 6; Moulin, *Matisse: Dessins* (1968), p. 11; Diehl, *Matisse* (1970), p. 57, under pl. 15 (ill.); Ferrier, "1907: 'Immensité intime'" (1970), pp. 41 (ill.), 42; Schneider, *Matisse centenaire* (1970), p. 26; Sutton, "Mozart of Painting" (1970), pp. 358, 360 (fig. 5); Taillandier, "Préhistoire du Bonheur" (1970), pp. 87–88; Aragon, *Matisse, roman* (1971), vol. 1, pp. 160 (pl. 19), 348; Elsen, *Sculpture of Matisse* (1972), pp. 56, 57 (pl. 64), 64, 108, 176; Jacobus, *Matisse* (1973), pp. 23–25, 26 (fig. 20), 28–29, 55, 116; Fourcade and Monod-Fontaine, *Matisse: Dessins et sculpture* (1975), pp. 25, 80, under no. 30; Milhau, "Matisse, Picasso et Braque" (1975), p. 98; Schneider, "Matisse's Lifelong Conflict" (1975), pp. 126, 128; Elderfield, *"Wild Beasts"* (1976), pp. 97, 102, 135 (ill.), 136–37, 159 n. 137; Oppler, *Fauvism Reexamined* (1976), p. 310, pl. 107; Gowing, *Matisse* (1979), pp. 60, 68, 100 (fig. 86), 208; Bock, *Matisse and Neo-Impressionism* (1981), pp. 93, 99, 151 n. 11; Carrà and Deryng, *Tout l'oeuvre peint de Matisse* (1982), pp. 7, 89 (ill.), 90, no. 90; Giry, *Fauvism* (1982), pp. 197, 199 (pl. 100); Mezzatesta, *Matisse, Sculptor/Painter* (1984), pp. 65, 69–70 (fig. 41), 73; Watkins, *Matisse* (1984), pp. 77, 110, 225; Flam, *Matisse: The Man and His Art* (1986), pp. 19, 211 (fig. 210), 296, 301, 321–22, 347, 499 n. 47; Guichard-Meili, *Matisse* (1986), pp. 20 (ill.), 113, 141; Guillaud and Guillaud, *Matisse: Rhythm and Line* (1987), pp. 23, 49 (pl. 38); Noël, *Matisse* (1987), p. 32; Brown, *Story of the Armory Show* (1988), pp. 127, 206, 210, 292, no. 407; Flam, *Matisse: A Retrospective* (1988), p. 77; Monod-Fontaine, *Matisse ou la couleur découpée* (1989), pp. 12, 40 (ill.); Monod-Fontaine, Baldassari, and Laugier, *Oeuvres de Matisse* (1989), pp. 32 (fig. b), 34–35, 46, 154, 158; Bois, *Painting as Model* (1990), pp. 20–21, 266 n. 46, 269 n. 68, 273 n. 104; Izerghina, *Matisse in Soviet Museums* (1990), pp. 167 (ill.), 168; Cauman, "Matisse's Letters to Pach" (1991), pp. 3, 4 (ill.), 5 (ill.); Néret, *Matisse* (1991), pp. 49 (fig. 73), 51–52, 97; Ferrier, *Les Fauves* (1992), pp. 30 (ill.), 32, 33 (ill.); Serritslev, *Arabesk og objekt* (1992), p. 68 (ill.); Girard, *Matisse: Une splendeur inouïe* (1993), p. 55; Herrera, *Matisse* (1993), pp. 85, 99, 109, pl. 6; Scavenius, *Se på verdenskunst i Danmark* (1993), p. 76; Bois, "On Matisse: The Blinding" (1994), pp. 89 n. 90, 105; Monneret, *Matisse* (1994), pp. 38, 92 (ill.), no. 111; Zürcher, *Les Fauves* (1995), pp. 142 (ill.), 189; Friis, *100 Mesterværker* (1996), pp. 156, 157 (ill.); Jensen, *De glade givere* (1996), pp. 259, 263 (photo) 326 (ill.); Læssøe, *Wilhelm Freddie* (1996), pp. 258 (ill.), 259; Néret, *Matisse* (1996), pp. 49 (ill.), 54–55, 92; Raaschou-Nielsen, *Fransk modernisme* (1996), pp. 101–3 (ill.), 153, no. 33; Reinvaldt, *Matisse* (1996), pp. 18, 20 (ill.); Benjamin, "Expression, Disfiguration" (1997), p. 103; Monrad, "Die Königliche Gemälde-und Skulpturensammlung in Kopenhagen" (1997), pp. 21, 22 (ill.); Zahle, *Billedvifte* (1997), pp. 115, 122 (ill.); Bois, *Matisse and Picasso* (1998), pp. 72, 112; Bois, "Matisse's Bathers with a Turtle" (1998), p. 9 (fig. 1.2); Bois, "Un silence de pierre" (1998), p. 23; Elderfield, "Moving Aphrodite" (1998), pp. 21, 22 (fig. 2.3), 23, 26–28, 43 n. 7, 44 n. 14; Spurling, *Unknown Matisse* (1998), p. 396 (ill.); Cauman, "Matisse and America" (2000), vol. 1, pp. 85, 92, 182–83, 193, 194 n. 10, vol. 2, fig. 1.36; Monod-Fontaine, "Paysages avec ou sans figures" (2000), pp. 138–39; Klein, *Matisse Portraits* (2001), p. 152; Schnell, *"Das rote Atelier"* (2001), pp. 32, 36, 70, 75–76, 155 (fig. 9); Percheron and Brouder, *Matisse: De la couleur à l'architecture* (2002), p. 96; Schneider, *Matisse* (2002), pp. 97–98, 103, 106, 266–67, 280, 283–84, 344, 372, 470; Werth, *Joy of Life* (2002), pp. 204, 223, 226; Amano et al., *Matisse: Processus/Variation* (2004), pp. 12, 46 (fig. 13), 56 (fig. 1); Wright, *Matisse and the Subject of Modernism* (2004), pp. 131, 150, 151 (pl. 77), 152; Aagesen et al., *Matisse: Masterpieces at Statens Museum for Kunst* (2005), pp. 9 (ill.), 12–13, 17, 20, 41, 135, 141–42, 147, 150, 154; Bois, "De luxe Experiment" (2005), pp. 109–30; Flam and Grammont in *Matisse-Derain* (2005), pp. 45, 47, 257 (ill.), 278, 283, no. 207; Labrusse and Munck, *Matisse, Derain* (2005), pp. 83, 108, 114, 117 (fig. 95), 146, 153, 166, 200; Müller-Tamm, *Matisse: Figur, Farbe, Raum* (2005), pp. 302, 306 (fig. 5); Jeancolas, *L'art fauve* (2006), pp. 146–47, 153 (ill.);

Fagioli, "Matisse, pittore e scultore" (2011), pp. 39, 41 (ill.); Segel and Jensen, "Le Luxe II by Matisse" (2012)

15

Seated Nude, 1909

Oil on canvas, 45½ x 35 in. (115.5 x 89 cm)
Pierre and Tana Matisse Foundation, New York
Not signed

Provenance: The artist (ca. 1909–d. 1954; his estate; to his son); Pierre Matisse, New York (until d. 1989); Pierre and Tana Matisse Foundation, New York (since 1989)

Exhibitions: *Matisse* (Aix-en-Provence 1960), no. 9; *La sculpture des peintres* (Saint-Paul-de-Vence 1997), no. 50; *Le nu au XXème siècle* (Saint-Paul-de-Vence 2000), no. 94; *Pierre Matisse: Passeur passionné* (Paris 2005–6), unnumbered cat., pp. 116 (ill.), 190; *Matisse* (Basel 2006), no. 30; *Matisse e Bonnard* (Rome 2006–7), no. 44; *Die Skulpturen der Maler* (Baden-Baden 2008), no. 52; *Matisse: La seduzione di Michelangelo* (Brescia 2011), unnumbered cat., pp. 110, 111 (ill.)

References: Werth, "Nude with a White Scarf" (2005), pp. 147, 148 (fig. 7), 149; D'Alessandro and Elderfield, *Matisse: Radical Invention* (2010), pp. 94 (fig. 6d), 95, under no. 6

16

Nude with a White Scarf, 1909

Oil on canvas, 45⅞ x 35 in. (116.5 x 89 cm)
Statens Museum for Kunst, Copenhagen, J. Rump Collection (KMSr81)
Signed and dated (lower right): Henri-Matisse 09

Provenance: [Galerie Bernheim-Jeune, Paris, purchased from the artist, June 2, 1909; stock no. 17563; at least until the end of 1912]; Guy de Cholet, Paris (until d. 1916; to his sister); Countess Vitali-Cholet (1916); Christian Tetzen-Lund, Copenhagen (1917–25; his sale, "Franske og Skandinaviske Billeder tilhørende Tetzen-Lund's Samlinger," Copenhagen, May 18–19, 1925, no. 88, to Rump); Johannes Rump, Copenhagen (1925–28; his gift to the Statens Museum for Kunst, Copenhagen, January 19, 1928)

Exhibitions: *Matisse* (Paris 1910), no. 56; *Sonderbund* (Düsseldorf 1910), no. 82; *Second Post-Impressionist Exhibition* (London 1912), no. 9; *Neue Kunst: Sommerschau* (Munich 1914), no. 45; *Matisse* (Copenhagen-Stockholm-Oslo 1924), no. 34 (shown only in Copenhagen); *Matisse* (Copenhagen 1970), no. 26; *Matisse Retrospective* (New York 1992–93), no. 118; *Johannes Rump* (Copenhagen 1994–95), no. 167; *Franske mestervoerker* (Aarhus 1996–97), no. 33; *Anri Matiss* (Saint Petersburg 1998), no. 21; *Matisse: Four Great Collectors* (Copenhagen 1999), no. 69; *Le Fauvisme* (Paris 1999–2000b), no. 122; *Matisse, Picasso* (London-Paris-New York 2002–3), no. 19 (London and New York), no. 16 (Paris); *Matisse &* (Copenhagen 2005), no. 9; *Matisse: Radical Invention* (Chicago-New York 2010), no. 6

References: Rivière, "Une exposition de Matisse [1910]" (1911), pp. 42–46; Apollinaire, "Matisse" (1918), n.p. (ill.); Danneskjold-Samsøe, "Fransk kunst i København" (1918), pp. 854, 863 (ill.); Häuser, "Ein dänischer Sammler" (1918), p. 164; Swane, "Matisse i Tetzen-Lunds samling" (1922), pp. 210 (ill.), 214; Swane, *J. Rumps Samling* (1929), p. 47, no. 81, pl. 18; Swane, "J. Rumps Samling" (1929–31), pp. 65, 73; Hoppe, "Fran Matisse till Segonzac (1930)," 1931 repr., p. 201 (ill.); Køedt, *Statusopgørelse i Malerkunsten* (1935), pp. 100 (ill.), 104; Swane et al., *Matisse* (1944), pp. 61, 89 (fig. 18); Wennberg, "Från Delacroix till Matisse" (1947), pp. 80 (ill.), 81, 87; Swane, *J. Rumps samling* (1948), pp. 86, 88 (ill.), no. 105; Barr, *Matisse: His Art and His Public* (1951), p. 132; Diehl and Humbert, *Matisse* (1958), p. 38; Finsen, *J. Rumps samling etc.* (1964), p. 55, no. R81, pl. R81; Werenskiold, *De norske Matisse-eleverne* (1972), pp. 14 (ill.), 50–51; Gordon, *Modern Art Exhibitions* (1974), vol. 1, pp. 176 (fig. 594), 315 (fig. 1835), vol. 2, pp. 419 (Düsseldorf 1910), 852 (Munich 1914); Gottlieb, "Tetzen-Lunds samling" (1984), pp. 44, 48; Werenskiold, *Concept of Expressionism* (1984), pp. 40, 172 n. 18, 212 n. 286, pl. 2; Flam, *Matisse: The Man and His Art* (1986), pp. 262, 266 (fig. 261), 282, 301, 310–11, 321, 343; Flam, *Matisse: Retrospective* (1988), p. 122; Scavenius, *Se på verdenskunst i Danmark* (1993), p. 76; Bois, "On Matisse: The Blinding" (1994), pp. 95 n. 110, 112 n. 148; Dauberville and Dauberville, *Matisse chez Bernheim-Jeune* (1995), vol. 1, pp. 78, 460, 461 (ill.), no. 92; Elderfield, *Pleasuring Painting* (1995), pp. 30 (fig. 20), 31–32, 58 n. 61; Schnell, *"Das rote Atelier"* (2001), pp. 33, 69, 75, 157 (fig. 11); Schneider, *Matisse* (2002), pp. 344, 348; Amano, "Processus et surface" (2004), p. 144 (fig. 3); Aagesen, "Matisse: Eight Takes" (2005), pp. 9 (ill.), 12, 13, 17, 20; Flam, "Goldfish" (2005), p. 173; Werth, "Nude with a White Scarf" (2005), pp. 133, 134 (ill.), 135–58; Elderfield, "La seduzione della pittura" (2011), p. 327 (ill.)

17

Seville Still Life I, 1910–11

Oil on canvas, 35⅜ x 46⅛ in. (90 x 117 cm)
The State Hermitage Museum, Saint Petersburg (6570)
Copenhagen only
Signed (lower right): Henri-Matisse

Provenance: Sergei Shchukin, Moscow (1911–18; commissioned from the artist, November 14, 1910, for 5,000 francs; confiscated by the Soviet authorities, November 5, 1918); First Museum of Modern Western Art, Moscow (1918–22); State Museum of Modern Western Art, Moscow (1922–48; Shchukin collection transferred in 1928 to the former Morosov mansion, then to Novossibirsk during WWII, then crated 1945–48); State Hermitage Museum, Leningrad/Saint Petersburg (from 1948)

Exhibitions: *French Art* (Moscow-Leningrad 1955–56), no. 39; *Exposition universelle* (Brussels 1958), no. 213; *Matisse* (Moscow-Leningrad 1969), no. 33; *Matisse ze sbírek sovetských muzeí* (Prague 1969–70), no. 11; *Matisse centenaire* (Paris 1970), no. 104; *French Artists from the Hermitage and the Pushkin* (Kyoto-Tokyo-Kamakura 1979), no. 31; *Matisse* (Zürich-Düsseldorf 1982–83), no. 31; *42 Capolavori dai musei sovietici* (Venice-Rome 1985), no. 35, pp. 104, 105 (misidentified ill.); *Matisse de los museos Pushkin y el Ermitage* (Barcelona-Madrid 1988–89), no. 13; *Matisse Retrospective* (Nagoya-Hiroshima-Kasama 1991), no. 27; *Matisse Retrospective* (New York 1992–93), no. 133; *Matisse* (Paris 1993), no. 81; *Anri Matiss* (Moscow-Saint Petersburg 1993), no. 37; *I cento capolavori dell'Ermitage* (Rome 1999–2000), no. 71; *Matisse: His Art and His Textiles* (Le Cateau-Cambrésis-London-New York 2004–5), no. 11 (shown only in London and New York); *Matisse and the Alhambra* (Granada 2010–11), no. 6

References: Shchukin collection, *Katalog kartin* (1913), no. 109; Migeon, "Impressions d'art en Russie" (1914), p. 3; Tugenkhol'd, "Frantsuzskoe sobranie Shchukina" (1914), p. 42; *Musée d'Art Moderne de Moscou* (1928), p. 67, no. 328; Réau, *Catalogue de l'art français dans les musées russes* (1929), p. 118, no. 942; Escholier, *Matisse* (1937), p. 49 (ill.); *Cahiers d'art*, "Musée d'Art Moderne Occidental à Moscou" (1950), p. 343, no. 328; Barr, *Matisse: His Art and His Public* (1951), pp. 24 (photo), 134, 143, 151, 372 (ill.), 537 (n. 7 under p. 134); Diehl and Humbert, *Matisse* (1958), pp. 52, 122; Hermitage, *Katalogu zhivopisi* (1958), p. 409; Sterling, *Great French Painting in the Hermitage* (1958), pp. 176, 240 n. 153; Marchiori, *Matisse* (1967), pp. 35 (fig. 30), 133; Diehl, *Matisse* (1970), p. 58, under pl. 18; Izerghina, Barskaya, and Zernov, *Hermitage: French 20th Century Masters* (1970), pl. 29; Rusakov, "Matisse in Russia" (1975), pp. 286, 288 n. 30; Gowing, *Matisse* (1979), pp. 111, 115 (fig. 100); Carrà and Deryng, *Tout l'oeuvre peint de Matisse* (1982), p. 92 (ill.), no. 143; Izerghina and Barskaya, *French Painting: The Hermitage* (1982), p. 14, pl. 171; Kean, *All the Empty Palaces* (1983), pp. 184, 192 (photos), 305; Watkins, *Matisse* (1984), pp. 103, 107 (pl. 89); Flam, *Matisse: The Man and His Art* (1986), pp. 294–96, 297 (fig. 294), 306, 497 n. 4; Kostenevich, *Matisse: Peintures et dessins du Pouchkine et de l'Ermitage* (1986), pp. 24, 56 (ill.), 57; Kostenevich, *Ot Mone do Pikasso* (1989), no. 205; Izerghina, *Matisse in Soviet Museums* (1990), pp. 13, 161 (ill.), no. 34 (ill.); Kostenevich in *From Poussin to Matisse* (1990), p. 140, no. 46; Barskaya and Kostenevich, *French Painting: Hermitage*

(1991), pp. 285 (ill.), 286, no. 194; Kostenevich and Semyonova, *Collecting Matisse* (1993), pp. 34 (photo), 114 (ill.), 117, 168 n. 3 to XXIV, 169, 170 n. 2 to XXVIII; Bois, "On Matisse: The Blinding" (1994), p. 81 n. 65; Monneret, *Matisse* (1994), p. 96 (ill.), no. 163; Brodskaya, *Fauves* (1995), pp. 61, 90, 91 (ill.), no. 39; Dauberville and Dauberville, *Matisse chez Bernheim-Jeune* (1995), vol. 1, pp. 490, 491 (ill.), no. 111; Kostenevich, "Un dialogo lungo" (1997), p. 45; Bois, *Matisse and Picasso* (1998), p. 112; Alaoui et al., *Le Maroc de Matisse* (1999), pp. 29, 162 (fig. 50), 170, 214; Kostenevich in Monrad, *Matisse: Four Great Collectors* (1999), no. 25 (ill.), 54 (ill.), 223, 224, no. 22; Schneider, Cowart, and Elderfield, *Matisse au Maroc* (1999), pp. 19, 204 (fig. 100), 226 (fig. 113); Percheron and Brouder, *Matisse: De la couleur à l'architecture* (2002), pp. 340–41 (fig. 368); Schneider, *Matisse* (2002), pp. 307 n. 30, 382 n. 29, 396; Amano et al., *Matisse: Processus/Variation* (2004), pp. 13, 37 (fig. 3), 47 (fig. 16); Monery, *Matisse: Émerveillement pour le sud* (2004), p. 60 (fig. 30); Spurling, *Matisse the Master* (2005), pp. 62, 473 n. 101, fig. 6; D'Alessandro and Elderfield, *Matisse: Radical Invention* (2010), pp. 25, 110, 111 (fig. 3), 123

18

***Seville Still Life II*, 1910–11**

Oil on canvas, 35¼ x 45¾ in. (89.5 x 116.3 cm)
The State Hermitage Museum, Saint Petersburg (9043)
Copenhagen only
Signed (lower right): Henri-Matisse

Provenance: Sergei Shchukin, Moscow (1911–18; commissioned from the artist, November 14, 1910, for 5,000 francs; confiscated by the Soviet authorities, November 5, 1918); First Museum of Modern Western Art, Moscow (1918–22); State Museum of Modern Western Art, Moscow (1922–48; Shchukin collection transferred in 1928 to the former Morosov mansion, then to Novossibirsk during WWII, then crated 1945–48); State Hermitage Museum, Leningrad/Saint Petersburg (from 1948)

Exhibitions: *Von Delacroix bis Picasso* (Berlin 1965), unnumbered cat., p. 51; *Masterpieces of Modern Painting from the USSR* (Tokyo–Kyoto 1966–67), no. 71; *Matisse* (Moscow–Leningrad 1969), no. 34; *Matisse* (Zürich–Düsseldorf 1982–83), no. 32; *Matisse* (Lille 1986), no. 13; *From Poussin to Matisse* (New York–Chicago 1990), no. 46; *Matisse Retrospective* (Nagoya–Hiroshima–Kasama 1991), no. 28; *Matisse Retrospective* (New York 1992–93), no. 134; *Matisse* (Paris 1993), no. 82; *Anri Matiss* (Moscow–Saint Petersburg 1993), no. 38; *Objects of Desire* (New York–London 1997–98), unnumbered cat., pp. 27–28, 38 (pl. 10), 223; *Matisse: Four Great Collectors* (Copenhagen 1999), no. 23; *I cento capolavori dell'Ermitage* (Rome 1999–2000), no. 70; *Matisse and the Alhambra* (Granada 2010–11), no. 7

References: Shuisky, "Matisse" (1911), fig. 5 (photo); Shchukin collection, *Katalog kartin* (1913), no. 116; Migeon, "Impressions d'art en Russie" (1914), p. 3; Tugenkhol'd, "Frantsuzskoe sobranie Shchukina" (1914), p. 42; *Musée d'Art Moderne de Moscou* (1928), p. 67, no. 329; Réau, *Catalogue de l'art français dans les musées russes* (1929), p. 118, no. 943; Kimball, "Discovery from America" (1948), p. 30 (photo); *Cahiers d'art*, "Musée d'Art Moderne Occidental à Moscou" (1950), p. 343, no. 329; Barr, *Matisse: His Art and His Public* (1951), pp. 25 (photo), 28 (photo), 134, 143, 151, 537; Diehl and Humbert, *Matisse* (1958), pp. 52, 122; Hermitage, *Katalogu zhivopisi* (1958), p. 409; Sterling, *Great French Painting in the Hermitage* (1958), pp. 176, 177, 191 (pl. 146), 240 n. 153; Conil Lacoste, "À Henri Matisse" (1970), p. 17; Alpatov, *Matisse* (1973), pp. 67, 71, pl. 10; Rusakov, "Matisse in Russia" (1975), pp. 286, 288 n. 30; Gowing, *Matisse* (1979), p. 111; Carrà and Deryng, *Tout l'oeuvre peint de Matisse* (1982), p. 92 (ill.), no. 144; Izerghina and Barskaya, *French Painting: Hermitage* (1982), p. 14, pl. 173; Kean, *All the Empty Palaces* (1983), pp. 184, 305; Watkins, *Matisse* (1984), p. 107; Flam, *Matisse: The Man and His Art* (1986), pp. 294–96, 298 (fig. 295), 306, 497 n. 4; Flam, *Matisse: A Retrospective* (1988), p. 106 (photo); Kostenevich, *Ot Mone do Pikasso* (1989), no. 206; Izerghina, *Matisse in Soviet Museums* (1990), pp. 13, 157, 158 (ill.), no. 35 (ill.); Kostenevich in *From Poussin to Matisse* (1990), pp. 139 (ill.), 140, 141 (ill.), 161, no. 46; Barskaya and Kostenevich, *French Painting: Hermitage* (1991), p. 286 (ill.), no. 195; Kostenevich and Semyonova, *Collecting Matisse* (1993), pp. 32 (photo), 35 (photo), 41 (photo), 54 (ill.), 116 (ill.), 117, 168 XXIV nn. 3, 7, 169 XXVI n. 4, 170 XXVIII n. 2; Bois, "On Matisse: The Blinding" (1994), p. 81 n. 65; Monneret, *Matisse* (1994), p. 96 (ill.), no. 164; Brodskaya, *Fauves* (1995), pp. 61, 90, 91 (ill.), no. 40; Dauberville and Dauberville, *Matisse chez Bernheim-Jeune* (1995), vol. 1, p. 492 (ill.), no. 112; Kostenevich, "Un dialogo lungo" (1997), p. 45; Bois, *Matisse and Picasso* (1998), p. 112; Alaoui et al., *Le Maroc de Matisse* (1999), pp. 29, 162, 163 (fig. 51), 170, 214; Schneider, Cowart, and Elderfield, *Matisse au Maroc* (1999), pp. 19, 204 (fig. 101), 226 (fig. 113); Essers, *Matisse: Master of Colour* (2002), pp. 36, 38 (ill.); Schneider, *Matisse* (2002), pp. 307 n. 30, 382 n. 29, 396, 399 (ill.); Amano et al., *Matisse: Processus/Variation* (2004), pp. 13, 37 (fig. 4), 47 (fig. 17); Dumas, *Matisse, His Art and His Textiles* (2004), pp. 55, 57, 58 (fig. 36), 181 (under no. 11); Flam, "Matisse and the Metaphysics of Decoration" (2004), pp. 39–40; Monery, *Matisse: Émerveillement pour le sud* (2004), p. 60 (fig. 31); Spurling, *Matisse the Master* (2005), pp. 62, 473 n. 101; Buschhoff, "'Der grosse Stil der Form'" (2007), p. 199 (fig. 9); D'Alessandro and Elderfield, *Matisse: Radical Invention* (2010), pp. 25, 110, 111 (fig. 4), 123

19

***Nasturtiums with the Painting "Dance" I*, 1912**

Oil on canvas, 75½ x 45⅜ in. (191.8 x 115.3 cm)
The Metropolitan Museum of Art, New York, Bequest of Scofield Thayer, 1982 (1984.433.16)
Signed (lower right): Henri-Matisse

Provenance: [Alfred Flechtheim, Düsseldorf, purchased from the artist in November 1913; sold to Moll]; Oskar and Margarete [Greta] Moll, Berlin, Paris, and Breslau (by 1920–23; sold in May 1923 for 2,000 dollars through Lutz and Flechtheim to Thayer); [Galerie Lutz, Berlin, and Alfred Flechtheim, Berlin, 1922–23, acting as agents for Thayer]; Scofield Thayer, New York and Vienna (1923–d. 1982; on extended loan at the Worcester Art Museum, Mass., 1931–82; his bequest to the Metropolitan Museum, 1984)

Exhibitions: *Second Post-Impressionist Exhibition* (London 1912), no. 22; *International Exhibition of Modern Art* [The Armory Show] (New York–Chicago–Boston 1913), no. 409 (New York), no. 246 (Chicago), no. 127 (Boston); *Beiträge zur Kunst des XIX. Jahrhunderts* (Düsseldorf 1913–14), unnumbered cat., pp. 97, 99 (ill.); "Loans from private collectors and dealers" (Berlin 1921–22), no cat. (lent by Moll); "Dial Folio 'Living Art'" (New York 1924a), no cat., unnumbered typed checklist (valued at $10,000); *Dial Collection* (Worcester 1924), no. 21; "Dial Collection" (Northampton 1924), no cat.; *Matisse Retrospective* (New York 1931), no. 22; *Henri-Matisse, "la danse": Sketch for the Moscow Decoration* (New York 1936a), no. 2; *Art of the Third Republic* (Worcester 1941), no. 23; *About 30 Years Ago* (New York 1943b), no. 7; *Matisse Retrospective* (Philadelphia 1948), no. 22; *"What They Said"* (New York 1949b), no. 14; *Five Modern Old Masters* (Providence 1950), no. 9; *Matisse* (New York and other cities 1951–52), no. 32; "Matisse" (Portland 1952), no cat., unnumbered typed checklist; *Modern French Masters* (Columbus–Akron–Worcester 1952–53), no. 21; *Dial and the Dial Collection* (Worcester 1959), no. 61; "Selections from the Dial Collection" (Worcester 1965), no cat., unnumbered typed checklist; "Dial Revisited" (Worcester 1971), no cat.; *"The Dial"* (Worcester 1981), no. 87; *20th Century Masters from the Metropolitan* (Canberra–Brisbane 1986), unnumbered cat., pp. 22, 23 (ill.); *Matisse Retrospective* (New York 1992–93), no. 149; *Matisse* (Paris 1993), no. 103; *Matisse* (Brisbane–Canberra–Melbourne 1995), no. 64; *Painters in Paris* (New York 2000–2001), unnumbered cat., pp. 77 (ill.), 123; *Matisse: Processus/Variation* (Tokyo 2004), no. 6; *Matisse: Figur, Farbe, Raum* (Düsseldorf 2005–6), no. 53

References: Brooke, *Cambridge Magazine* (1912), pp. 125–26; Hind, "Ideals of Post-Impressionism" (1912), p. 6; Cortissoz, "Post-Impressionist and Cubist Vagaries" (1913), sec. 2, p. 6; Greeley-Smith, "Go to the Cubist Show" (1913), p. 5 (caricature); MacChesney, "Talk with Matisse [June 1912]" (1913), p. 12 (ill.);

MacColl, "International Exhibition of Modern Art" (1913), p. 34; *The Sun*, "What Cesare Saw at the Armory" (1913), p. 41 (caricature); Braune, "Zu einem Gemälde von Matisse" (1920), pp. 197–98, ill. opp. p. 196; Schacht, *Matisse* (1922), p. 67 (ill.); Thayer, *Living Art* (1923), pl. 3; *Art News*, "'Living Art' Folio and Originals Seen" (1924), p. 5; Cary, "World of Art" (1924), p. SM10; Craven, "Living Art" (1924), pp. 181–82; Craven, " Matisse" (1924), p. 404; McBride, "Modern Art" (1924), p. 209; Einstein, *Kunst des 20. Jahrhunderts* (1926), pp. 24, 182 (ill.), 559; Schapiro, "Matisse and Impressionism" (1932), pp. 27–28; Davidson, "Matisse's Allegory of the Dance" (1936), p. 14; *New York Times*, "Matisse Art on Exhibition Here" (1936), p. 23; Smith, "Balancing to Date the Books on the French" (1941), p. 28; Hess, "Matisse: A Life of Color" (1948), p. 19 (ill.); Barr, *Matisse: His Art and His Public* (1951), pp. 127, 144, 149–50, 156–57, 174, 194, 199, 201, 383 (ill.), 539 (n. 5 under p. 144), 559; Trapp, "Paintings of Matisse" (1951), pp. 174–75 (fig. 127); *San Francisco Museum of Art Bulletin*, "Matisse Exhibition" (1952), p. 5 (photo); Diehl and Humbert, *Matisse* (1958), pp. 53, 101; Lassaigne, *Matisse* (1959), p. 69; Brown, *Story of the Armory Show* (1963), p. 267, no. 409; Sachs, "Reconstructing the 'Whirlwind of 26th Street'" (1963), p. 26; Trovato, *1913 Armory Show: 50th Anniversary* (1963), pp. 92 (fig. 409), 197, no. 409; Joost, *Scofield Thayer and the Dial* (1964), pp. 229, 237–38, ill.; Leymarie, "Evoluzione di Matisse" (1967), p. 46; Bowness, *Matisse and the Nude* (1968), p. 20, pl. 14; Moore, *Dialectic Norm* (1968), pp. 72–73, 83 (fig. 6); Aragon, *Matisse, roman* (1971), vol. 1, p. 301; Joost, "The Dial Collection" (1971), pp. 493 (fig. 9), 494; *Impressionist and Post-Impressionist Paintings from the U.S.S.R.* (1973), p. 72, under no. 25; Neff, "Matisse and Decoration" (1974), pp. 143–44, 180 n. 162, fig. 74; Neff, "Matisse and Decoration: Shchukin Panels" (1975), pp. 40, 41 (fig. 8), 44, 46 (fig. 15), 48 nn. 17, 23; Brenson, "Met Museum Given Major Private Collection" (1982), p. A1; Carrà and Deryng, *Tout l'oeuvre peint de Matisse* (1982), p. 92 (ill.), no. 148; Mannering, *Art of Matisse* (1982), pp. 49–50; Mezzatesta, *Matisse Sculptor/Painter* (1984), pp. 94, 95 (fig. 62), 96; Barbier, "Oeuvres réalisées à Issy-les-Moulineaux" (1985), no. 20; Messinger, "Thayer Bequest" (1985), pp. 46 (ill.), 47, cover ill.; Flam, *Matisse: The Man and His Art* (1986), pp. 345, 346 (fig. 347), 347, 500 nn. 41, 42, 501 n. 14; Hahnloser-Ingold, "Collecting Matisses of the 1920s in the 1920s" (1986), p. 273 n. 60; Lieberman, *20th Century Art* (1986), pp. 6, 20 (ill.), 21 (ill.), cover ill.; Lloyd, "Modern Masters from the Metropolitan" (1986), pp. 345, 348, cover ill.; Guillaud and Guillaud, *Matisse: Rhythm and Line* (1987), pp. 23, 67 (pl. 55); Richardson, "Life and Times of Scofield Thayer" (1987), p. 163 (ill.); Tinterow et al., *Modern Europe* (1987), pp. 102–3 (ill.); Bullen, *Post-Impressionists in England* (1988), pp. 367, 405; Flam, *Matisse: A Retrospective* (1988), p. 134 (reprint of MacChesney 1913); Bessonova in *From Poussin to Matisse* (1990), p. 144 under no. 48; Elderfield, "Matisse in Morocco: An Interpretive Guide" (1990), pp. 218, 219 (fig. 104), 222, 237 n. 76, 259; Cauman, "Matisse's Letters to Pach" (1991), pp. 3, 5–6; Bessonova in Költzsch, *Morozov and Shchukin* (1993), p. 416 (under no. 99, ill.); Kostenevich and Semyonova, *Collecting Matisse* (1993), pp. 134, 145; Martinez, "Mixed Reception for Modernism: 1913 Armory Show" (1993), p. 43; Bois, "On Matisse: The Blinding" (1994), p. 108; Monneret, *Matisse* (1994), p. 97 (ill.), no. 187; Benjamin, "Vital Sign" (1995), pp. 6 (ill.), 27, 195, 198 (ill.), no. 64; Néret, *Matisse* (1996), p. 63 (ill.); Kostenevich, "Un dialogo lungo" (1997), pp. 49, 54; Kropmanns, "Matisse und die Molls" (1997), pp. 82 (ill.), 83 (erroneous provenance); Elderfield, "Matisse au Maroc" (1999), pp. 203, 205 (fig. 104), 207; Kostenevich in Monrad, *Henri Matisse: Four Great Collectors* (1999), pp. 88, 232–33; Labrusse, "L'épreuve de Tanger" (1999), p. 42; O'Brian, *Ruthless Hedonism* (1999), p. 58; Persuy, "'Les sources du XXe siècle'" (1999), p. 63; Cauman, "Matisse and America" (2000), vol. 1, pp. 191–92 n. 3, 300 n. 26, 494, vol. 2, fig. 4.12; Golding in Cowling et al., *Matisse, Picasso* (2002), pp. 173, 353 nn. 1, 8, 10 (fig. 10), French ed.: pp. 175, 353 nn. 1, 8, 10 (fig. 51); Schneider, *Matisse* (2002), pp. 349, 431; Monod-Fontaine, "Variations autour d'un sujet" (2004), p. 47 (fig. 18); Bessonova, *Painting Collection: Pushkin* (2005), pp. 155, 157 (ill.); Bois, "De luxe Experiment" (2005), pp. 113, 115, 124 (fig. 7); Strobl, *Curt Glaser* (2006), p. 22 (erroneous provenance); Rewald in Tinterow et al., *Masterpieces of European Painting* (2007), pp. 200 (ill.), 274 (ill.), 275, no. 185; D'Alessandro and Elderfield, *Matisse: Radical Invention* (2010), pp. 43, 116, 119 n. 45, 141, 177 n. 6; Carbone, "Body Language" (2011), p. 47

20

Nasturtiums with the Painting "Dance" II, 1912

Oil on canvas, 76 x 44⅞ in. (193 x 114 cm)
The State Pushkin Museum of Fine Arts, Moscow (3301)
Not in exhibition
Signed (lower right): Henri-Matisse

Provenance: The artist (until end of July 1912; sold for 6,000 francs to Shchukin); Sergei Shchukin, Moscow (1912–18; probably received by Shchukin late summer 1913; confiscated by the Soviet authorities, November 5, 1918); First Museum of Modern Western Art, Moscow (1918–22); State Museum of Modern Western Art, Moscow (1922–48; Shchukin collection transferred in 1928 to the former Morosov mansion, then to Novossibirsk during WWII, then crated 1945–48); State Pushkin Museum, Moscow (since 1948)

Exhibitions: *Salon d'automne* (Paris 1912), no. 769 (erroneous lender's name); *Exposition universelle* (Brussels 1958), no. 210; *Chefs-d'oeuvre dans les musées de L'Ermitage et de Moscou* (Bordeaux 1965), no. 90; *Chefs d'oeuvre dans les musées de Leningrad et de Moscou* (Paris 1965–66), no. 90; *Terre des hommes* (Montreal 1967), no. 138; *Matisse* (Moscow–Leningrad 1969), no. 41; *Matisse ze sbirek sovětských muzeí* (Prague 1969–70), no. 12; *Van Van Gogh tot Picasso* (Otterlo 1972), no. 34; *Impressionist and Post-Impressionist Paintings* (Washington and other cities 1973), no. 25; *Matisse* (Tokyo–Kyoto 1981), no. 33; *Capolavori dai musei Sovietici* (Lugano 1983), no. 31; *42 Capolavori dai musei Sovietici* (Venice–Rome 1985), no. 37; *Impressionist to Early Modern Paintings from the U.S.S.R.* (Washington–Los Angeles–New York 1986), no. 31; *Tableaux de maîtres français de l'Union soviétique* (Quebec 1986), no. 31; *French Paintings from the USSR* (London 1988), no. 37; *Matisse* (Barcelona–Madrid 1988–89), no. 18; *From Poussin to Matisse* (New York–Chicago 1990), no. 48; *Matisse Retrospective* (New York 1992–93), no. 150; *Matisse* (Paris 1993), no. 104; *Anri Matiss* (Moscow–Saint Petersburg 1993), no. 46; *Morozov and Shchukin* (Essen–Moscow–Saint Petersburg 1993–94), no. 99; *Van Monet tot Matisse* (The Hague 1996), no. 31; *Da Monet a Picasso* (Milan 1996), no. 72; *Matisse, Picasso* (London–Paris–New York 2002–3), no. 81 (London), no. 72 (Paris), no. 81 (shown only in New York); *Old Masters, Impressionists, and Moderns* (Houston–Atlanta–Los Angeles 2002–3), no. 74

References: *American Art News*, "Autumn Salon" (1912), p. 5; Hind, "Ideals of Post-Impressionism" (1912), p. 6; Huneker, "Decade of the New Art Movement" (1912), p. SM12; Jean-Aubry, "Le Salon d'Automne" (1912), p. 320; Kahn, "Art" (1912), p. 881; Plée, "La vie artistique" (1912), p. 321; Vauxcelles, "Le Salon d'Automne" (1912), p. 2; MacChesney, "Talk with Matisse" (1913), p. 64; Shchukin collection, *Katalog kartin* (1913), pp. 28–29, no. 121; Tugenkhol'd, "Frantsuzskoe sobranie Shchukina" (1914), pp. 27–28, 42; Faure et al., *Henri-Matisse* (1920), pl. 11; Pertsov, *Shchukin Collection* (1921), p. 112, no. 121; *The Dial* 73, no. 1 (July 1922), p. 2 (ill.); Huneker, *Pathos of Distance* (1922), p. 152; Tugenkhol'd, *First Museum of Modern Western Painting* (1923), p. 143; *Musée d'Art Moderne de Moscou* (1928), p. 67, no. 331; Réau, *Catalogue de l'art français dans les musées russes* (1929), p. 118, no. 945; *Chroniques du jour*, "Pour ou contre Henri-Matisse" (1931), n.p. (ill.); Zervos, *Matisse* (1931), ill.; Becker, "Museum of Modern Western Painting in Moscow" (1932), p. 283; Courthion, *Matisse* (1934), p. 56, pl. 18; Romm, *Matisse* (1937), p. 29; *Cahiers d'art*, "Musée d'Art Moderne Occidental à Moscou" (1950), p. 343, no. 331; Barr, *Matisse: His Art and His Public* (1951), pp. 127, 144, 148, 156–57, 174, 194, 382 (ill.), 537 (n. 2 under p. 134), 539 (n. 5 under p. 144), 555; Diehl and Humbert, *Matisse* (1958), pp. 53, 101, 139, pl. 57; Sterling, *Great French Paintings in the Hermitage* (1958), pp. 180, 240 n. 161; Dresser, *Dial* (1959), p. 79; Langui, *50 Years* (1959), pp. 109 (ill.), 317, no. 205; Lassaigne, *Matisse* (1959), p. 69; Vipper, *Katalog kartinnoj galerei* (1961), p. 121, no. 3301;

Malitskaya, *Great Paintings from the Pushkin Museum* (1964), pl. 98; Leymarie, "Evoluzione di Matisse" (1967), pp. 45 (ill.), 46; Marchiori, *Matisse* (1967), pp. 42 (fig. 38), 58, 133; Moulin, *Matisse: Dessins* (1968), p. 16; Courthion, "Matisse et la danse" (1970), pp. 46, 47 (ill.) (both eds.); Diehl, *Matisse* (1970), pp. 20 (ill.), 58, under pl. 18; Aragon, *Matisse, roman* (1971), vol. 1, pp. 301, 323 (pl. 57), 351; Orienti, *Matisse* (1972), p. 32; Neff, "Matisse and Decoration" (1974), pp. 143–44, 180 n. 162, fig. 73; Neff, "Matisse and Decoration: Shchukin Panels" (1975), pp. 40, 41 (fig. 7), 44, 46 (fig. 15), 48 nn. 17, 23; Elderfield, *Matisse in the Museum of Modern Art* (1978), pp. 187–88 n. 38; Izerghina, *Matisse in Soviet Museums* (1978), pp. 19, 168 (ill.), 169–70, 172 (ill.), 173, no. 42; Gowing, *Matisse* (1979), pp. 96 (fig. 82), 103, 208; Kouznetsova and Georgievskaïa, *La peinture française au Musée Pouchkine* (1980), pp. 31, 391, no. 370, pl. 231; Antonova, *Masterpieces from the Pushkin Museum* (1982), pp. 190, 191 (pl. 87); Carrà and Deryng, *Tout l'oeuvre peint de Matisse* (1982), p. 92 (ill.), no. 147; Mannering, *Art of Matisse* (1982), pp. 49–50 (ill.); Barskaya and Bessonova, *Capolavori dai musei Sovietici* (1983), pp. 94, 95 (ill.), 129, no. 31; Kean, *All the Empty Palaces* (1983), pp. 124, 189 (ill.), 242, 296, 305; Mezzatesta, *Matisse Sculptor/Painter* (1984), pp. 94, 95 (fig. 61), 96; Watkins, *Matisse* (1984), pp. 115 (pl. 96), 119; Barbier, *L'Atelier d'Issy* (1985), no. 19; Messinger, "Thayer Bequest" (1985), pp. 46–47; Antonova, *Masterpieces from the Pushkin Museum* (1986), no. 82, ill.; Flam, *Matisse: The Man and His Art* (1986), pp. 344 (fig. 346), 345–48, 500 nn. 41, 42; Guichard-Meili, *Matisse* (1986), pp. 128, 132 (ill., flipped), 133, 143; Lieberman, *20th Century Art* (1986), p. 20; Babin et al., *French Paintings from the USSR* (1988), pp. 104 (ill.), 105, no. 37; Flam, *Matisse: A Retrospective* (1988), pp. 133–34, 160 (pl. 47); Izerghina, *Matisse in Soviet Museums* (1990), pp. 19, 172–73, no. 42 (ill.); Cowart et al., *Matisse in Morocco* (1990), pp. 218, 219 (fig. 105), 222, 237 n. 76, 247, 249, 253–54, 259, 265, no. 5, 267 n. 21, 268 n. 59; Fourcade and de Chassey, "Anthologie" (1993), pp. 488–90; Herrera, *Matisse: A Portrait* (1993), pp. 91 (ill.), 92; Kostenevich and Semyonova, *Collecting Matisse* (1993), pp. 33 (photo), 39, 129, 131 (ill.), 133–34, 172–73, 176; Bois, "On Matisse: The Blinding" (1994), p. 108; Lebovici and Peltier, "Lithophanies de Matisse" (1994), pp. 8, 38; Monneret, *Matisse* (1994), p. 97 (ill.), no. 186; Brodskaya, *Fauves* (1995), pp. 60, 93 (fig. 43); Flam, *Matisse on Art* (1995), pp. 67, 270 n. 5; Pushkin Museum *Katalog zhivopisi* (1995), pp. 378–79 (ill.), no. 3301; Girard, "Matisse und der Tanz" (1996), p. 28 (ill.); Kostenevich, "Un dialogo lungo" (1997), pp. 49, 54 (ill.); Alaoui et al., *Le Maroc de Matisse* (1999), pp. 16, 42, 46 (fig. 25), 217; Monrad, *Matisse: Four Great Collectors* (1999), pp. 26 (ill.), 61 (pl. 29), 76 (fig. 11), 232–33, no. 29; Schneider, Cowart, and Elderfield, *Matisse au Maroc* (1999), pp. 203, 205 (fig. 105), 207–8, 233 (fig. 118), 235, 238; Cauman, "Matisse and America" (2000), vol. 1, pp. 196 n. 12, 229, vol. 2, fig. 1.70; Antonova et al., *Old Masters, Impressionists, and Moderns* (2002), pp. 234–35 (ill.), 236, no. 74; Cook, "Rhythm Kings" (2002), pp. 30 (ill.), 31; Schneider, *Matisse* (2002), pp. 265 (ill.), 267, 302, 349, 431; Flam, *Matisse and Picasso* (2003), pp. 84, 85 (fig. 5.10), 132, 257; Amano et al., *Matisse: Processus/Variation* (2004), pp. 47 (fig. 19), 58 (fig. 2), 145; Bessonova and Georgievskaïa, *State Pushkin Museum of Fine Arts* (2005), pp. 155, 156 (ill.), 157–58, no. 125; Boehm, "Ausdruck und Dekoration" (2005), p. 279 (fig. 3); Bois, "De luxe Experiment" (2005), pp. 113, 115, 125 (fig. 8); Di Capua and Mattarella, "Il corpo in una stanza" (2006), p. 113 (fig. 11); Rewald in Tinterow et al., *Masterpieces of European Painting* (2007), p. 200 (under no. 185); D'Alessandro and Elderfield, *Matisse: Radical Invention* (2010), pp. 116 (fig. 13), 119 n. 45

21

***Palm Leaf, Tangier*, 1912**

Oil on canvas, 46¼ x 32¼ in. (117.5 x 81.9 cm)
National Gallery of Art, Washington, Chester Dale Fund (1978.73.1)
Signed (lower right): Henri-Matisse

Provenance: [Galerie Bernheim-Jeune, Paris, purchased from the artist, April 30, 1912; stock no. 19329, sold June 15, 1912, for 2,750 francs to Glaser]; [Curt Glaser, Berlin, 1912–13; to Moll by exchange for a Munch in 1913]; Oskar and Margarete [Greta] Moll, Berlin, Paris, and Breslau (1913–30); [Galerie Thannhauser (Justin K. Thannhauser), Berlin, by 1932]; [Valentine Gallery (F. Valentine Dudensing), New York]; [Eberhard Weyhe Gallery, New York, by the early 1940s–sold to Barr in 1948]; Mr. and Mrs. Alfred H. Barr Jr., New York (1948; on consignment with Thaw and Fourcade); [Eugene Victor Thaw and Co., New York, and Xavier Fourcade, Inc., New York, sold to National Gallery of Art, 1978]

Exhibitions: Possibly *Matisse: Tableaux du Maroc et sculpture* (Paris 1913), hors cat.; *Kollektionen: Matisse, Heckendorf, Kirchner, Leschnitzer* (Berlin 1913), no. 60; *Internationale Kunstausstellung* (Zürich 1925), no. 293; *Six Centuries of Landscape* (Montreal–Berlin 1952), no. 64; *Rétrospective Matisse* (Paris 1956), no. 32; *Dial and the Dial Collection* (Worcester 1959), no. 60; *Matisse centenaire* (Paris 1970), no. 114; *Matisse* (Zürich–Düsseldorf 1982–83), no. 35; *Orientalists* (London–Washington 1984), no. 99c (London), no. 77c (Washington); *Matisse* (Stockholm 1984–85), no. 20; "Matisse" (Humlebaek 1985), checklist no. 27; *Twentieth-Century Art* (Washington 1988–90), unnumbered cat., pp. 26, 27 (ill.), 150; *Matisse in Morocco* (Washington and other cities 1990–91a), no. 7; *Matisse* (Paris 1993), no. 98; "Matisse–Bonnard, une amitié" (Nice 1996), no cat.; *Matisse* (Rome 1997–98), no. 28; *Le Maroc de Matisse* (Paris 1999–2000a), no. 6; *Gärten* (Frankfurt am Main–Munich 2006–7), no. 118

References: Sembat, *Matisse* (1920), p. 10; Sembat, "Matisse und sein Werk" (1920), p. 194; Thayer, *Dial* (1925), ill. opp. p. 91; Barr, *Matisse: His Art and His Public* (1951), pp. 145, 154, 156–57, 381 (ill.), 540 (n. 2 under p. 154); Escholier, "Matisse et le Maroc" (1956), p. 710; Diehl and Humbert, *Matisse* (1958), p. 53; Salzmann and Salzmann, *Oskar Moll* (1975), p. 62; Gowing, *Matisse* (1979), p. 121; Carrà and Deryng, *Tout l'oeuvre peint de Matisse* (1982), p. 93 (ill.), no. 167; Flam, "Matisse in Morocco" (1982), pp. 82, 84 (ill.); Walker, *National Gallery of Art* (1984), p. 594, no. 923 (ill.); National Gallery, *European Paintings* (1985), p. 265 (ill.); Flam, *Matisse: The Man and His Art* (1986), pp. 349, 351 (fig. 351), 360, 419, 500 n. 50; Izerghina, *Matisse in Soviet Museums* (1990), p. 175 (ill.); Bois, "On Matisse: The Blinding" (1994), pp. 116, 117 (ill.), 118; Lebovici and Peltier, "Lithophanies de Matisse" (1994), pp. 7, 17–18, 38; Monneret, *Matisse* (1994), p. 97 (ill.), no. 182; Dauberville and Dauberville, *Matisse chez Bernheim-Jeune* (1995), vol. 1, pp. 508, 509 (ill.), no. 122; Kropmanns, "Matisse und die Molls" (1997), pp. 76 (ill.), 91–92; Schneider, Cowart, and Elderfield, *Matisse au Maroc* (1999) pp. 26, 31, 60–61 (ill.), 200, 255, 256 (no. 7, ill.), 257 (no. 7, ill.), 261–62, no. 75; Essers, *Matisse* (2002), p. 42; Schneider, *Matisse* (2002), pp. 450, 463 (ill.); Monod-Fontaine, "Variations autour d'un sujet" (2004), p. 47 (fig. 22); Strobl, *Curt Glaser* (2006), p. 22; D'Alessandro and Elderfield, *Matisse: Radical Invention* (2010), p. 343 (fig. 52b)

22

***Acanthus (Moroccan Landscape)*, 1912**

Oil on canvas, 45¼ x 31½ in. (115 x 80 cm)
Moderna Museet, Stockholm, Gift of Walther Halvorsen, 1917 (NM2070)
Signed (lower left): Henri-Matisse

Provenance: The artist (1912–13; sold on December 20, 1913, to Bernheim-Jeune); [Galerie Bernheim-Jeune, Paris, 1913–14; stock no. 20129, sold on March 4, 1914, for 5,000 francs, with two works by Van Dongen, to Rosenberg]; [Léonce Rosenberg, Paris, 1914–16; probably sold in December 1916 to Halvorsen]; [Walther Halvorsen, Paris and Oslo, 1916–17; his gift in 1917 to the Nationalmuseum, then Moderna Museet from 1958, Stockholm]

Exhibitions: *Den franske utstilling* (Oslo 1918), no. 45; *Matisse: Udstilling af hans arbejder* (Copenhagen–Stockholm–Oslo 1924), no. 38 (only shown in Copenhagen); *Fransk genombrottskonst från nittonhundratalet* (Stockholm and other cities 1931), no. 112; *Matisse* (Lucerne 1949), no. 51; *Matisse* (Nice 1950), no. 9; *Matisse* (New York and other cities 1951–52), no. 29; "Moderna Museet besøger Louisiana" (Humlebaek 1960), checklist, p. 32, no. 261; *Önskemuseet* (Stockholm 1963–64), no. 1; *Matisse centenaire* (Paris 1970), no. 113; *Matisse* (Copenhagen 1970), no. 32; "Moderna Museet besöker Liljevalchs" (Stockholm 1971), no cat.; "Moderna Museet på Liljevalchs Konsthall" (Stockholm 1975), no cat.; *Matisse* (Zürich–Düsseldorf 1982–83), no. 34; *Orientalists* (London–Washington 1984) no. 99a (London), no. 77a (Washington); *Matisse* (Stockholm 1984–85), no. 18; "Matisse" (Humlebaek 1985), no. 25, checklist pp. 44 (ill.), 57; *Matisse in Morocco* (Washington and other cities 1990–91a), no. 5; *Matisse* (Paris 1993), no. 96; *Monet to Matisse* (Edinburgh 1994), no. 123; *Matisse* (Brisbane–Canberra–Melbourne 1995), no. 62; *Moderna Museet Stockholm* (Bonn 1996–97), unnumbered cat., pp. 38, 39 (ill.), 297; *Moderna Klassiker* (Stockholm 2002–3), no. 40; "Den tidiga modernismen" (Malmö 2011), no cat.; "Change of Scenes" (Malmö 2011–12), no cat.

References: Sembat, "Matisse und sein Werk" (1920), p. 194; Zervos et al., *Matisse* (1931), p. 49 (fig. 36); Courthion, *Matisse* (1934), p. 56, pl. 21; Romm, *Matisse* (1937), pp. 8–9; Swane et al., *Matisse* (1944), p. 96, fig. 21; Raynal et al., *Modern Painting* (1950), pp. 46, 48 (ill.), 49–50; Barr, *Matisse: His Art and His Public* (1951), pp. 144–45, 154–56, 380 (ill.); Escholier, "Matisse et le Maroc" (1956), p. 710; Diehl and Humbert, *Matisse* (1958), p. 53; Lassaigne, *Matisse* (1959), pp. 72, 77–78; Escholier, *Matisse* (1960), pp. 89, 94, pl. 14; Brill, *Matisse* (1967), pp. 35–36, pl. 18; Guichard-Meili, *Matisse* (1967), pp. 73 (fig. 58), 79, 195, 246; Courthion, "La conquête de la lumiere" (1970), p. 54; Jacobus, *Matisse* (1972), pp. 31 (fig. 26), 32, 134; Fourcade and Monod-Fontaine, *Matisse: Dessins et sculpture* (1975), p. 90, under no. 42; Milhau, "Matisse, Picasso et Braque" (1975), p. 128; Gowing, *Matisse* (1979), p. 121; Carrà and Deryng, *Tout l'oeuvre peint de Matisse* (1982), p. 93 (ill.), no. 182, pl. XXVI; Flam, "Matisse in Morocco" (1982), pp. 82, 84, 85 (ill.); Watkins, *Matisse* (1984), pp. 112 (pl. 93), 114–15; Flam, *Matisse: The Man and His Art* (1986), pp. 314, 327, 331, 334 (fig. 336), 345, 349, 505 n. 4; Guichard-Meili, *Matisse* (1986), pp. 52 (ill.), 133, 141; Guillaud and Guillaud, *Matisse: Rhythm and Line* (1987), pp. 7 (fig. 3), 23, 63 (pl. 51); Flam, *Matisse: A Retrospective* (1988), pp. 140 (pl. 43), 302; Izerghina, *Matisse in Soviet Museums* (1990), p. 175 (ill.); Bjurström, *Nationalmuseum* (1992), p. 217 (ill.); Girard, *Matisse: Une splendeur inouïe* (1993), p. 77 (ill.); Herrera, *Matisse* (1993), pp. 106, 107 (ill.); Bois, "On Matisse: The Blinding" (1994), pp. 120 (ill.), 121; Monneret, *Matisse* (1994), p. 97 (ill.), no. 184; Dauberville and Dauberville, *Matisse chez Bernheim-Jeune* (1995), vol. 1, pp. 530, 531 (ill.), no. 139; Kostenevich, "Un dialogo lungo" (1997), pp. 51 (ill.), 52; Alaoui et al., *Le Maroc de Matisse* (1999), pp. 16, 40–41, 44 (fig. 22, sketch), 45 (fig. 23), 50, 62, 64, under no. 6, 182, 189, 228, 230; Domino, *Matisse et le Maroc* (1999), module 3 (ill.); Schneider, Cowart, and Elderfield, *Matisse au Maroc* (1999), pp. 26, 31, 56–57 (ill.), 195–98, 200, 202, 255, 256 (no. 5, ill.), 257 (no. 5, ill.), 260–61, no. 5; Klein, *Matisse Portraits* (2001), p. 198; Essers, *Matisse* (2002), pp. 40 (ill.), 42; Percheron and Brouder, *Matisse* (2002), p. 342; Schneider, *Matisse* (2002), pp. 450, 462 (ill.); Taube, *Kärleken och döden* (2002), pp. 38, 39 (ill.); Monod-Fontaine, "Variations autour d'un sujet" (2004), p. 47 (fig. 20); Bois, "De luxe Experiment" (2005), p. 126; Spurling, *Matisse the Master* (2005), pp. 113–14, 123; Hennig in Schulze, *Painter's Garden* (2006), p. 292, under no. 118; D'Alessandro and Elderfield, *Matisse: Radical Invention* (2010), pp. 115 (fig. 12), 117, 119 nn. 42, 43, 185, 187 n. 39

23

***Notre-Dame*, ca. 1900**

Oil on canvas, 18⅛ x 14¾ in. (46 x 37.5 cm)
Tate: Purchased 1949 (N05905)
Signed (lower right): Henri Matisse

Provenance: [Possibly with Ambroise Vollard, Paris, by 1904]; Alfred Klein, Paris and Le Cannet (ca. 1930–49; sold through the Galerie Rousso, Paris, in 1949, to the Tate)

Exhibitions: Possibly *Matisse* (Paris 1904), no. 22; *Matisse: Retrospective* (London 1968), no. 14; *Matisse* (Tokyo–Kyoto 1981), no. 11; *Monet to Matisse* (Edinburgh 1994), no. 59; *Matisse* (Brisbane–Canberra–Melbourne 1995), no. 9; *Cézanne to Picasso: Vollard* (New York–Chicago–Paris 2006–7), no. 132; *Bilder einer Metropole* (Essen 2010–11), no. 49

References: Hoppe, "På visit hos Matisse" (1919 interview with Matisse), 1931 repr., p. 193; Cooper, "Catalogue of the Courtauld Collection" (1954), p. 121; Escholier, *Matisse* (1960), pp. 12–13, pl. 1; Jacobus, *Matisse* (1972), pp. 96–97 (pl. 6); Fourcade, "Autres propos de Matisse" (1976), p. 93; Gosling, *Paris, 1900–1914* (1978), p. 33 (ill.); Gowing, *Matisse* (1979), pp. 29 (fig. 17), 30, 205; Siegel, "Matisse's *View of Notre Dame*" (1980), pp. 159 (ill.), 160; Alley, *Catalogue of the Tate* (1981), p. 492 (ill.), no. 5905; Watkins, *Matisse* (1984), pp. 15, 47 (pl. 27); Flam, *Matisse: The Man and His Art* (1986), pp. 98, 102 (fig. 84); Kostenevich, Rusakov, and Fukaya, *Matisse Retrospective* (1991), p. 58 (ill., under no. 8); Milner, *Matisse* (1994), p. 32 (ill.); Thomson, *Monet to Matisse* (1994), pp. 42, 43 (ill.), 192, no. 59; Flam, *Matisse on Art* (1995), p. 74; Freeman, *Fauves* (1995), p. 190 (fig. 1); Monod-Fontaine, "Variations autour d'un sujet" (2004), p. 47 (fig. 23); Blum, *Matisse: Rooms with a View* (2010), pp. 26, 27 (pl. 13), 29

24

***Notre-Dame*, 1914**

Oil on canvas, 57⅞ x 38⅝ in. (147 x 98 cm)
Kunstmuseum Solothurn, Dübi-Müller-Stiftung, Switzerland (C80.7)
Signed (lower left): Henri-Matisse

Provenance: [Galerie Bernheim-Jeune, Paris, purchased from the artist, July 28, 1914; stock no. 20429, sold to Lausanne branch, 1917]; [Galerie Bernheim-Jeune (Paul Vallotton), Lausanne, 1917; sold to Müller in August 1917]; Gertrud Müller, later Gertrud Dübi-Müller, Solothurn (1917–d. 1980; to her eponymous foundation in 1964; her bequest to the Dübi-Müller-Stiftung, 1980)

Exhibitions: *Ausstellung französischer Malerei* (Winterthur 1916), no. 103; *Januar-Ausstellung* (Basel 1917), no. 75; *Matisse* (Basel 1931), no. 32; *Matisse* (Lucerne 1949), no. 43; *Hundert Jahre Malerei aus Solothurner Privatbesitz* (Solothurn 1950), no. 132; *Chefs-d'oeuvre des collections suisses* (Lausanne 1964), no. 169; *Matisse centenaire* (Paris 1970), no. 125; *Matisse* (Zürich 1971), no. 7; *Matisse* (Basel 1980), no. 8; *Matisse* (Zürich-Düsseldorf 1982–83), no. 41 (shown only in Zürich); *Matisse Retrospective* (New York 1992–93), no. 176; *Kunst über Grenzen* (Munich 1999), no. 113; *Matisse: Processus/Variation* (Tokyo 2004), no. 2

References: Barth, *Matisse* (1917), pp. 4–5; Diehl and Humbert, *Matisse* (1958), p. 101, pl. 20; Diehl, *Matisse* (1970), p. 58; Elderfield, *Matisse in the Collection of the Museum of Modern Art* (1978), pp. 94, 96, 203 (fig. 76); Gowing, *Matisse* (1979), pp. 128 (fig. 113), 209; Siegel, "Matisse's *View of Notre-Dame*" (1980), p. 158 (ill.); Hauptman, "Notre-Dame de Paris" (1981), pp. 156–57 (ill.), no. 123; Carrà and Deryng, *Tout l'oeuvre peint de Matisse* (1982), p. 94 (ill.), no. 188, pl. XXIX; Flam, *Matisse: The Man and His Art* (1986), pp. 380, 381 (fig. 378), 502 nn. 7, 8, 505 n. 10; Hahnloser-Ingold, "Collecting Matisses of the 1920s in the 1920s (1986), p. 266; Ducrey and Ducrey, *La Galerie Paul Vallotton* (1988), p. 54 n. 8; Monneret, *Matisse* (1994), p. 99 (ill.), no. 217; Dauberville and Dauberville, *Matisse chez Bernheim-Jeune* (1995), vol. 1, p. 537 (ill.), no. 144; Blum, *Matisse: Rooms with a View* (2010), pp. 68, 69 (pl. 48); D'Alessandro and Elderfield, *Matisse: Radical Invention* (2010), p. 193 (fig. 23d)

25

***Notre-Dame*, 1914**

Oil on canvas, 58 x 37⅛ in. (147.3 x 94.3 cm)
The Museum of Modern Art, New York, Acquired through the Lillie P. Bliss Bequest, and the Henry Ittleson, A. Conger Goodyear, Mr. and Mrs. Robert Sinclair Funds, and the Anna Erickson Levene Bequest given in memory of her husband, Dr. Phoebus Aaron Theodor Levene, 1975 (116.75)
Stamped signature (lower left): H. Matisse

Provenance: The artist (1914–d. 1954; his estate, 1954–57; to his son); Pierre Matisse, New York (January 1957–75; sold through Eugene V. Thaw & Co., New York, to the Museum of Modern Art, 1975)

Exhibitions: *1914* (Baltimore 1964), no. 151; "Heroic Years: Paris" (Houston 1965), no cat.; *Matisse Retrospective* (Los Angeles–Chicago–Boston 1966), no. 37; *Matisse: 64 Paintings* (New York 1966), no. 27; *Matisse: Retrospective* (London 1968), no. 54; *Matisse centenaire* (Paris 1970), no. 126; *Matisse* (Copenhagen 1970), no. 35; *Matisse in the Collection of the Museum of Modern Art* (New York 1978–79), unnumbered cat., pp. 94, 95 (ill.), 96, 203–4; *Matisse* (Zürich–Düsseldorf 1982–83), no. 42; *Matisse Retrospective* (New York 1992–93), no. 177; *Matisse* (Paris 1993), no. 119; *Matisse: Masterworks from The Museum of Modern Art* (Atlanta 1996–97), unnumbered cat., pp. 76 (ill.), 77; *ModernStarts* (New York 1999–2000), unnumbered cat., pp. 260 (ill.), 262; *Le bleu de l'été* (Nice 2000), unnumbered cat., p. 41 (ill.); *Matisse, Picasso* (London–Paris–New York 2002–3), no. 63 (London and New York), no. 56 (Paris); *Heroic Century* (Houston 2003–4), unnumbered cat., p. 74 (ill.); *Das MoMA in Berlin* (Berlin 2004), unnumbered cat., p. 58 (ill.); *Matisse: Radical Invention* (Chicago–New York 2010), no. 23

References: Diehl and Humbert, *Matisse* (1954), p. 100; Greenberg, "Matisse in 1966" (1966), pp. 67, 71 (fig. 6); Seldis, "Magic of Matisse" (1966), p. 251; Russell, *World of Matisse* (1969), p. 119 (ill.); Mazars, "De la couleur avant toute chose" (1970), pp. 27 (ill.), 28; Roger-Marx, "Les dualités de Matisse" (1970), p. 32; Schneider, "Grand Palais: Matisse" (1970), p. 94; Aragon, *Matisse, roman* (1971), vol. 1, pp. 302, 332 (pl. 66), 351; Jacobus, *Matisse* (1972), p. 32 (fig. 27); Brice Marden in Lebensztejn, "Eight Statements" (1975), pp. 72–73; Russell, "Key Matisse Joins the Modern" (1975), p. 17 (ill.); Buck, "Ocean Park Paintings" (1976), pp. 43, 49 (fig. 69a); Laude, "Autour de la *Porte-fenêtre à Collioure* de Matisse" (1978), pp. 56, 58; Gowing, *Matisse* (1979), pp. 128 (fig. 114), 209; Gowing, *Matisse: Harmony of Light* (1979), pl. 13; Siegel, "Matisse's *View of Notre-Dame*" (1980), p. 159 (ill.); Carrà and Deryng, *Tout l'oeuvre peint de Matisse* (1982), p. 94 (ill.), no. 189; Hunter et al., *Museum of Modern Art* (1984), p. 72 (pl. 48); Flam, *Matisse: The Man and His Art* (1986), pp. 19, 380, 382 (fig. 379), 394, 407, 502 nn. 7–8, 505 n. 10; Guillaud and Guillaud, *Matisse: Rhythm and Line* (1987), pp. 23, 69 (pl. 57); Noël, *Matisse* (1987), pp. 41 (ill.), 43, 105; Flam, *Matisse: A Retrospective* (1988), p. 164 (pl. 51); Monod-Fontaine, *Matisse ou la couleur découpée* (1989), p. 45, slide no. 9; Monod-Fontaine, Baldassari, and Laugier, *Oeuvres de Matisse* (1989), pp. 38, 40 n. 3; Néret, *Matisse* (1991), pp. 84 (fig. 132), 87; Wilson, *Matisse* (1992), p. 74 (fig. 78); Fourcade and de Chassey, "Anthologie" (1993), p. 498, no. 119 (Sembat journal, 1914); Herrera, *Matisse* (1993), p. 115, pl. 16; Robinson and Bréda, *Matisse au Centre Pompidou* (1993), p. 74 (ill.); Bois, "On Matisse: The Blinding" (1994), pp. 66 (ill.), 67, 118; Lebovici and Peltier, "Lithophanies de Matisse" (1994), pp. 8, 29, 30 (ill.), 31–32, 38; Monneret, *Matisse* (1994), p. 99 (ill.), no. 218; Thomson, *Monet to Matisse* (1994), p. 43 (fig. 62); Bock-Weiss, *Matisse: Guide to Research* (1996), p. 311, no. 963; Néret, *Matisse* (1996), pp. 78 (ill.), 79, 92; Richardson, *Life of Picasso* (1996), p. 287; Kostenevich, "Un dialogo lungo" (1997), pp. 61, 62 (ill.); Cauman, "Matisse and America" (2000), vol. 1, p. 536; Monod-Fontaine, "Paysages avec ou sans figures" (2000), p. 139; Essers, *Matisse* (2002), pp. 44, 45 (ill.), 94; Marin-David, "Matisse, Picasso" (2002), p. 30 (ill.); Percheron and Brouder, *Matisse: De la couleur à l'architecture* (2002), p. 344; Schneider, *Matisse* (2002), pp. 133 (ill.), 320, 372, 381, 446, 479; Flam, *Matisse and Picasso* (2003), p. 101; Amano et al., *Matisse: Processus/Variation* (2004), pp. 14, 44, 47, 54 (fig. 1), 148, 260–61; Monod-Fontaine, "Question of Windows" (2005), pp. 193, 204 n. 11; Blum, *Matisse: Rooms with a View* (2010), pp. 68, 70 (pl. 49), 71, 77

26

Interior with Goldfish, 1914

Oil on canvas, 57⅞ x 38¼ in. (147 x 97 cm)
Centre Pompidou, Musée National d'Art Moderne, Paris, Bequest of Baronne Eva Gourgaud, 1965
(AM 4311 P)
Signed (lower left): Henri-Matisse

Provenance: The artist (1914–17; reserved for Shchukin in 1914 but never delivered due to the war; sold to Halvorsen in 1917); [private collection of Walther Halvorsen, Paris and Oslo, 1917–25; sold through Rosenberg in 1925]; [Galerie Paul Rosenberg, Paris, agent for Halvorsen; stock no. 1106, sold on June 3, 1925, for 40,000 francs to Gourgaud]; Baron Napoléon Gourgaud (d. 1944) and his wife, and later widow and executrix, née Eva Gebhard, Paris and New York (1925–her d. 1959; her estate, 1959–65; her bequest to the Musées Nationaux, 1965; assigned to the Musée National d'Art Moderne; at the Centre Pompidou since 1977)

Exhibitions: *Matisse* (New York 1915), no. 60; *La Triennale* (Paris 1916a), no. 87; *Den franske utstilling* (Oslo 1918), no. 44; *Utställning af fransk konst* (Stockholm 1918), no. 55; *Utställning af fransk konst* (Göteborg 1918), no. 51; *Fransk malerkunst* (Bergen 1918), no. 73; *Udstilling of fransk kunst* (Copenhagen 1919), no. 41; *Matisse* (Berlin 1930), no. 25; *Matisse* (Paris 1931), no. 27; *Matisse* (Basel 1931), no. 33; *Matisse Retrospective* (New York 1931), no. 26; *Matisse* (New York and other cities 1951–52), no. 35; *À la rencontre de Matisse* (Saint-Paul-de-Vence 1969), no. 9; *Matisse centenaire* (Paris 1970), no. 121; *Matisse* (Copenhagen 1970), no. 34; *Matisse Retrospective* (New York 1992–93), no. 169; *Matisse* (Paris 1993), no. 118; *Anri Matiss* (Moscow–Saint Petersburg 1993), no. 58; *Matisse* (Lyon 1998), unnumbered cat., pp. 7, 30 (ill.), 111; *Matisse: Processus/Variation* (Tokyo 2004), no. 75; *Matisse: Radical Invention* (Chicago–New York 2010), no. 24

References: Apollinaire, "Entrefilet" (1914); *Les Soirées de Paris*, "Sept reproductions" (1914), p. 264 (ill.); *New York Times*, "Matisse at the Montross Galleries" (1915), p. SM11 (ill.); Kahn, "Art" (1916), pp. 321–22; Faure et al., *Matisse* (1920), pl. 16; Joubin, "Jacques Doucet" (1930), p. 79 (fig. 5); McBride, *Matisse* (1930), p. 20; McBride, "Museum of Modern Art Gives a Matisse Exhibition" (1931); Barnes and De Mazia, *Art of Matisse* (1933), pp. 54, 90, 112, 437, no. 58; Kawashima, *Matisse* (1933); Besson, *La peinture française* (1934), fig. 27; Lipman, "Matisse Paintings in Clark Collection" (1934), pp. 139–40; Grünewald, *Matisse och Expressionismen* (1944), p. 44 (ill.); Barr, *Matisse: His Art and His Public* (1951), pp. 164, 168, 177, 179, 185, 188, 190–91, 203, 396 (ill.); Besson, *Matisse* (1954), pl. 35; Diehl and Humbert, *Matisse* (1958), pp. 51, 109, 122, pl. 71; Lassaigne, *Matisse* (1959), p. 76; Guichard-Meili, *Matisse* (1967), pp. 82 (fig. 70), 85, 247; Leymarie, "Evoluzione di Matisse" (1967), pp. 50, 52 (ill.); Diehl, *Matisse* (1970), pp. 21, 58, under pl. 27 (ill.); Fermigier, "Un barbare exquis" (1970), p. 41 (ill.); Fry, "Matisse" (1970), p. 21 (ill.); Aragon, *Matisse, roman* (1971), vol. 1, p. 302; Giraudy, "Correspondance Matisse–Camoin" (1971), p. 19 n. 97; Orienti, *Matisse* (1972), p. 91, pl. 15; Gordon, *Modern Art Exhibitions* (1974), vol. 1, p. 319 (fig. 1866), vol. 2, p. 863; Reff, "Matisse: Meditations on a Statuette and Goldfish" (1976), p. 113 (fig. 16); Elderfield, *Matisse in the Collection of the Museum of Modern Art* (1978), pp. 16 (ill.), 100, 205 (fig. 78); Laude, "Autour de la *Porte-fenêtre à Collioure*" (1978), p. 56; Monod-Fontaine, *Matisse* (1979), pp. 14 (ill.), 36, 37 (ill.), 38, no. 8; Carrà and Deryng, *Tout l'oeuvre peint de Matisse* (1982), p. 94 (ill.), no. 184, pl. XXXI; Watkins, *Matisse* (1984), pp. 124, 125 (pl. 107), 127, 130, 139; Flam, *Matisse: The Man and His Art* (1986), pp. 376, 378, 379 (fig. 377), 380, 397, 505 n. 10; Guichard-Meili, *Matisse* (1986), pp. 134, 135 (ill.), 143; Hahnloser-Ingold, "Collecting Matisses of the 1920s in the 1920s" (1986), p. 237 (fig. 6); Monod-Fontaine, "Matisse" (1986), pp. 410 (ill.), 411; Guillaud and Guillaud, *Matisse: Rhythm and Line* (1987), pp. 23, 68 (pl. 56); Flam, *Matisse: A Retrospective* (1988), p. 293 (translation of Kawashima 1933); Monod-Fontaine, Baldassari, and Laugier, *Oeuvres de Matisse* (1989), pp. 38, 39 (ill.), 40, no. 9; Izerghina, *Matisse in Soviet Museums* (1990), p. 165 (ill.); Fourcade and de Chassey, "Anthologie" (1993), pp. 497–98; Lebovici and Peltier, "Lithophanies de Matisse" (1994), pp. 8, 9 (ill.), 28, 31, 38; Monneret, *Matisse* (1994), pp. 58 (ill.), 59 (ill.), 99 (ill.), no. 214; Dauberville and Dauberville, *Matisse chez Bernheim-Jeune* (1995), vol. 1, pp. 211 (facsimile of Paris 1931), 267 (photo); Bois, *Matisse and Picasso* (1998), p. 65; Gaussen, *Le 5e arrondissement vu par les peintres* (1998), pp. 32, 33 (ill.); Kostenevich, "Sergei Shchukin" (1999), p. 89 (fig. 18); Monrad, *Matisse: Four Great Collectors* (1999), p. 172 (fig. 50); Cauman, "Matisse and America" (2000), vol. 1, pp. 257, 261, 268, 271, 274, 276, 494, vol. 2, fig. 2.6; Klein, *Matisse Portraits* (2001), pp. 184, 227; Percheron and Brouder, *Matisse*

(2002), pp. 346 (fig. 375), 347; Schneider, *Matisse* (2002), pp. 350, 419, 420 (ill.), 424, 474, 476, 479–80; Varnedoe in Cowling et al., *Matisse, Picasso* (2002), pp. 131, 350 (fig. 42), French ed.: p. 133; Monod-Fontaine, "Question of Windows" (2005), pp. 191, 204 n. 6; Pincemaille, *La Folie Gourgaud* (2009), pp. 82, 119, 128 (n. 108); Blum, *Matisse: Rooms with a View* (2010), pp. 64, 65 (pl. 45), 67

27

Goldfish and Palette, 1914

Oil on canvas, 57⅝ x 44¼ in. (146.5 x 112.4 cm)
The Museum of Modern Art, New York, Gift and bequest of Florene M. Schoenborn and Samuel A. Marx, 1964 (507.1964)
Signed (lower right): Henri-Matisse

Provenance: [Galerie Bernheim-Jeune, Paris, purchased from the artist, May 25, 1915; stock no. 20467, sold May 26, 1915, for 6,000 francs to Rosenberg]; [Léonce Rosenberg, Paris, May 26, 1915]; Jacques Doucet, Neuilly (purchased through Paul Guillaume, advised by André Breton, November 1923–d. 1929; to his widow); Mme Jacques Doucet, Neuilly (1929–39; on extended loan to the Museum of Modern Art, New York, April 21, 1939–January 31, 1947, E.L. 39.397; during which sold to de Hauke); [Cesar M. de Hauke, Paris, on behalf of Jacques Seligmann & Co., New York, 1939–47; purchased from Mme Doucet in 1939; delivered by the Museum of Modern Art to Knoedler for de Hauke on January 31, 1947]; [M. Knoedler & Co., Inc., New York, sold May 8, 1947, for 15,000 dollars to Matisse]; [Pierre Matisse Gallery, New York, purchased from Knoedler, May 8, 1947; stock no. 2225, sold on December 3, 1948, for 20,000 dollars to Marx]; Mr. and Mrs. Samuel A. Marx, Chicago (1948–64; their promised gift to the Museum of Modern Art in 1964; received through bequest of Florene May Schoenborn—Samuel A. Marx's widow, later Mrs. Wolfgang Schoenborn—in 1995)

Exhibitions: *Art in Our Time* (New York 1939), no. 94; *Modern Painting Isms* (Baltimore 1940), unnumbered cat.; "Refugee Art" (Detroit-Poughkeepsie 1941), no cat.; *Matisse Retrospective* (New York 1943a), no. 8; *Ivory Black in Modern Painting* (New York 1944), no. 10; *Matisse Retrospective* (Philadelphia 1948), no. 31; *Matisse* (New York and other cities 1951–52), no. 37; *Matisse* (Los Angeles 1952), no. 24; *Paintings from Private Collections* (New York 1955b), no. 90; *Rétrospective Matisse* (Paris 1956), no. 36; *School of Paris* (New York and other cities 1965–66), unnumbered cat., pp. 7, 10 (ill., flipped), 12; *Cézanne to Miró* (New York and other cities 1968), unnumbered cat., p. 29 (ill.); *Matisse Retrospective* (New York 1992–93), no. 179; *Matisse* (Paris 1993), no. 123; *Matisse* (Atlanta 1996–97), unnumbered cat., pp. 80–81; "Masterworks from the Schoenborn Bequest" (New York 1997), no cat.; *Objects of Desire* (New York–London 1997–98), unnumbered cat., pp. 90, 94, 95 (pl. 45), 223; *ModernStarts* (New York 1999–2000), unnumbered cat., p. 278 (ill.); *Matisse, Picasso* (London–Paris–New York 2002–3), no. 69 (London and New York), no. 61 (Paris); *Heroic Century* (Houston 2003–4), unnumbered cat., p. 75 (ill.); *Das MoMA in Berlin* (Berlin 2004), unnumbered cat., p. 59 (ill.); *Matisse: Radical Invention* (Chicago–New York 2010), no. 31

References: Salmon, *L'art vivant* (1920), pp. 228–29; Schwob, "Matisse" (1920), p. 195 (ill.); Einstein, *Kunst des 20. Jahrhunderts* (1926), pp. 183 (ill), 559; Zervos, "De l'importance de l'objet" (1930), p. 116 (ill.); Fry, "Matisse" (1931), p. 285 (fig. 53); Zervos et al., *Matisse* (1931), p. 63 (fig. 49); Zervos, *L'art contemporain* (1938), p. 163 (ill.); Barr, *Matisse: His Art and His Public* (1951), pp. 157, 164, 168, 169 (ill.), 171, 174, 181, 188, 190–91; Greenberg, *Matisse* (1955), pl. 13 and cover ill.; Hunter, *Matisse* (1956), fig. 10; Diehl and Humbert, *Matisse* (1958), p. 51; Revel, "Jacques Doucet" (1961), p. 45 (photo); Gottlieb, "Role of the Window in the Art of Matisse" (1964), pp. 398, 407 (fig. 8), 414–15, 418–19; Guichard-Meili, *Matisse* (1967), pp. 79 (fig. 67), 85, 247; Aragon, *Matisse, roman* (1971), vol. 1, pp. 96 (pl. 9), 302, 347; Cooper, *Cubist Epoch* (1971), pp. 206–7; Giraudy, "Correspondance Matisse–Camoin" (1971), p. 19; Jacobus, *Matisse* (1972), pp. 144–45 (pl. 30), 152, 154; Lyons, "Matisse: Work, 1914–1917" (1975), p. 75; Reff, "Matisse: Meditations on a Statuette and Goldfish" (1976), p. 113 (fig. 17); Elderfield, *Matisse in the Museum of Modern Art* (1978), pp. 100, 101 (ill.), 102, 204; Golding, *W. A. Cargill Memorial* (1978), p. 16; Gowing, *Matisse* (1979), pl. 14; Carrà and Deryng, *Tout l'oeuvre peint de Matisse* (1982), pp. 94, 95 (ill.), no. 202; Jacobus, *Matisse* (1982), pp. 144–45 (pl. 30); Chapon, *Mystère et splendeurs de Jacques Doucet* (1984), pp. 15, 293, 295, 333, 342–43, 381 n. 95; Hunter et al., *Museum of Modern Art* (1984), p. 72 (pl. 49); Watkins, *Matisse* (1984), p. 130 (pl. 114); Flam, *Matisse: The Man and His Art* (1986), pp. 397, 398 (fig. 397), 402–3, 405, 416, 441, 502 nn. 8, 10, 503 n. 47, 505 n. 10, and sketch p. 399 (fig. 398); Hahnloser-Ingold, "Collecting Matisses of the 1920s in the 1920s" (1986), pp. 242, 243 (photo); Cousins and Seckel, "Éléments pour une chronologie des *Demoiselles d'Avignon*" (1988), vol. 2, p. 587; Flam, *Matisse: A Retrospective* (1988), p. 166 (pl. 53); Monod-Fontaine, *Matisse ou la couleur découpée* (1989), p. 46, slide no. 10; Monod-Fontaine, Baldassari, and Laugier, *Oeuvres de Matisse* (1989), pp. 38, 40 (ill.), under no. 9; Fourcade and de Chassey, "Anthologie" (1993), pp. 501–2, no. 123 (1923 letter from Breton to Doucet); Girard, *Matisse: Une splendeur inouïe* (1993), p. 80 (ill.); Herrera, *Matisse: A Portrait* (1993), pp. 117, 118 (ill.), 119–21, 142; Bois, "On Matisse: The Blinding" (1994), p. 118; Cousins and Seckel, "Chronology of *Les Demoiselles d'Avignon*" (1994), p. 179; Lebovici and Peltier, "Lithophanies de Matisse" (1994), pp. 8, 14, 20–21, 26, 27 (ill.), 28–29, 32, 38; Monneret, *Matisse* (1994), pp. 52, 59, 99 (ill.), no. 220; Benjamin, "Vital Sign" (1995), pp. 29, 30 (fig. 16); Bernier, "Matisse, el conservador inspirado" (1995), pp. 38, 39 (ill.), 41; Dauberville and Dauberville, *Matisse chez Bernheim-Jeune* (1995), vol. 1, pp. 542, 543 (ill.), no. 148; Richardson, *Life of Picasso* (1996), pp. 386 (ill.), 387; Wolinski, "Les joyaux de l'héritage Doucet" (1996), pp. 94 (fig. 8), 95; Grammont, *Correspondence entre Camoin et Matisse* (1997), p. 67 (1914 postcard from Matisse to Camoin); Bois, *Matisse and Picasso*, exh. cat. (1998), pp. 11, 14 (fig. 5), 15; Cauman, "Matisse and America" (2000), vol. 1, pp. 386, 533 n. 7, vol. 2, fig. 3.12; Green, *Art in France* (2000), pp. 102, 103 (fig. 115); Schnell, *"Das rote Atelier"* (2001), pp. 36, 106, 134 (pl. 4); Carnielli and Loudon, "Chronology" (2002), p. 194 (installation photo, New York 1943a); Marin-David, "Matisse, Picasso" (2002), p. 34 (ill.); Schneider, *Matisse* (2002), pp. 350, 414, 418 (ill.), 419, 421–22, 434, 437–38, 481, 736; Werth, *Joy of Life* (2002), pp. 236, 301 no. 18; Flam, *Matisse and Picasso* (2003), pp. 102, 103 (fig. 6.7), 104, 106–7, 156, 257; Amano, "La peinture en procès" (2004), p. 17; Tanaka, "Le lieu de la production" (2004), pp. 95 (fig. 2), 96, 99; Flam, "Goldfish" (2005), pp. 165, 168 (fig. 4), 169, 179; Monod-Fontaine, "Question of Windows" (2005), pp. 190 (fig. 2), 191, 204 n. 7; Spurling, *Matisse, the Master* (2005), pp. 168, 186, 226, 256 (fig. 17); Chapon, *C'était Jacques Doucet* (2006), pp. 15, 274–75 (photo), 426, 429, 486, 499, 501; Blum, *Matisse: Rooms with a View* (2010), pp. 64, 66 (pl. 44), 67, 181

28

Marguerite in a Leather Hat, 1914

Oil on canvas, 32¼ x 25⅝ in. (82 x 65 cm)
Musée Matisse, Le Cateau-Cambrésis, Gift of Marie Matisse (2002-3)
Copenhagen only
Not signed

Provenance: The artist (1914–d. 1954; his estate; to his son); Jean Matisse, Pontoise (until d. 1976; to his widow); Marie Matisse, Pontoise (until d. 1999; gift from her estate to the Musée Matisse, Le Cateau-Cambrésis, 2002)

Exhibitions: "Matisse: L'atelier d'Issy-les-Moulinaux" (Le Cateau-Cambrésis 1986–87), no cat.; *Matisse et l'Italie* (Venice 1987), no. P25

References: Flam, *Matisse: The Man and His Art* (1986), pp. 434 (fig. 438, photo), 504 n. 1; *La Voix du Nord*, "Un Matisse exposé pour la première fois" (1986), p. 26 (ill.); Guillaud and Guillaud, *Matisse: Rhythm and Line* (1987), pp. 10 (pl. 5), 17; Malaurie, "Matissimo!" (1987), p. 57 (ill.); Néret, *Matisse* (1991), p. 95 (fig. 148); Néret, *Matisse* (1996), pp. 88 (ill.), 92; Monod-Fontaine, "La dation Marie Matisse" (2002), p. 16; Percheron and Brouder, *Matisse* (2002), pp. 266,

273 (fig. 293); Schneider, *Matisse* (2002), pp. 323 (ill.), 520 n. 6; Szymusiak, *Musée Matisse*" (2002), pp. 13, 101 (photo), 104 (ill.), 105; Monod-Fontaine, "Marguerite, Her Father's Model" (2008), p. 78; D'Alessandro and Elderfield, *Matisse: Radical Invention* (2010), pp. 236, 237 (fig. 30d), 239, 277, 333 n. 4

29

White and Pink Head, 1914–15

Oil on canvas, 29½ x 18½ in. (75 x 47 cm)
Centre Pompidou, Musée National d'Art Moderne, Paris, Purchase, 1976 (AM 1976-8)
Copenhagen only
Signed (lower right): Henri / Matisse

Provenance: [Galerie Bernheim-Jeune, Paris, 1915–19; purchased from the artist on December 21, 1915; returned in 1919 to the artist]; the artist (1919–d. 1954; his estate; to his son); Jean Matisse, Pontoise (until d. 1976; sold to Musée National d'Art Moderne, 1976; at the Centre Pompidou since 1977)

Exhibitions: *Exposition de peinture* (Paris 1916), no. 47; *Matisse Retrospective* (New York 1931), no. 27; *Matisse* (Providence 1931), no. 12; *Matisse* (Aix-en-Provence 1960), no. 13; *Matisse centenaire* (Paris 1970), no. 124; *Matisse* (Rome 1978–79), no. 7; *Paris en quatre temps* (Warsaw 1986–87), unnumbered cat., p. 55; *Matisse et l'Italie* (Venice 1987), no. P24; *Matisse Retrospective* (New York 1992–93), no. 180; *Matisse* (Paris 1993), no. 122; *Anri Matiss* (Moscow–Saint Petersburg 1993), no. 57; *Identity and Alterity* (Venice 1995), unnumbered cat., pp. 194, 195 (ill.); *La collection du Centre Pompidou* (Paris 1998–99), unnumbered cat., p. 26; *Le Musée qui n'existait pas* (Paris 2002), hors cat.; *Matisse: Processus/Variation* (Tokyo 2004), no. 8; *Matisse: Menschen Masken Modelle* (Stuttgart–Hamburg 2008–9), no. 24 (shown only in Stuttgart); *Matisse: Radical Invention* (Chicago–New York 2010), no. 30

References: Basler, *Matisse* (1924), ill. n.p.; Zervos, "L'art nègre" (1927), p. 257 (ill.); Zervos, *L'art contemporain* (1938), p. 155 (ill.); Wilenski, *Modern French* (1940), p. 258; Barr, *Matisse: His Art and His Public* (1951), pp. 181, 188, 194, 402 (ill.); Wilenski, *Modern French* (1954), p. 258; Escholier, *Matisse, ce vivant* (1956), pp. 173, 182; Diehl and Humbert, *Matisse* (1958), pp. 51, 101, 105, 108, 122, pl. 67; Selz, *Matisse* (1964), pp. 17, 39 (ill.), 47, 55; Brill, *Matisse* (1967), p. 36, pl. 19; Leymarie, "Evoluzione di Matisse" (1967), p. 78 (ill.); Laude, *La peinture française et l'art nègre* (1968), p. 237 (fig. 50); Diehl, *Matisse* (1970), pp. 19, 58, pl. 23; Esteban, "Une limpidité nécessaire" (1970), p. 74; Guichard-Meili, "Les odalisques" (1970), p. 64; Schneider, "Grand Palais: Matisse" (1970), pp. 90 (ill.), 94; Aragon, *Matisse, roman* (1971), vol. 1, pp. 302, 333 (pl. 67), 351; Cooper, *Cubist Epoch* (1971), pp. 206 (pl. 234), 207; Elsen, *Sculpture of Matisse* (1972), p. 138; Flam, *Norton Matisses* (1973), n.p.; Fourcade and Monod-Fontaine, *Matisse: Dessins et sculpture* (1975), p. 19; Lyons, "Matisse: Work, 1914–1917" (1975), pp. 74–75; Milhau, "Matisse, Picasso et Braque" (1975), p. 127; Musée National d'Art Moderne, *100 oeuvres nouvelles* (1977), pp. 93 (ill.), 94; Elderfield, *Matisse in the Collection of the Museum of Modern Art* (1978), pp. 100, 206 (fig. 81); Flam, *Matisse on Art* (1978), p. 14; Laude, "Autour de la *Porte-fenêtre à Collioure* de Matisse" (1978), pp. 56, 69 n. 4, 73 n. 41; Monod-Fontaine, *Matisse: Oeuvres* (1979), pp. 15 (ill.), 38, 39 (ill.), 40 (ill.), 41, no. 9; Carrà and Deryng, *Tout l'oeuvre peint de Matisse* (1982), p. 94 (ill.), no. 187; Daix, *Cubists and Cubism* (1982), pp. 132 (ill.), 134; Mezzatesta, *Matisse, Sculptor/Painter* (1984), pp. 100 (fig. 65), 101; Watkins, *Matisse* (1984), pp. 124, 126 (pl. 109), 226; Monod-Fontaine, *Sculpture of Matisse* (1984), p. 19 (fig. 19); Flam, *Matisse: The Man and His Art* (1986), pp. 400 (fig. 400), 402–3, 503 n. 47; Guichard-Meili, *Matisse* (1986), pp. 33, 37, 134; Monod-Fontaine, "Matisse" (1986), pp. 409, 412; Guillaud and Guillaud, *Matisse: Rhythm and Line* (1987), pp. 71, 72 (pl. 59); Noël, *Matisse* (1987), p. 43; Flam, *Matisse: A Retrospective* (1988), p. 153 (ill.); Monod-Fontaine, Baldassari, and Laugier, *Oeuvres de Matisse* (1989), pp. 46, 47 (ill.), 48 (ill.), 49, no. 11; Néret, *Matisse* (1991), pp. 94 (fig. 147), 97, 125; Wilson, *Matisse* (1992), p. 78 (fig. 84); Herrera, *Matisse: A Portrait* (1993), p. 119 (ill.); Lebovici and Peltier, "Lithophanies de Matisse" (1994), p. 26; Monneret, *Matisse* (1994), pp. 14, 99 (ill.), no. 216; Monod-Fontaine, "Black Light: Matisse" (1995), p. 92 (fig. 9); Richardson, *Life of Picasso*, vol. 2 (1996), pp. 286 (ill.), 287; Bois, *Matisse and Picasso* (1998), pp. 14 (fig. 6), 15; Cauman, "Matisse and America" (2000), vol. 1, p. 494, vol. 2, fig. 4.13; Klein, *Matisse Portraits* (2001), pp. 100, 101 (fig. 66), 222, 250, 264 n. 92; Percheron and Brouder, *Matisse: De la couleur à l'architecture* (2002), p. 344 (fig. 372); Schneider, *Matisse* (2002), pp. 322 (ill.), 328, 413, 474, 479, 486, 490, 520 n. 6, 735; Werth, *Joy of Life* (2002), p. 236; Monod-Fontaine, "Variations autour d'un sujet" (2004), pp. 45, 48 (fig. 32)

30

Goldfish, 1912

Oil on canvas, 32¼ x 36¾ in. (82 x 93.5 cm)
Statens Museum for Kunst, Copenhagen, J. Rump Collection (KMSr82)
Signed (lower left): Henri-Matisse

Provenance: [Galerie Bernheim-Jeune, Paris, 1912–17; purchased from the artist on May 24, 1912, for 1,553 francs; stock no. 19564, sold on May 1, 1917, for 7,000 francs to Halvorsen]; [Walther Halvorsen, Paris and Oslo, purchased on behalf of Tetzen-Lund, by March 1917; sale recorded May 1]; Johannes Tetzen-Lund, Copenhagen (by March 1917–25; his sale, "Franske og Skandinaviske Billeder tilhørende Tetzen-Lund's Samlinger," Copenhagen, May 18–19, 1925, no. 91, to Rump); Johannes Rump, Copenhagen (1925–28; his gift to the Statens Museum for Kunst, Copenhagen, January 19, 1928)

Exhibitions: *Second Post-Impressionist Exhibition* (London 1912), no. 29; *Prima esposizione internazionale d'arte della "Secessione"* (Rome 1913), no. 13; *Exposition de peinture, série C* (Paris 1916b), no. 48; *Den franske utstilling* (Oslo 1916), no. 30; *Moderne fransk kunst* (Copenhagen 1917), no. 1a or 2; *Matisse: Udstilling af hans arbejder* (Copenhagen–Stockholm–Oslo 1924), no. 43 (shown only in Copenhagen); *Matisse* (Copenhagen 1970), no. 33; *Matisse Retrospective* (New York 1992–93), no. 154; *Matisse* (Paris 1993), no. 100; *Johannes Rump* (Copenhagen 1994–95), no. 168; *Franske mesterværker* (Aarhus 1996–97), no. 34; *Age of Modernism* (Berlin 1997), no. 33; *Anri Matiss* (Saint Petersburg 1998), no. 22; *Matisse: Four Great Collectors* (Copenhagen 1999), no. 70; *Matisse &* (Copenhagen 2005), no. 17

References: *Gil blas*, "L'exposition postexpressioniste à la Grafton Gallery" (1912); *Politiken* (Denmark), April 1, 1917; Häuser, "Ein dänischer Sammler" (1918), p. 164; Swane, *J. Rumps Samling* (1929), pp. 47–48, no. 82, pl. 20; Swane, "J. Rumps Samling" (1929–31), pp. 65, 73; Swane, "Udstilling af moderne fransk kunst" (1931), p. 424; Zervos et al., *Matisse* (1931), pp. 26, 43 (fig. 32); Tetzen-Lund *Samling af moderne fransk malerkunst* (1934), p. 4, pl. 47; Zahle, *Fransk maleri efter 1900* (1938), p. 10, fig. 7; Zervos, *L'art contemporain* (1938), p. 150 (ill.); Madsen, *Från symbolism till Surrealism* (1939), p. 67 (ill.); Swane et al., *Matisse* (1944), pp. 62, 96, fig. 16; Wennberg, "Från Delacroix till Matisse" (1947), p. 87; Swane, *J. Rumps Samling* (1948), pp. 86, 89 (ill.), no. 106; Andersen, "Hos Matisse" (1950), p. 127; Barr, *Matisse: His Art and His Public* (1951), pp. 100, 127–28, 164, 190, 199, 348 (ill.); Finsen, "Kapellet in Vence" (1951), p. 59; Diehl and Humbert, *Matisse* (1958), p. 105, pl. 45; Halvorsen, "Kunstnerforbundet Exhibition in 1916" (1959); Lassaigne, *Matisse* (1959), p. 66; Escholier, *Matisse* (1960), pp. 12, 15, pl. 9; Finsen, *J. Rumps samling etc.* (1964), p. 56, no. R82, pl. R82; Marchiori, *Matisse* (1967), pp. 40 (fig. 36), 133; Bowness, *Matisse and the Nude* (1968), pl. 15; Diehl, *Matisse* (1970), p. 57, under pl. 14 (ill.); Schneider, *Matisse Centenaire* (1970), p. 38 (ill.); Sutton, "Mozart of Painting" (1970), p. 362 (pl. VII); Elsen, *Sculpture of Matisse* (1972), pp. 75, 78 (pl. 94); Jacobus, *Matisse* (1972), pp. 24 (fig. 17), 144; Orienti, *Matisse* (1972), p. 31; Gordon, *Modern Art Exhibitions* (1974), vol. 1, p. 248 (fig. 1232), vol. 2, pp. 626 (London 1912), 682 (Rome 1913, no. 13); Reff, "Matisse: Meditations on a Statuette and Goldfish" (1976), p. 111 (fig. 12); Elderfield, *Matisse in the Collection of the Museum of Modern Art* (1978), p. 197 n. 4 (fig. 60); Izerghina, *Matisse in Soviet Museums* (1978), pp. 155, 161 (ill.); Gowing, *Matisse* (1979), pp. 76, 77 (fig. 58), 207; Linker, "Meditation on a Goldfish Bowl" (1980), p. 66; Carrà and

Deryng, *Tout l'oeuvre peint de Matisse* (1982), pp. 90 (ill.), 91, no. 117; Barbier, "Oeuvres réalisées à Issy-les-Moulineaux" (1985), no. 21; Flam, *Matisse: The Man and His Art* (1986), pp. 342 (fig. 345), 343, 422, 499 nn. 32, 33; Guichard-Meili, *Matisse* (1986), pp. 104 (ill.), 133, 142; Guillaud and Guillaud, *Matisse: Rhythm and Line* (1987), pp. 23, 58 (pl. 47); Monod-Fontaine, Baldassari, and Laugier, *Matisse: Oeuvres* (1989), p. 321 n. 4, under no. 118; Izerghina, *Matisse in Soviet Museums* (1990), p. 165 (ill.); Néret, *Matisse* (1991), pp. 55 (fig. 83), 59; Ferrier, *Les Fauves* (1992), p. 53 (ill.); Wilson, *Matisse* (1992), p. 68 (fig. 63); Fergonzi, "Firenze 1910–Venezia 1920: Emilio Cecchi" (1993), pl. 2; Flam, "Matisse" (1993), p. 244 (fig. 3); Scavenius, *Se på verdenskunst i Danmark* (1993), p. 76; Monnerret, *Matisse* (1994), p. 95 (ill.), no. 153; Dauberville and Dauberville, *Matisse chez Bernheim-Jeune* (1995), vol. 1, pp. 500, 501 (ill.), no. 118; Jensen, *De glade givere* (1996), pp. 259, 263 (photo), 325 (ill.); Néret, *Matisse* (1996), p. 69 (ill.); Raaschou-Nielsen, *Fransk modernisme* (1996), pp. 104–5 (ill.), 106, 153, no. 34; Schneider, *Matisse* (2002), pp. 350, 420, 421 (ill.), 422, 468; Aagesen, "Matisse: Eight Takes" (2005), pp. 12–13, 17, 21; Flam, "Goldfish" (2005), pp. 160–33; Monod-Fontaine, "Question of Windows" (2005), p. 191; Perry, "Playing with Paint" (2005), pp. 100 (fig. 7), 101; Buschhoff, "'Der grosse Stil der Form'" (2007), pp. 198 (fig. 6), 199; Elderfield, "La seduzione della pittura" (2011), p. 326 (ill.)

31

***Sculpture and Vase of Ivy*, 1916**

Oil on canvas, 23⅝ x 28¾ in. (60 x 73 cm)
Centre Pompidou, Musée National d'Art Moderne, Paris, Gift of Adèle and George Besson, 1963 (AM 4224 P [6]). On extended loan to the Musée des Beaux-Arts et d'Archéologie, Besançon (DA. 970.1.75)
Signed (lower left): Henri Matisse

Provenance: [Galerie Bernheim-Jeune, Paris, purchased from the artist, February 6, 1917; stock no. 20835, sold February 26, 1917, to Besson]; Adèle and George Besson (1917–63; their gift to the French State; assigned to the Musée National d'Art Moderne, Paris, 1963; on extended loan to the Musée des Beaux-Arts et d'Archéologie in Besançon since January 19, 1972)

Exhibitions: *De Matisse à Segonzac* (Paris 1932), no. 30; *Matisse* (Paris 1950), no. 42; *Rétrospective Matisse* (Paris 1956), no. 38; *Cent tableaux de collections privées* (Paris 1960), no. 73; *Collection Besson* (Paris 1964–65), no. 127; *Matisse* (Stockholm 1984–85), no. 22; "Matisse" (Humlebaek 1985), checklist no 29; *La sculpture des peintres* (Saint-Paul-de-Vence 1997), no. 57; *Des nus & des nues* (Ornans 2003), unnumbered cat. pp. 70 (ill.), 71 (ill.); *Matisse: Figur Farbe Raum* (Düsseldorf 2005–6), no. 66; *Matisse: Figure, couleur, espace* (Basel 2006), no. 47; *Matisse e Bonnard* (Rome 2006–7), no. 11; *Die Skulpturen der Maler* (Baden-Baden 2008), no. 46; *Matisse, Rodin* (Nice–Paris 2009–10), no. 139; *Matisse: La seduzione di Michelangelo* (Brescia 2011), unnumbered cat., p. 177

References: Faure et al., *Matisse* (1920), pl. 17; Besson, *La peinture française au XXe siècle* (1949), vol. 1, fig. 8; Barr, *Matisse: His Art and His Public* (1951), p. 181; Besson, *Matisse* (1954), pl. 30; Reff, "Matisse: Meditations on a Statuette and Goldfish" (1976), pp. 114, 115 n. 22; Monod-Fontaine, *Sculpture of Matisse* (1984), p. 29 (fig. 37); Flam, *Matisse: The Man and His Art* (1986), pp. 422, 426 (fig. 430), 504 n. 33; Guichard-Meili, *Matisse* (1986), p. 137; Monod-Fontaine, Baldassari, and Laugier, *Matisse: Oeuvres* (1989), p. 321, under no. 118; Flam, "Matisse" (1993), pp. 250, 309 n. 2; Fourcade and de Chassey, "Anthologie" (1993), p. 506, no. 131 (1916 letter to Léonce Rosenberg); Dauberville and Dauberville, *Matisse chez Bernheim-Jeune* (1995), vol. 1, pp. 560, 561 (ill.), no. 161; Duthuit and Sèligny, *Matisse en France* (2004), pp. 26 (ill.), 72; Wright, *Matisse and the Subject of Modernism* (2004), pp. 170, 171 (pl. 85); D'Alessandro and Elderfield, *Matisse: Radical Invention* (2010), pp. 264, 265 (fig. 6)

32

***Sculpture and Vase of Ivy*, 1916–17**

Oil on canvas, 28¾ x 36¼ in. (73 x 92 cm)
Tikanoja Art Museum, Vaasa, Finland (TT44)
Signed (lower left): Henri-Matisse

Provenance: The artist (sold on May 1, 1917, for 6,300 francs to Halvorsen); [Walther Halvorsen, Paris and Oslo, 1917–18; sold to Stenman]; Gösta Stenman, Helsinki (1918–20; sold to Tikanoja); Frithjof Tikanoja, Vaasa (1920–51; his gift to his eponymous museum in Vaasa, 1951)

Exhibitions: *Den franske utstilling* (Oslo 1918), no. 44; *Utställning af fransk konst* (Stockholm 1918), no. 52; *Modern fransk konst* (Helsinki 1918), no. 67; *Eemu Myntti* (Helsinki 1930), no. 226; *Ulkomaista nykytaidetta Suomen kokoelmista* (Helsinki 1962), no. 103; *Occident–Orient* (Strasbourg 1972), no. 69; *Matisse* (Stockholm 1984–85), no. 23; "Matisse" (Humlebaek 1985), checklist no. 30, pp. 20 (ill.), 57; *Modernin taiteen klassikoita* (Tampere 1985), unnumbered cat., pp. 110–11 (ill.); *Matisse et l'Italie* (Venice 1987), no. P27; *Matisse Retrospective* (New York 1992–93), no. 190; *Matisse* (Paris 1993), no. 131; "Matisse-Bonnard, une amitié" (Nice 1996), no cat.; *Kunst-Welten im Dialog* (Cologne 1999–2000), no. 257; *Kleopatra blir Ariadne* (Stockholm 2003–4), no. 26; *Matisse: Figur, Farbe, Raum* (Düsseldorf 2005–6), no. 67; *Matisse: Figure, couleur, espace* (Basel 2006), no. 50; *Matisse e Bonnard* (Rome 2006–7), no. 10

References: Anon., *Samling Gösta Stenman* (1918), pp. 6, 39 (ill.); Hintze, *Modern konst* (1930), p. 22 (ill.); Barr, *Matisse His Art and His Public* (1951), p. 181; Reff, "Matisse: Meditations on a Statuette and Goldfish" (1976), p. 114 (fig. 21); Flam, *Matisse: The Man and His Art* (1986), pp. 422, 427 (fig. 431), 504 n. 33, 505 n. 4; Monod-Fontaine, Baldassari, and Laugier, *Oeuvres de Matisse* (1989), pp. 320 (fig. g), 321, under no. 118; Flam, "Matisse" (1993), pp. 250, 309 n. 2; Fourcade and de Chassey, "Anthologie" (1993), pp. 377 (ill.), 506, no. 131 (1916 letter to Léonce Rosenberg); Kostenevich and Semyonova, *Collecting Matisse* (1993), p. 104 (ill.); Dauberville and Dauberville, *Matisse chez Bernheim-Jeune* (1995), vol. 1, pp. 562, 563 (ill.), no. 162; Salin, *Tikanojan taidekodin kokoelmat* (2001), pp. 101–2; Schneider, *Matisse* (2002), p. 142 (ill.); Curuz, "Matisse e gli archetipi del codice Michelangelo" (2011), p. 338 (ill.)

33

***Bowl of Apples on a Table*, 1916**

Oil on canvas, 45¼ x 35¼ in. (114.9 x 89.5 cm)
Chrysler Museum of Art, Norfolk, Virginia, Gift of Walter P. Chrysler, Jr. (71.515)
Signed (lower left): Henri Matisse

Provenance: [Galerie Bernheim-Jeune, Paris, purchased from the artist, November 13, 1916; stock no. 20775, sold on November 18, 1916, for 7,000 francs to Vignier]; [Charles Vignier, Paris, 1916–31; his sale, Hôtel Drouot, Paris, May 21, 1931, no. 23, for 27,000 francs]; [probably purchased by Pierre Matisse, New York, in co-shares with F. Valentine Dudensing, in 1931]; [Valentine Galleries (F. Valentine Dudensing), New York, by 1936]; Walter P. Chrysler Jr. (by 1937–71; his gift to the Chrysler Museum, 1971)

Exhibitions: *Twenty Paintings by Matisse* (New York 1936b), no. 1; *Walter P. Chrysler, Jr. Collection* (Detroit 1937), no. 39; *Picasso, Matisse* (Boston 1938), no. 28; *Paintings by Matisse* (Chicago 1939), no. 5; *Seven Centuries of Painting* (San Francisco 1939–40), no. Y-186; *Collection of Walter P. Chrysler, Jr.* (Richmond–Philadelphia 1941), no. 121; *Inaugural Exhibition* (Provincetown 1958), no. 41; *French Paintings* (Dayton 1960), no. 116; *Controversial Century* (Provincetown–Ottawa 1962), unnumbered cat.; *Matisse centenaire* (Paris 1970), no. 142; *Matisse* (New York 1973), no. 11; "Homage to the Louvre" (Norfolk 1976), no cat.; *Treasures from the Chrysler Museum* (Nashville 1977), no. 49; *Veronese to Franz Kline* (New York 1978), no. 29; *Matisse, Sculptor/Painter* (Fort Worth 1984), no. 31; *French Paintings from The Chrysler Museum* (Raleigh–Birmingham 1986–87), no. 43; *Matisse Retrospective* (New York 1992–93), no. 185; *Cézanne and Beyond* (Philadelphia 2009), unnumbered cat., pp. 131 (pl. 18), 535; *Matisse: Radical Invention* (Chicago–New York 2010), no. 39.2

References: Davidson, "Magic Color of Matisse" (1936), pp. 14, 21; *Detroit Free Press*, October 3, 1937, part 3, p. 12; Lerch, "Walter P. Chrysler Jr.'s Collection" (1938), pp. 45 (ill.), 46; Bulliet, "Matisse 'Thrillers' of 1910" (1939), p. 25; Barr, *Matisse: His Art and His Public* (1951), p. 190; Russell, "Matisse-en-France" (1970), p. 23 (ill); McAllister, "Art Works Exchanged by Chrysler" (1972), p. B1; Greenberg, "Influences of Matisse" (1973), p. 29 (ill.); Carrà and Deryng, *Tout l'oeuvre peint de Matisse* (1982), pp. 94, 95 (ill.), no. 210; *Chrysler Museum: Selections* (1982), pp. 68, 69 (ill.); Mezzatesta, *Matisse, Sculptor/Painter* (1984), pp. 29 (ill.), 104 (ill.), 105–6, no. 31; Flam, *Matisse: The Man and His Art* (1986), pp. 423, 429 (fig. 433), 504 n. 31; L. Lieberman, "Select Offerings: Chrysler Museum" (1986), pp. 46–50; Harrison, *Chrysler Museum Handbook* (1991), pp. 174, 175 (ill.), no. 132; Monneret, *Matisse* (1994), p. 101 (ill.), no. 247; Dauberville and Dauberville, *Matisse chez Bernheim-Jeune* (1995), vol. 1, p. 557 (ill.), no. 159; Néret, *Matisse* (1996), pp. 84 (ill.), 85; Wood and Edelstein, *Art Institute of Chicago* (1996), p. 37; Percheron and Brouder, *Matisse: De la couleur à l'architecture* (2002), pp. 118, 119 (fig. 136); Schneider, *Matisse* (2002), pp. 372, 391, 446; Monod-Fontaine, "Variations autour d'un sujet" (2004), p. 48 (fig. 36); Harrison, *Collecting with Vision* (2007), p. 55 (pl. 55); Earle, *Legacy: Walter Chrysler Jr.* (2008), pp. 101–2

34

Apples, 1916

Oil on canvas, 46 x 35 in. (116.8 x 88.9 cm)
The Art Institute of Chicago, Gift of Florene May Schoenborn and Samuel A. Marx (1948.563)
Signed in reddish brown paint (lower right): Henri-Matisse

Provenance: [Galerie Bernheim-Jeune, Paris, purchased from the artist, November 13, 1916; stock no. 20776, sold on January 15, 1917, for 8,200 francs to Bernstein]; Henry Bernstein (January 15–December 13, 1917; resold to Bernheim-Jeune); [Galerie Bernheim-Jeune, Paris, December 13, 1917]; [Marius de Zayas, New York, sold on May 21, 1919, for 3,200 dollars to Quinn]; John Quinn, New York (1919–his d. 1924); Quinn estate (1924–27; his sale, "The John Quinn Collection," American Art Association, New York, February 9–11, 1927, no. 126; for 1,225 dollars to Dudensing and Matisse); [Valentine Gallery (F. Valentine Dudensing and Pierre Matisse in half shares), New York, February 1927–March 1931; sold for 1,225 dollars to Matisse]; [Pierre Matisse Gallery, New York, 1931–40; bought Dudensing's share in March 1931; stock no. 40, sold on December 20, 1940, for 6,500 dollars to Marx]; Mr. and Mrs. Samuel A. Marx, Chicago (1940–48; their gift to the Art Institute of Chicago, 1948)

Exhibitions: *Paintings by Courbet . . . Matisse* (New York 1919), no. 21; *Society of Independent Artists* (New York 1920a), no. 508; *Representative Modern Artists* (Philadelphia 1920), no. 150; "Paintings by Matisse" (New York 1920b), no cat.; *Contemporary French Art* (New York 1922), no. 84; *Works by Matisse* (New York 1924b), no. 7; "Modern French and American Paintings" (New York 1927), no cat.; *Matisse* (Paris 1931), no. 46; *Matisse* (Basel 1931), no. 48; *Matisse* (San Francisco 1936), no. 15; *Matisse Retrospective* (Philadelphia 1948), no. 38; *Matisse* (New York and other cities 1951–52), no. 38; *School of Paris* (New York and other cities 1965–66), unnumbered cat., pp. 11 (ill.), 12; *Matisse: Retrospective* (London 1968), no. 67; *Matisse centenaire* (Paris 1970), no. 141; *"Noble Buyer:" John Quinn* (Washington 1978), no. 50; *Ot Delakrua do Matissa* (Saint Petersburg–Moscow 1988), no. 51; *Matisse Retrospective* (New York 1992–93), no. 186; *Matisse* (Paris 1993), no. 129; *Objects of Desire* (New York–London 1997–98), unnumbered cat., pp. 50–51, 55 (pl. 21), 223 (shown only in New York); *Matisse: Radical Invention* (Chicago–New York 2010), no. 39.1

References: Gregg, "From Courbet to Matisse in One Art Exhibition" (1919), sec. 3, p. 10; McBride, "News and Comment in the World of Art" (1919), p. 12; McBride, "New Matisse Art on Exhibition" (1920), p. 4; Hind, *Art and I* (1921), pp. 153, 157–58; Watson, *John Quinn: Collection* (1926), pp. 5, 11, 73 (ill.); Quinn Sale, "Quinn Art in Five Session Sale" (Jan. 15, 1927), p. 2; Quinn Sale, "Last of Quinn Art to Go at Auction" (Jan. 16, 1927), p. E20; Quinn Sale, "Modern Art Brings $16,235 at Auction" (Feb. 10, 1927), p. 26; Quinn Sale, "Quinn Art Sale Nets $16,235 in First Session" (Feb. 10, 1927), p. 15; Quinn Sale, "Quinn's Art Collection Goes on Sale: $1,225 For a Matisse" (Feb. 10, 1927), p. 18; Quinn Sale, "Big Prices Keep Up in Quinn Sale" (Feb. 11, 1927), p. 15 (no. 126); Quinn Sale, "Sale of the Quinn Collection Is Completed" (Feb. 19, 1927), p. 7 (no. 126); Quinn Sale, "Detailed Statement of Sales: Quinn" (Mar. 1927), p. 6; Quinn Sale, "Collection of the Late John Quinn" (Mar. 1927), p. 6 (no. 126); McBride, "Modern French Masters at the Valentine Galleries" (Mar. 12, 1927), p. 5; *Art News*, "Modern Paintings: Valentine Galleries" (Mar. 26, 1927), p. 9; Zervos, "De l'importance de l'objet dans la peinture d'aujourd'hui" (1930), p. 118 (ill.); Zervos et al., *Matisse* (1931), p. 64 (fig. 51); Davidson, "Magic Color of Matisse" (1936), p. 14; Kimball, "Matisse: Recognition, Patronage, Collecting" (1948), p. 45; Kimball, "Discovery from America" (1948), p. 54; Barr, *Matisse: His Art and His Public* (1951), pp. 180–81, 189, 194, 263, 406 (ill.), 529; Diehl and Humbert, *Matisse* (1958), p. 53; Art Institute of Chicago, *Paintings* (1961), pp. 304, 466 (ill.); Speyer, "Twentieth-Century European Painting and Sculpture" (1966), p. 224 (fig. 3); Cunningham, *Instituto de Arte de Chicago* (1967), p. 38 (ill.); Guichard-Meili, *Matisse* (1967), p. 231; Okamoto, *Bonnard, Matisse* (1968), p. 110 (fig. 48); Reid, *Man from New York: John Quinn and His Friends* (1968), pp. 398, 499, 660; Maxon, *Art Institute of Chicago* (1970), pp. 116 (ill.), 117, 283; Samuels and Samuels, *Seeing with the Mind's Eye* (1975), p. 117 (ill.); Feldstein, *Art Institute of Chicago: 100 Masterpieces* (1978), pp. 138 (pl. 87), 139; Zilczer, "Dispersal of the John Quinn Collection" (1979), pp. 18, 19 (fig. 7); Speyer and Donnell, *Twentieth-Century European Paintings* (1980), pp. 14, 54 (no. 2F8); Carrà and Deryng, *Tout l'oeuvre peint de Matisse* (1982), pp. 94, 95 (ill.), no. 212; Mezzatesta, *Matisse, Sculptor/Painter* (1984), pp. 104, 105 (fig. 69), 107; Flam, *Matisse: The Man and His Art* (1986), pp. 423, 430 (fig. 434), 504 n. 31; Harrison, *French Paintings from the Chrysler Museum* (1986), p. 87 (fig. 42); Guichard-Meili, *Matisse* (1986), p. 129; Guillaud and Guillaud, *Matisse: Rhythm and Line* (1987), pp. 71, 81 (pl. 67); Noël, *Matisse* (1987), p. 106, cover ill.; Fourcade and de Chassey, "Anthologie" (1993), p. 506, no. 129 (repr. of Hind 1921); Monneret, *Matisse* (1994), p. 101 (ill.), no. 240; Dauberville and Dauberville, *Matisse chez Bernheim-Jeune* (1995), vol. 1, pp. 218 (facsimile of Paris 1931), 558, 559 (ill.), no. 160, and vol. 2, pp. 1433, 1459, 1463; Néret, *Matisse* (1996), p. 85 (ill.); Wood and Edelstein, *Art Institute of Chicago* (1996), pp. 37 (ill.), 159; Bois, *Matisse and Picasso* (1998), p. 65; Cauman, "Matisse and America" (2000), pp. 330, 333, 339, 347, 358–59, 378, 396, vol. 2, fig. 2.19; Rabinow, "Modern Art Comes to the Metropolitan" (2000), pp. 5, 9 nn. 19, 21; Cowling et al., *Matisse, Picasso* (2002), pp. 233, 355 (fig. 62), French ed.: p. 233; Schneider, *Matisse* (2002), pp. 372, 386 (ill.); Monod-Fontaine, "Variations autour d'un sujet" (2004), p. 48 (fig. 35); Jedlicka, *Mit Matisse in Paris* (2008), p. 7 (fig. 2)

35

Laurette in a Green Robe, Black Background, 1916

Oil on canvas, 28¾ x 21⅜ in. (73 x 54.3 cm)
The Metropolitan Museum of Art, New York, Jacques and Natasha Gelman Collection, 1998 (1999.363.43)
Signed and dated (lower right): H. Matisse 16

Provenance: The artist (1916–d. 1954); his estate (1954–57; to his son); [Pierre Matisse, New York; private collection, January 1957–69; consignment no. 9491, sold on October 24, 1969 for 100,000 dollars to Gelman]; Jacques and Natasha Gelman, Mexico City and New York (1969–his d. 1986); Natasha Gelman, Mexico City and New York (1986–d. 1998; her bequest to the Metropolitan Museum, 1999)

Exhibitions: Possibly *Matisse: Udstilling af hans arbejder* (Copenhagen–Stockholm–Oslo 1924), no. 46; likely *Internationale Kunstausstellung* (Zürich 1925), no. 296; *Matisse Retrospective* (New York 1931), no. 34; *Matisse* (Providence 1931), no. 15; *Masterpieces of Modern Painting and Sculpture* (New York 1937), no. 11; *Matisse* (Lucerne 1949), no. 48;

Matisse (Paris 1950), no. 43; *Matisse* (New York and other cities 1951–52), no. 46; *Matisse* (Los Angeles 1952), no. 29, *Salon d'automne* (Paris 1955b), no. 171; *Rétrospective Matisse* (Paris 1956), no. 44; *Matisse Retrospective* (Los Angeles–Chicago–Boston 1966), no. 43; *Matisse* (New York 1966), no. 30; *Matisse: Retrospective* (London 1968), no. 62; *Matisse centenaire* (Paris 1970), no. 132; *Matisse: En retrospektiv udstilling* (Copenhagen 1970), no. 40; *Matisse: Early Years in Nice* (Washington 1986–87), no. 8; *Matisse et l'Italie* (Venice 1987), no. P29; *Modern Masters: Gelman Collection* (New York–London 1989–90), unnumbered cat., p. 142 (ill.); *Matisse* (Paris 1993), no. 144; *De Matisse à Picasso: Collection Gelman* (Martigny 1994), unnumbered cat., p. 166; *Matisse, Picasso* (London–Paris–New York 2002–3), no. 101 (London and New York), no. 90 (Paris); *Matisse in Transition: Around Laurette* (West Palm Beach 2006), no. 9

References: Nirdlinger, "Matisse Way" (1931), p. 6; Fry, *Matisse* (1935), pl. 30; Mushakojo, *Matisse* (1939), p. 44 (fig. 80); Wilenski, *Modern French Painters* (1940), p. 259; Raynal, *Peintres du XX*ᵉ *siècle* (1947), pl. 11; Barr, *Matisse: His Art and His Public* (1951), pp. 191, 412 (ill.); Raynal, *Modern Painting* (1953), pp. 199 (ill.), 336; Escholier, *Matisse, ce vivant* (1956), p. 181; Diehl and Humbert, *Matisse* (1958), p. 54; Lassaigne, *Matisse* (1959), p. 77; Selz, *Matisse* (1964), p. 40 (ill.); Brill, *Matisse* (1967), p. 36, pl. 20; Guichard-Meili, *Matisse* (1967), pp. 89 (pl. 77), 247; Sutton, "Mozart of Painting" (1970), p. 359 (pl. VI); Aragon, *Matisse, roman* (1971), vol. 2, pp. 98, 101 (pl. 15), 360; Orienti, *Matisse* (1972), p. 35; Flam, *Norton Matisses* (1973), n.p.; Laude, "Les 'ateliers' de Matisse" (1974), pp. 19–20; Watkins, *Matisse* (1977), pl. 24; Carrà and Deryng, *Tout l'oeuvre peint de Matisse* (1982), no. 218, pl. XXXV; Mannering, *Art of Matisse* (1982), pp. 53–54 (ill.); Fourcade, "Matisse et Manet?" (1983), pp. 28, 29 (ill.), 32 n. 20; Watkins, *Matisse* (1984), pp. 137 (pl. 123), 138, 141; Addams Allen, "Exhibit Paints Matisse in a New Light" (1986), p. C2; Flam, *Matisse: The Man and His Art* (1986), pp. 441, 446 (fig, 450), 505 n. 9; Fourcade, "Crise du cadre" (1986), pp. 74–76, 77 (figs. 6, 7) 78 (fig. 8); Lebensztejn, "Constat amiable" (1986), pp. 84, 90–91; Noël, *Matisse* (1987), p. 45; Gowing, "Bonnard and the School of Paris in the Gelman Collection" (1989), p. 20; Lieberman, "Introduction," in Gelman Collection (1989), p. 2; Monod-Fontaine, Baldassari, and Laugier, *Oeuvres de Matisse* (1989), p. 50 (fig. a), under no. 12; Rewald, "Gelman Collection" (1989), pp. 142 (ill.), 143–44, 305 (ill.); Schneider, "Gelmans and the Fauves" (1989), pp. 29–30 n. 2; Elderfield, *Matisse Retrospective* (1992), p. 274 (ill.), no. 203; Monneret, *Matisse* (1994), p. 102 (ill.), no. 259; Benjamin, "Vital Sign" (1995), pp. 30–31; Monod-Fontaine, "Black Light" (1995), p. 92; Labrusse, "Catalogo delle opere" (1997), p. 188 (ill.); Monod-Fontaine, "Le paradoxe de l'odalisque" (1999), pp. 20 (ill.), 113, 116; Rewald, "Twentieth Century" (2000), pp. 54, 55 (ill.); Gilot, "Événement: Matisse/Picasso" (2002), p. 56 (ill.); Monod-Fontaine in Cowling et al., *Matisse, Picasso* (2002), pp. 190 (ill.), 191–93, 194 (pl. 101), French ed.: "Mélancolies," pp. 192 (ill.), 193–95, 197 (pl. 90); Schneider, *Matisse* (2002), pp. 428 (ill.), 437; Werth, *Joy of Life* (2002), p. 301 n. 18; Amano, "La peinture en procès" (2004), pp. 17, 37 (fig. 8), 260; Monod-Fontaine, "Matisse: Une pensée de la couleur" (2004), p. 28; Monod-Fontaine, "Question of Windows" (2005), pp. 187, 193, 204 n. 9; Spurling, *Matisse the Master* (2005), p. 222; D'Alessandro and Elderfield, *Matisse: Radical Invention* (2010), pp. 313, 314 (fig. 4)

36

***Laurette Seated on a Pink Armchair*, 1916–17**

Oil on canvas, 39⅜ x 28¾ in. (100 x 73 cm)
Private collection
New York only
Signed (lower right): Henri-Matisse

Provenance: [Galerie Bernheim-Jeune, Paris, 1917–19; purchased from the artist, December 10, 1917; sent to Swiss branches]; [Galerie Bernheim-Jeune & Cie (Paul Vallotton), Lausanne, early 1919]; [Galerie Bernheim-Jeune & Cie (Gottfried Tanner), Zürich, sold on July 1, 1919, to Hahnloser]; Arthur and Hedy Hahnloser, Winterthur (1919–52); Hans R. Hahnloser, Bern (by 1953); Dr. and Mrs. Paul Hahnloser, Fribourg (by 1986); private collection

Exhibitions: *Oeuvres récentes de Matisse* (Paris 1919a), no. 8; *Eröffnungausstellung* (Zürich 1919), no. 31; *Matisse* (Basel 1931), no. 39; *Werke aus der Sammlung Hahnloser* (Winterthur 1937), no. 85; *Die Hauptwerke der Sammlung Hahnloser* (Lucerne 1940), no. 68; *Winterthur Privatbesitz II* (Winterthur 1949), no. 142; *Europäische Kunst aus Berner Privatbesitz* (Bern 1953), no. 86; *Europäische Kunst* (Vienna 1955), no. 41; *Matisse centenaire* (Paris 1970), no. 146; *Künstlerfreunde* (Winterthur 1973), no. 158; *Matisse* (Zürich–Düsseldorf 1982–83), no. 52; *Matisse: Early Years in Nice* (Washington 1986–87), no. 9; *Matisse et l'Italie* (Venice 1987), no. P35; *Matisse* (Paris 1993), no. 147; *Matisse: Figur Farbe Raum* (Düsseldorf 2005–6), no. 79; *Matisse: Figure, couleur, espace* (Basel 2006), no. 45

References: Sembat, *Matisse* (1920), p. 29 (ill.); Courthion, "La collection Arthur Hahnloser" (1926), pp. 63 (ill.), 66; Courthion, *Matisse* (1934), p. 56, pl. 27; Mushakojo, *Matisse* (1939), p. 18 (fig. 29); Wilenski, *Modern French Painters* (1940), p. 259; Courthion, *Le visage de Matisse* (1942), pp. 63 (ill.), 131; Diehl and Humbert, *Matisse* (1958), p. 54; Haftmann, *Malerei im 20. Jahrhundert* (1965), pp. 210 (fig. 478), 411; Guichard-Meili, *Matisse* (1967), p. 88 (fig. 76), 247; Diehl, *Matisse* (1970), p. 59; Aragon, *Matisse, roman* (1971), vol. 2, p. 103; Carrà and Deryng, *Tout l'oeuvre peint de Matisse* (1982), pp. 95, 96 (ill.), no. 234; Schneider, "Matisse revisité" (1982), p. 7 (ill.); Flam, *Matisse: The Man and His Art* (1986), pp. 441, 448 (fig. 452); Malaurie, "Matissimo!" (1987), p. 57 (ill.); Ducrey and Ducrey, *La Galerie Paul Vallotton* (1988), p. 54 n. 3; Monneret, *Matisse* (1994), p. 102 (ill.), no. 270; Dauberville and Dauberville, *Matisse chez Bernheim-Jeune* (1995), vol. 1, p. 98 (facsimile of Paris 1919a); Monod-Fontaine, "Black Light" (1995), p. 92; Monod-Fontaine in Cowling et al., *Matisse, Picasso* (2002), p. 193, French ed.: "Mélancolies, " p. 194; Schneider, *Matisse* (2002), p. 482 (ill.); Flam, *Matisse in Transition* (2006), pp. 19, 32 n. 41; Hahnloser-Ingold et al., *Arthur and Hedy Hahnloser Collection* (2011), pp. 307, 308 (photo), 309 (ill.)

37

***Meditation (Portrait of Laurette)*, 1916–17**

Oil on canvas, 19½ x 13½ in. (49.5 x 34.3 cm)
The Museum of Fine Arts, Houston, Gift of Miss Ima Hogg (48.10)
Signed (upper left): Henri Matisse

Provenance: [Paul Guillaume, Paris]; Ima Hogg, Houston (1928–48; her gift to the Museum of Fine Arts, Houston, 1948)

Exhibitions: *55 Works of Modern Art Owned in Houston* (Houston 1947), no. 29; *Matisse: Early Years in Nice* (Washington 1986–87), no. 14; *Matisse* (Brisbane–Canberra–Melbourne 1995), no. 76; *Matisse in Transition: Around Laurette* (West Palm Beach 2006), no. 11

References: *Les Arts à Paris*, no. 16 (January 1929), p. 25 (ill.); Benjamin, "Vital Sign" (1995), pp. 30–31; Monod-Fontaine, "Black Light" (1995), pp. 92, 93 (fig. 7); Schneider, *Matisse* (2002), p. 482 (ill.); Kirkland, *Hogg Family and Houston* (2009), pp. 219, 223, 326 n. 80

38

***The Open Window (Room at the Hôtel Beau-Rivage)*, 1917–18**

Oil on canvas, 25¾ x 21½ in. (65.5 x 54.5 cm)
Private collection
Signed (lower right): Henri-Matisse

Provenance: [Galerie Bernheim-Jeune, Paris, purchased from the artist, March 18, 1918; stock no. 21123, sold to the Lausanne branch]; [Galerie Bernheim-Jeune & Cie (Paul Vallotton), Lausanne, sold October 31, 1918, to Purrmann]; Hans Purrmann, Berlin (1918; purchased for his brother-in-law, Rudolf Vollmoeller; signed by the artist after Purrmann's purchase); Rudolf Vollmoeller, Zürich (until d. 1941; to his daughter); Heidi Vollmoeller, Zürich (and thence by descent); private collection, Switzerland (acquired from the above); sale, "Impressionist and Modern Art," Christie's, London, February 4, 2008, no. 47, as Intérieur à Nice, for 3,156,500 pounds [6,211,992 dollars] to the present owner)

Exhibitions: *Matisse* (Paris 1931), hors cat.; *Matisse* (Basel 1931), no. 42; *Matisse* (Lucerne 1949), no. 52; *Matisse: Early Years in Nice* (Washington 1986–87), no. 29; *Matisse* (Madrid 2009), no. 2

References: Vildrac, *Nice 1921* (1922), preface (about the hotel room); Barnes and De Mazia, *Art of Matisse* (1933), pp. 209, 438, no. 75; Besson, "Arrivée de Matisse à Nice" (1939), pp. 41–42; Barr, *Matisse: His Art and His Public* (1951), pp. 195–96, 204–5, 420 (ill.); Escholier, *Matisse, ce vivant* (1956), p. 176; Diehl and Humbert, *Matisse* (1958), p. 57; Escholier, *Matisse: A Portrait of the Artist and the Man* (1960), p. 100; Fourcade, "Autres propos de Matisse" (1976), p. 102 n. 2 (1941 interview with Courthion); Carrà and Deryng, *Tout l'oeuvre peint de Matisse* (1982), p. 96 (ill.), no. 246; Flam, *Matisse: The Man and His Art* (1986), pp. 463, 469, 470 (fig. 483), 506 n. 28; Fourcade, "Uninterrupted Story" (1986), pp. 51, 98 (pl. 48); Shone, "Matisse: Intimate Splendor" (1987), p. 135 (ill.); Flam, *Matisse: A Retrospective* (1988), pp. 167–68 (trans. Besson 1939), 202 (trans. Vildrac 1922); Monod-Fontaine and Laugier, "Éléments de chronologie (1904–1918)" (1993), p. 125 (ill.); Bois, "On Matisse: The Blinding" (1994), pp. 70, 71 (ill.); Monneret, *Matisse* (1994), p. 103 (ill.), no. 275; Dauberville and Dauberville, *Matisse chez Bernheim-Jeune* (1995), vol. 1, p. 631 (ill.), no. 214; Monod-Fontaine, "Question of Windows" (2005), p. 204 n. 19; Spurling, *Matisse the Master* (2005), p. 205

39

Interior at Nice (Room at the Hôtel Beau-Rivage), 1918

Oil on canvas, 29 x 23¾ in. (73.7 x 60.3 cm)
Philadelphia Museum of Art, A. E. Gallatin Collection, 1952 (1952-61-79)
Signed (lower right): Henri-Matisse

Provenance: [Galerie Bernheim-Jeune, Paris, purchased from the artist, May 22, 1918; stock no. 21129]; Collection Josse and Gaston Bernheim-Jeune, Bois-Lurette, Villers-sur-Mer, Normandy (1918–21); [Galerie Bernheim-Jeune, Paris, 1921–27; sold to Swiss branch, April 29, 1927]; [L'Art Moderne (Bernheim-Jeune branch), Lucerne, April 29, 1927]; [Valentine Gallery (F. Valentine Dudensing), New York]; [Alex Reid & Lefèvre, London, sold in December 1932 to Gallatin]; A. E. Gallatin, New York (1932–52; on extended loan to the Philadelphia Museum of Art, 1943–d. 1952; his gift to the Philadelphia Museum of Art, 1952)

Exhibitions: *Oeuvres récentes de Matisse* (Paris 1919a), no. 10; possibly exhibited at L'Art Moderne, S.A., Lucerne, ca. 1927, no. 67; Gallery of Living Art, New York, presumably from 1933 to 1943; *Matisse: Early Years in Nice* (Washington 1986–87), no. 28; "Director's Choice" (Harrisburg 1987), no cat.; *Matisse Retrospective* (Nagoya-Hiroshima-Kasama 1991), no. 38; *Matisse Retrospective* (New York 1992–93), no. 219; *Côte d'Azur* (New York 2001), unnumbered cat., pp. 44–46; "Matisse and Modern Art on the French Riviera" (Philadelphia 2008–9 [this work shown through May 13, 2009]), no cat.; *Matisse* (Madrid 2009), no. 1; *Renoir in the Twentieth Century* (Paris–Los Angeles–Philadelphia 2009–10), hors cat. (shown only in Philadelphia)

References: Vildrac, *Nice 1921* (1922), preface; Gallatin, *Gallery of Living Art* (1933), no. 81, ill.; Gallatin, *Museum of Living Art* (1936), no. 81, ill.; Besson, "Arrivée de Matisse à Nice" (1939), pp. 41–42 (ill.); Gallatin, *Museum of Living Art* (1940), no. 83, ill.; Kimball, "Matisse: Recognition, Patronage, Collecting" (1948), p. 47; Kimball, "Discovery from America" (1948), p. 54; Barr, *Matisse: His Art and His Public* (1951), pp. 196, 543 (n. 5 under p. 196), 558; Gallatin, *Gallatin Collection* (1954), pp. 44, 112 (ill.), no. 115; Escholier, *Matisse: A Portrait* (1960), p. 100; Fourcade, "Autres propos de Matisse" (1976), p. 102 n. 2; Carrà and Deryng, *Tout l'oeuvre peint de Matisse* (1982), p. 96 (ill.), no. 247; Watkins, *Matisse* (1984), pp. 150 (pl. 134), 151, 162; Addams Allen, "Exhibit Paints Matisse in a New Light" (1986), p. C2; Flam, *Matisse: The Man and His Art* (1986), pp. 471 (fig. 484), 506 n. 28; Flam, *Matisse: A Retrospective* (1988), pp. 168 (trans. of Besson), 202 (trans. of Vildrac), 207 (pl. 62); Stavitsky, "Development, Institutionalization, and Impact of the Gallatin Collection" (1990), vol. 8, pp. 177–78; Herrera, *Matisse: A Portrait* (1993), pp. 136, 139, pl. 21; Bois, "On Matisse: The Blinding" (1994), pp. 70, 71 (ill.); Milner, *Matisse* (1994), p. 91 (ill.); Monneret, *Matisse* (1994), p. 104 (ill.), no. 291; Stavitsky, "A. E. Gallatin Collection" (1994), pp. 20, 21 (fig. 21); Dauberville and Dauberville, *Matisse chez Bernheim-Jeune* (1995), vol. 1, p. 632 (ill.), no. 215; Silver, *Making Paradise* (2001), pp. 44, 45 (fig. 9), 46; Golding in Cowling et al., *Matisse, Picasso* (2002), pp. 159, 352 (fig. 48), French ed.: p. 161; Monod-Fontaine, "A Question of Windows" (2005), pp. 197, 198 (fig. 5), 204 n. 19; Spurling, *Matisse the Master* (2005), p. 205; Blum, *Matisse: Rooms with a View* (2010), pp. 96, 97 (pl. 66), 102

40

Interior with a Violin (Room at the Hôtel Beau-Rivage), 1918

Oil on canvas, 45⅝ x 35 in. (116 x 89 cm)
Statens Museum for Kunst, Copenhagen, J. Rump Collection (KMSr83)
Signed (lower left): Henri-Matisse; inscribed in Matisse's hand (on back of the canvas): intérieur violon I

Provenance: The artist (submitted to Galerie Bernheim-Jeune, Paris, June 28, 1918; returned to the artist; sold to Halvorsen]; [Walther Halvorsen, Paris and Oslo, sold ca. 1922 for 40,000 francs (14,000 Kronen) to Langaard]; Johan H. Langaard, Oslo (ca. 1922–25; on extended loan to the Nasjonalgalleriet in Oslo, ca. 1923–25; sold to Rosenberg through Halvorsen's agency in 1925); [Galerie Paul Rosenberg, Paris, 1925; stock no. 1192, sold for 90,000 francs in November–December 1925 to Rump]; Johannes Rump, Copenhagen (1925–28; his gift to the Statens Museum for Kunst, Copenhagen, January 19, 1928)

Exhibitions: *La Triennale* (Paris 1919b), no. 87; *Matisse* (Copenhagen 1970), no. 44; *Matisse Retrospective* (New York 1992–93), no. 220; *Johannes Rump: Portraet af en samler* (Copenhagen 1994–95), no. 170; *Canto d'Amore* (Basel 1996), no. 60; *Franske mestervoerker* (Aarhus 1996–97), no. 35; *Anri Matiss* (Saint Petersburg 1998), no. 28; *Matisse: Four Great Collectors* (Copenhagen 1999), no. 76; *Méditerranée* (Paris 2000–2001), no. 45; *Matisse, Picasso* (London–Paris–New York 2002–3), no. 77 (London and New York), no. 68 (Paris); *Matisse &* (Copenhagen 2005), no. 18; *Rammens Kunst* (Copenhagen 2008), unnumbered cat., p. 85; *Matisse* (Madrid 2009), no. 4

References: Hoppe, "På visit hos Matisse" (1919 interview with Matisse), 1931 repr., p. 195 (ill.); Faure et al., *Matisse* (1920), pl. 28; Langaard, *Expressionisme og Kubisme i Frankrig* (1922), p. 23 (ill.); Basler, *Matisse* (1924), n.p. (ill.); Basler, "Matisse" (1924), p. 1004 (ill.); Kiersmeier, "La peinture française à Copenhague" (1929), p. 165; Swane, *J. Rumps samling af moderne fransk kunst* (1929), p. 48, no. 83, pl. 17; Swane, "J. Rumps Samling af moderne fransk Kunst i Kunstmuseet" (1929–31), pp. 63 (ill.), 65, 73–74; *Chroniques du jour*, "Pour ou contre Matisse" (1931), n.p. (ill.); Swane, "Rumps samling" (1932), pp. 406–7; Kødt, *Statusopgørelse i malerkunsten* (1935), p. 106; Zahle, *Fransk maleri efter 1900* (1938), p. 10, pl. 5, cover ill.; Besson, "Arrivée de Matisse à Nice" (1939), pp. 41–42; Swane et al., *Matisse* (1944), p. 102, pl. 2; Rostrup, "Matisse" (1947), pp. 7 (ill.), 9; Wennberg, "Från Delacroix till Matisse" (1947), p. 80; Swane, *J. Rumps Samling* (1948), pp. 90, 92 (ill.), no. 108; Duthuit, *Les Fauves* (1949), p. 11; Andersen, "Hos Matisse" (1950), p. 127; Raynal et al., *History of Modern Painting*, vol. 2 (1950), pp. 50, 52, 53 (ill.); Barr, *Matisse: His Art and His Public* (1951), pp. 196, 201, 204–5, 421 (ill.); Finsen, "Kapellet i Vence" (1951), p. 59; Raynal, *Modern Painting* (1953), pp. 202 (ill.), 336; Swane, *Ved mit vinduesspejl* (1955), p. 90; Schmalenbach, *Grosse Meister moderner Malerei* (1957), pl. 19; Diehl and Humbert, *Matisse* (1958), pp. 57, 59, 110, 123, pl. 83; Lassaigne, *Matisse* (1959), pp. 92 (ill.), 94; Ferrier, *Matisse* (1961), pl. 8; Finsen, *J. Rumps samling etc.* (1964), pp. 57–58, no. R83, ill.; Gottlieb, "Role of the Window in Art of Matisse" (1964), pp. 399, 409 (fig. 12), 415, 418–19; Leymarie, *Matisse* (1964), pl. IX; Haftmann, *Malerei im 20. Jahrhundert* (1965), pp. 210 (fig. 481), 411; Brill,

Matisse (1967), pp. 18, 36, pl. 24; Guichard-Meili, *Matisse* (1967), pp. 172 (fig. 166), 174, 198, 250; Marchiori, *Matisse* (1967), pp. 57 (fig. 52), 62, 134; Russell, *World of Matisse* (1969), p. 92 (ill.); Diehl, *Matisse* (1970), pp. 24 (ill.), 59; Schneider, *Matisse centenaire* (1970), pp. 37, 46 (ill.); Aragon, *Matisse, roman* (1971), vol. 2, pp. 136 (pl. 27), 361; Günther, *Akkorde der Palette* (1972), p. 93; Orienti, *Matisse* (1972), p. 35; Fourcade, "Autres propos de Matisse" (1976), pp. 94 n. 5 (1919 interview with Hoppe), 102 (1941 interview with Curthion); Flam, *Matisse on Art* (1978), pp. 14, 23, fig. 31; Beausire, "Matisse: Der 'Wilde' aus Flandern" (1982), p. 10 (ill.); Carrà and Deryng, *Tout l'oeuvre peint de Matisse* (1982), p. 97 (ill.), no. 262, pl. XLIV; Watkins, *Matisse* (1984), pp. 144 (pl. 126), 145, 227; Addams Allen, "Exhibit Paints Matisse in a New Light" (1986), p. C2; Cowart and Fourcade, *Matisse: Early Years in Nice* (1986), pp. 19, 52, 100 (pl. 50), 264; Flam, *Matisse: The Man and His Art* (1986), pp. 474, 482 (fig. 497), 506 n. 38; Guichard-Meili, *Matisse* (1986), pp. 53 (ill.), 133, 141; Monod-Fontaine, "Matisse" (1986), p. 411; Tono, *Matisse* (1986), fig. 38; Guillaud and Guillaud, *Matisse: Rhythm and Line* (1987), pp. 71, 101 (pl. 86); Flam, *Matisse: A Retrospective* (1988), pp. 167–68 (repr. of Besson 1939), 172 (reprint of Hoppe 1919), 189 (pl. 60); Monod-Fontaine, *Matisse ou la couleur découpée* (1989), p. 47, slide no. 11; Monod-Fontaine, Baldassari, and Laugier, *Oeuvres de Matisse* (1989), p. 186 (fig. a), under no. 63; Russell, "Matisse au MoMA" (1992), pp. 80 (ill.), 81; Wilson, *Matisse* (1992), pp. 18, 85 (fig. 100); Durozoi, *Matisse* (1993), pp. 112, 113 (ill.); Flam, "Matisse" (1993), p. 267 (fig. 3); Girard, *Matisse: "Une splendeur inouïe"* (1993), p. 94 (ill.); Herrera, *Matisse: A Portrait* (1993), p. 142, pl. 22; Robinson and Bréda, *Matisse au Centre Pompidou* (1993), pp. 78 (ill.), 114; Scavenius, *Se på verdenskunst i Danmark* (1993), p. 76; Monneret, *Matisse* (1994), p. 104 (ill.), no. 293; Bernier, "Matisse, el conservador inspirado" (1995), pp. 34, 35 (ill.); Flam, *Matisse on Art* (1995), pp. 75 (repr. of Hoppe 1919), 77 (fig. 15), 271 n. 3; Monod-Fontaine, "Black Light" (1995), p. 94 (fig. 11); Friis, *100 Mesterværker* (1996), pp. 166–67 (ill.); Jensen, *De glade givere* (1996), pp. 259, 263 (photo), 324 (ill.); Raaschou-Nielsen, *Fransk modernisme* (1996), pp. 107–9 (ill.), 153, no. 35; Zahle, *Billedvifte* (1997), p. 119; Bois, *Matisse and Picasso* (1998), p. 247 n. 147; Dolz, *Lo spendore delle cose* (2001), pp. 48 (ill.), 49; Marin-David, "Matisse, Picasso" (2002), pp. 32, 33 (ill.); Percheron and Brouder, *Matisse: De la couleur à l'architecture* (2002), p. 347 (fig. 376); Schneider, *Matisse* (2002), pp. 79 (ill.), 82, 148, 214, 339 n. 37, 451, 491; Aagesen, "Matisse: Eight Takes" (2005), pp. 9 (ill.), 11, 13, 21–22; Aagesen in Anderberg, *SMK Highlights* (2005), p. 129 (ill.); Monod-Fontaine, "Question of Windows: Interior with a Violin" (2005), pp. 185–204; Blum, *Matisse: Rooms with a View* (2010), pp. 98 (pl. 67), 99; D'Alessandro and Elderfield, *Matisse: Radical Invention* (2010), pp. 235, 350 (fig. 2)

41

***Interior at Nice (Room at the Hôtel Méditerranée)*, ca. 1919**

Oil on canvas, 26¼ x 21⅝ in. (66.7 x 54.9 cm)
Saint Louis Art Museum, Museum Purchase (74:1945)
Signed (lower left): Henri Matisse

Provenance: [Galerie Bernheim-Jeune, Paris, purchased from the artist on April 19, 1921; stock no. 22602, sold on May 23, 1921 for 11,500 francs to Hutchinson]; St. John Hutchinson, London (1921–at least 1928); [Guillaume and Davis, Ltd., London (Paul Guillaume and Brandon Davis), by 1929; sold in 1930 to Knoedler]; [M. Knoedler & Co., Inc., London and New York, 1930–40; sold in 1940 to the Albright Art Gallery]; Albright Art Gallery, Buffalo, New York (1940); [Theodore Schempp, New York, until 1945; sold on June 8, 1945, to Saint Louis Art Museum]

Exhibitions: *Contemporary Art Society* (London 1928), no. 7; *French Paintings* (London 1929), no. 22; *Matisse* (Paris 1931), no. 62; *State Fair of Texas* (Dallas 1933), no. 52; *French Painting* (San Francisco 1934), no. 208; "Seven Works by Matisse" (Saint Louis 1965), no cat.; "20th Century Masterworks" (Saint Louis 1973–74), no cat.; *Matisse e Bonnard* (Rome 2006–7), no. 130; *Matisse* (Madrid 2009), no. 7

References: Vildrac, *Nice 1921* (1922), preface (about the hotel room); *Town & Country*, "An Interior at Nice" 1931, p. 22 (ill.); Carco, *L'ami des peintres* (1944), pp. 262–63 (about Hôtel Méditerranée); City Art Museum of Saint Louis, *Handbook* (1953), pp. 184, 185 (ill.); Saint Louis Art Museum, *Handbook* (1975), p. 178 (ill.); Cowart, "Place of Silvered Light" (1986), pp. 23–24, 26 (about the hotel room); Hahnloser-Ingold, "Collecting Matisses of the 1920s in the 1920s" (1986), p. 258 (fig. 36); Flam, *Matisse: A Retrospective* (1988), p. 202 (trans. of Vildrac 1922); Shone, "Matisse in England" (1993), p. 482; Dauberville and Dauberville, *Matisse chez Bernheim-Jeune* (1995), vol. 2, p. 998 (ill.), no. 466; Korn, "Collecting Paintings by Matisse and by Picasso" (2004), p. 121

42

***Woman on a Divan (Room at the Hôtel Méditerranée)*, 1920–21**

Oil on canvas, 23¾ x 28⅞ in. (60.2 x 73.4 cm)
Kunstmuseum Basel, Bequest of Dr. h.c. Richard Doetsch-Benzinger, Basel, 1960 (G 1960.36)
Signed (lower right): Henri-Matisse

Provenance: [Galerie Bernheim-Jeune, Paris, purchased from the artist on April 19, 1921; stock no. 22601, sold on September 5, 1921, for 12,000 francs to Matsukata]; Baron Kojiro Matsukata, Paris and Tokyo (1921–probably ca. 1928); [Galerie Rosengart, Lucerne, in 1942]; Richard Doetsch-Benzinger, Basel (by 1956; his bequest to the Kunstmuseum Basel, 1960)

Exhibitions: *Sammlung Doetsch-Benziger* (Basel 1956), no. 21; *Matisse centenaire* (Paris 1970), no. 164; *Matisse: Early Years in Nice* (Washington 1986–87), no. 85; *Von Matisse bis Picasso* (Lucerne 1988), no. 41; *Matisse Retrospective* (New York 1992–93), no. 252; *Canto d'Amore* (Basel 1996), no. 67; *Painting on the Move* (Basel 2002), unnumbered cat., p. 68; *Matisse, la période niçoise* (Nantes 2003), no. 3; *Matisse: Figur, Farbe, Raum* (Düsseldorf 2005–6), no. 95; *Matisse: Figure, couleur, espace* (Basel 2006), no. 66; *Matisse: Menschen, Masken, Modelle* (Stuttgart-Hamburg 2008–9), no. 59 (shown only in Stuttgart); *Matisse* (Madrid 2009), no. 8

References: Vildrac, *Nice 1921* (1922), preface (about the hotel room); Courthion, *Matisse* (1934), p. 57, pl. 39; Courthion, *Le visage de Matisse* (1942), pp. 37 (ill.), 131; Carco, *L'ami des peintres* (1944), pp. 262–63 (about Hôtel Méditerranée); *Oeffentlichen Kunstsammlung Basel Jahresberichte* (1959–60), pp. 59, 89; Ferrier, *Matisse 1911–1930* (1961), pl. 11; Schmidt and Boerlin, *Oeffentliche Kunstsammlung Basel Katalog* (1961), p. 42 (ill.); Guichard-Meili, *Matisse* (1967), pp. 198, 199 (fig. 204), 251; Orienti, *Matisse* (1972), p. 91, pl. 23; Alpatov, *Matisse* (1973), p. 85, pl. 34; Fourcade and Monod-Fontaine, *Matisse: Dessins et sculpture* (1975), p. 21; Carrà and Deryng, *Tout l'oeuvre peint de Matisse* (1982), p. 101 (ill.), no. 359, pl. LII; Guichard-Meili, *Matisse* (1986), pp. 110 (ill.), 134, 142; Noël, *Matisse* (1987), pp. 65 (ill.), 105; Flam, *Matisse: A Retrospective* (1988), p. 202 (trans. of Vildrac 1922); Schmidt, *Kunstmuseum Basel: 150 Gemälde* (1988), pp. 148, 149 (ill.); Monneret, *Matisse* (1994), p. 109 (ill.), no. 369; Dauberville and Dauberville, *Matisse chez Bernheim-Jeune* (1995), vol. 2, pp. 996, 997 (ill.), no. 465; Katz, *Öffentliche Kunstsammlung Basel: 20. Jahrhundert* (1997), p. 164 (ill.); Schneider, *Matisse* (2002), p. 510

43

***Large Cliff—Two Rays*, 1920**

Oil on canvas, 36⅝ x 29 in. (93 x 73.7 cm)
Norton Museum of Art, West Palm Beach, Florida, Bequest of R. H. Norton (53.126)
Signed (lower right): Henri-Matisse

Provenance: [Galerie Bernheim-Jeune, Paris, purchased from the artist, November 1920; stock no. 22308, sold on November 6, 1920, for 12,000 francs to Marseille]; [Léon Marseille, Paris, 1920]; Lord Ivor Spencer Churchill, London (by 1927 until 1931); [Étienne Bignou, Paris and London, probably acquired in 1931; sold to Southam, likely in 1936];

Harry S. Southam, Ottawa (by 1937); [E. A. Silberman Galleries, New York, until 1945]; Ralph Hubbard Norton and Elizabeth Calhoun Norton, West Palm Beach (1945–his d. 1953; gift to their eponymous museum, West Palm Beach, 1953)

Exhibitions: *Matisse* (Paris 1920), no. 28; *Matisse* (Paris 1931), no. 66; *Matisse* (Basel 1931), no. 55; *Matisse Retrospective* (New York 1931), no. 54; *Modern French Classics* (London 1935), no. 11; *Modern French Paintings: The School of Paris* (Montreal 1936), no. 19; "Modern French Paintings: The School of Paris" (Ottawa 1936), no cat., checklist no. 15; *Matisse Retrospective* (Philadelphia 1948), no. 51; *Matisse* (New York and other cities 1951–52), no. 51; *Matisse* (Los Angeles 1952), no. 34; *Art of Matisse* (Palm Beach 1953), no. 21; *Paintings* (New York 1955b), no. 32; *Inaugural Exhibition* (Chicago 1960), no. 34; *Seashore: Paintings* (Pittsburgh 1965), no. 59; *Matisse: 64 Paintings* (New York 1966), no. 41; *Modern Masters* (Sydney–Melbourne–New York 1975), no. 70; *Masters from the Norton Gallery* (Saint Petersburg 1978), no cat.; "Modern European Masters" (Jacksonville 1981), no cat.; *Matisse: Early Years in Nice* (Washington 1986–87), no. 88; *Matisse Retrospective* (New York 1992–93), no. 244; *Masterworks from the Norton Museum* (Jacksonville 1995–96), unnumbered cat., p. 41 (ill.); *European Collection* (Yamagata and other cities 1996), no. 65; *Animal as Muse* (West Palm Beach–Naples 1998–99), no. 55; *Matisse* (Madrid 2009), no. 11; "Objects of Wonder" (Portland and other cities 2010–11), no cat.

References: *Art Digest*, "World's Greatest Exhibition of Matisse's Art Is Held Here" (1931), p. 5; Barnes and De Mazia, *Art of Matisse* (1933), pp. 26, 47, 50, 92, 119, 132, 297 (fig. 110), 441; Mushakojo, *Matisse* (1939), p. 61 (fig. 122); Barr, *Matisse: His Art and His Public* (1951), pp. 197, 209–10, 232, 433 (ill.); Norton Gallery and School of Art, *Collection of Painting and Sculpture* (1957), p. 20; Diehl and Humbert, *Matisse* (1958), pp. 59, 111, pl. 87; Escholier, *Matisse: Portrait of the Artist and the Man* (1960), pp. 10, 13, pl. 32; Norton Gallery and School of Art, *Paintings and Sculpture* (1963), p. 46 (ill.); Brill, *Matisse* (1967), p. 18; Marchiori, *Matisse* (1967), pp. 61 (fig. 56), 133; Courthion, "La conquête de la lumiere" (1970), p. 56 (ill.); Flam, *Norton Matisses* (1973), essay titled "Two Rays, 1920" and fig. 2; Norton Gallery and School of Art, *Catalogue of the Collection* (1979), p. 111, no. 257, pl. 21; Carrà and Deryng, *Tout l'oeuvre peint de Matisse* (1982), pp. 99 (ill.), 100, no. 333; Flam, *Matisse: A Retrospective* (1988), pp. 199, 234 (pl. 73); Wilson, *Matisse* (1992), p. 86 (fig. 101); Monneret, *Matisse* (1994), p. 109 (ill.), no. 368; Dauberville and Dauberville, *Matisse chez Bernheim-Jeune* (1995), vol. 1, pp. 105, 107 (facsimile of Paris 1920), 223 (ill.), 224 (facsimile of Paris 1931), 267 (photo), vol. 2, p. 909 (ill.), no. 414; Flam, *Matisse in the Cone Collection* (2001), p. 60 n. 21; Schneider, *Matisse* (2002), pp. 503–4 (on Étretat series); Korn, "Collecting Paintings by Matisse and by Picasso" (2004), p. 122; Boutilier, *Inspirational: The Collection of H. S. Southam* (2009), pp. 8 (fig. 1), 14 (fig. 5), 24

44

Large Cliff—Eel, 1920

Oil on canvas, 35⅞ x 28⅜ in. (91 x 72 cm)
Columbus Museum of Art, Ohio, Gift of Ferdinand Howald (1931.063)
Signed (lower left): Henri Matisse

Provenance: [Galerie Bernheim-Jeune, Paris, purchased from the artist on September 8, 1920; stock no. 22220, sold on September 24, 1920, for 12,750 francs to de Zayas]; [Marius de Zayas, Paris and New York, 1920; sold on October 21, 1920, for 30,000 francs (2,164 dollars) to Quinn]; John Quinn, New York (1920–d. 1924); Quinn estate (1924–26; sold to Dudensing); [Valentine Gallery (F. Valentine Dudensing), New York, 1926; sold on March 25, 1926, for 3,500 dollars to Howald]; Ferdinand Howald, Columbus, Ohio, and New York (1926–31; his gift to Columbus Gallery of Fine Arts, Ohio, 1931, later renamed Columbus Museum of Art)

Exhibitions: *Matisse* (Paris 1920), no. 29; *Impressionist and Post-Impressionist Paintings* (New York 1921), no. 70; *Matisse* (New York 1924b), no. 14; *Gallery of Living Art* (New York 1927–28), unnumbered cat.; *Inaugural Exhibition* (Columbus 1931), no. 153; "Howald Collection" (Pittsburgh 1952), no cat.; *Modern French Masters* (Columbus–Akron–Worcester 1952–53), no. 24; *Französische Malerei* (Munich 1961), no. 97; *From the Collection of Ferdinand Howald* (Columbus–Dayton–New York 1969–70), no. 18; *Selections from the Howald Collection* (San Antonio and other cities 1970–71), no. 51; *Ferdinand Howald: Avant-Garde Collector* (London–Dublin–Cardiff 1973), no. 35; *Ferdinand Howald: Avant-Garde Collector* (Palm Beach 1975), no. 9; *Ferdinand Howald: Avant-Garde Collector* (Madison 1977), no. 9; *Matisse: Early Years in Nice* (Washington 1986–87), no. 87; *Matisse Retrospective* (New York 1992–93), no. 243; *Masterpieces from the Columbus Museum of Art* (Columbus and other cities 1993), no. 35; *Matisse* (Madrid 2009), no. 12

References: Wehle, "Loan Exhibition of Modern French Paintings" (1921), p. 96; Watson, *Quinn Collection* (1926), p. 11; Barr, *Matisse: His Art and His Public* (1951), p. 209; Flam, *Norton Matisses* (1973), mentioned in "Two Rays, 1920"; Columbus Museum of Art, *Catalog of the Collection* (1978), p. 145; Zilczer, *Noble Buyer: John Quinn* (1978), p. 172; Dauberville and Dauberville, *Matisse chez Bernheim-Jeune* (1995), vol. 1, pp. 105, 107 (facsimile of Paris 1920), vol. 2, pp. 898, 899 (ill.), no. 407; Cauman, "Matisse and America" (2000), vol. 1, pp. 347–48, 360, 396 n. 144, 417, vol. 2, fig. 3.1; Flam, *Matisse in the Cone Collection* (2001), p. 60 n. 21; Schneider, *Matisse* (2002), pp. 503–4 (on Étretat series)

45

Large Cliff—Fish, 1920

Oil on canvas, 36½ x 29 in. (92.7 x 73.7 cm)
The Baltimore Museum of Art, The Cone Collection, formed by Dr. Claribel Cone and Miss Etta Cone of Baltimore, Maryland (BMA 1950.233)
Signed (lower right): Henri-Matisse

Provenance: [Georges Bernheim, Paris, purchased from the artist in 1920; sold on November 6, 1920, to Bernheim-Jeune]; [Galerie Bernheim-Jeune, Paris, 1920–23; stock no. 22359, sold on July 6, 1923, together with Matisse's *Standing Girl, Green Dress, White Shawl* (1921) for 25,000 francs to the Cone sisters]; Dr. Claribel Cone and Miss Etta Cone, Baltimore (1923–50; their bequest to the Baltimore Museum of Art, 1950)

Exhibitions: *Modern French Art* (Baltimore 1925), no. 69; *Cone Collection* (Baltimore 1930), no. 17 or 34 (both as *Étretat*); *Matisse* (Paris 1931), no. 86; *Cone Collection* (Baltimore 1934), no. 38; *Century of Baltimore Collecting* (Baltimore 1941), unnumbered cat., p. 83; "Selections from the Cone Collection" (Baltimore 1949), checklist no. 37; *Cone Memorial Exhibition* (Baltimore 1950), no. 48; *Cone Collection* (New York 1955a), no. 48; *Cone Collection* (New York 1974), no. 20; "Matisse and Master Drawings from the Baltimore Museum of Art" (New York 1979), no cat.; "Masterpieces from the Cone Collection" (Los Angeles–Fort Worth 1985–86), no cat.; *Matisse: Early Years in Nice* (Washington 1986–87), no. 89; "Matisse, Picasso and Impressionist Masters from the Cone Collection" (Boston 1991–92), no cat.; *Matisse Retrospective* (New York 1992–93), no. 245; "Van Gogh to Matisse" (Houston 1993–94), no cat.; *Matisse and Modern Masters from the Cone Collection* (Tokyo–Osaka 1996–97), no. 13; "Matisse from the Baltimore Museum of Art" (Denver–Birmingham–Toronto 2000–2001), no cat.; *Collecting Matisse and Modern Masters* (New York–Vancouver 2011–12), unnumbered cat., pp. 21, 37 (pl. 13), 74 (ill.), 76 (shown only in New York)

References: *Baltimore Sun*, "Baltimore Women Own Large Collection" (1924), p. M20; *Baltimore Sun*, "'Advanced' Works of Art Startle Some" (1925), p. 8 (ill.); *Le Mois*, July 1–August 1931, p. 224 (ill.); George, "Dualité de Matisse" (1931), ill. btw. pp. 94–95; *Art Digest*, "Baltimore Sees 52 Works by Matisse" (1934), p. 20 (ill.); Romm, *Matisse* (1937), no. 26 (ill.); Romm, *Matisse: A Social Critique* (1947), p. 95, and ill.; Barr, *Matisse: His Art and His Public* (1951), p. 209; Baltimore Museum of Art, *Cone Collection* (1955), p. 32, no. 48; Diehl and Humbert, *Matisse* (1958), p. 59; Lassaigne, *Matisse* (1959), p. 101; Pollack, *Collectors: Dr. Claribel and Etta Cone* (1962), photo of the Cone dining room; Baltimore Museum of Art, *Cone Collection* (1967), p. 66, no. 45; Flam, *Norton Matisses* (1973), n.p., mentioned under "Two Rays, 1920," fig. 10; Carrà and Deryng, *Tout l'oeuvre peint de Matisse* (1982), pp. 99, 100, 114 (ill.), no. 332; Hohl, "Matisse und Picasso" (1982), p. 45 (fig. 23, photo); Richardson, *Dr. Claribel & Miss Etta* (1985), pp. 26 (photo), 94, 120 (photo), 173, 174 (ill.), 197; Richardson, "Dr. Claribel and Miss Etta Cone" (1987), pp. 294, 307 (fig. 307, photo); Ducrey and Ducrey, *La Galerie Paul Vallotton depuis 1913* (1988), pp. 66 (ill.), 67, 76 n. 31; Girard, *Les chefs-d'oeuvre du Musée Matisse* (1991), p. 56 (ill.); Monneret, *Matisse* (1994), p. 109 (ill.), no. 367; Dauberville and Dauberville, *Matisse chez Bernheim-Jeune* (1995), vol. 1, p. 233 (facsimile of Paris 1931), and vol. 2, p. 916 (ill.), no. 418; O'Brian, *Ruthless Hedonism* (1999), p. 82 (fig. 32, photo); Cauman, "Matisse and America" (2000), vol. 1, pp. 416–17, vol. 2, fig. 3.15; Flam, *Matisse in the Cone Collection* (2001), pp. 55, 59 (pl. 22), 60; Cowling et al., *Matisse, Picasso* (2002), p. 375 (fig. 96, reprint of ill. from *Le Mois* 1931); Schneider, *Matisse* (2002), pp. 503–4 (on Étretat series); Brettell and Eisenman, *Nineteenth-Century Art in the Norton Simon Museum* (2006), vol. 1, pp. 180–81 (fig. 45d), 573; Hirschland and Ramage, *Cone Sisters of Baltimore* (2008), pp. 104 (fig. 5.10), 105, 136 (photo)

46

***Still Life with Yellow Curtain, Anemones, and Fruit*, 1925**

Oil on canvas, 31½ x 39⅜ in. (80 x 100 cm)
Private collection
New York only
Signed and dated (lower right): Henri-Matisse 25

Provenance: [Pierre Matisse Gallery, New York, on consignment from the artist, October 3, 1933; inventory C134; stock no. 619; sold on May 20, 1937, for 9,200 dollars to Ittleson; signed and dated by the artist in summer 1937]; Mr. and Mrs. Henry Ittleson Jr., New York (1937–his d. 1973); by descent to heirs; sale, "Impressionist and Modern Art, Part I," Sotheby's, London, December 8, 1997, no. 13; private collection

Exhibitions: *Matisse* (Berlin 1930), no. 67; possibly *29th International Exhibition of Paintings* (Pittsburgh 1930), no. 216; possibly *Matisse* (Basel 1931), no. 95; likely *Paintings: Matisse* (New York 1934), no. 17; *French Painting* (San Francisco 1934), no. 209; *Paintings by Matisse* (New York 1954), no. 11; *Paintings from Private Collections* (New York 1962), no. 42; *Matisse: Early Years in Nice* (Washington 1986–87), no. 142; *Matisse Retrospective* (New York 1992–93), no. 262

References: Guadagnini, *Matisse* (1993), p. 194 (ill.); Schneider, *Matisse* (2002), p. 512 (ill.)

47

***Still Life with Candied Pineapple, Anemones, and Fruit*, 1925**

Oil on canvas, 31¾ x 39¼ in. (80.6 x 99.7 cm)
Philadelphia Museum of Art, Gift of Henry P. McIlhenny, 1964 (1964-77-1)
Signed (lower left): Henri-Matisse

Provenance: [Galerie Bernheim-Jeune, Paris, purchased from the artist, April 20, 1925; stock no. 24258, sold on May 6, 1925, for 50,000 francs to Pacquement]; Charles Pacquement, Paris (1925–32; his sale, Galerie Georges Petit, Paris, December 12, 1932, no. 48, as *L'ananas*, to Dudensing); [Valentine Gallery (F. Valentine Dudensing), New York, 1932–33; stock no. 707, sold for 7,500 dollars on March 14, 1933, to McIlhenny]; Henry P. McIlhenny, Philadelphia (1933–64; his gift to the Philadelphia Museum of Art, 1964)

Exhibitions: *Matisse* (Basel 1931), no. 74; *Twenty Paintings by Matisse* (New York 1936b), no. 9; "French Artists of the 18th and 19th Centuries" (Philadelphia 1937), no cat.; *Picasso, Matisse* (Boston 1938), no. 35; *Masterpieces of Philadelphia Private Collections* (Philadelphia 1947), no. 76; *Matisse Retrospective* (Philadelphia 1948), no. 64; *McIlhenny Collection* (San Francisco 1962), no. 28; *French Masterpieces from the McIlhenny Collection* (Allentown 1977), unnumbered cat., pp. 94, 95 (ill.); "From the McIlhenny Collection" (Pittsburgh 1979), no cat., unnumbered typed checklist; *McIlhenny Collection* (Atlanta 1984), no. 39; *Matisse: Early Years in Nice* (Washington 1986–87), no. 143; *Masterpieces from the Philadelphia Museum of Art* (Kyoto–Tokyo 2007), no. 44; "Matisse and Modern Art on the French Riviera" (Philadelphia 2008–9), no cat.; *Manet to Picasso* (Seoul–Busan–Taipei 2009–10), unnumbered cat., p. 153

References: Mauny, "Pacquement Collection" (1928), p. 14; *Art News*, "Pacquement Sale" (1932), pp. 5 (ill.), 8; Huyghe, *L'art contemporain* (1935), p. 106 (fig. 122); Barr, *Matisse: His Art and His Public* (1951), p. 212; Bernier, "Le musée privé d'un conservateur" (1957), pp. 26–27 (ill.); G[ardiner], "Matisse . . . *Still Life on Table*" (1965), p. 7 (ill.); Carrà and Deryng, *Tout l'oeuvre peint de Matisse* (1982), p. 103 (ill.), no. 433; Rishel, *McIlhenny Collection* (1987), pp. 40–41 (ill.); Monneret, *Matisse* (1994), p. 115 (ill.), no. 466; Bernier, "Matisse en persona" (1995), p. 31 (ill.); Dauberville and Dauberville, *Matisse chez Bernheim-Jeune* (1995), vol. 2, pp. 1234, 1235 (ill.), no. 641; Sotheby's, London, *Impressionist and Modern Art, Part I*, December 8, 1997, pp. 38, 40 (fig. 3), under no. 13; Naudin et al., *Matisse* (1998), p. 69 (photo reconstructing the still life)

48

***Still Life with "Histoire Juive,"* 1924**

Oil on canvas, 32⅛ x 39½ in. (81.6 x 100.3 cm)
Philadelphia Museum of Art, The Samuel S. White 3rd and Vera White Collection, 1967 (1967-30-56)
Signed (lower left): Henri-Matisse; inscribed on books: HISTOIR[E] / JUIVE; L'AMO / ROMA; PHILO / SOPH / IE

Provenance: [Galerie Bernheim-Jeune, Paris, purchased from the artist, April 15, 1924; stock no. 23900, sold on January 31, 1925, for 2,200 dollars to White]; Mr. and Mrs. Samuel S. White 3rd, Ardmore, Pennsylvania (1925–his d. 1952; to his widow); Vera White (1952–d. 1966; her bequest to the Philadelphia Museum of Art, 1967)

Exhibitions: *Matisse* (Paris 1924), no. 12; *Inaugural Exhibition* (Philadelphia 1928), p. 15; *Matisse* (Paris 1931), no. 114; *Matisse Retrospective* (New York 1931), no. 65; *Matisse* (Providence 1931), no. 30; *Century of Progress* (Chicago 1933), no. 396; "White Collection" (Philadelphia 1933–34), no cat.; *Matisse* (San Francisco 1936), no. 26; *Picasso, Matisse* (Boston 1938), no. 34; *Masterpieces of Philadelphia Private Collections* (Philadelphia 1947), no. 75; *Matisse Retrospective* (Philadelphia 1948), no. 63; "White Collection" (Philadelphia 1950), no cat.; "White Collection" (Philadelphia 1962–66), no cat.; *World of Flowers* (Philadelphia 1963), p. 160; *Peale Club Collectors Show* (Philadelphia 1965), no. 18; *White Collection* (Philadelphia 1968), no. 26; *Matisse: Early Years in Nice* (Washington 1986–87), no. 137; "Matisse and Modern Art on the French Riviera" (Philadelphia 2008–9), no cat.

References: Brown, "Matisse Exhibition" (1932), p. 3 (ill.); Barnes and de Mazia, *Art of Matisse* (1933), pp. 26, 32, 34, 36, 56–57, 67, 87, 92–93, 102–3, 108, 119, 134, 146, 156, 167, 196, 330 (ill.), 445, no. 154; Mushakojo, *Matisse* (1939), p. 87 (fig. 183); Hess, "Matisse: A Life of Color" (1948), p. 18 (ill.); Kimball, "Matisse: Recognition, Patronage, Collecting" (1948), p. 47; Kimball, "Discovery from America" (1948), p. 54; Goudy, "Four Collectors in Philadelphia" (1950), p. 28 (photo); Barr, *Matisse: His Art and His Public* (1951), p. 212; Diehl and Humbert, *Matisse* (1958), p. 60; Carrà and Deryng, *Tout l'oeuvre peint de Matisse* (1982), p. 103 (ill.), no. 411; Monneret, *Matisse* (1994), p. 114 (ill.), no. 445; Dauberville and Dauberville, *Matisse chez Bernheim-Jeune* (1995), vol. 1, pp. 250 (facsimile of Paris 1931), 251 (ill.), vol. 2, p. 1197 (ill.), no. 612; Sotheby's, London, *Impressionist and Modern Art, Part I*, December 8, 1997, pp. 38, 40 (fig. 2), under no. 13; Cauman, "Matisse and America" (2000), vol. 1, p. 475; Schneider, *Matisse* (2002), p. 27

49

***Reclining Odalisque*, 1926**

Oil on canvas, 15⅛ x 21⅝ in. (38.4 x 54.9 cm)
The Metropolitan Museum of Art, New York, Bequest of Miss Adelaide Milton de Groot (1876–1967), 1967 (67.187.82)
Copenhagen only
Signed (lower left): Henri Matisse

Provenance: [Valentine Gallery (F. Valentine Dudensing), New York, in 1930]; Mme Guy du Manoir; Adelaide Milton de Groot, New York (by 1936–d. 1967; on loan to the Metropolitan Museum, 1936; her bequest to the Museum, 1967)

Exhibitions: Likely *Twenty Paintings by Matisse* (New York 1936b), no. 16; *Twentieth Century Painting* (Hartford 1955), no. 33; *Masterpieces from the Collection of Adelaide Milton de Groot* (New York 1958), no. 15; *Masterpieces from the Adelaide Milton de Groot Collection* (Columbus 1958–59), no. 24; *Matisse* (New York 1973), no. 30; *Inventive Clothes* (New York–Kyoto 1973–75), hors cat.; *5000 Years of Art* (Bellingham 1976–77), no. 77; *Le Maroc de Matisse* (Paris 1999–2000a), no. 56; *Painters in Paris* (New York 2000–2001), unnumbered cat., p. 47 (ill.); *Picasso and the School of Paris* (Kyoto–Tokyo 2002–3), no. 49; *Matisse, His Art and His Textiles* (Le Cateau-Cambrésis–London–New York 2004–5), no. 23; *Matisse and the Alhambra* (Granada 2010–11), no. 22; *Matisse: Drawing Life* (Brisbane 2011–12), no. 296

References: Gros, "Matisse" (1927), p. 274 (ill.); Fels, *Matisse* (1929), p. 43 (ill.); *Creative Art*, "Art Market" (1930), suppl. p. 66 (ill.); Kawashima, *Matisse* (1936), ill.; Wehle, "Loan of Paintings" (1936), p. 209; Dauberville and Dauberville, *Matisse chez Bernheim-Jeune* (1995), vol. 2, pp. 1282, 1283 (ill.), no. 680; Schneider, *Matisse* (2002), p. 527

50

***Odalisque in Gray Harem Pants*, 1926–27**

Oil on canvas, 21¼ x 25⅝ in. (54 x 65 cm)
Musée de l'Orangerie, Paris, Collection Jean Walter and Paul Guillaume (RF 1963-67)
Copenhagen only
Signed (lower left): Henri-Matisse

Provenance: [Paul Guillaume, Paris, by 1929–d. 1934]; Juliette Lacaze (Mme Paul Guillaume, later Mme Jean Walter), Paris (1934–63; sold to the French State, retaining life-interest, in 1963–d. 1977; at the Musée de l'Orangerie since 1984)

Exhibitions: *Salon d'automne* (Paris 1927), no. 1055; "Collection Paul Guillaume" (Paris 1929), no cat.; *Matisse* (Paris 1931), no. 139; *Twenty Paintings by Matisse* (New York 1936b), no. 15; *Collection Jean Walter—Paul Guillaume* (Paris 1966), no. 62; *Matisse* (Rome 1978–79), no. 17; *Matisse* (Stockholm 1984–85), no. 52; "Matisse" (Humlebaek 1985), checklist no. 63; *Matisse Retrospective* (New York 1992–93), no. 279; *Matisse* (Brisbane–Canberra–Melbourne 1995), no. 113; *Chefs-d'oeuvre du Musée de l'Orangerie* (Tokyo and other cities 1998–99), no. 49; *Chefs-d'oeuvre du Musée de l'Orangerie* (Taipei-Kaohsiung 1999–2000), no. 49; *From Renoir to Picasso* (Montreal–Fort Worth 2000–2001), no. 47; *Renoir to Picasso* (Brisbane–Sydney–Melbourne 2001), no. 47; *De Renoir a Picasso* (Barcelona 2002), no. 47; *Matisse* (Taipei 2002–3), unnumbered cat., p. 83; *Matisse: La période niçoise* (Nantes 2003), no. 19; *Matisse, Picasso 1920* (Grenoble–Marseille 2003–4), unnumbered cat., pp. 36–37, Marseille ed.: pp. 40–41 (ill.), 50; *Matisse, His Art and His Textiles* (Le Cateau-Cambrésis–London–New York 2004–5), no. 25; *Matisse* (Madrid 2009), no. 42

References: Gros, "Matisse" (1927), p. 270 (ill.); Guenne, "Salon d'Automne" (1927), pp. 869, 884–85 (ill.); George, *La grande peinture contemporaine à la collection Paul Guillaume* (1929), pp. 78, 80 (ill.); McBride, *Matisse* (1930), no. 3, ill.; *Chroniques du jour*, "Pour ou contre Matisse" (1931), ill.; George, "Dualité de Matisse" (1931), ill. btw. pp. 94–95; Barnes and De Mazia, *Art of Matisse* (1933), pp. 33, 39, 57, 62, 72, 93, 118, 127, 138, 155, 164, 173, 196, 446, no. 174; Davidson, "Magic Color" (1936), pp. 14 (ill.), 21; Cassou, *Matisse* (1939), p. 15; Cassou, *Matisse* (1948), pl. 14; Escholier, "Matisse et le Maroc" (1956), p. 712 (ill.); Diehl and Humbert, *Matisse* (1958), pp. 61, 112, pl. 100; Carrà and Deryng, *Tout l'oeuvre peint de Matisse* (1982), p. 104 (ill.), no. 450; Guillaud and Guillaud, *Matisse: Rhythm and Line* (1987), pp. 188, 206 (pl. 201); Guicharnaud in Hoog, *Musée de l'Orangerie: Catalogue* (1990), pp. 138, 139 (ill.), no. 59; Bois, "On Matisse: The Blinding" (1994), p. 120; Monneret, *Matisse* (1994), pp. 72 (ill.), 73 (detail ill.), 116 (ill.), no. 483; Dauberville and Dauberville, *Matisse chez Bernheim-Jeune* (1995), vol. 2, pp. 1270, 1271 (ill.), no. 674; Golan, *Modernity and Nostalgia* (1995), pp. 108, 109 (fig. 114); Néret, *Matisse* (1996), p. 137 (ill.); Bois, *Matisse and Picasso* (1998), pp. 34, 35 (fig. 19), 244 n. 82; Monod-Fontaine in Alaoui et al., *Le Maroc de Matisse* (1999), p. 136, under no. 56; Green, *Art in France* (2000), pp. 220 (fig. 263), 221; Percheron and Brouder, *Matisse* (2002), p. 354 (fig. 383); Schneider, *Matisse* (2002), p. 527; Weid, *Musée de l'Orangerie: Guide* (2006), p. 62 (ill.); Monod-Fontaine, "Matisse aux carreaux" (2010), pp. 48, 49 (ill.)

51

***Seated Nude with Foliage, Sketch*, 1936**

Oil on canvas, 28½ x 23⅞ in. (72.5 x 60.5 cm)
Musée Matisse, Nice, Gift of the Estate of Mrs. Henri Matisse, 1960 (63.2.3)
Copenhagen only
Monogrammed and dated (lower right): H.M. 37 [see Jack Flam's discussion of the dating on pp. 138, 191 n. 2, in this volume]

Provenance: The artist (1936–d. 1954; his estate); to his widow, Amélie Matisse (until d. 1958; gift of the artist's children in keeping with their mother's verbal bequest to the city of Nice, 1960)

Exhibitions: *Matisse centenaire* (Paris 1970), no. 190; *L'art moderne dans les musées de province* (Paris 1978), no. 196; *Matisse* (Madrid 1980), no. 33; *Matisse et ses amis* (Hiroshima and other cities 1981), no. 6; *Matisse* (Zürich–Düsseldorf 1983), no. 81; *Matisse* (Stockholm 1984–85), no. 60; "Matisse" (Humlebaek 1985), checklist no. 74; *Matisse et l'Italie* (Venice 1987), no. P50; *Chefs-d'oeuvre du Musée Matisse* (Tokyo and other cities 1987–88), no. 37; *Chefs-d'œuvre du Musée Matisse* (Dijon 1991), unnumbered cat., pp. 76, 77 (ill.), 78; *Matisse: Capolavori dal Museo Matisse di Nizza* (Rome–Milan 1991–92), no. 13; *Matisse: Image into Sign* (Saint Louis 1993a), no. 6; *Matisse: Le grand atelier* (Nice 1994), unnumbered cat., p. 2 (ill.); *Matisse: Femmes et fleurs* (Nice 1998), p. 15 (ill.); *Lydia D* (Le Cateau-Cambrésis–Nice 2010), unnumbered cat., pp. 65 (ill.), 214; *Matisse: La seduzione di Michelangelo* (Brescia 2011), unnumbered cat., pp. 152, 153 (ill.)

References: Schneider, "Grand Palais: Matisse" (1970), p. 95 (ill.); Aragon, *Matisse, roman* (1971), vol. 1, p. 137 (fig. 73); Carrà and Deryng, *Tout l'oeuvre peint de Matisse* (1982), p. 106 (ill.), no. 477; Delectorskaya, *L'apparente facilité* (1986), pp. 31, 201 (ill.); Guichard-Meili, *Matisse* (1986), p. 43 (ill.); Milner, *Matisse* (1994), p. 114 (ill.); Monneret, *Matisse* (1994), p. 119 (ill.), no. 522; Delectorskaya, *Matisse: Contre vents et marées* (1996), p. 414 (photo); Girard, *Matisse in Nice* (1996), p. 77 (ill.)

52

***Draped Nude*, 1936**

Oil on canvas, 18 x 14¾ in. (45.7 x 37.5 cm)
Tate: Purchased 1959 (T00306)
Copenhagen only
Signed and dated (lower left): Henri / Matisse 36

Provenance: The artist (1936–37; Bernheim-Jeune photograph no. 8610, March 1937; sold to Rosenberg); [Paul Rosenberg, Paris, 1937; stock no. 3724]; [Rosenberg & Helft, London, 1937; sold to Willoughby]; Hugh Willoughby, Cheltenham (1937); [Rosenberg and Helft, London, 1937; sold to Edwards]; Mrs. M. L. Edwards, Gloucester (ca. 1937–59; sold to Tate, London, 1959)

Exhibitions: *Oeuvres récentes de Matisse* (Paris 1937a), no. 3; *Recent Works of Matisse* (London 1937), no. 3; *Matisse, Picasso, Braque, Laurens* (Oslo-Copenhagen-Stockholm 1938), no. 25; "Body in 20th Century Art" (Norwich 2002), no cat.; *Matisse: Menschen Masken Modelle* (Stuttgart–Hamburg 2008–9), no. 83 (shown only in Stuttgart); *Lydia D.* (Le Cateau-Cambrésis–Nice 2010), unnumbered cat., pp. 50, 51 (ill.), 214

References: Alley, *Tate Collection of Modern Art* (1981), p. 500 (ill.), no. T.306; Delectorskaya, *L'apparente facilité* (1986), pp. 31, 202 (ill.); Guichard-Meili, *Matisse* (1986), pp. 40 (ill.), 141; Girard, *Les chefs-d'œuvre du Musée Matisse* (1991), pp. 78, 79 (ill.); Dauberville and Dauberville, *Matisse chez Bernheim-Jeune* (1995), vol. 2, p. 1344 (ill.), no. 730; Schneider, *Matisse* (2002), p. 636; Korn, "Collecting Paintings by Matisse and by Picasso" (2004), p. 123

53

***The Large Blue Dress*, 1937**

Oil on canvas, 36½ x 29 in. (92.7 x 73.7 cm)
Philadelphia Museum of Art, Gift of Mrs. John Wintersteen, 1956 (1956-23-1)
Signed (lower left): Henri Matisse / 37

Provenance: [Paul Rosenberg, Paris; acquired from the artist, June 1937; stock no. 3788]; [with Rosenberg & Helft, London, July 1937; sold to McIlhenny, July 1937]; Henry P. McIlhenny, Philadelphia (1937; gift to his sister); Bernice (Bonnie) McIlhenny Wintersteen (Mrs. John Wintersteen), Villanova, Penn. (July 1937–56; her gift to the Philadelphia Museum of Art, 1956)

Exhibitions: *Oeuvres récentes de Matisse* (Paris 1937a), no. 15; *Recent Works by Matisse* (London 1937), no. 15; *Picasso, Matisse* (Boston 1938), no. 39; *Art of the Third Republic* (Worcester 1941), no. 24; *Masterpieces of Philadelphia Private Collections* (Philadelphia 1947), no. 92; *Matisse Retrospective* (Philadelphia 1948), no. 79; *Paintings by Matisse* (New York 1954), no. 15; *Matisse Retrospective* (Los Angeles–Chicago–Boston 1966), no. 77; *Collection of Mrs. John Wintersteen* (San Francisco–Santa Barbara 1966), no. 19; *Matisse: 64 Paintings* (New York 1966), no. 53 (on view only September 1–25); *Matisse Retrospective* (London 1968), no. 110; *Matisse: Retrospective* (New York 1992–93), no. 317; *Matisse: Image into Sign* (Saint Louis 1993a), no. 7; *Matisse: Le grand atelier* (Nice 1994), unnumbered cat., pp. 10 (ill.), 34, cover ill.; *Matisse* (Brisbane–Canberra–Melbourne 1995), no. 161; *Fabric of Vision* (London 2002), no. 62; *Matisse: Fabric of Dreams* (Le Cateau-Cambrésis–London–New York 2004–5), no. 47 (shown only in London); *Masterpieces from the Philadelphia Museum of Art* (Kyoto–Tokyo 2007), no. 46; *Repeating Image* (Baltimore–Phoenix 2007–8), no. 65 (and photos of nine stages, figs. 21–30) (shown only in Phoenix); "Matisse and Modern Art on the French Riviera" (Philadelphia 2008–9), no cat. (work shown beginning June 29); *Cézanne and Beyond* (Philadelphia 2009), unnumbered cat., pp. 134 (pl. 21), 535, cover ill.

References: *Magazine of Art*, "Evolution of a Painting" (1939), pp. 414 (ill., stages), 415 (ill.); Smith, "Balancing the Books" (1941), p. 27 (ill.); Besson, *Matisse* (1943), pl. 20 (early stage); Frankfurter, "Is He the Greatest?" (1948), p. 22 (photos of 10 stages of the painting); Barr, *Matisse: His Art and His Public* (1951), pp. 234 (early stage), 235 (ill.), 251–53, 263; Peckham, "Triumph of Romanticism" (1952), pp. 292 (ill., stages), 293 (ill.); Besson, *Matisse* (1954), pl. 44; Greenberg, *Matisse* (1955), pl. 27; Hunter, *Matisse* (1956), fig. 22; Escholier, *Matisse: A Portrait* (1960), p. 14, pl. 49; Werner, "Earthly Paradise of Matisse" (1966), p. 33 (ill.); Brill, *Matisse* (1967), p. 38, pl. 35; Leymarie, "Evoluzione di Matisse" (1967), pp. 62 (ill.), 70; Okamoto, *Bonnard, Matisse* (1968), pl. 64; Russell, *World of Matisse* (1969), p. 116 (ill.); Aragon, *Matisse, roman* (1971), vol. 2, pp. 86 (pl. 10), 118, 359; Jacobus, *Matisse* (1972), pp. 38 (fig. 41), 39; Orienti, *Matisse* (1972), p. 39; Flam, "Jazz" (1977), pp. 39, 40 (fig. 22), 41; Watkins, *Matisse* (1977), pp. 12, 16, pl. 42; Gowing, *Matisse* (1979), pp. 170, 171 (fig. 158), 173, 211; Gowing, *Matisse: Harmony of Light* (1979), pp. 13–14; Beausire, "Matisse" (1982), p. 12 (ill.); Watkins, *Matisse* (1984), pp. 183, 185 (pl. 175), 186–87, 202, 216; Delectorskaya, *L'apparente facilité* (1986), pp. 31, 231 (photos), 232–33 (ills.), 234 (photos), 235 (ill.); Rishel, *Henry P. McIlhenny Collection* (1987), pp. 40 (ill.), 68; Flam, *Matisse: A Retrospective* (1988), pp. 280 (pl. 87), 353 (excerpt of Barr 1951); Kostenevich, Rusakov, and Fukaya, *Matisse* (1991), p. 156, under no. 57 (ill.); Néret, *Matisse* (1991), pp. 178 (fig. 266), 189; Wilson, *Matisse* (1992), p. 105 (fig. 141); Flam, "Matisse: Image into Sign" (1993), pp. 7–8, 9 (fig. 3, A–D), 10, 22 (pl. 7); Girard, *Matisse: Une splendeur inouïe* (1993), pp. 117, 119 (ill.); Girard, *Matisse: Le grand atelier* (1994), pp. 10 (ill.), 11–12, 14; Milner, *Matisse* (1994), pp. 6, 12, 115 (ill.), frontis.; Philadelphia Museum of Art, *Paintings from Europe and the Americas* (1994), p. 393.8 (ill.); Benjamin, "Vital Sign" (1995), p. 35 (fig. 22); Dauberville and Dauberville, *Matisse chez Bernheim-Jeune* (1995), vol. 2, p. 1369 (ill.), no. 755; Temkin in Philadelphia Museum of Art, *Handbook* (1995), p. 325 (ill.); Néret, *Matisse* (1996), pp. 182 (ill.), 183, 195; Klein, *Matisse Portraits* (2001), pp. 12, 16 (detail ill.), 23, 25 (fig. 10); Essers, *Matisse* (2002), pp. 73 (ill.), 74, 95; Percheron and Brouder, *Matisse: De la couleur à l'architecture* (2002), pp. 356, 357 (fig. 386); Schneider, *Matisse* (2002), pp. 441, 569, 642; Flam, *Matisse and Picasso* (2003), pp. 171 (fig. 8.15), 176, 259; Amano, "Processus et surface" (2004), pp. 148, 149 (fig. 18); Kropmanns, "Matisse à Vence" (2007), p. 62; Llorens, *Matisse* (2009), pp. 148 (fig. 38), 149, 221; Blum, *Matisse: Rooms with a View* (2010), p. 134 (pl. 92)

54

***The Dream*, 1940**

Oil on canvas, 31⅞ x 25⅝ in. (81 x 65 cm)
Private collection
Signed and dated (lower left): Henri Matisse 9/40

Provenance: The artist (1940–d. 1954; his estate; to his daughter); Marguerite Duthuit, Paris (until d. 1982; to her son); Claude Duthuit (until d. 2011); private collection

Exhibitions: *Salon d'automne* (Paris 1945a), no. XIX; *Matisse* (Paris 1945b), no. 3 (exhibited with 12 photos of successive stages of the painting); *Matisse, Picasso* (Brussels 1946), no. 12 (with 14 photos); *Peintures et sculptures contemporaines* (Avignon 1947), no. 127; *Matisse Retrospective* (Philadelphia 1948), no. 82; *Matisse* (Lucerne 1949), no. 102; *XXVe Biennale* (Venice 1950), no. 39; *Mostra di Matisse* (Milan 1950), no. 28; *Matisse* (Hamburg-Düsseldorf-Munich 1951), no. 20; *Matisse. Thèmes et Variations: Le rêve—la chapelle* (Stockholm 1951–52), unnumbered cat. (with 13 photos); *Matisse* (Lund 1952), no. 2 (with 13 photos); *Sculpture of Matisse and 3 Paintings with Studies* (London 1953), no. 53 (with 7 studies and 13 photos); *Matisse* (Copenhagen 1953), no. 48 (with 13 photos); *Matisse* (Oslo 1954), no. 49 (with 13 photos); *Matisse* (Rotterdam 1954), no. 50 (with 7 studies and 13 photos); *Matisse* (Ottawa and other cities 1954–55), no. 50 (with 7 studies and 13 photos); *Matisse* (Houston 1955), no. 50 (11 studies and 13 photos); *Matisse* (Boston 1955), no. 50 (with 7 studies and 13 photos); *Matisse* (Aix-en-Provence 1960), no. 25; *Documenta III* (Kassel 1964), p. 78, no. 2; *Matisse Retrospective* (Los Angeles–Chicago–Boston 1966), no. 81; *Matisse: Retrospective* (London 1968), no. 112; *Matisse* (Moscow–Leningrad 1969), hors cat.; *Matisse centenaire* (Paris 1970), no. 192; *Matisse* (Copenhagen 1970), no. 58; *Matisse* (Madrid 1980), no. 34; *Matisse* (Tokyo-Kyoto 1981), no. 85; *Matisse Retrospective* (Nagoya-Hiroshima-Kasama 1991), no. 62; *Matisse Retrospective* (New York 1992–93), no. 334; *Matisse: Image into Sign* (Saint Louis 1993a), no. 13; *Matisse: "La révélation m'est venue de l'Orient"* (Rome 1997–98), no. 94; *Matisse and Picasso* (Fort Worth 1999), unnumbered cat., pp. 72, 136, 137 (fig. 126), 139 (fig. 128), 183 (photo), 184, 253 n. 258, 311 n. 319; Matisse: *Processus/Variation* (Tokyo 2004), no. 67; *Matisse: The Fabric of Dreams* (Le Cateau-Cambrésis–London–New York 2004–5), no. 51 (shown only in New York)

References: Besson, *Matisse* (1943), pl. 51; Besson, *Matisse* (1945), pl. 51; Degand, "Matisse à Paris" (1945), pp. 1, 4; Parrot, "Matisse au Salon d'automne" (1945), p. 2 (ill.); Aragon, *Apologie du luxe* (1946),

60

***Interior in Venetian Red*, 1946**

Oil on canvas, 36¼ x 25⅝ in. (92 x 65 cm)
Royal Museums of Fine Arts of Belgium, Brussels (6412)
Signed and dated (upper right): H Matisse 46

Provenance: The artist (1946–48; sold to Royal Museums of Fine Arts of Belgium through M. Robert Giron, Brussels, 1948)

Exhibitions: *Gloires de la peinture moderne* (Ostende 1949), no. 105; *Rétrospective Matisse* (Paris 1956), no. 92; *Meesterwerken van het Museum voor Schone Kunsten te Brussel* (Bruges 1961), no. 62; *À la rencontre de Matisse* (Saint-Paul-de-Vence 1969), no. 26; *Matisse* (Zürich–Düsseldorf 1982–83), no. 90 (shown in Zürich only); *Matisse Retrospective* (New York 1992–93), no. 375; *Matisse: "La révélation m'est venue de l'Orient"* (Rome 1997–98), no. 112; *Matisse, une seconde vie* (Paris–Humlebaek 2005), no. 107 (Paris), no. 96 (Humlebaek); *Matisse: Figur, Farbe, Raum* (Düsseldorf 2005–6), no. 185; *Matisse: Figure, couleur, espace* (Basel 2006), no. 116; *De l'impressionnisme au fauvisme en Belgique* (Yamanashi and other cities 2009–10), no. 67; *Matisse: La seduzione di Michelangelo* (Brescia 2011), unnumbered cat., pp. 228, 229

References: Besson, *Matisse* (1954), pl. 48; Guichard-Meili, *Matisse* (1967), pp. 205 (fig. 212), 251; Leymarie, "Evoluzione di Matisse" (1967), p. 71; Aragon, *Matisse, roman* (1971), vol. 2, pp. 333 (pl. 61), 363; Monod-Fontaine, *Matisse: Oeuvres* (1979), p. 90 (fig. a); Watkins, *Matisse* (1984), p. 212; Monod-Fontaine, Baldassari, and Laugier, *Matisse: Oeuvres* (1989), p. 108 (fig. a); Mirabdolbaghi, "Incursions champêtres" (1997), p. 112; Museum voor Moderne Kunst, *Een keuze* (2001), pp. 192–93 (both eds.); Monod-Fontaine and Tanaka in Amano et al., *Matisse: Processus/Variation* (2004), pp. 28, 202 (fig. 1); Kropmanns, "Matisse à Vence" (2007), p. 73 (photo); Monod-Fontaine, "Grenades et palmiers" (2007), pp. 32, 36; Blum, *Matisse: Rooms with a View* (2010), pp. 158 (pl. 111), 159

61

***Interior with an Egyptian Curtain*, 1948**

Oil on canvas, 45¾ x 35⅛ in. (116.2 x 89.2 cm)
The Phillips Collection, Washington, D.C. (1305)
New York only
Signed and dated (lower right): Matisse 48

Provenance: [Pierre Matisse Gallery, New York, 1948–50, on consignment from the artist, December 1948; consignment no. 1939; stock no. 2327, sold on February 8, 1950, for 20,000 dollars to Phillips]; Duncan Phillips, Washington D.C. (1950–d. 1966; on view in his mansion—opened to the public as a museum as of 1930—from 1950)

Exhibitions: *Matisse* (New York 1949a), no. 8; *Matisse: Oeuvres récentes* (Paris 1949), no. 8; *Pittsburgh International* (Pittsburgh 1950), no. 128; *Matisse* (New York and other cities 1951–52), no. 73; *Art of Matisse* (Palm Beach 1953), no. 29; *Paintings by Matisse* (New York 1954), no. 18; *Man and His Years* (Baltimore 1954), no. 121; *Rétrospective Matisse* (Paris 1956), no. 95; *Matisse: 64 paintings* (New York 1966), no. 61; *Matisse* (New York 1973), no. 55; *Matisse* (Rome 1978–79), no. 29; *Master Paintings from the Phillips Collection* (San Francisco and other cities 1981–82), unnumbered cat., pp. 84, 85 (ill.); *Matisse* (Zürich–Düsseldorf 1982–83), no. 96; *Matisse* (Stockholm 1984–85), no. 75; "Matisse" (Humlebaek 1985), checklist no. 88; *Matisse Retrospective* (New York 1992–93), no. 385; *Matisse and Picasso* (Fort Worth 1999), unnumbered cat., pp. 178 (fig. 164), 204, 231, 255 n. 384; *Art Beyond Isms* (Houston and other cities 2002–5), unnumbered cat. pp. 18, 102, 103 (ill.), 154; *Chefs-d'oeuvre de la Phillips Collection* (Martigny 2004), no. 39; *La Collection Phillips à Paris* (Paris 2005–6), no. 54

References: *Verve*, "Vence, 1944–48" (1948), n.p. (ill.); Zervos, "À propos de l'exposition Matisse" (1949), p. 168 (ill.); Barr, *Matisse: His Art and His Public* (1951), pp. 238–39 (ill.), 260, 262, 266, 276–77; Phillips Collection, *Catalogue* (1952), p. 68, pl. 139; Tériade, "Matisse Speaks" (1952), p. 77 (ill.); Hunter, *Matisse* (1956), fig. 23; Diehl and Humbert, *Matisse* (1958), pp. 115, 124, pl. 133; Lassaigne, *Matisse* (1959), p. 117; Escholier, *Matisse: A Portrait* (1960), p. 14, pl. 58; Brill, *Matisse* (1967), pp. 16, 39, pl. 44; Guichard-Meili, *Matisse* (1967), pp. 201 (fig. 206), 232, 251; Leymarie, "Evoluzione di Matisse" (1967), p. 68 (ill.); Fermigier, "Un barbare exquis" (1970), p. 42; Schneider, *Matisse centenaire* (1970), p. 47 (ill.); Greenberg, "Influences of Matisse" (1973), p. 31; Jacobus, *Matisse* (1973), pp. 45 (fig. 54), 47, 102; Gowing, *Matisse* (1979), pp. 181 (fig. 171), 182–83, 212; Gowing, *Matisse: Harmony of Light* (1979), p. 14; Carrà and Deryng, *Tout l'oeuvre peint de Matisse* (1982), pp. 8, 107 (ill.), no. 515; Phillips, *Duncan Phillips and His Collection* (1982), p. 237; Watkins, *Matisse* (1984), pp. 212, 213 (pl. 214); Carey and Martin, *Phillips Collection* (1985), p. 152 (ill.), no. 1183; Richardson, *Dr. Claribel & Miss Etta* (1985), p. 147; Guichard-Meili, *Matisse* (1986), pp. 47, 49 (ill.), 129, 141; Guillaud and Guillaud, *Matisse: Rhythm and Line* (1987), pp. 387 (pl. 421), 402; Noël, *Matisse* (1987), pp. 66 (ill.), 106; Richardson, "Dr. Claribel and Miss Etta Cone" (1987), pp. 310–11; Flam, *Matisse: A Retrospective* (1988), pp. 333 (pl. 105), 356; Monod-Fontaine, *Matisse ou la couleur découpée* (1989), p. 59, slide no. 20; Monod-Fontaine, Baldassari, and Laugier, *Matisse: Oeuvres* (1989), p. 115 (fig. c), under no. 30; Bois, *Painting as Model* (1990), p. 28; Bernier, *Matisse, Picasso, Miró* (1991), pp. 23, 24 (ill.); Girard, *Les chefs-d'oeuvre du Musée Matisse* (1991), pp. 100, 102 (ill.); Néret, *Matisse* (1991), p. 228 (fig. 324); Wilson, *Matisse* (1992), p. 114 (fig. 162); Herrera, *Matisse: Portrait* (1993), p. 190, pl. 27; Girard, *Matisse: Le grand atelier* (1994), pp. 23 (ill.), 24; Milner, *Matisse* (1994), pp. 13, 124 (ill.); Monneret, *Matisse* (1994), p. 122 (ill.), no. 566; Benjamin, "Vital Sign" (1995), p. 36; Bernier, "Matisse en persona" (1995), pp. 32, 34, 39 (ill.); Girard, *Matisse in Nice* (1996), p. 78 (ill.); Néret, *Matisse* (1996), pp. 224 (ill.), 229; Labrusse, "Catalogo delle opere" (1997), p. 242 (ill.); Phillips Collection, *Master Paintings* (1998), pp. 142, 143 (ill.); Furth in Passantino, *Eye of Duncan Phillips* (1999), pp. 204, 206, 207 (ill.), 208, 727 nn. 31, 32, no. 110; Essers, *Matisse: Master of Colour* (2002), pp. 83, 86 (ill.); Percheron and Brouder, *Matisse: De la couleur à l'architecture* (2002), pp. 364, 365 (fig. 393); Schneider, *Matisse* (2002), pp. 21 (ill.), 83, 163, 172, 448, 450, 650; Séligny and Kropmanns, *Matisse, Vence* (2007), pp. 32, 38, 41 (ill.), 64; Blum, *Matisse: Rooms with a View* (2010), pp. 168 (pl. 119), 169; Jarauta Marión et al., *Matisse and the Alhambra* (2010), p. 14 (fig. 3)

62

***Interior with Black Fern*, 1948**

Oil on canvas, 45⅝ x 35 in. (116 x 89 cm)
Fondation Beyeler, Basel (79.1)
Signed and dated (lower center; incised in black surface, sideways): Matisse / Vence / 1948

Provenance: The artist (1948–49; sold through Pierre Matisse Gallery, New York, in February 1949, for 18,000 dollars to Block); Mr. and Mrs. Leigh B. Block, Chicago (from 1949); [with Soho Gallery, London, by 1965]; Mr. and Mrs. Otto Preminger, New York (by 1966–at least 1970); [Richard Feigen Gallery, New York; sold in October 1979 to Beyeler]; Ernst Beyeler, Basel (from 1979; Fondation Beyeler since 1997)

Exhibitions: *Matisse* (New York 1949a), no. 13; *Matisse: Oeuvres récentes* (Paris 1949), no. 12; *Matisse Retrospective* (Los Angeles–Chicago–Boston 1966), no. 91; *Matisse: 64 Paintings* (New York 1966), no. 60; *Matisse: Retrospective* (London 1968), no. 123; *Matisse centenaire* (Paris 1970), no. 200; *Matisse* (Basel 1980), no. 44; *Matisse* (Madrid 1980), no. 40; *Matisse* (Bielefeld 1981), no. 12; *Matisse* (Zürich–Düsseldorf 1982–83), no. 93; *La grande parade* (Amsterdam 1984–85), no. 156; *Monet to Matisse* (Jerusalem 1988–89), unnumbered cat., p. 117 (ill.); *L'éternel féminin* (Basel 1989–90), no. 39; *Matisse Retrospective* (New York 1992–93), no. 384; *Wer hat Angst vor Rot?* (Basel 1995), no. 50; *Ornament and Abstraction* (Basel 2001), no. 118; *Matisse, une seconde vie* (Paris–Humlebaek 2005), no. 99 (Humlebaek only); *Matisse: Figur Farbe Raum* (Düsseldorf 2005–6), no. 192; *Matisse: Figure, couleur, espace* (Basel 2006), no. 122

References: Besson, *Matisse* (1954), cover ill.; Haftmann, *Malerei im 20. Jahrhundert* (1965), pp. 212 (fig. 489), 411; Diehl, *Matisse* (1970), p. 60, under pl. 43; Aragon, *Matisse, roman* (1971), vol. 2, p. 340, pl. 79; Jacobus, *Matisse* (1973), pp. 45 (fig. 53), 47; Carrà and Deryng, *Tout l'oeuvre peint de Matisse* (1982), p. 107 (ill.), no. 517; Guichard-Meili, *Matisse* (1986), p. 47; Bernier, *Matisse, Picasso, Miró* (1991), pp. 22, 23 (ill.); Monneret, *Matisse* (1994), p. 122 (ill.), no. 568; Bernier, "Matisse en persona" (1995), pp. 32, 34 (ill.); Delectorskaya, *Matisse: Contre vents et marées* (1996), pp. 457 (ill.), 552; Néret, *Matisse* (1996), pp. 222 (ill.), 229; Essers, "Eine schöpferische Selbstbefragung" (2005), p. 26 (ill.); Blum, *Matisse: Rooms with a View* (2010), pp. 160, 162 (pl. 114), 163–64

63

***Interior with View of a Palm Tree*, 1948**

Ink on paper, 41⅜ x 29½ in. (105 x 75 cm)
Private collection
Copenhagen only
Signed and dated (lower right): H. Matisse 48

Provenance: The artist; private collection, Paris; private collection

Exhibitions: *Matisse Retrospective* (Los Angeles–Chicago–Boston 1966), no. 217; *130 dessins de Matisse* (Marseille 1974), section titled "hors cat.," no. 122; *Matisse* (Rome 1978–79), no. 31; *Matisse: Figur, Farbe, Raum* (Düsseldorf 2005–6), no. 189; *Matisse: Figure, couleur, espace* (Basel 2006), no. 120

References: Volboudt, "La ligne à la recherche de la forme" (1970), p. 109; Monod-Fontaine, *Matisse: Oeuvres* (1979), p. 101 (ill.); Carrà and Deryng, *Tout l'oeuvre peint de Matisse* (1982), p. 107 (ill.), no. D41; Girard, *Matisse: Photographies* (1986), pp. 102–3 (photo); Monod-Fontaine, Baldassari, and Laugier, *Matisse: Oeuvres* (1989), p. 112 (fig. a), under no. 30; Elderfield, Kernan, and Cousins, "Plates and Chronology" (1992), p. 416 (photo); Amano et al., *Matisse: Processus/Variation* (2004), p. 205 (figs. 1, 2); Wenzel, "Virtuose der linie" (2005), p. 60 (ill.); Monod-Fontaine, "Grenades et palmiers" (2007), p. 40 (photo); Séligny, "Nature morte aux grenades" (2007), p. 20 (photo); Séligny and Kropmanns, *Matisse, Vence: L'espace d'un atelier* (2007), p. 53 (ill.)

64

***Large Red Interior*, 1948**

Oil on canvas, 57½ x 38¼ in. (146 x 97 cm)
Centre Pompidou, Musée National d'Art Moderne, Paris, State purchase, 1950 (AM 2964 P)
Signed and dated (lower left): Matisse 48

Provenance: The artist (1948–50; sold to the French State and assigned to the Musée National d'Art Moderne, Paris, 1950; at the Centre Pompidou since 1977)

Exhibitions: *Matisse* (New York 1949a), no. 12; *Matisse* (Paris 1949), no. 13; *XXVe Biennale* (Venice 1950), "Francia" section, no. 45; *Mostra di Matisse* (Milan 1950), no. 34; *L'école de Paris* (London 1951), no. 43; *Matisse* (New York and other cities 1951–52), no. 72; *10 ans de peinture française* (Grenoble 1956), no. 71; *XXXIe Biennale* (Venice 1962), no. 17; *Matisse Retrospective* (Los Angeles–Chicago–Boston 1966), no. 90; *Matisse: 64 Paintings* (New York 1966), no. 59; *Matisse: Retrospective* (London 1968), no. 124; *Matisse* (Moscow–Leningrad 1969), hors cat.; *Matisse centenaire* (Paris 1970), no. 203; *Matisse: En retrospektiv udstilling* (Copenhagen 1970), no. 64; *Modern Masters: Manet to Matisse* (Sydney–Melbourne–New York 1975), no. 73; *Matisse* (Tokyo–Kyoto 1981), no. 93; *Matisse* (Zürich–Düsseldorf 1982–83), no. 95 (shown only in Zürich); "Chefs d'oeuvre du Musée National d'Art Moderne" (Toulouse 1984), no cat.; *La France à Venise* (Venice 1990), unnumbered cat., pp. 32, 150, 151 (ill.); *Matisse Retrospective* (New York 1992–93), no. 387; *Anri Matiss* (Moscow–Saint Petersburg 1993), no. 74; *Jean Cassou* (Paris 1995), no. 298; "Made in France" (Paris 1997), assoc. pub., p. 10 (ill.); *La collection du Centre Pompidou* (Tokyo 1997), no. 77; *Matisse* (Lyon 1998), unnumbered cat., pp. 7, 76–77 (ill.); *Matisse and Picasso* (Fort Worth 1999), unnumbered cat. pp. 206, 209 (fig. 197); *Matisse, Picasso* (London–Paris–New York 2002–3), no. 157 (London and New York), no. 138 (Paris); *Matisse: Processus/Variation* (Tokyo 2004), no. 104; *Matisse: Figure, couleur, espace* (Basel 2006), no. 124; *Arcadie* (Seoul–Taipei–Kaohsiung 2008–9), no. 31; *Chefs-d'oeuvre* (Metz 2010–11), unnumbered cat., pp. 75 (ill.), 547

References: *Verve*, "Vence 1944–48" (1948), ill.; *L'Âge nouveau*, "Présence de Matisse" (1949), ill.; *Art News*, "Reviews and Previews: Matisse" (1949), p. 45 (ill.); Greenberg, "Review" (1949), pp. 284–85; Zervos, "À propos de l'exposition Matisse" (1949), p. 170 (ill.); Barr, *Matisse: His Art and His Public* (1951), pp. 260, 262, 266, 277, 507 (ill.); Dorival, "Chronique de l'art" (1952), p. 253 (ill.); Salles, "Visit to Matisse" (1952), p. 80 (ill.); Besson, *Matisse* (1954), pl. 49; Cassou, Dorival, and Homolle, *Catalogue-guide* (1954), p. 112; Greenberg, *Matisse* (1955), pl. 28; Hunter, *Matisse* (1956), fig. 24; Neumayer, *Fauvismus* (1956), pp. 30, 31 (pl. 8); Diehl and Humbert, *Matisse* (1958), pp. 67, 115, 124, pl. 137; Dorival, *Twentieth Century Painters* (1958), pp. 71 (ill.), 72; Lassaigne, *Matisse* (1959), p. 117; Escholier, *Matisse: Portrait* (1960), p. 14, pl. 54; Dorival, *L'École de Paris* (1961), pp. 132, 133 (ill.); Aragon, "Matisse ou le peintre français" (1963), p. 13 (ill.); Cocteau, "Matisse et Picasso" (1963), ill.; Leymarie, *Matisse* (1964), pls. XIV, XV; *Newsweek*, "Matisse" (1966), pp. 52 (ill.), 53; *Time Magazine*, "Distiller of Sunshine" (1966), p. 82 (ill.); Brill, *Matisse* (1967), p. 39, pl. 43; Guichard-Meili, *Matisse* (1967), pp. 197 (fig. 202), 210, 251; Lévêque, "Matisse 1" (1967), p. 25 (ill.); Leymarie, "Evoluzione di Matisse" (1967), pp. 66 (ill.), 71; Marchiori, *Matisse* (1967), pp. 79, 88–89, 100, 101 (ill.), 103, 115; Ogawa and Yanaihara, *Matisse, Rouault* (1967), pl. 33; Lévêque, *Matisse* (1968), p. 48 (ill.); Okamoto, *Bonnard, Matisse* (1968), p. 115 (ill.); Russell, *World of Matisse* (1969), p. 140 (ill.); Diehl, *Matisse* (1970), pp. 28, 60, pl. 46; Fermigier, "Un barbare exquis" (1970), p. 42; Taillandier, "Préhistoire du bonheur" (1970), p. 92 (ill.); Aragon, *Matisse, roman* (1971), vol. 2, pp. 304, 342 (pl. 71), 363; Carlson, *Matisse as a Draughtsman* (1971), p. 19; Orienti, *Matisse* (1972), pp. 40, 91, pl. 40; Alpatov, *Matisse* (1973), p. 111; Milhau, "Matisse, Picasso et Braque" (1975), p. 133; Flam, *Matisse on Art* (1978), p. 15, fig. 44; Gowing, *Matisse* (1979), pp. 180 (fig. 170), 181–82, 211; Gowing, *Matisse: Harmony of Light* (1979), p. 14; Monod-Fontaine, *Matisse: Oeuvres* (1979), pp. 16 (ill.), 98 (ill.), 99–100, no. 28; *Aftermath France, 1945–54* (1982), p. 36 (ill.), pl. II; Carrà and Deryng, *Tout l'oeuvre peint de Matisse* (1982), p. 107 (ill.), no. 514; Mezzatesta, *Matisse, Sculptor/Painter* (1984), pp. 139, 140 (fig. 92); Watkins, *Matisse* (1984), pp. 201 (pl. 197), 212–13, 215, 221; Guichard-Meili, *Matisse* (1986), pp. 47, 114 (ill.), 135, 142; Monod-Fontaine, "Matisse" (1986), p. 416 (ill.); Guillaud and Guillaud, *Matisse: Rhythm and Line* (1987), pp. 389 (pl. 422), 402; Noël, *Matisse* (1987), pp. 84 (ill.), 85, 106; Flam, *Matisse: A Retrospective* (1988), pp. 336 (pl. 108), 356 (excerpt of Barr 1951); Monod-Fontaine, Baldassari, and Laugier, *Matisse: Oeuvres* (1989), pp. 112, 113 (ill.), 114, 115 (fig. c), no. 30; Bernier, *Matisse, Picasso, Miró* (1991), pp. 19, 20 (ill.), 21; Girard, *Les chefs-d'œuvre du Musée Matisse* (1991), p. 100; Wilson, *Matisse* (1992), pp. 26, 114 (fig. 163); Robinson and Bréda, *Matisse Centre Pompidou* (1993), pp. 82 (ill.), 83–84, 86–87, 117, cover ill.; Monneret, *Matisse* (1994), pp. 18, 80 (ill.), 81 (ill., detail), 122 (ill.), no. 565; Benjamin, "Vital Sign" (1995), p. 36; Bernier, "Matisse en persona" (1995), pp. 32, 33 (ill.);; Delectorskaya, *Matisse: Contre vents et marées* (1996), pp. 456 (ill.), 552; Girard, *Matisse in Nice* (1996), p. 76 (ill.); Néret, *Matisse* (1996), pp. 223 (ill.), 229; Cauman, "Matisse and America" (2000), vol. 1, p. 534; Schnell, *"Das rote Atelier" des Matisse* (2001), pp. 94, 137 (pl. 7); Essers, *Matisse: Master of Colour* (2002), pp. 83, 85 (ill.); Marin-David, "Matisse, Picasso" (2002), pp. 60 (ill.), 64; Percheron and Brouder, *Matisse: De la couleur à l'architecture* (2002), pp. 364 (fig. 392), 366; Schneider, *Matisse* (2002), pp. 424, 442, 569, 650, 652, 653 (ill.); Grammont and Finsen in Finsen, *Matisse: A Second Life* (2005), pp. 168, 170; Monod-Fontaine, "Vence: Interior/Exterior Studio Visits" (2005), pp. 46 (ill.), 47–48; Monod-Fontaine in Léal, *Collection art moderne* (2006), p. 455 (ill.); Kropmanns, "Matisse à Vence" (2007), pp. 64, 65 (photo); Séligny, "Nature morte aux grenades" (2007), pp. 19, 20 (photo), 21 (ill.); Blum, *Matisse: Rooms with a View* (2010), pp. 164, 165 (pl. 116)

BIBLIOGRAPHY

Our understanding of Matisse's repeated images is indebted to the many scholars who have previously considered the issue. Among the earliest was Alfred H. Barr Jr., the first director of the Museum of Modern Art, New York. In *Matisse: His Art and His Public* (1951), Barr uses terms such as "versions," "pairs," "twin canvases," and "trios" to describe the relationships among Matisse's paintings. Dividing the pairs into first, intuitive attempts and subsequent, purified versions, he contends that the artist moved from naturalistic to abstract modes of representation. While later generations have considered Barr's interpretation overly schematic, his analysis of the complex internal connections in Matisse's work remains highly influential.

Over the past fifty years, a number of scholars—among them, Yve-Alain Bois, Jack Cowart, John Elderfield, Jack Flam, Dominique Fourcade, Isabelle Monod-Fontaine, and Pierre Schneider—have examined the issue of repetition within the larger context of Matisse's production. In *Matisse: The Man and His Art, 1869–1918* (1986), for example, Flam writes that "one of the most striking features of Matisse's oeuvre is the constant interaction of recurrent subjects and formal motifs, so that the meanings of individual works are related in various ways to the thematic and pictorial concerns of his oeuvre as a whole" (p. 22). While Flam agrees with Barr that stylistic difference is key to understanding the pairs, he draws a more radical conclusion: "Matisse's variety of visual modes is a paradigm of modernist ambivalence in the face of experience, an expression of the conviction that there is no single true way of seeing reality and thus no possibility of a single style" (p. 19). More recently, scholars have reexamined Matisse's work within historical and critical contexts and studied how meaning can be extrapolated from his artistic process. Bois, for instance, presents a detailed study of the relationship between *Le Luxe I* and *II* in *Matisse: Masterpieces at Statens Museum for Kunst* (2005). He concludes that the artist's early practice of painting in pairs developed into a theory of color that culminated in *Dance II* and *Music* (1910; The State Hermitage Museum, Saint Petersburg).

Three recent exhibition catalogues have further elucidated Matisse's use of repeated images. An important Japanese-language publication, *Henri Matisse: Processus / Variation* (Tokyo: National Museum of Western Art, 2004), posits that repetition and variation were of crucial importance to the artist's creative process. Among its many strengths is an essay by Chika Amano discussing Matisse's employment of photography to document his work, as well as his 1945 exhibition at the Galerie Maeght, in which his paintings appeared along with their photographed "stages." *The Repeating Image: Multiples in French Painting from David to Matisse* (Baltimore: The Walters Art Museum, 2007) is a broad survey that offers a historical context in which to consider this aspect of Matisse's oeuvre. Of particular note is its essay by Jeffrey Weiss on Matisse and photography. Three years later, Stephanie D'Alessandro and John Elderfield presented "Matisse: Radical Invention 1913–1917," an exhibition devoted to Matisse's "methods of modern construction." Drawing on new technical studies as well as archival research, their catalogue (Chicago: The Art Institute of Chicago, 2010) offers a scientifically sustained investigation of the formative principles in Matisse's oeuvre during the years in which he was working on *Bathers by a River* (fig. 56). The authors identify "two broad and connected ways in which works of the period relate to one another. One is through stylistic alternation, the other through replication" (p. 25). Our discussions of certain pairs are indebted to the discoveries put forth in this meticulously researched catalogue.

These sources, as well as many others listed below, have shaped our thinking to a large extent as we prepared this volume. We eagerly await a complete catalogue raisonné of Matisse's painting, which will significantly enhance the understanding of Matisse's work as a whole and in particular his use of pairs, trios, and series.

Dorthe Aagesen and Rebecca Rabinow

EXHIBITIONS CITED

1900–1909

Paris 1904. *Exposition des oeuvres du peintre Henri Matisse.* Galerie Vollard, Paris, June 1–18, 1904. Catalogue. Paris, 1904.

Paris 1905. *Salon de la Société des Artistes Indépendants: 21e exposition.* Grandes Serres de la Ville de Paris, March 24–April 30, 1905. Catalogue. Paris, 1905.

Paris 1906. *Exposition Henri Matisse.* Galerie Druet, Paris, March 19–April 7, 1906. Catalogue. Paris, 1906.

Paris 1907. *Salon d'Automne.* Grand Palais des Champs Élysées, Paris, October 1–22, 1907. *Catalogue des ouvrages de peinture, sculpture, dessin, gravure, architecture et art décoratif.* Paris, 1907.

Paris 1908. *Salon d'Automne.* Grand Palais des Champs Élysées, Paris, October 1–November 8, 1908. *Catalogue des ouvrages de peinture, sculpture, dessin, gravure, architecture et art décoratif.* Paris, 1908.

Odessa and other cities 1909–10. *Internatsional'noi vystavki kartin, skul'ptury, graviury i risunkov* (organizator "Salona" Vladimir Izdebskii) [International exhibition of paintings, sculpture, prints, and drawing (Izdebsky Salon)]. Unknown venue, Odessa, December 17, 1909–February 6, 1910; unknown venue, Kiev, February 25–March 27, 1910; unknown venue, Saint Petersburg, May 2–June 7, 1910; unknown venue, Riga, June 25–July 20, 1910. Catalogue. Saint Petersburg, 1909.

1910–1919

Paris 1910. *Exposition Henri Matisse.* Galerie Bernheim-Jeune, Paris, February 14–March 5, 1910. Catalogue. Paris, 1910.

Düsseldorf 1910. *Ausstellung des Sonderbundes Westdeutscher Kunstfreunde und Künstler.* Städtischer Kunstpalast am Kaiser-Wilhelm-Park, Düsseldorf, July 16–October 9, 1910. Catalogue. Düsseldorf, 1910.

Paris 1912. *Salon d'Automne.* Grand Palais des Champs-Elysées, Paris, October 1–November 8, 1912. *Catalogue des ouvrages de peinture, sculpture, dessin, gravure, architecture et art décoratif.* Paris, 1912.

London 1912. *Second Post-Impressionist Exhibition.* Grafton Galleries, London, October 5–December 31, 1912. Catalogue introduction by Roger Fry; essays by Clive Bell and Boris von Anrep. London, 1912.

New York–Chicago–Boston 1913. *International Exhibition of Modern Art* [The Armory Show]. Armory of the 69th Regiment, New York, February 15–March 15, 1913; The Art Institute of Chicago, March 24–April 16, 1913; Copley Hall, Copley Society of Boston, April 28–May 19, 1913. Catalogue and supplement. New York, 1913. Other eds.: Chicago and Boston, 1913.

Rome 1913. *Prima esposizione internazionale d'arte della "Secessione."* Rome, March–June 1913. Catalogue. Rome, 1913.

Paris 1913. *Exposition Henri-Matisse: Tableaux du Maroc et sculpture.* Galerie Bernheim-Jeune, Paris, April 14–19, 1913. Catalogue. Paris, 1913.

Berlin 1913. *Kollektionen: Henri Matisse, Franz Heckendorf, E.L. Kirchner, Georg Leschnitzer.* Kunst-Salon Fritz Gurlitt, Berlin, November 1913. Catalogue. Berlin, 1913.

Düsseldorf 1913–14. *Beiträge zur Kunst des XIX. Jahrhunderts und unserer Zeit.* Galerie Alfred Flechtheim, Düsseldorf, December 21, 1913–January 1914. Catalogue by Paul Mahlberg. Düsseldorf, 1913.

Rome 1914. *Seconda esposizione internazionale d'arte della "Secessione."* Sala 8, Rome, February–June 1914. Catalogue. Rome, 1914.

Munich 1914. *Neue Kunst: Sommerschau.* Galerie Neue Kunst Hans Goltz, Munich, summer 1914. Catalogue. Munich, 1914.

Berlin 1914. *Henri Matisse (Sammlung des Herrn Michael Stein in Paris).* Kunstsalon Fritz Gurlitt, Berlin, July–August 1914. Catalogue. Berlin, 1914.

New York 1915. *Henri Matisse Exhibition.* Montross Gallery, New York, January 20–February 27, 1915. Catalogue. New York, 1915.

Paris 1916a. *La Triennale: [2e] exposition d'art français au profit de la Fraternité des artistes.* Salle du Jeu de Paume, Paris, March 1–April 15, 1916. Catalogue. Paris, 1916.

Paris 1916b. *Exposition de peinture, série C.* Galerie Bernheim-Jeune, Paris, June 19–30, 1916. Catalogue. Paris, 1916.

Winterthur 1916. *Ausstellung französischer Malerei.* Kunstverein, Winterthur, Switzerland, October 29–November 26, 1916. Catalogue. Winterthur, 1916.

Oslo 1916. *Den franske utstilling.* Kunstnerforbundet, Christiania (Oslo), November 18–December 10, 1916. Catalogue prefaces by Jean Cocteau, Guillaume Apollinaire, and André Salmon. [Oslo], 1916.

Basel 1917. *Januar-Ausstellung.* Kunsthalle, Basel, January 10–February 4, 1917. Catalogue. Basel, 1917.

Copenhagen 1917. *Moderne fransk kunst: Samtlige Billeder tilhører Herr Tetzen-Lund.* Grønningen, Copenhagen, March 31–April 1917. Catalogue. Copenhagen, 1917.

Oslo 1918. *Den franske utstilling.* Kunstnerforbundet, Christiania (Oslo), January 18–February 1918. Catalogue. [Oslo], 1918.

Stockholm 1918. *Utställning af fransk konst.* Svensk-Franska Konstgalleriet, Stockholm, April–May 1918. Catalogue. Stockholm, 1918.

Göteborg 1918. *Utställning af fransk konst.* Valand's, Göteborg, September 1918. Catalogue. Göteborg, 1918.

Bergen 1918. *Fransk malerkunst: Fortegnelse over malerier—akvareller—pasteller—tegninger af franske kunstnere.* Bergens Kunstforening, Bergen, October 1918. Catalogue. [Copenhagen], 1918.

Helsinki 1918. *Modern fransk konst.* Stenmans Konstsalong, Helsinki, October 2–20, 1918. [Helsinki, 1918.]

Copenhagen 1919. *Udstilling of fransk kunst.* Danske Kunsthandel, Copenhagen, January 16–February 2, 1919. Catalogue. Copenhagen, 1919.

Paris 1919a. *Oeuvres récentes d'Henri-Matisse.* Galerie Bernheim-Jeune, Paris, May 2–16, 1919. Catalogue. Paris, 1919.

Paris 1919b. *La Triennale: Troisiéme exposition d'art français.* École des Beaux-Arts, Paris, May 5–June 30, 1919. Catalogue. Paris, 1919.

Zürich 1919. *Eröffnungsausstellung.* Galerie Bernheim-Jeune & Cie, Zürich, June 25–August 20, 1919. Catalogue. Zürich, 1919.

New York 1919. *Exhibition of Paintings by Courbet, Manet, Degas, Renoir, Cézanne, Seurat, Matisse.* Marius de Zayas Gallery, New York, November 17–December 6, 1919. Catalogue. New York, 1919.

1920–1929

New York 1920a. *Fourth Annual Exhibition of the Society of Independent Artists.* Waldorf Astoria, New York, March 11–April 1, 1920. Catalogue. New York, 1920.

Philadelphia 1920. *Exhibition of Paintings and Drawings by Representative Modern Artists.* Pennsylvania Academy of the Fine Arts, Philadelphia, April 17–May 9, 1920. Catalogue. Philadelphia, 1920.

Copenhagen 1920. "Matisse in the Tetzen-Lund and Sagen Collections." Tetzen-Lund Apartment, Copenhagen, early October (two days), 1920. No catalogue published. Reviewed by Carl Petersen in *Politiken,* October 2, 1920.

Paris 1920. *Exposition Henri-Matisse.* MM. Bernheim-Jeune & Cie., Paris, October 15–November 6, 1920. Catalogue. Paris, 1920.

Barcelona 1920. *Exposició d'art francès d'avantguarda.* Galeries Dalmau, Barcelona, October 26–November 15, 1920. Catalogue. Barcelona, 1920.

New York 1920b. "Paintings by Matisse." Marius de Zayas Gallery, New York, December 6–25, 1920. No catalogue published.

New York 1921. *Loan Exhibition of Impressionist and Post-Impressionist Paintings.* The Metropolitan Museum of Art, New York, May 3–September 15, 1921. Catalogue. New York, 1921.

Berlin 1921–22. Loans from private collectors and dealers. Kronprinzen-Palais (Nationalgalerie), Berlin, June 21, 1921–October 1922. No catalogue published.

New York 1922. *Exhibition of Contemporary French Art.* The Sculptor's Gallery, New York, March 24–April 10, 1922. Catalogue. New York, 1922.

Copenhagen 1924. *Grønningens udstilling.* Den Frie Udstillings Bygning, Copenhagen, January–February 1924. Catalogue. Copenhagen, 1924.

New York 1924a. "Original Paintings, Drawings, and Engravings Being Exhibited with the Dial Folio 'Living Art.'" Montross Gallery, New York, January 26–February 14, 1924. No catalogue published; unnumbered typed checklist.

New York 1924b. *Exhibition of Works by Henri Matisse.* Joseph Brummer Galleries, New York, February 25–March 22, 1924. Catalogue. New York, 1924.

Worcester 1924. *Exhibition of the Dial Collection of Paintings, Engravings, and Drawings by Contemporary Artists.* Worcester Art Museum, March 5–30, 1924. Catalogue. Worcester, Mass., 1924.

Northampton 1924. "The Dial Collection." Hillyer Art Gallery, Smith College, Northampton, Mass., spring 1924. No catalogue published.

Paris 1924. *Henri Matisse.* Galerie Bernheim-Jeune, Paris, May 6–20, 1924. Catalogue. Paris, 1924.

Copenhagen–Stockholm–Oslo 1924. *Henri Matisse: Udstilling af hans arbejder.* Ny Carlsberg Glyptotek, Copenhagen, September 1924;

Nationalmuseum, Stockholm, October 1924; Nasjonalgalleriet, Oslo, November–December 1924. Catalogue. Copenhagen, 1924. Swedish ed. (same numeration): *Henri Matisse: Utställning av has arbeten.* Stockholm, 1924. No separate catalogue for Oslo.

Baltimore 1925. *An Exhibition of Modern French Art.* Baltimore Museum of Art, January 9–February 1, 1925. Catalogue. Baltimore, 1925.

Zürich 1925. *Internationale Kunstausstellung.* Kunsthaus, Zürich, August–September 1925. Catalogue. Zürich, 1925.

Paris 1926. *Trente ans d'art indépendant, 1884–1914.* Grand Palais des Champs-Elysées, Paris, February 20–March 21, 1926. Catalogue. Paris, 1926.

New York 1927. "Group Exhibition of Modern French and American Paintings." Pierre Matisse and F. Valentine Dudensing, New York, March–June 1927. No catalogue published.

Paris 1927. *Salon d'Automne.* Grand Palais des Champs-Élysées, Paris, November 5–December 18, 1927. *Catalogue des ouvrages de peinture, dessin, sculpture, gravure, architecture et art decoratif.* Paris, 1927.

New York 1927–28. *Gallery of Living Art: Opening Exhibition.* New York University, Gallery of Living Art, New York, December 13, 1927–January 25, 1928. Catalogue. New York, 1927.

London 1928. *The Contemporary Art Society: Second Loan Exhibition of Foreign Paintings.* M. Knoedler & Co., London, February 1928. London, 1928.

Philadelphia 1928. *Inaugural Exhibition.* Philadelphia Museum of Art, March 1928. Catalogue published as "The New Museum of Art Inaugural Exhibition." *Pennsylvania Museum Bulletin* 23, no. 119 (March 1928), pp. 2–31.

Paris 1929. "Collection particulière de M. Paul Guillaume." MM. Bernheim-Jeune, Paris, May 27–June 7, 1929. No catalogue published.

London 1929. *Exhibition of French Paintings.* Paul Guillaume Galleries, London, December 1929. Catalogue by P. G. Konody. [London], 1929.

1930–1939

Helsinki 1930. *Eemu Myntti: Retrospektiivinen näyttely: Ulkomaista taidetta kauppaneuvos F. Tikanojan kokoelmasta* [Retrospective exhibition: International art from the Frithjof Tikanojas collection]. Kunsthalle Helsinki, opened February 8, 1930. Catalogue. Helsinki, 1930.

Berlin 1930. *Henri Matisse.* Galerien Thannhauser, Berlin, February 15–March 19, 1930. Catalogue by Hans Purrmann. Berlin, 1930.

Baltimore 1930. *Cone Collection of Modern Paintings and Sculpture.* The Baltimore Museum of Art, April 1–December 1, 1930. Catalogue. Baltimore, 1930.

Pittsburgh 1930. *29th International Exhibition of Paintings.* Carnegie Institute, Pittsburgh, October 16–December 7, 1930. Catalogue. Pittsburgh, 1930.

Columbus 1931. *Inaugural Exhibition.* Columbus Gallery of Fine Arts, January–February 1931. Catalogue. [Columbus, 1931.]

Stockholm and other cities 1931. *Fransk genombrottskonst från nittonhundratalet.* Exhibitions in Stockholm, Oslo, Gothenburg, and Copenhagen, March–June 1931. Catalogue by Ragnar Hoppe, introduction by Tor Hedberg. Stockholm, 1931.

Paris 1931. *Henri Matisse: Exposition organisée au profit de l'Orphelinat des arts.* Galeries Georges Petit, Paris, June 16–July 25, 1931. Catalogue. Paris, 1931.

Basel 1931. *Henri-Matisse.* Kunsthalle, Basel, August 9–September 15, 1931. Catalogue. Basel, 1931.

New York 1931. *Henri-Matisse: Retrospective Exhibition.* Museum of Modern Art, New York, November 3–December 6, 1931. Catalogue by Alfred H. Barr Jr. New York, 1931.

Providence 1931. *Henri Matisse.* Rhode Island School of Design, Providence, December 14–28, 1931. Catalogue by J. N. Brown published in *Bulletin of the Rhode Island School of Design* 20, no. 1 (January 1932).

Paris 1932. *De Matisse à Segonzac.* Galerie d'Art Braun & Cie, Paris, May 2–21, 1932. Catalogue. Paris, 1932.

Dallas 1933. *State Fair of Texas. 1933 Exhibition, Showing the Changes in Painting for the Last Hundred Years in Europe and America.* Fair Park Gallery, Dallas, 1933. Catalogue. Dallas, 1933.

Chicago 1933. *A Century of Progress: Exhibition of Paintings and Sculpture Lent from the American Collections.* Art Institute of Chicago, June 1–November 1, 1933. Catalogue. Chicago, 1933.

Philadelphia 1933–34. "The White Collection." Philadelphia Museum of Art, 1933–34. No catalogue published.

New York 1934. *Paintings: Henri Matisse.* Pierre Matisse Gallery, New York, January 23–February 24, 1934. Catalogue. New York, 1934.

Baltimore 1934. *The Cone Collection of Baltimore, Maryland.* Baltimore Museum of Art, May 12–October 1, 1934. Catalogue by Etta Cone and George Boas. Baltimore, 1934.

San Francisco 1934. *Exhibition of French Painting from the Fifteenth Century to the Present Day.* California Palace of the Legion of Honor, San Francisco, June 8–July 8, 1934. Catalogue. San Francisco, 1934.

London 1935. *Modern French Classics.* Alex Reid & Lefevre, London, February–March 1935. Catalogue. London, 1935.

San Francisco 1936. *Henri-Matisse: Paintings, Drawings, Sculpture.* San Francisco Museum of Art, January 11–February 24, 1936. Catalogue. San Francisco, 1936.

Montreal 1936. *Exhibition of Modern French Paintings: The School of Paris.* W. Scott & Sons, Montreal, October 1936, organized with Alex Reid & Lefevre, London. Catalogue. Montreal, 1936.

New York 1936a. *Henri-Matisse, "la danse": Sketch for the Moscow Decoration.* Pierre Matisse Gallery, New York, October 27–November 21, 1936. Checklist. New York, 1936.

Ottawa 1936. "Exhibition of Modern French Paintings: The School of Paris." James Wilson & Co., Ottawa, November 1936. No catalogue published.

New York 1936b. *Twenty Paintings by Henri Matisse.* Valentine Gallery, New York, November 23–December 19, 1936. Catalogue. New York, 1936.

Philadelphia 1937. "French Artists of the 18th and 19th Centuries." Philadelphia Museum of Art, 1937. No catalogue published.

New York 1937. *Masterpieces of Modern Painting and Sculpture.* Pierre Matisse Gallery, New York, January 5–30, 1937. New York, [1937].

Winterthur 1937. *Ausstellung im Museum: Werke aus der Sammlung Dr. Arthur Hahnloser.* Kunstverein, Winterthur, April 18–May 30, 1937. Catalogue. Winterthur, 1937.

Paris 1937a. *Oeuvres récentes de Henri-Matisse.* Galerie Paul Rosenberg, Paris, June 1–29, 1937. Catalogue. Paris, 1937.

London 1937. *Recent Works by Henri Matisse.* Rosenberg and Helft Gallery, London, July 5–31, 1937. Catalogue. London, 1937.

Paris 1937b. *Origines et développement de l'art international indépendant.* Musée du Jeu de Paume, Paris, July 30–October 31, 1937. Catalogue. Paris, 1937.

Detroit 1937. *Selected Exhibition of the Walter P. Chrysler, Jr. Collection.* Detroit Institute of Arts, October 5–31, 1937. Catalogue. Detroit, 1937.

Oslo–Copenhagen–Stockholm 1938. *Matisse, Picasso, Braque, Laurens.* Kunstnernes Hus, Oslo, January 1938; Statens Museum for Kunst, Copenhagen, February 1938; Liljevalchs Konsthall, Stockholm, March 1938. Catalogue by Walther Halvorsen. Oslo, 1938.

Boston 1938. *Picasso, Henri Matisse.* Boston Museum of Modern Art, October 19–November 11, 1938. Catalogue. Boston, 1938.

Chicago 1939. *Paintings by Henri Matisse.* Arts Club of Chicago, March 30–April 18, 1939. Catalogue. Chicago, 1939.

New York 1939. *Art in Our Time. 10th Anniversary Exhibition.* Museum of Modern Art, New York, May 11–October 1, 1939 (on the occasion of the 1939 New York World's Fair). Catalogue. New York, 1939.

San Francisco 1939–40. *Seven Centuries of Painting: A Loan Exhibition of Old and Modern Masters.* California Palace of the Legion of Honor and M. H. de Young Memorial Museum, San Francisco, December 29, 1939–January 28, 1940. Catalogue. San Francisco, 1939.

1940–1949

Lucerne 1940. *Die Hauptwerke der Sammlung Hahnloser, Winterthur*. Kunstmuseum Lucerne, 1940. Catalogue by Hedy Hahnloser-Bühler. Basel, [1940].

Baltimore 1940. *Modern Painting Isms and How They Grew*. Baltimore Museum of Art, January 12–February 11, 1940. Brochure. Baltimore, 1940.

Detroit–Poughkeepsie 1941. "Refugee Art." Detroit Institute of Art, January 1941; Vassar College, Poughkeepsie, April 18–May 1941. No catalogue published.

Richmond–Philadelphia 1941. *Collection of Walter P. Chrysler, Jr.* Virginia Museum of Fine Arts, Richmond, January 16–March 4, 1941; Philadelphia Museum of Art, March 29–May 11, 1941. Catalogue essay by Henry McBride. Richmond, 1941.

Worcester 1941. *The Art of the Third Republic: French Painting 1870–1940*. Worcester Art Museum, Worcester, Mass., February 22–March 16, 1941. Catalogue. Worcester, Mass., 1941.

Baltimore 1941. *A Century of Baltimore Collecting 1840–1940: An Exhibition at the Baltimore Museum of Art.* Baltimore Museum of Art, June 6–September 1, 1941. Catalogue. Baltimore, 1941.

New York 1943a. *Henri Matisse Retrospective: Exhibition of Paintings, 1898–1939.* Pierre Matisse Gallery, New York, February 9–27, 1943. Catalogue. New York, 1943.

New York 1943b. *About 30 Years Ago: An Exhibition Reviewing Some of the Works of the Leaders of French Modern Painting in Its Youth*. Pierre Matisse Gallery, New York, April 13–May 1, 1943. Catalogue. New York, 1943.

Philadelphia 1943. "The A. E. Gallatin Collection: Inaugural Exhibition." Philadelphia Museum of Art, May 14–November 3, 1943. No catalogue published.

Paris 1943. *Salon d'Automne*. Société du Salon d'Automne, Palais des Beaux-Arts de la Ville de Paris, September 25–October 31, 1943. Catalogue. Paris, 1943.

New York 1944. *Ivory Black in Modern Painting.* Pierre Matisse Gallery, New York, March 21–April 15, 1944. Catalogue. New York, 1944.

Paris 1945a. *Salon d'Automne.* Palais des Beaux-Arts de la Ville de Paris, September 28–October 29, 1945. *Catalogue des ouvrages de peinture, sculpture, dessin, gravure, architecture et art décoratif*. Paris, 1945.

London 1945. *Exhibition of Paintings by Picasso and Matisse / Exposition Picasso–Matisse*. Victoria and Albert Museum, London, December 1945. Catalogue by Yves Sjöberg, Jean Cassou, and Christian Zervos. London, 1945.

Paris 1945b. *Henri Matisse*. Galerie Maeght, Paris, December 7–29, 1945. Catalogue. Paris, 1945.

Amsterdam 1946. *Picasso, Matisse: Pablo Picasso in het Stedelijk Museum Amsterdam / Henri Matisse in het Stedelijk Museum Amsterdam*. Stedelijk Museum, Amsterdam, 1946. Catalogue. Amsterdam, 1946.

Nice 1946. "Henri Matisse." Nice, January–February 1946. No catalogue published.

Glasgow–Birmingham 1946. *Picasso, Matisse Exhibition*. Glasgow and Birmingham, Arts Council of Great Britain, [January–February] 1946. Catalogue. London, 1946.

Brussels 1946. *Matisse, Picasso.* Palais des Beaux-Arts, Brussels, May 1946. Catalogue. Brussels, 1946.

Paris 1946. *Salon d'Automne*. Société du Salon d'Automne, Musée des Beaux-Arts de la Ville de Paris, October 4–November 10, 1946. *Catalogue: Peinture, sculpture, dessin, gravure, livre, arts appliqués*. Paris, 1946.

Houston 1947. *55 Works of Modern Art Owned in Houston*. Museum of Fine Arts, Houston, January 12–February 3, 1947. Brochure. Houston, 1947.

Philadelphia 1947. *Masterpieces of Philadelphia Private Collections*. Philadelphia Museum of Art, May 30–September 14, 1947. Catalogue published in *Philadelphia Museum Bulletin* 42, no. 214 (May 1947), pp. 65–88.

Avignon 1947. *Peintures et sculptures contemporaines*. Palais des Papes, Avignon, June 27–September 30, 1947. Catalogue. Paris, 1947.

Philadelphia 1948. *Henri Matisse: Retrospective Exhibition of Paintings, Drawings, and Sculpture Organized in Collaboration with the Artist.* Philadelphia Museum of Art, April 3–May 9, 1948. Catalogue. Philadelphia, 1948.

York 1948. *French Paintings from the Kessler Collection*. City of York Art Gallery, May 1948. Catalogue. York, 1948.

London 1948. *The Kessler Collection: 19th and 20th Century French Masters*. Wildenstein & Co. Ltd., London, October–November 1948. Catalogue. London, 1948.

New York 1949a. *Henri Matisse: Paintings, Papiers découpés, Drawings, 1945–1948*. Pierre Matisse Gallery, New York, February 1949. Pamphlet. New York, 1949.

Paris 1949. *Henri Matisse: Oeuvres récentes 1947–1948*. Musée National d'Art Moderne, Paris, June–September 1949. Catalogue. Paris, 1949.

Lucerne 1949. *Henri Matisse*. Musée des Beaux-Arts, Lucerne, July 9–October 2, 1949. Catalogue. Lucerne, 1949.

Ostende 1949. *Gloires de la peinture moderne: Hommage à James Ensor*. Palais des Thermes, Ostende, July 23–August 22, 1949. Catalogue by Em. Langui. Brussels, 1949.

Winterthur 1949. *Winterthur Privatbesitz II: Werke des 20. Jahrhunderts*. Kunstmuseum Winterthur, August 28–November 20, 1949. Catalogue. Winterthur, 1949.

Baltimore 1949. "Selections from the Cone Collection." Baltimore Museum of Art, October 7–December 31, 1949. Checklist published in *News: The Baltimore Museum of Art* 12 (October 1949), p. 12.

New York 1949b. *"What They Said": Postscript to Art Criticism. For the Benefit of the Museum of Modern Art on Its 20th Anniversary*. Durand Ruel Galleries, New York, November 28–December 17, 1949. Catalogue. New York, 1949.

1950–1959

Philadelphia 1950. "S. S. White, 3rd, Collection." Philadelphia Museum of Art, 1950. No catalogue published.

Nice 1950. *Henri Matisse*. Galerie des Ponchettes, Nice, January–March 1950. Catalogue. Nice, 1950.

Baltimore 1950. *Cone Memorial Exhibition.* Baltimore Museum of Art, January 13–March 5, 1950. Catalogue. Baltimore, 1950.

Bern 1950. *Les Fauves: Braque, Derain, Dufy, Friesz, Manguin, Marinot, Marquet, Matisse, Valtat, van Dongen, Vlaminck. . . .* Kunsthalle Bern, April 29–May 29, 1950. Catalogue by Arnold Rüdinger. Bern, 1950.

Venice 1950. *XXV Biennale di Venezia*. Venice, June 8–October 15, 1950. Catalogue. Venice, 1950.

Paris 1950. *Henri Matisse: Chapelle, peintures, dessins, sculptures*. Maison de la Pensée Française, Paris, July 5–September 24, 1950. Catalogue. Paris, 1950.

Solothurn 1950. *Hundert Jahre Malerei aus Solothurner Privatbesitz: Ausstellung zur Hundertjahrfeier des Solothurner Kunstvereins.* Museum der Stadt Solothurn, September 23–November 26, 1950. Catalogue by Gottlieb Loertscher. Solothurn, 1950.

Pittsburgh 1950. *The Pittsburgh International Exhibition of Paintings*. Carnegie Institute, Pittsburgh, October 19–December 21, 1950. Catalogue. Pittsburgh, 1950.

Providence 1950. *Five Modern Old Masters*. Museum of Art, Rhode Island School of Design, Providence, October 25–November 26, 1950. Catalogue. Providence, R.I., 1950.

Milan 1950. *Mostra di Matisse: Con il concorso dell'Association Française d'Action Artistique e per gentile concessione dell'ente "La Biennale Veneziana."* Comune di Milano, Milan, November 1–21, 1950. Folded brochure. Milan, 1950.

New York 1950. *Les Fauves*. Sidney Janis Gallery, New York, November 13–December 23, 1950. Catalogue. New York, 1950.

London 1951. *L'École de Paris, 1900–1950*. The Royal Academy of Arts, London, January 13–March 7, 1951. Catalogue. London, 1951.

Hamburg–Düsseldorf–Munich 1951. *Matisse: Gemälde, Skulpturen, Handzeichnungen, Graphik*. Kunstverein, Hamburg, February 17–March 18, 1951; Kunstmuseum, Düsseldorf, April 14–May 6, 1951; Haus der Kunst, Munich, May 11–June 3, 1951. Catalogue. Hamburg, 1951.

Tokyo–Osaka–Okayama 1951. *Henri Matisse, 1951.* National Museum, Tokyo, March 3–May 13, 1951; Municipal Museum, Osaka, May 23–June 17, 1951; Museum Ohara, Okayama, June 19–25, 1951. Catalogue in Japanese and French published in the journal *Yomiuri*, 1951. Tokyo, 1951.

Paris 1951. *Le Fauvisme.* Musée National d'Art Moderne, Paris, June–September 1951. Catalogue by Jean Cassou. Paris, 1951.

New York 1951. *Selections from Five New York Private Collections.* Museum of Modern Art, New York, June 26–September 9, 1951. Catalogue. New York, 1951.

New York and other cities 1951–52. *Henri Matisse.* Museum of Modern Art, New York, November 13, 1951–January 13, 1952; Cleveland Museum of Art, February 5–March 16, 1952; Art Institute of Chicago, April 1–May 4, 1952; San Francisco Museum of Art, May 22–July 6, 1952. Catalogue. New York, 1951.

Baltimore 1951. *From Ingres to Gauguin: French Nineteenth Century Paintings Owned in Maryland.* Baltimore Museum of Art, November 13–December 30, 1951. Catalogue by George Heard Hamilton. Baltimore, 1951.

Stockholm 1951–52. *Henri Matisse. Thèmes et variations: Le rêve—la chapelle.* Galerie Samlaren, Stockholm, December 31, 1951–January 31, 1952. Catalogue. Stockholm, 1951.

Pittsburgh 1952. "The Howald Collection from the Columbus Gallery of Fine Arts, Museum of Art." Carnegie Institute, Pittsburgh, February 28–April 13, 1952. No catalogue published.

Montreal–Berlin 1952. *Six Centuries of Landscape.* Montreal Museum of Fine Arts, March 7–April 13, 1952; Nationalgalerie, Berlin, 1952. Catalogue. Montreal, 1952.

Lund 1952. *Henri Matisse.* Skånska Konstmuseum, Lund, opened April 6, 1952. Catalogue. Lund, 1952.

Saint Louis 1952. *St. Louis Collects: An Exhibition Selected from Private Collections.* City Art Museum of Saint Louis, Missouri, April 7–May 5, 1952. Catalogue published as *Bulletin of the City Art Museum of St. Louis* 37 (April 7–May 5, 1952). Saint Louis, 1952.

Amsterdam–Brussels 1952. *Cent chefs-d'oeuvre du Musée National d'Art Moderne de Paris.* Stedelijk Museum, Amsterdam, April 18–May 26, 1952; Palais des Beaux-Arts, Brussels, May 31–July 14, 1952. Catalogue. Paris, [1952]. Dutch ed.: *Honderd meesterwerken: Uit het Nationaal Museum voor Moderne Kunst te Parijs.* Amsterdam, [1952].

Los Angeles 1952. *Henri Matisse: Exhibition Organized by the Museum of Modern Art.* Los Angeles Municipal Art Department, July 24–August 17, 1952; Catalogue. Los Angeles, 1952.

Portland 1952. "Henri Matisse." Portland Art Museum, Portland, Ore., September 12–October 12, 1952. No catalogue published; unnumbered typed checklist.

New York and other cities 1952–53. *Les Fauves.* Museum of Modern Art, New York, October 8, 1952–January 4, 1953; Minneapolis Institute of Arts, January 21–February 22, 1953; San Francisco Museum of Art, March 13–April 12, 1953; Art Gallery of Toronto, May 1–31, 1953. Catalogue by John Rewald. New York, 1952.

Columbus–Akron–Worcester 1952–53. *Modern French Masters.* Columbus Gallery of Fine Arts, November 28–December 31, 1952; Akron Art Institute, January 13–February 16, 1953; Worcester Art Museum, March 5–April 12, 1953. Catalogue. Columbus, Ohio, 1952.

London 1953. *An Exhibition of the Sculpture of Matisse and 3 Paintings with Studies.* Tate Gallery, London, January 9–February 22, 1953. Catalogue. London, 1953.

Palm Beach 1953. *The Art of Henri Matisse.* Society of the Four Arts, Palm Beach, February 6–March 1, 1953. Catalogue. Palm Beach, Fla., 1953.

Bern 1953. *Europäische Kunst aus Berner Privatbesitz.* Kunsthalle Bern, July 31–September 20, 1953. Catalogue. Bern, 1953.

New York 1953a. *5th Anniversary Exhibition.* Sidney Janis Gallery, New York, September 29–October 31, 1953. Catalogue. New York, 1953.

Copenhagen 1953. *Henri Matisse: Skulpturer, malerier, farveklip.* Ny Carlsberg Glyptotek, Copenhagen, November 6–December 6, 1953. Copenhagen, 1953.

New York 1953b. *Seurat and His Friends: For the Benefit of the Scholarship Fund of L'Alliance Française de New York.* Wildenstein Gallery, New York, November 18–December 26, 1953. Catalogue by John Rewald. New York, 1953.

Oslo 1954. *Henri Matisse.* Kunstnernes Hus, Oslo, February 20–March 7, 1954. Catalogue. Oslo, 1954.

New York 1954. *Loan Exhibition of Paintings by Henri Matisse.* Paul Rosenberg & Co., New York, April 5–May 1, 1954. Catalogue. New York, 1954.

Rotterdam 1954. *Matisse: Bronzen, tekeningen, schilderijen, schetsen.* Museum Boymans, Rotterdam, April 16–June 8, 1954. Catalogue by J. C. Ebbinge Wubben. Rotterdam, 1954.

Baltimore 1954. *Man and His Years.* Baltimore Museum of Art, October 19–November 21, 1954. Catalogue. Baltimore, 1954.

Ottawa and other cities 1954–55. *Matisse: Sculptures, Paintings, and Drawings.* National Gallery of Canada, Ottawa, [December 1954]; circulated January 2–June 5, 1955, to Toronto, Vancouver, and Boston. Catalogue. Ottawa, 1954.

New York 1955a. *The Cone Collection.* M. Knoedler & Co., New York, January 24–February 19, 1955. Catalogue. New York, 1955.

Paris 1955a. *Salon des Indépendants.* Société des Artistes Indépendants, Grand Palais des Champs-Elysées, Paris, April 15–May 8, 1955. *Catalogue de la 66e exposition.* Paris, 1955.

New York 1955b. *Paintings from Private Collections.* Museum of Modern Art, New York, May 31–September 5, 1955. Catalogue. New York, 1955.

Vienna 1955. *Ausstellung europäische Kunst gestern und heute.* Österreichisches Museum für Angewandte Kunst, Vienna, June 6–July 6, 1955. Catalogue. Vienna, 1955.

Houston 1955. *Henri Matisse: Exhibition of Sculptures, Paintings, and Drawings.* Museum of Fine Arts, Houston, September 18–October 16, 1955. Catalogue. Houston, 1955.

New York 1955c. *An Exhibition of Paintings.* E. and A. Silberman Galleries, New York, October 12–November 1, 1955. Catalogue by Edna Perkel. New York, 1955.

Hartford 1955. *Twentieth Century Painting from Three Cities: New York, New Haven, Hartford.* Wadsworth Atheneum, Hartford, October 19–December 4, 1955. Catalogue foreword by C. C. Cunningham. Hartford, 1955.

Moscow–Leningrad 1955–56. *Vystavka frantsuzskogo iskusstva XII–XX v.v.* [French art of the 12th–20th centuries]. State Pushkin Museum of Fine Arts, Moscow, opened November 1955; Hermitage, Leningrad, 1956. Catalogue by A. G. Barskaya et al. Moscow, 1956.

Boston 1955. *Matisse: Sculptures, Paintings, and Drawings.* Museum of Fine Arts, Boston, November 1–27, 1955. Catalogue. Boston, 1955.

Paris 1955b. *Salon d'Automne. Exposition rétrospective d'oeuvres de Henri Matisse (1869–1953).* Grand Palais des Champs-Élysées, Paris, November 5–30, 1955. Catalogue. Paris, 1955.

Basel 1956. *Sammlung Richard Doetsch-Benziger: Malerei, Zeichnung und Plastik des 19. und 20. Jahrhunderts.* Kunstmuseum Basel, June 9–July 8, 1956. Catalogue. Basel, 1956.

Grenoble 1956. *10 ans de peinture française, 1945–1955.* Musée de Grenoble, July 1–September 23, 1956. Catalogue. Grenoble, 1955.

Paris 1956. *Rétrospective Henri Matisse.* Musée National d'Art Moderne, Paris, July 28–November 18, 1956. Catalogue by Gabrielle Vienne. Paris, 1956.

Paris 1957. *Cent chefs-d'oeuvre de l'art français, 1750–1950.* Galerie Charpentier, Paris, 1957. Catalogue by Raymond Nacenta. Paris, 1957.

London 1957. *An Exhibition of Paintings from the Musée d'Art Moderne, Paris.* R.B.A. Galleries, London, April 13–May 18, 1957. Catalogue. London, 1957.

Provincetown 1958. *Chrysler Art Museum of Provincetown Inaugural Exhibition.* Provincetown, Mass., 1958. Catalogue by Bertina Suida Manning. Provincetown, Mass., 1958.

London 1958. *Paintings by XX Century French Masters*. Lefevre Gallery, London, March 1958. Catalogue. London, 1958.

New York 1958. *Masterpieces from the Collection of Adelaide Milton de Groot.* Perls Galleries. New York, April 14–May 3, 1958. Catalogue. New York, 1958.

Brussels 1958. *Exposition universelle et internationale: 50 ans d'art moderne.* Palais International des Beaux-Arts, Brussels, April 17–July 21, 1958. Catalogue. Brussels, 1958.

Zürich 1958. *Sammlung Emil G. Bührle, Festschrift zu Ehren von Emil G. Bührle zur Eröffnung des Kunsthaus-Neubaus und Katalog der Sammlung Emil G. Bührle*. Kunsthaus Zürich, June 7–late September 1958. Catalogue. Zürich, 1958.

Liège 1958. *Léger, Matisse*. Musée de l'Art Wallon, Liège, July 1–September 30, 1958. Catalogue. Liège, 1958.

Berlin 1958. *Französische Malerei von Manet bis Matisse aus der Sammlung Emil G. Bührle, Zürich*. Schloss Charlottenburg, Berlin, October 5–November 23, 1958. Catalogue. N.p., 1958.

Columbus 1958–59. *Masterpieces from the Adelaide Milton de Groot Collection.* Columbus Gallery of Fine Arts, Columbus, Ohio, December 2, 1958–March 1, 1959. Catalogue. Columbus, Ohio, 1958.

Munich 1958–59. *Hauptwerke der Sammlung Emil Georg Bührle, Zürich*. Haus der Kunst, Munich, December 5, 1958–February 15, 1959. Catalogue. Munich, 1958.

Worcester 1959. *The Dial and the Dial Collection*. Worcester Art Museum, April 30–September 8, 1959. Catalogue. Worcester, Mass., 1959.

Schaffhausen–Berlin 1959. *Triumph der Farbe: Die europäischen Fauves*. Museum zu Allerheiligen, Schaffhausen, Switz., July 5–September 13, 1959; Orangerie des Schlosses Charlottenburg, Berlin, September 20–November 15, 1959. Catalogue. Berlin, 1959.

1960–1969

Paris 1960. *Cent tableaux de collections privées de Bonnard à de Staël*. Galerie Charpentier, Paris, 1960. Catalogue. Paris, 1960.

Dayton 1960. *French Paintings 1789–1929 from the Collection of Walter P. Chrysler, Jr.* Dayton Art Institute, Dayton, Ohio, March 25–May 22, 1960. Catalogue. Dayton, 1960.

Aix-en-Provence 1960. *Matisse*. Pavillon de Vendôme, Aix-en-Provence, July 9–August 31, 1960. Catalogue. Aix-en-Provence, 1960.

Humlebaek 1960. "Moderna Museet besøger Louisiana." Louisiana Museet, Humlebaek, September 23–November 6, 1960. Checklist published in *Louisiana Revy* 1, no. 1 (September 1960).

Paris 1960–61. *Les sources du XXème siècle: Les arts en Europe de 1884 à 1914*. Musée National d'Art Moderne, Paris, November 4, 1960–January 23, 1961. Catalogue. Paris, 1960.

Chicago 1960. *Inaugural Exhibition*. The Art Gallery, McCormick Place, Chicago, November 18–December 23, 1960. Catalogue. [Chicago, 1960.]

Bruges 1961. *Meesterwerken van het Museum voor Schone Kunsten te Brussel*. Stedelijk Museum voor Schone Kunsten (Groeningemuseum), Bruges, February 18–March 19, 1961. Catalogue. N.p., 1961.

Munich 1961. *Französische Malerei von Delacroix bis Picasso.* Stadthalle Wolfsburg, April 8–May 31, 1961. Catalogue by Max Huggler. Munich, 1961.

Albi 1961. *Exposition Henri Matisse, 1869–1954: Peintures, dessins, gouaches, sculptures, gravures*. Musée Toulouse-Lautrec, Albi, July 11–September 15, 1961. Catalogue. Albi, 1961.

Philadelphia 1962–66. "The Samuel S. White, 3rd, and Vera White Collection." Philadelphia Museum of Art, 1962–66. No catalogue published.

Provincetown–Ottawa 1962. *The Controversial Century 1850–1950.* Chrysler Art Museum of Provincetown, Mass.; National Gallery of Canada, Ottawa, 1962. Catalogue. Provincetown, Mass., 1962.

Paris 1962. *Les Fauves*. Galerie Charpentier, Paris, March 7–June 15, 1962. Catalogue by Raymond Nacenta. Paris, 1962.

San Francisco 1962. *The Henry P. McIlhenny Collection: Paintings, Drawings, and Sculpture*. California Palace of the Legion of Honor, San Francisco, June 15–July 31, 1962. Catalogue. San Francisco, 1962.

Venice 1962. *XXXI esposizione Biennale internazionale d'arte, Venezia*. Venice, June 16–October 7, 1962. Catalogue. Venice, 1962.

New York 1962. *Paintings from Private Collections: Summer Loan Exhibition*. The Metropolitan Museum of Art, New York, July 3–September 6, 1962. Catalogue. New York, 1962.

Helsinki 1962. *Ulkomaista nykytaidetta Suomen kokoelmista*. [Foreign contemporary art collections in Finland]. Ateneum, Helsinki, November 16–December 9, 1962. Catalogue by Göran Schildt. Text in Finnish and Swedish. Helsinki, 1962.

Utica–New York 1963. *1913 Armory Show: 50th Anniversary Exhibition, 1963*. Munson-Williams-Proctor Institute, Utica, February 17–March 31, 1963; Armory of the Sixty-ninth Regiment, New York, April 6–28, 1963. Catalogue edited by Joseph S. Trovato. New York, 1963.

Philadelphia 1963. *A World of Flowers*. Philadelphia Museum of Art, May 2–June 9, 1963. Catalogue by Henry Clifford and Carl Zigrosser, published as *Philadelphia Museum of Art Bulletin* 58, no. 277 (Spring 1963), pp. 93, 97–243.

Berlin 1963. *Die Ile de France und ihre Maler*. Nationalgalerie, Schloss Charlottenburg, Orangerie, Berlin, September 29–November 24, 1963. Catalogue. Berlin, 1963.

Stockholm 1963–64. *Önskemuseet / The Museum of Our Wishes / Notre musée tel qu'il devrait être / Museum unserer Wünsche.* Moderna Museet, Stockholm, December 26, 1963–February 16, 1964. Catalogue by Olle Granath, K.G. Hultén et al. Stockholm, 1963.

Los Angeles 1964. *From the Ludington Collection*. Dickson Art Center, University of California, Los Angeles, March 16–April 12, 1964. Catalogue. Los Angeles, 1964.

Lausanne 1964. *Chefs-d'oeuvre des collections suisses: De Manet à Picasso*. Palais de Beaulieu, Lausanne, May 1–October 25, 1964. Catalogue by François Daulte. Lausanne, 1964.

Kassel 1964. *Documenta III. Internationale Ausstellung*. Alte Galerie, Kassel, June 27–October 5, 1964. Catalogue by Klaus Förster, edited by Siegfried Hagen und Alfred Nemeczek. 2 vols. Cologne, 1964.

Baltimore 1964. *1914: An Exhibition of Paintings, Drawings and Sculpture, in Celebration of the 50th Anniversary of the Baltimore Museum of Art*. Baltimore Museum of Art, October 6–November 15, 1964. Catalogue by George Boas. Baltimore, 1964.

Paris 1964–65. *Collection George et Adèle Besson*. Musée du Louvre, Paris, December 11, 1964–February 8, 1965. Catalogue. Paris, 1964.

Saint Louis 1965. "Seven Works by Henri Matisse." City Art Museum of Saint Louis, February 1965. No catalogue published.

Bordeaux 1965. *Chefs-d'oeuvre de la peinture française dans les musées de L'Ermitage et de Moscou*. Musée des Beaux-Arts, Bordeaux, May 14–September 6, 1965. Catalogue by Gilberte Martin-Méry et al. Bordeaux, 1965.

Berlin 1965. *Von Delacroix bis Picasso: Ein Jahrhundert französischer Malerei*. Nationalgalerie, Berlin, September–October 1965. Catalogue. Berlin, 1965.

Philadelphia 1965. *Peale Club Collectors Show*. Peale House Galleries, Philadelphia, September 23–October 31, 1965. Catalogue. Philadelphia, 1965.

Paris 1965–66. *Chefs d'oeuvre de la peinture française dans les musées de Leningrad et de Moscou*. Musée du Louvre, Paris, September 24, 1965–January 1966. Catalogue by Marie-Thérèse Lemoyne de Forges et al. Paris, 1965.

Paris 1965. *La cage aux fauves du Salon d'Automne 1905*. Galerie de Paris, October 12–November 6, 1965. Catalogue with text by Pierre Cabanne. Paris, 1965.

Houston 1965. "The Heroic Years: Paris, 1908–1914." Museum of Fine Arts, Houston, October 20–December 8, 1965. No catalogue published.

Pittsburgh 1965. *The Seashore: Paintings of the 19th and 20th Centuries*. Museum of Art, Carnegie

Institute, Pittsburgh, October 22–December 5, 1965. Catalogue. Pittsburgh, 1965.

New York and other cities 1965–66. *The School of Paris: Paintings from the Florene May Schoenborn and Samuel A. Marx Collection.* Museum of Modern Art, New York, November 1, 1965–January 2, 1966; Art Institute of Chicago, February 11–March 27, 1966; City Art Museum of Saint Louis, April 26–June 13, 1966; Museo de Arte Moderno, Mexico City, July 2–August 7, 1966; San Francisco Museum of Art, September 2–October 2, 1966. Catalogue by Alfred H. Barr Jr., James Thrall Soby, and Lucy R. Lippard. New York, 1965.

Worcester 1965. "Selections from the Dial Collection." Worcester Art Museum, Worcester, Mass., November 13–30, 1965. No catalogue published; unnumbered typed checklist.

Paris 1966. *Collection Jean Walter—Paul Guillaume.* Musée de l'Orangerie, Paris, January–September 1966. Catalogue. Paris, 1966.

Los Angeles–Chicago–Boston 1966. *Henri Matisse: Retrospective.* UCLA Art Gallery, Los Angeles, January 5–February 27, 1966; Art Institute of Chicago, March 11–April 24, 1966; Museum of Fine Arts, Boston, May 11–June 26, 1966. Catalogue by Jean Leymaire, Herbert Read, and William S. Lieberman. [Los Angeles], 1966; Boston, 1966.

Paris–Munich 1966. *Le fauvisme français et les débuts de l'expressionnisme allemand / Der französische Fauvismus und der deutsche Frühexpressionismus.* Musée National d'Art Moderne, Paris, January 15–March 6, 1966; Haus der Kunst, Munich, March 26–May 15, 1966. Catalogue by Michel Hoog and Leopold Reidemeister. Paris, 1966.

Kansas City 1966. "Washington University Collection of Modern Paintings and Sculpture." William Rockhill Nelson Gallery of Art–Mary Atkins Museum of Fine Arts, Kansas City, Mo., April 8–May 8, 1966. No catalogue published.

Hamburg 1966. *Matisse und seine Freunde: Les Fauves.* Kunstverein, Hamburg, May 25–July 10, 1966. Catalogue. Hamburg, 1966.

San Francisco–Santa Barbara 1966. *The Collection of Mrs. John Wintersteen: An Exhibition of Paintings, Drawings and Sculpture.* California Palace of the Legion of Honor, San Francisco, June 10–July 24, 1966; Santa Barbara Museum of Art, Santa Barbara, August 2–September 4, 1966. Catalogue. [San Francisco], 1966.

New York 1966. *Henri Matisse: 64 Paintings.* Museum of Modern Art, New York, July 18–September 25, 1966. Catalogue by Lawrence Gowing. New York, 1966.

Tokyo–Kyoto 1966–67. *Masterpieces of Modern Painting from the USSR. The Hermitage, the Pushkin, the Russian, and the Tretyakov Museums in Leningrad and Moscow.* National Museum of Western Art, Tokyo, October 15–December 25, 1966; Municipal Museum, Kyoto, January 14–February 28, 1967. Catalogue. Tokyo, 1966.

Montreal 1967. *Terre des hommes / Man and His World, International Fine Arts Exhibition.* Expo 67, National Gallery of Canada, Montreal, April 28–October 27, 1967. Catalogue in French and English. Montreal, 1967.

Washington–Los Angeles 1967. *100 European Paintings & Drawings from the Collection of Mr. and Mrs. Leigh B. Block.* National Gallery of Art, Washington, D.C., May 4–June 11, 1967; Los Angeles County Museum of Art, September 21–November 2, 1967. Catalogue. Washington, D.C., 1967.

New York 1968. *Neo-Impressionism.* Solomon R. Guggenheim Museum, New York, February–April 1968. Catalogue by Robert L. Herbert. New York, 1968.

Washington and other cities 1968. *Painting in France, 1900–1967.* National Gallery of Art, Washington, D.C., February 18–March 17, 1968; The Metropolitan Museum of Art, New York, April 6–May 5, 1968; Museum of Fine Arts, Boston, May 18–June 10, 1968; Art Institute of Chicago, July 13–August 18, 1968; M. H. de Young Memorial Museum, San Francisco, September 7–October 13, 1968. Catalogue. Washington, D.C., 1968.

New York and other cities 1968. *Cézanne to Miró: Masters of Modern Painting.* Museum of Modern Art, New York, April 23–May, 1968. New York, 1968. Museo Nacional de Bellas Artes, Buenos Aires, May 15–June 5, 1968; Museo de Arte Contemporáneo de la Universidad de Chile, Santiago, June 26–July 17, 1968; Museo de Bellas Artes, Caracas, August 4–25, 1968. Catalogue. New York, 1968. Spanish ed.: *De Cézanne a Miró: Una exposición organizada bajo los auspicios del International Council of the Museum of Modern Art, New York.* New York, 1968.

Philadelphia 1968. *The Samuel S. White, 3rd, and Vera White Collection.* Philadelphia Museum of Art, opened May 31, 1968. Catalogue, edited by Henry G. Gardiner, published in *Philadelphia Museum of Art Bulletin* 63, no. 296–97 (1968).

London 1968. *Matisse, 1869–1954: A Retrospective Exhibition.* Hayward Gallery, London, July 4–September 8, 1968. Catalogue by Lawrence Gowing. London, 1968.

Paris 1968–69. *Baudelaire.* Petit Palais, Paris, November 23, 1968–March 17, 1969. Catalogue by Arlette Calvet. Paris, 1968.

Moscow–Leningrad 1969. *Matiss: Zhivopis', skul'ptura, grafika, pis'ma / Matisse: Painting, Sculpture, Graphic Art, Letters.* State Pushkin Museum of Fine Arts, Moscow, March–June 1969, Hermitage, Leningrad / Saint Petersburg, September–October 1969. Catalogue by A. N. Izerghina. Leningrad / Saint Petersburg, 1969.

Saint-Paul-de-Vence 1969. *À la rencontre de Matisse.* Fondation Maeght, Saint-Paul-de-Vence, July 16–September 30, 1969. Catalogue. Saint-Paul-de-Vence, 1969.

Columbus–Dayton–New York 1969–70. *From the Collection of Ferdinand Howald: 19th and 20th Century Paintings.* Columbus Gallery of Fine Arts, Columbus, Ohio, October 10–December 31, 1969; Dayton Art Institute, Dayton, Ohio, January 11–February 16, 1970; Wildenstein & Co., New York, May 19–July 3, 1970. Catalogue. Columbus, Ohio, 1969.

Prague 1969–70. *Henri Matisse ze sbirek sovětských muzeí.* National Gallery, Prague, December 1969–February 1970. Catalogue. Prague, 1969.

1970–1979

Paris 1970. *Henri Matisse: Exposition du centenaire.* Galeries Nationales du Grand Palais, Paris, April 22–September 22, 1970. Catalogue edited by Pierre Schneider, with Tamara Prèaud. Paris, 1970.

San Antonio and other cities 1970–71. *Selections from the Ferdinand Howald Collection.* Witte Memorial Museum, San Antonio, September 20–October 18, 1970; Cummer Gallery, Jacksonville, Fla., January 2–31, 1971; Georgia Museum of Art, Athens, Ga., February 21–March 21, 1971; Phoenix Art Museum, April 11–May 9, 1971; Milwaukee Art Center, Wisc., May 30–June 27, 1971. Catalogue. New York, 1970.

Copenhagen 1970. *Matisse: En retrospektiv udstilling.* Statens Museum for Kunst, Copenhagen, October 10–November 29, 1970. Catalogue by Hanne Finsen. Copenhagen, 1970.

Baltimore–San Francisco–Chicago 1971. *Matisse as a Draughtsman.* Baltimore Museum of Art, January 12–February 21, 1971; California Palace of the Legion of Honor, San Francisco, March 20–May 9, 1971; Art Institute of Chicago, May 26–July 10, 1971. Catalogue by Victor I. Carlson. Baltimore, 1971.

Tel Aviv 1971. *Maîtres français du XXe siècle: Tapisseries françaises comtemporaines.* Muze'on Tel Aviv, April 19–July 1, 1971. Catalogue. Tel Aviv, 1971.

Stockholm 1971. "Moderna Museet besöker Liljevalchs." Liljevalchs Konsthall, Stockholm, May 19–September 5, 1971. No catalogue published.

Worcester 1971. "The Dial Revisited." Worcester Art Museum, Worcester, Mass., June 29–August 22, 1971. No catalogue published.

Zürich 1971. *Henri Matisse: Zwanzig auserlesene Werke / Twenty Important Paintings.* Marlborough Galerie, Zürich, September–October 1971. Catalogue. Zürich, 1971.

Otterlo 1972. *Van Van Gogh tot Picasso: Schilderijen en tekeningen uit de negentiende en twintigste eeuw uit het Poesjkin Museum te Moskou en de Hermitage te Leningrad / From Van Gogh to Picasso: Nineteenth and Twentieth-Century Paintings and Drawings from the Pushkin Museum in Moscow and The Hermitage in Leningrad.* Rijksmuseum Kröller-Müller, Otterlo, April 30–July 16, 1972. Catalogue by A. G. Barskaya et al., in Dutch and English. N.p., 1972.

Strasbourg 1972. *Occident-Orient: L'art moderne et l'art islamique*. L'Ancienne Douane, Strasbourg, May 15–September 15, 1972. Catalogue. Strasbourg, 1972.

Washington and other cities 1973. *Impressionist and Post-Impressionist Paintings from the U.S.S.R., Lent by the Hermitage Museum, Leningrad, and the Pushkin Museum, Moscow*. National Gallery of Art, Washington D.C., March 31–April 29, 1973; M. Knoedler & Co. Gallery, New York, May 3–26, 1973; Los Angeles County Museum of Art, June 15–July 8, 1973; Art Institute of Chicago, July 18–August 12, 1973; also traveled to Kimbell Art Museum, Fort Worth, August 22–September 16, 1973; Institute of Art, Detroit, 1973. Catalogue by John Richardson and Alice Jackson Myers. Washington, D.C., 1973.

London–Dublin–Cardiff 1973. *Ferdinand Howald: Avant-Garde Collector*. Wildenstein & Co., London, June 20–July 21, 1973; National Gallery of Ireland, Dublin, August 3–September 16, 1973; National Museum of Wales, Cardiff, September 28–October 28, 1973. Catalogue. London, 1973.

Winterthur 1973. *Künstlerfreunde um Arthur und Hedy Hahnloser-Bühler*. Kunstmuseum Winterthur, September 23–November 11, 1973. Catalogue edited by Rudolf Koella. Winterthur, 1973.

New York 1973. *Henri Matisse*. Acquavella Galleries, New York, November 2–December 1, 1973. Catalogue. New York, 1973.

Saint Louis 1973–74. "20th Century Masterworks from St. Louis Collections." Saint Louis Art Museum, December 1, 1973–February 3, 1974. No catalogue published.

New York–Kyoto 1973–75. *The 10s, the 20s, the 30s: Inventive Clothes, 1909–1939.* The Metropolitan Museum of Art, New York, December 13, 1973–September 3, 1974; National Museum of Modern Art, Kyoto, March 25–May 25, 1975. Catalogue by Diana Vreeland. New York, 1973.

Okayama–Hiroshima–Tokyo 1974. *Gustave Moreau et ses élèves / Morō to sono deshitachi ten.* Magasin Teyaman, Okayama, February 15–March 6, 1974; Magasin Teyaman, Hiroshima, March 15–30, 1974; Magasin Tobu, Tokyo, April 6–23, 1974. Catalogue. Bordeaux, 1974.

New York 1974. *Cone Collection from the Baltimore Museum of Art: A Benefit Exhibition*. Wildenstein Galleries, New York, March 29–May 4, 1974. Pamphlet. New York, 1974.

Marseille 1974. *130 dessins de Matisse*. Musée Cantini, Marseille, June 15–September 15, 1974. Catalogue. Marseille, 1974.

Palm Beach 1975. *Ferdinand Howald: Avant-Garde Collector*. Society of the Four Arts, Palm Beach, February 7–March 2, 1975. Catalogue. [Palm Beach, 1975.]

Sydney–Melbourne–New York 1975. *Modern Masters: Manet to Matisse.* Art Gallery of New South Wales, Sydney, April 10–May 11, 1975; National Gallery of Victoria, Melbourne, May 28–June 22, 1975; Museum of Modern Art, New York, August 4–September 1, 1975. Catalogue edited by William S. Lieberman. New York, 1975.

Stockholm 1975. "Moderna Museet på Liljevalchs Konsthall, Stockholm." Liljevalchs Konsthall, Stockholm, May 15–September 28, 1975. No catalogue published.

Paris 1975. *Henri Matisse: Dessins, sculpture*. Musée National d'Art Moderne, Paris, May 29–September 7, 1975. Catalogue by Dominique Fourcade and Isabelle Monod-Fontaine. Paris, 1975.

Brussels 1975. *Henri Matisse: Dessins, sculpture / Tekeningen en sculpturen*. Palais des Beaux-Arts, Brussels, September 29–October 29, 1975. Catalogue by Dominique Bozo et al. Brussels, 1975.

New York–San Francisco–Fort Worth 1976. *The "Wild Beasts": Fauvism and Its Affinities*. Museum of Modern Art, New York, March 26–June 1, 1976; San Francisco Museum of Modern Art, June 29–August 15, 1976; Kimbell Art Museum, Fort Worth, September 11–October 31, 1976. Catalogue by John Elderfield. New York, 1976.

Norfolk 1976. "Homage to the Louvre." Chrysler Museum, Norfolk, Va., May–September 1976. No catalogue published.

Bellingham 1976–77. *5000 Years of Art: An Exhibition from the Collections of The Metropolitan Museum of Art*. Whatcom Museum of History and Art, Bellingham, Wash., December 4, 1976–October 2, 1977. Catalogue by Thomas Schlotterback. Bellingham, Wash., 1976.

Paris 1977a. *Acquisitions du Cabinet d'Art Graphique, 1971–1976*. Musée National d'Art Moderne, Paris, January 31–March 28, 1977. Catalogue by Pierre Georgel. Paris, 1977.

Madison 1977. *Ferdinand Howald: Avant-Garde Collector*. Elvehjem Art Center, University of Wisconsin, Madison, April 21–June 5, 1977. Catalogue. [Madison, Wisc., 1977.]

Allentown 1977. *French Masterpieces of the 19th Century from the Henry P. McIlhenny Collection.* Allentown Art Museum, Allentown, Pa., May 1–September 18, 1977. Catalogue. Allentown, 1977.

Paris 1977b. *Paris, New York*. Centre Pompidou, Musée National d'Art Moderne, Paris, June 1–September 19, 1977. Catalogue by Hélène Seckel, Daniel Abadie, and Alfred Pacquement. Paris, 1977.

Nashville 1977. *Treasures from the Chrysler Museum at Norfolk and Walter P. Chrysler, Jr.* Tennessee Fine Arts Center at Cheekwood, Nashville, June 12–September 5, 1977. Catalogue by Mario Amaya and Eric M. Zafran. Norfolk, Va., 1977.

Washington–Detroit–Saint Louis 1977–78. *Henri Matisse: Paper Cut-Outs*. National Gallery of Art, Washington, D.C., September 10–October 23, 1977; Detroit Institute of Arts, November 23, 1977–January 8, 1978; Saint Louis Art Museum, January 29–March 12, 1978. Catalogue by Jack Cowart et al. Saint Louis, 1977.

Saint Louis 1977–78. "Selections from the Permanent Collection." Washington University Gallery of Art, Saint Louis, December 1, 1977–February 12, 1978. No catalogue published.

Paris 1978. *L'art moderne dans les musées de province*. Grand Palais, Paris, February 3–April 24, 1978. Catalogue by Henri de Cazals. Paris, 1978.

New York 1978. *Veronese to Franz Kline: Masterworks from the Chrysler Museum at Norfolk, for the Benefit of The Chrysler Museum Art Reference Library*. Wildenstein & Co., New York, April 13–May 13, 1978. Catalogue by Mario Amaya and Eric Zafran. Norfolk, Va., 1978.

Saint Petersburg 1978. "Masters from the Norton Gallery." Museum of Fine Arts, St. Petersburg, Fla., April 16–May 21, 1978. No catalogue published.

Bordeaux 1978. *La nature morte de Brueghel à Soutine*. Galerie des Beaux-Arts, Bordeaux, May 5–September 1, 1978. Catalogue edited by Gilberte Martin-Méry. N.p., [1978].

Washington 1978. *"The Noble Buyer:" John Quinn, Patron of the Avant-Garde*. Hirshhorn Museum and Sculpture Garden, Smithsonian Institution, Washington, D.C., June 1–August 6, 1978. Catalogue by Judith Zilczer. Washington, D.C., 1978.

New York 1978–79. *Matisse in the Collection of the Museum of Modern Art: Including Remainder-Interest and Promised Gifts*. Museum of Modern Art, New York, October 27, 1978–January 30, 1979. Catalogue by John Elderfield, with William S. Lieberman and Riva Castleman. New York, 1978.

Rome 1978–79. *Henri Matisse*. Académie de France, Villa Medici, Rome, November 24, 1978–January 28, 1979. Catalogue edited by Isabelle Monod-Fontaine; texts by Jean Leymarie, Giulio Carlo Argan, and Henri Matisse. Rome, 1978.

Kyoto–Tokyo–Kamakura 1979. *Sorenpō Shozō no Furansu kindai kaiga ten: Pūshikin. Erumitāju ryo bijutsukan kara [Exhibition of French Modern Painting from the Collections of the U.S.S.R: Pushkin and Hermitage Museums.]* Kyoto National Museum of Modern Art, April 17–May 27, 1979; Tokyo Metropolitan Museum of Art, June 7–July 1, 1979; Kamakura Museum of Modern Art, July 5–August 5, 1979. Catalogue edited by Hijikata Teiichi and others. Tokyo, 1979.

Pittsburgh 1979. "From the Henry P. McIlhenny Collection." Carnegie Institute, Pittsburgh, May 10–July 1, 1979. Unnumbered typed checklist.

New York 1979. "Matisse and Master Drawings from the Baltimore Museum of Art." Solomon R. Guggenheim Museum, New York, August 24–October 14, 1979. No catalogue published.

London 1979–80. *Post-Impressionism: Cross-Currents in European Painting*. Royal Academy of Arts, London, November 17, 1979–March 16, 1980. Catalogue edited by John House and Mary Anne Stevens. London, 1979.

1980–1989

Basel 1980. *Matisse: Huiles, gouaches découpées, dessins, sculptures*. Galerie Beyeler, Basel, June–September 1980. Catalogue. Basel, 1980.

Saint Louis 1980. "Cubist, Expressionist, and Surrealist Paintings and Sculptures." Washington University Gallery of Art, Saint Louis, September 20–November 2, 1980. No catalogue published.

Madrid 1980. *Matisse: Oleos, dibujos, gouaches, découpées, esculturas y libros*. Fundación Juan March, Madrid, October–December 1980. Catalogue. Madrid, 1980.

Paris 1980–81. *Cinq années d'enrichissement du patrimoine national, 1975–1980: Donations, dations, acquisitions*. Galeries Nationales du Grand Palais, Paris, November 15, 1980–March 2, 1981. Catalogue. Paris, 1980.

Jacksonville 1981. "Modern European Masters." Jacksonville Art Museum, Jacksonville, Fla., January 7–March 29, 1981. No catalogue published.

Worcester 1981. *"The Dial": Arts and Letters in the 1920s. An Anthology of Writings from "The Dial" Magazine, 1920–29*. Worcester Art Museum, Worcester, Mass., March 7–May 10, 1981. Catalogue edited by Gaye L. Brown. Worcester, Mass., 1981.

Hiroshima and other cities 1981. *Matisse et ses amis*. Museum of Fine Arts, Hiroshima, March 14–April 5, 1981; Otani Museum of Fine Arts, Nishinomiya, April 10–May 5, 1981; Museum of Fine Arts, Kumamoto, May 9–31, 1981; House of Regional Culture, Tokushima Prefecture, June 6–28, 1981. Catalogue. Kobe, 1981.

Tokyo–Kyoto 1981. *Machisu ten / Matisse.* National Museum of Modern Art, Tokyo, March 20–May 17, 1981; National Museum of Modern Art, Kyoto, May 26–July 19, 1981. Catalogue (in Japanese). Osaka, 1981.

Saint Louis 1981. "The Centennial Exhibition." Washington University Gallery of Art, Saint Louis, May 15–October 11, 1981. Catalogue, *Illustrated Checklist of the Collection. Paintings, Sculpture and Works on Paper*. Saint Louis, 1981.

San Francisco and other cities 1981–82. *Master Paintings from the Phillips Collection*. Fine Arts Museum of San Francisco, July 4–November 1, 1981; Dallas Museum of Fine Arts, November 22, 1981–February 16, 1982; Minneapolis Institute of Arts, March 14–May 30, 1982; High Museum of Art, Atlanta, June 24–September 16, 1982. Catalogue by Eleanor Green et al. Fort Lee, N.J., 1981.

Bielefeld 1981. *Matisse: Das Goldene Zeitalter*. Kunsthalle Bielefeld, October 18–December 13, 1981. Catalogue by Ulrich Weisner. Bielefeld, 1981.

Zürich–Düsseldorf 1982–83. *Henri Matisse.* Kunsthaus Zürich, October 15, 1982–January 16, 1983; Städtische Kunsthalle Düsseldorf, January 29–April 4, 1983. Catalogue edited by Felix Baumann Margit Hahnloser-Ingold, and Klaus Schrenk. Zürich, 1982.

Saint Louis 1983a. "Capsule of Modern Art." Washington University Gallery of Art, Saint Louis, January 9–March 6, 1983. No catalogue published.

Saint Louis 1983b. "Cubists, Surrealists, and Expressionists." Washington University Gallery of Art, Saint Louis, May 15–September 4, 1983. No catalogue published.

Washington 1983. *The John Hay Whitney Collection*. National Gallery of Art, Washington, D.C., May 29–September 5, 1983. Catalogue by John Rewald. Washington, D.C., 1983.

Lugano 1983. *Capolavori impressionisti e postimpressionisti dai musei Sovietici*. Collection Thyssen-Bornemisza, Villa Favorita, Lugano, June 14–October 15, 1983. Catalogue. Lugano, 1983.

London–Washington 1984. *The Orientalists: Delacroix to Matisse; European Painters in North Africa and the Near East*. Royal Academy of Arts, London, March 24–May 27, 1984; National Gallery of Art, Washington, D.C., July 1–October 28, 1984. Catalogue edited by Mary Anne Stevens. London, 1984. Washington ed.: *The Orientalists: Delacroix to Matisse; the Allure of North Africa and the Near East*. New York, 1984.

Atlanta 1984. *The Henry P. McIlhenny Collection: Nineteenth Century French and English Masterpieces*. High Museum of Art, Atlanta, May 25–September 30, 1984. Catalogue. Atlanta, 1984.

Fort Worth 1984. *Henri Matisse, Sculptor / Painter: A Formal Analysis of Selected Works*. Kimbell Art Museum, Fort Worth, May 26–September 2, 1984. Catalogue by Michael P. Mezzatesta. Fort Worth, 1984.

Toulouse 1984. "Chefs d'oeuvre du Musée National d'Art Moderne à Toulouse." Réfectoire des Jacobins, Toulouse, September–December 1984. No catalogue published.

London–New York 1984–85. "The Sculpture and Drawings of Henri Matisse," Hayward Gallery, London, October 4, 1984–January 6, 1985; "The Drawings of Henri Matisse," Museum of Modern Art, New York, February 27–May 14, 1985. Catalogue, *The Drawings of Henri Matisse*, essay by John Elderfield; entries by Magdalena Dabrowski. New York, 1984.

Stockholm 1984–85. *Henri Matisse*. Moderna Museet, Stockholm, November 3, 1984–January 6, 1985. Catalogue. Stockholm, 1984.

Amsterdam 1984–85. *La grande parade: Hoogtepunten van de schilderkunst na 1940 / Highlights in Painting after 1940.* Stedelijk Museum, Amsterdam, December 15, 1984–April 15, 1985. Catalogue edited by Alexander van Grevenstein, Edy de Wilde, and Karel Schampers. Amsterdam, 1984.

Humlebaek 1985. "Henri Matisse." Louisiana Museum, Humlebaek, January 18–April 14, 1985. Checklist published in *Louisiana revy* 25, no. 2 (January 1985).

Venice–Rome 1985. *Da Cézanne, Monet, Renoir, Gauguin, van Gogh, Matisse, Picasso: 42 Capolavori dai musei Sovietici*. Museo Correr ala Napoleonica, Venice, February 23–April 14, 1985; Musei Capitolini, Rome, April 23–June 10, 1985. Catalogue by Albert Grigorevich Kostenevich et al. Translated from Russian to Italian by Michaela Böhmig et al. Milan, 1985.

Los Angeles–Fort Worth 1985–86. "Masterpieces from the Cone Collection of the Baltimore Museum of Art." Los Angeles County Museum of Art, October 6–November 24, 1985; Kimbell Art Museum, Fort Worth, December 14, 1985–February 9, 1986. No catalogue published.

Tampere 1985. *Bonnard, Braque, Gris, Léger, Matisse, Picasso: Modernin taiteen klassikoita / Classics of Modern Art*. Sara Hildénin Taidemuseo, Tampere, October 12–December 8, 1985. Catalogue. Tampere, 1985.

Lille 1986. *Matisse: Peintures et dessins du Musée Pouchkine et du Musée de l'Ermitage*. Musée des Beaux-Arts, Lille, 1986. Catalogue. Lille, 1986.

Canberra–Brisbane 1986. *20th Century Masters from The Metropolitan Museum of Art, New York*. Australian National Gallery, Canberra, March 1–April 27, 1986; Queensland Art Gallery, Brisbane, May 7–July 1, 1986. Catalogue. Canberra and Brisbane, 1986.

Washington–Los Angeles–New York 1986. *Impressionist to Early Modern Paintings from the U.S.S.R.: Works from the Hermitage Museum, Leningrad, and the Pushkin Museum of Fine Arts, Moscow*. National Gallery of Art, Washington D.C., May 1–June 15, 1986; Los Angeles County Museum of Art, June 26–August 12, 1986; The Metropolitan Museum of Art, New York, August 22–October 5, 1986. Catalogue. Los Angeles, 1986.

Raleigh–Birmingham 1986–87. *French Paintings from the Chrysler Museum*. North Carolina Museum of Art, Raleigh, May 31–September 14, 1986; Birmingham Museum of Art, November 6, 1986–January 18, 1987. Catalogue by Jefferson C. Harrison. Norfolk, Va., 1986.

Nice 1986. *Matisse Photographies*. Musée des Beaux-Arts Jules Chéret, Nice, July 4–September 30, 1986. Catalogue by Jean-François Chevrier; introduction by Xavier Girard. Nice, 1986.

Le Cateau-Cambrésis 1986–87. "Matisse: L'atelier d'Issy-les-Moulineaux, 1909–1917." Musée Départemental Matisse, Le Cateau-Cambrésis, October 1986–March 1987. No catalogue published.

Toulouse–Nice 1986–87. *Matisse: Ajaccio–Toulouse, 1898–1899: Une saison de peinture*. Musée Paul-Dupuy, Toulouse, October 9–December 15, 1986; Galerie des Ponchettes, Nice, December 19, 1986–January 30, 1987. Catalogue. Nice and Toulouse, 1986.

Warsaw 1986–87. *4 x Paryz / Paris en quatre temps.* Galeria Zacheta, Warsaw, October 12, 1986–February 12, 1987. Catalogue. Warsaw, 1986.

Quebec 1986. *Tableaux de maîtres français impressionnistes et post-impressionnistes de l'Union soviétique*. Musée du Québec, October 18–November 23, 1986. Catalogue. Quebec, 1986.

Washington 1986–87. *Henri Matisse: The Early Years in Nice 1916–1930*. National Gallery of Art, Washington, D.C., November 2, 1986–March 29, 1987. Catalogue by Jack Cowart and Dominique Fourcade. Washington, D.C., 1986.

Venice 1987. *Henri Matisse: Matisse et l'Italie*. Museo Correr, Venice, May 30–October 18, 1987. Catalogue edited by Pierre Schneider. Milan, 1987.

Harrisburg 1987. "Director's Choice: An Exhibition for the Governor's Residence." Governor's Home, Harrisburg, Pa., June 10–September 8, 1987. No catalogue published.

Tokyo and other cities 1987–88. *Machisu-Ten / Les chefs-d'oeuvre du Musée Matisse et les Matisses de Matisse*. Isetan Museum of Art, Tokyo, October 22–November 17, 1987; Yamaguchi Prefectural Museum, November 20–December 27, 1987; Daimaru Museum of Art, Osaka, January 3–18, 1988; Sogo Museum of Art, Yokohama, February 10–March 27, 1988. Catalogue. Tokyo, 1987.

Philadelphia 1987–88. *The Henry P. McIlhenny Collection: An Illustrated History.* Philadelphia Museum of Art, November 22, 1987–January 17, 1988. Catalogue by Joseph J. Rishel. Philadelphia, 1987.

Saint-Étienne 1987–88. "L'art en Europe: Les années decisives, 1945–1953." Musée d'Art Moderne de Saint-Étienne, December 1, 1987–February 28, 1988. No catalogue published.

Saint Petersburg–Moscow 1988. *Ot Delakrua do Matissa: Shedevry frantsuzskoi zhivopisi XIX-nachala XX veka, iz Muzeia Metropoliten v Niulorke i Khudozhestvennogo Institua v Chikago.* State Hermitage Museum, Saint Petersburg, March 15–May 10, 1988; State Pushkin Museum of Fine Arts, Moscow, June 10–July 30, 1988. Catalogue. Leningrad / Saint Petersburg, 1988.

London 1988. *French Paintings from the USSR: From Watteau to Matisse*. National Gallery, London, June 15–September 18, 1988. Catalogue by Alexander A. Babin et al.; translated by Irene Gore and Catherine Matthews. London, 1988.

Lucerne 1988. *Von Matisse bis Picasso. Hommage an Siegfried Rosengart.* Kunstmuseum Luzern, Lucerne, June 19–September 11, 1988. Catalogue edited by Angela Rosengart and Martin Kunz. Stuttgart, 1988.

Jerusalem 1988–89. *Monet to Matisse: Modern Masters from Swiss Private Collections*. The Israel Museum, Jerusalem, October 1988–January 1989. Catalogue edited by Stephanie Rachum. Jerusalem, 1988.

Barcelona–Madrid 1988–89. *Henri Matisse: Pinturas y dibujos de los museos Pushkin de Moscú y el Ermitage de Liningrado*. Museo Picasso, Barcelona, October 12–December 11, 1988; Centro de Arte Reina Sofia, Madrid, December 19, 1988–February 15, 1989. Catalogue. Barcelona, 1988.

Washington 1988–89. *Places of Delight: The Pastoral Landscape*. The Phillips Collection and the National Gallery of Art, Washington, D.C., November 6, 1988–January 22, 1989. Catalogue by Robert C. Cafritz, Lawrence Gowing, and David Rosand. Washington, D.C., 1988.

Washington 1988–90. *Twentieth-Century Art: Selections for the Tenth Anniversary of the East Building*. National Gallery of Art, Washington, D.C., December 13, 1988–December 31, 1990. Catalogue. Washington, D.C., 1988.

Moscow–Saint Petersburg 1989. "L'art en France: Un siècle d'inventions, du fauvisme aux années quatre-vingt." State Pushkin Museum of Fine Arts, Moscow, March 27–May 9, 1989; State Hermitage Museum, Saint Petersburg, June 1–September 1, 1989. No catalogue published.

Basel 1989–90. *L'éternel féminin*. Galerie Beyeler, Basel, November 1989–January 1990. Catalogue by Urs Albrecht. Basel, 1989.

New York–London 1989–90. *Twentieth Century Modern Masters: The Jacques and Natasha Gelman Collection*. The Metropolitan Museum of Art, New York, December 12, 1989–April 1, 1990; Royal Academy of Arts, London, April 19–July 15, 1990. Catalogue by Sabine Rewald et al. New York, 1989.

1990–1999

Washington and other cities 1990–91a. *Matisse in Morocco: The Paintings and Drawings, 1912–1913*. National Gallery of Art, Washington, D.C., March 18–June 3, 1990; Museum of Modern Art, New York, June 20–September 4, 1990; State Pushkin Museum of Fine Arts, Moscow, September 28–November 20, 1990; State Hermitage Museum, Leningrad / Saint Petersburg, December 15, 1990–February 15, 1991. Catalogue by Jack Cowart et al. Washington, D.C., 1990.

Washington and other cities 1990–91b. *The Passionate Eye: Impressionist and Other Master Paintings from the Collection of Emil G. Bührle, Zürich*. National Gallery of Art, Washington, D.C., May 6–July 15, 1990; Montreal Museum of Fine Arts, August 3–October 14, 1990; Yokohama Museum of Art, November 2, 1990–January 13, 1991; Royal Academy of Arts, London, February 1–April 9, 1991. Catalogue. Zürich, 1990.

New York–Chicago 1990. *From Poussin to Matisse: The Russian Taste for French Painting. A Loan Exhibition from the USSR.* The Metropolitan Museum of Art, New York, May 20–July 29, 1990; Art Institute of Chicago, September 8–November 25, 1990. Catalogue. Chicago, 1990.

Venice 1990. *La France à Venise: Le Pavillon français de 1948 à 1988. XLIVème Biennale de Venise*. Peggy Guggenheim Collection, Solomon R. Guggenheim Foundation, Venice, May 23–September 30, 1990. Catalogue by Annick Spay and Laurence Waurin. Paris and Rome, 1990.

Fréjus 1990. "L'art en France, 1945–1990." Fondation Daniel Templon, Fréjus, July 3–September 16, 1990. No catalogue published.

Essen–Amsterdam 1990–91. *Vincent van Gogh und die Moderne*. Museum Folkwang, Essen, August 10–November 4, 1990; Van Gogh Museum, Amsterdam, November 16, 1990–February 18, 1991. Catalogue edited by Georg-W. Költzsch, Ronald de Leeuw, and Inge Bodesohn-Vogel. Freren, 1990. Eng. ed.: *Vincent van Gogh and the Modern Movement, 1890–1914*. Translated by Eileen Martin.

Los Angeles–New York–London 1990–91. *The Fauve Landscape*. Los Angeles County Museum of Art, October 4–December 30, 1990; The Metropolitan Museum of Art, New York, February 19–May 5, 1991; Royal Academy of Arts, London, June 10–September 1, 1991. Catalogue by Judi Freeman et al. New York, 1990.

Paris 1990–91. *De Manet à Matisse: Sept ans d'enrichissements au Musée d'Orsay*. Musée d'Orsay, Paris, November 12, 1990–March 10, 1991. Catalogue. Paris, 1990.

Dijon 1991. *Les chefs-d'oeuvre du Musée Matisse, Nice, Cimiez*. Musée des Beaux-Arts de Dijon, July 6–October 6, 1991. Catalogue by Xavier Girard. Dijon, 1991.

Nagoya–Hiroshima–Kasama 1991. *Machisu ten / Matisse Retrospective*. Nagoya City Art Museum, August 24–September 29, 1991; Hiroshima Museum of Art, October 5–November 4, 1991; Kasama Nichido Museum, November 9–December 8, 1991. Catalogue by Albert Kostenevich, Y. A. Rusakov, and Katsunori Fukaya. Nagoya, 1991.

Boston 1991–92. "Matisse, Picasso and Impressionist Masters from the Cone Collection." Museum of Fine Arts, Boston, October 2, 1991–January 19, 1992. No catalogue published.

Rome–Milan 1991–92. *Henri Matisse: Capolavori dal Museo Matisse di Nizza.* Académie de France, Rome, October 17–December 29, 1991; Palazzo Reale, Milan, January 22–March 29, 1992. Catalogue by Xavier Girard. N.p., 1991.

Saint Louis 1991–92. "Selections from the Permanent Collection." Washington University Gallery of Art, Saint Louis, November 1, 1991–May 1, 1992. No catalogue published.

Le Cateau-Cambrésis 1992. *Matisse et Baudelaire: Les Fleurs du mal.* Musée Matisse, Le Cateau-Cambrésis, June 27–September 27, 1992. Catalogue. Le Cateau-Cambrésis, 1992.

Tokyo–Osaka 1992–93. *Keishō no hazama ni: Gendai bijutsu e no shiten / Among the Figures: A Perspective on Contemporary Art*. National Museum of Modern Art, Tokyo, September 22–November 8, 1992; National Museum of Art, Osaka, December 12, 1992–January 31, 1993. Catalogue (in Japanese and English). Tokyo, 1992.

New York 1992–93. *Henri Matisse: A Retrospective.* Museum of Modern Art, New York, September 24, 1992–January 12 (extended to January 19), 1993. Catalogue by John Elderfield. New York, 1992.

Saint Louis 1993a. *Matisse: Image into Sign.* Saint Louis Art Museum, February 19–April 25, 1993. Catalogue by Jack Flam. Saint Louis, 1993.

Paris 1993. *Henri Matisse, 1904–1917.* Centre Pompidou, Musée National d'Art Moderne, Paris, February 25–June 21, 1993. Catalogue edited by Dominique Fourcade and Isabelle Monod-Fontaine. Paris, 1993.

Columbus and other cities 1993. *Masterpieces of Impressionism and European Modernism from the Columbus Museum of Art.* Columbus Museum of Art, Columbus, Ohio, opened March 1, 1993; Daimaru Museum Umeda, Osaka, April 21–May 10, 1993; Chiba Sogo Museum of Art, Chiba, May 21–June 8, 1993; Hokkaido Obihiro Museum of Art, Obihiro, June 26–August 8, 1993; Museum of Fine Arts, Gifu, August 27–October 11, 1993; Bunkamura Museum of Art, Tokyo, October 16–November 28, 1993; The Miyagi Museum of Art, Miyagi, December 3–26, 1993. Catalogue by Charles F. Stuckey et al. Columbus, Ohio, 1993.

Saint Louis 1993b. "Selections from the Permanent Collection." Washington University Gallery of Art, Saint Louis, March 1–May 15, 1993. No catalogue published.

Essen–Moscow–Saint Petersburg 1993–94. *Morozov and Shchukin, the Russian Collectors: Monet to Picasso.* Museum Folkwang, Essen, June 25–October 31, 1993; State Pushkin Museum of Fine Arts, Moscow, November 30, 1993–January 30, 1994; State Hermitage Museum, Saint Petersburg, February 16–April 16, 1994. Catalogue edited by Georg-W. Költzsch. Cologne, 1993.

Moscow–Saint Petersburg 1993. *Anri Matiss, 1869–1954: Zhipovis', risunok, dekupazhi.* State Pushkin Museum of Fine Arts, Moscow, July 12–August 27, 1993; State Hermitage Museum, Saint Petersburg, September 18–November 23, 1993. Catalogue by A. G. Kostenevich et al. Moscow, 1993.

Saint-Étienne 1993–94. "Entre la sérénité et l'inquiétude." Musée d'Art Moderne de Saint-Étienne, November 19, 1993–January 30, 1994. No catalogue published.

Houston 1993–94. "Van Gogh to Matisse: Impressionist and Modern Masters from the Cone Collection of the Baltimore Museum of Art." Museum of Fine Arts, Houston, November 21, 1993–January 30, 1994. No catalogue published.

Martigny 1994. *De Matisse à Picasso: Collection Jacques et Natasha Gelman.* Fondation Pierre Gianadda, Martigny, June 18–November 1, 1994. Catalogue (bilingual reprint of catalogue for New York–London 1989–90) by Sabine Rewald et al. Martigny and New York, 1994.

Nice 1994. *Matisse: Le grand atelier, 1935–1948.* Musée Matisse, Nice, June 25–October 2, 1994. Catalogue by Xavier Girard published as *Cahiers du musée Matisse*, no. 12. Nice, 1994.

Edinburgh 1994. *Monet to Matisse: Landscape Painting in France, 1874–1914.* National Gallery of Scotland, Edinburgh, August 11–October 23, 1994. Catalogue by Richard Thomson. Edinburgh, 1994.

Copenhagen 1994–95. *Johannes Rump: Portraet af en Samler.* Statens Museum for Kunst, Copenhagen, October 29, 1994–January 15, 1995. Catalogue edited by Lennart Gottlieb and Villads Villadsen. Copenhagen, 1994.

Paris 1995. *Jean Cassou 1897–1986: Un musée imaginé.* Galerie Mansart, Bibliothèque Nationale de France, Paris, March 15–June 18, 1995. Catalogue edited by Florence de Lussy. Paris, 1995.

Brisbane–Canberra–Melbourne 1995. *Matisse.* Queensland Art Gallery, Brisbane, March 29–May 16, 1995; National Gallery of Australia, Canberra, May 27–July 9, 1995; National Gallery of Victoria, Melbourne, July 19–September 3, 1995. Catalogue edited by Caroline Turner and Roger Benjamin. Brisbane, 1995.

Basel 1995. *Wer hat Angst vor Rot . . . ? / Who Is Afraid of Red . . . ?* Galerie Beyeler, Basel, June–September 1995. Catalogue. Basel, 1995.

Venice 1995. *Identity and Alterity: Figures of the Body 1895 / 1995. La Biennale di Venezia, 46.* Palazzo Grassi, Venice, June 8–October 15, 1995. Catalogue. Venice, 1995.

Jacksonville 1995–96. *Masterworks from the Norton Museum of Art, West Palm Beach* ["European Masterworks" section]. Cummer Museum of Art and Gardens, Jacksonville, Fla., October 20, 1995–February 4, 1996. Catalogue by Henry Adams, Marianne Berardi, and Sally Metzler. Jacksonville, Fla., 1995.

Copenhagen 1996a. *Fransk modernisme: Hovedvaerker på Statens Museum for Kunst.* Statens Museum for Kunst, Copenhagen, 1996. Catalogue by Inge Vibeke Rasschou-Nielsen. Copenhagen, 1996.

Saint Louis 1996. "Selections from the Permanent Collection." Washington University Gallery of Art, Saint Louis, February 1–March 31, 1996. No catalogue published.

Milan 1996. *Da Monet a Picasso: Capolavori impressionisti e postimpressionisti dal Museo Puškin di Mosca.* Palazzo Reale, Milan, February 21–June 30, 1996. Catalogue by Marina Bessonova. Milan, 1996.

Yamagata and other cities 1996. *The European Collection, Selected Works from the Norton Museum of Art.* Yamagata Museum, April 18–May 19, 1996; Asahikawa Museum of Art, May 25–June 23, 1996; Chiba Sogo Museum of Art, June 29–August 4, 1996; Mitaka City Art Gallery, August 10–September 8, 1996; Kumamoto Prefectural Museum, September 13–October 20, 1996; Ashikaga Museum of Art, October 26–November 24, 1996. Catalogue. West Palm Beach, 1996.

Basel 1996. *Canto d'Amore: Classicism in Modern Art and Music, 1914–1935.* Kunstmuseum Basel, April 27–August 11, 1996. Catalogue edited by Gottfried Boehm, Ulrich Mosch, and Katharina Schmidt. Basel, 1996.

Nice 1996. "Matisse-Bonnard, une amitié." Musée Matisse, Nice, June–October, 1996. No catalogue published.

Copenhagen 1996b. *100 Mesterværker.* Statens Museum for Kunst, Copenhagen, June 23–August 4, 1996. Catalogue edited by Eva Friis. Copenhagen, 1996.

Antibes 1996. *1946: L'art de la reconstruction.* Musée Picasso, Antibes, France, June 28–October 20, 1996. Catalogue by Maurice Fréchuret, Laurence Bertrand Dorléac, Serge Guibaut, and Jean-Pierre Rioux. Antibes, 1996.

Bonn 1996–97. *Moderna Museet Stockholm zu Gast in Bonn.* Kunst- und Ausstellungshalle der Bundesrepublik Deutschland, Bonn, July 4, 1996–January 12, 1997. Catalogue by Dorothee von Drachenfels and Petra Kruse. Bonn and Ostfildern-Ruit, 1996.

The Hague 1996. *Van Monet tot Matisse: Franse meesters uit Poesjkin Museum in Moskou.* Haags Gemeentemuseum, The Hague, July 13–October 13, 1996. Catalogue by Jonieke van Es and Patty Wageman. The Hague, 1996.

Tokyo–Osaka 1996–97. *Kon korekushon ten katarogu / Matisse and Modern Masters from the Cone Collection of The Baltimore Museum of Art.* Isetan Museum of Art, Tokyo, October 3–December 28, 1996; Osaka Municipal Museum of Art, January 8–February 11, 1997. Catalogue. N.p., 1996.

Atlanta 1996–97. *Henri Matisse: Masterworks from the Museum of Modern Art.* High Museum, Atlanta, November 2, 1996–January 19, 1997. Catalogue by John Elderfield. New York, 1996.

Münster–Grenoble–Weimar 1996–97. *Farben des Lichts: Paul Signac und der Beginn der Moderne von Matisse bis Mondrian.* Westfälisches Landesmuseum für Kunst und Kulturgeschichte, Münster, December 1, 1996–February 16, 1997; Musée de Grenoble, March 9–May 25, 1997; Kunstsammlung zu Weimar, June 15–August 31, 1997. Catalogue edited by Erich Franz. Ostfildern, 1996. French ed.: *Signac et la libération de la couleur: De Matisse à Mondrian.* Paris, 1997.

Aarhus 1996–97. *Franske mesterværker: Fra Matisse til Picasso.* Aarhus Kunstmuseum, Aarhus, December 14, 1996–March 9, 1997. Catalogue by Villads Villadsen. Copenhagen, 1996.

Paris 1997. "Made in France: 1947–1977–1997." Centre Pompidou, Musée National d'Art Moderne, Paris, January 30–September 29, 1997. A special edition of *Connaissance des arts* [hors série, no. 103 (1997)], was published on the occasion. Paris, 1997.

New York 1997. "Masterworks from the Florene May Schoenborn Bequest." The Museum of Modern

Art, New York, February 4–March 30, 1997. No catalogue published.

London 1997. *Modern Art in Britain, 1910–1914*. Barbican Art Gallery, London, February 20–May 26, 1997. Catalogue by Anna Gruetzner Robins. London, 1997.

Berlin 1997. *The Age of Modernism: Art in the 20th Century*. Martin-Gropius-Bau, Berlin, May 7–July 27, 1997. Catalogue edited by Christos M. Joachimides and Norman Rosenthal. Ostfildern, 1997. German ed.: *Die Epoche der Moderne: Kunst im 20. Jahrhundert*. Ostfildern, 1997.

New York–London 1997–98. *Objects of Desire: The Modern Still Life*. Museum of Modern Art, New York, May 25–August 26, 1997; Hayward Gallery, London, October 9, 1997–January 4, 1998. Catalogue by Margit Rowell. New York, 1997.

Vence 1997. *Incursions champêtres*. Château de Villeneuve, Fondation Émile Hugues, Vence, June 28–October 19, 1997. Held in conjunction with exhibitions at 12 other venues in France, under the joint title: *1918–1958, La Côte d'Azur et la modernité*. Catalogue. Paris, 1997.

Saint-Paul-de-Vence 1997. *La Sculpture des peintres: Honoré Daumier . . . et al.* Fondation Maeght, Saint-Paul-de-Vence, July 2–October 19, 1997. Catalogue by Jean-Louis Prat. Saint-Paul-de-Vence, 1997.

Rome 1997–98. *Matisse: "La révélation m'est venue de l'Orient."* Musei Capitolini, Rome, September 20, 1997–January 20, 1998 (extended to February 1). Catalogue by Claude Duthuit et al. Florence, 1997.

Tokyo 1997. *La collection du Centre Georges Pompidou: Les chefs-d'oeuvre du Musée National d'Art Moderne*. Museum of Contemporary Art, Tokyo, September 20–December 14, 1997. Catalogue (in Japanese). Tokyo, 1997.

Saint Petersburg 1998. *Anri Matiss i vydaiushchiesia datskie sobirateli* [Henri Matisse and great Danish collectors]. State Hermitage Museum, Saint Petersburg, March 3–July 5, 1998. Catalogue edited by Kasper Monrad. Copenhagen, 1998.

Lyon 1998. *Matisse: La collection du Centre Georges Pompidou, Musée National d'Art Moderne*. Musée des Beaux-Arts de Lyon, April 4–June 28, 1998. Catalogue by Isabelle Monod-Fontaine et al. Paris, 1998.

West Palm Beach–Naples 1998–99. *Animal as Muse: A Not So Peaceable Kingdom*. Norton Museum of Art, West Palm Beach, Fla., May 16–August 23, 1998; Philharmonic Center for the Arts, Naples, Fla., February 9–April 2, 1999. Catalogue by Neil Watson. West Palm Beach, Fla., 1998.

Nice 1998. *Matisse: Femmes et fleurs*. Musée Matisse, Nice, June 11–August 30, 1998. Catalogue. Cologne, 1998.

Paris 1998–99. *La Collection du Centre Georges Pompidou: Un parcours au Musée d'Art Moderne de la Ville de Paris*. Musée d'Art Moderne de la Ville de Paris, June 18, 1998–September 19, 1999. Catalogue. Paris, 1998.

London 1998. *Henri Matisse: Twenty Paintings & Drawings*. Lumley Cazalet Ltd., London, June 23–July 31, 1998. Catalogue preface by Hilary Spurling. London, 1998.

Saint Louis 1998. "Early Modern European and American Art." Washington University Gallery of Art, Saint Louis, September 8–October 12, 1998. No catalogue published.

Zürich–Saint Louis 1998–99. *Max Beckmann und Paris: Matisse, Picasso, Braque, Léger, Rouault*. Kunsthaus, Zürich, September 25, 1998–January 3, 1999; Saint Louis Art Museum, February 6–May 9, 1999. Catalogue. Cologne, 1998.

New York 1998–99. *Rendezvous: Masterpieces from the Centre Georges Pompidou and The Guggenheim Museums*. Solomon R. Guggenheim Museum, New York, October 16, 1998–January 24, 1999. Catalogue by Bernard Blistène, Lisa Dennison, et al. Paris and New York, 1998.

Tokyo and other cities 1998–99. *Shi ji feng hua: Ju Yuan Meishu Guan zhen cang zhan / Chefs-d'oeuvre du Musée de l'Orangerie: Collection Jean Walter et Paul Guillaume*. Bunkamura Museum of Art, Tokyo, November 14, 1998–February 14, 1999; Nagoya City Art Museum, February 23–April 7, 1999; Hiroshima Museum of Art, April 17–June 27, 1999; Niigata Prefectural Museum of Modern Art, July 10–September 12, 1999; National Museum of Modern Art, Kyoto, September 21–November 14, 1999. Catalogue. Tokyo, 1998.

Copenhagen 1999. *Henri Matisse: Four Great Collectors*. Statens Museum for Kunst, Copenhagen, January 22–May 24, 1999. Catalogue edited by Kasper Monrad. Copenhagen, 1999.

Fort Worth 1999. "Matisse and Picasso: A Gentle Rivalry." Kimbell Art Museum, Fort Worth, January 31–May 2, 1999. Catalogue, *Matisse and Picasso*, by Yve-Alain Bois. New York, 1998.

Munich 1999. *Kunst über Grenzen: Die Klassische Moderne von Cézanne bis Tinguely und die Weltkunst, aus der Schweiz gesehen*. Haus der Kunst, Munich, March 7–May 30, 1999. Catalogue edited by Christoph Vitali and Hubertus Gassner. Munich and New York, 1999.

New York 1999–2000. *ModernStarts: People, Places, Things*. Museum of Modern Art, New York, October 7, 1999–March 14, 2000. Catalogue edited by John Elderfield. New York, 1999.

Paris 1999–2000a. *Le Maroc de Matisse*. Institut du Monde Arabe, Paris, October 19, 1999–January 30, 2000. Catalogue by Brahim Alaoui et al. Paris, 1999.

Paris 1999–2000b. *Le Fauvisme; ou, "l'épreuve du feu": Éruption de la modernité en Europe*. Musée d'Art Moderne de la Ville de Paris, October 29, 1999–February 27, 2000. Catalogue. Paris, 1999.

Cologne 1999–2000. *Kunst-Welten im Dialog: von Gauguin zur globalen Gegenwart*. Museum Ludwig, Cologne, November 5, 1999–March 19, 2000. Catalogue by Marc Scheps, Yilmaz Dziewior, and Barbara M. Thiemann. Cologne, 1999.

Taipei–Kaohsiung 1999–2000. *Shi ji feng hua: Ju Yuan Meishu Guan zhen cang zhan / Chefs-d'oeuvre du Musée de l'Orangerie: Collection Jean Walter et Paul Guillaume*. Taipei Fine Arts Museum, December 4, 1999–March 1, 2000; Kaohsiung Museum of Fine Arts, March 10–April 23, 2000. Catalogue. Taipei, 1999.

Rome 1999–2000. *I cento capolavori dell'Ermitage: Impressionisti e avanguardie alle Scuderie Papali al Quirinale*. Scuderie Papali al Quirinale, Rome, December 22, 1999–June 11, 2000. Catalogue by A. G. Kostenevich. Milan, 1999.

2000–2009

New York 2000–2001. *Painters in Paris: 1895–1950*. The Metropolitan Museum of Art, New York, March 8, 2000–January 14, 2001. Catalogue by William S. Lieberman. New York, 2000.

Denver–Birmingham–Toronto 2000–2001. "Matisse from the Baltimore Museum of Art." Denver Art Museum, March 11–June 25, 2000; Birmingham Museum of Art, July 23–September 17, 2000; Art Gallery of Ontario, Toronto, October 10, 2000–January 28, 2001. No catalogue published.

Paris 2000a. *1900*. Galeries Nationales du Grand Palais, Paris, March 14–June 26, 2000. Catalogue. Paris, 2000.

Montreal–Fort Worth 2000–2001. *From Renoir to Picasso: Masterpieces from the Musée de l'Orangerie*. Montreal Museum of Fine Arts, June 1–October 15, 2000; Kimbell Art Museum, Fort Worth, November 12, 2000–February 25, 2001. Catalogue. Montreal, 2000.

Saint-Paul-de-Vence 2000. *Le nu au XXe siècle*. Fondation Maeght, Saint-Paul-de-Vence, July 4–October 30, 2000. Catalogue edited by Jean-Louis Prat. Saint-Paul-de-Vence, 2000.

Nice 2000. *Le Bleu de l'été*. Musée Matisse, Nice, July 8–September 25, 2000. Paris, 2000.

Düsseldorf 2000. "Unser 20. Jahrhundert: Meisterwerke von Picasso bis Beuys." Kunstsammlung Nordrhein-Westfalen, Düsseldorf, July 15–October 29, 2000. For journal published on the occasion of this exhibition, see Kruszynski, *Vernissage* (2000).

Paris 2000b. *Paris sous le ciel de la peinture*. Hôtel de Ville de Paris, September 14–December 17, 2000. Catalogue. Paris, 2000.

Paris 2000–2001. *Méditerranée: De Courbet à Matisse*. Galeries Nationales du Grand Palais, Paris, September 19, 2000–January 15, 2001. Catalogue edited by Françoise Cachin. Paris, 2000.

Brisbane–Sydney–Melbourne 2001. *Renoir to Picasso: Masterpieces from the Musée de l'Orangerie, Paris*. Queensland Art Gallery, Brisbane, March 29–May 20, 2001; Art Gallery of

New South Wales, Sydney, June 1–July 29, 2001; National Gallery of Victoria, Melbourne, August 10–September 30, 2001. Catalogue edited by Suzanne Grano. Brisbane, 2001.

New York 2001. *Côte d'Azur: Art, Modernity, and the Myth of the French Rivera.* AXA Gallery, New York, April 27–July 14, 2001. Catalogue, *Making Paradise: Art, Modernity, and the Myth of the French Riviera*, edited by Kenneth E. Silver. New York, 2001.

Basel 2001. *Ornament and Abstraction: The Dialogue between non-Western, Modern and Contemporary Art.* Fondation Beyeler, Basel, June 10–October 7, 2001. Catalogue edited by Markus Brüderlin. Basel, 2001.

Madrid 2001–2. *Forma: El ideal clásico en el arte moderno.* Museo Thyssen-Bornemisza, Madrid, October 8, 2001–January 13, 2002. Catalogue edited by Tomàs Llorens. Madrid, 2001.

Norwich 2002. "The Body in 20th Century Art." Norwich Castle Museum and Art Gallery, Norfolk, England, February 11–April 21, 2002. No catalogue published.

New York 2002. *Pierre Matisse and His Artists.* The Pierpont Morgan Library, New York, February 14–May 19, 2002. Catalogue by William M. Griswold and Jennifer Tonkovich. New York, 2002.

New York–Saint Louis 2002. *H. W. Janson and the Legacy of Modern Art at Washington University in St. Louis.* Salander-O'Reilly Galleries, New York, March 12–April 6, 2002; Washington University Gallery of Art, Saint Louis, August 30–December 6, 2002. Catalogue by Sabine Eckmann et al. Saint Louis, 2002.

Barcelona 2002. *De Renoir a Picasso: Obres mestres del Musée de l'Orangerie, Paris.* Fundació "La Caixa," Barcelona, April 11–June 30, 2002. Catalogue. Barcelona, 2002.

London–Paris–New York 2002–3. *Matisse, Picasso.* Tate Modern, London, May 11–August 18, 2002; Galeries Nationales du Grand Palais, Paris, September 25, 2002–January 6, 2003; Museum of Modern Art, New York, February 13–May 19, 2003. Catalogue by Elizabeth Cowling et al. Eng. eds.: London and New York, 2002; French ed.: Paris, 2002.

Basel 2002. *Painting on the Move.* Kunstmuseum Basel, May 26–September 8, 2002. Catalogue. Basel, 2002.

London 2002. *Fabric of Vision: Dress and Drapery in Painting.* National Gallery, London, June 19–September 8, 2002. Catalogue by Anne Hollander. London, 2002.

Paris 2002. *Le musée qui n'existait pas.* Musée National d'Art Moderne, Centre Pompidou, Paris, June 26–September 23, 2002. Catalogue, *Daniel Buren, 1997–1999*, edited by Annick Boisnard and Daniel Buren. Le Bourget and Paris, 2002.

Kyoto–Tokyo 2002–3. *Picasso and the School of Paris: Paintings from The Metropolitan Museum of Art, New York.* Kyoto Municipal Museum of Art, September 14–November 24, 2002; Bunkamura Museum of Art, Tokyo, December 7, 2002–March 9, 2003. Catalogue in Japanese and English edited by William S. Lieberman. N.p., 2002.

Houston and other cities 2002–5. *Art Beyond Isms: Masterworks from El Greco to Picasso in the Phillips Collection.* Museum of Fine Arts, Houston, September 22, 2002–January 5, 2003; Phoenix Art Museum, January 23–May 4, 2003; Albright-Knox Art Gallery, Buffalo, May 23–September 1, 2003; Denver Art Museum, October 2, 2003–January 4, 2004; Frist Center for the Visual Arts, Nashville, February 6–May 16, 2004; also traveled to Los Angeles County Museum of Art, October 17, 2004–January 2, 2005; Cleveland Museum of Art, February 20–May 29, 2005; Mori Arts Center, Tokyo, June 17–September 4, 2005; Museo di Arte Moderna e Contemporanea di Trento e Rovereto, September 17–November 13, 2005. Catalogue by Eliza E. Rathbone and Johanna Halford-MacLeod. London and Washington, D.C., 2002. For other venues, see Martigny 2004 and Paris 2005–6.

Stockholm 2002–3. *Moderna Klassiker.* Moderna Museet c/o Prins Eugens Waldemarsudde, Stockholm, September 28, 2002–February 16, 2003. Catalogue. Stockholm, 2002.

Taipei 2002–3. *Matisse: L'émotion du trait, le don de l'espace.* National Museum of History, Taipei, November 19, 2002–February 16, 2003. Catalogue. Taipei, 2002.

Houston–Atlanta–Los Angeles 2002–3. *Old Masters, Impressionists, and Moderns: French Masterworks from the State Pushkin Museum, Moscow.* Museum of Fine Arts, Houston, December 15, 2002–March 9, 2003; High Museum of Art, Atlanta, April 5–June 29, 2003; Los Angeles County Museum of Art, July 27–October 13, 2003. Catalogue by Irina Antonova with Charlotte Eyerman, Eugenia Georgievskaïa, and Elena Sharnova. New Haven and Houston, 2002.

Nantes 2003. *Matisse, la période niçoise 1917–1929.* Musée des Beaux-Arts de Nantes, March 7–June 2, 2003. Catalogue edited by Vincent Rousseau and Céline Rincé-Vaslin. Paris, 2003.

Ornans 2003. *Des nus & des nues; ou, Les aventures de la Percheronne.* Musée Gustave Courbet, Ornans, June 21–September 28, 2003. Catalogue by Jean-Jacques Fernier. Ornans, 2003.

Grenoble–Marseille 2003–4. *Matisse, Picasso 1920: 12 chefs-d'oeuvre du Musée de l'Orangerie.* Musée de Grenoble, June 21–September 21, 2003; Musée Cantini, Marseille, March 13–June 13, 2004. Catalogue by Pierre Georgel, Guy Tosatto, and Christine Poullain. Grenoble and Marseille, 2003.

Houston 2003–4. "The Heroic Century: The Museum of Modern Art's Masterpieces, 200 Paintings and Sculptures." Museum of Fine Arts, Houston, September 21, 2003–January 4, 2004. Catalogue, *Visions of Modern Art: Painting and Sculpture from the Museum of Modern Art*, edited by John Elderfield. New York, 2003.

Stockholm 2003–4. *Kleopatra blir Ariadne: Identitet och förvandling.* Prins Eugens Waldemarsudde, Stockholm, October 11, 2003–February 8, 2004. Catalogue by Hans Henrik Brummer. Stockholm, 2003.

Berlin 2004. *Das MoMA in Berlin: Meisterwerke aus dem Museum of Modern Art, New York.* Neue Nationalgalerie, Berlin, February 20–September 19, 2004. Catalogue edited by John Elderfield and Angela Schneider. Ostfildern-Ruit, 2004.

Martigny 2004. *Chefs-d'oeuvre de la Phillips Collection, Washington.* Fondation Pierre Gianadda, Martigny, May 27–September 27, 2004. Catalogue. Martigny, 2004.

Nice 2004. *Matisse en France.* Musée Matisse, Nice, July 8–September 21, 2004. Catalogue by Claude Duthuit and Marie-Thérèse Pulvénis de Séligny. Paris and Nice, 2004.

Saint-Tropez 2004. *Henri Matisse: Émerveillement pour le Sud.* L'Annonciade, Musée de Saint-Tropez, July 10–October 11, 2004. Catalogue edited by Jean-Paul Monery. Saint-Tropez, 2004.

San Antonio 2004. "Picasso to Pollock: H.W. Janson and the Legacy of Modern Art at Washington University in St. Louis." Marion Koogler McNay Art Museum, San Antonio, Texas, August 17–October 24, 2004. No catalogue published.

Tokyo 2004. *Matisu ten / Matisse: Processus / Variation.* National Museum of Western Art, Tokyo, September 10–December 12, 2004. Catalogue (in Japanese) by Tanaka Masayuki et al. Tokyo, 2004.

Le Cateau-Cambrésis–London–New York 2004–5. *Matisse, His Art and His Textiles: The Fabric of Dreams.* Musée Matisse, Le Cateau-Cambrésis, October 23, 2004–January 25, 2005; Royal Academy of Arts, London, March 5–May 30, 2005; The Metropolitan Museum of Art, New York, June 23–September 25, 2005. Catalogue by Ann Dumas et al. London, 2004.

Rüsselsheim and other cities 2004–6. *Exil und Moderne: H. W. Janson und die Sammlung der Washington University in St. Louis.* Stiftung Opelvillen, Zentrum fur Kunst, Rüsselsheim, Germany, November 19, 2004–March 28, 2005; Angermuseum, Erfurt, April 9–August 21, 2005; Museen für Kunst und Kulturgeschichte der Hansestadt Lübeck, St. Annen-Museum, Lübeck, September 4, 2005–January 29, 2006; Museum für Neue Kunst, Freiburg, February 18–June 24, 2006. Catalogue. Berlin, 2004.

Paris 2005. *Le néo-impressionnisme de Seurat à Paul Klee.* Musée d'Orsay, Paris, March 14–July 10, 2005. Catalogue. Paris, 2005.

Paris–Humlebaek 2005. *Matisse: Une seconde vie.* Musée du Luxembourg, Paris, March 16–July 17, 2005; Louisiana Museum for Moderne Kunst,

Humlebaek, August 12–December 4, 2005. Catalogue published as "Matisse: Et nyt liv," *Louisiana Revy* 46, no. 1 (August 2005).

Céret–Le Cateau-Cambrésis 2005–6. *Matisse-Derain: Collioure 1905, un été fauve*. Musée d'Art Moderne, Céret, June 18–October 2, 2005; Musée Matisse, Le Cateau-Cambrésis, October 22, 2005–January 22, 2006. Catalogue by Joséphine Matamoros et al. Paris, 2005.

Copenhagen 2005. *Matisse & Jesper Just, Aino Kannisto, Malene Landgren*. Statens Museum for Kunst, Copenhagen, August 13–December 4, 2005. Catalogue by Tine Nygaard. Copenhagen, 2005.

Paris 2005–6. *Pierre Matisse: Passeur passionné. Un marchand d'art et ses artistes*. Mona Bismarck Foundation, Paris, October 20, 2005–January 14, 2006. Catalogue. Paris, 2005.

Düsseldorf 2005–6. *Henri Matisse: Figur, Farbe, Raum*. Kunstsammlung Nordrhein-Westfalen, Düsseldorf, October 29, 2005–February 19, 2006. Catalogue edited by Pia Müller-Tamm. Ostfildern-Ruit, 2005.

Paris 2005–6. *La Collection Phillips à Paris*. Musée du Luxembourg, Paris, November 30, 2005–March 26, 2006. Catalogue. Milan, 2005.

West Palm Beach 2006. *Matisse in Transition: Around Laurette*. Norton Museum of Art, West Palm Beach, January 28–April 16, 2006. Catalogue by Jack D. Flam. West Palm Beach, 2006.

Saint Louis 2006. "Permanent Collection Exhibition Spring 2006." Mildred Lane Kemper Art Museum, Washington University in Saint Louis, opened February 16, 2006. No catalogue published.

Basel 2006. *Henri Matisse: Figure, couleur, espace*. Fondation Beyeler, Basel, March 19–July 9 (extended to July 23), 2006. Catalogue by Ernst Beyeler et al. Basel, 2006.

Paris 2006. "¡Almodovar Exhibition!" Cinémathèque Française, Paris, April 5–July 31, 2006. No catalogue published.

Nancy 2006. *Roger Marx, un critique aux côtés de Gallé, Monet, Rodin, Gauguin*. Musée des Beaux-Arts, Nancy, May 6–August 28, 2006. Catalogue. Versailles and Nancy, 2006.

New York–Chicago–Paris 2006–7. *Cézanne to Picasso: Ambroise Vollard, Patron of the Avant-Garde*. The Metropolitan Museum of Art, New York, September 13, 2006–January 7, 2007; Art Institute of Chicago, February 17–May 13, 2007; Musée d'Orsay, Paris, June 18–September 16, 2007. Catalogue by Rebecca Rabinow et al. New York, 2006.

Rome 2006–7. *Matisse e Bonnard: Viva la pittura!* Complesso del Vittoriano, Rome, October 6, 2006–February 4, 2007. Catalogue edited by Philippe Cros, Maria Teresa Benedetti, and Sandro Barbagallo. Milan, 2006.

Paris–Le Cateau-Cambrésis 2006–7. *Rouault, Matisse: Correspondances*. Musée d'Art Moderne de la Ville de Paris, October 26, 2006–February 15, 2007; Musée Matisse, Le Cateau-Cambrésis, March 24–June 17, 2007. Catalogue. [Paris, 2006.]

Frankfurt am Main–Munich 2006–7. *Gärten: Ordnung—Inspiration—Glück*. Städel Museum, Frankfurt am Main, November 24, 2006–March 11, 2007; Städtische Galerie im Lenbachhaus, Munich, April 5–July 8, 2007. Catalogue by Sabine Schulze and Andreas Beyer. Ostfildern, 2006. English ed.: *The Painter's Garden: Design, Inspiration, Delight*. Translated by Paul Aston, John S. Southard, and Stephen Telfer. Ostfildern, 2006.

Paris 2006–7. "Présentation des collections permanentes (collections modernes)." Musée National d'Art Moderne, Paris, December 15, 2006–December 15, 2007. No catalogue published. See Léal, *Collection art moderne* (2006).

Kyoto–Tokyo 2007. *Masterpieces from the Philadelphia Museum of Art: Impressionism and Modern Art*. Kyoto Municipal Museum of Art, July 14–September 24, 2007; Tokyo Metropolitan Art Museum, October 10–December 24, 2007. Catalogue by Yoichiro Ide and Anne d'Harnoncourt, in English and Japanese. Tokyo, 2007.

Baltimore–Phoenix 2007–8. "Déjà vu? Revealing Repetition in French Masterpieces." Walters Art Museum, Baltimore, October 7, 2007–January 1, 2008; Phoenix Museum of Art, January 20–May 4, 2008. Catalogue, *The Repeating Image: Multiples in French Painting from David to Matisse*, edited by Eik Kahng. Baltimore, 2007.

Copenhagen 2008. *Rammens Kunst*. Statens Museum for Kunst, Copenhagen, March 8–September 7, 2008. Catalogue by Henrik Bjerre et al. Copenhagen, 2008.

Paris 2008–9. "Présentation des collections permanentes (collections modernes)." Musée National d'Art Moderne, Paris, June 2, 2008–June 2, 2009. No catalogue published.

Baden-Baden 2008. *Die Skulpturen der Maler: Malerei und Plastik im Dialog*. Museum Frieder Burda, Baden-Baden, July 5–October 26, 2008. Catalogue by Jean-Louis Prat et al. Baden-Baden, 2008.

Nagoya–Tokyo–Kobe 2008–9. *Masterpieces of the Kunstsammlung Nordrhein-Westfalen*. Nagoya City Art Museum; The Bunkamura Museum of Art, Tokyo; Hyogo Prefectural Museum of Art, Kobe, 2008–9. Catalogue. [Tokyo, 2008.]

Stuttgart–Hamburg 2008–9. *Matisse: Menschen, Masken, Modelle*. Staatsgalerie, Stuttgart, September 27, 2008–January 11, 2009; Bucerius Kunst Forum, Hamburg, January 31–April 19, 2009. Catalogue by Ortrud Westheider et al. Munich, 2008. English ed., *Matisse: People, Masks, Models*. Munich, 2008.

New York 2008–9. *The Philippe de Montebello Years: Curators Celebrate Three Decades of Acquisitions*. The Metropolitan Museum of Art, New York, October 24, 2008–February 1, 2009. Related electronic material available at www.metmuseum.org.

Seoul–Taipei–Kaohsiung 2008–9. *Shiwai taoyuan / Arcadie: Dans les collections du Centre Pompidou*. Seoul Museum of Art, November 21, 2008–March 22, 2009; Taipei Fine Arts Museum, April 18–July 12, 2009; Kaohsiung Museum of Fine Arts, July 30–October 30, 2009. Catalogue by Yu Siying and Fang Meijing. Taipei, 2009.

Philadelphia 2008–9. "Henri Matisse and Modern Art on the French Riviera." Philadelphia Museum of Art, December 13, 2008–October 25, 2009. No catalogue published; Electronic resource: www.philamuseum.org/exhibitions/334.html

Philadelphia 2009. *Cézanne and Beyond*. Philadelphia Museum of Art, February 26–May 31, 2009. Catalogue by Joseph J. Rishel and Katherine Sachs; essays by Roberta Bernstein et al. Philadelphia, 2009.

Yamanashi and other cities 2009–10. *Berugi kindai kaiga no ayumi / De l'impressionnisme au fauvisme en Belgique*. Yamanashi Prefectural Museum of Art, April 18–July 5, 2009; Prefectural Museum, Tottori, July 20–August 30, 2009; Seiji Togo Memorial Sompo Japan Museum of Art, Tokyo, September 12–November 23, 2009; Matsuzakaya Art Museum, December 12, 2009–February 14, 2010. Catalogue by Noémie Goldman. Tokyo, 2009.

Madrid 2009. *Matisse: 1917–1941*. Museo Thyssen-Bornemisza, Madrid, June 9–September 20, 2009. Catalogue by Tomàs Llorens. Madrid, 2009.

Nice–Paris 2009–10. *Matisse, Rodin*. Musée Matisse, Nice, June 19–September 28, 2009; Musée Rodin, Paris, October 23, 2009–February 28, 2010. Catalogue. Paris, 2009.

Schleswig 2009. *Die Kunstsammlung Nordrhein-Westfalen zu Gast in Gottorf: Picasso, Klee, Beckmann, Matisse und weitere Künstler in Schloß Gottorf*. Landesmuseum für Kunst und Kulturgeschichte, Stiftung Schleswig-Holsteinische Landesmuseen, Schloss Gottorf, Schleswig, July 19–October 25, 2009. Catalogue by Herwig Guratzsch. Schleswig, 2009.

São Paulo 2009. *Matisse hoje / aujourd'hui: Diálogos com cinco artistas franceses contemporâneos*. Pinacoteca do Estado de São Paulo, September 5–November 1, 2009. Catalogue by Emilie Ovaere; dialogues with Cecile Bart, Christophe Cuzin, Frédérique Lucien, Philippe Richard, and Pierre Mabille. São Paulo, 2009.

Paris–Los Angeles–Philadelphia 2009–10. *Renoir in the Twentieth Century*. Galeries Nationales du Grand Palais, Paris, September 23, 2009–January 4, 2010; Los Angeles County Museum of Art, February 14–May 9, 2010; Philadelphia Museum of Art, June 17–September 6, 2010.

Catalogue edited by Claudia Einecke and Silvie Patry. Ostfildern, 2010.

Seoul–Busan–Taipei 2009–10. *Manei dao Bikasuo / Manet to Picasso: Masterpieces from the Philadelphia Museum of Art.* Seoul Arts Center, Seoul, South Korea, December 16, 2009–March 28, 2010; Busan Museum of Art, Busan, South Korea, April 2–June 2, 2010; Taipei Fine Arts Museum, Taipei, Taiwan, June 25–September 26, 2010. Catalogue. Taipei, 2010.

2010–

Portland and other cities 2010–11. "Objects of Wonder: Four Centuries of Still Life from the Norton Museum of Art." Portland Museum of Art, Portland, Maine, February 4–June 6, 2010; Montgomery Museum of Art, Montgomery, Ala., July 3–October 10, 2010; Dixon Gallery & Gardens, Memphis, Tenn., October 16, 2010–January 9, 2011; Hyde Collection, Glens Falls, N.Y., January 21–April 21, 2011. No catalogue published.

Zürich 2010. "Van Gogh, Cézanne, Monet: Die Sammlung Bührle zu Gast im Kunsthaus Zürich." Kunsthaus Zürich, February 12–May 16, 2010. No catalogue published.

Le Cateau-Cambrésis–Nice 2010. *Lydia D.: Lydia Delectorskaya, muse et modèle de Matisse.* Musée Matisse, Le Cateau-Cambrésis, February 27–May 30, 2010; Musée Matisse, Nice, June 18–September 27, 2010. Catalogue by Dominique Szymusiak et al. Paris, 2010.

Chicago–New York 2010. *Matisse: Radical Invention, 1913–1917.* The Art Institute of Chicago, March 20–June 20, 2010; Museum of Modern Art, New York, July 18–October 11, 2010. Catalogue by Stephanie D'Alessandro and John Elderfield. Chicago, 2010.

Giverny 2010. *L'impressionnisme au fil de la Seine.* Musée des Impressionnismes, Giverny, April 1–July 18, 2010. Catalogue. Milan, 2010.

Metz 2010–11. *100 chefs-d'oeuvre du XXe siècle dans les collections du Centre Pompidou.* Centre Pompidou-Metz, May 12, 2010–August 29, 2011. Catalogue edited by Laurent Le Bon. Metz, 2010.

Essen 2010–11. *Bilder einer Metropole: Die Impressionisten in Paris.* Museum Folkwang, Essen, October 2, 2010–January 30, 2011. Catalogue by Hartwig Fischer and Sandra Gianfreda. Göttingen, 2010.

Granada 2010–11. *Matisse and the Alhambra, 1910–2010.* Fine Arts Museum of Granada, The Alhambra, Palace of Charles V, October 15, 2010–February 28, 2011. Catalogue by Francisco Jarauta Marión et al. Madrid, 2010.

Brescia 2011. *Matisse: La Seduzione di Michelangelo.* Museo di Santa Giulia, Brescia, February 11–June 12 (extended to June 26), 2011. Catalogue edited by Claudia Beltramo Ceppi Zevi. Florence, 2011.

Malmö 2011. "Den tidiga modernismen, 1900–1920, ur Moderna Museets samling" [Early Modernism, 1900–1920, from the Moderna Museet Collection]. Moderna Museet Malmö, March 19–October 2, 2011. No catalogue published.

New York–Vancouver 2011–12. *Collecting Matisse and Modern Masters: The Cone Sisters of Baltimore.* Jewish Museum, New York, May 6–September 25, 2011; Vancouver Art Gallery, May 26–September 30, 2012. Catalogue by Karen Levitov. New York and New Haven, 2011.

San Francisco–Paris–New York 2011–12. *The Steins Collect: Matisse, Picasso, and the Parisian Avant-garde.* San Francisco Museum of Modern Art, May 21–September 6, 2011; Galeries Nationales du Grand Palais, Paris, October 5, 2011–January 16, 2012; The Metropolitan Museum of Art, New York, February 21–June 3, 2012. Catalogue edited by Rebecca Rabinow, Janet Bishop, and Cécile Debray. San Francisco, 2011. French ed.: *Matisse, Cézanne, Picasso: L'aventure des Stein.* Paris, 2011.

Nice 2011. *Henri Matisse, la dissolution du trait et de la couleur: Autour de la donation de la céramique "La Piscine."* Musée Matisse, Nice, July 1–October 2, 2011. Catalogue. Paris, 2011.

Malmö 2011–12. "Change of Scenes: Works from the Moderna Museet Collection by Dardel, Matisse, Abdul-Hâdi, Hjertén, Léger, among Others." Moderna Museet Malmö, October 15, 2011–February 5, 2012. No catalogue published.

Brisbane 2011–12. *Matisse: Drawing Life.* Queensland Art Gallery, Gallery of Modern Art, Brisbane, December 3, 2011–March 4, 2012. Catalogue by Céline Chicha and Emilie Ovaere. South Brisbane, 2011.

REFERENCES CITED

Aagesen, Dorthe. "Henri Matisse 1905–1918: Eight Takes on Eight Paintings." In Dorthe Aagesen et al., *Matisse: Masterpieces at Statens Museum for Kunst*, pp. 11–22. Copenhagen, 2005.

Aagesen, Dorthe, et al. *Matisse: Masterpieces at Statens Museum for Kunst.* Copenhagen, 2005.

Addams Allen, Jane. "Exhibit Paints Matisse in a New Light." *The Washington Times*, October 30, 1986, pp. C1, C2.

Aftermath France, 1945–54: New Images of Man. Exh. cat. London, 1982.

L'Âge nouveau. Anonymous. "Présence de Matisse." *L'Âge nouveau*, no. 39 (June 1949), n.p.

Alaoui, Brahim, Tahar Ben Jelloun, Claude Duthuit, Rémi Labrusse, Isabelle Monod-Fontaine, Pierre Schneider, et al. *Le Maroc de Matisse.* Exh. cat. Paris, 1999.

Alley, Ronald. *Catalogue of The Tate Gallery's Collection of Modern Art, Other Than Works by British Artists.* London, 1981.

Alliez, Éric, and Jean-Claude Bonne. *La pensée-Matisse: Portrait de l'artiste en hyperfauve.* 2 vols. Paris, 2005.

Alpatov, Mikhail V. *Henri Matisse.* Dresden, 1973. First published in Moscow, 1969.

Amano, Chika. "L'exposition Henri Matisse à la galerie Maeght." In *Matisu ten / Henri Matisse: Processus / Variation*, pp. 128–33. Exh. cat. Tokyo, 2004.

——. "La peinture en procès." In *Matisu ten / Henri Matisse: Processus / Variation*, pp. 8–24. Exh. cat. Tokyo, 2004.

——. "Processus et surface." In *Matisu ten / Henri Matisse: Processus / Variation*, pp. 144–51. Exh. cat. Tokyo, 2004.

Amano, Chika, et al. *Matisu ten / Henri Matisse: Processus / Variation.* Exh. cat. Tokyo, 2004.

American Art News. R. R. M. "The Autumn Salon, Oct. 9, 1912." *American Art News* 11, no. 2 (October 19, 1912), pp. 1–8.

Anderberg, Brigitte, et al. *SMK Highlights: Statens Museum for Kunst.* Edited by Peter Nørgaard Larsen and Sven Bjerkhof; translated by René Lauritsen. Copenhagen, 2005.

Andersen, Mogens. "Hos Matisse. . . ." *Aarstiderne* 7 (March 1950), pp. 126–28.

Anonymous. *Samling Gösta Stenman.* Helsingfors, 1918.

Antonova, Irina A. *Masterpieces from the Pushkin Museum of Fine Arts, Moscow.* Moscow, 1982.

——. *Shedevry Gosudarstvennogo Muzeia Izobrazitel'nykh Iskusstv Imeni A. S. Pushkina* [Masterpieces from the Pushkin Museum of Fine Arts]. Moscow, 1986.

Antonova, Irina A., Charlotte Nalle Eyerman, E. B. Georgievskaia, and Elena Sharnova. *Old Masters, Impressionists, and Moderns: French Masterworks from the State Pushkin Museum, Moscow.* Exh. cat. New Haven, 2002.

Apollinaire, Guillaume. "Henri Matisse." *La Phalange* (December 15, 1907). Reprinted in Leroy C. Breunig, ed. *Apollinaire on Art: Essays and Reviews.* Translated by Susan Suleiman. New York, 1972, pp. 36–39, 479.

——. "Entrefilet." *Paris-Journal*, May 15, 1914.

——. "Henri Matisse." *Klingen* 1, no. 11–12 (August–September 1918), n.p.

Apollonio, Umbro. *Fauves e cubisti.* Bergamo, 1959.

Aragon, Louis. "Matisse-en-France." In Henri Matisse, *Dessins: Thèmes et variations.* Paris, 1943.

——. *Apologie du luxe.* Geneva, 1946.

——. "Henri Matisse ou le peintre français." *Jardin des arts* no. 106 (September 1963), pp. 2–13.

——. "Henri Matisse" (3 chapters of Aragon's forthcoming book, *Henri Matisse: Roman*). *Les lettres françaises*, no. 1330 (April 15–21, 1970), pp. 3–30.

——. *Henri Matisse, roman.* 2 vols. Paris, 1971.

——. *Henri Matisse, a Novel.* 2 vols. Translated by Jean Stewart. New York, 1972.

Art Digest. Anonymous. "World's Greatest Exhibition of Matisse's Art Is Held Here." *Art Digest* 6 (November 15, 1931), p. 5.

——. Anonymous. "Baltimore Sees 52 Works by Henri Matisse." *Art Digest* (combined with the

Argus of San Francisco: The News-Magazine of Art) 8, no. 20 (September 1, 1934), p. 20.
——. Anonymous. "Art of the Third Republic—When France Was Free and Creative." *Art Digest* 15, no. 11 (March 1, 1941), pp. 16, 30.
Art Institute of Chicago. *Paintings in the Art Institute of Chicago: A Catalogue of the Picture Collection*. Chicago, 1961.
Art News. Anonymous. "'Living Art' Folio and Originals Seen." Art News 22, no. 17 (February 2, 1924), p. 5.
——. Anonymous. "Modern Paintings: F. Valentine Dudensing Galleries." *Art News* 25 (March 26, 1927), p. 9.
——. Anonymous. "Pacquement Sale of French Art to Be Notable Event." *Art News* 31 (November 19, 1932), pp. 3, 5, 8–9.
——. B. K. "Reviews and Previews: Henri Matisse." *Art News* 47 (February 1949), pp. 44–45.
Asano, Toru. "Fauvism and Modern Japanese Painting—The Roles Played by Yori Saito and Kotaro Takamura." In *Fauvism and Modern Japanese Painting*, pp. 26–31, 267–72. Exh. cat. Nagoya, 1992.
Babin, Alexander A., et al. *French Paintings from the USSR: Watteau to Matisse*. Translated by Irene Gore and Catherine Matthews. Exh. cat. London, 1988.
Baldwin, Carl R. "The Fauves: Reflections on an Exhibition, a Catalogue, and a History." *Arts* 50 (June 1976), pp. 98–102.
Baltimore Museum of Art. *Cone Collection: A Handbook with a Catalogue of Paintings and Sculpture*. Baltimore, 1955.
——. *Paintings Sculpture and Drawings in the Cone Collection*. Rev. ed. of 1955. Baltimore, 1967.
Baltimore Sun. Anonymous. "Baltimore Women Own Large Collection of Matisse Works." *Baltimore Sun*, December 14, 1924, p. M20.
——. Anonymous. "'Advanced' Works of Art Startle Some." *Baltimore Sun*, January 18, 1925, p. 8.
Barbier, Agnès. "Oeuvres réalisées à Issy-les-Moulineaux." In *Henri Matisse: L'atelier d'Issy, 1909–1917*. Exh. cat. Issy-les-Moulineaux, 1985.
Barnes, Albert C., and Violette de Mazia. *The Art of Henri-Matisse*. New York and London, 1933.
Barr, Alfred H., Jr. *Matisse: His Art and His Public*. New York, 1951.
——. "Matisse, Picasso and the Crisis of 1907." *Magazine of Art* 44 (May 1951), pp. 163–70.
Barskaya, A. G., and M. A. Bessonova. *Capolavori impressionisti e postimpressionisti dai musei Sovietici*. Exh. cat. Lugano and Milan, 1983.
Barskaya, A. G., and Albert G. Kostenevich. *French Painting, mid-Nineteenth to Twentieth Centuries*. The Hermitage Catalogue of Western European Painting 12. Florence, 1991.
B[arth], W[ilhelm]. *Henri Matisse*. Beitrage zur zeitgenössischen Kunst, vol. 1. Basel, 1917.
Basler, Adolphe. "Henri Matisse." *Der Cicerone* 13, no. 1 (January 1921), pp. 16–20. Reprinted under alias Philippe Marcel in *L'Art d'aujourdhui*, summer 1924, and as Charles Kunstler in *La peinture indépendante en France*, vol. 2 (1929). The 1924 version is excerpted and translated in Flam, *Matisse: A Retrospective* (1988), pp. 219–22.
——. "Henri Matisse." *Der Cicerone* 16 (1924), pp. 1001–5.
——. *Henri Matisse*. Leipzig, 1924.
Baumann, Felix, Margit Hahnloser-Ingold, and Klaus Schrenk, eds. *Henri Matisse*. Exh. cat. Zürich, 1982.
Beaumelle, Agnès de la. *Collection art graphique. La collection du Centre Pompidou, Musée National d'Art Moderne: Centre de création industrielle*. Paris, 2008.
Beausire, Marguerite. "Henri Matisse: Der 'Wilde' aus Flandern." *Pan*, no. 1 (January 1982), pp. 4–21.
Becker, John. "The Museum of Modern Western Painting in Moscow," 2 parts. *Creative Art: Magazine of Fine and Applied Art*, March 1932, pp. 190–200; April 1932, pp. 278–83.
Bell, Clive. *Modern French Painting: The Cone Collection*. Baltimore, 1951.
Beltramo Ceppi Zevi, Claudia, ed. *Matisse: La seduzione di Michelangelo*. Exh. cat. Florence, 2011.
Benedetti, Maria Teresa. "Colore e luce nell'arte di Matisse e di Bonnard." In *Matisse e Bonnard: Viva la pittura!*, pp. 77–105. Exh. cat. Rome, 2006.
Benjamin, Roger. *Matisse's "Notes of a Painter": Criticism, Theory, and Context, 1891–1908*. Ann Arbor, Mich., 1987.
——. "Recovering Authors: The Modern Copy, Copy Exhibitions and Matisse." *Art History* 12 (June 1989), pp. 176–201.
——. "Fauves in the Landscape of Criticism: Metaphor and Scandal at the Salon." In Judi Freeman et al., *The Fauve Landscape*, pp. 241–68. Exh. cat. Los Angeles, 1990.
——. "The Decorative Landscape, Fauvism, and the Arabesque of Observation." *Art Bulletin* 75 (June 1993), pp. 295–316.
——. "Orientalist Excursions: Matisse in North Africa." In *Matisse*, edited by Caroline Turner and Roger Benjamin, pp. 71–83. Exh. cat. Brisbane, 1995.
——. "The Vital Sign: An Overview of Matisse's Painting." In *Matisse*, edited by Caroline Turner and Roger Benjamin, pp. 19–39. Exh. cat. Brisbane, 1995.
——. "Expression, Disfiguration: Matisse, the Female Nude and the Academic Eye." In *In Visible Touch: Modernism and Masculinity*, edited by Terry Smith, pp. 75–105. Chicago, 1997.
——. "Landscape near Collioure: Study for The Joy of Life." In Dorthe Aagesen et al., *Matisse: Masterpieces at Statens Museum for Kunst*, pp. 24–44. Copenhagen, 2005.
Benois, Alexandre. "The 'Salon' and Bakst's School." *Rech'* [Speech], May 1, 1910. English translation in Dorontchenkov, *Russian and Soviet Views of Modern Western Art* (2009), p. 100.
Bernier, Rosamund. "Le Musée privé d'un conservateur." *L'Oeil*, no, 27 (March 1957), pp. 20–29.
——. *Matisse, Picasso, Miró: As I Knew Them*. New York, 1991.
——. "Matisse en persona." *Saber ver lo contemporáneo del arte*, no. 22 (May–June 1995), pp. 12–75.
——. "Matisse, el conservador inspirado." *Saber ver lo contemporáneo del arte*, no. 23 (July–August 1995), pp. 8–73.
Besset, Maurice. *Art of the Twentieth Century*. London, 1976.
Besson, George. *La peinture française au XXe siècle*. Paris, 1934.
——. "Arrivée de Matisse à Nice." In "Matisse," special issue of *Le Point* (Colmar), no. 21 (July 1939), pp. 41–42. Translated as "Matisse's Arrival in "Nice," in Flam, *Matisse: A Retrospective* (1988), pp. 167–68.
——. *Matisse*. Paris, 1945. First published 1943.
——. *La peinture française au XXe siècle*. 2 vols. Paris, 1949.
——. *Matisse*. Paris, 1954. Earlier editions: 1943, 1945.
Bessonova, Marina Aleksandrovna, and Georgievskaia, Eugenia. *France, Second Half 19th–20th Century, Painting Collection: State Pushkin Museum of Fine Arts*. Moscow, 2005.
Bishop, Janet. "Sarah and Michael Stein, Matisse, and America." In *The Steins Collect: Matisse, Picasso, and the Parisian Avant-garde*, edited by Rebecca Rabinow, Janet Bishop, and Cécile Debray, pp. 129–49. Exh. cat. San Francisco, 2011.
Bjurström, Per. *Nationalmuseum, 1792–1992*. Stockholm, 1992.
Blistène, Bernard, and Lisa Dennison, eds. *Rendez-vous: Masterpieces from the Centre Georges Pompidou and the Guggenheim Museums*. Exh. cat. Paris and New York, 1998.
Blum, Shirley Neilsen. *Henri Matisse: Rooms with a View*. New York, 2010.
Bock, Catherine C. *Henri Matisse and Neo-Impressionism, 1898–1908*. Ann Arbor, 1981. Originally the author's PhD diss., UCLA, 1977.
Bock-Weiss, Catherine. *Henri Matisse: A Guide to Research*. New York and London, 1996.
Boehm, Gottfried. "Henri Matisse." In *Canto d'Amore: Classicism in Modern Art and Music, 1914–1935*, edited by Gottfried Boehm, Ulrich Mosch, and Katharina Schmidt, pp. 410–16. Exh. cat. Basel, 1996.
——. "Ausdruck und Dekoration: Henri Matisse auf dem Weg zu sich Selbst." In *Henri Matisse: Figur, Farbe, Raum*, pp. 277–89. Exh. cat. Ostfildern-Ruit, 2005.
Bois, Yve-Alain. "Henri Matisse: Dessins." *Art Press*, July 1975, pp. 18–20.
——. *Painting as Model*. Cambridge, Mass., 1990.
——. "L'aveuglement." In *Henri Matisse 1904–1917*, edited by Dominique Fourcade and Isabelle Monod-Fontaine, pp. 12–57. Exh. cat. Paris, 1993.

——. "On Matisse: The Blinding. For Leo Steinberg." Translated by Greg Sims. *October* 68 (spring 1994), pp. 60–121.
——. *Matisse and Picasso*. Published in conjunction with the exhibition "Matisse and Picasso: A Gentle Rivalry," Kimbell Art Museum, Fort Worth. New York, 1998.
——. "Matisse's 'Bathers with a Turtle.'" *Saint Louis Art Museum Bulletin* 22, no. 3 (fall 1998), pp. 8–19.
——. "Un silence de pierre: Baigneuses à la tortue (1908) de Henri Matisse." *Les Cahiers du Musée national d'art moderne*, no. 65 (fall 1998), pp. 22–37.
——. "A De luxe Experiment: Le Luxe, II." In Dorthe Aagesen et al., *Matisse: Masterpieces at Statens Museum for Kunst*, pp. 109–30. Copenhagen, 2005.
——. "Cézanne and Matisse: From Apprenticeship to Creative Misreading." In *Cézanne and Beyond*, pp. 103–35. Exh. cat. Philadelphia, 2009.
Bonnet, Éric, and Dominique Szymusiak. *Henri Matisse et la sensation d'espace: Actes du colloque organisé les 10 et 11 octobre 2003 au Musée Matisse, Le Cateau-Cambrésis*. Valenciennes, 2007.
Borovaia, T. A. *French Painting of the 20th Century: Pushkin Museum of Fine Arts Collection, Moscow*. In English and Russian. Leningrad, 1972.
Boutilier, Alicia, ed. *Inspirational: The Collection of H. S. Southam*. Exh. cat. Hamilton, Ont., 2009.
Bowness, Alan. *Matisse and the Nude*. New York, 1968.
Braune, Heinz. "Zu einem Gemälde von Henri Matisse." *Genius* 2 (1920), pp. 196–98.
Brenson, Michael. "Met Museum Given Major Private Collection." *New York Times*, August 25, 1982, p. A1.
Breshko-Breshkovskii, Nikolai. "The Salon." *Birzhevye vedomosti* [Stock Exchange Gazette], April 21, 1910. English translation in Dorontchenkov, *Russian and Soviet Views of Modern Western Art* (2009), p. 100.
Brettell, Richard R., and Stephen F. Eisenman, eds. *Nineteenth-Century Art in the Norton Simon Museum*. Vol. 1. New Haven, 2006.
Brill, Frederick. *Matisse*. London, 1967.
Brodskaya, Natalia. *The Fauves: The Hermitage, St. Petersburg, the Pushkin Museum of Fine Arts, Moscow*. Bournemouth, 1995.
Brooke, Rupert. In *Cambridge Magazine*, November 23, 1912, pp. 125–26. Reprinted in Bullen, *Post-Impressionists in England* (1988), p. 405.
Brown, J. N. "Matisse Exhibition." *Bulletin of the Rhode Island School of Design* 20 (January 1932), pp. 3–5.
Brown, Milton W. *The Story of the Armory Show*. 2nd ed. New York, 1988. First published Greenwich, Conn., 1963.
Buck, Robert T. Jr. "The Ocean Park Paintings." In *Richard Diebenkorn: Paintings and Drawings, 1943–1976*, pp. 42–49. Exh. cat. Buffalo, 1976.
Bullen, J. B., ed. *Post-Impressionists in England*. London and New York, 1988.
Bulliet, C. J. "Around the Galleries: Matisse 'Thrillers' of 1910." *Chicago Daily News*, April 1, 1939, p. 25.
Buschhoff, Anne. "'Der grosse Stil der Form verlangt auch einen grossen Stil der Farbe': Stilleben mit Früchten, Blumenstücke und Figurendarstellungen vor Blumengrund." In *Paula Modersohn-Becker und die Kunst in Paris um 1900: Von Cézanne bis Picasso*, pp. 192–204. Exh. cat. Munich, 2007.
Büttner, Philippe. "Sans visage dans un intérieur: Un leitmotiv de Matisse, entre surface et représentation." In *Henri Matisse: Figure, couleur, espace*, pp. 19–23. Exh. cat. Basel, 2006.
Cachin, Françoise. *Paul Signac*. Paris, 1971.
——. "C'est l'éden retrouvé." In *Méditerranée de Courbet à Matisse*, pp. 17–108. Exh. cat. Paris, 2000.
——. "Néo-impressionnisme et fauvism." In *Le néo-impressionnisme de Seurat à Paul Klee*, pp. 82–93. Exh. cat. Paris, 2005.
[Caffin, Charles H.]. "The International—Yes—But Matisse and Picabia? Work of Leading Spirits in Modern Movement is Discussed in Contrast." *New York American*, March 3, 1913, p. 8.
——. "Matisse's Career Is Shown in Representative Exhibition." *New York American*, January 25, 1915, p. 8.
Cahiers d'art. C. A. "L'art moderne français dans les collections des musées étrangers, I: Musée d'Art Moderne Occidental à Moscou." *Cahiers d'art* 25, no. 2 (1950), pp. 334–48.
Campaux, François, dir. *Un grand peintre français: Henri Matisse*. N.p.: La Compagnie Générale Cinématographique, 1946. 16-mm, black-and-white film, 25 min. Four excerpts are available online at http://www.artic.edu/aic/exhibitions/matisse/video1mat.html.
Canaday, John. *Mainstreams of Modern Art*. New York, 1959.
——. "Art: Museum Stresses Early Matisse: 40 of Show's 64 Items Are Youthful Works." *New York Times*, July 19, 1966, p. 35.
Carbone, Teresa A. "Body Language: Liberation and Restraint in Twenties Figuration." In *Youth and Beauty: Art of the American Twenties*, edited by Teresa A. Carbone, pp. 15–111. Exh. cat. New York and Brooklyn, 2011.
Carco, Francis. "Souvenir d'atelier: Conversation avec Matisse" (1941). *Die Kunst-Zeitung* (Zürich) 8 (August 1943). Reprinted in Carco, *L'ami des peintres* (1944). Translated in Flam, *Matisse on Art* (1995), pp. 132–42.
——. *L'ami des peintres: Souvenirs*. Geneva, 1944. 2nd ed. Paris, 1953.
——. "Conversations avec Matisse." In Francis Carco, *L'ami des peintres: Souvenirs*, pp. 251–76. Geneva, 1944.
Carey, Martha, and Sarah Martin. *The Phillips Collection: A Summary Catalogue*. Washington, D.C., 1985.
Carlson, Victor I. *Matisse as a Draughtsman*. Exh. cat. Baltimore, 1971.
——. *Matisse Drawings*. Boston, 1975.
Carnielli, Alessandra, and Margaret Loudon. "Chronology." In *Pierre Matisse and His Artists*. Exh. cat. New York, 2002.
Carrà, Massimo, and Xavier Deryng. *Tout l'oeuvre peint de Matisse, 1904–1928*. Introduction by Pierre Schneider; translated by Simone Darses. Paris, 1982. Rev. ed. of Luzi and Carrà, *L'opera di Matisse* (1971).
[Cary, Elizabeth Luther]. "The World of Art: Modern Art of One Kind and Another." *New York Times,* January 27, 1924, pp. SM10–11.
Caspers, Frank. "Philadelphia Honors Henri Matisse with Impressive Retrospective." *Art Digest* 22, no. 14 (April 15, 1948), pp. 9, 34.
Cassou, Jean. *Matisse*. Couleurs des maîtres, 1. Paris, 1939. Eng. ed.: *Paintings and Drawings of Matisse*. Paris and New York, 1939.
——. *Matisse*. London, 1948.
——. *Matisse: The Faber Gallery*. London, 1958.
——. "Une homme de lumière" and "Le Grand Palais Salle par Salle." In "Spécial Matisse," *Figaro littéraire* 48, no. 2222 (April 23, 1970), pp. B1, B2, C17.
Cassou, Jean, Bernard Dorival, and Geneviève Homolle. *Catalogue-Guide: Musée National d'Art Moderne*. 2nd ed. Paris, 1950.
——. *Catalogue-guide, Musée national d'art moderne*. Paris, 1954.
Cauman, John. "Henri Matisse's Letters to Walter Pach." *Archives of American Art Journal* 31, no. 3 (1991), pp. 2–14.
——. "Matisse and America, 1905–1933." 2 vols. PhD diss., City University of New York, 2000.
Chalumeau, Jean-Luc. *Fauvisme*. Paris, 2004.
Chapon, François. *Mystère et splendeurs de Jacques Doucet, 1853–1929*. Paris, 1984.
——. *C'était Jacques Doucet*. Paris, 2006.
Chassé, Charles. *Les Fauves et leur temps*. Paris, 1963.
de Chassey, Eric. "Signac und die 'Fauves.'" In *Farben des Lichts: Paul Signac und der Beginn der Moderne von Matisse bis Mondrian*, pp. 143–77. Exh. cat. Ostfildern, 1996.
Chastel, André. "Le grand été de Matisse." *Le Monde*, July 28, 1956, p. 7.
Childs, Elizabeth C., and John Klein. "Oceanic Escapes: Travel, Memory and Decoration in the Art of Matisse." In *Matisse*, edited by Caroline Turner and Roger Benjamin, pp. 122–35. Exh. cat. Brisbane, 2005.
Choffel, Dominique, and Véronique Sulzer, eds. "La chronique des arts: Principales acquisitions des musées en 1985." *Gazette des beaux-arts* 57 (March 1986), suppl. pp. 1–57.

Chroniques du jour. "Pour ou contre Henri-Matisse: Enquête, opinions, documents." *Chroniques du jour* 2, no. 9 (April 1931).

The Chrysler Museum: Selections from the Permanent Collection. Norfolk, Va., 1982.

City Art Museum of Saint Louis. *Handbook of the Collections: The City Art Museum of St. Louis*. Saint Louis, 1953.

Cocteau, Jean. "Matisse et Picasso." *Le Matin* (Antwerp), May 16, 1963.

Collection de la "Peau de l'Ours": Oeuvres de Bernard, Bonnard, Cross, Denis, Derain, Van Dongen, Dufrenoy, Filiger, Flandrin, Forain, R. de la Fresnaye, Friesz, Gauguin, Girieud, Van Gogh, Grass-Mick, Guys, Henri-Matisse, Herbin, Hervier, Lacoste, Laprade, Marie Laurencin, Maillol, Manguin, Marquet, Mme. Marval, Metzinger, Picasso, Puy, Ranson, Od. Redon, Rouault, Roussel, Dunoyer de Segonzac, Seruzier, Signac, Utrillo, Vallotton, Verhoeven, de Vlaminck, Vuillard etc. Sale cat., Hôtel Drouot, Paris, February 28–March 1, 1914.

Columbus Museum of Art. *Catalog of the Collection*. Columbus, Ohio, 1978.

Cone, Etta. *The Cone Collection of Baltimore, Maryland: Catalogue of Paintings, Drawings, Sculpture of the Nineteenth and Twentieth Centuries*. Baltimore, 1934.

Conil Lacoste, Michel. "À Henri Matisse: Les éblouissements raisonnés du peintre." *Le Monde*, April 23, 1970, p. 17.

Conzen, Ina. "The True Image: On Spirituality in Henri Matisse's Portraits." In *Matisse: People, Masks, Models*, pp. 12–35. Exh. cat. Munich, 2008.

Cook, Christopher. "Rhythm Kings." *Tate: The Art Magazine*, no. 29 (summer 2002), pp. 30–31.

Cooper, Douglas, "Catalogue of the Courtauld Collection." *Burlington Magazine* 96 (April 1954), pp. 119–22.

——. *Cubist Epoch*. London and Los Angeles, 1971.

Coret, Nöel. *Fauvisme: La couleur en heritage*. Paris, 2005.

C[ortissoz], R[oyal]. "The Post-Impressionist and Cubist Vagaries." *New York Tribune*, February 23, 1913, section 2, p. 6.

Courthion, Pierre. "La collection Arthur Hahnloser." *L'Amour de l'art* 7 (1926), pp. 62–68.

——. *Panorama de la peinture française contemporaine*. 5th ed. Paris, 1927.

——. *Henri-Matisse*. Paris, 1934.

——. *Le visage de Matisse*. Lausanne, 1942.

——. "La conquête de la lumière." In "Hommage à Henri Matisse," special issue of *XX*[e] *siècle*, edited by Gualtieri Di San Lazzaro, pp. 51–62. Paris, 1970. Also English ed.

——. "Matisse et la danse." In "Hommage à Henri Matisse," special issue of *XX*[e] *siècle*, edited by Gualtieri Di San Lazzaro, pp. 45–49. Paris, 1970. Also English ed.

Cousins, Judith, and Hélène Seckel. "Éléments pour une chronologie de l'histoire des *Demoiselles d'Avignon*." In *Les Demoiselles d'Avignon*, vol. 2. Exh. cat. Paris, 1988.

——. "Chronology of *Les Demoiselles d'Avignon*, 1907 to 1939." In *Les Demoiselles d'Avignon*, by William Rubin, Hélène Seckel, and Judith Cousins. Studies in Modern Art, 3. New York, 1994.

Cowart, Jack. "The Place of Silvered Light: An Expanded, Illustrated Chronology of Matisse in the South of France, 1916–1932." In Jack Cowart and Dominique Fourcade, *Henri Matisse: The Early Years in Nice, 1916–1930*, pp. 15–45. Exh. cat. Washington, D.C., 1986.

Cowart, Jack, et al. *Matisse in Morocco: Paintings and Drawings, 1912–1913*. Exh. cat. Washington, D.C., 1990.

Cowart, Jack, Jack Flam, Dominique Fourcade, and John H. Neff. *Henri Matisse: Paper Cut-outs*. Exh. cat. Saint Louis, 1977.

Cowart, Jack, and Dominique Fourcade. *Henri Matisse: The Early Years in Nice, 1916–1930*. Exh. cat. Washington, D.C., 1986.

Cowling, Elizabeth, et al. *Matisse, Picasso*. Exh. cat. London, 2002.

Craven, Thomas. "Living Art." *Dial* 76 (February 1924), pp. 180–83.

——. "Henri Matisse." *Dial* 76 (May 1924), pp. 404–6.

Creative Art. Anonymous. "The Art Market." *Creative Art* 7 (November 1930), supplement, pp. 65–70.

Crespelle, Jean-Paul. *Les Fauves*. Neuchâtel, 1962.

Cunningham, Charles C., et al. *Instituto de Arte de Chicago*. Buenos Aires, 1967.

Curuz, Maurizio Bernadelli. "Matisse e gli archetipi del codice Michelangelo." In *Matisse: La seduzione di Michelangelo,* edited by Claudia Beltramo Ceppi Zevi, pp. 338–42. Exh. cat. Florence, 2011.

Daix, Pierre. *Cubists and Cubism*. Translated by R. F. M. Dexter. New York, 1982.

——. *La grande histoire de la peinture moderne*. Vol. 2, *Le temps des revolutions, 1900–1914: Fauvism, expressionism, cubism, futurism*. Edited by Jean-Luc Daval. Paris, 1982.

D'Alessandro, Stephanie. "The Challenge of Painting." In D'Alessandro and Elderfield, *Matisse: Radical Invention*, pp. 262–69. Chicago, 2010.

——. "Interruptions and Returns." In D'Alessandro and Elderfield, *Matisse: Radical Invention*, pp. 222–31. Chicago, 2010.

D'Alessandro, Stephanie, and John Elderfield. *Matisse: Radical Invention 1913–1917*. Exh. cat. Chicago, 2010.

Danneskjold-Samsøe, Sophus. "Fransk kunst i København i efteraaret 1918." *Vor Tid* (1918), pp. 849–55.

Dauberville, Guy-Patrice, and Michel Dauberville. *Matisse: Henri Matisse chez Bernheim-Jeune*. 2 vols. Paris, 1995.

Daval, Jean-Luc. *Journal de l'art moderne, 1884–1914*. Geneva, 1973.

Davidson, Martha. "Matisse's Allegory of the Dance." *Art News* 35, no. 6 (November 7, 1936), pp. 13–14.

——. "The Magic Color of Matisse." *Art News* 35, no. 10 (December 5, 1936), pp. 14, 21.

Degand, Léon. "Matisse à Paris." *Les Lettres françaises* 6 (October 1945), pp. 1, 4. Translated in Flam, *Matisse on Art* (1995), pp. 159–65.

Delectorskaya, Lydia. *L'apparente facilité . . . Henri Matisse: Peintures de 1935–1939*. Paris, 1986.

——. *With Apparent Ease . . . Henri Matisse: Paintings from 1935–1939*. Translated by Olga Tourkoff. Paris, 1988.

——. "'Thèmes et Variations', Album didactique de Henri Matisse." In *Henri Matisse: Zeichnungen und Gouaches découpées*, pp. 135–36. Exh. cat. Stuttgart, 1993.

——. *Henri Matisse: Contre vents et marées: Peinture et livres illustrés de 1939 à 1943*. Introduction by Isabelle Monod-Fontaine. Paris, 1996.

Denis, Maurice. "La réaction nationaliste." *L'Ermitage*, May 15, 1905. Reprinted in Maurice Denis, *Théories, 1890–1910: Du symbolism et de Gauguin vers un nouvel ordre classique*, pp. 187–98. Paris, 1920.

Di Capua, Marco, and Lea Mattarella. "Il corpo in una stanza." In *Matisse e Bonnard: Viva la pittura!*, pp. 107–17. Exh. cat. Milan, 2006.

Diehl, Gaston. *H. Matisse*. Paris, 1970.

——. *The Fauves*. New York, 1975.

Diehl, Gaston, and Agnès Humbert. *Henri Matisse*. Paris, 1954.

——. *Henri Matisse*. Paris and New York, 1958.

Dittière, Monique. "Henri Matisse; ou, Le bonheur de vivre." *L'Aurore*, April 22, 1970, p. 16.

Dittmann, Lorenz. *Matisse begegnet Bergson: Reflexionen zu Kunst und Philosophie*. Cologne, 2008.

Dolz, Michele. *Lo spendore delle cose: Appunti di arte e di spirito*. Milan, 2001.

Domino, Christophe. *Matisse et le Maroc*. Paris, 1999.

Dorival, Bernard. "Musée d'Art Moderne: Peintures de maîtres contemporains." *Bulletin des musées de France* 11 (April 1946), pp. 15–20.

——. "Musée d'Art Moderne: Trois mois d'activité (Octobre–Novembre 1948)." *Musées de France*, no. 6 (July–August 1949), pp. 154–61.

——. "Chronique de l'art ancien et moderne: Le XXe siècle." *La Revue des arts* 2 (December 1952), pp. 252–55.

——. *Twentieth Century Painters*. Vol. 1, *Nabis, Fauves, Cubists*. Translated by W. J. Strachan. New York, [1958]. French ed.: Paris, 1957.

——. *L'École de Paris au Musée National d'Art Moderne*. Paris, 1961.

Dorontchenkov, Ilia ed. *Russian and Soviet Views of Modern Western Art: 1890s to Mid-1930s*. Translated by Charles Rougle. Berkeley, 2009.

Dorr, Charles Henry. "Cubists and Futurists Have Reached America." *World*, February 23, 1913, sect. 2, p. 2.

Dresser, Louisa. In *The Dial and the Dial Collection*. Exh. cat. Worcester, 1959.

Ducrey, Marina, and Guy Ducrey. *La Galerie Paul Vallotton depuis 1913*. Lausanne, 1988.
Dumas, Ann, ed. *Matisse, His Art and His Textiles: The Fabric of Dreams*. Exh. cat. London, 2004.
Durozoi, Gérard. *Matisse*. Translated by John Greaves. London, 1993.
Duthuit, Claude, et al. *Matisse: "La révélation m'est venue de l'Orient."* Exh. cat. Florence, 1997.
Duthuit, Claude, and Marie-Thérèse Pulvénis de Séligny. *Matisse en France*. Exh. cat. Paris, 2004.
Duthuit, Georges. "Le fauvisme." *Cahiers d'art* 4, no. 10 (1929), pp. 429–35.
——. *Les Fauves: Braque, Derain, Van Dongen, Dufy, Friesz, Manguin, Marguet, Matisse, Puy, Vlaminck*. Geneva, 1949.
——. *Matisse: Période fauve*. Paris, 1956. Eng. ed.: *Matisse: Fauve Period*. New York, 1956.
——. *Écrits sur Matisse*. Edited by Rémi Labrusse. Paris, 1992.
Earle, Peggy. *Legacy: Walter Chrysler Jr. and the Untold Story of Norfolk's Chrysler Museum of Art*. Charlottesville and London, 2008.
Einstein, Carl. *Die Kunst des 20. Jahrhunderts*. Berlin, 1926.
Eisendrath, William N., Jr. "The Washington University Collections." *Art Journal* 23 (summer 1964), pp. 292–94, 296.
Elderfield, John. *The "Wild Beasts": Fauvism and Its Affinities*. Exh. cat. New York, 1976.
——. *Matisse in the Collection of the Museum of Modern Art, Including Remainder-Interest and Promised Gifts*. Additional texts by William S. Lieberman and Riva Castleman. New York, 1978.
——. *The Drawings of Henri Matisse*. Catalogue entries by Magdalena Dabrowski. Exh. cat. New York, 1984.
——. "Matisse in Morocco: An Interpretive Guide." In Jack Cowart et al., *Matisse in Morocco: The Paintings and Drawings, 1912–1913*, pp. 201–39. Exh. cat. Washington, D.C., 1990.
——. *Henri Matisse: A Retrospective*. Exh. cat. New York, 1992.
——. *Pleasuring Painting: Matisse's Feminine Representations*. London, 1995.
——. *Henri Matisse: Masterworks from The Museum of Modern Art*. Exh. cat. New York, 1996.
——. "Moving Aphrodite: On the Genesis of 'Bathers with a Turtle' by Henri Matisse." *Saint Louis Art Museum Bulletin* 22, no. 3 (fall 1998), pp. 20–49.
——. "Matisse au Maroc: Guide d'interprétation." In *Matisse au Maroc: Peintures et dessins, 1912–1913*, pp. 187–225. Paris, 1999. Translation of 1990 essay.
——. "Drawings at an Exhibition." In *Matisse*, edited by Caroline Turner and Roger Benjamin, pp. 52–69. Exh. cat. Brisbane, 2005.
——. "Construction by Means of Color." In Stephanie D'Alessandro and John Elderfield. *Matisse: Radical Invention*, pp. 108–19. Exh. cat., Chicago, 2010.
——. "La seduzione della pittura: Rappresentazioni femminili in Matisse." In *Matisse: La seduzione di Michelangelo*, edited by Claudia Beltramo Ceppi Zevi, pp. 308–35. Exh. cat. Florence, 2011.
Elderfield, John, Beatrice Kernan, and Judith Cousins. "Plates and Chronology." In *Henri Matisse: A Retrospective*, pp. 79–469. Exh. cat. New York, 1992.
Elliott, Patrick. "Il Fauvismo e il Midi." In *L'oro e l'azzurro: I colori del Sud da Cézanne a Bonnard*, edited by Marco Goldin, pp. 221–32. Exh. cat. Conegliano, 2003.
Elsen, Albert Edward. *The Sculpture of Henri Matisse*. New York, 1972.
Escholier, Raymond. *Henri Matisse*. Paris, 1937.
——. *Matisse, ce vivant*. Paris, 1956.
——. "Matisse et le Maroc." *Le Jardin des arts* 24 (October 1956), pp. 705–12.
——. *Matisse: A Portrait of the Artist and the Man*. New York, 1960.
Essers, Volkmar. *Henri Matisse, 1869–1954: Master of Colour*. Cologne, 2002.
——. "Eine schöpferische Selbstbefragung: Das Bild eigener Werke im Bild." In "Kunstsammlung Nordrhein-Westfalen, Düsseldorf," *Vernissage: Die Zeitschrift zur Ausstellung* 13, no. 16 (2005), pp. 20–27.
Essers, Volkmar, et al. *Einblicke: Das 20. Jahrhundert in der Kunstsammlung Nordrhein-Westfalen, Düsseldorf*. Düsseldorf, 2000.
——. *K20, K21: Kunstsammlung Nordrhein-Westfalen*. Munich, 2003.
Esteban, Claude. "Une limpidité nécessaire." *Nouvelle Revue française* 18, no. 211 (July 1970), pp. 72–77.
Fagioli, Marco. "Henri Matisse, pittore e scultore." In *Matisse: La seduzione di Michelangelo*, edited by Claudia Beltramo Ceppi Zevi, pp. 34–93. Exh. cat. Florence, 2011.
Faider-Thomas, Thérèse. *Anna Boch und Eugène Boch: Werke aus den Anfängen der modernen Kunst*. Exh. cat. Mettlach, 1971.
Faure, Élie, Jules Romains, Charles Vildrac, and Léon Werth. *Henri Matisse*. Paris, 1920.
Feldstein, Janice J., ed. *The Art Institute of Chicago: 100 Masterpieces*. Chicago, 1978.
Fels, Florent. *Henri-Matisse*. Paris, 1929.
Fergonzi, Flavio. "Firenze 1910–Venezia 1920: Emilio Cecchi, i quadri francesi e le difficoltà dell'impressionismo." *Bollettino d'arte*, ser. 6, no. 79 (May–June 1993), pp. 1–26.
Fermigier, André. "Un barbare exquis." *Le Nouvel Observateur*, April 20–26, 1970, pp. 40–42.
——. "Matisse à Marseille." *Le Monde*, July 10, 1974, p. 1.
——. "Matisse à la Villa Medicis: Le faune et le lion." *Le Monde*, January 4, 1979, p. 11.
Ferretti Bocquillon, Marina. "Matisse et le néo-impressionnisme: 'Extirper tout ce que la division du ton avait dans la peau.'" In *Henri Matisse: Émerveillement pour le sud*, edited by Jean-Paul Monery, pp. 31–43. Exh. cat. Saint-Tropez, 2004.
Ferrier, Jean-Louis. *Matisse, 1911–1930*. Paris, 1961.
——. "1907: 'Immensité intime' et simplification du tableau." In "Hommage à Henri Matisse," special issue of *XXe siècle*, edited by Gualtieri Di San Lazzaro, pp. 39–43. Paris, 1970. Also English ed.
——. *Les Fauves: Le règne de la couleur*. Paris, 1992.
Fiala, Vlastimil. *Henri Matisse*. Prague, 1967.
Fineberg, Jonathan. "The Innocent Eye." *Art News* 94 (April 1995), pp. 118–25.
——. *The Innocent Eye: Children's Art and the Modern Artist*. Princeton, 1997.
Finsen, Hanne. "Kapellet i Vence." *Aarstiderne* 9 (1951), pp. 58–64.
——. *Moderne udenlandsk kunst: J. Rumps samling, etc., Statens Museum for Kunst*. 4th ed. Copenhagen, 1964. First published 1958.
——. *Matisse: En retrospektiv udstilling*. Exh. cat. Copenhagen, 1970.
——. *Matisse, Rouveyre Correspondance*. Paris, 2001.
——, ed. *Matisse: A Second Life*. Exh. cat. Paris, 2005.
FitzGerald, Michael C. *Making Modernism: Picasso and the Creation of the Market for Twentieth-Century Art*. New York, 1995.
Flam, Jack. *The Norton Matisses: The Rose, Lorette, Two Rays*. Norton Gallery Studies 2. Palm Beach, 1973.
——, ed. *Matisse on Art*. New York, 1973; New York 1978. Rev. ed., 1995.
——. "Jazz." In *Henri Matisse: Paper Cut-outs*, pp. 37–47. Exh. cat. Saint Louis, 1977.
——. "Matisse in Morocco." *Connoisseur* 211 (August 1982), pp. 74–86.
——. "Matisse and the Fauves." In *"Primitivism" in 20th Century Art: Affinity of the Tribal and the Modern*, edited by William Rubin, vol. 1, pp. 211–39. Exh. cat. New York, 1984.
——. *Matisse: The Man and His Art, 1869–1918*. Ithaca, N.Y., and London, 1986.
——, ed. *Matisse: A Retrospective*. New York, 1988.
——. "Henri Matisse." In Richard J. Wattenmaker and Anne Distel, *Great French Paintings from the Barnes Foundation: Impressionist, Post-Impressionist, and Early Modern*, pp. 226–93. Exh. cat. New York, 1993.
——. "Matisse: Image into Sign." In *Matisse: Image into Sign*, pp. 5–13. Saint Louis, 1993.
——. *Henri Matisse, 1869–1954*. Cologne, 1994.
——. *Matisse on Art*. Rev. ed. Berkeley and Los Angeles, 1995. First published 1973.
——. *Matisse in the Cone Collection: The Poetics of Vision*. Baltimore, 2001.
——. *Matisse and Picasso: The Story of Their Rivalry and Friendship*. Cambridge, Mass., 2003.
——. "Matisse and the Metaphysics of Decoration." In *Matisse, His Art and His Textiles*, edited by Ann Dumas, pp. 34–45. Exh. cat. London, 2004.
——. "Goldfish." In Dorthe Aagesen et al., *Matisse: Masterpieces at Statens Museum for Kunst*, pp. 160–83. Copenhagen, 2005.
——. "Matisse à Collioure, evolution du style et datation des tableaux." In *Matisse–Derain: Collioure*

1905, un été fauve, pp. 30–47, 290–91. Exh. cat. Paris, 2005.
——. *Matisse in Transition: Around Laurette*. Exh. cat. West Palm Beach, 2006.
Fourcade, Dominique, ed. *Henri Matisse: Écrits et propos sur l'art*. Paris, 1972.
——, ed. "Autres propos de Matisse." *Macula* 1 (1976), pp. 92–115. Interview with Courthion on pp. 101–3.
——. "Matisse et Manet?" In Catherine David et al., *Bonjour Monsieur Manet*, pp. 25–32. Exh. cat. Paris, 1983.
——. "Crise du cadre." *Cahiers du Musée National d'Art Moderne*, no. 17 / 18 (1986), pp. 68–83.
——. "An Uninterrupted Story." In *Henri Matisse: The Early Years in Nice 1916–1930*, edited by Jack Cowart and Dominique Fourcade, pp. 47–57. Exh. cat. Washington, D.C., 1986.
——. "An Uninterrupted Story: The Work of Henri Matisse Between 1916 and 1930." In *Canto d'Amore: Classicism in Modern Art and Music, 1914–1935*, edited by Gottfried Boehm, Ulrich Mosch, and Katharina Schmidt, pp. 388–409. Exh. cat. Basel, 1996.
Fourcade, Dominique, and Eric de Chassey. "Anthologie." In *Henri Matisse, 1904–1917*, pp. 419–516. Exh. cat. Paris, 1993.
Fourcade, Dominique, and Isabelle Monod-Fontaine, eds. *Henri Matisse: Dessins et sculpture*. Exh. cat. Paris, 1975.
——, eds. *Henri Matisse 1904–1917*. Exh. cat. Paris, 1993.
Francastel, Pierre. *Histoire de la peinture française*. Vol. 2, *Du classicism au cubism*. Paris, 1955.
Frankfurter, Alfred M. "Is He the Greatest?" *Art News* 47, no. 2 (April 1948), pp. 21–22.
——. "International Report" (Matisse exhibit at the Venice Biennale). *Art News* 49, no. 5 (September 1950), pp. 5, 14–19, 57.
Franz, Erich. "Paul Signac und die Befreiung der Farbe—von Matisse bis Mondrian." In *Farben des Lichts: Paul Signac und der Beginn der Moderne von Matisse bis Mondrian*, pp. 19–50. Exh. cat. Ostfildern, 1996.
Frèches-Thory, Claire. "After 1900." In *Painting in the Musée d'Orsay*, pp. 147–57. London, 1986.
Freeman, Judi. "Documentary Chronology" and "Far from the Earth of France: The Fauves Abroad." In Judi Freeman et al., *The Fauve Landscape*, pp. 59–122, 177–214. Exh. cat. Los Angeles, 1990.
——. *Fauves*. Exh. cat. Sydney, 1995.
Freeman, Judi, et al. *The Fauve Landscape*. Exh. cat. Los Angeles, 1990.
Friis, Eva, ed. *100 Mestervoerker* [Statens Museum for Kunst]. Copenhagen, 1996.
From Poussin to Matisse: The Russian Taste for French Painting. Exh. cat. Chicago, 1990.
Frontisi, Claude G. "L'Estaque entre Cézanne et Braque: Du sujet du tableau au motif pictural." In *L'Estaque: Naissance du paysage moderne, 1870 / 1910*, pp. 84–99. Exh. cat. Marseille, 1994.
Fry, Roger. "Henri-Matisse." *Cahiers d'art* 6 (1931), pp. 283–88.
——. *Henri-Matisse*. New York, 1935.
——. "Matisse et le renouveau de l'expression plastique." In "Hommage à Henri Matisse," special issue of *XXe siècle*, edited by Gualtieri Di San Lazzaro, pp. 11–20. Paris, 1970. Also English ed.
Funch, Bjarne Sode. *The Psychology of Art Appreciation*. Copenhagen, 1997.
Galerie jardin des arts. Anonymous. "Ici commence l'art moderne." *Galerie jardin des arts*, no. 139 (July–August 1974), pp. 67–82.
Gallatin, A. E. *Gallery of Living Art: A. E. Gallatin Collection, 100 Washington Square East, New York*. Contributions by Jean Hélion, J. J. Sweeney, and George L. K. Morris. New York, 1933.
——. *Museum of Living Art: A. E. Gallatin Collection, New York University*. Contributions by Jean Hélion, J. J. Sweeney, and George L. K. Morris. New York, 1936.
——. *Museum of Living Art: A. E. Gallatin Collection, New York University*. Contributions by Jean Hélion, J. J. Sweeney, and George L. K. Morris. New York, 1940.
——. *A. E. Gallatin Collection: "Museum of Living Art."* Philadelphia, 1954.
G[ardiner], H[enry] G. "Henri Matisse . . . *Still Life on Table, 1925*." In "A Selection of Works Given to the Museum," *Philadelphia Museum of Art Bulletin* 60, no. 283–84 (winter 1965), p. 7.
Gaussen, Frédéric. *Le 5e arrondissement vu par les peintres*. Paris, 1998.
Gazette de l'Hôtel Drouot. "Revue des ventes: Collections de la 'Peau de l'Ours.'" *Gazette de l'Hôtel Drouot* 23, no. 26 (March 3, 1914), n.p.
——. "Collection Jules Chavasse." *Gazette de l'Hôtel Drouot* 81, no. 75 (June 24, 1922), n.p.
Gee, Malcolm. *Dealers, Critics, and Collectors of Modern Painting: Aspects of the Parisian Art Market Between 1910 and 1930*. New York, 1981. Originally the author's thesis, University of London, 1977.
George, Waldemar. *La grande peinture contemporaine à la collection Paul Guillaume*. Paris, [1929].
——. "Psychanalyse de Matisse—Lettre à Raymond Cogniat." *Chroniques du jour*, no. 9 (April 1931), pp. 6–8.
——. "Dualité de Matisse." *Formes*, no. 16 (June 1931), pp. 94–95.
Georges-Michel, Michel. "Tra Fauves e Cubisti." *La Biennale di Venezia*, no. 2 (October 1950), pp. 9–10.
Gil Blas. Anonymous. "L'Exposition postexpressioniste à la Grafton Gallery de Londres." *Gil Blas*, October 4, 1912.
Gilot, Françoise. "Événement: Matisse / Picasso." *Beaux-Arts*, no. 220 (September 2002), pp. 48–57.
Girard, Xavier. *Matisse: Photographies*. Exh. cat., Musée des Beaux-Arts, Jules Chéret. Nice, 1986.
——. *Les chefs-d'oeuvre du Musée Matisse, Nice, Cimiez*. Exh. cat. Musée des Beaux-Arts de Dijon. Dijon, 1991.
——. *Matisse: "Une splendeur inouïe."* Paris, 1993.
——. *Matisse: Le grand atelier, 1935–1948*. Cahiers Henri Matisse, no. 12. Exh. cat. Nice, 1994.
——. *Matisse in Nice, 1917–1954*. London, 1996.
——. "Matisse und der Tanz." In *Tanz in der Moderne: Von Matisse bis Schlemmer*. Exh. cat. Cologne, 1996.
——. *Matisse: "Une splendeur inouïe."* Rev. ed. Paris, 2008.
Giraudy, Danièle. "Correspondance Henri Matisse–Charles Camoin." *Revue de l'art*, no. 12 (1971), pp. 7–34.
Girieud, Maxime. "Au Salon des Indépendants." *Le Soir*, April 11, 1905, p. 1. Reprinted in Fourcade and de Chassey, "Anthologie" (1993), pp. 419–20.
Giry, Marcel. *Le fauvisme: Ses origines, son évolution*. Neuchâtel, 1981.
——. *Fauvism: Origins and Development*. New York, 1982.
Gloor, Lukas, and Marco Goldin, eds. *Foundation E. G. Bührle Collection, Zürich: Catalogue*. 3 vols. Conegliano, 2003–5. German ed.: *Stiftung Sammlung E. G. Bührle, Zürich: Katalog*. 3rd ed. 3 vols. Conegliano, 2003–5. Italian ed.: *La Fondazione Collezione E. G. Bührle a Zurigo: Catalogo delle opere*. 3rd ed. 3 vols. Conegliano, 2003–5.
Golan, Romy. *Modernity and Nostalgia: Art and Politics in France between the Wars*. New Haven, 1995.
Goldin, Marco, ed. *L'oro e l'azzurro: I colori del Sud da Cézanne a Bonnard*. Exh. cat. Conegliano, 2003.
Golding, John. *W. A. Cargill Memorial Lectures in Fine Arts: Matisse and Cubism*. Glasgow, 1978.
Golson, L. M. "The Michael Steins of San Francisco: Art Patrons and Collectors." In *Four Americans in Paris: The Collections of Gertrude Stein and Her Family*, pp. 35–49. Exh. cat. New York, 1970.
Gordon, Donald E. *Modern Art Exhibitions 1900–1916: Selected Catalogue Documentation*. 2 vols. Munich, 1974.
Gosling, Nigel. *Paris, 1900–1914: The Miraculous Years*. London, 1978.
Gottlieb, Carla. "The Role of the Window in the Art of Matisse." *Journal of Aesthetics and Art Criticism* 22, no. 4 (summer 1964), pp. 393–423.
Gottlieb, Lennart. "Tetzen-Lunds samling: Om dens historie indhold og betydning." *Kunst og museum* 19 (1984), pp. 18–49.
——, ed. *Johannes Rump: Portræt af en samler*. Exh. cat. Copenhagen, 1994.
Goudy, Alice M. "Four Collectors in Philadelphia." *Artnews* 49 (summer 1950), pp. 28–31, 65–66.
Gowing, Lawrence. *Henri Matisse: 64 Paintings*. Exh. cat. New York, 1966.
——. *Matisse, 1869–1954: A Retrospective Exhibition*. Exh. cat. London, 1968.
——. *Matisse*. World of Art series. New York, 1979.

——. *Matisse: The Harmony of Light.* Medaenas Monographs on the Arts. New York, 1979.
——. "The Modern Vision." In *Places of Delight: The Pastoral Landscape*, pp. 182–248. Exh. cat. Washington, D.C., 1988.
——. "Bonnard and the School of Paris in the Gelman Collection." In Sabine Rewald et al., *Twentieth-Century Modern Masters: The Jacques and Natasha Gelman Collection,* pp. 18–23. Exh. cat. New York, 1989.
Grammont, Claudine, ed. *Correspondance entre Charles Camoin et Henri Matisse*. Lausanne, 1997.
——. "Matisse aux portes de l'Orient: Une chronique." In *Le Maroc de Matisse*, pp. 228–35. Exh. cat. Paris, 1999.
——. "'L'attitude lyrique contemporaine': Les fauves et le milieu néo-symboliste." In *Éclats du fauvisme*, pp. 31–38. Exh. cat. Saint-Tropez, 2005.
——. "Chronologie. L'atelier du sud: Henri Matisse à Collioure 1905–1914." In *Matisse–Derain: Collioure 1905, un été fauve*, pp. 270–88, 292–93. Exh. cat. Paris, 2005.
——. "Matisse as Religion: The 'Mike Steins' and Matisse, 1908–1918." In *The Steins Collect: Matisse, Picasso, and the Parisian Avant-garde*, edited by Rebecca Rabinow, Janet Bishop, and Cécile Debray, pp. 151–65. Exh. cat. San Francisco, 2011.
Greeley-Smith, Nixola. "An Alienist Will Charge You $5,000 to Tell You If You're Crazy; Go to the Cubist Show and You'll Be Sure of It for a Quarter." *Evening World*, February 22, 1913, p. 5 (caricature).
Green, Christopher. *Art in France: 1900–1940*. New Haven, 2000.
Greenberg, Clement. "Review of an Exhibition of Henri Matisse" (Paris 1949). *The Nation*, March 5, 1949. pp. 284–85. Reprinted in *Clement Greenberg: The Collected Essays and Criticism,* vol. 2, edited by John O'Brian, pp. 293–94. Chicago, 1986.
——. *Henri Matisse (1869–1954)*. New York, 1955. First published 1953.
——. "Influences of Matisse." *Art International* 17 (November 1973), pp. 28–31, 39.
——. "Matisse in 1966." *Boston Museum Bulletin* 64, no. 336 (1966), pp. 66–76.
Greentree Foundation Sale. *Property of the Greentree Foundation from the Collection of Mr. & Mrs. John Hay Whitney, Impressionist & Modern Art*. Sale, Sotheby's, New York, May 5, 2004.
Gregg, Frederick James. "From Courbet to Matisse in One Art Exhibition." *New York Herald*, November 23, 1919, sec. 3, p. 10.
Grohé, Stefan. "Körperbeherrschung: Der Maler Matisse zitiert den Bildhauer Matisse." In *Henri Matisse: Figur, Farbe, Raum*, pp. 305–10. Exh. cat. Ostfildern-Ruit, 2005.
Gros, G. J. "Henri Matisse." *Cahiers d'art* 2, nos. 7–8 (1927), suppl. pp. 268–74.
Grünewald, Isaac. *Matisse och Expressionismen*. Stockholm, 1944.
Guadagnini, Walter. *Matisse*. Translated by Richard Pierce. Milan and New York, 1993.
Guenne, Jacques. "Le XXe Salon d'Automne." *L'Art vivant* 3 (November 1927), pp. 865–73.
Guichard-Meili, Jean. *Matisse.* Translated by Caroline Moorehead. New York, 1967. French ed.: *Henri Matisse: Son oeuvre, son univers*. Paris, 1967.
——. "Les odalisques." In "Hommage à Henri Matisse," special issue of *XXe siècle*, edited by Gualtieri Di San Lazzaro, pp. 63–69. Paris, 1970. Also English ed.
——. *Matisse.* Paris, 1986.
Guillaud, Jacqueline, and Maurice Guillaud. *Matisse, Rhythm and Line*. Translated by Jack Flam, Timothy Bent, and Eleanor Levieux. Paris and New York, 1987. French ed.: *Matisse: Le rythme et la ligne*. Paris and New York, 1987.
Günther, Herbert. *Akkorde der Palette:10 grosse franz. Maler*. Munich, 1972.
Haftmann, Werner. *Painting in the Twentieth Century*. Translated by Ralph Manheim. Rev. ed. 2 vols. New York, 1961.
——. *Malerei im 20. Jahrhundert: Eine Bild-Enzyklopädie*. Munich, 1965. Earlier eds.: Munich, 1954–55, 1957.
Hahnloser-Ingold, Margrit. "Collecting Matisses of the 1920s in the 1920s." In Jack Cowart and Dominique Fourcade, *Henri Matisse: Early Years in Nice*, pp. 235–74. Exh. cat. Washington, D.C., 1986.
Hahnloser-Ingold, Margrit, et al. *The Arthur and Hedy Hahnloser Collection: An Eye for Art Shared with Artists*. Translated by Jean-Marie Clarke. New York, 2011.
Halvorsen, Walther. "The Kunstnerforbundet's Exhibition of French Modern Art [in Oslo] in 1916." *Aftenposten*, December 14, 1959.
Harrison, Jefferson C. *French Paintings from the Chrysler Museum.* Exh. cat. Norfolk, Va., 1986.
——. *The Chrysler Museum Handbook of the European and American Collections: Selected Paintings, Sculpture, and Drawings*. Norfolk, Va., 1991.
——. *Collecting with Vision: Treasures from the Chrysler Museum of Art*. London, 2007.
Hauptman, William. "Notre-Dame de Paris." In *Dübi-Müller-Stiftung, Josef Müller-Stiftung*, pp. 156–57. Kataloge Schweizer Museen und Sammlungen, vol. 6. Solothurn, 1981.
Häuser, Henrik. "Ein dänischer Sammler." *Der Cicerone* 10 (May 1918), pp. 159–67.
Herbert, James D. "Painters and Tourists: Matisse and Derain on the Mediterranean Shore." In Judi Freeman et al., *The Fauve Landscape*, pp. 153–76. Exh. cat. Los Angeles, 1990.
——. *Fauve Painting: The Making of Cultural Politics*. New Haven, 1992.
——. "Reconsiderations of Matisse and Derain in the Classical Landscape." In *Framing France: The Representation of Landscape in France, 1870–1914*, edited by Richard Thomson, pp. 173–93. Exh. cat. Manchester, 1998.
The Hermitage. *Otdel Zapadnoevropeiskogo iskusstva: Katalogu zhivopisi* [The Department of Western European Art: Catalogue of paintings]. Vol. 1. Leningrad and Moscow, 1958.
Herrera, Hayden. *Matisse: A Portrait*. New York, 1993.
Hess, Thomas B. "Matisse: A Life of Color." *Art News* 47, no. 2 (April 1948), pp. 16–19, 56–58.
Hind, Charles Lewis. "Ideals of Post-Impressionism." *Daily Chronicle*, October 5, 1912, p. 6. Reprinted in *Post-Impressionists in England*, edited by J. B. Bullen, pp. 365–68. London, 1988.
——. *Art and I.* New York and London, 1921.
Hintze, Bertel. *Modern konst: 1900–talet*. Helsinki, 1930.
Hirschland, Ellen B., and Nancy Hirschland Ramage. *The Cone Sisters of Baltimore: Collecting at Full Tilt*. Evanston, Ill., 2008.
Hohl, Reinhold. "Matisse und Picasso." In *Henri Matisse*, edited by Felix Baumann, pp. 26–63. Zürich, 1982.
"Hommage à Henri Matisse." Special issue of *XXe siècle*. Edited by Gualtieri Di San Lazzaro. Paris, 1970. English ed.: "Homage to Henri Matisse." New York, 1970.
Hoog, Michael. *Musée de l'Orangerie: Catalogue de la collection Jean Walter et Paul Guillaume*. 3rd ed. Paris, 1990. First published 1984.
Hoppe, Ragnar. "På visit hos Matisse" (1919 interview with Matisse). Reprinted in Ragnar Hoppe, *Städer och Konstnärer: Resebrev och essäer om Konst*, pp. 193–95. Stockholm, 1931. Translated in Flam, *Matisse on Art* (1995), pp. 73–77.
——. "Fran Matisse till Segonzac (1930)." In Ragnar Hoppe, *Städer och konstnärer: Resebrev och essäer om konst*, pp. 200–225. Stockholm, 1931.
Hughes, Robert. *The Portable Matisse*. New York, 2002.
Huneker, James. "Decade of the New Art Movement Shows Big Changes." *New York Times*, November 10, 1912, p. SM12.
——. *Pathos of Distance: A Book of a Thousand and One Moments*. New York, 1922. First published 1913.
Hunter, Sam. *Henri Matisse, 1869–1954*. The Metropolitan Museum of Art Miniatures: Album XM. New York, 1956.
Hunter, Sam, et al. *The Museum of Modern Art: The History and The Collection*. New York, 1984.
Huyghe, René, ed. *Histoire de l'art contemporain: La peinture*. Paris, 1935.
Impressionist and Post-Impressionist Paintings from the U.S.S.R., Lent by the Hermitage Museum, Leningrad, and the Pushkin Museum, Moscow. Exh. cat. New York, 1973.
Impressionist to Early Modern Paintings from the U.S.S.R.: Works from The Hermitage Museum, Leningrad, and The Pushkin Museum, Moscow. Exh. cat. Los Angeles, 1986.

Izerghina, A. N. *Henri Matisse: Paintings and Sculptures in Soviet Museums*. Translated by R. J. Rosengrant et al. Leningrad, 1978.
——. *Henri Matisse: Paintings and Sculptures in Soviet Museums*. Translated by R. J. Rosengrant et al. New ed. Leningrad, 1990. German ed.: *Henri Matisse: Gemälde und Plastiken in den Museen der Sowjetunion*. Leningrad, 1990.
Izerghina, A. N., and A. G. Barskaya. *French Painting, Second Half of the 19th to the Early 20th Century: The Hermitage*. 2nd ed. Translated by Philippa Hentgès and Yuri Pamfilov. Leningrad, 1982.
Izerghina, A. N., A. G. Barskaya, and B. A. Zernov. *The Hermitage, Leningrad: French 20th Century Masters*. Prague, 1970.
Jacobus, John M. *Henri Matisse*. New York, 1972.
——. *Henri Matisse*. London, 1973.
——. *Henri Matisse*. Concise ed. New York, 1982.
Jarauta Marión, Francisco, et al. *Matisse and the Alhambra, 1910–2010*. Exh. cat. Granada, 2010.
Jean-Aubry, Georges. "La peinture au Salon d'Automne." *L'Art moderne*, no. 43 (October 27, 1907). Reprinted in Fourcade and de Chassey, "Anthologie" (1993), p. 443.
Jeancolas, Claude. *L'art fauve*. Paris, 2006.
Jedlicka, Gotthard. *Der Fauvismus*. Zürich, 1961.
——. *Henri Matisse: La coiffure*. Stuttgart, 1965.
——. *Mit Henri Matisse in Paris, 1931*. Basel, 2008.
Jensen, Knud W. *De glade givere*. Copenhagen, 1996.
Joachimides, Christos M., and Norman Rosenthal, eds. *The Age of Modernism: Art in the 20th Century*. Exh. cat. Berlin, 1997.
Joost, Nicholas. *Scofield Thayer and* The Dial*: An Illustrated History*. Carbondale and Edwardsville, Ill., 1964.
Josephson, Ragnar. "Kvinnorna från Collioure och kvinnorna från Avignon." *Tidsskrift för Konstvetenskap* 26 (1947), pp. 9–46.
Joubin, André. "Jacques Doucet, 1853–1929." *Gazette des beaux-arts*, ser. 6, 3 (1st semester 1930), pp. 69–82.
Jouffroy, Alain. "Henri Matisse: Cette exposition rétrospective montre que le peintre de la joie de vivre était un homme et un artiste inquiet." *Beaux-Arts*, July 25–31, 1956, p. 10.
Jover, Manuel. "From Fauvism to Pop Art, Sixty Years of Creativity." In *Great Museums: The National Museum of Modern Art, Georges Pompidou Center*, pp. 16–49. Paris, [1990].
Kahn, Gustave. "Art [Le Salon d'automne]." *Mercure de France*, October 16, 1912, pp. 879–84. Reprinted in Fourcade and de Chassey, "Anthologie" (1993), p. 488.
——. "Art." *Mercure de France*, March 16, 1916, pp. 320–24. Reprinted in Fourcade and de Chassey, "Anthologie" (1993), p. 488.
Katz, Katharina, ed. *Öffentliche Kunstsammlung Basel: 20. Jahrhundert*. Basel, 1997.
Kauffmann, Arthur. *Stiftung Sammlung E. G. Bührle / Foundation E. G. Bührle Collection / Fondation Collection E. G. Bührle*. Zürich, 1971.
Kawashima, R[iichiro]. *Matisse*. Tokyo, 1933. Translated in Flam, *Matisse: A Retrospective* (1988), pp. 291–94.
Kay, Jane H. "Matisse: Triumphant Exhibition." *Christian Science Monitor*, May 5, 1966, p. 6.
Kean, Beverly Whitney. *All the Empty Palaces: The Merchant Patrons of Modern Art in Pre-Revolutionary Russia*. London, 1983.
Kiersmeier, Carl. "La peinture française à Copenhague." *L'Amour de l'art* 10 (1929), pp. 162–66.
Kimball, Fiske. "Matisse: Recognition, Patronage, Collecting." *Philadelphia Museum Bulletin* 43, no. 217 (March 1948), pp. 34–47.
——. "Discovery from America." *Art News* 47, no. 2 (April 1948), pp. 29–31, 54.
Kirkland, Kate Sayen. *The Hogg Family and Houston: Philanthropy and the Civic Ideal*. Austin, 2009.
Klein, John. "Book Reviews." *Art Journal* 45, no. 4 (winter 1985), pp. 359–61, 363, 365, 367.
——. "Objects of Desire and Irresistible Forces: Matisse between Patrons, Collectors, and War." In *Henri Matisse: Four Great Collectors*, edited by Kasper Monrad, pp. 11–32. Exh. cat. Copenhagen, 1999.
——. *Matisse Portraits*. New Haven, 2001.
——. "Henri Matisse, *Still Life with Oranges (II)*, c. 1899." Spotlight Series Essay, April 2011. Saint Louis: Mildred Lane Kemper Art Museum. http://kemperartmuseum.wustl.edu/files/spotlightApr11.pdf.
Kødt, M. Peschcke. *Statusopgørelse i malerkunsten*. Copenhagen, 1935.
Kold, Anders, and Kirsten Strømstad, eds. *Richard Mortensen: Maleri 1929–1993*. Exh. cat. Copenhagen, 1994.
Kolpinsky, IU. D. "Painting and Drawing of the 20th Century" [in Russian/cyrillic]. In *Vseobshchaia istoriia iskusstv*, vol. 6, part 2, pp. 81–82. Moscow, 1965.
Költzsch, Georg-W., ed. *Morozov and Shchukin, the Russian Collectors: Monet to Picasso*. Exh. cat. Cologne, 1993.
Korn, Madeleine. "Collecting Paintings by Matisse and by Picasso in Britain before the Second World War." *Journal of the History of Collections* 16, no. 1 (2004), pp. 111–29.
Kostenevich, Albert. *Matisse: Peintures et dessins du Musée Pouchkine et du Musée de l'Ermitage*. Exh. cat. Lille, 1986.
——. *Ot Mone do Pikasso: Frantsuzskaia zhivopis' vtoroĭ poloviny XIX-nachala XX veka v Ermitazhe*. Leningrad, 1989.
——. "Un dialogo lungo mezzo secolo: Incontriti con l'Oriente." In Claude Duthuit et al., *Matisse: "La révélation m'est venue de l'Orient,"* pp. 23–79. Exh. cat. Florence, 1997.
——. "Sergei Shchukin—An Unsurpassed Collector with a Sense for the Unique and the Epoch-making." In *Henri Matisse: Four Great Collectors*, edited by Kasper Monrad, pp. 71–92. Exh. cat. Copenhagen, 1999.
Kostenevich, Albert, Y. A. Rusakov, and Katsunori Fukaya. *Machisu ten / Matisse Retrospective*. Exh. cat. Nagoya, 1991.
Kostenevich, Albert, and Natalia Semyonova. *Collecting Matisse*. Translated from Russian by Andrew Bromfield. Paris, 1993.
Kouznetsova, Irina, and Eugenia Georgievskaïa. *La peinture française au musée Pouchkine*. Paris and Léningrad, 1980.
Kropmanns, Peter. "Matisse und die Molls, seine bedeutendsten deutschen Sammler." In *Oskar Moll: Gemälde und Aquarelle*, pp. 76–92. Exh. cat. Cologne, 1997.
——. "Matisse à Vence: Les peintures, 1943–1948." In Marie-Thérèse Pulvenis de Séligny and Peter Kropmanns, *Henri Matisse; Vence: L'espace d'un atelier*, pp. 58–74. Exh. cat. Paris, 2007.
——. "A Women's Painter and Men: Matisse's Male Models and Sitters." In *Matisse: People, Masks, Models*, pp. 58–71. Exh. cat. Munich, 2008.
——. "Matisse au fil de l'eau." In *Henri Matisse: La dissolution du trait et de la couleur*, pp. 12–21. Exh. cat. Nice, 2011.
Kruszynski, Anette. "Die Malerei der Fauves und des Expressionismus." *Kunstsammlung Nordrhein-Westfalen, Düsseldorf. Vernissage. Die Zeitschrift zur Ausstellung* 71, no. 13 (2000), pp. 6–13. Published on the occasion of "Unser 20. Jahrhundert: Meisterwerke von Picasso bis Beuys" (Düsseldorf 2000).
Küster, Ulf. "Henri Matisse ou *Le chef d'oeuvre inconnu*." In *Henri Matisse: Figure, couleur, espace*, pp. 11–16. Exh. cat. Basel, 2006.
Kuznetsova, Irina Aleksandrovna, and E. B. Georgievskaïa. *La peinture française au Musée Pouchkine*. Paris, 1980.
La Beaumelle, Agnès de, and Nadine Pouillon, eds. *La collection du Musée National d'Art Moderne: Catalogue*. Paris, 1986.
Labrusse, Rémi. "Catalogo delle opere." In Claude Duthuit et al., *Matisse: "La révélation m'est venue de l'Orient,"* pp. 97–319. Exh. cat. Rome, 1997.
——. "L'épreuve de Tanger." In *Le Maroc de Matisse*, pp. 28–53. Exh. cat. Paris, 1999.
——. *Matisse: La condition de l'image*. Paris, 1999.
——. "'What Remains Belongs to God': Henri Matisse, Alois Riegl, and the Arts of Islam." In *Matisse, His Art and His Textiles: The Fabric of Dreams*, edited by Ann Dumas, pp. 46–61. Exh. cat. London, 2004.
——. "Das Ende des Bilderkultes: Bemerkungen zu den 'Symphonischen Interieurs' (1911)." In *Henri Matisse: Figur, Farbe, Raum*, pp. 290–304. Exh. cat. Ostfildern-Ruit, 2005.
Labrusse, Rémi, and Jacqueline Munck. *Matisse, Derain: La vérité du fauvisme*. Paris, 2005.
Laessøe, Rolf. *Wilhelm Freddie*. Copenhagen, 1996.
Lagerkvist, Bengt. "Henri-Matisse." *Manadsjournalen* 11 (November 1984), pp. 53–63.
Langaard, Johan H. *Expressionisme og kubisme i Frankrig*. Kristiania (Oslo), 1922.

Langui, Émile. *50 Years of Modern Art*. Translated by Geoffrey Sainsbury and James Oliver. New York, 1959.

Lassaigne, Jacques. "Expériences de Matisse." *Panorama des arts 1946* (1947), pp. 13–16.

——. *Matisse: Biographical and Critical Study*. Translated by Stuart Gilbert. [Geneva], 1959.

Laude, Jean. *La peinture française (1905–1914) et l'art nègre*. Paris, 1968.

——. "Les 'ateliers' de Matisse." *Colóquio: Artes* (Lisbonne), no. 18 (June 1974), pp. 16–25.

——. "Autour de la *Porte-fenêtre à Collioure* de Matisse." In *D'un espace à l'autre: La fenêtre; oeuvres du XXe siècle*, pp. 55–74. Exh. cat. Saint-Tropez, 1978.

Léal, Brigitte, ed. *Collection art moderne: La collection du Centre Pompidou, Musée National d'Art Moderne*. Paris, 2006.

Lebensztejn, Jean-Claude. "Eight Statements [on Matisse]." *Art in America* 63, no. 4 (July–August 1975), pp. 67–75.

——. "Constat amiable." *Cahiers du Musée National d'Art Moderne*, no. 17 / 18 (1986), pp. 84–91.

Lebovici, Elisabeth, and Philippe Peltier. "Lithophanies de Matisse." *Cahiers du Musée National d'Art Moderne*, no. 49 (autumn 1994), pp. 5–39.

Lécuyer-Corthis, Gilberte. "Peintres et naïades." *Le Jardin des arts*, no. 22 (August 1956), pp. 597–604.

Legg, Alicia. *The Sculpture of Matisse*. New York, 1972.

Lejard, André. *Matisse*. Paris, 1952. First published Paris, 1948.

Lemoine, Serge, ed. *Paintings in the Musée d'Orsay*. London, 2004.

Lerch, John. "Walter P. Chrysler Jr.'s Collection of Twentieth Century Masterpieces." *Country Life and the Sportsman* 74 (May 1938), pp. 44–47, 94, 97–98.

Lévêque, Jean-Jacques. "Matisse 1." *Galerie des arts* no. 44 (May 1967), pp. 16–25.

——. *Matisse*. [Paris], 1968.

Leymarie, Jean. *Fauvism: Biographical and Critical Study*. Translated by James Emmons. Lausanne, 1959.

——. *Henri Matisse*. Milan, 1964.

——. "Evoluzione di Matisse." *L'arte moderna* 10, no. 83 (1967), pp. 41–80.

——. "Il Fauvismo." *L'arte moderna* 3, no. 25 (1967), pp. 241–80 ("La formazione del movimento"); no. 26 (1967), pp. 281–320 ("La piena maturità").

——. *Braque: Les ateliers*. Aix-en-Provence, 1995. Italian ed.: *Braque: Ateliers*. Translated by Chiara Formis. I contemporanei. Milan, 1995.

Leymarie, Jean, Herbert Read, and William S. Lieberman. *Henri Matisse: Retrospective*. Exh. cat. [Los Angeles], 1966.

Lieberman, Laura C. "Select Offerings: French Paintings from the Chrysler Museum." *Southern Accents* 9, no. 6 (November 1986), pp. 46–50.

Lieberman, William S. *20th Century Art: Selections from the Collection of The Metropolitan Museum of Art, New York*. Vol. 1, *Painting, 1905–1945*. New York, 1986.

——. "Introduction: A Chronicle." In Sabine Rewald et al., *Twentieth Century Modern Masters: The Jacques and Natasha Gelman Collection*, pp. 1–17. Exh. cat. New York, 1989.

Linker, Kate. "Meditation on a Goldfish Bowl: Autonomy and Analogy in Matisse." *Artforum* 19, no. 2 (October 1980), pp. 65–73.

Lipman, Jean. "Matisse Paintings in the Stephen C. Clark Collection." *Art in America* 22 (October 1934), pp. 134–44.

Llorens, Tomàs. *Matisse: 1917–1941*. Exh. cat. Madrid, 2009.

Lloyd, Michael. "Modern Masters from the Metropolitan." *Art and Australia* 23, no. 3 (autumn 1986), pp. 343–49.

Lobstein, Dominique. *Les salons au XIXe siècle: Paris, capitale des arts*. Paris, 2006.

Lyons, Lisa. "Matisse: Work, 1914–1917." *Arts Magazine* 49, no. 9 (May 1975), pp. 74–75.

MacChesney, Clara Taggart. "A Talk with Matisse, Leader of Post-Impressionists" (June 1912 interview, published on the occasion of the Armory show in New York). *New York Times Magazine*, March 9, 1913, p. 12. Reprinted in Flam, *Matisse: A Retrospective* (1988), pp. 132–34; Fourcade and de Chassey, "Anthologie" (1993), pp. 488–89; and Flam, *Matisse on Art* (1995), pp. 64–69.

MacColl, W. D. "The International Exhibition of Modern Art: An Impression." *Forum* 50 (July 1913), pp. 24–36.

Madsen, Herman. *Från Symbolism till Surrealism: Problem och gestalter i den moderna målarkonsten*. Stockholm, 1939.

Magazine of Art. Anonymous. "Evolution of a Painting." *Magazine of Art* 32, no. 7 (July 1939), pp. 414–15.

Malaurie, Guillaume. "Matissimo!" *L'Express*, June 12, 1987, pp. 55–57.

Malitskaya, K. M. *Great Paintings from the Pushkin Museum, Moscow*. New York, 1964.

Malpel, Charles. "Le Salon d'Automne à Paris." *Le Télégramme* (Toulouse), fall 1907. Reprinted in Malpel, *Notes sur l'art d'aujourd'hui et peut-être de demain* (Toulouse, 1910), vol. 2, pp. 154–55, and Fourcade and de Chassey "Anthologie" (1993), p. 444.

Mannering, Douglas. *The Art of Matisse*. London, 1982.

Marchiori, Giuseppe. *Matisse*. New York, [1967].

Marin-David, Sophie. "Matisse, Picasso: Exposition au Grand Palais." *Dossier de l'art*, no. 90 (October 2002). Issued in conjunction with the exhibition held at the Grand Palais 2002–3.

Martinez, Andrew. "A Mixed Reception for Modernism: The 1913 Armory Show at the Art Institute of Chicago." In "One Hundred Years at the Art Institute: A Centennial Celebration," *Art Institute of Chicago Museum Studies* 19, no. 1, (1993), pp. 30–57, 102–5.

Matamoros, Joséphine. "L'incidence du site de Collioure et du paysage dans l'oeuvre de Matisse et de Derain." In *Matisse-Derain: Collioure 1905, un été fauve*, pp. 12–25, 289. Exh. cat. Paris, 2005.

Matisse, Henri. "Notes d'un peintre." *La Grande Revue* 2, no. 24 (December 25, 1908), pp. 731–45. Reprinted in Fourcade, *Henri Matisse: Écrits et propos sur l'art* (1972), pp. 40–53; English translation "Notes of a Painter," in Flam, *Matisse on Art* (1995), pp. 37–43.

——. *Portraits*. Monte-Carlo, 1954.

Mauny, Jacques. "The Charles Pacquement Collection." *Arts* 13, no. 1 (January 1928), pp. 5–17.

Maurer, Emil. *Stiftung Sammlung E. G. Bührle, Zürich*. Bern, 1992.

Maxon, John. *The Art Institute of Chicago*. New York, 1970.

Mazars, Pierre. "De la couleur avant toute chose." *Le Figaro littéraire*, no. 1248 (April 20–26, 1970), pp. 27–28.

McAllister, Bill. "Art Works Exchanged by Chrysler." *Virginian-Pilot*, October 25, 1972, pp. B1, B8.

McBride, Henry. "News and Comment in the World of Art." *New York Sun*, November 23, 1919, sec. 7, p. 12.

——. "New Matisse Art on Exhibition." *New York Herald*, December 12, 1920, sec. 3, p. 4.

——. "Modern Art." *Dial* 76 (February 1924), pp. 207–9.

——. "Modern French Masters at the Valentine Galleries." *New York Sun*, March 12, 1927, p. 5.

——. *Matisse*. Modern Art. New York, 1930.

——. "The Museum of Modern Art Gives a Matisse Exhibition." *New York Sun*, November 7, 1931. Reprinted in Fourcade and de Chassey, "Anthologie" (1993), p. 497.

Messinger, Lisa M. "Twentieth-Century Art: The Scofield Thayer Bequest." In *Metropolitan Museum of Art: Notable Acquisitions, 1984–1985, Selected by Philippe de Montebello, Director*, pp. 44–51. New York, 1985.

Mezzatesta, Michael P. *Henri Matisse, Sculptor / Painter: A Formal Analysis of Selected Works*. Exh. cat. Fort Worth, 1984.

Micha, René. "Matisse à Zürich." *Art International* (April–June 1983), pp. 3–14, 88.

Migeon, Gaston. "Impressions d'art en Russie." *Le Journal des débats*, January 29, 1914, p. 3.

Milhau, Denis. "Matisse, Picasso et Braque, 1918–1926, y-a-t-il un retour à l'ordre?" In *Le retour à l'ordre dans les arts plastiques et l'architecture, 1919–1925*, pp. 95–142. Saint-Étienne, 1975.

Milner, Frank. *Henri Matisse*. London, 1994.

Mirabdolbaghi, Zia. "Incursions champêtres." In *1918–1958: La Côte d'Azur et la modernité*, pp. 111–17. Paris, 1997.

Monery, Jean-Paul, ed. *Henri Matisse: Émerveillement pour le sud*. Exh. cat. Saint-Tropez, 2004.

Monneret, Sophie. *Matisse: L'homme, la vie, l'oeuvre*. Paris, 1994.
Monnier, Geneviève. *Ruvuru Bijutsukan to Pari no sobyo* [Master Drawings from the Louvre and National Museums in Paris]. Vol. 5. Tokyo, 1997.
Monod-Fontaine, Isabelle. *Matisse: Oeuvres de Henri Matisse (1869–1954)*. Collections du Musée National d'Art Moderne. Paris, 1979.
——. *The Sculpture of Henri Matisse*. Exh. cat. New York, 1984.
——. "Henri Matisse, 1869–1954." In *La Collection du Musée National d'Art Moderne*, edited by Agnès de la Beaumelle and Nadine Pouillon, pp. 408–19. Paris, 1986.
——. *Henri Matisse, ou, la couleur découpée*. Paris, 1989.
——. "Matisse: Les années fauves (1904–1907)." In *Fauvism and Modern Japanese Painting*, pp. 21–25, 264–66. Exh. cat. Tokyo, 1992.
——. "A Black Light: Matisse (1914–1918)." In *Matisse*, edited by Caroline Turner and Roger Benjamin, pp. 84–95. Exh. cat. Brisbane, 1995.
——. "Le paradoxe de l'odalisque." In *Le Maroc de Matisse*, pp. 111–56. Exh. cat. Paris, 1999.
——. "Paysages avec ou sans figures (Matisse, Derain et Braque, 1905–1908)." In *Méditerranée de Courbet à Matisse*, pp. 131–43. Exh. cat. Paris, 2000.
——. "La dation Marie Matisse entre dans les collections du Centre Georges Pompidou, Musée National d'Art Moderne." *Revue du Louvre* 52, no. 1 (February 2002), pp. 16–20.
——. "Henri Matisse: Une pensée de la couleur" and "Variations autour d'un sujet." In *Matisu ten / Henri Matisse: Processus / Variation*, by Chika Amano et al., pp. 25–30, 44–51. Exh. cat. Tokyo, 2004.
——. "A Question of Windows: Interior with a Violin." In Dorthe Aagesen et al., *Matisse: Masterpieces at Statens Museum for Kunst*, pp. 185–204. Copenhagen, 2005.
——. "Vence 1943–1948: Interior / Exterior Studio Visits." In *Matisse, a Second Life*, edited by Hanne Finsen, pp. 43–53. Exh. cat. Paris, 2005.
——. "Grenades et palmiers." In *Henri Matisse; Vence: L'espace d'un atelier*, pp. 30–41. Exh. cat. Paris, 2007.
——. "Marguerite, Her Father's Model." In *Matisse: People, Masks, Models*, pp. 72–83. Exh. cat. Munich, 2008.
——. "Matisse aux carreaux (The Odalsique Motif from 1921 to 1935)." In *Matisse and the Alhambra, 1910–2010*, pp. 45–51. Exh. cat. Granada, 2010.
Monod-Fontaine, Isabelle, et al. Matisse: *La collection du Centre Georges Pompidou, Musée National d'Art Moderne*. Exh. cat. Paris, 1998.
Monod-Fontaine, Isabelle, Anne Baldassari, and Claude Laugier. *Matisse: Oeuvres de Henri Matisse*. Collections du Musée National d'Art Moderne. Paris, 1989.
Monod-Fontaine, Isabelle, and Claude Laugier. "Éléments de chronologie (1904–1918)." In *Henri Matisse, 1904–1917*, pp. 61–126. Exh. cat. Paris, 1993.
Monrad, Kasper. "Die Königliche Gemälde-und Skulpturensammlung in Kopenhagen." In *Meisterwerke des Kopenhagener Statens Museum for Kunst im Kunsthistorischen Museum Wien*, edited by Wilfried Seipel, pp. 11–24. Exh. cat. Vienna, 1997.
——. ed. *Henri Matisse: Four Great Collectors*. Exh. cat. Copenhagen, 1999.
Moore, Richard A. *The Dialectic Norm of Nineteenth and Twentieth Century Art*. Georgia State College. School of Arts and Sciences Research Paper, no. 20. Atlanta, 1968.
Morice, Charles. "Art moderne: Exposition Henri Matisse." *Mercure de France* 51 (August 1904), pp. 533–34.
——. "Le XXIe Salon des Indépendants." *Mercure de France*, April 15, 1905, pp. 542–43. Reprinted in Fourcade and de Chassey, "Anthologie" (1993), p. 420.
Moulin, Raoul-Jean. *Henri Matisse: Dessins*. Paris, 1968.
Mousseigne, Alain. "Toulouse . . . la couleur." In *Matisse: Ajaccio–Toulouse, 1898–1899, une saison de peinture*, pp. 51–99. Exh. cat. Nice, 1986.
Muller, Joseph-Émile. *Fauvism*. Translated by Shirley E. Jones. Enl. ed. New York, 1967.
Müller-Tamm, Pia, ed. *Henri Matisse: Figur, Farbe, Raum*. Exh. cat. Ostfildern-Ruit, 2005.
Munier, Geneviève. *100 chefs-d'oeuvre du XXe siècle dans les collections du Centre Pompidou*. Paris, 2010.
Musée d'Art Moderne de Moscou: Catalogue illustré. Moscow, 1928.
Musée National d'Art Moderne, Paris. *100 oeuvres nouvelles, 1974–1976*. Introduction by Pontus Hulten. Paris, 1977.
Museum voor Moderne Kunst. *Een keuze*. Brussels, 2001. French ed.: Musée d'Art Moderne. *Oeuvres choisies*. Brussels, 2001.
Mushakojo. *Henri Matisse 1890–1939*. Tokyo, 1939.
Myers, Bernard S. "Matisse and the Fauves." *American Artist* 15, no. 10 (December 1951), pp. 70–72, 86.
Naesgaard, Ole. "Matisse's Luxe." *Aarstiderne* 9 (August 1952), pp. 65–68.
National Gallery of Art. *European Paintings: An Illustrated Catalogue*. Washington, D.C., 1985.
Naudin, Jean-Bernard, et al. *Matisse: A Way of Life in the South of France*. New York, 1998.
Neff, John Hallmark. "Matisse and Decoration, 1906–1914: Studies of the Ceramics and the Commissions for Paintings and Stained Glass." PhD diss., Harvard University. Cambridge, Mass., 1974.
——. "Matisse and Decoration: The Shchukin Panels." *Art in America* 63, no. 4 (July–August 1975), pp. 38–48.
Negri, Renata. *Matisse e i Fauves*. Milan, 1969.
Neidhardt, Jane E., ed. *A Gallery of Modern Art at Washington University in St. Louis*. Saint Louis, 1994.
Néret, Gilles. *Matisse*. New ed. Paris, 1991.
——. *Henri Matisse*. English ed. Cologne, 1996. French ed.: Paris, 1996.
Neumayer, Heinrich. *Fauvismus*. Vienna, 1956.
Newsweek. Anonymous. "Henri Matisse." *Newsweek*, January 17, 1966, pp. 50–53.
New York Times. Anonymous. "Art at Home and Abroad: News and Comment. Matisse at the Montross Galleries." *New York Times*, January 24, 1915, p. SM11.
——. H. D. "Henri Matisse Art on Exhibition Here: First Sketch for One of His Famous Works, 'La Danse,' Is Brought to Light" (review of exh. at Pierre Matisse Gallery). *New York Times*, October 28, 1936, p. 23.
Nirdlinger, Virginia. "The Matisse Way: Forty Years in the Evolution of an Individualist." *Parnassus* 3 (November 1931), pp. 4–6, 37.
Noël, Bernard. *Matisse*. Rev. ed. Paris, 1987. First published 1983.
Norton Gallery and School of Art. *Norton Collection of Painting and Sculpture*. West Palm Beach, 1957.
——. *Paintings and Sculpture in the Norton Gallery*. West Palm Beach, 1963.
——. *Catalogue of the Collection*. West Palm Beach, 1979.
O'Brian, John. *Ruthless Hedonism: The American Reception of Matisse*. Chicago, 1999.
Öffentliche Kunstsammlung Basel: 20. Jahrhundert. Basel, 1997.
Ogawa, Masataka, and Isaku Yanaihara. *Matisse, Rouault*. Tokyo, 1967.
Okamoto Kenjiro. *Bonaru, Matisu / Bonnard, Matisse*. L'art du monde, vol. 16. Tokyo, 1968.
Oppler, Ellen C. *Fauvism Reexamined*. New York, 1976.
Orienti, Sandra. *Henri Matisse*. Florence, 1971. Eng. ed.: *Matisse*. London, 1972.
Otten, Liam. "A Bold, Modern Art Collection." *Washington University in St. Louis Magazine* 72 (spring 2002), pp. 18–21.
Pach, Walter. "Why Matisse?" *Century Magazine* 89 (February 1915), pp. 633–36.
Palermo, Charles. "A Project for Wholeness." In *Picasso and Braque: The Cubist Experiment, 1910–1912*, pp. 15–37. Exh. cat. Santa Barbara, 2011.
Parker, Robert McD. "Catalogue of the Stein Collections." In *The Steins Collect: Matisse, Picasso, and the Parisian Avant-garde*, edited by Rebecca Rabinow, Janet Bishop, and Cécile Debray, pp. 394–457. Exh. cat. San Francisco, 2011.
Parrot, Louis. "Matisse au Salon d'Automne." *Labyrinthe* (Paris), no. 13, October 15, 1945, pp. 2–3.
Passantino, Erika D., ed. *The Eye of Duncan Phillips: A Collection in the Making*. Washington, D.C., 1999.
The Passionate Eye: Impressionist and Other Master Paintings from the Collection of Emil G. Bührle, Zürich. Exh. cat. Zürich, 1990.
Peckham, Morse. "The Triumph of Romanticism." *Magazine of Art* 45, no. 7 (November 1952), pp. 291–99.

Percheron, René, and Christian Brouder. *Matisse: De la couleur à l'architecture*. Paris, 2002.

Pernoud, Régine. "Il faut regarder toute la vie avec des yeux d'enfants." *Le Courrier de l'U.N.E.S.C.O.* 6 (October 1953). Interview with Matisse, reprinted in Fourcade, *Henri Matisse: Écrits et propos sur l'art* (1972), pp. 321–23.

Perry, Gill. "Playing with Paint: 'Pink Onions.'" In Dorthe Aagesen et al., *Matisse: Masterpieces at Statens Museum for Kunst*, pp. 88–106. Copenhagen, 2005.

Persuy, Sandra. "'Les sources du XXe siècle': Une vision européenne et pluridisciplinaire de l'art moderne." *Les Cahiers du Musée National d'Art Moderne* 67 (spring 1999), pp. 31–63.

Pertsov, Petr. *Shchukinskoe sobranie frantsuzskoi zhivopisi: Muzei Novoi Zapadnoi Zhivopisi, Moskva* [The Shchukin collection of French paintings: The Museum of Modern Western Painting, Moscow]. Moscow, 1921.

Petersen, Carl V. "Henri Matisse: Den Stein'ske Samling hos Tetzen-Lund." *Politiken*, October 2, 1920. Review of Copenhagen 1920 (in Danish). Reprinted in Gottlieb, "Tetzen-Lund samling" (1984), p. 25.

Philadelphia Museum of Art. *Paintings from Europe and the Americas in the Philadelphia Museum of Art: A Concise Catalogue*. Philadelphia, 1994.

——. *Handbook of the Collections*. Philadelphia, 1995.

Phillips, Marjorie. *Duncan Phillips and His Collection*. Rev. ed. New York, 1982. First published 1970.

Phillips Collection. *The Phillips Collection: A Museum of Modern Art and Its Sources. Catalogue*. Washington, D.C., 1952.

——. *Master Paintings: The Phillips Collection*. Essay by Robert Hughes. Washington, D.C., 1998.

Pincemaille, Christophe. *La Folie Gourgaud: Les musées nationaux de l'Île-d'Aix*. Paris, 2009.

Plée, Léon. "La vie artistique: Le futuro-cubisme et le Salon d'automne." *Les Annales politiques et littéraires*, October 13, 1912, pp. 320–21.

Pollack, Barbara. *The Collectors: Dr. Claribel and Miss Etta Cone*. Indianapolis, Ind., 1962.

Purrmann, Hans. "Aus der Werkstatt Henri Matisses." *Kunst und Künstler* 20 (February 1922), pp. 167–76.

——. "From the Workshop of Henri Matisse," translated by Kenneth Burke. *The Dial* 73 (July 1922), pp. 32–40.

Pushkin Museum. *Gosudarstvenny Muzey Izobrazitelnykh Iskusstv imeni A.S. Pushkina: Katalog kartinnoy galerei; zhivopis, skulptura, miniatyura* [State Pushkin Museum of Fine Arts: Catalogue of the picture gallery; Painting, sculpture, miniatures]. Moscow, 1986.

——. *Katalog zhivopisi: Gosudarstvennyi muzei izobrazitel'nykh iskusstv imeni A. S. Pushkina* [Catalogue of painting, State Pushkin Museum of Fine Arts]. Moscow, 1995.

Puy, Jean. "Souvenirs." In "Matisse," special issue of *Le Point*, no. 21 (July 1939), pp. 16–37.

Puy, Michel. "Les Fauves." *La Phalange*, November 15, 1907. Translated in Flam, *Matisse: A Retrospective* (1988), pp. 69–70.

Quinn Sale. Anonymous. "Quinn Art in Five Session Sale." *Art News* 25 (January 15, 1927), pp. 1–2.

——. Anonymous. "Last of Quinn Art to Go at Auction." *New York Times*, January 16, 1927, sec. 2, p. E20.

——. Anonymous. "Modern Art Brings $16,253 at Auction." *New York Times*, February 10, 1927, p. 26.

——. Anonymous. "Quinn Art Sale Nets $16,235 in First Session." *New York Herald Tribune*, February 10, 1927, p. 15.

——. Anonymous. "Quinn's Art Collection Goes on Sale: $1,225 for a Matisse." *New York World*, February 10, 1927, p. 18.

——. Anonymous. "Big Prices Keep Up in Quinn Sale." *New York American*, February 11, 1927, p. 15.

——. Anonymous. "Sale of the Quinn Collection Is Completed." *Art News* 25, no. 20 (February 19, 1927), pp. 1, 6, 7, 10, 11.

——. Anonymous. "Detailed Statement of Sales: Quinn." *American Art Sales* 7 (March 1927), pp. 3–14.

——. Anonymous. "Paintings, Drawings and Sculpture, the Modern Art Collection of the Late John Quinn." *American Art Sales* 7, 4 (March 1927), p. 6.

Raaschou-Nielsen, Inge Vibeke. *Fransk modernisme: Hovedværker på Statens Museum for Kunst*. Exh. cat. Copenhagen, 1996.

Rabinow, Rebecca. "The Legacy of la rue Férou: *Livres d'artistes* created for Tériade by Rouault, Bonnard, Matisse, Léger, Le Corbusier, Chagall, Giacometti, and Miró." PhD diss., Institute of Fine Arts, New York University, 1995.

——. "Modern Art Comes to the Metropolitan: The 1921 Exhibition of 'Impressionist and Post-Impressionist Paintings.'" *Apollo* 152, no. 464 (October 2000), pp. 3–12.

——. "Vollard and Matisse." In *Cézanne to Picasso: Ambroise Vollard, Patron of the Avant-Garde*, edited by Rebecca Rabinow, pp. 130–41. Exh. cat. New York, 2006.

Rabinow, Rebecca, Janet Bishop, and Cécile Debray, eds. *The Steins Collect: Matisse, Picasso, and the Parisian Avant-garde*. Exh. cat. San Francisco, 2011.

Rathsman, Siri. "Pariskrönika." *Konstrevy* 22, no. 1–2 (1946), pp. 45–55.

Raver, Anne. "Where Plants Are Indolent as Odalisques." *New York Times*, December 17, 1992, p. C7.

Raynal, Maurice. *Peintres du XXe siècle*. Geneva, 1947.

——. *Modern Painting*. Geneva, 1953.

Raynal, Maurice, et al. *History of Modern Painting*. Vol. 2, *Matisse, Munch, Rouault: Fauvism, Expressionism*. Geneva, 1950. French ed.: *Histoire de la peinture moderne*. Vol. 2, *Matisse, Munch, Rouault: Fauvisme et expressionisme*. Geneva, 1950.

Réau, Louis. *Catalogue de l'art français dans les musées russes*. Paris, 1929.

Reff, Theodore. "Matisse: Meditations on a Statuette and Goldfish." *Arts Magazine* 51, no. 3 (November 1976), pp. 109–15.

Reid, Benjamin Lawrence. *The Man from New York: John Quinn and His Friends*. New York, 1968.

Reidemeister, Leopold. *Auf den Spuren der Maler der Ile de France: Topographische Beiträge zur Geschichte der französischen Landschaftsmalerei von Corot bis zu den Fauves*. Berlin, 1963.

Reidemeister, Leopold, et al. *Stiftung Sammlung Emil G. Bührle / Foundation Collection Emil G. Bührle / Foundation Emil G. Bührle Collection*. Zürich, 1973.

——. *Stiftung Sammlung Emil G. Bührle / Foundation Collection Emil G. Bührle / Foundation Emil G. Bührle Collection*. 2nd ed. Zürich, 1986.

Reinvaldt, Henrik, ed. *Matisse, 1869–1954*. Translated by Anne Mette Bering. Copenhagen, 1996.

Revel, Jean-Francois. "Jacques Doucet, couturier et collectionneur." *L'Oeil*, no. 84 (December 1961), pp. 44–51, 81, 106.

Rewald, John. *The John Hay Whitney Collection*. Exh. cat. Washington, D.C., 1983.

——. *Studies in Post-Impressionism*. New York, 1986.

Rewald, Sabine. "The Jacques and Natasha Gelman Collection." In Sabine Rewald et al., *Twentieth Century Modern Masters: The Jacques and Natasha Gelman Collection*, pp. 53–291. Exh. cat. New York, 1989.

——. "A Sailor's Yarn." *Art in America* 87 (October 1999), pp. 118–23.

——. "Twentieth Century" [Gelman Matisses]. In "Recent Acquisitions: A Selection, 1999–2000," *Metropolitan Museum of Art Bulletin* 58 (autumn 2000), pp. 54–55.

Richardson, Brenda. *Dr. Claribel & Miss Etta: The Cone Collection of the Baltimore Museum of Art*. Baltimore, 1985.

——. "Dr. Claribel and Miss Etta Cone." In Guillaud and Guillaud, *Matisse: Rhythm and Line* (1987), pp. 290–314, 324–25.

Richardson, John. "Rediscovering an Early Modern Vision: The Dial Collection Recalls the Life and Times of Scofield Thayer." *House & Garden* 159, no. 2 (February 1987), pp. 158–63.

——. *A Life of Picasso*. Vol. 2, *1907–1917*. New York, 1996.

Rishel, Joseph J. *The Henry P. McIlhenny Collection: An Illustrated History*. Philadelphia, 1987.

Rivière, Jacques. "Une exposition de Henri Matisse [1910]." In Jacques Rivière, *Études*, 2nd ed., pp. 42–46. Paris, 1911. Translated in Flam, *Matisse: A Retrospective* (1988), pp. 121–22.

Robinson, Anette, and Isabelle Bréda. *Matisse au Musée National d'Art Moderne, Centre Georges Pompidou*. Tableaux choisis. Paris, 1993.

Roger-Marx, Claude. "À propos de la présentation de quelques toiles d'Henri Matisse." *Arts et spectacles*, December 5–20, 1945, p. 1.

——. "Le nu et la mer." *Jardin des arts* no. 11 (September 1955), pp. 658–64.

——. "Les dualités de Matisse." *Le Figaro littéraire*, no. 1248 (April 20–26, 1970), p. 32.

Romm, Alexander Georgievich. *Henri Matisse*. Translated by Chen I-Wan. Moscow, 1937.

——. *Matisse: A Social Critique*. Translated by Jack Chen. New York, 1947.

Rosenthal, Gertrude. *Paintings, Sculpture and Drawings in the Cone Collection*. Rev. ed. Baltimore, 1967. First published as Adelyn Breeskin and George Boas, *Cone Collection: A Handbook with a Catalogue of Paintings and Sculpture*. Baltimore, 1955.

Rostrup, Havard. "Matisse." *Aarstiderne* 6 (November 1947), pp. 2–19.

Rusakov, Yu. A. "Matisse in Russia in the Autumn of 1911." *Burlington Magazine* 117 (May 1975), pp. 284–91.

Russell, John. *The World of Matisse: 1869–1954*. New York, 1969.

——. "Matisse en France." *L'Oeil*, no. 184 (April 1970), pp. 16–25, 66.

——. "A Key Matisse Joins the Modern." *New York Times*, April 26, 1975, p. 17.

——. "The Birth of a Wild Beast." *Horizon* 18 (summer 1976), pp. 4–17.

——. "A Monumental Show of Matisse's Work." *New York Times*, December 3, 1978, p. 35.

——. "The Dial: Showcase of a Pioneer Collector." *New York Times*, May 3, 1981, p. D27.

——. "Even Now, Fresh Insights into Matisse." *New York Times*, January 2, 1983, pp. H1, H21.

——. "Impressionist Show at Met from Soviet." *New York Times*, August 22, 1986, pp. C1, C20.

——. "Matisse au MoMA." *Connaissance des arts*, no. 487 (1992), pp. 76–85.

Sachs, Samuel, II. "Reconstructing the 'Whirlwind of 26th Street.'" *Art News* 61, no. 10 (February 1963), pp. 26–28, 57–58.

Saint Louis Art Museum. *The St. Louis Art Museum: Handbook of the Collections*. Saint Louis, 1975.

Salé, Marie-Pierre. "Le mythe de l'âge d'or et le retour à la nature." In *1900*, pp. 314–43. Exh. cat. Paris, 2000.

Salin, Anne-Maj. *Tikanojan taidekodin kokoelmat / Tikanojas konsthems samlingar*. Vaasa, 2001.

Salles, Georges. "Visit to Matisse." *Art News Annual* 21 (1952), pp. 37–39, 79–81.

Salmon, André. *L'art vivant*. Paris, 1920.

——. *Souvenirs sans fin: Deuxième époque, 1908–1920*. Paris, 1956.

Salzmann, Dorothea, and Siegfried Salzmann. *Oskar Moll: Leben und Werk*. Munich, 1975.

Samuels, Mike, and Nancy Samuels. *Seeing with the Mind's Eye: The History, Techniques, and Uses of Visualization*. New York, 1975.

San Francisco Museum of Art Quarterly Bulletin. Anonymous. "The Henri Matisse Exhibition." *San Francisco Museum of Art Quarterly Bulletin*, ser. 2, 1, no. 1–2 (1952), p. 5.

Sarradin, Édouard. "Le Salon des Indépendants." *Journal des débats*, March 26, 1905, p. 3.

Scavenius, Bente. *Se på verdenskunst i Danmark*. Copenhagen, 1993.

Schacht, Roland. *Henri Matisse*. Dresden, 1922.

Schapiro, Meyer. "Matisse and Impressionism." *Androcles* 1 (February 1932), pp. 21–36. Reprinted in Fourcade and de Chassey, "Anthologie" (1993), pp. 489–90.

Scharf, Susanne. "Vis-à-Vis: Short Biographies of Matisse's Models and Sitters." In *Matisse: People, Masks, Models*, pp. 204–9. Exh. cat. Hamburg, 2008.

Scheiwiller, Giovanni. *Henri Matisse*. Milan, 1933.

——. *Henri Matisse*. Milan, 1947.

Schmalenbach, Werner. *Grosse Meister moderner Malerei*. Lucerne, 1957.

——. *Bilder des 20. Jahrhunderts: Die Kunstsammlung Nordrhein-Westfalen, Düsseldorf*. Munich, 1986.

——. *Die Lust auf das Bild: Ein Leben mit der Kunst*. Berlin, 1996.

Schmidt, Georg. *Kunstmuseum Basel: 150 Gemälde, 12.–20 Jahrhundert*. 6th ed. Basel, 1988.

Schmidt, Georg, and Paul Boerlin. *Oeffentliche Kunstsammlung Basel*. Vol. 3, *Von Impressionismus bis sur Gegenwart*. Basel, 1961.

Schneider, Pierre. "Galeries Nationales du Grand Palais—Henri Matisse." *La Revue du Louvre et des musées de France* 20, no. 2 (1970), pp. 87–96.

——, ed. *Henri Matisse: Exposition du centenaire*. Exh. cat. Paris, 1970.

——. "Matisse à Marseille." *L'Express*, July 1–7, 1974.

——. "Matisse's Lifelong Conflict: Drawing vs. Color." *Vogue*, August 1975, pp. 126–28, 168, 174–75.

——. "Matisse revisité." *L'Express*, November 5, 1982, pp. 6–7.

——, ed. *Henri Matisse: Matisse et l'Italie*. Exh. cat. Milan, 1987.

——. "The Gelmans and the Fauves." In Sabine Rewald et al., *Twentieth-Century Modern Masters: The Jacques and Natasha Gelman Collection*, pp. 24–31. Exh. cat. New York, 1989.

——. "The Moroccan Hinge." In Jack Cowart et al., *Matisse in Morocco*, pp. 17–56. Exh. cat. Washington, D.C., 1990.

——. "La charnière marocaine." In Brahim Alaoui et al., *Matisse au Maroc: Peintures et dessins, 1912–1913*, pp. 9–43. Exh. cat. Paris, 1999.

——. *Matisse*. New ed. Paris, 2002. First ed., Paris, 1984; Eng. ed., New York, 1984.

——. "Les lumières de Matisse." In *Henri Matisse: Émerveillement pour le sud*, pp. 11–19. Exh. cat. Saint-Tropez, 2004.

Schneider, Pierre, Jack Cowart, and John Elderfield. *Matisse au Maroc: Peintures et dessins, 1912–1913*. Translation by Anne Michel and Gilles Courtois of 1990 ed. Paris, 1999.

Schnell, Werner. *"Das rote Atelier" des Henri Matisse: Ein Bild und seine Verwandten*. Berlin, 2001.

Schulze, Sabine, ed. *The Painter's Garden: Design, Inspiration, Delight*. Exh. cat. Ostfildern and Frankfurt am Main, 2006.

Schwob, René. "Henri Matisse." *L'Amour de l'art*, no. 6 (October 1920), pp. 192–95. Translated in Flam, *Matisse: A Retrospective* (1988), pp. 182, 191–93.

Seckel, Hélène. "27 rue de Fleurus, 58 rue Madame: Les Stein à Paris." In *Paris, New York*, pp. 182–205. Exh. cat. Paris, 1977.

Segel, Kathrine, and Ole Nørregaard Jensen. "Le Luxe II by Henri Matisse." *SMK Art Journal 2010–11* (Copenhagen) 2012. Forthcoming.

Seipel, Wilfried, ed. *Meisterwerke des Kopenhagener Statens Museum for Kunst*. Exh. cat. Vienna, 1997.

Seldis, Henry J. "The Magic of Matisse." *Apollo* 83 (April 1966), pp. 244–55.

Séligny, Marie-Thérèse Pulvenis de. "Nature morte aux grenades (1947)" and "Les grenades." In Marie-Thérèse Pulvenis de Séligny and Peter Kropmanns, *Henri Matisse; Vence: L'espace d'un atelier*, pp. 18–25, 42–55. Exh. cat. Paris, 2007.

——. "Henri Matisse: De la fluidité à la dissolution du trait et de la couleur." In *Henri Matisse: La dissolution du trait et de la couleur*, pp. 22–37. Exh. cat. Nice, 2011.

Séligny, Marie-Thérèse Pulvenis de, and Peter Kropmanns, eds. *Henri Matisse, Vence: L'espace d'un atelier. Nature morte aux grenades*. Exh. cat. Paris, 2007.

Selz, Jean. *Matisse*. Translated by A. P. H. Hamilton. New York, [1964]. Rev. ed.: *Henri Matisse*. Translated by A. P. H. Hamilton. New York, 1990.

Sembat, Marcel. *Henri Matisse: Trente reproductions de peintures et dessins précédées d'une étude critique*. Les peintres français nouveaux, no. 1. Paris, 1920. Also Paris, 1921.

——. "Matisse und sein Werk." *Genius* 2, part 2 (1920), pp. 190–96.

Serritslev Petersen, Lise. *Arabesk og objekt 1890–1940: Essays om Billeder*. Copenhagen, 1992.

Shchukin collection. *Katalog kartin sobraniia S. I. Shchukina / Catalogue des tableaux de la collection de M-r Serge Stschoukine*. Moscow, 1913.

Shone, Richard. "Matisse: An Intimate Splendor." *House and Garden*, March 1987, pp. 133–39.

——. "Matisse in England and Two English Sitters." *Burlington Magazine* 135 (July 1993), pp. 479–84.

Shuisky, B. "Henri Matisse." *Zerkalo* [The mirror] (Moscow), no. 45 (1911). Reprinted in Kostenevich and Semyonova, *Collecting Matisse* (1993), pp. 53–55.

Siegel, Jeanne. "Henri Matisse's *View of Notre-Dame*, Spring 1914." *Arts Magazine* 54, no. 5 (January 1980), pp. 158–61.

Silver, Kenneth E. *Making Paradise: Art, Modernity, and the Myth of the French Riviera*. Exh. cat. Cambridge, Mass., 2001.

Smith, Huldah M. "Balancing to Date the Books on the French: The Art of the Third Republic, 1870–1940." *Art News* 40, no. 1 (February 15–28, 1941), pp. 27–29, 44.

Les Soirées de Paris. Anonymous. "Sept reproductions d'après les oeuvres récentes d'Henri-Matisse." *Les Soirées de Paris*, no. 24 (May 15, 1914), p. 264.

Spar, Francis, ed. *Annuaire du collectionneur, répertoire des prix des tableaux . . . estampes, sculptures vendus à Paris et en province durant la saison 1950–1951*. Paris, 1951.

Speyer, A. James. "Twentieth-Century European Painting and Sculpture." *Apollo* 84, no. 55 (September 1966), pp. 222–25.

Speyer, A. James, and Courtney Graham Donnell. *Twentieth-Century European Paintings*. Chicago, 1980.

Spurling, Hilary. *The Unknown Matisse: A Life of Henri Matisse; the Early Years, 1869–1908*. New York, 1998.

——. "Material World: Matisse, His Art and His Textiles." In *Matisse, His Art and His Textiles: The Fabric of Dreams*, edited by Ann Dumas, pp. 14–33. London, 2004.

——. *Matisse, the Master: A Life of Henri Matisse; the Conquest of Colour, 1909–1954*. London and New York, 2005.

Stavitsky, Gail. "The Development, Institutionalization, and Impact of the A. E. Gallatin Collection of Modern Art." PhD diss., New York University, 1990.

——. "The A. E. Gallatin Collection: An Early Adventure in Modern Art." *Philadelphia Museum of Art Bulletin* 89 (winter–spring 1994), pp. 1, 4–47.

Stein, Leo. *Appreciation: Painting, Poetry, and Prose*. New York, 1947. Reprint ed., 1996.

Sterling, Charles. *Musée de l'Ermitage: La peinture française de Poussin à nos jours*. Paris, 1957.

——. *Great French Paintings in the Hermitage*. Translated by Christopher Ligota. New York, 1958.

Strobl, Andreas. *Curt Glaser: Kunsthistoriker—Kunstkritiker—Sammler. Eine deutsch-jüdische Biographie*. Cologne, 2006.

The Sun. Anonymous. "What Cesare Saw at the Armory Art Show." *The Sun*, February 23, 1913, p. 41 (caricature).

Sutton, Denys. "Aspects of the Venice Biennale: 1. The Fauves." *Burlington Magazine* 92 (September 1950), pp. 262–65.

——. "The Mozart of Painting." *Apollo* 92 (November 1970), pp. 358–65.

Swane, Leo. "Matisse i Tetzen-Lunds samling." *Tilskueren* 39, no. 2 (1922), pp. 206–16.

——. *Katalog over J. Rumps samling af moderne fransk kunst*. Copenhagen, 1929.

——. "J. Rumps Samling af moderne fransk Kunst i Kunstmuseet." *Kunstmuseets Aarsskrift* 16–18 (1929–31), pp. 61–80.

——. "Udstilling af moderne fransk kunst i 'Den Frie.'" *Tilskueren* 1 (1931), pp. 421–30.

——. "Kunstmuseet. Provinsmuseer: Rumps samling." *Tilskueren* 2 (December 1932), pp. 402–7.

——. *Katalog over J. Rumps samling af moderne fransk kunst*. 2nd ed. Copenhagen, 1948.

——. *Ved mit vinduesspejl*. Copenhagen, 1955.

Swane, Leo, et al. *Henri Matisse*. Stockholm, 1944.

——. *Matisse*. Copenhagen, 1945.

Sykora, Katharina. "Durch das Fenster sehen: Schwellenraum und Weiblichkeit in den 'Zimmern mit Aussicht' von Henri Matisse." In *Henri Matisse: Figur, Farbe, Raum*, pp. 57–74. Exh. cat. Ostfildern-Ruit, 2005.

Szymusiak, Dominique, ed. *Matisse et Baudelaire: Les Fleurs du mal*. Exh. cat. Le Cateau-Cambrésis, 1992.

——, ed. *Musée Matisse Le Cateau-Cambrésis: Les collections Henri Matisse, Auguste Herbin, Abstraction géométrique, Tériade, éditeur d'art*. Le Cateau-Cambrésis, 2002.

Taillandier, Yvon. "Matisse et la préhistoire du bonheur." In "Hommage à Henri Matisse," special issue of *XXe siècle*, edited by Gualtieri Di San Lazzaro, pp. 85–95. Paris, 1970. Also English ed.

Tanaka, Masayuki. "Le lieu de la production." In *Matisu ten / Henri Matisse: Processus / Variation*, by Chika Amano et al., pp. 94–101. Exh. cat. Tokyo, 2004.

Taube, Maria. *Kärleken och döden: Konst på Moderna Museet*. Stockholm, 2002.

Tériade, E. "Constance du fauvisme." *Minotaure* 2, no. 9 (October 15, 1936), pp. 3, 6–8. Translated in Flam, *Matisse on Art* (1995), pp. 122–23.

——. "Matisse Speaks." *Art News Annual* 21 (1952), pp. 40–77. Reprinted in Flam, *Matisse on Art* (1995), pp. 199–207, 299–301.

Tetzen-Lund, Christian. *Chr. Tetzen-Lund samling af moderne fransk malerkunst*. Copenhagen, 1934.

Thayer, Scofield. *Living Art*. New York, 1923.

Thomson, Richard. *Monet to Matisse: Landscape Painting in France, 1874–1914*. Exh. cat. Edinburgh, 1994.

——, ed. *Framing France: The Representation of Landscape in France, 1870–1914*. Exh. cat. Manchester, 1998.

Time Magazine. Anonymous. "Art: Beauty and the Beast." *Time Magazine*, April 5, 1948, pp. 52–57.

——. Anonymous. "Painting: Distiller of Sunshine." *Time Magazine* 87, no. 8 (February 25, 1966), pp. 79–82.

Tinterow, Gary, et al. *The Metropolitan Museum of Art*. Vol. 8, *Modern Europe*. New York, 1987.

——. *Masterpieces of European Painting, 1800–1920, in The Metropolitan Museum of Art*. New York, 2007.

Tono, Yoshiaki. *Matisu / Matisse*. Vol. 10 of *Gendai sekai no bijutsu*. Tokyo, 1986.

Town & Country. Anonymous. "An Interior at Nice." *Town & Country* 86 (June 15, 1931), p. 22.

Trachtman, Paul. "Matisse & Picasso." *Smithsonian Magazine*, February 2003, electronic ed.: www.smithsonianmag.com.

Trapp, Frank. "The Paintings of Henri Matisse: Origins and Early Development (1890–1917)." PhD diss., Harvard University, Cambridge, Mass., 1951.

Trovato, Joseph S., ed. *1913 Armory Show: 50th Anniversary Exhibition, 1963*. Exh. cat. New York, 1963.

Tugenkhol'd, Ia[kov]. "Frantsuzskoe sobranie S. I. Shchukina" [The French collection of S. I. Shchukin]. *Apollon* 5, no. 1–2 (January–February 1914), pp. 5–46.

——. *Pervyi muzei novoi zapadnoi zhivopisi* [First Museum of Modern Western Painting]. Moscow, 1923.

Turner, Caroline, and Roger Benjamin, eds. *Matisse*. Exh. cat. Brisbane, 1995.

Vallier, Dora. "Matisse et la Russie en 1911: Influences textuelles et influences contextuelles." In *Matisse aujourd'hui*, pp. 55–71. Cahiers Henri Matisse, no. 5. Nice, 1992.

Vallotton, Félix. "Au Salon d'Automne." *La Grande Revue*, October 25, 1907, p. 920. Reprinted in Fourcade and de Chassey, "Anthologie" (1993), p. 443.

Van Gelder, Lawrence. "Footlights: Legacy." *New York Times*, March 12, 2002, p. E1.

Vauxcelles, Louis. "Le Salon des Indépendants." *Gil Blas*, March 23, 1905, n.p. Reprinted in Flam, *Matisse: A Retrospective* (1988), pp. 45–46.

——. "Le Salon d'automne." *Gil Blas*, September 30, 1912, pp. 1–3. Reprinted in Fourcade and de Chassey, "Anthologie" (1993), p. 488.

"La Vente de la Peau de l'Ours." *La Revue française politique et littéraire*, March 1914. Reproduced in Monod-Fontaine and Laugier, "Éléments de chronologie" (1993), p. 112.

Verve. "De la couleur," special issue with contributions by André Rouveyre and Henri Matisse. *Verve* 4, no. 13 (1945).

——. "Vence, 1944–48," special issue. *Verve* 6, no. 21–22 (1948).

Vienne, Gabrielle. *Rétrospective Henri Matisse*. Exh. cat. Paris, 1956.

Vildrac, Charles. *Nice 1921: Seize reproductions d'après les tableaux de Henri Matisse*. Paris, 1922.

Vipper, B. R. *Katalog kartinnoj galerei: Zîvopis' skul'ptura* [The State Pushkin Museum of Fine Arts. Catalogue of the Picture Gallery: Painting, Sculpture]. Moscow, 1961.

Vogel, Carol. "The Art Market." *New York Times*, February 5, 1993, p. C24.

Vogue. Anonymous. "Matisse: A Rare Collection Record; Cone Collection. *Vogue* 125 (March 1, 1955), pp. 132–35.

La Voix du Nord. J.-Y. N. "Un Matisse exposé pour la première fois au monde." *La Voix du Nord*, October 23, 1986, p. 26.

Volboudt, Pierre. "La ligne à la recherché de la forme." In "Hommage à Henri Matisse," special issue of *XXe siècle*, edited by Gualtieri Di San Lazzaro, pp. 97–112. Paris, 1970. Also English ed.

Wadley, Nicholas. *Cubism*. London, 1970.

——. *Cézanne and His Art*. London and New York, 1975.

Walker, John. *National Gallery of Art, Washington*. Rev. ed. New York, 1984.

Wanscher, Wilhelm. "Grønningen." *Politiken*, January 29, 1924.

Washington University Magazine. Anonymous. "The University Collections." *Washington University Magazine* 34 (fall 1963), pp. 17–28.

——. Anonymous. "Art Museum Centennial: First Museum of the Mississippi." *Washington University Magazine* 51 (fall 1981), pp. 2–3.

Watanabe, Junichi, Chuji Ikegami, and Shuji Takashina. *Matisse*. Tokyo, 1973.

Watkins, Nicholas. *Matisse*. Oxford, 1977.

——. *Matisse*. Oxford, 1984.

Watson, Forbes. *John Quinn 1870–1925: Collection of Paintings, Water Colors, Drawings, and Sculpture*. Huntington, N.Y., 1926.

Wattenmaker, Richard J., and Anne Distel. *Great French Paintings from the Barnes Foundation: Impressionist, Post-Impressionist, and Early Modern*. New York, 1993.

Wehle, Harry B. "Loan Exhibition of Modern French Paintings." *Metropolitan Museum of Art Bulletin* 16, no. 5 (May 1921), pp. 93–96.

——. "A Loan of Paintings." *Metropolitan Museum of Art Bulletin* 31 (October 1936), pp. 209–10.

Weid, Jean-Noël von der. *Musée de l'Orangerie: Guide de visite*. [Paris], 2006.

Weiss, Jeffrey. "The Matisse Grid." In *The Repeating Image: Multiples in French Painting from David to Matisse*, edited by Eik Kahng, pp. 173–93. Exh. cat. Baltimore, 2007.

Wennberg, Bo. "Från Delacroix till Matisse." *Tidsskrift för konstvetenskap* 26 (1947), pp. 47–94.

Wenzel, Angela. "Virtuose der linie: Henri Matisse als Zeichner." In "Kunstsammlung Nordrhein-Westfalen, Düsseldorf," *Vernissage. Die Zeitschrift zur Ausstellung* 13, no. 16 (2005), pp. 52–61.

Werenskiold, Marit. *De norske Matisse-elevene: Laeretid og gjenombrudd, 1908–1914*. Oslo, 1972.

——. *The Concept of Expressionism: Origin and Metamorphoses*. Translated by Ronald Walford. Oslo, 1984.

Werner, Alfred. "The Earthly Paradise of Henri Matisse." *Arts Magazine* 40 (January 1966), pp. 30–35.

Werth, Margaret. *The Joy of Life: The Idyllic in French Art, circa 1900*. Berkeley and Los Angeles, 2002.

——. "Nude with a White Scarf: A Thick and Full Material." In Dorthe Aagesen et al., *Matisse: Masterpieces at Statens Museum for Kunst*, pp. 133–58. Copenhagen, 2005.

Wescher, Paul. *La prima idea*. Munich, 1960.

Westheider, Ortrud. "The Portrait as Manifesto: Matisse as Portraitist." In *Matisse: People, Masks, Models*, pp. 84–89. Exh. cat. Munich, 2008.

Whitfield, Sarah. *Fauvism*. London, 1991.

Wilenski, R. H. *Modern French Painters*. New York, 1940.

——. *Modern French Painters*. 3rd ed. London, 1954.

Wilson, Sarah. *Matisse*. New York, 1992.

Wolinski, Natasha. "Les joyaux de l'héritage Doucet." *Beaux-Arts* 151 (December 1996), pp. 91–95.

Wood, James N., and Teri J. Edelstein. *The Art Institute of Chicago: Twentieth-Century Painting and Sculpture*. Chicago, 1996.

Wright, Alastair. *Matisse and the Subject of Modernism*. Princeton, 2004.

Zahle, Erik. *Fransk maleri efter 1900*. Copenhagen, 1938.

Zahle, Grete. *Billedvifte*. Copenhagen, 1997.

Zervos, Christian. "L'art nègre." *Cahiers d'art* 2, nos. 7–8 (1927), pp. 229–58.

——. "De l'importance de l'objet dans la peinture d'aujourd'hui." *Cahiers d'art* 5, 3 (1930), pp. 113–20.

——. "Henri-Matisse. Notes on the Formation and Development of His Work." In Christian Zervos et al., *Henri Matisse*, pp. 9–32. Paris and New York, 1931.

——. "Notes sur la formation et le développement de l'oeuvre de Henri-Matisse." *Cahiers d'art* 6 (1931), pp. 229–52.

——. *Histoire de l'art contemporain*. Paris, 1938.

——. "À propos de l'exposition Matisse au Musée d'Art Moderne de Paris." *Cahiers d'art* 24, no. 1 (1949), pp. 159–70.

Zervos, Christian, et al. *Henri-Matisse*. Paris and New York, 1931.

Ziegler, Frank-Thomas. "Henri Matisse: Biography." In *Matisse: People, Masks, Models*, pp. 210–23. Exh. cat. Munich, 2008.

Zilczer, Judith. *"The Noble Buyer": John Quinn, Patron of the Avant-Garde*. Washington, D.C., 1978.

——. "The Dispersal of the John Quinn Collection." *Archives of American Art Journal* 19, no. 3 (1979), pp. 15–21.

Zürcher, Bernard. *Les Fauves*. Paris, 1995.

PHOTOGRAPH CREDITS

Cats. 1–64, jacket front and back: © 2012 Succession H. Matisse / Artists Rights Society (ARS), New York

Figs. 1–8, 12, 14–17, 19, 21, 22, 27, 31, 32–38, 40–42, 44, 46, 48–52, 54–63, 67–77, 81, 82, 84, 86, 91: © 2012 Succession H. Matisse / Artists Rights Society (ARS), New York
Fig. 43: © 2012 Artists Rights Society (ARS), New York / ADAGP, Paris
Fig. 45: © 2012 Estate of Pablo Picasso / Artists Rights Society (ARS), New York
Fig. 89: © Estate Brassaï-Réunion des Musées Nationaux / Art Resource, NY

Cat. 7: Réunion des Musées Nationaux / Art Resource, NY
Cats. 11, 19: The Sherman Fairchild Paintings Conservation Center, The Metropolitan Museum of Art
Cat. 12: © CNAC / MNAM / Dist. Réunion des Musées Nationaux / Art Resource, NY
Cats. 16, 30: © SMK Photo
Cats. 25, 27: Digital Image © The Museum of Modern Art / Licensed by SCALA / Art Resource, NY
Cat. 38: Private collection, c/o Christie's
Cat. 50: Scala / Art Resource, NY

Figs. 3, 64: Scala / Art Resource, NY
Figs. 4, 5, 42, 52, 55, 61: Digital Image © The Museum of Modern Art / Licensed by SCALA / Art Resource, NY
Figs. 6, 8, 58: Photograph © 2012 The Barnes Foundation
Fig. 7: © Musée d'Art Moderne / Roger-Viollet
Fig. 13: Erich Lessing / Art Resource, NY
Fig. 14: Photo by Bernard C. Meyers
Figs. 15, 16: © The Bridgeman Art Library
Fig. 19: © Courtesy of Sotheby's Picture Library
Fig. 20: Réunion des Musées Nationaux / Art Resource, NY
Fig. 23: Bridgeman-Giraudon / Art Resource, NY
Figs. 25, 26: Photo: Kathrine Segel
Figs. 27, 37, 40, 43, 51: © The State Hermitage Museum / photos by Vladimir Terebenin, Leonard Kheifets, Yuri Molodkovets
Figs. 28, 33: The Sherman Fairchild Paintings Conservation Center, The Metropolitan Museum of Art
Fig. 46: © Archives Camoin, Paris
Fig. 80c, page vi: © Archives Henri Matisse
Fig. 92, frontispiece: Michel Sima—Rue des Archives / The Granger Collection

CONTRIBUTORS TO THE CATALOGUE

DORTHE AAGESEN, Curator, Senior Researcher, Statens Museum for Kunst, Copenhagen

STEPHANIE D'ALESSANDRO, Gary C. and Frances Comer Curator of Modern Art, The Art Institute of Chicago

CÉCILE DEBRAY, Curator of Modern Collections, Centre Pompidou, Musée National d'Art Moderne, Paris

ISABELLE DUVERNOIS, Associate Conservator, The Sherman Fairchild Paintings Conservation Center, The Metropolitan Museum of Art, New York

JACK FLAM, President of the Dedalus Foundation and Distinguished Professor Emeritus of Art and Art History, Brooklyn College and the Graduate Center, City University of New York

CLAUDINE GRAMMONT, independent art historian and researcher

RÉMI LABRUSSE, Professor of Art History, Université Paris Ouest–Nanterre

DOÏNA LEMNY, Assistant Curator of Modern Collections, Centre Pompidou, Musée National d'Art Moderne, Paris

ISABELLE MONOD-FONTAINE, Former Deputy Director, Centre Pompidou, Musée National d'Art Moderne, Paris

KASPER MONRAD, Chief Curator, Statens Museum for Kunst, Copenhagen

REBECCA RABINOW, Curator, Department of Modern and Contemporary Art, The Metropolitan Museum of Art, New York

SAMANTHA RIPPNER, Associate Curator, Department of Drawings and Prints, The Metropolitan Museum of Art, New York

KATHRINE SEGEL, independent conservator

HILARY SPURLING, author of *The Unknown Matisse. A Life of Henry Matisse*, vol. 1, 1869–1908 (Knopf, 1995), and *Matisse the Master. A Life of Henri Matisse*, vol. 2, 1909–1954 (Knopf, 2005)

ALASTAIR WRIGHT, University Lecturer and Tutorial Fellow, St. John's College, University of Oxford